Guide to Wireless Communications

Third Edition

Jorge L. Olenewa

COURSE TECHNOLOGY
CENGAGE Learning·

Australia • Brazil • Japan • Korea • Mexico • Singapore • Spain • United Kingdom • United States

COURSE TECHNOLOGY
CENGAGE Learning

Guide to Wireless Communications, Third Edition

Jorge L. Olenewa

Vice President, Careers & Computing: Dave Garza

Executive Editor: Stephen Helba

Acquisitions Editor: Nick Lombardi

Director, Development-Careers & Computing: Marah Bellegarde

Product Development Manager: Juliet Steiner

Senior Product Manager: Michelle Ruelos Cannistraci

Developmental Editor: Kent Williams

Editorial Assistant: Sarah Pickering

Brand Manager: Kristin McNary

Senior Market Development Manager: Mark Linton

Senior Production Director: Wendy Troeger

Production Manager: Andrew Crouth

Content Project Manager: Allyson Bozeth

Art Director: GEX

Technology Project Manager: Joe Pliss

Media Editor: William Overocker

Cover Image: ©iStockphoto.com/andersboman

Library of Congress Control Number: 2012951455

ISBN-13: 978-1-111-30731-8

ISBN-10: 1-111-30731-8

Course Technology
20 Channel Center Street
Boston, MA 02210
USA

Cengage Learning is a leading provider of customized learning solutions with office locations around the globe, including Singapore, the United Kingdom, Australia, Mexico, Brazil, and Japan. Locate your local office at: **international.cengage.com/region**

Cengage Learning products are represented in Canada by Nelson Education, Ltd.

For your lifelong learning solutions, visit **www.cengage.com/coursetechnology**

Purchase any of our products at your local college store or at our preferred online store **www.cengagebrain.com**

Visit our corporate website at **cengage.com.**

Printed in the United States of America
1 2 3 4 5 6 7 16 15 14 13 12

Brief Contents

Table of Contents

Introduction

We live in a wireless world! All the technologies and standards that have been released in the past six years, along with the ones that will be released between now and 2014, mean that almost everything we do—every aspect of our lives—has a wireless component. In fact, wireless data communications is omnipresent today—in the cordless phones we use in our homes and offices, in the nearly 6 billion cellular phones that roam the world, even in warehouses, where wireless is used to keep track of inventory. Today, we can even purchase products or board a flight with our cellular phones and tablets, thanks to wireless. Furthermore, homes, businesses, even whole towns are now equipped with wireless networks that allow residents, employees, and visitors to access the Internet from anywhere using laptop computers, mobile phones, and tablets.

Whether you are a manager who needs a better understanding of the implementation of wireless communication devices, an IT professional looking to enhance your understanding of the field by adding wireless data communications, or a student taking an introductory course in this topic, *Guide to Wireless Communications*, Third Edition, will help you gain a basic understanding of the technical and business aspects of wireless data communications technologies and prepare you for more in-depth learning.

Approach

Since the introduction, in mid-1995, of infrared interfaces in laptop computers, which allowed two computers to communicate without wires, along with the publication, in 1997, of the first IEEE 802.11 wireless local area network standards, the field of wireless data communications has expanded dramatically. This book takes you on a virtual tour of all the wireless data communication technologies, covering the basics of radio frequency transmissions, antennas, infrared, Bluetooth, the IEEE 802.15.4 (ZigBee) standard for low-rate wireless personal area networks, the IEEE 802.15.3c standard for high-rate wireless personal area networks, ultra wide band (UWB), WiGig, WirelessHD, Wireless Home Digital Interface, IEEE 802.11a/b/g/n wireless local area networks, IEEE 802.16 (WiMAX), free-space optics, LMDS and MMDS wireless metropolitan area networks, cellular and satellite wireless wide area networks, and, finally, radio frequency identification (RFID). Coexistence (the ability of two or more of these technologies to work in the same physical space) is also discussed, as are the basic implementation and security issues for each of the mentioned technologies as well as the various business and residential applications.

Using straightforward language, this text introduces the most important technical aspects of each technology and can be used in either classroom settings or for distance education. It features extensive linking to Web sites, where the reader can find additional materials. Please note, however, that although the addresses of these Web sites were accurate at the time this book was printed, some of them may no longer be available.

This text's pedagogical materials include Real-World Exercises, which further your learning outside the classroom setting, and Hands-On Projects, which take you through the often step-by-step process of performing tasks relevant to working in wireless communications. The Hands-On Projects, which can be performed in the lab or at home, use inexpensive, consumer-class equipment as well as freeware and demo versions of popular software. Finally, there are Challenge Case Projects, team-based research projects that help expand the student's knowledge of the technologies discussed and direct him or her to additional learning resources.

Intended Audience

Guide to Wireless Communications, Third Edition, is intended to meet the needs of students and professionals who want to gain a better understanding of the fundamental concepts, scope, and penetration of wireless data communications technologies. It assumes a basic knowledge of computers and networks at a CompTIA A+ and Network+ level. The pedagogical features provide a realistic, interactive learning experience to help prepare students for the challenges of working in the field of wireless data communications.

Chapter Descriptions

Here is a summary of the topics covered in each chapter of this book:

Chapter 1, Introduction to Wireless Communications, provides an overview of a range of applications of wireless data communications in personal, local, metropolitan, and wide area networks. This chapter follows the way the industry is classifying wireless data communications today and looks at the advantages and disadvantages of wireless data communications.

Chapter 2, Wireless Data Transmission, introduces you to wireless data transmission techniques by discussing various techniques used with infrared light and radio waves to transmit data without wires.

Chapter 3, Radio Frequency Communications, looks at the individual components and design of radio systems and how they are used to transmit data. It also provides an overview of standards and their role in the wireless data communications industry.

Chapter 4, How Antennas Work, takes a simplified but in-depth look at antennas and the important role they have in the successful implementation of a wireless data communications system.

Chapter 5, Wireless Personal Area Networks, looks at the first two technologies developed for short-range wireless data communications: Bluetooth, and ZigBee (IEEE 802.15.4).

Chapter 6, High-Rate Wireless Personal Area Networks, wraps up the discussion of short-range wireless data communications with IEEE 802.15.3c, a technology developed for interconnecting multimedia devices and entertainment systems in homes and businesses, WiGig from the Wireless Gigabit Alliance, WirelessHD, and WHDI. It also looks at ultra wide band (UWB) technology and the impact it has in wireless communications in general.

Chapter 7, Low-Speed Wireless Local Area Networks, introduces the IEEE 802.11 WLAN technology, including its infrared variant, and IEEE 802.11b for transmission at up to 11 megabits-per-second.

Chapter 8, High-Speed WLANs and WLAN Security, discusses IEEE 802.11a, the different frequency bands that 802.11 networks operate in, as well as all the enhancements to 802.11 technology designed to boost its data transmission speed and usability. It also introduces 802.11ac and 802.11ad multi-Gigabit wireless standards, as well as the security techniques and issues in WLANs.

Chapter 9, Wireless Metropolitan Area Networks, addresses medium-range wireless data communications, from infrared free-space optics to the latest WiMAX (IEEE 802.16) technology.

Chapter 10, Wireless Wide Area Networks, takes a look at cellular and satellite technologies and how they are used to extend the reach of wireless data communications networks across the entire world.

Chapter 11, Radio Frequency Identification and Near-Field Communication, describes the RFID technology that is being used today to help identify, count, and track everything from small packaged products to the entire contents of large warehouses automatically and without wires. The chapter then introduces NFC, the technology that enables wireless payments, enables wireless information exchange between cellular phones and tablets, and enables handheld devices to read RFID tags.

Chapter 12, Wireless Communications in Business, outlines the advantages and challenges of wireless data communications and discusses the steps that a typical business must go through to identify, evaluate, and implement the wireless data communications technology that is the best solution for its needs, including developing RFI, RFP, and RFQ documents as well as performing wireless site surveys.

Appendix A, History of Wireless Communications, details the history of wireless communications in addition to the histories of television, radar, and cellular technologies.

Features

This book includes many features designed to enhance your understanding of wireless data communications technology:

- **Chapter Objectives**—Each chapter begins with a detailed list of the concepts to be mastered within that chapter. This list provides you with both a quick reference to the chapter's contents and a useful study aid.

- **Illustrations and Tables**—Numerous illustrations of wireless LAN concepts and technologies help you visualize theories and concepts. In addition, the tables provide details and comparisons of practical and theoretical information.

- **Chapter Summaries**—Each chapter's text is followed by a summary of the concepts introduced in that chapter. These summaries provide a helpful way to review the ideas covered in each chapter.

- **Key Terms**—The important terminology introduced in each chapter is summarized in a list at the end of each chapter. The Key Term list includes definitions for each term.

- **Review Questions**—The end-of-chapter assessment begins with a set of review questions (including multiple choice, fill-in-the-blank, and true/false) that reinforces the ideas introduced in each chapter. These questions help you evaluate and apply the material you have learned. Answering these questions will ensure that you have mastered the important concepts.

- **Hands-On Projects**—Although it is important to understand the theory behind wireless networking technology, nothing can improve on real-world experience. Toward this end, each chapter provides several Hands-On Projects that provide you with a practical wireless network experience. Some of these projects require Internet and library research to investigate concepts covered in the chapter; others let you put into practice the chapter's content using Linksys and D-Link equipment and the Windows XP operating systems as well as software downloaded from the Internet.

- **Real-World Exercises**—In these extensive exercises, students implement the skills and knowledge gained in the chapter by doing research and working on real design and implementation scenarios.

- **Challenge Case Projects**—These group exercises take students even further, posing questions that emulate real-life situations, thereby helping students apply their knowledge, initiative, and in-depth research.

New To This Edition

This edition covers a number of standards and technologies that were not yet approved when the second edition was published. It also covers several new topics and provides enhanced coverage of ongoing topics. New areas include:

- IEEE 802.11n, IEEE 802.11ac, and IEEE 802.11ad
- IEEE 802.15.3c WiGig, WirelessHD, and WHDI
- IEEE 802.16m and WiMAX
- Expanded coverage of cellular technologies such as HSPA, HSPA+, and LTE
- Near-Field Communication (NFC) technology

Text and Graphic Conventions

Wherever appropriate, additional information has been added to help you better understand the topic at hand. The following icons are used throughout the text to alert you to additional materials:

The Note icon indicates helpful material related to the subject being described.

The Tip icon indicates helpful pointers on completing particular tasks.

The Hands-On Project icon indicates lab-setting projects that provide practical wireless network experience.

The Challenge Case Projects icon indicates group exercises that promote further learning by emulating real-life scenarios.

Instructor's Materials

Instructor Resources CD (ISBN: 9781111307578)

Please visit *login.cengage.com* and log in to access instructor-specific resources. To access additional course materials, please visit *www.cengagebrain.com*. At the CengageBrain.com home page, search for the ISBN of your title (from the back cover of your book) using the search box at the top of the page. This will take you to the product page where these resources can be found.

The following supplemental materials are available when this book is used in a classroom setting. All the supplements available with this book are provided to the instructor on a single CD-ROM as well as online at the textbook's Web site.

Electronic Instructor's Manual. The Instructor's Manual that accompanies this textbook includes additional instructional material to assist in class preparation, including suggestions for lecture topics, recommended lab activities, tips on setting up a lab for the Hands-On Projects, and solutions to all end-of-chapter materials.

ExamView Test Bank. This cutting-edge Windows-based testing software helps instructors design and administer tests and pretests. In addition to generating tests that can be printed and administered, this full-featured program has an online testing component that allows students to take tests at the computer and have their exams graded automatically.

PowerPoint Presentations. This book comes with a set of Microsoft PowerPoint slides for each chapter. These slides are meant to be used as a teaching aid for classroom presentations, to be made available to students on the network for chapter review, or to be printed for classroom distribution. Instructors are also at liberty to add their own slides for other topics introduced.

Figure Files. All the figures in the book are reproduced on the Instructor Resource CD, in bit-mapped format. Similar to the PowerPoint presentations, these are included as a teaching aid for classroom presentation, to make available to students for review, or to be printed for classroom distribution.

Solutions. Answers to the end-of-chapter material are provided. These include the answers to the Review Questions and to the Hands-On Projects (when applicable).

Syllabus. To help prepare for class, a sample syllabus is provided.

About the Author

Jorge L. Olenewa has been working in and teaching data communications since 1970. With a passion for learning and teaching, Jorge has spent the past 12 years developing and teaching courses in wireless data communications at George Brown College in Toronto, Ontario, Canada. Prior to this, he worked for several large and small IT organizations, beginning with Burroughs (today Unisys), in Brazil, where he supported and trained data communications technologists throughout South and Central America. Olenewa is also the author of the second edition of *Guide to Wireless Communications* and the accompanying lab manual. In addition, he is actively involved in applied research at George Brown College, working in the field of energy management, and helping industry adopt and develop new wired and wireless data communications products for building and residential control systems.

Acknowledgments

Writing a textbook, especially one covering so many different technologies, is a huge undertaking that requires the involvement of a large team of people. The folks at Cengage/Course Technology are undoubtedly one of the very best teams I have ever worked with. Acquisitions Editor Nick Lombardi again demonstrated his excellent vision and insight by crafting the direction of the book to meet the needs of the readers. Product Manager Michelle Ruelos Cannistraci was wonderful in keeping this project on track and was always helpful and supportive, especially when my daytime job required that I be out of the country or when my teaching schedule left few hours during the day for writing. Developmental Editor Kent Williams is a master at his job. If you find this book useful or perhaps even enjoyable, it is due to Kent's incredible language skills and his insightful comments. Kent deserves full credit for helping to turn my random thoughts into readable text. John Freitas is an extremely thorough Technical Editor. He caught many of my "slips" and made excellent suggestions. I hope to get a chance to work with these two fellows again in a future book. Production Editor Allyson

Bozeth was instrumental in getting all the graphics right and being so patient with the delays. A very special thank you is also due to Ylber Ramadani, Chair of the School of Computer Technology at George Brown College in Toronto, Ontario, Canada, for his support; Bob Moroz from RFID Canada in Markam, Ontario, for his time and his assistance with tags and readers; Henry White of Bell Mobility in Mississauga, Ontario, Canada, for his help with cellular technology; and Jeff Mulvey of Redline Communications Inc. of Markham, Ontario, Canada, for his assistance with revising the WiMAX content. Carolyn Duarte, from Nelson Canada, our Cengage representative, also deserves a special mention here, for caring and being supportive of this project. In addition, we would like to thank our team of peer reviewers, who evaluated each chapter and provided very helpful suggestions and contributions:

Shawn Batt—Wichita Technical Institute

Kenneth J. Dreistadt—Lincoln Technical Institute

Carl Meyer—Lincoln Technical Institute

Ylber Ramadani—George Brown College

Tom Vaughn—Lincoln Technical Institute

The entire Cengage/Course Technology staff was always helpful and worked very hard to create this finished product. I feel privileged and honored to be part of such an outstanding group of professionals, and to these people and everyone on the team I extend a very sincere thank you.

I also want to thank my sons Marcelo and Ricardo for their continuous encouragement and support. Finally, I want to thank my wife Elisabeth and my best friend, our dog Charlie, whose love and patience are reflected in literally every page of this text.

Writing about such a diverse range of wireless data communications technologies also demands many hours of reading, research, and experimentation. Translating the technical language and standards into text that can be read by virtually anyone with an interest in the field is made far easier when you can count on the assistance of people who work with the various technologies every day and who can provide invaluable help with examples, equipment, and many of the pictures used to illustrate this edition. I would like to especially acknowledge Bob Moroz, the president of RFID Canada, Jeff Mulvey of Redline Communications, Henry White of Bell Mobility, Hisham Alasady from George Brown College, and Allison Csanyi from fSona Networks, for their time and their contributions.

Lab Requirements

To the User

This book is intended to be read in sequence, from beginning to end. Each chapter builds on preceding chapters to provide a solid understanding of wireless data communications.

Hardware and Software Requirements

Here are the hardware and software requirements needed to perform the end-of-chapter Hands-On Projects:

- Built-in or USB Bluetooth adapter (supported by Windows XP or Windows 7)
- Any consumer-class wireless residential gateway or access point, such as Linksys or DLink
- Wi-Fi-certified IEEE 802.11a/b/g/n wireless network adapter (the adapter standard should ideally match that of the access point or wireless router)
- Windows XP Professional or preferably Windows 7
- An Internet connection and the most current version of a Web browser application

Specialized Requirements

Whenever possible, the need for specialized equipment was kept to a minimum. However, Chapter 5 requires the following specialized hardware:

- Laptop computers with USB version 2.0+ ports, a Wi-Fi adapter, and Bluetooth (USB Bluetooth is acceptable)

Free downloadable software is required for some of the Hands-On Projects. Instructions for downloading the software are given in each chapter, as required:

- AirMagnet Bluesweep
- MetaGeek inSSIDer
- Ixia QCheck
- Ekahau HeatMapper

To my three grandsons, Tristan, Nathanael, and Logan, who unknowingly inspire me to carry on, and to my best friend, Charlie, our toy poodle, for his constant companionship and affection.

chapter 1

Introduction to Wireless Communications

After reading this chapter and completing the exercises, you will be able to:

- Describe how wireless communications technologies are used today
- List various applications of wireless communications technology
- Outline the advantages and disadvantages of wireless communications technology
- List several types of wireless technologies and their purposes

We all know that wireless communications technologies have had a huge impact around the world, especially in the last five years. Today, wireless communications affects almost everything we do on a daily basis, from using the ever-present cellular phones to making voice calls and accessing information, to the counting of inventory in large retail stores, to buying public transit system tickets, to locating hotspots for Internet access and wireless remote sensors installed in locations that are difficult to access, to using credit and debit cards that just need to be placed near a device instead of swiped or inserted, and many, many other uses. There should be no question in anyone's mind that the use of wireless devices will continue to expand into virtually every aspect of our lives.

Wireless communications has completely revolutionized the way we live, just as personal computers forever altered how we worked in the 1980s and the Internet dramatically changed how we obtained and accessed information in the 1990s. Lately, the Internet has also changed how we communicate around the world. Using wireless devices to send and receive short messages as well as to browse the Internet and access corporate applications and databases from any location in the world is now an integral part of our daily lives. And numerous devices—notebook computers, tablets, digital still picture and video cameras, printers, portable digital music players, even refrigerators, washing and drying machines, and electricity meters—are equipped with the ability to communicate without wires.

Today, we can all be in touch with the digital resources we need, no matter where we may find ourselves. Nearly everyone has experienced dramatic changes based on wireless technologies, to the extent that we don't even think about what we are doing, we just expect devices to work without being connected by a cable.

Using an electronic book reader or e-reader, you can view the cover, sample some pages, and purchase a book simply by visiting an online bookstore. On an Amazon Kindle device, for example, all you need is access to either a wireless network or to the cellular telephone network (in over 100 different countries), depending on which model you have. The book will be automatically downloaded to your reader within a couple of minutes. See *www.amazon.com/kindle*.

How Wireless Technology Is Used

Before we continue, let's define precisely what we mean by *wireless communications*. The term *wireless* is often used to describe all types of devices and technologies not connected by a wire. A garage door opener and a television remote control can be called "wireless devices," but they have little in common with the technologies discussed in this book. Because the term *wireless* is sometimes used to refer to any device that has no wires, people can be puzzled about the exact meaning of *wireless communications*. A cordless phone can be considered a wireless communications device—for communicating with the human voice, that is. But for the purposes of this book, **wireless communications** is defined as the transmission of digital data without the use of wires, meaning devices that can be interconnected using some kind of data networking technology. Digital data may include e-mail messages, spreadsheets, and messages transmitted to or from a digital cellular phone. However, note that devices that use a computer network to transmit voice conversations are also included here.

One example of a device that can be used to transmit voice conversations over a computer network is an Apple iPod Touch. This device is generally used to listen to music but can also be used to make calls to telephone numbers anywhere in the world while it's connected to a wireless network, using an application such as Skype. (Go to *www.apple.com/ipodtouch*. Also go to *www.skype.com*, place the mouse cursor over Get Skype, then click iPhone.) When using such devices, your voice is first converted to digital data and then transmitted first over a wireless network and then over the Internet. At the receiving end, the stream of data that is your voice is converted back to sound. You will read more about this in Chapter 10.

The next section talks about the various forms that wireless data communications can take. You will learn about Bluetooth, WirelessHD, WiGig, satellite, cellular, **Wi-Fi**-based wireless LANs, and fixed broadband wireless communications technologies. The specific details of each of these technologies are covered in later chapters. Let's take a look at a day in the life of a typical couple, Joseph and Ann Kirkpatrick, which will provide a quick overview of some of today's wireless communications and how they can be used.

A Wireless World

Joseph and Ann get ready for a typical day. Before Ann leaves for the office, she must first print a copy of a spreadsheet that she finished working on late last night. Because there are several computers in their house, the Kirkpatricks have set up a wireless network that uses a specific networking standard to allow all the digital-data-enabled devices around the house to communicate with one another. Computers and other devices that are compatible with the standards can be as far as roughly 330 feet (100 meters) apart from each other and can send and receive data at speeds up to 300 million bits per second (300 megabits per second or Mbps), depending on which specific standard they are compatible with. The devices that can be part of the network include not only computer equipment but also **Voice over Internet Protocol (VoIP)** telephones, which carry digitized voice over the Internet, home entertainment and gaming equipment, and even some digital music players, such as an Apple iPod Touch.

To get a better idea of the speed of wireless transmission of data, consider that each alphanumeric character transmitted typically uses 16 bits of data. This means that at 300 Mbps, which is the speed of the fastest wireless network today, a computer can transmit over 9,000 letter-sized pages per second, with approximately 2,000 letters and spaces in each. Can you read that fast?

Ann pulls a tablet computer out of her briefcase and opens a spreadsheet. She then selects the print command. A device called a **wireless network interface card** (or **wireless NIC**) is built in on the tablet computer. This interface card sends the data over radio waves directly to the wireless-enabled laser printer downstairs, which has its own wireless NIC. This wireless network is ideal for the Kirkpatricks. They can have all their home computing and electronic devices interconnected without the trouble and expense of installing cables; this network enables all of their devices to share printers, files, and even the home Internet connection. Figure 1-1 illustrates the home wireless network.

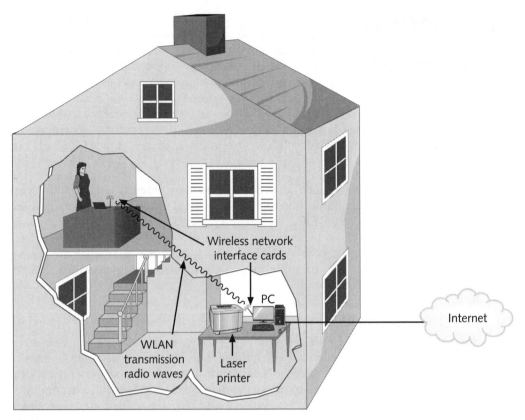

Figure 1-1 Home wireless network (WLAN)

© Cengage Learning 2014

Ann places a call to her office to pick up her messages using her **smartphone,** a combination of a mobile phone and **personal digital assistant (PDA)** that also provides an appointment calendar, a to-do list, a phone book, and a notepad as well as many other useful business and entertainment applications. Although most mobile phones today include some of these features, smartphones can connect to other devices, such as personal computers, and synchronize the data between the two devices; they can also electronically store and transmit business cards and other types of information, even word-processing files and spreadsheets. In addition, almost all models of smartphones today can connect directly to the same kind of wireless network that we use to interconnect computers. Because Ann is inside the home, the smartphone automatically connects to the wireless network to access and store data. While they are inside the house, both Ann and Joseph's smartphones can use software that enables them to make calls using VoIP over their wireless network and the Internet instead of their cellular provider. They even have separate phone numbers that people can dial to call them from a landline phone. After Joseph and Ann leave home, their mobile phones disconnect when they are out of range of the wireless network; then they use the cellular network to make and receive voice calls. Being able to use VoIP over the Wi-Fi network helps them save money by cutting down on their cellular phone bills.

As early as 2004, runners in the Boston Marathon covered the 26.2-mile course with tiny wireless chips clipped to their shoelaces. The chips transmit an identification code that is detected at several stations along the marathon course, and the code is used to track the runners' times as well as to e-mail updates to the runners' friends and relatives regarding their locations and progress. For a full description of the technology employed, search the Internet using the keywords "Boston marathon wireless."

Shortly after finishing their breakfast in the kitchen, Joseph hears a short beep and notices that a shopping list has been e-mailed to his smartphone from the refrigerator. A computer system installed in the refrigerator door automatically generates a grocery list by scanning the **radio frequency identification (RFID)** tags attached to almost every product package. RFID tags are small chips containing radio transponders that can be used to identify products and track inventory. At predetermined dates and times, the refrigerator computer compares the remaining food items with a list of minimum quantities for those items. If the items are running out, it adds them to a list and sends an e-mail over the Internet to both Ann and Joseph, which they receive on their smartphones. Joseph or Ann can also use the wireless network to connect to the refrigerator's computer and find out what they need to buy. Because the refrigerator is also connected to the Internet, the same function can be accomplished regardless of where they are, at any time.

To watch a video demonstration of a refrigerator computer in action, search the Internet or YouTube using the keywords "Samsung Internet fridge." The refrigerator in this video does not include RFID, but it allows you to manage a family calendar, leave notes for family members, send e-mails and tweets, and connect to Facebook. You can also access recipes online, create a shopping list, etc.

Bluetooth and Other Short-Range Wireless Technologies

Bluetooth is a wireless standard designed to transmit data at very short ranges—typically, from a few inches to 33 feet (10 meters). The main purpose of short-range technologies such as Bluetooth is to eliminate cables between devices such as smartphones and computers, which allows data to be transmitted wirelessly between, say, a computer and a printer or a mobile telephone and a music player or a computer and a smartphone. Figure 1-2 shows two examples of Bluetooth headsets that are typically used with mobile phones or digital music players like the iPod Touch but that can also be used with computers. Bluetooth communicates using small, low-power transceivers called **radio modules**, which are built into tiny circuit boards and contain very small microprocessors. Bluetooth devices use a **link manager**, which is software that helps it identify other Bluetooth devices, create a link between them, and send and receive music and voice in the form of digital data; it can also send other types of data.

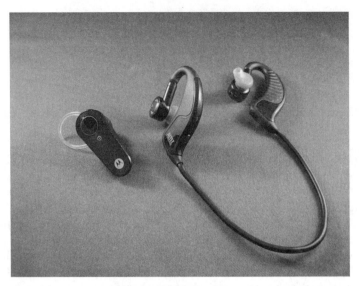

Figure 1-2 Two examples of Bluetooth headsets: mono (left) and stereo (right)

© Cengage Learning 2014

There are other short-range wireless technologies designed for use primarily in the home, which are similar to Bluetooth but can handle a lot more data at much higher speeds. For example, **WirelessHD** and **WiGig** can send CD-quality audio and DVD or Blu-ray disk high-definition video to multiple receivers around the house at the same time. Most Bluetooth devices can transfer a maximum of between 1 Mbps and 3 Mbps at distances of up to 33 feet (10 meters), but the latest version covers transmission at data rates up to 24 Mbps. WirelessHD and WiGig can transfer video and sound at speeds between 7 Gbps and 10 Gbps (gigabits or billions of bits per second) using a radio transmission technology called **Ultra Wide Band** (**UWB**). Bluetooth can send data through physical barriers like walls. These wireless devices don't even have to be aimed at each other the way a TV remote control usually has to be aimed at the TV set when changing channels or adjusting the sound. UWB WirelessHD and WiGig generally have a range of up to 10 meters, but only within a room with few or no obstacles between devices. In addition, the greater the distance, the slower the transmission. The gigabit per second speeds above can only be achieved at distances of up to 6 feet (approximately 1.8 meters). Plus, the more obstacles, including people, that there are in a room, the shorter the transmission range of UWB.

Nearly 14,000 different computer, telephone, and peripheral vendors create products based on the Bluetooth standard. Both WirelessHD and WiGig also have an impressive list of well-known member companies.

To check out the range of available products, visit the WirelessHD Consortium Web site at *www.wirelesshd.org*. When the main page opens, place the mouse cursor over the Consumers tab, then click Product Listing.

Joseph and Ann both work for Federated Package Express (FPE), a package delivery service. To send a package, a customer telephones the local FPE call center. An FPE customer service representative receives the call using her VoIP telephone handset, which is connected to the

WLAN and to a Bluetooth telephone headset. Ann doesn't even have to be at her desk; her Bluetooth device automatically establishes a connection with the wireless telephone handset as soon as both devices are turned on. She can immediately answer a call by simply tapping a small button on the headset, without having to pick up the receiver. In addition, the tablet computer she carries around keeps her connected to the office network at all times, no matter where she is in the building. For example, the address list and calendar that Ann updated last night at home are transmitted to the office, and the information is immediately refreshed.

The automatic connection between various Bluetooth devices creates a **piconet**, also sometimes called a **wireless personal area network (WPAN)**. A piconet consists of two or more Bluetooth devices that are exchanging data with each other. Up to seven devices can belong to a single Bluetooth WPAN.

The customer service representative at FPE answers the call while she is moving around her cubicle, without having her movements not limited by a telephone wire. She can also enter the package pickup information on her computer or, when she is not at her desk, on her tablet. Figure 1-3 illustrates a Bluetooth wireless network.

Bluetooth is named after the tenth-century Danish King Harald Bluetooth, who was responsible for unifying Scandinavia. You can read more of his story on the Internet by searching for the king's name.

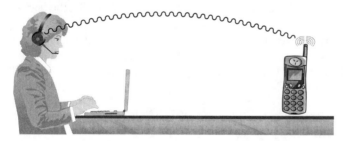

Figure 1-3 Bluetooth network (piconet) or WPAN between a cordless handset and a headset

© Cengage Learning 2014

Satellite Networks

FPE, the company that Joseph and Ann work for, has connectivity needs that go far beyond the walls of its headquarters building. The company uses a combination of a satellite-based network and the cellular wireless network to stay in touch with its delivery vehicles while they are on the road. Where cellular networks (discussed in the next section) are not available, the drivers can use satellite phones to connect their handheld computers to FPE's head office.

After the FPE customer service representative has entered the pickup information into the computer, the data needs to get to the pickup driver—in this case, Joseph. FPE's satellite network is sometimes responsible for this data transmission. From the main head-office computer, the pickup data is transmitted to a satellite orbiting the Earth and then back down to the handheld satellite phone and finally to Joseph's handheld computer. Figure 1-4 shows a satellite retransmitting the signal between the main office and the satellite phone in Joseph's van.

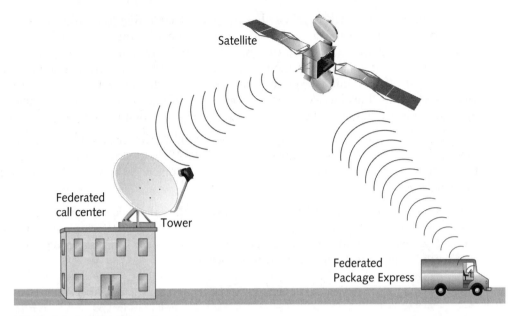

Figure 1-4 Satellite data network

© Cengage Learning 2014

In satellite communications, a device called a **repeater** is located in the satellite itself. A repeater simply "repeats" the same signal to another location down on the surface. An Earth station transmits to the satellite at one frequency band, and the satellite regenerates and transmits (repeats) the signal back to Earth on a different frequency. The transmission time needed to repeat a signal from one Earth station to another can be up to 250 milliseconds. This is illustrated in Figure 1-5.

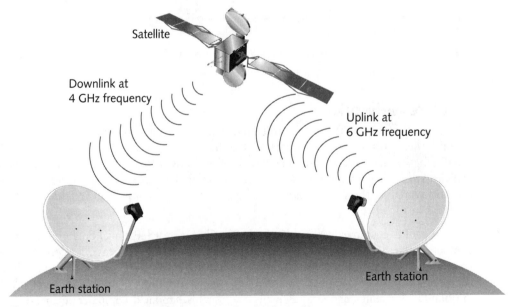

Figure 1-5 Satellite repeating a signal to another Earth station

© Cengage Learning 2014

FPE uses an outside vendor that provides international satellite communications.

The first satellite to orbit Earth successfully, called Sputnik, was launched by the Soviet Union in 1957. Today, there are more than 900 operational satellites in orbit around the planet and reportedly over 5000 that are no longer functional. It's only due to some truly amazing mathematical calculations that they don't continually crash into one another, but on February 10, 2009, a nonoperational Russian satellite did crash into the Iridium 33 communications satellite, which is used for satellite phones.

Cellular Networks

Cellular digital technology provides another link between the various components that make up the FPE package pickup process. A modern cellular telephone network is built around the concept of low-power transmitters, with each "cell" handling a number of users. With transmission towers spread throughout a city, the same radio frequency channel can be used by towers located a few miles away from each other, thereby avoiding interference. This concept maximizes the use of a limited range of frequency channels and is made possible by low-power digital transmission technology, which permits another transmitter to use the same frequency a relatively short distance away, without causing interference problems. This topic is discussed in greater detail in Chapter 10. Figure 1-6 shows examples of two smartphones.

Figure 1-6 Smartphones—Blackberry Bold (left) and Apple iPhone (right)

© Cengage Learning 2014

Joseph is equipped with a handheld smart wireless terminal, and his truck is equipped with a wireless printer. Joseph's handheld terminal receives the pickup order via the cellular phone network and can also receive time-sensitive information, such as route alerts warning of traffic delays or changes in pickup schedules; Joseph can also access route maps online. The van's engine computer, which monitors engine performance and other vehicle systems, can perform diagnostic checks and transmit the results back to FPE over the same cellular connection. GPS tracking technology installed in the truck allows FPE to monitor the location of the delivery trucks, sending pickup orders to the one that is closest to the customer.

With the pickup order transmitted through the cellular network to the handheld terminal, Joseph swings onto the highway and reaches the address in about 15 minutes. He leaves the van carrying his handheld terminal, and then walks into the building to retrieve the package. The customer has already filled out a package label called a *waybill* that includes the sender's information as well as the recipient's name, address, and other information. A unique, 12-digit tracking number is printed on the waybill along with a barcode that corresponds to the tracking number. Using his smart terminal, which includes a barcode scanner and keyboard, Joseph scans the barcode on the waybill and then types in the destination of the package, the type of service delivery (such as Priority or Standard Overnight), and the delivery deadline. If necessary, when Joseph returns to the van, the terminal connects to the printer and can output a more detailed routing label that contains all this information, which Joseph can then place on the package before putting it in the back of his truck.

The information Joseph enters on his handheld terminal after picking up the package is immediately transmitted back to the office using wireless digital cellular technology. The data is actually transmitted to a cellular tower, which retransmits the data to the office via the cellular carrier's central office and eventually through the Internet. This cellular technology is based on a standard commonly known as **4G (fourth generation)** technology, which uses 100 percent digital transmission for both voice and data. On a 4G cellular phone, the technology allows the user to make a voice call at the same time data is being transmitted or received.

 Check out the range of RFID-equipped and barcode-scan-equipped mobile computers at the Motorola Solutions Web site—for example, the MC65 model at *www.motorola.com* or the Intermec 70 series
TIP devices (that can be used for parcel delivery and pick-up) at *www.intermec.com*. Some of these devices can also be used as a cellular phone anywhere in the world. For portable wireless printers, check out *www.maxatec-europe.com* or *www.zebra.com*. You can also search the Internet using the terms in this tip to find other products.

4G sends data at rates that can theoretically reach over 150 Mbps when the devices are not moving and located in an area with few concurrent users, over 45 Mbps for slow-moving pedestrians, and over 20 Mbps in a fast-moving vehicle. 4G technologies are expected to harmonize all the different digital cellular specifications used around the world into a single standard. If Joseph happens to be located in an area outside the reach of the current 4G cellular networks, the terminal can use the interim technology known as **3G (third generation)**, which has a theoretical maximum data transmission rate of up to 21 Mbps and can realistically reach speeds between 3 to 11 Mbps. The latest cellular technology standard that is being deployed by carriers around the world is capable of even higher speeds and will be discussed in greater detail in Chapter 10. A digital cellular network is illustrated in Figure 1-7.

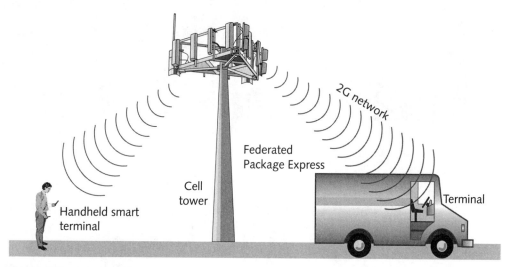

Figure 1-7 Digital cellular network

© Cengage Learning 2014

Wireless Local Area Networks

Joseph pulls his van into the FPE distribution warehouse, where packages are unloaded and sorted for delivery. His handheld terminal may still contain a large amount of important data, including shipping receipts and electronic customer signatures for deliveries. As soon as he pulls the van up to the loading dock, the terminal begins communicating with the computer network in the warehouse through a **wireless local area network (WLAN)**. A WLAN is an extension of a wired LAN, connecting to it through a device called a **wireless access point** (also **AP** or **wireless AP**). The AP relays data signals among all the devices on the wired network, including file servers, printers, and even other access points and the wireless devices connected to them. Each computer on the WLAN has a wireless network interface card (NIC). This card performs the same basic functions and looks similar to a traditional NIC except that it does not have a cable that connects it to a network jack in the wall. Instead, the wireless NIC has an antenna built into it. The AP is fixed in one place, although it can be moved when necessary, whereas the computing devices with wireless NICs have the freedom to move around the office area or sometimes an entire campus complex. An access point and wireless NIC are illustrated in Figure 1-8, but keep in mind that the wireless NIC in Joseph's handheld terminal is built in and is much smaller.

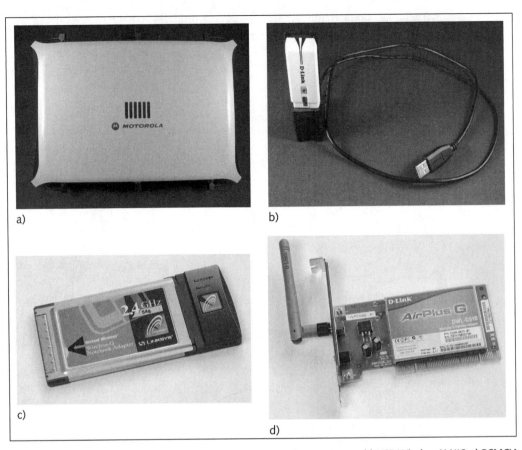

Figure 1-8 Clockwise from top left: a) access point with built-in antennas, b) USB Wireless N NIC, c) PCMCIA, and d) PCI Wireless NICs

© Cengage Learning 2014

WLANs operate based on networking standards established by the Institute of Electrical and Electronics Engineers (IEEE). The IEEE has published a series of standards, including the more recent **IEEE 802.11n-2009** (more commonly known as **IEEE 802.11n**), which provides for data transmission speeds of up to 600 Mbps and distances much greater than those of earlier versions of the standard. Depending on the standard used, most WLANs can transmit at speeds anywhere from 1 Mbps to 300 Mbps and cover distances of up to 375 feet (114 meters), under ideal conditions. In fact, even with some inexpensive 802.11n devices, today's WLANs can reach speeds of up to 450 Mbps. See Table 1-1 on page 18 of this chapter for a breakdown of the standards and their capabilities.

Throughout this book, "IEEE 802.11," "802.11," and "Wi-Fi" are used interchangeably, with or without a letter after the main standard number, 802.11. Although this may not be the most correct way to refer to these standards, it is the way everyone in the industry usually refers to them.

FPE currently uses an 802.11g network and is in the process of updating its WLAN to the higher capacity and faster 802.11n standard. The transmission of data from the handheld smart terminal, which includes all the important information regarding each pickup, is completed before the first package is unloaded from Joseph's van (see Figure 1-9).

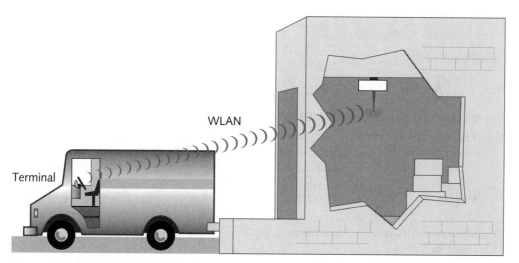

Figure 1-9 Warehouse WLAN

© Cengage Learning 2014

Joseph's wife, Ann, who also works for FPE, uses WLANs at her office, too. She does not have a desktop computer in her cubicle. Instead, FPE provides employees with portable notebook computers or tablet computers that they use while traveling, at home, and in the office. None of the notebook computers and tablets in the office are connected to the local area network by cables or wires. Instead, a WLAN provides connectivity among devices.

The WLAN renders devices portable. When Ann turns on her notebook computer at her desk, it establishes an automatic, preconfigured connection with the access point. She can now perform any network activity as if she were connected to the network with a cable. She can bring her notebook to a conference room for meetings. Once there, her notebook is still connected to the network, as are the notebooks of the other staff members in the meeting. Figure 1-10 illustrates the office WLAN.

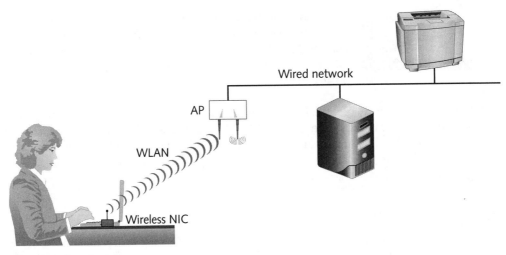

Figure 1-10 Office WLAN

© *Cengage Learning 2014*

Fixed Broadband Wireless

FPE's offices are spread over three locations: the main office, which is downtown; the warehouse, which is in a small industrial park; and the call center, which is at the edge of town. Through the years, FPE has tried a variety of connection types to link the three sites. Initially, FPE used expensive transmission lines leased from the local telephone company. **Integrated Services Digital Networks (ISDN)**, which transmits at up to 256 Kbps over regular phone lines, was soon replaced with T1 lines, which transmit at 1.544 Mbps, which was itself replaced with **optical fiber**. However, both of these types of communication lines cost several thousands of dollars per month. Technologies such as **cable modems**, which use a television cable connection, are generally only available in or near residential areas. **Digital subscriber lines (DSL)**, which use either regular or special telephone lines, are sometimes available, but the speed is dependent on the distance between FPE's main office and the nearest telephone switching office (CO, for "central office").

The best and lowest-cost way for FPE to link its office locations was to use a **wireless metropolitan area network (WMAN)**. A single WMAN link can cover an area of about 25 square miles, and it can be used to carry data, voice, and video signals. WMANs today are mostly based on the **IEEE 802.16 WiMAX Fixed Broadband Wireless** standard and use radio waves for data communications instead of optical or telephone wires. These networks use small custom antennas on the roof of each building in the WMAN. The signal is transmitted to the antenna of the receiving building. The transmission speed can be as high as 75 Mbps at distances of up to 4 miles (6.4 km), and 17 to 50 Mbps (depending on link quality) at distances over 6 miles (10 km) in a straight line, which is enough to interconnect all of FPE's offices. Newer versions of the IEEE 802.16m standard, which should be approved by the time this book is published, can achieve average speeds up to 100 Mbps, and up to 1 Gbps in a point-to-point link. The use of antennas substantially reduces the cost when compared to traditional wired connections, which require an infrastructure under city roads, are more prone to damage, and are more expensive to maintain.

Ironman triathlons, which can encompass a wide geographical area, can now be viewed live online using an IEEE 802.16 WMAN to connect cameras along the race route to the competition's Web site. Several channels of video are sent out, allowing enthusiasts to check what is happening at different race checkpoints simultaneously.

FPE has antennas on each of its three buildings in the area. Once the data from Joseph's van is transmitted to the network in the warehouse, it is sent to the main office by fixed broadband wireless. This process is illustrated in Figure 1-11.

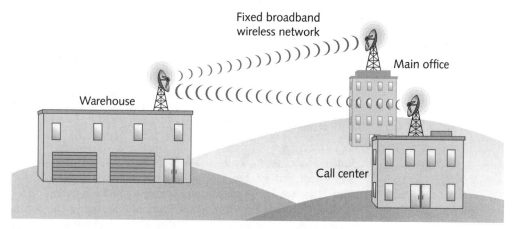

Figure 1-11 IEEE 802.16 wireless metropolitan area network (WMAN)

© Cengage Learning 2014

Wireless Wide Area Network

Personal computers use Web browsers to display Internet data. Based on user input, a Web browser requests Web pages to be displayed on the user's computer screen. The requested page is transmitted from a file server to the user's Web browser in **Hypertext Markup Language (HTML)**, the standard language for displaying content from the Internet. This model is illustrated in Figure 1-12.

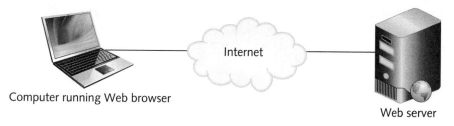

Figure 1-12 Browsing the World Wide Web on a PC

© Cengage Learning 2014

As Joseph's van is unloaded, he takes his afternoon break. Joseph pulls out his smartphone to surf the Internet. He can do this because his phone is a late model that includes an HTML version 5-compatible Web browser, which displays Web content the same way a computer does. Older cellular phones may be equipped with a **microbrowser**, a miniaturized version of a Web browser program that is based on version 1 of the **Wireless Application Protocol (WAP)** and cannot display graphics or pictures. Newer types of phones that are not smartphones use the **Wireless Application Protocol version 2.0 (WAP2)**, which provides a standard way to transmit, format, and display Internet data for small wireless devices such as cellular phones.

WAP2 follows the standard Internet model, allowing compatible cellular phones to display Internet content directly. The microbrowser in a WAP2-compatible cellular phone is a tiny program much like the browser on a PC, but the Web pages can be reformatted by the microbrowser for cellular phone screens, which usually have much less space. WAP2 is compatible with HTTP, the protocol used by Web server software to format data into Web pages, but it uses an earlier, simpler version (1.1) of HTTP rather than the version (4.1) in use by most of today's full-featured browsers. Most smartphones are also equipped with WAP2 browsers, which are used when they cannot access high-speed digital cellular services but still need to be able to access the World Wide Web.

 When a Web server sends a Web page back to a PC, it is sending HTML code and any files (such as graphics) required to assemble the page. The Web browser application program on the receiving device is responsible for interpreting the code and displaying the results on the screen; in other words, the Web server does not send a fully formatted image of the page. Rather, it sends only HTML code and text along with formatting instructions, images and graphics, and the relative positions where they should be displayed on the screen. It is the receiving device itself that is responsible for formatting and displaying the Web pages.

Some newer cellular phones can even display live television and can be used to access a variety of business applications. Most cellular phones today still use a version of **J2ME (Java 2 Micro Edition)** and are designed and optimized to display text, graphics, and even some limited animations on the small screens, as seen in Figure 1-13. Several business applications that support common file formats such as Microsoft Word or Excel spreadsheets can be downloaded and displayed on some mobile devices or can be available on demand on the Web. Using cellular phone technologies, companies can create a **wireless wide area network (WWAN)** that enables employees to access corporate data and applications from virtually anywhere—across the country, an entire continent, or, depending on the type of cellular phone or mobile device, anywhere around the world.

Figure 1-13 Displaying Web content on a smartphone

© Cengage Learning 2014

Joseph uses his cellular phone to connect to a Web server. Actually, the cellular phone connects to the nearest cell tower, which connects to the local telephone company, which in turn connects to an Internet provider and completes the link to the Web server. The contents of the Web page are then sent back and displayed on the screen of Joseph's phone.

The previous version of Wireless Application Protocol (WAP) allowed Web browsing from cellular phones using text only, and it required a gateway server between the Web server and the cellular phone. In the original version of WAP, the text information (but not the images) contained in a Web page was extracted and translated by the WAP gateway (or WAP proxy) server from HTTP into a WAP-specific format called Wireless Markup Language (WML) and broken down into a series of pages called "cards." These cards could be displayed on the small screen of a cellular phone, one at a time.

The Wireless Landscape

Most of the Kirkpatrick's activities, in a typical day, could not be attempted—much less completed—without wireless technology. It's clear that wireless communication is no longer reserved only for high-end users. Instead, it has become a standard means of communication for people in many occupations and circumstances, as shown in Figure 1-14. As new wireless communications technologies are introduced, they will become even more integral to our lifestyle and will continue to change how we live. Table 1-1 summarizes these technologies; Figure 1-15 compares their capabilities.

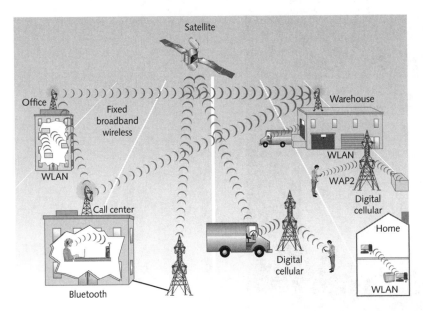

Figure 1-14 Wireless communications

© Cengage Learning 2014

Wireless Technology	Range (Transmission Distance)	Maximum (Average) Speed
RFID	1 inch (2.5 centimeters) to 300 feet (100 meters), depending on frequency and type of tag	A few thousand bits-per-second (Kbps)
Bluetooth version 4	Class 3: 3.3 feet (1 meter) Class 2: 33 feet (10 meters) Class 1: 330 feet (100 meters)	1 Mbps (721.2 Kbps) to 24 Mbps (version 4 only)
WiGig and WirelessHD	150 feet (50 meters)	7–10 Gbps (3–5 Gbps)
WLAN 802.11n	375 feet (114 meters)	300–600 Mbps (140–400 Mbps)
WLAN 802.11g	300 feet (90 meters)	54 Mbps (22–26 Mbps)
WMAN 802.16 WiMAX	35 miles (56 kilometers)	75 Mbps (20–40 Mbps)
WMAN 802.16m WiMAX	35 miles (56 kilometers)	100 Mbps (40–60 Mbps) to 1 Gbps (point-to-point)
3G digital cellular	16 miles (up to 25 kilometers to tower), then anywhere in the world via other networks	21 Mbps (2–11 Mbps)
4G digital cellular	Typically, 16 miles (up to 25 kilometers) to tower, then anywhere in the world via other networks	20 Mbps–150 Mbps (4–25 Mbps)
Satellite	Worldwide	Greatly varying speeds, with each transmission experiencing about a quarter second (250 milliseconds) delay

Table 1-1 Wireless data communications technologies

© Cengage Learning 2014

The speeds of wireless networks vary greatly, depending on the number of users connected, the amount of data traffic, the amount of interference present at the time, and many other factors that will be discussed in later chapters.

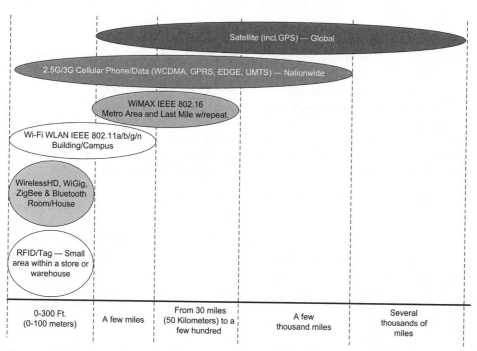

Figure 1-15 Comparing wireless communications technologies

© Cengage Learning 2014

Just as the number of wireless devices will dramatically increase, so will the number of job opportunities to support these new technologies. Professionals such as wireless engineers, wireless local area network managers, and wireless technical support personnel will be needed to build wireless networks and assist wireless users. The job market for these new careers is exploding and will continue to grow.

NOTE Worldwide expansion of wireless has surpassed all expectations. This has made it difficult for market research companies to provide accurate estimates of growth. In areas of central Africa, for example, where banking systems and a communications infrastructure practically do not exist, customers do not have a credit history, and the majority of the population survives on less than $1.00 a day, a cellular phone operator estimated it might have 36,000 customers by the end of one year. Instead, it had 38,000 subscribers within three weeks.

NOTE A team of anthropologists recently studied wireless device usage among people around the world. They noted several cultural differences in how wireless products were perceived. In Sweden, wireless phone devices become an extension of users' personalities. In France, users are more concerned about how the phone looks than the underlying technology or what it can do. In Great Britain, shy people find wireless devices help them overcome their reticence and reach out to others. In Japan, wireless usage helps citizens break through social barriers, a common obstacle in that culture. In the United States, there's concern about people developing information overload from being available 24 hours a day. And in India, many business appointments and even major transactions are often accomplished using text messaging on cellular phones.

Digital Convergence

Users are constantly demanding more functionality from their computers, and as a result, wireless devices such as cellular phones and PDAs are being combined into single devices, what we today call smartphones. These devices have also continued to add capabilities. Whereas they were initially used only as appointment calendars, phonebooks, and phones, today they can play computer games with sophisticated graphics, play both short- and full-length movies, and play music as well as provide Web access and run business and utility software while connecting via the cellular network or WLANs. Some carriers even provide users with the ability to watch live television programs on their smartphones.

Digital convergence refers to the power of digital devices—such as desk and laptop computers and wireless handhelds like smartphones—to combine voice, video, and text-processing capabilities as well as to be connected to business and home networks and to the Internet. The same concept applies to the development of VoIP networks, which use the same protocols and media (both wired and wireless) that once carried only data to carry two-way voice conversations. Wireless networks in general play an important part in digital convergence as users demand to be connected to their data and voice networks at all times, wherever they may be. Cellular providers in North America and Europe are beginning to introduce TV programming; depending on the device, we can even have access to on-demand movies and Internet radio.

The recent and upcoming advances in wireless technology and standards discussed in this book will enable an ever-wider range of applications for wireless devices. There are now smartphones that incorporate all voice and data communications in addition to providing entertainment functions and allowing the user to make payments and debits directly from a bank or prepaid account, and many more devices with these same capacities will be introduced in the near future. Today, people in Finland can purchase a ticket, pay for a bus or streetcar ride, buy a drink from a pop machine, order movie tickets, and so forth just using their cellular phones. They don't need to carry a wallet.

In China and many other Asian countries, more people use cellular phones than computers to access the Internet and e-mail, check news reports, and watch movies.

Wireless Applications

Almost every type of business needs a computer network, but many are unable to install traditional cabled networks because of the physical limitations of such systems. Wireless networks can go where regular wired networks couldn't. Wireless applications—the use of wireless communications technologies in conducting day-to-day business activities—can be found in any industry whose employees need the mobility and freedom to conduct business without being confined to a specific location. Industries and fields such as education, construction, and health care are among those using wireless technologies to make a number of activities occur more quickly and conveniently.

Education

Wireless technology is ideal for schools. An instructor can create a classroom presentation on a notebook computer in his home or school office, then carry the computer right into the classroom. He does not have to plug and unplug cables to attach to the campus network. Instead, the notebook automatically connects to the classroom network as soon as the instructor walks into the room; it can even connect to multimedia display projectors without using wires. Teachers can also distribute handouts directly to students who have brought their own wireless devices to class, and they can conduct pop quizzes in which students submit their answers directly and immediately.

The wireless connection also frees students from having to go to a specific computer lab or the library to get on the school's computer network. They can access the school network wirelessly from almost any location on campus. As students move to different classrooms in different buildings, they remain connected to the network. Wireless education makes computing resources available to students and teachers from anywhere at any time.

Wireless technology translates into a cost savings for colleges. Traditional classrooms become fully accessible computer labs without the expense of additional wiring and infrastructure. And colleges no longer have to consider the expense of adding open computer labs for students because everyone can access the resources from any building on campus or, in some cases, while outdoors.

You can search YouTube for a video called "Classroom of the Future." This short video provides an overview of many of the wireless advances being employed in today's schools.

Home Entertainment

Since 2006, a number of manufacturers have introduced products designed to enhance the home entertainment experience by enabling people to distribute all forms of digital media throughout the home. From wireless speakers to media players, game consoles, DVD players, televisions, digital video recorders (DVR), and multimedia personal computers, several large manufacturers are adding wireless networking capability to their products. Multimedia PCs enable movie and audio enthusiasts to download, distribute, and control all forms of digital entertainment from anywhere in the house. The specialized wireless networking software and hardware simplifies processing of sound, video, and pictures. You can send music, movies, or pictures to a stereo receiver, TV set, portable device, or PC located anywhere in the house. Begin watching a movie in the family room, if you wish, then move to the bedroom and finish watching the show from there. You can also download the files to your digital media portable devices, such as MP3 and video players, which can be used while roaming throughout the house.

Although there are many such multimedia-capable devices on the market today, three notable ones are Apple TV, WD TV Live Plus, and Boxee. Both Apple TV and Boxee come with built-in wireless, and WD TV Live Plus is compatible with a wide range of USB wireless NICs. Once connected to a television and a WLAN, these devices are able to access and play media stored in networked disk drives or computers, display Internet content directly, and allow users to rent or purchase movies and music from a variety of sources. You can search the Web for more information on these products.

Home Control Systems

In addition to multimedia, several manufacturers are making wireless systems that enable us to control lights, heating, ventilation, air conditioning, drapes, alarms, door locks, and various home appliances from locations throughout the home or even from a smartphone or tablet anywhere in the world. These systems, several of which use the **ZigBee Alliance** communications protocols and the IEEE 802.15.4 standard, enable devices like light switches and wall sockets to communicate with one another, thereby allowing us to control the entire home environment. This can help keep the home secure by turning lights on and off at preset times or by randomly increasing and decreasing the time by up to a half hour, to make the home look "lived-in." It can also make the environment more comfortable when we get home from work. And, finally, it's more "green," given that lights and devices can be automatically turned off and the temperature can be adjusted when no one is home.

Health Care

Administering the correct medication is a major concern in the health care industry. It is estimated that incorrectly administered medication results in hundreds of thousands of medical emergencies annually. Typically, printouts of prescriptions are posted in the pharmacy area of a health care facility. As the medications are dispensed for delivery to a patient, they are crossed off the list. However, because the paper record cannot always be updated immediately, there is a possibility that a patient will get an extra dose of medication before an order for a new or changed medication has been processed. This potential problem necessitates duplicate documentation, with nurses first checking the printout to determine the medication and dosage to be given, then noting on paper that the medication was actually given, then later entering the data into the hospital's database.

Wireless point-of-care computer systems based on smartphones, tablet computers, or wireless-equipped computers mounted on movable carts allow medical staff to access and update patient records immediately. Many hospitals are using portable devices with barcode scanners or RFID and a wireless connection. Without connecting and disconnecting cables, health care professionals can immediately document a patient's medication administration in the computer while moving from room to room. Nurses and doctors can identify themselves to the computer system or be automatically detected by a real-time location system. The patient's barcoded or RFID-enabled armband is then scanned, and all medications that are currently due for that patient are brought up on the screen. The medications to be administered are sealed in pouches that can be read by a device connected to the computer. Nurses identify the medications before opening the package. An alert immediately appears on the screen if the wrong medication or incorrect amount is selected. After administration, the nurse indicates through the wireless network that the medication has been given, electronically signing the distribution form. A hard copy can be printed out as needed.

The system immediately verifies that medication is being administered to the correct patient in the correct dosage, which eliminates potential errors and documentation inefficiencies. The documentation process now takes place at the bedside, where care is delivered, which improves accuracy. In addition, all hospital personnel have real-time access to the latest medication and patient status information.

 Select medical groups are now beginning to provide their physicians smartphone software, a portable printer, and prescription-writing software. This technology is intended to reduce errors associated with illegible handwritten prescriptions and can transmit drug orders to the pharmacy via the hospital's WLAN or the Internet.

Even telephones are now being connected to hospital IEEE 802.11 WLANs, employing VoIP technology. Doctors and nurses no longer have to be paged over the PA system, nor do they have to be in an office or nursing station to access lab results. Doctors can also consult with specialists while at a patient's bedside, and the specialists can be more easily reached, no matter where they are in the hospital. Cellular phones have been banned from health care facilities due to their potential for interfering with diagnostic equipment, but handsets that can connect to an IEEE 802.11 WLAN and use VoIP are allowed, and they are making hospitals far more efficient.

 Wireless real-time location systems are also being implemented in hospitals around the world to track equipment, staff, patients, and doctors, and to identify the potential spread of contagious diseases in hospitals, a major problem that is made worse by the advent of antibiotic-resistant bacteria (see *www.aeroscout.com*, *www.sonitor.com*, and *www.infonaut.ca*). Some of these wireless systems are also being connected to hand-washing stations and hand-sanitizer stations to track whether doctors and nurses are complying with hospital and government regulations dealing with hand hygiene.

Doctors can now monitor a patient's vital signs remotely. A graphical application running on a smartphone can display a patient's heart rate and electrocardiogram and can monitor a patient's blood pressure and other vital signs. This can be done via Wi-Fi if the doctor is in the hospital, or through the cellular network after she leaves the facility, or from anywhere in the world where cellular phone service is available (see *www.airstriptech.com*).

Government

Many cities around the world are deploying broadband and Wi-Fi wireless networks that let residents, city employees, contractors, and utility staff access the Internet, collect and transmit data to central databases, and so forth. For example, building inspectors can update permit data while at the construction site. City employees can locate and monitor municipal vehicles. Police officers can watch live streaming video feeds to help them fight crime. And visitors to the city can access the Internet in key areas, which promotes tourism and stimulates the local economy. Nearly every day, there's another news report that a city is either planning or deploying a wireless network.

Allegany County in western Maryland has been reaping the benefits of an IEEE 802.16 network since before the 802.16 standards were ratified. The county's $4.7 million AllCoNet2 project uses 16 radio towers configured in a ring to deliver broadband connectivity to schools, libraries, and government buildings. To avoid conflict with Internet service providers, the city allows them to resell the excess capacity of the county's broadband network at a reduced rate to commercial users, which further stimulates economic development in the region.

Many other cities use wireless technology to provide free Internet access to residents and to attract visitors and businesspeople. The city of Fredericton in the Canadian province of New

Brunswick deployed a system that covers the entire downtown business district and uses a mix of technologies. IEEE 802.16 wireless broadband connects all the major points, and an IEEE 802.11 WLAN is available in the major downtown streets as well as in restaurants, bars, and many other retail businesses. These options provide residents with free Internet access from notebook computers, tablets, and smartphones. In 2005, the city won a major award for innovation as a result of this project. The city of Hamilton in Ontario, Canada uses an IEEE 802.11 WLAN to read smart electrical meters. These meters monitor business and residential hourly electricity consumption and report back to the city's utilities commission.

Military

Military forces around the world use a large variety of both commercial and dedicated wireless communications devices. The latest devices allow military personnel in the field to use voice and the Internet as well as receive and transmit full-motion video, maneuver remote control survey drones, use digital battlefield maps, and so on. Most military technology is considered part of national security, and detailed information about it is generally available only to military personnel or to those with the proper security clearances.

Office Environments

Thanks to wireless technologies, employees in all lines of work never have to be away from the data they need to help them make decisions. In addition to the accessibility of networked data, wireless technologies allow businesses to create an office where the traditional infrastructure doesn't exist. Typically, an office space must be wired with computer cables for network connections and telephone wires for telephones. With wireless technologies such as WLAN and Bluetooth, that expensive cabling infrastructure, which is difficult to troubleshoot and modify, is no longer necessary. This means that an office can be created in a very short period of time with minimum expense. For example, a hotel conference room that may not have the infrastructure to support a wired network can quickly be turned into a wireless networked office environment. During office renovations or reorganization, employees can move to another location in the building or to a completely different place and can be connected immediately, saving businesses the expense of rewiring the entire office.

Event Management

Managing spectators attending a sporting event or concert can be a daunting task. Each attendee has a ticket, and there are special passes for the press and team officials. However, tickets can be lost, stolen, or counterfeited. Attempting to identify a stolen or counterfeit ticket as thousands of spectators are waiting to be admitted has until now been almost impossible. But several large arenas and stadiums are now turning to wireless systems to facilitate this process.

Event tickets are printed with a unique barcode and have an RFID tag embedded that is then scanned at the venue's point of entry using handheld or integrated turnstile hardware, which in turn is connected to a wireless network. The network instantly validates the ticket and then sends a signal back to the turnstile that permits the patron to enter the arena. This technology is very difficult to reproduce, can prevent the use of counterfeit tickets and can also be used to identify stolen or duplicated tickets.

The wireless point-of-entry turnstiles can provide organizers with a real-time look at traffic flow, thus helping a venue effectively manage its staff and determine where additional people are needed. Advertisers can also tailor their marketing based on who is entering at which gate on wireless display screens installed near the entry points.

In addition, wireless technologies are changing the entertainment experience itself. In several major stadiums, wireless transmissions of in-progress game statistics are available to any fan in the stadium with a wireless device, such as a notebook or tablet computer, or even with a portable media player or video-enabled smartphone. Fans can also view instant replays of the event they are attending or watch replays from other games around the country. In the Arizona Cardinals' football stadium, fans can use their wireless devices to play fantasy football or order concessions and have them delivered to their seats.

Travel

Because wireless technology creates mobility, the travel industry was one of the first to embrace it widely. Wireless global positioning systems (GPS) that tie into emergency roadside assistance have become standard features on many automobiles sold today. **Satellite radio** transmission of over 150 music and talk stations solves the problem of losing a station outside its transmission range. Satellite radio is a subscription service, meaning that users pay a monthly fee for the privilege of listening to the stations without any commercial interruptions. The OnStar roadside assistance service uses GPS and cellular technology to link the vehicle and driver to a central service center. Users can also use the system to make phone calls using the cellular network. Although the system has been exclusively available to GM vehicle owners for several years, electronics and auto accessory retailers now sell it to the general public as OnStar FMV (For My Vehicle), with a user interface built into the rearview mirror (see Figure 1-16).

Figure 1-16 OnStar user interface mounted on the rearview mirror

Source: Courtesy of General Motors

Airport terminals are likewise turning to wireless technologies. Most large airport terminals in North America transmit wireless signals that passengers can pick up on their wireless notebook and tablet computers or smartphones while waiting for their flights. For a nominal fee (or at no cost in some airports, such as Pearson International in Toronto, Canada), they can also surf the Internet or read e-mail as well as check or change flight schedules, and so forth.

Even the airplanes themselves are being equipped with wireless data access. Several large airlines—Lufthansa, Scandinavian Airlines, Singapore Airlines, China Airlines, Korean Air, and many others—are offering wireless Internet capabilities to passengers on cross-country or long-haul flights. Like their Earth-bound counterparts, these passengers can access the Internet or view their corporate data and e-mail from their seats while in flight. Air Canada began a pilot project to offer wireless Internet access on short flights between Toronto, Montreal, and New York City.

City transit systems are also "going wireless." People in Finland can purchase bus, train, and movie tickets (not to mention a can of soda) without ever needing to show a piece of paper. The cost is debited automatically from their bank accounts, and in most cases they simply present a two-dimensional barcode on their phone screens when entering the cinema or bus. Tram tickets in Amsterdam, Holland are equipped with an RFID chip and antenna. Although they look and feel like a regular cardboard ticket, to use them you simply wave the ticket by a box placed near the doors when you board and exit the tram. The unit makes a sound to indicate that your ticket is still valid (usually for one hour) or to let you know that you will need to purchase a new one if your current one has expired.

Construction

Although at first glance the construction industry may not seem to be a prime candidate for wireless technologies, in reality it benefits greatly. Special rugged tablet computers are being manufactured to allow engineers and architects to review drawings and plans at the job site. One challenge for builders is that each construction phase must be completed before the next can begin. For example, if the concrete footings for a new building cannot be poured, then the entire project must be put on hold. This series of events often means idle construction employees and last-minute schedule adjustments. Information from the job site, such as a tardy subcontractor or a problem with materials, could be relayed back to the main office for rescheduling of workers to other sites to prevent idle time.

Because foremen are often at multiple sites during a day's work, filing daily payroll paperwork can be a challenge. Payroll clerks often wrestle with scrawled or illegible notes and are unable to contact the foreman on the job for clarification. The paperwork problems can be eliminated when foremen enter time sheet information on a tablet computer and transmit it to the main office.

Construction equipment such as bulldozers and earth graders also participate in wireless networks by being fitted with wireless terminals, turning them into "smart" equipment. A GPS on a bulldozer can provide location information accurate to within a foot or, in some cases, an inch. The exact location of the dig coordinates can be transmitted to a terminal on the bulldozer, which displays a color-coded map to guide the operator. Smart equipment can be connected through wireless transmissions back to the home office, which tracks engine hours and equipment location. Wireless terminals in the engine's diagnostic system can send an alert when the oil needs to be changed or other maintenance operations are due.

Warehouse Management

Managing a warehouse stocked with inventory can be a nightmare. New products arrive continually and must be inventoried and stored. When products are shipped out of the warehouse, they must be located and then transferred to the correct loading dock so they can be placed on the right truck. Then, employees must update the stock database to reflect the outgoing shipment. A mistake in any one of these steps can result in a warehouse stocked with products that it cannot locate, irate customers receiving the wrong items, or a store running out of goods to sell.

Implementing wireless technology is essential in many warehouse operations. By equipping all of the warehouse's machinery and personnel with wireless networking devices, managers can use warehouse management system (WMS) software to supervise all the activities, from receiving through shipping. And because this network is tied into the front-office computer system, managers can have statistics that are always current.

Pallet loads arriving from locations outside the receiving warehouse come with barcoded pallet labels. The bar coding includes product identification numbers, product code dates or expiration dates, originating plants and lines of manufacture, and sequentially assigned serial numbers. As pallets arrive, a forklift operator scans the barcode label with his portable wireless device. This device sends the data to the wireless network, where the warehouse software immediately designates a storage location for the pallet and relays the information back to the computer on the forklift. A warehouse employee prints out a barcode and fixes it to the pallet. The forklift operator then transports the pallet to the designated storage location. A barcode label suspended from the ceiling for floor locations or attached to a rack face identifies every storage location. The operator scans that barcode to confirm that the pallets are being put in the correct location before depositing the load.

In the front office, orders for merchandise to ship out are received and entered into the computer that connects to the WLAN in the warehouse. The WMS software manages order picking, balances workloads, and selects pick sequences for forklift operators. The dock control module of the WMS then releases orders for picking. A forklift operator locates the correct storage location, scans the barcode of the pallet, and then ferries it to the shipping dock to be loaded onto a truck.

In the near future, most of the barcode functions, including inventory counting, will be replaced by RFID tags, removing the need for printing and affixing labels. Many large retailers already have instructed their suppliers to implement RFID in all the products they purchase. Some highly sophisticated warehouses are operating with fully automated pallet machines and forklifts that can process the storing and retrieving of products completely without human intervention.

Environmental Research

One of the most challenging aspects of documenting research while in the field is that it is difficult and dangerous to extend long cables or install heavy equipment inside, say, deep caves or on the tops of trees. Today, in places that were previously difficult to access and monitor, scientists are using small, battery-powered or solar-cell-powered sensors that can connect to a WLAN. For example, transmitter-equipped sensors located at the tops of tall trees monitor the effects that ultraviolet rays are having on our forests due to the holes in the ozone layer. The computer equipment that records the sensor readings can be installed in a much more accessible location nearby, along with large, heavy batteries or generators, and it can communicate with the sensors using wireless technology. This capability has proven to be a major breakthrough in many scientific fields and has helped collect data that, until recently, was very difficult—if not impossible—to record.

Industrial Control

Because of their size and complexity, large manufacturing facilities, such as automotive assembly plants, find that it is often impossible to install a full-featured network using very long cables. If machines need to be monitored, it can take hours or even days for a technician to access every machine and record or download the status of each piece of equipment. Wireless networking can solve that problem. Remote sensors called **motes** can connect to a WLAN, then collect data and transmit it to a central location. Manufacturing managers can monitor their equipment from an office, detecting problems instantly. Technicians in a control room can monitor the status of every machine or device and dispatch a technician to perform work on the equipment when necessary.

Wireless Advantages and Disadvantages

As with any new technology, wireless communications offers both advantages and disadvantages.

Advantages of Wireless Networking

There are many advantages to using wireless technology compared to wired networks. These include mobility, ease of installation and lower cost, increased reliability, and more rapid disaster recovery.

Mobility The freedom to move about without being tethered by wires is certainly the principal advantage of a wireless network. Mobility enables users to stay connected to the network no matter where they roam within the network's range. Many workers who can't stay tied to a desk—such as police officers who need to access vehicle registration and infraction records or inventory clerks who work in large stores or warehouses—are finding that wireless data communications has become vital to the performance of their jobs.

Wireless technology is also permitting many industries to shift toward an increasingly mobile workforce. Many employees spend large portions of their time away from a desk—whether they are in meetings, working on a hospital floor, or conducting research. Notebook computers—and, more recently, tablet computers, smartphones, and other portable devices—allow these employees to enjoy added convenience, including access to the company network and business applications.

One characteristic of today's business world is "flatter" organizations, meaning there are fewer management levels between top executives and regular employees. Much of the work is done in teams that cross both functional and organizational boundaries, requiring many team meetings away from the employees' desks. The need for immediate access to network resources exists even while these meetings are taking place. WLANs are again the solution to the problem. They give team-based workers the ability to access the network resources they need while collaborating in a team environment.

Easier and Less Expensive Installation Installing network cabling in older buildings can be a difficult, slow, and costly task. Facilities constructed prior to the mid-1980s were built without any thought given to running computer wiring in each room. Thick masonry walls and plaster ceilings are difficult (and messy and loud) to drill holes through and snake cabling around. Some older buildings have asbestos—a potentially cancer-causing insulation material—that has to be completely removed before cabling can be installed. And there are often restrictions on modifying older buildings that have historical value.

In all these instances, a WLAN is the ideal solution. Historical buildings can be preserved, dangerous asbestos doesn't need to be disturbed, and difficult drilling can be avoided by using a wireless system. And, of course, eliminating the need to install cabling can result in significant cost savings for companies.

WLANs also make it easier for any office—in either an old or a new building—to be modified with new cubicles or furniture. No longer does the design for a remodeled office first have to consider the location of the computer jack in the wall when relocating furniture. Instead, the focus can be on creating the most effective work environment for the employees.

The amount of time required to install network cabling is generally significant. Although the cable itself is not very expensive, installers must pull wires through the ceiling and then drop cables down walls to network outlets. This can usually take days or even weeks to complete, and in countries where labor costs are high, this can make it very expensive. And except in the case of brand-new buildings, employees must somehow continue their work in the midst of the construction zone, which is often difficult to do. Using a WLAN eliminates any such disruption.

 Using your favorite search engine, look for "installing wireless in a castle." There are a couple of interesting articles by Motorola and Aruba Networks, two of the most successful manufacturers, about their ventures into networking old buildings.

Increased Reliability Network cable failures may be the most common source of network problems. Moisture from a leak during a thunderstorm or a coffee spill can erode metallic conductors. A user who shifts the computer on her desk may break the network connection. When cables are installed in the ceiling or behind walls, a cable splice that is done incorrectly can result in unexplainable errors that are very difficult to identify and locate. Using wireless technology eliminates these types of cable failures and increases the overall reliability of the network.

Disaster Recovery Accidents happen every day. Fires, tornados, and floods can occur with little, if any, warning. Any organization that is not prepared to recover from such disasters will find itself quickly out of business. A documented disaster recovery plan is vital to every business if it is to get back to work quickly after a calamity.

Because the computer network is such a vital part of the daily operation of a business, the ability to have the network up and working after a disaster is critical. Many businesses are turning to WLANs as a major piece of their disaster recovery plans, in addition to using IEEE 802.11n wireless networking as the main connectivity solution. Savvy planners keep laptop computers with wireless NICs and access points in reserve along with backup network servers. Then, in the event of a disaster, managers can quickly relocate the office without needing to find a new facility with network wiring. Instead, the network servers are installed in the building along with the access points, and the laptop computers are distributed to the resettled employees.

Future Applications Digital wireless communications has expanded almost beyond human imagination since the second edition of this book was published in 2006, and this trend will continue at a very fast pace. Wireless networks have overcome most of the speed limitations since the original standards were approved. At one time, paperless tablet devices like the ones you may have seen in old Star Trek movies were practically unthinkable. Today, they're becoming commonplace in homes and offices and are being used for a very wide range of applications. Patients can swallow tiny wireless cameras installed in capsules that enable doctors to conduct examinations inside a person's body without the need for exploratory surgery. It is virtually impossible to make predictions or to cover every single application here. Every day, a new application for wireless data transmission is thought of or implemented.

Disadvantages of Wireless Networking

Along with the many advantages of wireless technology, there are disadvantages and concerns, including radio signal interference, security issues, and possible health risks.

Radio Signal Interference Because wireless devices operate using radio signals, the potential for two signals to interfere with each other exists. Virtually any wireless device can be a source of interference for other devices.

Several common office devices emit signals that may interfere with the receivers in a WLAN. These devices include microwave ovens, elevator motors, and other heavy electrical equipment, such as manufacturing machines, photocopiers, certain types of outdoor lighting systems, theft protection systems, and cordless telephones. These may cause errors to occur in the transmission between a wireless device and an access point. In addition, Bluetooth, WLAN 802.11b/g/n, and ZigBee devices can all operate in the same radio frequency, potentially resulting in interference between such devices in spite of efforts to design these radios to automatically avoid interference.

Interference is nothing new for a computer data network. Even when using cables to connect network devices, interference from fluorescent light fixtures and electric motors can sometimes disrupt the transmission of data. The solution for wireless devices is the same as that for standard cabled network devices: locate the source of the interference and eliminate it. This can usually be resolved by moving a photocopier or microwave oven across the room or to another room. Most wireless devices can identify that an error has occurred in the transmission and retransmit the data as necessary.

   Outside interference from AM or FM radio stations, TV broadcast stations, or other large-scale transmitters is not an issue because they operate on vastly different frequencies and power levels. However, GPS and satellite transmissions can sometimes affect Bluetooth and WLAN transmissions outdoors.

Security Because a wireless device emits radio signals that can cover a wide area, security becomes a major concern. It is possible for an intruder to be lurking outdoors with a notebook computer and a wireless NIC with the intent of intercepting the signals from a nearby wireless network. Because much of a business's network traffic may contain sensitive information, this is a real concern for many users.

However, some wireless technologies can provide added levels of security. A special coded number can be programmed into an authorized wireless device, which must then transmit this special number prior to gaining access to the network; otherwise, it is denied access. Network managers can also limit access to a wireless network by programming it with a list of approved wireless devices. Only those devices on the list will be allowed access. As a further protection, data transmitted between the access point and the wireless device can also be encrypted or encoded in such a way that only the recipient can decode the message. If an unauthorized user were to intercept the radio signals being transmitted, he or she could not read the messages being sent.

Health Risks

Health Risks Wireless devices contain radio transmitters and receivers that emit radio frequency (RF) energy. Typically, these wireless devices emit low levels of RF while being used. Scientists know that high levels of RF can produce biological damage through heating effects (this is how a microwave oven is able to cook food). However, it is not known if lower levels of RF can cause adverse health effects. Although some research has been done to address these questions, no clear picture of the biological effects of this type of radiation has been found to date.

Most wireless devices also emit very low levels of RF energy when in stand-by mode. These levels are considered insignificant and do not appear to have health consequences.

In the United States, the Food and Drug Administration (FDA) and the Federal Communications Commission (FCC) set policies and procedures for some wireless devices, such as cellular telephones. However, only the World Health Organization (WHO) currently conducts and sponsors research on this topic. In May 2011, the WHO indicated that these devices can be "carcinogenic" but also included a statement that no adverse health effects had been established yet. The announcement was related to the use of cellular handsets, which place the transmitter antenna very close to the user's head during a call. One of the easiest ways to address this issue is to always use a headset when talking on a cellular device.

The FCC and FDA, along with the Environmental Protection Agency (EPA), established RF exposure safety guidelines for wireless phones back in 1996. Before a wireless phone is available for sale to the public, it must be tested by the manufacturer and certified that it does not exceed specific limits. One of the limits is expressed as a specific absorption rate (SAR). SAR relates to the measurement of the rate of absorption of RF energy by a wireless phone user. The FCC requires that the SAR of handheld wireless phones not exceed 1.6 watts per kilogram, averaged over 1 gram of tissue.

Science today does not yet permit anyone to draw a definitive conclusion about the safety of wireless mobile devices. Although there is no proof that using mobile wireless devices has adverse health effects, it is wise to be aware of the possibility and monitor ongoing scientific research.

Chapter Summary

- Wireless communications has become commonplace today and is quickly becoming the standard in the business world. Remote wireless Internet connections and entire wireless computer networks are making many network-based business activities faster and more convenient.

- Wireless networks and devices are found in all circles of life today. Home users can implement WLANs to connect different devices. Meanwhile, Bluetooth, WirelessHD and WiGig are beginning to be implemented on consumer devices, making it possible to connect many different types of home audio and video equipment over short distances. The WAP2 protocol is used along with programming languages such as J2ME to access Web sites and private networks from cellular phones, but HTML version 5 is already being introduced in all new models. WLANs are also becoming the standard in business networks. Fixed broadband wireless is used to transmit data at distances up to 35 miles (56 kilometers), and satellite transmissions can send data around the world. Digital cellular networks are used to transmit data at up to 21 Mbps.

- Wireless wide area networks will enable companies of all sizes to interconnect their offices without the high cost charged by telephone carriers for their landline connections.

- WLAN applications are found in a wide variety of industries and organizations, including the military, education, business, entertainment, travel, construction, warehouse management, and health care.

- Remote sensors capable of communicating using wireless technologies are used in large manufacturing facilities to monitor equipment and for scientific research.

- Mobility—the ability to move around without being connected to the network by a cable—is the primary advantage of a WLAN. Other advantages include easier and less expensive installation, increased network reliability, and support for disaster recovery.

- There are some disadvantages to a WLAN. Radio signal interference, security issues, and health risks may slow down the growth of these technologies for a while, but there are so many advantages that use of wireless data will very likely continue to grow and to be an integral part of our lives.

Key Terms

3G (third generation)   A digital cellular technology that can send data at up to 21 Mbps over the cellular telephone network.

4G (fourth generation)   A digital cellular technology that can transmit and receive data at theoretical speeds up to 20 Mbps when users are moving fast and up to 150 Mbps (theoretically) when users are moving slowly or are stationary.

access point (AP or wireless AP)   A device that receives the signals and transmits signals back to wireless network interface cards (NICs).

Bluetooth   A wireless standard that enables devices to transmit data at up to 721.2 Kbps over a typical maximum distance of 33 feet. Bluetooth can transmit data farther, but devices that can use this capability are rare.

cable modem   A technology used to transmit data over a television cable connection.

digital convergence   The power of digital devices such as desktop computers and wireless handhelds to combine voice, video, and text-processing capabilities as well as to be connected to business and home networks and to the Internet.

digital subscriber line (DSL)   A technology used to transmit data over a telephone line.

Hypertext Markup Language (HTML)   The standard language for displaying Web pages.

Institute of Electrical and Electronic Engineers (IEEE) 802.11n-2009   A set of standards that allows WLAN computers to transmit data at speeds ranging from 1 Mbps to a maximum of 600 Mbps. 802.11n (or 802.11n-2009, as the specification is now called) can also make use of the 5 GHz band in addition to the 24 GHz band.

Institute of Electrical and Electronic Engineers (IEEE) 802.16 Fixed Broadband Wireless   A set of standards, some established and some still under development, for fixed and mobile broadband wireless communications that allows computers to communicate at up to 75 Mbps and at distances of up to 35 miles (56 km) in a point-to-point configuration. This set of standards also allows the use of both licensed and unlicensed frequencies.

Integrated Services Digital Networks (ISDN)   A technology that transmits data over telephone lines at a maximum of 256 Kbps.

J2ME (Java 2 Micro Edition)   A variation of the Java programming language designed for use in portable devices such as PDAs and cellular phones.

link manager   Special software in Bluetooth devices that helps identify other Bluetooth devices, creates the links between them, and sends and receives data.

microbrowser   A tiny browser program that runs on a WAP or WAP2 cellular phone.

motes   Remote sensors used for collecting data from manufacturing equipment or for scientific research, which can communicate using wireless technology.

optical fiber   A glass strand, about the thickness of a human hair, that carriers data signals encoded in a laser beam.

personal digital assistant (PDA)   A handheld computer device used for taking notes, making appointments, creating to-do lists, and communicating with other devices.

piconet   A small network composed of two or more Bluetooth devices that are exchanging data with each other.

radio frequency identification (RFID)   A small tag placed on product packaging and boxes that can be remotely activated and read by remote sensors. The data about the product is then transferred directly to an information-processing system for inventory control, location tracking, and item counting.

radio modules   Small radio transceivers built onto microprocessor chips and embedded into Bluetooth devices, which enable them to communicate.

repeater   A device commonly used in satellite communications that simply "repeats" the signal to another location.

satellite radio   A pay-for-service radio broadcast system that transmits digital programming directly from satellites to a network of ground-based repeaters and that holds the signal regardless of the listener's location. Users must purchase special receivers and pay a monthly subscription fee to listen to commercial-free music channels. Because the digital transmission is decoded at the receivers, the sound quality is also much better than conventional FM radio.

smartphone   A device that combines a cellular phone with the capabilities of a personal digital assistant (PDA). These devices provide the user with the ability to enter appointments in a calendar, write notes, send and receive e-mail, and browse Web sites, among other functions.

T1   A technology used to transmit data over special telephone lines at 1.544 Mbps.

Ultra Wide Band (UWB)   A wireless communications technology that allows devices to transmit data at hundreds of megabits or even gigabits per second at short distances—up to 6 feet (2 meters) at the higher speeds and up to 150 feet (50 meters) at lower speeds.

Voice over Internet Protocol (VoIP)   A technology that allows voice telephone calls to be carried over the same network used to carry computer data.

Wi-Fi   A certification label awarded to IEEE 802.11 WLAN-compatible wireless devices that pass all interoperability tests performed by an organization called the Wi-Fi Alliance. The acronym is often thought to stand for Wireless Fidelity, but this is a common misconception. The name was chosen by the alliance purely for marketing reasons and is not an acronym at all.

WiGig   An alliance of companies involved in developing a common wireless specification for connecting computers, communication, and entertainment devices over short ranges, using the 60 GHz band at multi-gigabit speeds.

Wireless Application Protocol (WAP or WAP2)   A standard for transmitting, formatting, and displaying Internet data on cellular phones. WAP can display only text. WAP2 supports HTML and can display color and pictures.

wireless communications   The transmission of user data between devices without the use of wires.

WirelessHD   A specification for the wireless transmission of high-definition video (HD), multichannel audio and data between consumer devices such as televisions, stereo systems, and Blu-ray players, using the 60 GHz frequency band.

wireless local area network (WLAN)   A local area network that is not connected by wires but instead uses wireless technology. Its range extends to approximately 100 meters and has a maximum data rate of 600 Mbps. Today's WLANs are based on IEEE 802.11a/b/g/n standards.

wireless metropolitan area network (WMAN)   A wireless network that covers a large geographical area such as a city or suburb. The technology is usually based on the IEEE 802.16 set of standards and can span an entire city, covering distances of up to 35 miles (56 km) between transmitters and receivers or repeaters.

wireless network interface card (wireless NIC)   A device that connects to a PC to transmit and receive network data over radio waves. It includes an antenna for wireless communication between networked devices.

wireless personal area network (WPAN)   A very small network that typically extends to 10 meters or less. Due to its limited range, WPAN technology is used mainly as a replacement for cables. *See also* piconet and Ultra Wide Band.

wireless wide area network (WWAN)   A WAN that uses cellular phone technologies and encompasses any geographical region, including the entire globe.

ZigBee Alliance   An organization that creates protocols and specifications for devices used to wirelessly control lighting, as well as security and energy systems, for home and industry.

Review Questions

1. Ultra Wide Band technology is used primarily for _____.

    a. displaying Web pages on a cellular phone

    b. connecting devices inside the home at very high speeds

    c. finding the location of a car within a city

    d. transmitting data at distances of up to 35 miles

2. Bluetooth devices communicate using small radio transceivers called _____ that are built onto microprocessor chips.

    a. receivers

    b. transponders

    c. radio modules

    d. link managers

3. _____ provides a standard way to transmit, format, and display Internet data on cellular phones.

    a. WLAN

    b. WAP2

    c. HTML

    d. WML

4. IEEE 802.11n devices can be as far as 375 feet apart and can send and receive data at rates up to _____ million bits per second (Mbps).

    a. 75

    b. 600

    c. 100

    d. 54

5. Each Bluetooth device uses a _____, which is special software that helps identify other Bluetooth devices.

    a. frame

    b. link manager

    c. repeater

    d. bridge

6. Bluetooth can send data through physical barriers, like walls. True or False?

7. Most Bluetooth devices can transmit data at up to 1 Mbps over a distance of 33 feet (10 meters). True or False?

8. A wireless network interface card performs basically the same functions and looks similar to a traditional network interface (NIC) card. True or False?

9. An Earth station transmits to a satellite at one frequency, and the satellite regenerates and transmits the signal back to Earth at another frequency. True or False?

10. Eliminating installation costs is a disadvantage of a WLAN. True or False?

11. The automatic connection between various Bluetooth devices creates a network called a(n) _____.

    a.   micronet

    b.   small net

    c.   piconet

    d.   Intranet

12. The new fourth generation (4G) cellular technology will allow data to be transmitted at a maximum speed of _____.

    a.   2 Mbps

    b.   1 Gbps

    c.   20 Mbps

    d.   150 Mbps

13. An 802.11 wireless NIC, when configured to communicate with a wired network, sends its signals through invisible radio waves to _____.

    a.   another computer directly

    ,b.   an access point

    c.   a wireless server

    d.   the Internet

14. _____ uses wireless transmissions for data communications as much as 35 miles apart.

    a.   Wi-Fi

    b.   WirelessHD

    c.   WiGig

    d.   WiMAX

15. "WAP2" stands for _____.

    a.   Wireless Access Protected version 2

    b.   Wi-Fi Access Protocol 2

    c.   Wireless Application Protocol version 2

    d.   Wireless Protected Access II

16. Explain the role of an access point (AP) in a WLAN.

17. Explain how a WAP cellular phone sends and receives Internet data.

18. Explain how a WLAN can be used in a classroom.

19. Describe how wireless networks can reduce installation time.

20. Explain how implementing a wireless network can be helpful in case of disaster recovery.

Hands-On Projects

Project 1-1

Understanding the terminology and being able to explain what something means to a person who does not work in the same field is an essential part of any support technician's job today. Although many of the following terms will be discussed and reviewed in later chapters, you should become familiar with as many of them as possible. Research these terms and write a one-paragraph description of each of them, in your own words.

HSPA+	Ultra Wide Band (UWB)	Parity check
Frequency channel	WiGig	Bandwidth
Free-space optics	Wireless repeater	Wi-Fi protected access
Spread spectrum	Frequency hopping	Yagi
RFID	Personal area network	Metropolitan area network
Wireless bridge	Data encryption	Data integrity

Project 1-2

To be successful in today's job market, wireless technicians and engineers must be familiar with the industry and have a broad knowledge of the various products available. For example, you may have heard about the Verizon Palm Pre smartphone, but who actually makes this phone? If you needed a full set of specifications for this device, you would have to contact Hewlett-Packard because Verizon does not actually manufacture it and may not provide you with all the data that you need. Using the Internet, research one or two manufacturers (not distributors or resellers) of the products listed below, then provide links to information about the products.

Wireless controllers	Enterprise-class access point
RFID tags	RFID readers
Bluetooth access point	Wireless bridge
ZigBee development kits	WiMAX sector controller
Wi-Fi antennas	Free-space optics transceivers
Smartphones	Bluetooth class 1 adapter (300 feet/100 meter range)

Project 1-3

Following the news about the wireless industry is a very good way to learn who uses a particular technology and for what purpose. Use local news services or the Internet to find a school, hospital, manufacturing plant, warehouse, or other business in your area that is switching to wireless technology. If possible, try to interview some of the people involved to determine why they are making the change. Ask what benefits and drawbacks they considered. Write a one-page paper describing what you find out.

Project 1-4

Because a wireless device transmits radio signals over a broad area, security becomes a major concern. What are some of the security concerns with using a WLAN? What security options are available? Write a one-page paper that addresses these concerns. Use the Internet and information from hardware and security vendors as additional resources.

Project 1-5

Using the Internet, find the latest information about health concerns using wireless technologies. What studies are currently under way? What issues are of concern? What are the official positions of the government departments on these issues? Write a one-page paper about your findings.

Real-World Exercises

Tenbit Wireless Inc. (TWI) is a company consisting of 50 wireless networking specialists who assist organizations and businesses with network planning, design, implementation, and problem solving. You have recently been hired by TWI to work with one of its new clients, Vincent Medical Center (VMC), a large health care facility, concerning their wireless needs.

Each day, doctors and nurses throughout VMC's facility attend to patients, update medical records, issue prescriptions, and order medical exams. VMC has deployed a sophisticated suite of medical software that stores all patient records, exam results, and diagnoses. The system is also fully integrated with VMC's pharmacy and can process purchase orders, payments, and receipts as well as inventory and shipments, and it meets the tightest patient information protection regulations established by the federal government.

Exercise 1-1

VMC is interested in learning about the possibilities of upgrading its infrastructure and deploying a wireless network to allow doctors, nurses, and all staff members to access information from anywhere within the medical facility (two buildings). VMC does not want to spend money installing additional network cabling connections to every patient room. VMC has asked you to make a presentation to its administrator regarding the use of a WLAN. Create a presentation to deliver to the staff about WLANs. Be sure to cover the following points:

- Greater mobility for doctors and nurses
- Ease and cost of installation

- Easier network modifications
- Increased network reliability
- Radio signal interference
- Security

Exercise 1-2

VMC would like to know about potential interference that medical equipment such as X-ray machines and CT and MRI scanners might cause on the WLAN, or vice versa. Prepare a report to present to the hospital administrators addressing their concerns.

Exercise 1-3

After your presentation, the physicians and nurses seem very interested in the potential of the WLAN. However, VMC also has an outdated telephone system that provides mobile cordless handsets but is no longer supported by the manufacturer. Without the ability to use voice communications from anywhere in the facility, the staff cannot see how a wireless network alone will solve their dilemma. Create a presentation that expands on your first one and proposes a solution based on the existing WLAN.

Exercise 1-4

Although some doctors have notebook computers already equipped with wireless NICs, VMC is also interested in providing other staff members with portable data communication equipment, but at a lower cost than notebooks. The devices should be able to transmit prescriptions directly to the central system. The pharmacy would then deliver medications to patients right away. VMC would also like to be able to check on the status of these pharmacy orders. VMC administrators have asked your opinion regarding using smartphones on the WLAN or tablet computers, and they have told you that their software can handle these requirements through a Web server. Prepare to present your recommendations to VMC's management team.

Challenge Case Project

A syndicated magazine is writing an article about Bluetooth technology and has asked Tenbit Wireless Inc. for information. Form a team of three or four consultants and research Bluetooth technology. Focus on the current specifications and on the future of Bluetooth. Provide information regarding its problems and concerns by some vendors. Also provide estimates regarding how you envision Bluetooth or any other proposed technology will be used in home, office, and personal applications.

chapter 2

Wireless Data Transmission

After reading this chapter and completing the exercises, you will be able to:

- Discuss the two types of wireless transmission
- Explain the properties of a wave, such as amplitude, wavelength, frequency, and phase
- Describe the basic concepts and techniques related to the transmission of data by radio waves

Consider the wireless cellular telephone that may now be in your pocket or sitting on your desk. If you were to take that telephone apart, you would find an array of pieces: chips, a microphone, a speaker, resistors, capacitors, and other parts. Yet much more than that mobile cordless telephone is needed to complete a call. Some of the other elements involved are the cellular towers, the equipment that manages your call as you move from one cell to another, and all the equipment at the telephone company's central office that directs your call to the correct recipient. Moreover, if you're calling someone overseas, additional equipment, such as satellites or underwater cables, may be used to complete the international connection.

Trying to make sense of a modern communications system is truly mind-boggling because of the sheer number of components that are involved. How can we begin to understand how it all works?

One approach is the bottom-up method, which looks first at the individual elements or components that make up a system, then ties them all together to show how the system works. This chapter uses the bottom-up approach to set the foundation for our exploration of wireless communications and networks. You will apply the concepts covered in this chapter to more specific technologies discussed in later chapters. If you are studying or working in the IT field, you already know how data is represented inside a computer or digital device. In this chapter, you will learn how the various types of wireless signals are used to transmit data. Finally, we'll delve a little deeper into how data is transmitted using radio waves.

To keep things simple, we will use the **American Standard Code for Information Interchange** (or **ASCII** code), which uses only eight bits to represent all the letters of the alphabet, all the numerals, and several symbols. In this book's Appendix, you will find a complete ASCII table showing the hexadecimal value for all the characters and symbols.

Recall that all numbers—such as street-address numbers or any other numbers that are not intended to be used by the computer in calculations—are stored as text (i.e., as character data, without numerical value). In this case, the number is stored in ASCII code. For example, the decimal value 47 is normally stored as its binary equivalent (00101111) in the computer memory. When using ASCII code, the decimal number 4 is stored as hexadecimal 34 (0x34), which uses one byte (00110100 in binary); and the number 7 is stored in another byte in the computer memory using the ASCII code 0x37 (00110111 in binary). See Table 2-1.

First byte	Hexadecimal	3				4			
	Binary	0	0	1	1	0	1	0	0
Second byte	Hexadecimal	3				7			
	Binary	0	0	1	1	0	1	1	1

Table 2-1 ASCII code for 47 as stored in computer memory

© Cengage Learning 2014

One of the limitations of ASCII is that there are not enough codes for all the symbols used by foreign languages. Another coding scheme, called Unicode, is therefore used today. Unicode can represent 65,535 different characters because it uses 16 bits, or two bytes, instead of eight bits, or a single byte, to represent each character. In addition, when one bit out of every byte is used for error control (parity), the ASCII code can only represent 128 different characters.

Wireless Signals

Wired communications uses either copper wires or fiber-optic cables to send and receive data. Wireless transmissions, of course, do not use these or any other visible media. Instead, data signals travel on electromagnetic waves. All forms of electromagnetic energy—gamma rays, radio waves, even light—travel through space in the form of waves. The light from a flashlight or the heat from a fire also moves through space as waves. These waves, known as electromagnetic waves, don't require any special medium (such as air) or any type of conductor (such as a copper wire or optical fiber). Instead, they travel freely through space at the speed of light: 186,000 miles per second (300,000 kilometers per second).

Practically everything in the universe emits or absorbs electromagnetic radiation. Figure 2-1 illustrates the electromagnetic spectrum, which lets you compare each of the properties of electromagnetic radiation—such as the lengh of an electromagnetic wave—with the sizes of some common objects and items. The middle portion of the figure shows the commonly used names for these waves, and the bottom portion shows the range of frequencies—that is, how many waves occur in one second—along with where these waves usually originate. For example, in the visible light emitted by a light bulb, the number of waves that occur in one second is higher than 10^{13}, and each wave is about the size of a bacteria—that is, 0.000001 meters (3.281×10^{-6} feet). In this chapter, you will learn about each of these wave properties and the significance it has in wireless data communications.

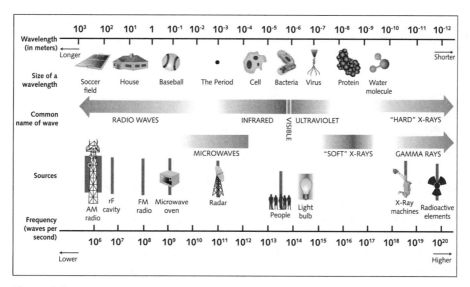

Figure 2-1 Electromagnetic spectrum

© Cengage Learning 2014

NOTE Many people, when asked what type of medium is used to send and receive wireless transmissions, answer "airwaves." If this were the case, radio signals would not propagate in space, where there is no air. Wireless transmissions use electromagnetic (EM) waves as the medium, not air or empty space.

Infrared Light

There are two basic types of waves by which wireless data are sent and received: infrared light and radio waves. For centuries, flashes of light have been used to transmit information. Bonfires set on top of hills were once used to relay messages. Ocean vessels sent signals from ship to ship or from ship to shore using light. In 1880, Alexander Graham Bell demonstrated an invention called the photophone, which used light waves to transmit voice information. Transmitting modern computer or network data using light follows the same basic principle.

Because computers and data communication equipment use binary code, it is easy to transmit information with light. Just as binary code uses only two digits (0 and 1), light has only two properties (off and on). Sending a 1 in binary code could result in a light quickly flashing on; sending a 0 could result in the light remaining off. For example, the letter "A" (ASCII 0x41 or 01000001) could be transmitted by light as *off-on-off-off-off-off-off-on*. This concept is illustrated in Figure 2-2.

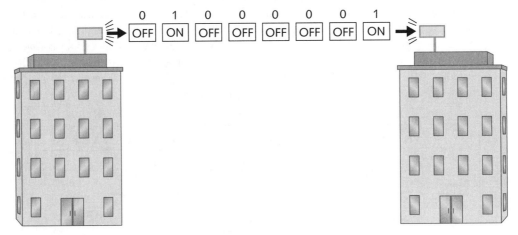

Figure 2-2 Transmitting a message using visible light

© Cengage Learning 2014

What type of light should be used to transmit these signals? Transmitting data using visible light flashes, such as a strobe light, would be very unreliable because other lights could be mistaken for the transmission signal or another bright light could wash out the light flashes. In addition, visible light (and even some frequencies that are invisible to the human eye) can be blocked by various obstacles—fog, heavy rain, etc.—and is therefore not a reliable medium for data transmissions.

However, visible light is only one type of light. All the different types of light that travel from the Sun to the Earth make up the **light spectrum,** and visible light is just a small part of that entire spectrum. Some of the other forms of energy within the light spectrum, such as X-rays, ultraviolet rays, and microwaves, are also invisible to the human eye. **Infrared light,** some of which is invisible, has many of the characteristics that visible light has because it is adjacent to visible light on the light spectrum. Yet, it is a much better medium for data transmission because it is less susceptible to interference from other sources of visible light.

Each wavelength within the spectrum of visible light represents a particular color. This is because the differing wavelengths of light waves bend at a different angle when passed through a prism, which in turn produces different colors. The colors that visible light produces are red (R), orange (O), yellow (Y), green (G), blue (B), indigo (I), and violet (V). Visible light is sometimes referred to as ROYGBIV.

Infrared wireless systems require that each device have two components: an **emitter**, which transmits a signal, and a **detector**, which receives the signal. (These two components are almost always combined into one device.) An emitter is usually a laser diode or a light-emitting diode (LED). Infrared wireless systems send data by the intensity of the light wave instead of whether the light signal is on or off. To transmit a 1, the emitter increases the intensity of the electrical current and, consequently, the intensity of the infrared light, which indicates a pulse to the receiver. The detector senses the higher-intensity pulse of light and produces a proportional electrical current (see Figure 2-3).

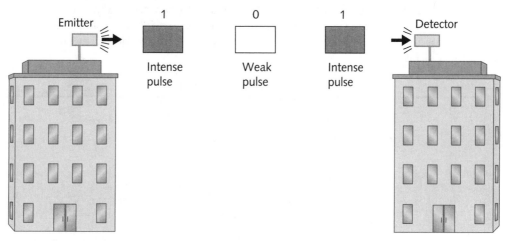

Figure 2-3 Light pulses

© Cengage Learning 2014

Infrared wireless transmission can be either directed or diffused. A **directed transmission** requires that the emitter and detector be directly aimed at one another (called the **line-of-sight** principle), as shown in Figure 2-4. The emitter sends a narrowly focused beam of infrared light. The detector has a small receiving or viewing area. A television remote control, for example, uses directed transmission, and this is the reason that most of us point the remote at the TV or other remote-controlled devices.

Although TV remote controls generally use directed transmission, with a fresh set of batteries you should be able to point the remote at a white wall directly across from the TV set and use it to change channels, increase the volume, and so on—as long as nothing else is blocking the path of the invisible infrared light.

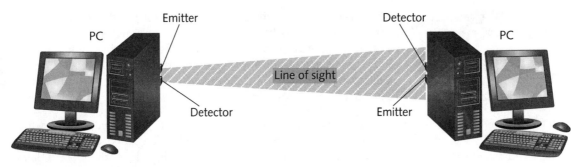

Figure 2-4 Directed infrared transmission

© Cengage Learning 2014

A **diffused transmission** relies on reflected light. With diffused transmissions, the emitters have a wide-focused beam instead of a narrow beam. For example, the emitter might be pointed at the ceiling of a room and use it as a reflection point. When the emitter transmits an infrared signal, the signal bounces off the ceiling and fills the room with the signal. The detectors are pointed at the same reflection point and can detect the reflected signal, as shown in Figure 2-5.

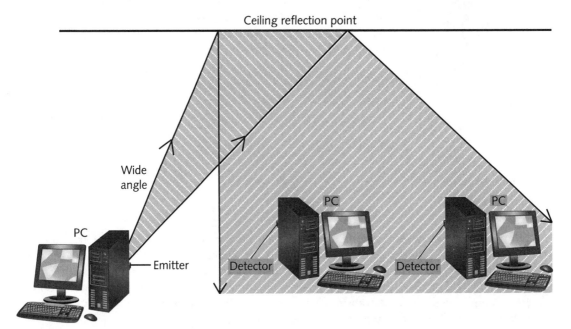

Figure 2-5 Diffused infrared transmission

© Cengage Learning 2014

Infrared wireless systems have several advantages. Infrared light neither interferes with other types of communications signals (such as radio signals) nor is it affected by other signals, except light. In addition, because infrared light does not penetrate walls, the signals are kept inside a room. This makes it impossible for someone elsewhere to listen in on the transmitted signal.

However, there are several serious limitations to infrared wireless systems. The first limitation involves the lack of mobility. Directed infrared wireless systems use a line-of-sight principle, which makes it challenging for mobile users because the alignment between the emitter and the detector would have to be continually adjusted. The second limitation is the range of coverage. Directed infrared systems, which require line of sight, cannot be placed in an environment where there is the possibility that anything could get in the way of the infrared beam (think of someone standing in front of your remote control while you are trying to change TV channels). This means that devices using infrared transmissions must be placed close enough to one another to eliminate the possibility of something moving between them. Due to the angle of deflection, diffused infrared can cover a range of only 50 feet (15 meters). And because diffused infrared requires a reflection point, it can only be used indoors. These restrictions limit the range of coverage.

Another significant limitation of an infrared system is the speed of transmission. Diffused infrared can send data at maximum speeds of only 4 Mbps. This is because the wide angle of the beam loses energy as it reflects. The loss of energy results in a weakening signal. The weak signal cannot be transmitted over long distances, nor does it have sufficient energy to maintain a high transmission speed, resulting in a lower data rate.

Because of these limitations, infrared wireless systems are generally used in specialized applications, such as data transfers between notebook computers, digital cameras, handheld data collection devices, PDAs, electronic books, and other similar mobile devices. In the past, laptop computers were almost always equipped with infrared interfaces; sadly, this is no longer true. If you still need an infrared interface today, you must purchase one that plugs into a USB port on the computer. Figure 2-6 shows an example of such a device.

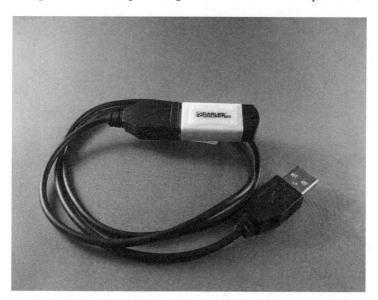

Figure 2-6 USB infrared adapter with extension cable

© Cengage Learning 2014

Some specialized wireless local area networks are based on the infrared method of transmitting data signals. These are used in situations where radio signals would interfere with other equipment, such as in hospital operating rooms, or when security is a concern, such as in some government and military installations.

Like other types of electromagnetic waves (such as visible light and heat), infrared light has limitations. Light waves, for example, cannot penetrate through most materials like wood or concrete, and heat rays are absorbed by most objects, including human skin (we feel infrared waves as heat). Solid objects and even dust and humidity (water molecules in the atmosphere) can limit the distance that light and infrared waves can travel. See Figure 2-7.

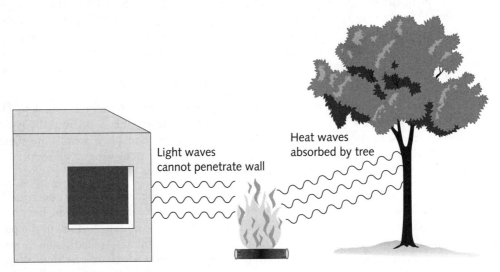

Figure 2-7 Limitations of light and heat waves

© Cengage Learning 2014

Is there a wave in the electromagnetic spectrum that does not have the distance limitations of light or infrared? The answer is yes: radio waves.

Radio Waves

The second means of transmitting a wireless signal is by using radio transmission. Radio waves provide the most common and effective means of wireless communications today. To understand the basic properties of radio waves, imagine that you are watering your lawn with a garden hose. As you move your hand up and down, the water creates what look like waves that are also moving up and down, as shown in Figure 2-8.

Figure 2-8 Simulating a radio wave using a garden hose

© Cengage Learning 2014

The waves created by the garden hose have a shape that is similar to that of electromagnetic waves. Recall that energy travels through space or air in electromagnetic waves. Infrared light, visible light from a flashlight, and heat from a fire also move through empty space or through the air in the atmosphere as electromagnetic waves.

Another type of electromagnetic wave that travels in this fashion is called a **radio wave** (**radiotelephony**). When an electric current passes through a wire, it creates a magnetic field in the space around the wire. As this magnetic field radiates, it creates radio waves. Because radio waves, like light and heat waves, are electromagnetic waves, they move outward, usually in all directions.

Radio waves are free from some of the limitations that affect light and heat. Unlike heat waves, radio waves can travel great distances. Radio waves can also penetrate most solid objects (with the exception of metallic ones), whereas light waves cannot penetrate anything opaque or solid. Visible light waves and heat waves can be seen and felt, but radio waves are invisible. These characteristics are illustrated in Figure 2-9. Because of these characteristics, radio waves are an excellent means to transmit data without wires.

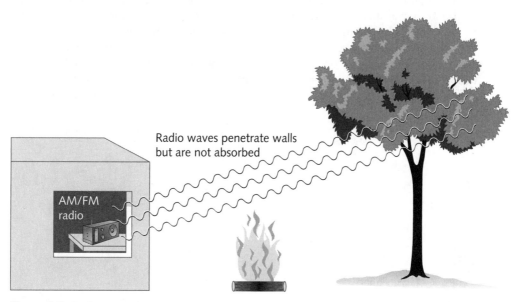

Radio waves penetrate walls but are not absorbed

AM/FM radio

Figure 2-9 Radio waves can penetrate most solid objects

© Cengage Learning 2014

How Radio Data Is Transmitted

Radio waves can be used to transmit data over long distances without the need for wires. The method by which these waves transport data involves several concepts. We will start by discussing the ways that analog and digital data are transmitted over radio waves.

Analog and Digital

When you create waves using a garden hose, the waves are continuous as long as the water is turned on and you keep moving your hand up and down. These waves represent an analog signal. An **analog signal** is one in which the intensity of the waves (**voltage** or **amplitude**) varies and is broadcast continuously—in other words, the signal has no breaks in it. Figure 2-10 illustrates an analog signal. Audio, video, voice, and even light are all examples of analog signals. An audio signal that contains a tone or a song is continuously flowing and doesn't start and stop until the tone or song is over.

Figure 2-10 Analog signal

© *Cengage Learning 2014*

Now, suppose that instead of moving the hose up and down, you were to hold it steady, place your thumb over the end of the garden hose for a second and then remove it. Water would stop flowing while your thumb was over the hose and then start flowing again when you removed your thumb. This on-off activity, shown in Figure 2-11, is similar to a digital signal. A **digital signal** consists of discrete or separate pulses, as opposed to an analog signal, which is continuous. A digital signal has numerous starts and stops throughout the signal stream—Morse code, for example, with its series of dots and dashes. Figure 2-12 illustrates a digital signal.

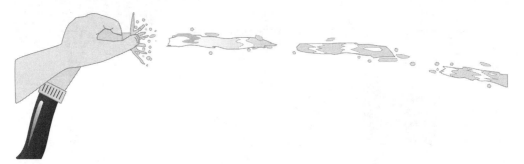

Figure 2-11 Simulating a digital signal with a garden hose

© *Cengage Learning 2014*

Figure 2-12 Digital signal

© *Cengage Learning 2014*

Computers operate using digital signals. If analog data, such as a video image or an audio sound, needs to be stored on the computer, it must be converted into a digital format before it can be stored and processed or interpreted by a computer.

Various techniques are used to convert the different types of analog data to digital data. For CD-quality stereophonic music (2-channels), the analog signal is measured (sampled) at the rate of 44,100 times per second; each sample is then stored in a digital format, using a minimum of 16 bits per sample. Using a number of other techniques, computers also compress digitized signals to minimize the total amount of storage space or the amount of data that needs to be transmitted.

To transmit a digital signal over an analog medium, as when two computers communicate over an analog telephone line or TV cable, a device known as a **modem** (**MOdulator/ DEModulator**) is used. A modem takes the distinct digital signals from a computer and encodes them into a continuous analog signal for transmission over analog phone lines. The process of encoding the digital signals (bits) onto an analog wave is called **modulation**. The modem at the other end of the connection then reverses the process by receiving an analog signal, decoding it, and converting it back into a digital signal.

Frequency and Wavelength

Now, think about holding a garden hose and slowly moving your hand up and down. You will create long waves, as shown in Figure 2-13. If you rapidly move your hand up and down, the waves become shorter, as shown in Figure 2-14. Depending on how fast you move your hand up and down, the peaks of the waves will be closer together or farther apart. This illustrates another property of waves, called the **wavelength**. The wavelength is the distance between any point in one wave **cycle** and the same point in the next wave cycle.

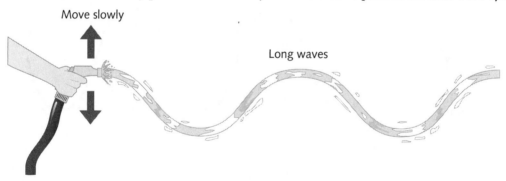

Figure 2-13 Long waves

© Cengage Learning 2014

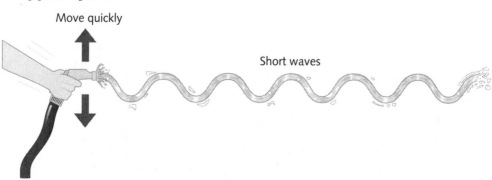

Figure 2-14 Short waves

© Cengage Learning 2014

The same variations occur with radio waves. The rate at which a radio circuit creates the waves (like moving the garden hose up and down faster or slower) will result in a different number of radio waves being created each second and the peaks becoming either closer or farther apart. This rate is a radio wave's **frequency**. That is, the number of times a cycle (which is composed of one top [positive] and one bottom [negative] peak) occurs within one second equals the frequency of a wave.

The wavelength is inversely proportional to the frequency, which means that when the frequency is high, the wavelength is short or small, and when the frequency is low, the wavelength is long.

Radio transmitters send what is known as a **carrier signal**. This is a **continuous wave (CW)** of constant amplitude (measured in volts) and frequency. This is essentially an up-and-down wave called an **oscillating signal** or a **sine wave**, as illustrated in Figure 2-15. A CW carries no useful information by itself. Only after it is modulated does it contain some kind of information signal, such as music, voice, or data; then, it is correctly called a carrier signal or carrier wave. A receiver is adjusted (or tuned) to the frequency of the carrier, and it ignores all the other frequencies.

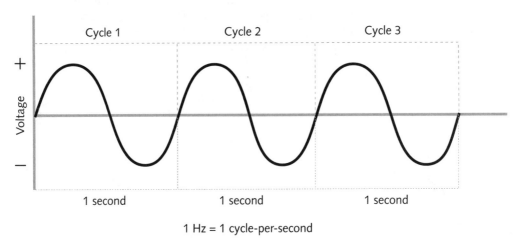

Figure 2-15 Sine wave (analog wave) and frequency

© *Cengage Learning 2014*

Notice in Figure 2-15 that the wave starts at zero, moves up to the maximum voltage (+), then down to the minimum voltage (−), and finally returns to its starting point (0) before beginning all over again. Whenever the wave completes its trip up, then down, and returns back to the starting point, it has finished one cycle. Recall that frequency is defined as the number of times a wave completes a cycle in one second.

Figure 2-16 illustrates two different frequencies. Notice that both the lower frequency and the higher frequency alternate to the same maximum and minimum voltage. A change in voltage does not create a change in frequency. Instead, changes in frequency result from how long it takes to reach the maximum, fall back to the minimum, and then return to neutral to complete a cycle.

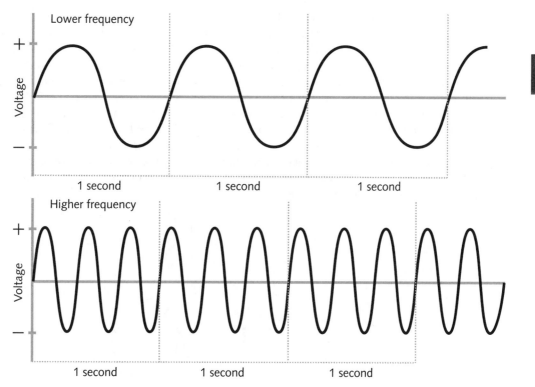

Figure 2-16 Two different frequencies; same amplitude

© Cengage Learning 2014

In electrical terms, the cycle produces what is known as an alternating current (AC) because it flows between negative (−) and positive (+). AC is the type of current that runs to the electrical outlets in a house, and it usually has a frequency of 60 Hz. Direct current (DC) is found in batteries. With DC, the current flows only from one terminal (−) to the other (+) and does not alternate. This lack of fluctuating movement also means that DC cannot be directly transmitted via an analog medium and cannot carry any data.

Although frequencies are measured by counting the number of complete wave cycles that occur in one second, the term **Hertz (Hz)** is used instead of cycles-per-second. A radio wave measured as 710,000 Hz means that its frequency is 710,000 cycles per second. Because of the high number of cycles in radio waves, metric prefixes are used when referring to frequencies. A **Kilohertz (KHz)** is 1,000 Hertz, a **Megahertz (MHz)** is 1,000,000 Hertz, and a **Gigahertz (GHz)** is 1,000,000,000 Hertz. The wave measured as 710,000 Hz is referred to as 710 KHz.

Frequency is an important part of music also. The frequency of the musical note A is 440 Hz, and middle C is 262 Hz. This means that when middle C is played, 262 pockets of higher air pressure pound against your eardrum each second.

Radio waves are usually transmitted and received using an **antenna**. An antenna is a length of copper wire, or similar material, with one end free and the other end connected to a receiver or transmitter. When transmitting, the radio waves created by the electronic circuit of the transmitter are fed to this antenna wire. This sets up an electrical pressure (voltage) along the wire, which will cause a small electrical current to flow into the antenna. Because the current is alternating, it flows back and forth in the antenna at the same frequency as the radio waves. When the electricity moves back and forth in the antenna at the same frequency as the radio waves, it creates both a magnetic field and an electrical field around the antenna. This continuous (analog) combination of magnetism and electrical pressure moves away (propagates) from the antenna the same way that water waves move away from the point of impact when you throw a rock in a pond. The result is an **electromagnetic wave (EM wave)**, as illustrated in Figure 2-17.

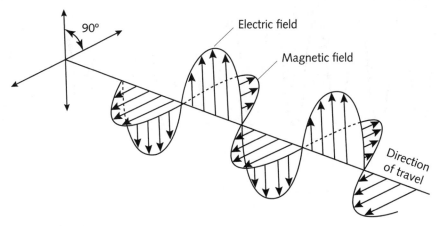

Figure 2-17 Electromagnetic wave consisting of electrical and magnetic fields

© Cengage Learning 2014

Antennas are also used to pick up transmitted radio signals. A very small amount of electricity moves back and forth in the receiving antenna in response to the radio signal (EM wave) reaching it. This results in a very small amount of current flowing from the antenna into the receiver, as shown in Figure 2-18. In Chapter 3, you will learn what needs to be done to this small current so that the receiver can demodulate it and retrieve the data that was transmitted.

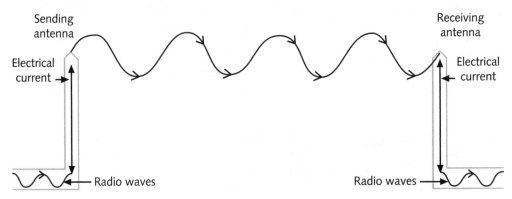

Figure 2-18 Radio antennas transmitting and receiving signals

© Cengage Learning 2014

Transmission Speed

Several different terms are used when referring to the transmission speed of radio waves. The electromagnetic waves themselves always travel at the speed of light, which is 186,000 miles per second (300,000 kilometers per second). When digital information is transmitted using radio waves, the speed of transmission is usually shown in **bits per second (bps)**, since the primary concern is how efficiently the data can be moved from one place to another.

Another term used in measuring the speed of radio transmission is *baud rate*. Recall that radio transmissions send out a carrier signal and that this signal can be changed or modulated. A **baud** is a change in that signal, and every time the signal changes, as you will learn later in this chapter, it defines the boundary of a signal unit. **Baud rate**, then, refers to the number of signal units (changes) per second that are required to represent the bits transmitted. The fewer signal units required, the better the system works, since the range of frequencies required for transmitting the signal is smaller.

Sometimes the terms *bps* and *baud rate* are used interchangeably, although they are not synonymous. This confusion originated with early computer modems. The first modems, for example, had speeds of 300, 600, and 1200 baud. These early modems used a simple modulation technique and were capable of transmitting at a maximum of one signal unit per bit transmitted; therefore, their speed in bps was the same as the baud rate, or 300, 600, and 1200 bps. For example, to transmit the letter U (0x55 ASCII or 01010101), it would take eight signal changes, one for each bit. Thus, the number of bits transmitted per signal unit (baud) was 1.

However, with later modems, it became possible to have a change in signal (a baud) represent more than one bit. A signal can be changed in several different ways, as explained later in this textbook; different changes result in different combinations of two bits (there can be up to four), each being assigned to one of four different signal changes. This is illustrated in Table 2-2.

Signal Change (Baud)	Bit Combination Represented
Signal W	00
Signal X	01
Signal Y	10
Signal Z	11

Table 2-2 **Bit representation of four signal changes**

© *Cengage Learning 2014*

The letters in Table 2-2 are simply used to differentiate four different types of signal changes. Today's analog modems transmit at a maximum rate of 4,800 baud, which is the maximum number of signal changes per second that a typical phone line can support. However, by using more complex modulation techniques, along with compression of the data, current modems can transmit data at speeds of up to 33,600 bps and receive data at up to 56,200 bps.

56 Kbps modems are a little different from 33.6 Kbps modems in that one end of the connection must be a digital connection. To achieve 56 Kbps download speed from the ISP, the signal conversion from analog to digital or from digital to analog must only happen at one end of the phone line. Because of this limitation, these modems achieve a high downstream speed (from the ISP side to the modem) of 56 Kbps. The maximum speed from the modem side to the ISP side, or upstream, is 33.6 Kbps.

A signal unit—that is, the change that is made to the signal that represents two bits—is known as a **dibit**. When a signal unit can represent three bits, it is called a **tribit**. If 16 different signal units are used, then four bits per signal unit can be represented (known as a **quadbit**). These characteristics are summarized in Table 2-3.

Name	Number of Signal Changes	Number of Bits Encoded Per Baud
Standard	1	1
Dibit	4	2
Tribit	8	3
Quadbit	16	4

Table 2-3 Signal changes (baud) vs. number of bits represented

© Cengage Learning 2014

Another term used when referring to transmission speed is **bandwidth**. Although this term is often used to refer to the maximum data transmission capacity, this is accurate only when referring to purely digital systems. Strictly speaking, in analog systems, bandwidth is defined as the range of frequencies that can be transmitted by a particular system or medium. In simple terms, bandwidth is the difference between the higher frequency and the lower frequency. Suppose a transmission for a human voice could be sent between 300 Hz and 3,400 Hz. The difference between the two frequencies (3,400 Hz minus 300 Hz) is 3,100 Hz, which happens to be the bandwidth of a human voice that is transmitted during a telephone conversation.

Digital Subscriber Line (DSL) modems usually transmit at speeds ranging from a few hundred Kbps to about 25 Mbps on a telephone line, at a distance of up to 2.5 miles (4 kilometers). The usable bandwidth of the pair of copper wires in a modern phone line is about 1 Megahertz. DSL takes advantage of the higher frequencies that can be transmitted on a phone line but that are not used for voice (above 4,000 Hz); it divides these into a large number of separate frequencies and transmits data bits at a few bps over several of them at the same time, resulting in the high data rates described earlier. Full coverage of DSL technology is beyond the scope of this book, but later chapters cover technologies that work in a very similar fashion.

Analog Modulation

Recall that the carrier signal sent in analog radio transmissions is simply a continuous electrical signal. It carries no information and is more correctly referred to as a CW. Only after information is added to it by modulation should it be called a carrier. **Analog modulation** is the representation of analog information by an analog signal. There are three types of modulation that can be applied to an analog signal to enable it to carry information: the height of the signal, the frequency of the signal, and the relative starting point, or **phase**, of the signal. Let's look at each type of modulation separately.

The height, frequency, and relative starting point of a signal (phase) are sometimes called the "three degrees of freedom."

Amplitude Modulation (AM) The height of a wave, known as the **amplitude**, can be measured in volts (electrical pressure). This is illustrated in Figure 2-19 with a typical sine wave. In **amplitude modulation (AM)**, the height of the wave is changed in accordance with the height of another analog signal, called the modulating signal. In the case of an AM radio station, the modulating signal is the voice of the announcer or the music, which is also an analog signal. The carrier wave's frequency and phase remain constant.

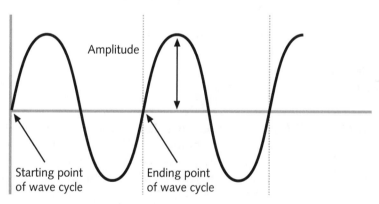

Figure 2-19 Amplitude of a signal

© Cengage Learning 2014

Amplitude modulation is used by broadcast radio stations. Because pure AM is very susceptible to interference from outside sources, such as lightning, it is not generally used for data transmissions. Figure 2-20 shows a carrier wave and a sine wave being used to modulate the carrier. The bottom portion of the figure shows the carrier wave after it has been modulated.

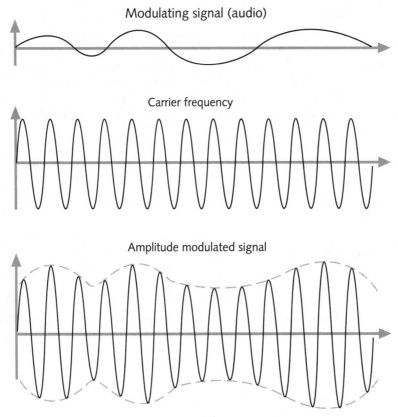

Figure 2-20 Amplitude modulation (AM)

© *Cengage Learning 2014*

Frequency Modulation (FM) In **frequency modulation** (FM), the number of waves that occur during one second undergoes change based on the amplitude of the modulating signal while the amplitude and the phase of the carrier remain constant. Figure 2-21 illustrates an FM signal and a simple modulating sine wave. The bottom portion of the figure shows the result of modulating the FM carrier in frequency. Note how the frequency changes proportionally, based on the change in amplitude of the input signal, which effectively allows the receiver to reproduce the signal with the correct amplitude (or the volume of the sound). In addition, the rate of change of the modulated signal also follows the rate of change of the input signal, which, in turn, allows the receiver to reproduce the frequency (pitch or tone) at the output.

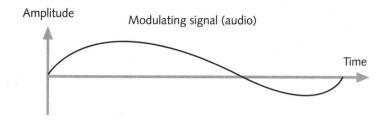

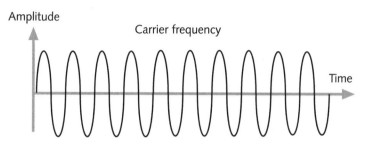

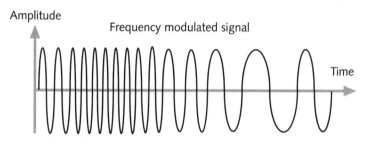

Figure 2-21 Frequency modulation (FM)

© Cengage Learning 2014

Like amplitude modulation, frequency modulation is often used by broadcast radio stations. However, FM is not as susceptible to interference from outside sources and is most commonly used to broadcast music programs. In addition, an FM carrier has a wider bandwidth, which allows it to carry Hi-Fi as well as stereophonic signals, with two separate sound channels.

 In most countries, FM radio stations broadcast between 88 MHz and 108 MHz, whereas AM stations transmit between 535 KHz and 1,700 KHz.

Phase Modulation (PM) In contrast to AM, which changes the height of the wave, and FM, which increases the number of waves per cycle, **phase modulation (PM)** changes the starting point of the cycle, while the amplitude and frequency of the carrier remain constant. Phase modulation is not generally used to represent analog signals.

A signal composed of sine waves has a phase associated with it. This phase is measured in degrees, and one complete wave cycle covers 360 degrees. A phase change is always measured with reference to some other signal. Because it would be very difficult to ensure that the wave cycles of a reference signal in two separate devices—the transmitter and the receiver—remain perfectly synchronized (in phase), PM systems almost always use the previous wave cycle as the reference signal. Figure 2-22 shows an example of four different phase shifts with respect to a reference signal shown at the top of the figure.

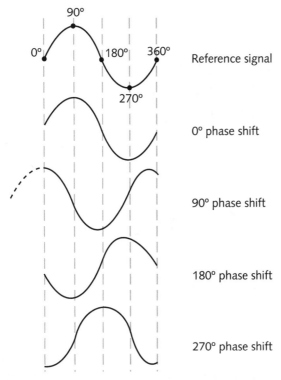

Figure 2-22 Visual representation of phase shift

© Cengage Learning 2014

 Although radio broadcasts use either amplitude modulation (AM) or frequency modulation (FM), television broadcasts actually use AM, FM, and phase modulation (PM). A television video signal uses amplitude modulation, the sound uses frequency modulation, and the color information uses phase modulation.

Digital Modulation

How can digital data be transmitted by an analog carrier signal when the medium used for transmission cannot be used with digital signals? The simple answer is that it can be done by modulating the analog signal or changing it to represent a 1 bit or a 0 bit.

Most modern wireless systems use **digital modulation,** which is the method of encoding a digital signal onto an analog wave for transmission over a medium that does not support digital signals, such as the atmosphere or the vacuum of space. In an analog system, the carrier signal is continuous, and amplitude, frequency, and phase changes also occur continuously because the input or modulating signal is still analog and therefore continuous. However, in a digital system that uses binary signals, the changes are distinct, which results in one of two states: a 1 or a 0, a constant positive or a constant negative voltage, on or off. For a computer to be able to understand these signals, each bit must have a fixed duration to represent a 1 or a 0 (more on digital signals later). Otherwise, the computer would not be able to determine when one bit ends and another one begins.

There are four primary advantages of digital modulation over analog modulation:

- It makes better use of the bandwidth available.
- It requires less power to transmit.
- It performs better when the signal experiences interference from other signals.
- Its error-correcting techniques are more compatible with other digital systems.

With digital modulation, as with analog modulation, there are three basic changes that can be made to the signal to enable it to carry information: the height, the frequency, and the relative starting point (phase) of the signal. However, with the need for faster transmission speeds, more binary signals (or bits) have to be crammed into the same number of wave cycles. The result is that in wireless communications there are now dozens of different types of modulation. For the most sophisticated modulations, it is practically impossible to show a graphic example of what the signals look like. This chapter covers a few basic methods of digital modulation; these methods serve as the basis for more sophisticated modulation techniques.

Binary Signals
Recall that with an analog signal the carrier wave alternates between the positive and negative voltage in a continuous cycle—that is, it doesn't stop. A binary signal can alternate between positive and zero volts or between a positive and a negative voltage. Data transmissions are typically sent in bursts of bits, meaning that some bits are transmitted, then the transmission momentarily stops. When there are no bits to be transmitted, no signal is transmitted. In analog systems, even when a radio station is not transmitting any sound, the carrier wave continues to be transmitted; in this case, your radio receiver simply does not detect any modulation of the carrier and therefore does not extract the original signal. Consequently, the receiver does not reproduce any sound even though the continuous carrier signal is still being transmitted.

Three types of binary signaling methods can be used. The **return-to-zero (RZ)** technique calls for the signal to rise (the voltage to increase) to represent a 1 bit. A 0 bit is represented by the absence of voltage, or 0 volts. This is illustrated in Figure 2-23. Notice that the voltage is reduced to 0 before the end of the period for transmitting a 1 bit. Also notice that the signal does not quite fill the bit period; this transition of the signal in the middle of a bit period is used to synchronize the transmitter and receiver.

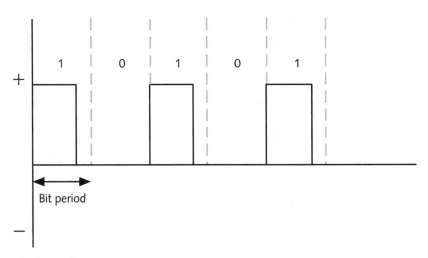

Figure 2-23 Return-to-zero (RZ)

© Cengage Learning 2014

The second method is known as the **non-return-to-zero (NRZ)** technique. With non-return-to-zero, the voltage signal remains positive (high) for the entire length of the bit period. In addition, if the next bit to be transmitted is the same as the previous bit, the signal does not change, remaining high for a 1 and low (0 volts or no voltage) for a 0. This effectively reduces the number of signal transitions (baud) required to transmit the message. As with RZ, there is no voltage when transmitting a 0 bit (see Figure 2-24).

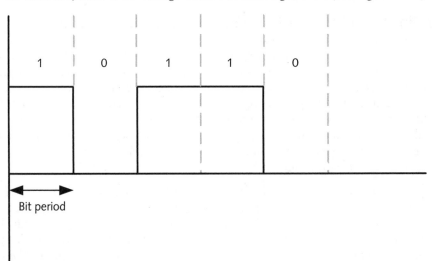

Figure 2-24 Non-return-to-zero (NRZ)

© Cengage Learning 2014

The final method, **polar non-return-to-zero (polar NRZ)**, raises the signal (increases the voltage) to represent a 1 bit and drops the signal (reduces the voltage to a negative amount) to represent a 0 bit. This technique is more commonly referred to as **non-return-to-zero-level (NRZ-L)** because the signal never returns to the 0 volts level. NRZ-L is illustrated in Figure 2-25.

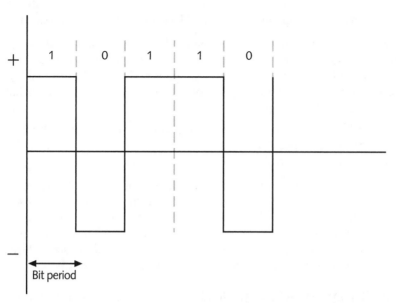

Figure 2-25 Polar non-return-to-zero (non-return-to-zero level or NRZ-L)

© Cengage Learning 2014

 The difference between NRZ and polar NRZ is that polar uses two voltage levels (positive and negative).

A variation of NRZ-L is **non-return-to-zero, invert-on-ones (NRZ-I)**. This is also used to reduce the baud rate required to transmit a digital signal. In NRZ-I, a change in voltage level represents a 1 bit, whereas no change in voltage level indicates that the next bit is a 0. NRZ-I is illustrated in Figure 2-26.

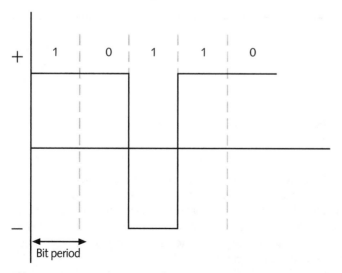

Figure 2-26 Non-return-to-zero, invert-on-ones (NRZ-I)

© Cengage Learning 2014

Why are there so many binary signaling methods? Here are two important reasons:

- Digital electronic circuits tend to average the level of a signal that exhibits a lot of transitions. The result is that the more transitions the signal has, the greater the chance that the circuits will lower the maximum amplitude of the signal, thus making it harder for the receiver to detect the transitions. Using bipolar signals helps but does not eliminate the problem completely.

- Transmitters and receivers have a tendency of getting out of synchronization with each other. If the transmitter sends a long string of 1s or a long string of 0s, the lack of transitions makes it difficult to keep both devices in sync.

Therefore, while trying to minimize the number of transitions, we must also be concerned with having enough of them to ensure good synchronization between the transmitter and the receiver. The methods described above are the most basic ones that are employed when transmitting at lower speeds. Many more sophisticated and complex methods of transmitting digital signals over wires and cables exist, but they are beyond the scope of this book. You will certainly learn about them in later, more advanced courses and books.

Amplitude Shift Keying (ASK)   **Amplitude shift keying (ASK)** is a binary modulation technique similar to amplitude modulation in that the height of the carrier signal can be changed to represent a 1 bit or a 0 bit. However, instead of both a 1 bit and a 0 bit having a carrier signal, as with amplitude modulation, ASK usually employs NRZ coding. This means that the presence of a carrier signal represents a 1 bit (positive voltage), whereras the absence of a carrier signal represents a 0 bit (zero voltage). Figure 2-27 illustrates the letter A (ASCII 0x41 or 01000001) being transmitted using ASK.

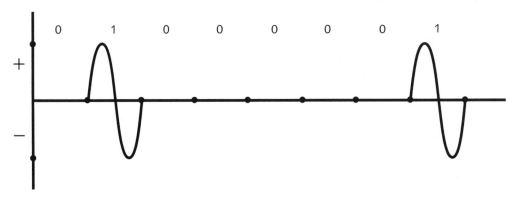

Figure 2-27   Amplitude shift keying (ASK)

© *Cengage Learning 2014*

The signals for transmission using digital binary modulation are still shown here as sine waves because wireless transmissions use a medium (electromagnetic waves) that can only support analog signals. Note that the direct transmission of purely digital signals (discrete pulses) can only be done using a medium that conducts electricity, such as copper wiring.

Frequency Shift Keying (FSK) Similar to frequency modulation, **frequency shift keying (FSK)** is a binary modulation technique that changes the frequency of the carrier signal. Because it is sending a binary signal, the carrier signal does start and stop as the data transmission stops. As an example, when using FSK, more wave cycles are needed to represent a 1 bit and, respectively, fewer wave cycles are needed to represent a 0 bit. Figure 2-28 illustrates the letter A (ASCII 0x41 or 01000001) being transmitted using FSK. In this example, the number of wave cycles used to represent a 1 bit is double that of the number of wave cycles used to represent a 0 bit.

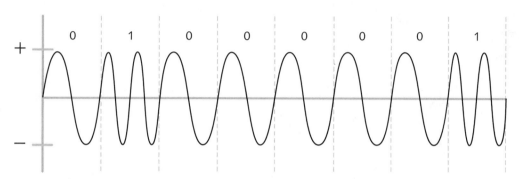

Figure 2-28 Frequency shift keying (FSK)

© *Cengage Learning 2014*

Phase Shift Keying (PSK) **Phase shift keying (PSK)** is a binary modulation technique, similar to phase modulation, in which the transmitter varies the starting point of the wave. The difference is that the PSK signal starts and stops because it is a binary signal. Figure 2-29 illustrates the letter A (ASCII 0x41 or 01000001) being transmitted using PSK.

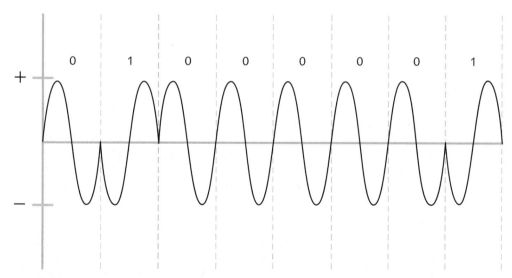

Figure 2-29 Phase shift keying (PSK)

© *Cengage Learning 2014*

Notice that whenever a bit being transmitted changes from 1 to 0 (or 0 to 1), the starting point (i.e., the direction of the wave) changes. For example, after the first 0 bit is represented by a "normal" carrier wave cycle, the next bit is a 1 bit. However, instead of this being indicated by another normal carrier wave cycle in which the signal goes into the positive range (goes up on the sine wave), it starts by going into the negative range. The change in starting point (going down instead of up) represents a change in the bit being transmitted (0 to 1).

In the preceding example, the change in the starting point of the wave means that the wave will start moving in the opposite direction—in this case, 180 degrees from the original direction. Note that phase modulation can change the starting point at various points (angles), as shown in Figure 2-30.

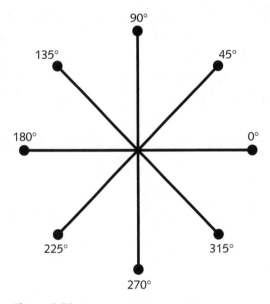

Figure 2-30 Phase modulation angles

© *Cengage Learning 2014*

In this case, there are eight possible starting points for a signal (0 degrees, 45 degrees, 90 degrees, 135 degrees, 180 degrees, 225 degrees, 270 degrees, and 335 degrees), with each dot in the figure representing a different starting point. You will recall that to transmit a tribit (3 bits per signal change or baud), eight different signals are needed. Using phase modulation with 45-degree angles can result in eight different signals. However, in wireless communications today, phase modulation is combined with amplitude modulation, which is easier for receivers to detect than very small phase changes and can provide 16 or more different signals.

In Figure 2-31, each dot represents a different signal, for a total of 16 different combinations that can be used to transmit quadbits. This technique of combining amplitude and phase modulation is called **quadrature amplitude modulation (QAM)**. Due to the potential complexity of the resulting signal, most graphic representations of QAM only show the starting point of each wave with a dot. This representation is called a **constellation diagram**.

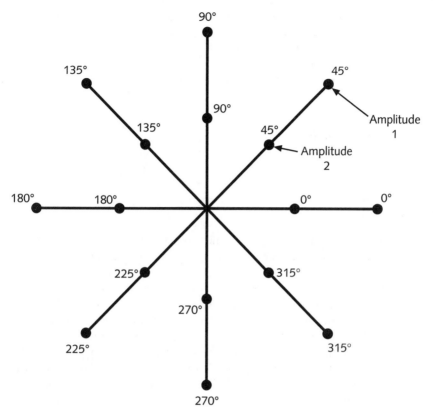

Figure 2-31 Constellation diagram (QAM—quadrature amplitude modulation)

© Cengage Learning 2014

In the presence of background electromagnetic noise (interference), receivers can detect a phase change much more reliably than a frequency or amplitude change. Noise may be detected as a spike or sudden change in the amplitude of the signal and can also be detected as a change to a higher frequency at a particular point, although the latter happens less frequently. Because the phase of a signal is always referenced to the phase of the last wave cycle that was correctly detected, it is much less likely that noise will occur at the same time in a wave and at an amplitude level that would make the receiver detect it as a phase change; that's because noise is random. These benefits make PSK-based systems more attractive for high-speed wireless communications.

A variation of the PSK modulation technique previously described combines amplitude modulation with PSK. This variation, called **binary phase shift keying (BPSK)**, can be used to transmit dibits (four signal changes equals 2 bits per signal change). Figure 2-32 shows an approximate representation of the resulting waveform of this modulation technique for sending a series of 10 bits. It would be practically impossible to visualize this signal with any kind of electronic instrument, such as an oscilloscope, but simple modulations like this one allow us to demonstrate graphically (as in Figure 2-32) what it would look like.

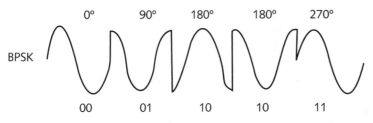

Figure 2-32 Transmitting dibits using BPSK

© Cengage Learning 2014

Spread Spectrum

Radio signal transmissions are, by nature, **narrow-band transmissions**. This means that each signal transmits on one radio frequency or a very narrow range of frequencies. An FM broadcast radio station, for example, might tell its listeners to "tune to 90.3 MHz" because this is the frequency on which it broadcasts. The next-lower frequency that listeners would be able to tune to would be 90.1 MHz; and 90.5 MHz would be the station with the next-higher frequency. This ensures that the station at 90.3 MHz can broadcast roughly between 90.2 and 90.4 MHz without interfering with other stations. The actual bandwidth used by FM stations is less than the difference between 90.2 and 90.4 MHz, allowing for some unused "frequency space" between the highest frequency used by the next-lower station on the FM band, the station you are tuned to, and the next station operating at a higher frequency.

Narrow-band transmissions are vulnerable to outside interference from another signal. Another signal that is transmitted at or near the broadcast frequency—90.3, in this case—can easily render the radio signal inoperable or make it difficult to detect and decode the information contained in the signal.

Broadcast radio stations work effectively with narrow-band transmissions because each station is allowed to transmit on only one frequency in a specific area. Radio stations broadcast using high-powered transmitters and use different frequencies, which are licensed by the Federal Communications Commission (FCC) in the United States. In contrast, most WLAN devices use the same frequency band but transmit at very low power levels. This means that the signals have a short useful range, helping to ensure that minimum interference occurs.

An alternative to narrow-band transmission is **spread spectrum transmission**. Spread spectrum is a technique that takes a narrow band signal and spreads it over a broader portion of the radio frequency band, as shown in Figure 2-33. Spread spectrum transmissions are more resistant to outside interference because any noise is likely to affect only a small portion of the signal instead of the entire signal. As an analogy, although an accident in one lane of an eight-lane freeway is inconvenient, there are still seven other lanes that traffic can use. Likewise, spread spectrum results in less interference and fewer errors. Two common methods used in spread spectrum transmissions are frequency hopping and direct sequence.

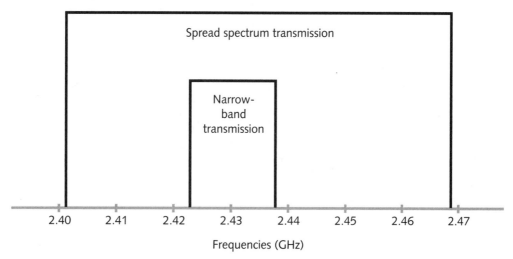

Figure 2-33 Spread spectrum vs. narrow-band transmission

© Cengage Learning 2014

Frequency Hopping Spread Spectrum (FHSS)

Instead of transmitting on just one frequency, **frequency hopping spread spectrum (FHSS)** uses a range of frequencies and changes the frequency of the carrier several times during the transmission. With FHSS, a short burst of data is transmitted in one frequency, and then another short burst is transmitted at another frequency, and so on until the transmission is completed.

NOTE Hedy Lamarr, a well-known film actress during the 1940s, and George Antheil, who had experience synchronizing the sounds of music scores with motion pictures, conceived the idea of frequency hopping spread spectrum during the early part of World War II. Their goal was to keep the Germans from jamming the equipment that guided U.S. torpedoes against German warships. Lamarr and Antheil received a U.S. patent in 1942 for their idea.

Figure 2-34 shows how an FHSS transmission starts by sending a burst of data at the 2.44 GHz frequency for 1 microsecond. Then the transmission switches to the 2.41 GHz frequency and transmits for the next microsecond. During the third microsecond, the transmission takes place at the 2.42 GHz frequency. This continual switching of frequencies takes place until the entire transmission is complete. The sequence of changing frequencies is called the **hopping code**. In the example shown in Figure 2-34, the hopping code is 2.44–2.41–2.42–2.40–2.43. The receiving station must also know the hopping code in order to correctly receive the transmission. The hopping codes are predefined and are usually part of the standard that defines how the radio circuit will be designed and implemented. Hopping codes can change so that multiple radios can each use a different sequence of frequencies within the same area and never interfere with one another, but the transmitter and receiver have to agree beforehand on which sequence to use.

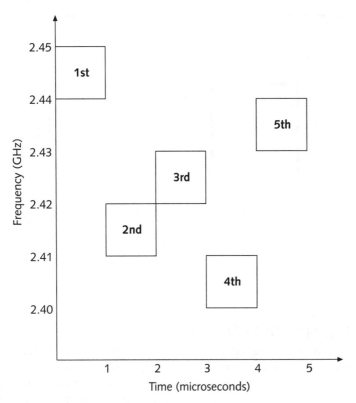

Figure 2-34 Frequency hopping spread spectrum (FHSS) transmission

© Cengage Learning 2014

If interference is encountered while transmitting with FHSS on a particular frequency, only a small part of the message is lost. Figure 2-35 shows an example in which the second transmission has been affected by interference. Each block of data transmitted in FHSS is only about 400 bytes long, and FHSS systems can detect errors at the lower protocol layers and request retransmission before passing the data to higher protocol layers. Some technologies make use of forward error correction (FEC), a technique that sends redundant data to minimize the need for retransmission of the messages. Error handling and error detection and correction at the lower protocol layers are discussed in later chapters.

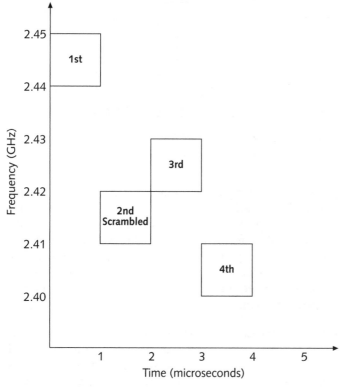

Figure 2-35 FHSS error detection

© *Cengage Learning 2014*

Frequency hopping can reduce the impact of interference from other radio signals. An interfering signal will affect the FHSS signal only when both are transmitting at the same frequency and at the same time. Because FHSS transmits short bursts over a wide range of frequencies, the extent of any interference will be very small, the error can be detected through error checking, and the message can be easily retransmitted. In addition, FHSS signals exert minimal interference on other signals. To an unintended receiver, FHSS transmissions appear to be of a very short duration (similar to noise), and unless the receiver knows the exact hopping sequence of frequencies, it is extremely difficult to eavesdrop on the message.

A variety of devices use FHSS. Several of these devices are consumer-oriented products, because FHSS devices are relatively inexpensive to manufacture. Cordless phones, including multi-handset units for small businesses, typically use FHSS. Bluetooth, which is covered in Chapter 5, also uses FHSS.

Direct Sequence Spread Spectrum (DSSS)

The other type of spread spectrum technology is **direct sequence spread spectrum (DSSS)**. DSSS uses an expanded redundant code to transmit each data bit and then a modulation technique such as **quadrature phase shift keying (QPSK)**. This means that a DSSS signal is effectively modulated twice. The first step before transmission is shown in Figure 2-36. At the top of the figure are two original data bits to be transmitted: a 0 and a 1.

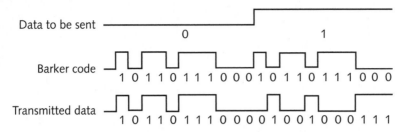

Figure 2-36 Encoding before modulation in a DSSS transmission

© Cengage Learning 2014

However, instead of simply encoding these two bits over a carrier wave for transmission, the value of each data bit is first added to each individual 1 and 0 in a sequence of binary digits called a Barker code. A **Barker code** (or **chipping code**) is a particular sequence of 1s and 0s that has properties that make it ideal for modulating radio waves as well as for being detected correctly by the receiver. These 1s and 0s are called *chips-* instead of bits to avoid confusing them with the actual data bits. The chipping code is sometimes called a **pseudo-random code** because it is usually derived through a number of mathematical calculations as well as through practical experimentation.

The term *Barker code* is correctly used only when referring to 802.11 transmissions at 1 and 2 Mbps. When referring to most other spreading codes used in DSSS-based systems—such as CDMA cellular phones—the terms *pseudo-random code, PN code, spreading code,* and *chipping code* may be used interchangeably.

The result of the addition is the actual set of 1s and 0s (the chips) that will be modulated over a carrier wave and transmitted (as seen in the bottom line of Figure 2-36). Let's take another look at how this sequence of chips is created. If a 1 bit is to be transmitted, then a 1 is added to each bit of the chipping code:

Bit to be transmitted: 1	1	1	1	1	1	1	1	1	1	1	1
Add Barker code:	1	0	1	1	0	1	1	1	0	0	0
Resulting signal sent:	0	1	0	0	1	0	0	0	1	1	1

If a 0 data bit is to be transmitted, then a 0 is added to each bit of the chipping code:

Bit to be transmitted: 0	0	0	0	0	0	0	0	0	0	0	0
Add Barker code:	1	0	1	1	0	1	1	1	0	0	0
Resulting signal sent:	1	0	1	1	0	1	1	1	0	0	0

The adding of the chipping code and the specific value to be added are arrived at by the Boolean operation of "exclusive or" (XOR) on a bit-by-bit basis, which is equivalent to a modulo 2 addition. In modulo 2 addition, there is no carryover, which means that 1 + 1 = 0 and a 1 is not carried over to the next digit to the left. Other than that, a modulo 2 addition works exactly like a normal sum of two digits. See "Boolean Operations, XOR (Exclusive Or)" at *www.cplusplus.com/doc/papers/boolean.html*.

Instead of transmitting a single 1 or 0, a DSSS system transmits these combinations of chips. The 11 chips are transmitted at a rate 11 times faster than the data rate; in other words, the data rate does not change. However, the result of transmitting at a higher rate is the spreading of the signal over a much wider frequency band than that of the channel. In the case of 802.11, to continue with the example given earlier, the signal is spread 11 MHz to each side of the center frequency and ends up occupying a total bandwidth of 22 MHz. Figure 2-37 illustrates the results.

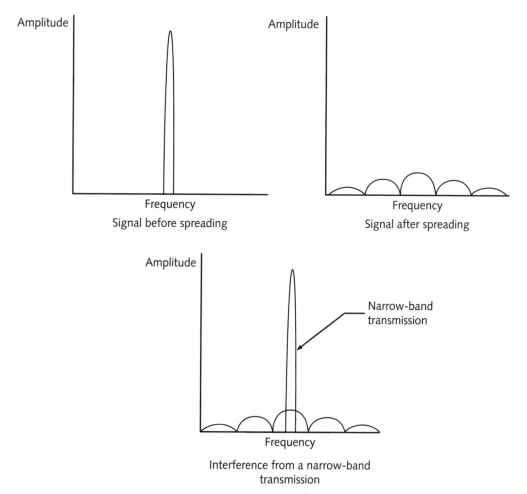

Figure 2-37 Spreading the signal over a wider range of frequencies

© Cengage Learning 2014

This spread signal has three important characteristics:

- The frequency of the signal's digital component (or chipping rate) is much higher than that of the original data.

- A plot of the signal's frequency spectrum looks similar to random noise.

- All the information contained in the original signal (a 0 bit or a 1 bit) is still there.

The most important aspect of this, however, is not the spreading of the signal but the fact that the power level (amplitude), *at any given frequency*, has dropped significantly. In similar fashion to FHSS, a DSSS signal appears to an unintended narrow-band receiver to be low-powered noise, which is one major advantage of this method.

At the receiver, the signal is first demodulated and then de-spread. One of the techniques the receiver uses to detect which bit was transmitted is to count the number of 0 chips. If the pattern of chips received contains six 0s, the value of the data bit is 1. Conversely, if the pattern contains six 1s, the value of the data bit is 0.

Another major advantage of using DSSS with a chipping code is that in conventional narrow-band transmissions, any interference, even if it caused the loss of only one bit, would require the entire message to be re-sent, which takes time. In DSSS, if there is any noise or other type of narrow-band interference that may cause some of the chips to change value, the receiver can employ embedded statistical techniques—mathematical algorithms that are used to recover the original data bit, thus avoiding the need for retransmission.

Devices that use DSSS are typically higher-end products because they are more expensive to manufacture than FHSS systems, but they also have many advantages over FHSS, as previously described. WLANs use DSSS along with products that interconnect networks located in several buildings that comprise a campus setting, such as a school, a large corporation, a manufacturing plant, or a convention center.

FHSS and DSSS are not the only transmission techniques used for spread spectrum transmission. There are other techniques that are even more resistant to interference and to different kinds of phenomena that can cause data loss or reduce the performance of this type of wireless transmission. Some of the techniques are based on variations of DSSS; others are completely different. Later chapters of this book discuss some of the more sophisticated techniques as well as the types of problems that can affect wireless transmissions.

Chapter Summary

- One of the arbitrary coding schemes, which uses the numbers from 0 to 127, is called the American Standard Code for Information Interchange (ASCII). A character that will be stored or transmitted by the computer is first converted to its ASCII equivalent, then that number is stored as a byte in binary.

- Whereas traditional wired communications use copper wires or fiber-optic cables to send and receive data, wireless transmissions do not use a visible medium. Instead, they travel on electromagnetic waves. There are two basic types of waves by which wireless signals are sent and received: infrared light and radio waves.

- Infrared light, which is next to visible light on the light spectrum, has many of the same characteristics as visible light. Infrared wireless transmission can be either directed or diffused. A directed transmission sends a narrowly focused beam of infrared light from the emitter to the detector. A diffused transmission relies on reflected light.

- The second means of transmitting a wireless signal is by using radio transmission. Radio waves provide the most common and effective means of wireless communications today. Radio waves have fewer limitations than light waves.

- Radio transmissions use a carrier signal, which is a continuous wave (CW) of constant amplitude (voltage) and frequency. This signal is essentially an up-and-down wave called an oscillating signal or sine wave. The carrier signal sent by analog radio transmissions is simply a continuous electrical signal that carries no information.

- The carrier signal can undergo three types of modulation (i.e., change) to enable it to carry information: the height of the signal, the frequency of the signal, and the relative starting point. Amplitude modulation (AM) changes the signal height. Frequency modulation (FM) changes the number of wave cycles that occur in one second. Phase modulation (PM) changes the starting point of the cycle.

- In digital modulation, there are also three types of changes that can be made to the carrier to enable it to carry information: the height of the signal, the frequency of the signal, and the relative starting point. Amplitude shift keying (ASK) changes the height of the carrier to represent a 1 bit or a 0 bit. A carrier is transmitted for a 1 bit, and no signal is transmitted for a 0 bit. Frequency shift keying (FSK) is a modulation technique that changes the frequency of the carrier signal. Phase shift keying (PSK) is a modulation technique similar to phase modulation. The difference is that the PSK signal starts and stops because it is a binary signal.

- Radio signals are by nature a narrow-band type of transmission, which means that they transmit on one radio frequency or a very narrow spectrum of frequencies. An alternative to narrow-band transmissions is spread spectrum transmission. Spread spectrum is a technique that takes a narrow signal and spreads it over a broader portion of the radio frequency band.

- Spreading the signal over a wide range of frequencies and reducing the amplitude has the advantage of making the signal look like noise to an unintended narrow-band receiver, reducing the effects of interference.

- One of the most common spread spectrum methods is frequency hopping spread spectrum (FHSS). Instead of sending on just one frequency, frequency hopping uses a range of frequencies and changes frequencies during the transmission. The other method is direct sequence spread spectrum (DSSS). DSSS uses an expanded redundant code to transmit each data bit.

Key Terms

American Standard Code for Information Interchange (ASCII)   An arbitrary coding scheme that uses the numbers from 0 to 127 to represent alphanumeric characters and symbols.

amplitude   The height of a carrier wave.

amplitude modulation (AM)   A technique that changes the height of a carrier wave in response to a change in the height of the input signal.

amplitude shift keying (ASK)   A digital modulation technique whereby a 1 bit is represented by the existence of a carrier signal, whereas a 0 bit is represented by the absence of a carrier signal.

analog modulation   A method of encoding an analog signal onto a carrier wave.

analog signal   A signal in which the intensity (amplitude or voltage) varies continuously and smoothly over a period of time.

antenna A copper wire, rod, or similar device that has one end up in the air and the other end connected to the ground through a receiver.

bandwidth The range of frequencies that can be transmitted.

Barker code (chipping code) A bit pattern used in a DSSS transmission. The term *chipping code* is used because a single radio bit is commonly referred to as a *chip*.

baud A change in a carrier signal.

baud rate The number of times that a carrier signal changes per second.

binary phase shift keying (BPSK) A simple digital modulation technique that uses four phase changes to represent 2 bits per signal change.

bits per second (bps) The number of bits that can be transmitted per second.

carrier signal A signal of a particular frequency that is modulated to contain either analog or digital data.

constellation diagram A graphical representation that makes it easier to visualize signals using complex modulation techniques such as QAM. It is generally used in laboratory and field diagnostic instruments and analyzers to aid in design and troubleshooting of wireless communications devices.

continous wave (CW) An analog or sine wave that is modulated to eventually carry information, becoming a carrier wave.

cycle An oscillating sine wave that completes one full series of movements.

detector A diode that receives a light-based transmission signal.

dibit A signal unit that represents 2 bits.

diffused transmission A light-based transmission that relies on reflected light.

digital modulation A method of encoding a digital signal onto an analog carrier wave for transmission over media that does not support direct digital signal transmission.

digital signal Data that is discrete or separate.

direct sequence spread spectrum (DSSS) A spread spectrum technique that uses an expanded, redundant code to transmit each data bit.

directed transmission A light-based transmission that requires the emitter and detector to be directly aimed at one another.

electromagnetic wave (EM wave) A signal composed of electrical and magnetic forces that in radio transmission usually propagates from an antenna and can be modulated to carry information.

emitter A laser diode or a light-emitting diode that transmits a light-based signal.

frequency A measurement of radio waves that is determined by how frequently a cycle occurs.

frequency hopping spread spectrum (FHSS) A spread spectrum technique that uses a range of frequencies and changes frequencies during the transmission.

frequency modulation (FM) A technique that changes the number of wave cycles in response to a change in the amplitude of the input signal.

frequency shift keying (FSK) A digital modulation technique that changes the frequency of the carrier signal in response to a change in the binary input signal.

Gigahertz (GHz) 1,000,000,000 Hertz.

Hertz (Hz) The number of cycles per second.

hopping code The sequence of changing frequencies used in FHSS.

infrared light   Light that is next to visible light on the light spectrum and that has many of the same characteristics as visible light.

Kilohertz (KHz)   1,000 Hertz.

light spectrum   All the different types of light that travel from the Sun to the Earth.

line of sight   The direct alignment as required in a directed transmission.

Megahertz (MHz)   1,000,000 Hertz.

modem (MOdulator/DEModulator)   A device used to convert digital signals into an analog format, and vice versa.

modulation   The process of changing a carrier signal.

narrow-band transmissions   Transmissions that use one radio frequency or a very narrow portion of the frequency spectrum.

non-return-to-zero (NRZ)   A binary signaling technique that increases the voltage to represent a 1 bit but provides no voltage for a 0 bit.

non-return-to-zero, invert-on-ones (NRZ-I)   A binary signaling technique that changes the voltage level only when the bit to be represented is a 1.

non-return-to-zero level (NRZ-L)   *See* polar non-return-to-zero.

oscillating signal   A wave that illustrates the change in a carrier signal.

phase   The relative starting point of a wave, in degrees, beginning at zero degrees.

phase modulation (PM)   A technique that changes the starting point of a wave cycle in response to a change in the amplitude of the input signal. This technique is not used in analog modulation.

phase shift keying (PSK)   A digital modulation technique that changes the starting point of a wave cycle in response to a change in the binary input signal.

polar non-return-to-zero (polar NRZ)   A binary signaling technique that increases the voltage to represent a 1 bit but drops to negative voltage to represent a 0 bit.

pseudo-random code   A code that is usually derived through a number of mathematical calculations as well as practical experimentation.

quadbit   A signal unit that represents 4 bits.

quadrature amplitude modulation (QAM)   A combination of phase modulation with amplitude modulation to produce 16 different signals.

quadrature phase shift keying (QPSK)   A digital modulation technique that combines quadrature amplitude modulation with phase shift keying.

radio wave (radiotelephony)   An electromagnetic wave created when an electric current passes through a wire and creates a magnetic field in the space around the wire.

return-to-zero (RZ)   A binary signaling technique that increases the voltage to represent a 1 bit, but the voltage is reduced to 0 before the end of the period for transmitting the 1 bit, and there is no voltage for a 0 bit.

sine wave   A wave that illustrates the change in a carrier signal.

spread spectrum transmission   A technique that takes a narrow signal and spreads it over a broader portion of the radio frequency band.

tribit   A signal unit that represents 3 bits.

voltage   Electrical pressure.

wavelength   The length of a wave as measured between two positive or negative peaks or between the starting point of one wave and the starting point of the next wave.

Review Questions

1. Which range of the electromagnetic spectrum is less susceptible to interference from sources of visible light?

   a. ultraviolet

   b. gamma light

   c. infrared

   d. yellow light

2. The distance between one positive peak and the next positive peak of a wave is called _____.

   a. frequency

   b. wavelength

   c. elasticity

   d. intensity

3. Which type of transmission is used when human voice is modulated directly onto a carrier wave?

   a. analog

   b. digital

   c. diffused

   d. directed

4. Why do computers and data transmission equipment use binary?

   a. They are electrical devices, and electricity has only two states.

   b. Base 2 is too difficult to use.

   c. Base 10 was developed before binary.

   d. Binary is the next step beyond quadecimal.

5. Eight binary digits grouped together form which of the following?

   a. byte

   b. bit

   c. binary

   d. 2x quad

6. The American Standard Code for Information Interchange (ASCII) can represent up to 1024 characters. True or False?

7. Letters of the alphabet and symbols are stored using the ASCII code, but not numbers used in calculations. True or False?

8. Infrared light, though invisible, has many of the characteristics of visible light. True or False?

9. Infrared wireless systems require that each device needs to have only one component: either an emitter that transmits a signal or a detector that receives the signal. True or False?

10. Infrared wireless systems send data by the intensity of the light wave instead of whether the light signal is on or off. True or False?

11. Infrared wireless transmission can be either directed or _____.

    a. analog

    b. digital

    c. diffused

    d. detected

12. Radiotelephony or radio travels in waves known as _____ waves.

    a. electromagnetic

    b. analog

    c. magnetic

    d. electrical

13. Unlike a digital signal, a(n) _____ signal is a continuous signal with no "breaks" in it.

    a. magnetic

    b. visible

    c. light

    d. analog

14. Changing a signal to encode data onto it is known as _____.

    a. baud

    b. demodulation

    c. modulation

    d. continuity

15. PSK is an example of _____.

    a. ASCII encoding

    b. unicoding

    c. phase modulation

    d. digital modulation

16. Explain how a radio antenna works when transmitting a signal.

17. Explain the difference between bps and baud rate.

18. Explain the difference between amplitude modulation, frequency modulation, and phase modulation.

19. What is quadrature amplitude modulation (QAM) and how does it work?

20. List and describe the three different types of binary signaling techniques.

Hands-On Projects

Project 2-1

In this project, you will write your name in both hexadecimal and binary.

1. Using the ASCII chart found in the Appendix of this book, look up the hexadecimal ASCII value for each of the letters of your last name. (Note that the ASCII table contains codes for both uppercase and lowercase letters.) Here is what my last name looks like in hexadecimal, with a dash placed between successive letters, to make it easier to read:

   O–l–e–n–e–w–a = 4F–6C–65–6E–65–77–61

2. Convert each hexadecimal value to binary. The easiest way to do this is to break the hexadecimal code for each character into two separate digits. In the case of an uppercase O, this would be 4 and F. Each digit represents four bits out of one byte (also called a nibble).

3. Convert each digit to its binary equivalent in the range 0000 (0x0) to 1111 (0xF). Put the two groups of four bits together into a byte. For the purposes of this project, the most significant bit, which is generally used for parity, will always be a 0.

4. Write your full last name in binary. Again, use a dash between each group of eight bits to make it easier to read. Here is what my last name looks like:

   01001111–01101100–01100101–01101110–01100101–01110111–01100001

   You will use these results in the following projects.

Project 2-2

This project helps you develop an appreciation for the topic of modulation and what it takes to transmit data—analog or digital—over the wireless medium. As you know, this book introduces many different wireless technologies that use various modulation techniques. In this project, you perform amplitude modulation.

1. In Figure 2-38, an analog input signal is shown at the top of the grid. To draw a wave that is modulated in amplitude, begin by copying the input signal to the top two rows of the grid shown in Figure 2-38. The goal is to create an "envelope" to guide you and make it easier to draw the carrier wave, showing what it will look like after it is modulated. Use a dashed line to draw the input signal.

2. Complete the envelope by drawing a mirror-image (vertically inverted) version of the input signal in the bottom two rows of the grid. Again, use a dashed line.

3. You are now ready to draw the modulated carrier. Considering a carrier with a frequency of 4 Hz, so that it will be easier to draw and visualize, draw a sine wave with four complete cycles for each second. The wave must fit inside and follow the contour of the envelope you created in the previous two steps. The frequency of the modulated carrier must remain constant at 4 Hz for each one-second interval on the grid. The high and low peaks of the modulated carrier must reach all the way to the upper and lower guides you just drew, the envelope.

4. Check your results with your instructor, or see Figure 2-20 to make sure you got it right.

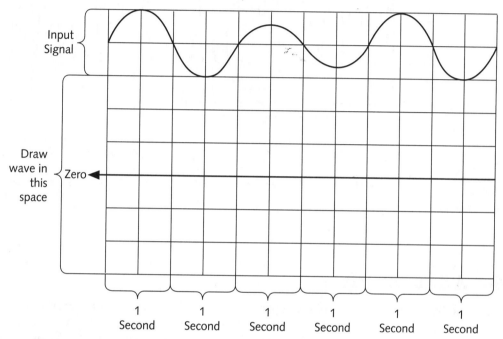

Figure 2-38 Analog modulation grid

© Cengage Learning 2014

Project 2-3

As you have learned, digital modulation makes it possible to transmit a digital signal using an analog medium such as an electromagnetic wave. In this project, you draw a waveform to show how a digital signal can be encoded onto a carrier using one bit per phase change (PSK).

1. In Figure 2-39, a grid and an analog reference wave are shown without an input signal. Input the binary ASCII code for the first letter of your last name in the spaces provided at the top of the grid.

2. The modulated carrier wave should have the same amplitude as the original carrier. Begin at the 0 level indicated on the left side of the grid and draw a 4 Hz carrier to represent the first bit, a 0.

3. At the end of the first second, continue drawing the carrier but change the phase if the second most significant bit is a 1. If not, continue drawing the carrier at the same phase.

4. Keep drawing the 4 Hz carrier wave, changing phase as required to show a change from a bit with a value of 1 or 0.

5. After you have drawn the carrier wave for all eight bits of the ASCII code, compare your results with Figure 2-39 to make sure it looks correct.

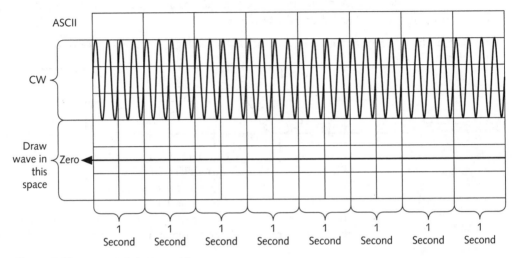

Figure 2-39 Phase shift keying grid

Real-World Exercises

The Baypoint Group (TBG), a company of 50 consultants who assist organizations and businesses with issues involving network planning and design, has hired you as a consultant. One of their oldest clients, Woodruff Medical Group, needs your help with the following tasks.

Exercise 2-1

Woodruff Medical has been approached by a vendor who is trying to sell it an infrared WLAN for its office. Because the equipment is proprietary, the cost is quite high, and this is one of their main concerns. Although none of the networking equipment will be placed around sensitive medical equipment, the office manager prefers infrared because he believes that other types of wireless networking equipment could interfere with the medical equipment in another hospital campus building that is located about 125 meters away.

Exercise 2-2

Prepare a PowerPoint presentation outlining how infrared and radio wireless transmissions work. This will be presented to the office manager, who is not technically inclined, and the LAN manager, who has a strong technology background. Be sure to list the advantages and disadvantages of both. The presentation should contain at least 10 slides. You will only have 20 minutes to explain both technologies.

Exercise 2-3

After listening to your presentation, the office manager has several questions. One of the questions involves wireless transmission speeds. The office manager has a "good 56 Kbps baud" dial-up data modem at home and wants to know how its transmission speed compares with that of an infrared and RF WLAN. He also does not understand the difference between *baud* and *bps*, two terms that he has been hearing a lot about lately, but none of the explanations has satisfied him yet. For this, the office manager wants a written report instead of a presentation. Write a one-page summary regarding different transmission speeds. Be sure to include information about the difference between bps, baud, baud rate, and bandwidth. Also, show how bps is not always identical to baud.

Challenge Case Project

CASE PROJECTS

A local community college has contacted The Baypoint Group for information about modulation for a networking class, and TBG has passed this request on to you. Form a team of two or three consultants and research AM, FM, PM, ASK, FSK, and PSK. Specifically, pay attention to how they are used, as well as their strengths and weaknesses. Provide your conclusions regarding which of these methods, or combination of methods, is now the dominant player in wireless data transmission and why you think this is the case.

chapter 3

Radio Frequency Communications

After reading this chapter and completing the exercises, you will be able to:

- List the components of a radio system
- Describe the factors that affect the design of a radio system
- Discuss why standards are beneficial and list the major telecommunications standards organizations
- Explain the radio frequency spectrum

Radio frequency (RF) communications is the most common type of wireless communications. It comprises all the types of radio communications that use radio frequency waves, from radio broadcasting to wireless computer networks. In this book, we focus primarily on wireless data communications. Due to the convergence of technologies—for example, data transmission over cellular phones and satellites—we also cover these types of RF communications.

Unlike light-based communications, which is also wireless and is briefly discussed in this chapter, RF communications can cover long distances and is not always blocked by objects in the path of the signal, as light-based communications can be. RF is also a mature communications technology, the first radio transmission having been sent over 100 years ago.

RF communications can be very complex, but this chapter attempts to demystify the subject. First, we explore the basic components of RF communications. Then, we look at the issues regarding the design and performance of an RF system. Next, we explore the national and international organizations that create and enforce RF standards. Finally, we examine the RF spectrum allocation.

Components of a Radio System

Several hardware components are common to all radio systems, even though the functions of the radio systems may vary. These components include filters, mixers, amplifiers, and antennas. The first three are covered in this chapter. The fourth component, antennas, is important enough to warrant a chapter of its own (Chapter 4), especially given the accelerated growth of the wireless data communications field.

Filters

A **filter** does exactly what its name indicates: It gets rid of all the RF signals that are not wanted. The world around us is filled with RF signals that cover virtually every frequency in the electromagnetic spectrum (refer back to Figure 2-1). Most of these signals are generated by transmission equipment, such as cellular phones, communications satellites, and radio and television station transmitters; some reach us from outer space. After radio receivers have picked up these RF waves that are "flying" around us, a filter sifts out the frequencies that we do not want to receive. Think of a home-based water filter that removes particles and other impurities, or an automotive oil filter that prevents large contaminants from reaching the engine while allowing the oil itself to pass through. An RF filter either passes or rejects a signal based on the signal's frequency. The block diagram symbol for a filter is shown in Figure 3-1.

The block diagram symbols are universal and are commonly used to illustrate radio frequency as well as microwave components.

Figure 3-1 Filter symbol

© Cengage Learning 2014

There are three types of RF filters: low-pass, bandpass, and high-pass. With a **low-pass filter**, a maximum frequency threshold is set and all signals below that value are allowed to pass through, as shown in Figure 3-2.

Maximum threshold: 900 MHz

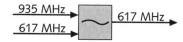

Figure 3-2 Low-pass filter

© Cengage Learning 2014

A **high-pass filter**, instead of setting a maximum frequency threshold level, as a low-pass filter does, sets a minimum frequency threshold. All signals above the minimum threshold are allowed to pass through, whereas those below the minimum threshold are blocked. In addition, the process of modulating a signal with data to be transmitted creates "stray" signals called **harmonics**, which fall outside the range of frequencies we wish to transmit; these must also be filtered out. A high-pass filter is shown in Figure 3-3.

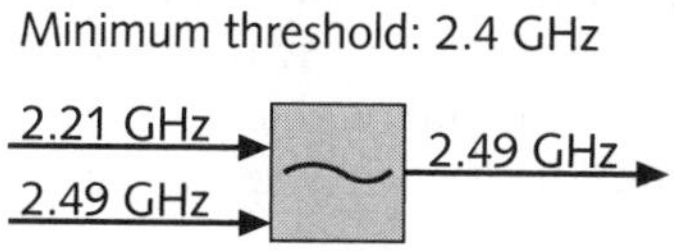

Minimum threshold: 2.4 GHz

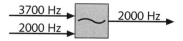

Figure 3-3 High-pass filter

© Cengage Learning 2014

A **bandpass filter**, instead of setting either a minimum or maximum frequency threshold, sets a range called a **passband**, which includes both a minimum and a maximum threshold. Signals that fall within the passband are allowed through the bandpass filter. This is shown in Figure 3-4.

Passband: 300 Hz to 3400 Hz

Figure 3-4 Bandpass filter

© Cengage Learning 2014

 Some of the figures depicting filters show multiple inputs. This is for the purpose of clarity only. A filter usually has a single input.

Filters are also found in transmitters, where they are used to eliminate unwanted frequencies called harmonic oscillations, which result from the process of modulating the signal before transmission. The way a filter functions in a transmitter is shown in Figure 3-5, which is a partial block diagram. The input is the information that needs to be sent; it can take the form of audio, video, or data. The transmitter takes the input data and modulates the signal (through analog or digital modulation) by changing the amplitude, frequency, or phase of the sine wave (see Chapter 2 to refresh your memory of RF signal modulation). The output from the modulation process is known as the **intermediate frequency (IF)** signal; it includes the frequencies between 8 MHz and 112 MHz. The IF signal is then filtered through a bandpass filter to remove any undesired high-frequency or low-frequency signals and produce an output with a frequency range of between 10 MHz and 100 MHz.

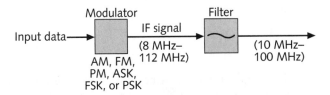

Figure 3-5 Filter function in a radio transmitter

© Cengage Learning 2014

Mixers

The purpose of a **mixer** is to combine two inputs to create a single output. The mixer symbol is shown in Figure 3-6. The single output of a mixer is in the range of the highest sum and the lowest difference of the two frequencies. In Figure 3-7, the input signal—the information to be transmitted—is between 300 Hz and 3400 Hz, and the carrier frequency is 20,000 Hz.

Figure 3-6 Mixer symbol

© Cengage Learning 2014

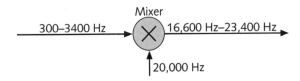

Figure 3-7 Mixer output

© Cengage Learning 2014

The mixer adds the input frequencies to the mixed-in frequency to produce the sums:

$$
\begin{array}{cc}
20{,}000 \text{ Hz} & 20{,}000 \text{ Hz} \\
+\ 300 \text{ Hz} & +3{,}400 \text{ Hz} \\
\hline
20{,}300 \text{ Hz} & 23{,}400 \text{ Hz}
\end{array}
$$

In this example, 23,400 Hz is the highest sum. The mixer also determines the lowest difference between the input frequencies and the mixed-in frequency, for example:

$$
\begin{array}{cc}
20{,}000 \text{ Hz} & 20{,}000 \text{ Hz} \\
-\ 300 \text{ Hz} & -3{,}400 \text{ Hz} \\
\hline
19{,}700 \text{ Hz} & 16{,}600 \text{ Hz}
\end{array}
$$

In this example, the lowest difference frequency would be 16,600 Hz. Therefore, the output from the mixer would be a frequency from 16,600 Hz to 23,400 Hz. The sum and the difference are known as the **sidebands** of the frequency carrier because they fall above and below the center frequency of the carrier signal.

One way to think about sidebands is by considering AM radio signals. AM broadcast radio is confined to a frequency range of 535 KHz to 1605 KHz. In an AM broadcast radio signal, the sidebands are typically 7.5 KHz wide, so a radio station on the AM dial uses a total of about 15 KHz of bandwidth to transmit a single audio channel or voice. An example of sidebands is shown in Figure 3-8.

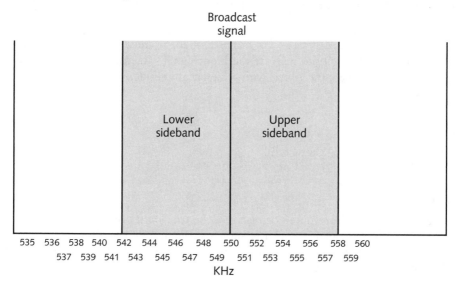

Figure 3-8 AM radio sidebands

© *Cengage Learning 2014*

Mixers are used to convert an input frequency to a specific desired output frequency. For example, let's say that you wish to transmit data using an 800 MHz carrier. Figure 3-9 illustrates how a mixer functions in a radio transmitter. The transmitter takes the input data and modulates the signal to produce an IF signal. In this example, the output from the modulator is a range of frequencies from 8 MHz to 112 MHz, which also includes some undesirable harmonic frequencies. This signal is then put through a bandpass filter to produce the desired IF signal range of 10 MHz to 100 MHz. This IF signal then becomes the input to the mixer along with the desired carrier frequency of 800 MHz. The output of the mixer is a signal with a frequency range between 698 MHz and 903 MHz, which is finally run through another bandpass filter to remove any frequencies outside the transmission range—in other words, those that fall outside the intended sideband limits.

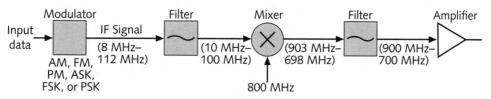

Figure 3-9 Mixer function in a radio transmitter

© *Cengage Learning 2014*

Amplifiers

An **amplifier** increases the amplitude of an RF signal. Figure 3-10 shows the symbol for an amplifier. In Figure 3-9, the amplifier is the last stage in a radio circuit and its function is to boost the power of the signal received from the last filter stage before it is transmitted. Amplifiers are critical components in a radio system because RF signals tend to lose intensity (amplitude) when they move through circuits or through air or space. Filters and mixers are passive devices, meaning that they do not add power to a signal; instead, they take power away from the signal. Likewise, when an electromagnetic wave carrying a modulated signal leaves the antenna and travels from the transmitter to the receiver antenna, a large portion of its power is lost or attenuated (reduced in amplitude) when it is absorbed by water particles in the air, walls, trees, and so on.

The amplifier is an active device. To work, though, it must be supplied with electricity. Amplifiers use this electricity to increase the input signal's intensity or strength and then output an exact copy of the input signal with a higher amplitude.

Figure 3-10 Amplifier symbol

© Cengage Learning 2014

Antennas

For an RF signal to be transmitted or received, the transmitter or receiver must be connected to an antenna, the symbol for which is shown in Figure 3-11. Table 3-1 shows the list of radio system components along with their functions and block diagram symbols. Antennas will be discussed in greater detail in Chapter 4.

Figure 3-11 Antenna symbol

© Cengage Learning 2014

Component Name	Function	Block Diagram Symbol
Filter	Accept or block RF signal	
Mixer	Combine two radio frequency inputs to create a single output	
Amplifier	Boost signal strength	
Antenna	Send or receive an electromagnetic wave	

Table 3-1 Radio system components and their symbols

© Cengage Learning 2014

Design of a Radio System

Filters, mixers, amplifiers, and antennas are necessary components of all radio systems, but designers need to consider how the systems will be used. In radio signal broadcasting, this may be as straightforward as determining the size and location of the antenna as well as a signal that will be strong enough to cover a very large area. However, in a radio system that incorporates two-way communications—for example, cellular phones connected via a wireless network—there are other considerations, including multiple user access, transmission direction, switching, and signal strength.

Multiple Access

Because the number of frequencies available for radio transmission is limited, conserving the use of frequencies is important. One way to do this is by sharing a particular frequency among multiple users, which reduces the number of frequencies needed. In Figure 3-12, a group of people is using walkie-talkies, all the users participating on the same channel. If the three people on the left transmit at the same time, the three on the right will not be able to understand the messages. The only way for all the users to share a channel is if they take turns transmitting.

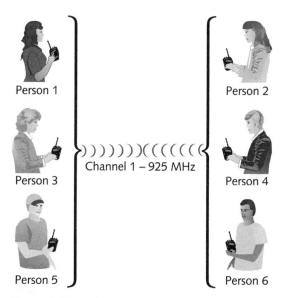

Person 1

Person 3

Channel 1 – 925 MHz

Person 2

Person 4

Person 5

Person 6

Figure 3-12 Multiple access

© Cengage Learning 2014

Another example of multiple access is when employees of a company send multiple envelopes or packages from one office to another office. All the envelopes and packages are shipped at the same time and share space in the same courier truck on the same trip (multiple access). But when the truck arrives at the other office, the envelopes and packages are sorted and delivered to their respective recipients.

Several methods allow multiple access. The most significant, in terms of wireless communications, are Frequency Division Multiple Access (FDMA), Time Division Multiple Access (TDMA), and Code Division Multiple Access (CDMA).

Frequency Division Multiple Access (FDMA) Frequency Division Multiple Access (FDMA) divides the bandwidth of a channel (a range of frequencies) into several smaller frequency bands (narrower ranges of frequencies, or channels). For example, a transmission band with a 50,000 Hz bandwidth can be divided into 1,000 channels, each with a bandwidth of 50 Hz. Each channel can then be dedicated to one specific user. This concept is illustrated in Figure 3-13. FDMA is most often used with analog transmissions.

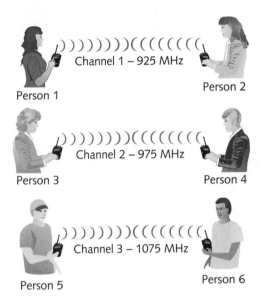

Person 1 — Channel 1 – 925 MHz — Person 2

Person 3 — Channel 2 – 975 MHz — Person 4

Person 5 — Channel 3 – 1075 MHz — Person 6

Figure 3-13 Frequency Division Multiple Access (FDMA)

© Cengage Learning 2014

Cable television is transmitted using FDMA over coaxial cable. Each analog television signal uses 6 MHz of the 500 MHz bandwidth of the cable.

NOTE

Think back to the example in Figure 3-12. If each of the three people on the left uses a different portion of the same frequency band by selecting a different channel on the walkie-talkie and if each of the three people on the right select one of the three transmitting channels, the people on the left can transmit simultaneously and each of the people on the right will receive the different transmissions.

One of the drawbacks of FDMA is that when signals are sent at frequencies that are grouped closely together, an errant signal from one frequency may encroach on its neighbor's frequency. This phenomenon, known as **crosstalk**, causes interference on the other frequency and may disrupt the transmission.

Time Division Multiple Access (TDMA) To overcome the problem of crosstalk, Time Division Multiple Access (TDMA) was developed. Whereas FDMA divides the bandwidth into several frequencies, TDMA divides the transmission time into several slots. Each user is assigned the entire frequency for a fraction of time on a fixed, rotating basis. Because the duration of each time slot is short, the delays that occur while others are using the frequency are not noticeable. Figure 3-14 illustrates TDMA for six users. TDMA is most often used with digital transmissions.

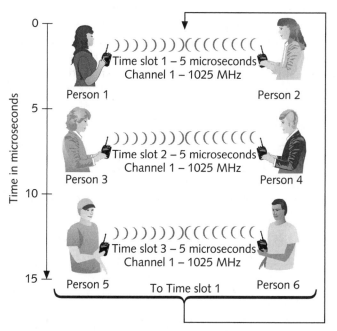

Figure 3-14 Time Division Multiple Access (TDMA)

© Cengage Learning 2014

In traditional TDMA, if a user has no data to transmit during his or her assigned time slot with TDMA, the frequency remains idle—in other words, no one else uses that frequency. In more modern systems, the unused time slots can be assigned to users that are currently communicating.

Some types of cellular phones based on GSM technology, which until recently were the most common cellular technology used in Europe, transmit and receive using the TDMA method.

TDMA has two significant advantages over FDMA. First, it uses the bandwidth more efficiently. Studies indicate that when using a 25 MHz bandwidth, TDMA can achieve over 20 times the capacity of FDMA, meaning it can handle a much larger number of transmitters sharing the same frequency band. Second, TDMA allows data and voice transmissions to be mixed using the same frequency.

Code Division Multiple Access (CDMA) Code Division Multiple Access (CDMA) is another transmission method used in cellular telephone communications. Rather than separate RF frequencies or channels, CDMA uses direct sequence spread spectrum (DSSS) technology with a unique digital spreading code (called a **PN code**) to differentiate the multiple transmissions in the same frequency range. Before transmission occurs, the high-rate

PN code is combined with the data to be sent; this step spreads the signal over a wide frequency band.

CDMA is very similar to the spread spectrum transmission technique described in Chapter 2. What's different about CDMA is that, to implement multiple access, the transmission to each user begins on a subsequent chip of the PN code. Recall that, in DSSS, the 1s and 0s of the spreading code are referred to as "chips" to avoid confusing them with the data bits; this imprints a unique address on the data. Each "address" is then used only by one of the receivers sharing a frequency. Figure 3-15 illustrates the concept of the spreading code.

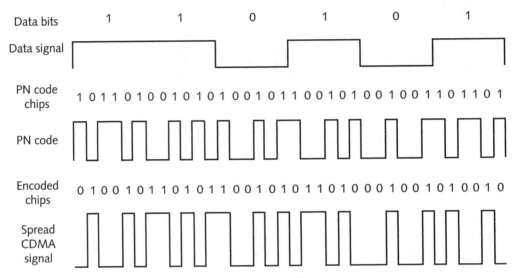

Figure 3-15 CDMA spreading of a data signal by a PN code

© Cengage Learning 2014

The unique-address concept works this way:

Channel 1: 1 0 0 1 1 0 1

Channel 2: 0 0 1 1 0 1 1

Channel 3: 0 1 1 0 1 1 0

and so on, until the sequence of chips wraps around.

Note that each of these codes starts on a different chip of the same sequence of 1s and 0s. The code for channel 2 begins on the second chip of channel 1. The code for channel 3 begins on the second chip of channel 2, and so on, until there are no more unique codes available and the sequence of chips wraps around. The longer the code is, the larger the number of users who will be able to share a channel. In the previous unique-address example, there are seven chips per code, which allows for seven unique codes.

The number of chips in the code determines the amount of spreading or bandwidth that the transmitted signal will occupy. Because the amount of spreading is limited by the bandwidth allocated to the system, the length of the spreading code also determines the number of unique code sequences and, consequently, the number of users that can share that frequency band.

In CDMA technology, the spreading code is called a pseudo-random code (PN code), because the code appears to be a random sequence of 1s and 0s, but it actually repeats itself over and over.

The spreading process is reversed at the receiver, and the code is de-spread to extract the original data bit transmitted. Because all receivers are on the same frequency, they all receive the same transmission. The PN code is designed so that when a receiver picks up a signal that was spread with the PN code that's being used by another receiver and then attempts to recover the original data, the decoded signal still looks like a high-frequency signal instead of data, so it is ignored. Figure 3-16 illustrates the decoding of the data in CDMA, and Figure 3-17 shows an example of what happens when a receiver attempts to de-spread another receiver's signal and recover the data bits.

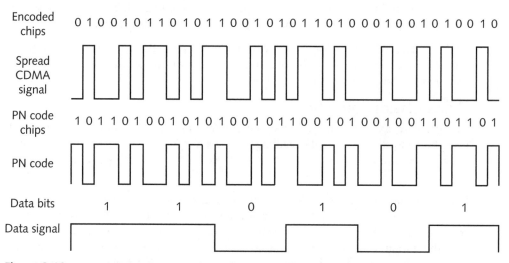

Figure 3-16 De-spreading a CDMA signal to recover the data bits

© Cengage Learning 2014

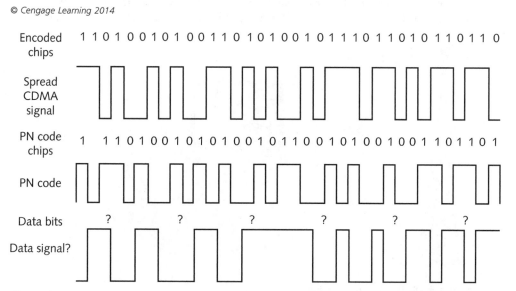

Figure 3-17 Attempting to de-spread another receiver's CDMA signal

© Cengage Learning 2014

To understand CDMA, imagine a room with 20 people in it who are having 10 simultaneous one-on-one conversations. Now suppose that all the pairs are talking at the same time but in different languages. Ignoring the issue of the noise level in the room, because none of the listeners understands any language other than that of the individual with whom they are speaking, the other nine conversations don't bother them.

There are several advantages to CDMA:

- It can carry up to three times the amount of data as TDMA.
- Transmissions are much harder to eavesdrop on, because a listener would have difficulty picking out a single conversation spread across the entire spectrum.
- A would-be eavesdropper must know the exact chip in which a particular transmission starts, and the PN code changes if the user is moving when his cellular phone connects to a different tower, thus making eavesdropping extremely difficult.

CDMA-based cellular technology is extremely complex. Because this book is not specifically focused on CDMA technology, the preceding description is included merely to provide an overview of this multiple access method.

Transmission Direction

In most wireless communications systems, data must flow in both directions, and the flow must be controlled so that the sending and receiving devices know when data will arrive or when it needs to be transmitted. There are three types of data flow: simplex, half-duplex, and full-duplex.

Simplex transmission occurs in only one direction, from device 1 to device 2, as shown in Figure 3-18. A broadcast radio station is an example of simplex transmission: The signal goes from the radio transmitter to the listener's radio, but the listener has no way of communicating with the station using the same radio signal. Except for broadcast radio and television, simplex is rarely used in wireless data communications today. That's because the receiver is unable to give the sender any feedback regarding the transmission, such as whether it was received correctly or if it needs to be resent. Such reliability is essential for successful data exchange.

Figure 3-18 Simplex transmission

Half-duplex transmission occurs in both directions, but only one way at a time, as shown in Figure 3-19. This type of communications is typically used in consumer devices such as citizens band (CB) radios or walkie-talkies. In order for User A to transmit a message to User B, he must hold down the "talk" button while speaking. While the button is being pressed, User B can only listen and not talk. User A must release the "talk" button before User B can press her "talk" button. Both parties can send and receive information, but only one at a time.

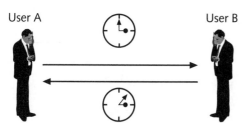

Figure 3-19 Half-duplex transmission

© Cengage Learning 2014

Full-duplex transmission occurs in both directions simultaneously, as shown in Figure 3-20. A telephone system is a type of full-duplex transmission. Both parties to a telephone call can speak at the same time, and they are able to hear each other throughout the call. Most modern wireless systems, such as cellular telephones, use full-duplex transmission.

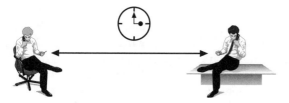

Figure 3-20 Full-duplex transmission

© Cengage Learning 2014

If the same antenna is used for wireless transmission and reception, a filter can be used to handle full-duplex transmissions. Most RF communications equipment that works in full-duplex mode sends and receives on different frequencies. A transmission picked up by the antenna on the receiving frequency passes through a filter and is sent to the receiver, while the transmission signal on the sending frequency is passed on to the same antenna. This is shown in Figure 3-21.

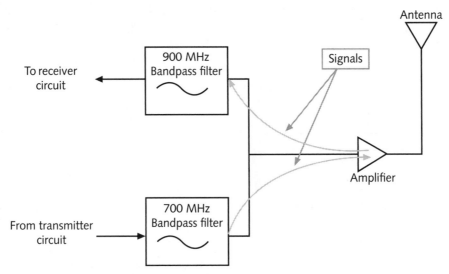

Figure 3-21 Using a single antenna in full-duplex RF communications

© *Cengage Learning 2014*

Switching

The concept of **switching** is essential to all types of telecommunications, wireless as well as wired. Switching involves moving the signal from one wire or frequency to another. Consider for a moment the telephone in your home. You can use that one telephone to call a friend across the street, a classmate in another town, a store in a distant state, or anyone else who also has a phone. How can one single telephone be used to call any other telephone in the world? This is accomplished through a switch at the telephone company's central office. The signal from your phone goes out your telephone's wire all the way to a telephone company's switching office and is then switched or moved to the wire of the telephone that belongs to your friend across the street. This process is shown in Figure 3-22.

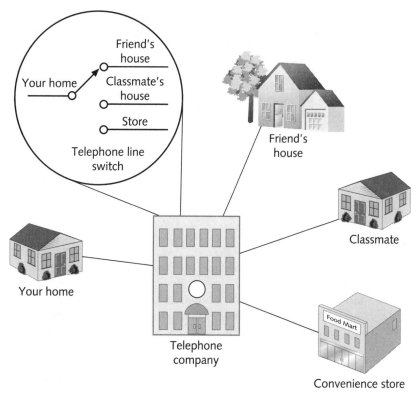

Figure 3-22 Telephone call switching

© Cengage Learning 2014

 The first telephone switches were not automatic. Human operators connected (switched) each two lines manually. Today, the telephone system is known as the Public Switched Telephone Network (PSTN), and the collection of equipment used in this network, including the home telephone sets, is commonly referred to in the data communications field as the Plain Old Telephone System (POTS).

To better understand why switches are necessary, imagine a telephone network in which each telephone must be wired to every other telephone without using switches. If this network had 500 telephones, each telephone would require 499 cables to connect to all the others, and a total of 124,750 cables would be needed to connect all the telephones to one another. If you draw a simple network of five telephones on a piece of paper, you'll notice that you need 10 cables to interconnect all of them. This type of connection is called a "mesh network."

 You can quickly calculate how many cables would be required to interconnect several telephones or computers in a mesh network by using the formula $n(n-1)/2$, where n is the total number of devices you want to connect. Of course, this is not a very practical solution. To connect all the telephone sets in a city with 100,000 telephones would require that each be connected to an enormously large number of wires.

The type of switching used by telephone systems today is known as **circuit switching**. When a telephone call is placed, a direct physical connection is made, through the switch, between the caller and the recipient of the call. While the telephone call is taking place, the connection is "dedicated" and remains open only to these two users. Ignoring, for the moment, some of the advanced features available in today's telephone networks, such as call waiting and conference calling, no other calls can be made from or received by the two connected phones while this conversation is taking place, and anyone who calls that phone will receive a busy signal. This direct connection lasts until the end of the call, at which time the switch drops the connection and makes the two telephone lines available once more to receive or make calls.

Circuit switching is used for both wired telephone systems and second-generation wireless cellular telephone systems.

Circuit switching is ideal for voice communications. However, it is not efficient at transmitting data, because data transmission occurs in "bursts," with periods of delay in between. The delay would result in wasted time while nothing is transmitted. Instead of using circuit switching, data networks use **packet switching**. Packet switching requires that the data transmission be broken into small units called **packets**. Each packet is then sent independently through the network to reach the destination, as shown in Figure 3-23.

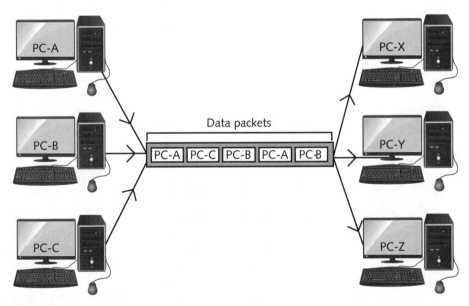

Figure 3-23 Packet switching

© Cengage Learning 2014

Packet switching has a couple of important advantages for data transmissions. One advantage is that it allows better utilization of the network. In Figure 3-23, if PC-A does not have any data to send, PC-B and PC-C can use the available bandwidth on the network to send more data. Circuit switching ties up the communications line until the transmission is complete, whereas packet switching allows multiple computers to share the same line or frequency. That's because packets from several different computers can be intermingled while being sent. Another advantage has to do with error correction. If a transmission error occurs, it usually affects only one or a few packets. Only those packets affected must be resent, not the entire message.

Signal Strength

In a radio system, a signal's strength must be sufficient for the signal to reach its destination with enough amplitude for it to be picked up by the antenna and for the information to be extracted from it. Managing signal strength is much more complicated in a wireless system than in a wired network. Because the signal is not confined to a pair of wires, many types of electromagnetic interference can wreak havoc with the transmission. In addition, many types of objects, both stationary and moving, can impact the signal by blocking it or causing it to reflect. Examples of electromagnetic interference include high-voltage power lines, various types of radiation emitted by the sun, and lightning (see Figure 3-24).

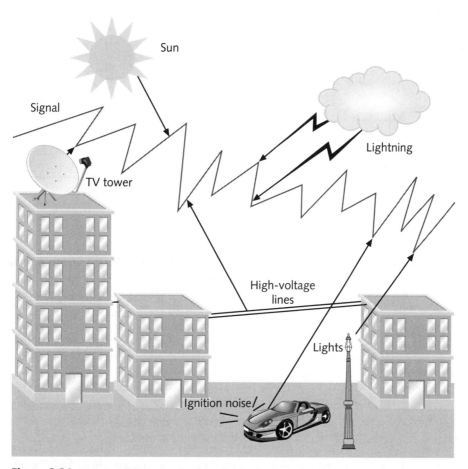

Figure 3-24 Sources of EMI or noise (interference)

© Cengage Learning 2014

Electromagnetic interference (EMI) is also called **noise**. Consider a room with 20 people in it who are having 10 one-on-one conversations. If everyone talks freely, there is a great deal of "racket" or background noise, which interferes with all conversations. With radio waves, background electromagnetic "noise" of various types can impede a signal.

A measurement called **signal-to-noise ratio (SNR)** compares the signal strength with the background noise (see Figure 3-25). When signal strength falls close to or below the level of noise, interference can take place. However, when the strength of the signal is well above the noise, interference can be easily filtered out. Consider again the example of the room with 20 people having 10 conversations. Someone who moves closer to her partner so she can be heard above the background noise is trying to achieve a higher SNR.

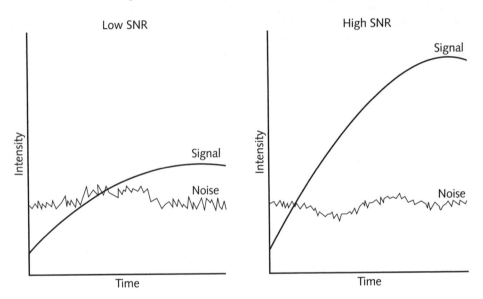

Figure 3-25 Signal-to-noise ratio (SNR)

© Cengage Learning 2014

There are various ways to reduce the interference caused by noise, thereby creating an acceptable SNR. You can use more powerful amplifiers to boost the signal strength, you can filter the signal on the receiving end, or you can use techniques such as frequency hopping spread spectrum.

With a highly complex and expensive device, such as an extremely sensitive radio telescope receiver, the temperature of the circuits is lowered to −459 degrees Fahrenheit to maximize the performance and minimize the noise and attenuation generated by the circuits themselves. Recall that filters and mixers are passive devices that tend to reduce the amplitude or strength of the signal. Cooling these circuits down to −459 degrees Fahrenheit virtually eliminates the attenuation and dramatically reduces the noise. However, it is not practical to do this in a handheld transmitting device.

Loss of signal strength, or **attenuation**, is caused by various factors, but objects in the path of the signal, including man-made objects such as walls, are what cause the most attenuation. Table 3-2 shows examples of different building materials and their effects on radio transmissions. Amplifying a signal both before it is transmitted (to increase the power level) and after it is received helps to minimize attenuation.

Type of Material	Use in a Building	Impact on Radio Waves
Wood	Office partition	Low
Plaster	Inner walls	Low
Glass	Windows	Low
Bricks	Outer walls	Medium
Concrete	Floors and outer walls	High
Metal	Elevator shafts and cars	Very high

Table 3-2 **Materials and their effects on radio waves**

© Cengage Learning 2014

 At certain frequencies, attenuation can also be caused by precipitation, such as rain or snow. Consequently, attenuation decreases as the altitude increases because of the decrease in air and water vapor density at higher altitudes.

As a radio signal is transmitted, the electromagnetic waves spread out. Some of these waves may reflect off distant surfaces and continue toward the receiver. This results in the same signal being received not only from several different directions but also at different times, since it takes longer for the wave that bounced off a distant surface to reach the receiver (see Figure 3-26).

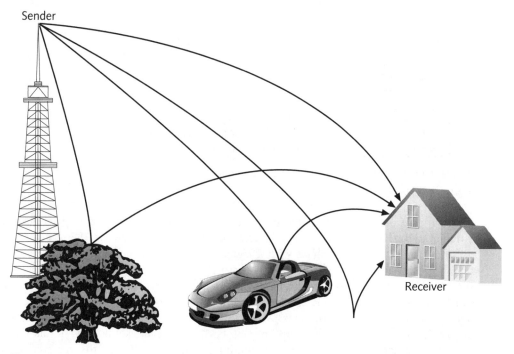

Figure 3-26 Multipath interference or distortion

© Cengage Learning 2014

This phenomenon, known as **multipath distortion,** can cause interference problems that affect the strength of the signal. This can prevent the receiver from picking up a signal strong enough for reliable reception (see Figure 3-27).

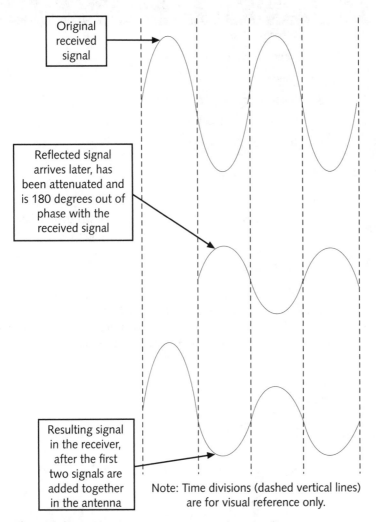

Original received signal

Reflected signal arrives later, has been attenuated and is 180 degrees out of phase with the received signal

Resulting signal in the receiver, after the first two signals are added together in the antenna

Note: Time divisions (dashed vertical lines) are for visual reference only.

Figure 3-27 Effect of multipath distortion in a signal

© Cengage Learning 2014

Multipath distortion gets its name from the fact that some of the waves get reflected, travel different paths between the transmitter and the receiver, and arrive at the receiver antenna at different times and out of phase with a signal that travels a more direct path. The resulting signal at the input of the receiver gets distorted because the peaks of the waves of both signals—one positive and one negative, for example—get added to each other. The result can be a reduction or an increase in the amplitude of the signal at the receiver's antenna, both of which can cause problems. Multipath distortion is a very complex topic, and a full discussion of it is beyond the scope of this book. However, some new standards—such as 802.11n—actually take advantage of multiple signals arriving at the receiver at different times to improve reception.

There are various ways to minimize multipath distortion, including using a **directional antenna,** or multiple receiver radios and antennas, where possible, or changing the height of the transmitter antenna to provide a stronger signal with a clear line of sight to the receiver's antenna. Directional antennas radiate the electromagnetic waves in one direction only and can help reduce or eliminate the effect of multipath distortion if there is a clear line of sight between the receiver and transmitter antennas. Other methods include using a more powerful amplifier in front of the receiver circuit to help increase the SNR, or transmitting the same signal on separate frequencies (see the discussion about OFDM in Chapter 8). Multipath distortion is particularly problematic in cities with large buildings and structures where the receiver is in constant motion, such as in cellular telephony.

Multipath distortion affects FM reception as well, particularly in the downtown districts of metropolitan areas. FM stations are usually free from noise; however, if you have ever been riding in an automobile in the downtown area of a large city you may have noticed occasional static-like noise while listening to an FM station. This noise is caused by the signal reflecting off large buildings and reaching the receiver out of phase, sometimes canceling the signal for very brief moments.

Multipath distortion in RF communications works very similarly to the way an echo affects sound. A good way to simulate multipath distortion is to use an audio editor such as Audacity (on a computer running Windows) or Garageband (on an Apple Macintosh running OS X) to record a sentence like "This is what happens when multipath affects a wireless transmission," then add an echo effect to the recording. Experiment with different degrees of echo. When you play the recording with a lot of echo, try to pick out the individual words in the middle of the sentence.

Understanding Standards

In place almost from the beginning of the telecommunications industry, standards have played an important role in its rapid growth. Today, a knowledge of which standards apply (and how they apply) to the wireless communications systems you are working on will enhance your ability to read and understand industry news, technical articles, and system specifications as well as design and deploy multi-vendor systems that offer excellent compatibility and scalability.

Need for Standards

Some IT people believe that the standards set for computer technologies stifle growth in this fast-paced field—that waiting for standards to catch up slows everything down. Nevertheless, standards do ultimately benefit both manufacturers and consumers. The very nature of the telecommunications industry, in which pieces of equipment from one manufacturer interact with equipment from other manufacturers, requires that standards exist for the design, implementation, test, and operation of the equipment. For example, using your laptop computer on virtually any network worldwide would be next to impossible without standards.

 The world's first telecommunications standard was published by the International Telegraph Union (ITU) in 1885. The standard originated from a desire by the governments of many countries to have a compatible telegraph operation. It took 20 years for the first telegraph standard to be created and published.

Advantages and Disadvantages of Standards

There are pros and cons to developing and applying standards in the telecommunications industry. The advantages have to do with interoperability and corporate competition, whereas the disadvantages are primarily political in nature.

Advantages of Standards One advantage of telecommunications standards is the guarantee that devices from one vendor will interoperate with those from other vendors. Devices that are not based on standards may not be able to connect and communicate with similar devices from other vendors. Standards ensure that a transmitter purchased from Vendor A can be seamlessly integrated into a communications network that contains a receiver from Vendor B.

A second advantage of standards is that they create competition. Standards are open to everyone; any vendor who wants to enter a marketplace can do so. Thus, standards can result in competition between vendors; and competition has several benefits. It results in lower costs for consumers and better-developed products. A vendor who has created a proprietary device gains no benefit from reducing his prices because he has no competition. Instead, with a captive market, he may raise prices at will. However, vendors making products based on the same standards may reduce their prices in order to compete in the marketplace. The competition usually results in lower costs to consumers.

Competition also results in lower costs for manufacturers. Because standards have already been established, manufacturers do not have to invest large amounts of capital in research and development. Instead, they can use the standards as a blueprint for their manufacturing. This reduces startup costs as well as the amount of time needed to bring a product to the market. Also, because standards increase the market for products that follow those standards, manufacturers tend to employ mass production techniques and gain economies of scale in manufacturing and engineering. As a result, production costs stay low, and these savings are passed on to the consumer.

A third advantage of standards is that they help consumers protect their investments in equipment. It is not uncommon for a manufacturer of a proprietary device to phase out a product line of equipment. Businesses that purchased that line are left with two choices. They can continue to support this now-obsolete legacy system, although the costs will dramatically escalate as replacement parts (and support specialists) become more difficult to locate. Or they can throw everything away and buy an up-to-date system. Both choices are very expensive.

Standards can help create a migration path. The organization that creates the initial standards continues to incorporate new technologies by regularly revising its standards. Generally, these revisions are backward-compatible, which reduces the risk of obsolete "orphan" systems that are incompatible with newer technologies.

Disadvantages of Standards International standards can be perceived as a threat to large countries such as the United States because their domestic markets become subjected to overseas competition. Manufacturers in smaller countries may have lower overhead costs, allowing them to produce a device more cheaply than larger manufacturers. Standards allow those manufacturers to produce and sell their products abroad, often threatening a domestic manufacturer's market share. Another way to look at this, of course, is that standards can benefit industries in smaller countries.

Another disadvantage of standards is that although they are intended to create unity, they can have the opposite effect. Periodically, a country will create a standard and offer it to other countries as a global standard. However, another country, for political reasons having nothing to do with technology, may reject the standard and attempt to create its own. Television broadcasting standards provide an example of this. Countries around the world have created various standards as a way of protecting their internal markets as well as their cultural heritages. With the advent of the Internet and global commerce, this type of protectionism appears to be on the way out, but multiple TV standards continue to be in effect, forcing many manufacturers to design and produce television sets and video recorders that support multiple standards. The consumer ultimately has to pay the cost of maintaining these more complex devices.

Most experts agree that the advantages of standards far outweigh the disadvantages and that standards are vital in industries such as telecommunications.

Types of Standards

There are two major types of standards in the telecommunications industry: de facto standards and de jure standards. A third type, consortia standards, is increasingly influencing how standards are set.

De Facto Standards De facto standards are not official standards. They are simply common practices that the industry follows for various reasons—because they're easy to use, perhaps, or because they've traditionally been used or they're what the majority of users have adopted. For the most part, de facto standards are established by their success in the marketplace. For example, most industry experts would agree that Microsoft Windows has become the de facto standard for personal-computer operating systems. By one estimate, approximately 85 percent of computer users worldwide run Windows on their computers (as of November 2011). No organization proclaimed Windows the standard; its widespread use has created what amounts to a standard.

 The term "de facto" comes from Latin and means "from the fact." As it applies to computer and communications technologies, those technologies that are adopted by the market voluntarily become known as de facto standards.

De Jure Standards De jure standards, also called **official standards**, are those that are controlled by an organization or body that has been entrusted with that task. Each standards group has its own rules regarding membership. You will read about some of these groups in the next section.

The process for creating standards can be very involved. Generally, the organization develops subcommittees responsible for specific technologies. Each subcommittee is composed of different working groups, which are teams of industry experts given the task of creating the initial draft of a standard's documentation. The draft is then published to the members, both individuals and companies, and requests for comments (RFCs) are solicited. These members are developers, potential users, and other people with an interest in the field. The original committee reviews the comments and revises the draft. This final draft is then reviewed by the entire organization and is usually put to a vote before the final standards are officially published and made available to the public.

De facto standards sometimes become de jure standards by being approved by a committee. The TCP/IP network communications protocol that is so widely used today is an example of a de facto standard that later became an official standard, when the Internet Engineering Task Force (IETF) became an official standards body.

Consortia One of the major complaints against de jure standards is the amount of time it takes for a standard to be completed. For example, the initial standard for wireless local area networks took seven years to complete. In the telecommunications and IT industries, this represents an extremely long period of time before products can be brought to the marketplace; and, in some cases, manufacturers release products long before the standards are approved, as was the case with the latest high-speed WLAN standard.

Responding to this criticism, consortia are often used today to create standards. **Consortia** are industry-sponsored organizations with the goal of promoting a specific technology. Unlike with de jure standards bodies, membership in consortia is not open to everyone. Instead, specific high-profile companies create and serve on consortia. The goal of consortia is to develop a standard that promotes their specific technology in a shorter period of time than what official standards organizations take.

One of the most well-known consortia is the World Wide Web Consortium (W3C), which is composed of industry giants such as Microsoft, Netscape, Sun, and IBM. The W3C is responsible for creating the standards that are widely used on the Internet today, including hypertext markup language (HTML), cascading style sheets (CSS), and the Document Object Model (DOM).

Telecommunications Standards Organizations

In the telecommunications field, standards organizations exist at the national, multinational, and international levels. The following sections discuss each of these levels.

National Standards Organizations In the United States, there are several standards organizations, each of which plays a role in setting telecommunications standards. The **American National Standards Institute (ANSI)** functions largely as a clearinghouse for all kinds of standards development in the United States. Most ANSI standards are developed by one of its over 270 affiliated organizations, which include diverse groups such as the Water Quality Association and the Telecommunications Industry Association, as well as the group that originally created the ASCII code for use in computers and data communications. As of 2011, ANSI represents the interests of over 125,000 companies and 3.5 million professionals.

One of the ANSI-affiliated organizations is the **Telecommunications Industries Association (TIA)**. It is made up of industry vendors from telecommunications, electronic components, consumer electronics, and electronic information. Working with vendors, the TIA publishes Recommended Standards (RS) for the industry to follow. For example, the TIA developed and published a standard that defines how a computer's serial port, connector pin-outs, and electrical signaling should function. This standard is generally known as TIA RS-232. More information on the TIA can be found at *www.tiaonline.org*.

The TIA represents more than 600 companies that manufacture or supply the products and services used in global communications. The function of the TIA is to advocate policies to legislative bodies and to establish standards in five areas: user-premises equipment, network equipment, wireless communications, fiber optics, and satellite communications.

Two other organizations play roles in establishing national standards for telecommunications technology. The **Internet Engineering Task Force (IETF)** is a large, open (to anyone interested in joining) community of network designers, operators, vendors, and researchers concerned with the evolution of the Internet's architecture and the smooth operation of the Internet. Although it is a United States organization, it accepts members from any country in the world and focuses on the upper layers of telecommunications protocols; it is the organization that designs and develops practically all of the protocols used on the Internet. The IETF existed informally for many years, and it was not an official standards body until 1986, when it was formalized by the **Internet Architecture Board (IAB)**.

The IAB is responsible for defining the overall architecture of the Internet; it also serves as the technology advisory group for the **Internet Society (ISOC)**, a professional-membership organization of Internet experts that comments on policies and practices and oversees a number of other boards and task forces dealing with network policy issues. You can find out more about the IETF and its parent organizations at *www.ietf.org*.

The **Institute of Electrical and Electronics Engineers (IEEE)**, like the IETF, establishes standards for telecommunications. However, it also establishes a wide range of other IT standards. The IEEE's most well-known standards include IEEE 802.3, which covers local area network Ethernet transmissions, and IEEE 802.11, which covers the lower protocol layers of wireless local area network transmissions.

NOTE You can learn more about the IEEE at *www.ieee.org*. You can also obtain a no-cost copy of the IEEE 802 standards that relate to networking and wireless networking, provided that these have been published for longer than six months, at the following Web site: *standards.ieee.org/getieee802/portfolio.html*.

Multinational Standards Organizations

Multinational standards organizations span more than one country; many of them are based in Europe. For example, the **European Telecommunications Standards Institute (ETSI)** develops telecommunications standards for use throughout Europe. Its membership consists primarily of European companies and European government agencies, but they also interface with organizations in other countries, including the United States. You can learn more about ETSI at *www.etsi.org*.

International Standards Organizations Because telecommunications technology is truly global, there are also global organizations that set industry standards. The best known is the **International Telecommunication Union (ITU)**, an agency of the United Nations that is responsible for telecommunications. The ITU is composed of over 200 governments and private companies that coordinate global telecommunications networks and services. Unlike other bodies that set standards, the ITU is actually a treaty organization. The regulations set by the ITU are legally binding on the nations that have signed the treaty.

Two of the ITU's subsidiary organizations prepare recommendations on telecommunications standards. The ITU-T focuses on telecommunications networks, and the ITU-R focuses on RF-based communications, including the radio frequencies that should be used and the radio systems that support them. Although these recommendations are not mandatory and are not binding on the countries that have signed other treaties, almost all of the countries elect to follow the ITU recommendations, and these essentially function as worldwide standards. You can learn more about the ITU at *www.itu.int*.

ITU-T replaced a standards body known as the CCITT, whose origins date back to work on standards for telegraphs in the 1860s.

The **International Organization for Standardization (ISO)** is based in Geneva, Switzerland. (Note that it uses the acronym "ISO" instead of "IOS." That's because "iso" means "equal" in Greek, and the organization wanted to use the same acronym worldwide, regardless of language.) Started in 1947, the ISO promotes international cooperation and standards in the areas of science, technology, and economics. Today, groups from over 100 countries belong to the ISO. You can learn more about it at *www.iso.org*.

Several of the groups that belong to the ISO are actually national standards bodies. For example, the TIA interfaces with the ISO.

It might seem like there are too many standards organizations, but all these organizations, including the ones in the United States, tend to cooperate with one another, seldom stepping over one another's authority or geographical jurisdiction. You will read more about this cooperation in the upcoming chapters.

Regulatory Agencies

Although setting standards is important for telecommunications, enforcing telecommunications regulations is equally important. In a sense, the nature of national and international commerce enforces some standards. A company that refuses to abide by standards for cellular telephone transmissions will find that nobody buys its products. Telecommunications regulations, however, must be enforced by an outside regulatory agency, whose role is to ensure that all participants adhere to the prescribed standards. These regulations typically involve defining who can use a specific frequency when broadcasting a signal. Almost all countries have a national organization that functions as the regulatory agency to determine and enforce telecommunications policies. Some small countries simply adopt the regulations used by another country.

In the United States, the **Federal Communications Commission (FCC)** serves as the primary regulatory agency for telecommunications. The FCC is an independent government agency that is directly responsible to Congress. It was established by the Communications Act of 1934 and is charged with regulating interstate and international communications by radio, television, wire, satellite, and cable. The FCC's jurisdiction covers the 50 states, the District of Columbia, and U.S. territories.

In order to preserve its independence, the FCC is directed by five commissioners who are appointed by the President and confirmed by the Senate for five-year terms. Only three commissioners may be members of the same political party, and none of them can have a financial interest in any FCC-related business.

The FCC's responsibilities are very broad. In addition to developing and implementing regulatory programs, it processes applications for licenses and other filings, analyzes complaints, conducts investigations, and takes part in congressional hearings. The FCC also represents the United States in negotiations with foreign nations about telecommunications issues.

The FCC plays an important role in wireless communications. It regulates radio and television broadcast stations as well as cable and satellite stations. It also oversees the licensing, compliance, implementation, and other aspects of cellular telephones, pagers, and two-way radios. The FCC regulates the use of radio frequencies to fulfill the communications needs of businesses, local and state governments, public safety service providers, aircraft and ship operators, as well as individuals.

The RF spectrum is a limited resource, meaning that only a certain range of frequencies can be used for radio transmissions. Because of this limitation, frequencies are often licensed by regulatory agencies in the different countries around the world. In the United States, the regulatory agency is the FCC, which has the power to allocate portions of the spectrum. Broadcasters are required to transmit only in the frequency or frequencies for which they obtained a license. Commercial companies such as radio and television stations must pay fees (which are sometimes quite large) for the right to use a frequency; and, naturally, they do not want anyone else to be allowed to transmit on the same frequency within their coverage area. The FCC and other countries' agencies continually monitor transmissions to ensure that no one is using a frequency without a license or is transmitting with more power than their license allows.

Radio Frequency Spectrum

The **radio frequency spectrum** is the entire range of all radio frequencies that exist, from 10 KHz to over 30 GHz. The spectrum is divided into 450 different sections, or **bands**. Table 3-3 lists the major bands, their corresponding frequencies, and some typical uses.

Band (Acronym)	Frequency	Common Uses
Very low frequency (VLF)	10 KHz to 30 KHz	Maritime ship-to-shore
Low frequency (LF)	30 KHz to 300 KHz	Radio location such as LORAN (Long Range Navigation) Time signals for clock synchronization (WWVB)
Medium frequency (MF)	300 KHz to 3 MHz	AM radio
High frequency (HF)	3 MHz to 30 MHz	Short wave radio, CB radio
Very high frequency (VHF)	30 MHz to 144 MHz 144 MHz to 174 MHz 174 MHz to 328.6 MHz	TV channels 2–6, FM radio Taxi radios TV channels 7–13
Ultra high frequency (UHF)	328.6 MHz to 806 MHz 806 MHz to 960 MHz 960 MHz to 2.3 GHz 2.3 GHz to 2.9 GHz	Public safety: Fire, Police, etc. Cellular telephones Air traffic control radar WLANs (802.11b/g/n)
Super high frequency (SHF)	2.9 GHz to 30 GHz	WLANs (802.11a/n)
Extremely high frequency (EHF)	30 GHz and above	Radio astronomy

Table 3-3 Radio frequency bands

© Cengage Learning 2014

Radio frequencies of other common devices include:

- Garage door openers, alarm systems: 40 MHz
- Baby monitors: 49 MHz
- Radio-controlled airplanes: 72 MHz
- Radio-controlled cars: 75 MHz
- Wildlife tracking collars: 215 MHz–220 MHz
- Global positioning system (GPS): 1.227 GHz and 1.575 GHz

The United States is obligated to comply with the international spectrum allocations established by the ITU. However, the United States' use of its domestic spectrum may differ from the international allocations as long as those uses do not conflict with international regulations or agreements.

Until 1993, the ITU held conferences at 20-year intervals to review the international spectrum allocations. Since then, ITU conferences are convened every two to three years.

The U.S. Commerce Department's National Telecommunications and Information Administration (NTIA), serves as the principal advisor to the President on domestic and international communications and information issues. It also represents the views of the executive branch before Congress, the Federal Communications Commission, foreign governments, and international organizations.

Although a license from the FCC is required to send and receive on a specific frequency, there is a notable exception. This is known as the **license exempt spectrum**, or **unregulated bands**. Unregulated bands are, in effect, radio spectra that are available to any users nationwide without charge and without a license. Devices that use these bands can be either fixed or mobile. The FCC designated the unregulated bands to promote the development of a broad range of new devices and stimulate the growth of new industries.

 The FCC does impose power limits on devices using the unregulated bands, which in effect reduces their ranges. This prevents manufacturers of devices such as long-range walkie-talkies from using these frequencies instead of the regulated frequencies intended for these products.

Table 3-4 outlines a subset of the unregulated bands used by many of the technologies discussed in this book. The ITU-R has published recommendations for many additional unregulated bands; but as you learned earlier, not every country's domestic market follows all of the ITU-R's recommendations. One unregulated band is the **Industrial, Scientific and Medical (ISM) band**, which was approved by the FCC in 1985. Today, devices such as WLANs that transmit at speeds between 1 Mbps and 300 Mbps use this band. Another unlicensed band is the **Unlicensed National Information Infrastructure (U-NII)**, approved in 1996. The U-NII band is intended for devices that provide short-range, high-speed wireless digital communications. U-NII devices provide a means for educational institutions, libraries, and health care providers to connect to basic and advanced telecommunications services. Wireless networks working in unlicensed frequency bands are already helping to improve the quality and reduce the cost of medical care by allowing medical staff to obtain on-the-spot patient data, X-rays, and medical charts, and by giving health care workers access to telecommunications services.

Unlicensed Band	Frequency	Total Bandwidth	Common Uses
Industrial, Scientific and Medical (ISM)	902–928 MHz 2.4–2.4835 GHz 5.725–5.875 GHz	259.5 MHz	Cordless phones, WLANs, wireless public branch exchanges
Unlicensed Personal Communications Systems	1910–1930 MHz	20 MHz	WLANs, wireless public branch exchanges
Unlicensed National Information Infrastructure (U-NII)	5.15–5.25 GHz 5.15–5.25 (Low) 5.25–5.35 GHz (Mid) 5.47–5.725 (Worldwide) 5.725–5.825 GHz (Upper)	555 MHz	WLANs, wireless public branch WLANs wireless public branch exchanges, campus applications, long outdoor links
Millimeter Wave	59–64 GHz	5 GHz	In-home networking applications

Table 3-4 Unregulated bands

© Cengage Learning 2014

Two recent developments have had an impact on the crowded radio frequency spectrum. The first involves the direction of radio signals. Currently, when radio signals leave the sender's antenna, they spread or radiate out (the word "radio" comes from the term "radiated energy") and can be picked up by multiple recipients. A new technique known as **adaptive array processing** replaces a traditional antenna with an array of antenna elements. These elements deliver RF signals to one specific user instead of sending signals out in a scattered pattern. This helps prevent eavesdropping by unapproved listeners and also allows more transmissions to take place in a given range of frequencies.

The second development is known as **ultra-wideband transmission (UWB)**. UWB does not use a traditional radio signal carrier sending signals in the regulated frequency spectrum. Instead, UWB uses low-power, precisely timed pulses of energy that operate in the same frequency spectrum as low-end noise, such as that emitted by computer chips, TV monitors, automobile ignitions, and fans. UWB is currently used in limited radar and position-location devices. The IEEE has ratified standards for its use in wireless network communications. One example is IEEE 802.15.3c, which is used in WirelessHD and WiGig.

Chapter Summary

- Several hardware components are essential for communicating using radio frequencies (RF): filters, mixers, amplifiers, and antennas. A version of each of these components is found on all radio systems.

- A filter is used to either accept or block a radio frequency signal. With a low-pass filter, a maximum frequency threshold is set. All signals that are below that maximum threshold are allowed to pass through. Instead of setting a maximum frequency threshold, as with a low-pass filter, a high-pass filter sets a minimum frequency threshold. All signals that are above the minimum threshold are allowed to pass through, whereas those below the minimum threshold are turned away. A bandpass filter sets a passband, which is both a minimum and maximum threshold.

- The purpose of a mixer is to combine two inputs to create a single output. The single output is the highest sum and the lowest difference of the frequencies.

- An amplifier increases a signal's intensity or strength, whereas an antenna converts an RF signal from the transmitter into an electromagnetic wave, which carries the information through the air or empty space.

- Although filters, mixers, amplifiers, and antennas are all necessary components for a radio system, there are other design considerations that must be taken into account when creating a radio system. Because there are only a limited number of frequencies available, conserving the use of frequencies is important. One way to conserve is by sharing a frequency among several individual users.

- Frequency Division Multiple Access (FDMA) divides the bandwidth of the frequency into several narrower frequencies. Time Division Multiple Access (TDMA) divides the bandwidth into several time slots. Each user is assigned the entire frequency band for his transmission but only for a small fraction of time on a fixed, rotating basis. Code Division Multiple Access (CDMA) uses spread spectrum technology and unique digital spreading codes called PN codes, rather than separate RF frequencies or channels, to differentiate between the different transmissions.

- The direction in which data travels on a wireless network is important. There are three types of data flow. Simplex transmission occurs in only one direction. Half-duplex transmission sends data in both directions, but only one way at a time. And full-duplex transmission enables data to flow in both directions simultaneously.

- Switching involves moving the signal from one wire or frequency to another. Telephone systems use a type of switching known as circuit switching. When a telephone call is made, a dedicated and direct physical connection is made between the caller and the recipient of the call through the switch. Instead of using circuit switching, data networks use packet switching. Packet switching requires that the data transmission be broken into smaller units called packets, and each packet is then sent independently through the network to reach the destination.

- Managing a signal's strength is much more complicated in a wireless system than in a wired system. Electromagnetic interference (EMI), sometimes called noise, comes from a variety of man-made and natural sources. The signal-to-noise ratio (SNR) refers to the measure of signal strength relative to the background noise. A loss of signal strength is known as attenuation. Attenuation can be caused by a variety of factors (such as walls) that can decrease the signal's strength. As a radio signal is transmitted, the electromagnetic waves spread out. Some of these waves may reflect off surfaces and slow down. This results in the same signal being received not only from several different directions but at different times. This is known as multipath distortion.

- Telecommunications standards have been in place almost since the beginning of the industry and have played an important role in the rapid growth of the field. There are several advantages of having standards, including interoperability, lower costs, and a migration path. De facto standards are not standards per se, just common practices that the industry follows. Official standards (also called de jure standards) are those that are controlled by an organization or body that has been entrusted with that task. Consortia are often used today to create standards. Consortia are industry-sponsored organizations that have the goal of promoting a specific technology.

- Some standards organizations span more than one country. And because telecommunications is a truly global phenomenon, there are also multinational organizations that set standards. In the United States, the Federal Communications Commission (FCC) serves as the primary regulatory agency for telecommunications. The FCC is an independent government agency that is directly responsible to Congress.

- The radio frequency spectrum is the entire range of all radio frequencies that exist. This range extends from 10 KHz to over 30 GHz and is divided into 450 different bands. Although a license from the FCC is normally required to send and receive on a specific frequency, unregulated bands are available for use without a license in the United States and many other countries. Two unregulated bands are the Industrial, Scientific and Medical (ISM) band and the Unlicensed National Information Infrastructure (U-NII).

- Two recent developments have had an impact on the crowded radio frequency spectrum. A new technique known as adaptive array processing replaces a traditional antenna with an array of antenna elements. These elements deliver RF signals to one specific user instead of sending signals out in a scattered pattern. Ultra-wideband transmission (UWB) does not use a traditional radio signal carrier to send signals in the regulated frequency spectrum. Instead, it uses low-power, precisely timed pulses of energy that operate in the same frequency spectrum as low-end noise, such as that emitted by computer chips and TV monitors.

Key Terms

adaptive array processing   A radio transmission technique that replaces a traditional antenna with an array of antenna elements.

American National Standards Institute (ANSI)   A clearinghouse for standards development in the United States.

amplifier   A component that increases a signal's intensity.

attenuation   A loss of signal strength.

bandpass filter   A filter that passes all signals that are between the maximum and minimum threshold.

circuit switching   A switching technique in which a dedicated and direct physical connection is made between two transmitting devices—for example, between two telephones during a call.

Code Division Multiple Access (CDMA)   A technique that uses spread spectrum technology and unique digital codes to send and receive radio transmissions.

consortia   Industry-sponsored organizations that have the goal of promoting a specific technology.

crosstalk   Signals from close frequencies that may interfere with other signals.

de facto standards   Common practices that the industry follows for various reasons.

de jure standards   Standards that are controlled by an organization or body.

directional antenna   An antenna that radiates the electromagnetic waves in one direction only. As a result, it can help reduce or eliminate the effect of multipath distortion if there is a clear line of sight between the two antennas.

electromagnetic interference (EMI)   Interference with a radio signal; also called noise.

European Telecommunications Standards Institute (ETSI)   A standards body that develops telecommunications standards for use throughout Europe.

Federal Communications Commission (FCC)   The primary U.S. regulatory agency for telecommunications.

filter   A component that is used to either accept or block a radio frequency signal.

Frequency Division Multiple Access (FDMA)   A radio transmission technique that divides the bandwidth of the frequency into several smaller frequency bands.

full-duplex transmission   Transmissions in which data flows in either direction simultaneously.

half-duplex transmission   Transmission that occurs in both directions but only one way at a time.

high-pass filter   A filter that passes all signals that are above a maximum threshold.

harmonics   Stray oscillations that result from the process of modulating a wave and that fall outside the range of frequencies used for transmission. Harmonics also occur when a signal goes through a mixer and must be filtered out at several points before the signal is finally fed to the antenna for transmission.

Industrial, Scientific and Medical (ISM) band   An unregulated radio frequency band approved by the FCC in 1985.

Institute of Electrical and Electronics Engineers (IEEE)   A standards body that establishes standards for telecommunications.

intermediate frequency (IF)   The output signal that results from the modulation process.

International Organization for Standardization (ISO)   An organization to promote international cooperation and standards in the areas of science, technology, and economics.

International Telecommunication Union (ITU)   An agency of the United Nations that sets international telecommunications standards and coordinates global telecommunications networks and services.

Internet Architecture Board (IAB)   The organization responsible for defining the overall architecture of the Internet, providing guidance and broad direction to the IETF. The IAB also serves as the technology advisory group to the Internet Society and oversees a number of critical activities in support of the Internet.

Internet Engineering Task Force (IETF)   A standards body that focuses on the lower levels of telecommunications technologies.

Internet Society (ISOC)   A professional-membership organization of Internet experts that comments on policies and practices and oversees a number of other boards and task forces dealing with network policy issues.

license exempt spectrum   Unregulated radio frequency bands that are available in the United States to any users without a license.

low-pass filter   A filter that passes all signals that are below a maximum threshold.

mixer   A component that combines two inputs to create a single output.

multipath distortion   What occurs when the same signal reflects and arrives at the receiver's antenna from several different directions and at different times.

noise   Interference with a signal.

official standards   *See* de jure standards.

packet   A smaller segment of the transmitted signal.

packet switching   Data transmission that is broken into smaller units.

passband   A minimum and maximum threshold that spells out which range of frequencies will pass through a filter.

PN code   Pseudo random code; a code that appears to be a random sequence of 1s and 0s but actually repeats itself. Used in CDMA cellular telephone technology.

radio frequency (RF) communications   All types of radio communications that use radio frequency waves.

radio frequency spectrum   The entire range of all radio frequencies that exist.

sidebands   The sum and the differences of the frequency carrier that serve as buffer space around the frequency of the transmitted signal.

signal-to-noise ratio (SNR)   The measure of signal strength relative to the background noise.

simplex transmission   Transmission that occurs in only one direction.

switching   Moving a signal from one wire or frequency to another.

Telecommunications Industries Association (TIA)   A group of more than 600 companies that manufacture or supply the products and services used in global communications.

Time Division Multiple Access (TDMA) A transmission technique that divides the bandwidth into several time slots.

ultra-wideband transmission (UWB) Low-power, precisely timed pulses of energy that operate in the same frequency spectrum as low-end noise, such as that emitted by computer chips and TV monitors.

Unlicensed National Information Infrastructure (U-NII) An unregulated band approved by the FCC in 1996 to provide for short-range, high-speed wireless digital communications.

unregulated bands *See* license exempt spectrum.

Review Questions

1. Each of the following is a type of RF filter except _____.
   a. low-pass
   b. high-pass
   c. passband
   d. bandpass

2. A(n) _____ combines two inputs to create a single output.
   a. mixer
   b. codex
   c. filter
   d. amplifier

3. A(n) _____ actively increases a signal's intensity or strength.
   a. transmitter
   b. demodulator
   c. amplifier
   d. antenna

4. The result of using a PN code is that _____.
   a. it adds a unique address to the signal
   b. it spreads the signal over a wider range of frequencies
   c. it mixes the signal with the IF
   d. it decodes the signal

5. _____ is a method of transmission in which the information is broken up into smaller units.
   a. Error correction
   b. Circuit switching
   c. Electromagnetic interference
   d. Packet switching

6. A passband has both a minimum and maximum threshold. True or False?

7. The resulting output from the modulation process is known as the middle frequency (MF) signal. True or False?

8. When mixing two signals, the highest sum and the smallest difference between the carrier frequency and the range of frequencies at the other input define two limits known as the sidebands of the frequency carrier. True or False?

9. TDMA can carry three times the amount of data that CDMA can. True or False?

10. Without switching, 1,225 cables would be required to interconnect 50 telephones. True or False?

11. When using the same antenna for full-duplex communications, the same frequency can be used for transmitting and receiving simultaneously. True or False?

12. _____ divides the bandwidth of the frequency into several narrower frequencies. Each user then transmits using its own narrower frequency channel.

    a. TDMA

    b. OFDM

    c. FDMA

    d. CDMA

13. When signals are sent at frequencies that are closely grouped together, an errant signal may encroach on a close frequency, causing _____.

    a. frequency conflict

    b. crosstalk

    c. time conflict

    d. channel mixing

14. Which of the following divides the bandwidth of the frequency channel into several time slots?

    a. FDMA

    b. OFDM

    c. CDMA

    d. TDMA

15. A _____ transmission uses spread spectrum technology and unique spreading codes for each user.

    a. CDMA

    b. FDMA

    c. TDMA

    d. OFDM

16. List and describe the three types of data flow.

17. List and discuss the advantages of standards.

18. What is switching? What type of switching is used with telephone transmissions, and what type is used for data transmissions?

19. Explain multipath distortion and how it can be minimized.

20. What does the Federal Communications Commission do regarding the licensing of radion frequencies?

Hands-On Projects

Project 3-1

In Figure 3-28, fill in the dashed lines on the right with the resulting output frequency ranges from the various filters. Begin by converting the input frequencies to a common unit: KHz, MHz, or GHz. Then, show the results in the unit of your preference. (Recall that filters usually have only a single input but are shown here, for reasons of clarity, with two inputs.)

Maximum Threshold = 600 KHz

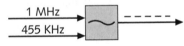

Low-pass filter

Minimum Threshold = 1,800 MHz

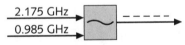

High-pass filter

Passband = 1,800 MHz–1900 MHz

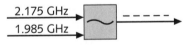

Bandpass filter

Figure 3-28 Filters (1)

© Cengage Learning 2014

Project 3-2

In Figure 3-29, fill in the dashed lines at the right with the resulting output frequencies or ranges. Begin by converting the input frequencies to a common unit: KHz, MHz, or GHz. Then, show the results in the unit of your preference.

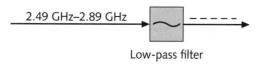

Maximum Threshold = 2.312 GHz

2.49 GHz–2.89 GHz

Low-pass filter

Minimum Threshold = 800 MHz

0.725 GHz–0.985 GHz

High-pass filter

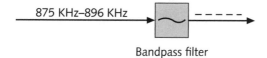

Passband = 0.852 MHz–0.986 MHz

875 KHz–896 KHz

Bandpass filter

Figure 3-29 Filters (2)

© Cengage Learning 2014

Project 3-3

In Figure 3-30, fill in the dashed lines at the right with the resulting output frequency ranges. Begin by converting the frequencies to a common unit: KHz, MHz, or GHz. Then, show the results in the unit of your preference.

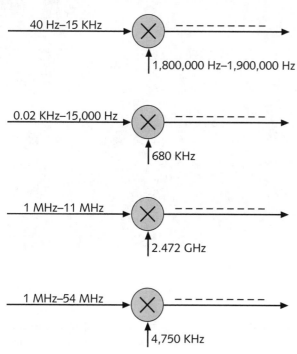

40 Hz–15 KHz

1,800,000 Hz–1,900,000 Hz

0.02 KHz–15,000 Hz

680 KHz

1 MHz–11 MHz

2.472 GHz

1 MHz–54 MHz

4,750 KHz

Figure 3-30 Mixers

© Cengage Learning 2014

Project 3-4

Both natural and man-made objects located in a radio signal's path can cause attenuation—that is, a loss of signal strength. For this project, you will need a notebook computer equipped with a wireless LAN interface that is connected to an AP or wireless residential gateway. You will download, install, and configure inSSIDer to monitor the signal strength of the network that your computer is connected to.

1. In a Web browser, enter the address **www.metageek.net**.

2. Click **Downloads**. The inSSIDer download page should open automatically. If it doesn't, click **inSSIDer** in the menu on the left side of the page.

3. Save the file in the location of your preference, then locate the file inSSIDer-Installer-*x.x.x.x*.exe, in which *x.x.x.x* is the latest version of the program. Double-click the file to install the utility on your computer. Accept all the default settings.

4. Once the program has finished installing, click **Start, All Programs, Metageek,** then click **inSSIDer**.

5. inSSIDer will open and display a screen similar to the one in Figure 3-31. Maximize the inSSIDer application window. By default, inSSIDer will detect and display a list of all the wireless networks your computer has detected around your current location.

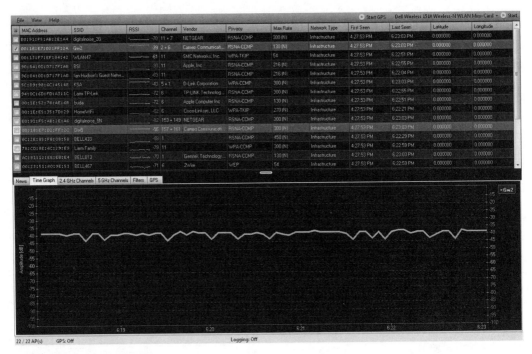

Figure 3-31 inSSIDer window

Source: MetaGeek, LLC

6. Click the box to the left of "MAC Address" (just below the menu bar in the inSSIDer window) to remove the checkmarks in the column below. In the next project, you will monitor only the wireless network to which your computer is connected.

7. If you don't know it yet, ask your instructor to provide you with the SSID of the network. Locate it in the SSID column of the inSSIDer window and click the box to the left of the MAC Address of your network's SSID. A checkmark should appear in the box, with the row highlighted.

8. In the middle of the inSSIDer window, you will find a series of tabs. Click the **Time Graph** tab.

You will use inSSIDer in the following projects as well as in other chapters of this book.

NOTE

HANDS-ON PROJECTS

Project 3-5

In this project, you will use inSSIDer to monitor the signal strength of your AP.

1. The line in the Time Graph graph tab at the bottom of the inSSIDer window (see Figure 3-31) displays the strength of the signal that your computer is receiving from the AP. It will appear near the top of the graph if the signal strength is high and near the bottom of the graph if the signal strength is low.

Don't worry about the meaning of the numbers on either side of the inSSIDer Time Graph window for now. You will learn what they mean and how to use them in Chapter 4.

NOTE

2. Monitor the strength of the signal while roaming away from the access point with the computer. Try to determine how far you can move from the access point before the signal is too weak for the connection to work reliably. To do this, you will need to attempt to open a Web page or download a file.

You can estimate the distance between you and the AP by any method available to you, such as counting tiles on the floor and multiplying by the size of the tiles or measuring your stride and counting the number of paces between the notebook computer and the AP.

TIP

3. As you move away from the AP, record all the obstacles between the computer and the AP, such as walls, doors, windows, and partitions. As you monitor the signal strength, record which items appear to have the greatest impact on the strength of the signal.

4. Record the distance at which the connection to the AP drops or becomes too slow or unreliable, such as when you can no longer access Web pages or when a file download appears to stop for a minute or longer.

5. Monitor the strength of the signal while standing between 50 ft. (15 meters and 100 ft. (30 meters) from the AP and covering the antenna of the network interface card with the following items:

- your hand (for a short period of time)
- a piece of aluminum foil
- a sheet of paper
- a sheet of plastic (like a shopping bag)
- a purse or briefcase with some metalic objects inside

If the NIC is built into the notebook computer, try using both hands to cover the back of the screen or the bottom of the computer until you see a definite reduction in the strength of the signal.

TIP

HANDS-ON PROJECTS

Project 3-6

Research the Web sites of the organizations listed in the left column of the table below and list some of the standards that they publish. Using Row 1 as a guide, identify other types of standards published by the same organization.

ISO – International Organization for Standardization *www.iso.org*	Screw threads, freight containers, computer protocols
IEEE – Institute of Electrical and Electronic Engineers *www.ieee.org*	
ITU – International Telecommunication Union *www.itu.int*	
ANSI – American National Standards Institute *www.ansi.org*	
ETSI – European Telecommunications Standards Institute *www.etsi.org*	

Real-World Exercises

The Baypoint Group (TBG), a company of 50 consultants who work with organizations and businesses on issues involving network planning and design, has again requested your services as a consultant. This time, the Good Samaritan Center, which assists needy citizens in the area, needs to modernize its office facilities. As part of its community outreach program, TBG has asked you to donate your time to help the Good Samaritan Center.

The Good Samaritan Center wants to install a wireless network in its offices. One local vendor has been trying to sell the center a proprietary system based on five-year-old technology that does not follow any current standards. The price given for the product and its installation is low and is therefore attractive to the center. However, managers at the center have asked TBG for advice.

Exercise 3-1

Create a PowerPoint slide presentation that outlines the different types of standards, the advantages and disadvantages of standards, and why they are needed. Include examples of products that did not follow standards and have vanished from the marketplace. Because the Good Samaritan Center is on the verge of buying the product, TBG has asked you to be very persuasive in your presentation. You are told that presenting the facts is not enough at this point; you must convince them why they should purchase a product that follows standards before you leave the room.

Exercise 3-2

Your presentation casts a shadow of doubt over the vendor's proprietary product, but the Good Samaritan Center is still not completely convinced it should go with a standard product. TBG has just learned that the vendor's proprietary product uses a licensed frequency that will require the center to secure and pay for a license from the FCC. TBG has asked you to prepare another presentation regarding the advantages and disadvantages of unregulated frequency bands. Because an engineer who sits on the Board of the Good Samaritan Center will be there, this PowerPoint presentation should be detailed and technical in its scope. Avoid focusing on the disadvantages of the vendor's proposal. Be prepared to answer questions related to potential interference by other wireless network users in nearby offices and what measures can be taken either to avoid such interference altogether or to deal with any problems that may arise.

Challenge Case Project

CASE PROJECTS

A local engineering user's group has contacted The Baypoint Group requesting a speaker to discuss multiple access technologies (FDMA, TDMA, and CDMA). Form a team of two or three consultants and research these technologies in detail. Specifically, pay attention to how they are used, and address their strengths and weaknesses. Provide an opinion about which technology will become the dominant player in the future of wireless.

chapter 4

How Antennas Work

After reading this chapter and completing the exercises, you will be able to:

- Define decibels, gain, and loss
- Explain the purpose of an antenna
- List the different antenna types, shapes, and sizes as well as their applications
- Explain RF signal strength and direction
- Describe how antennas work

So far, we have looked at the properties of radio frequency signals, most of the components that are required to generate these signals, and how to load these signals (modulation) with some kind of meaningful information, whether analog (like music or voice) or digital data (which is what this book is about). The last component required for transmission of these signals is an antenna, and this is such a vast topic that it deserves its own chapter.

Antennas mystify even some RF engineers and technicians, for they are responsible for the "magic" of RF communications. The purpose of an antenna is to convert electricity into electromagnetic waves, which then radiate or move away from the antenna at the transmitting end. At the receiving end, antennas convert the EM waves back into an electrical current.

The field of wireless communications is growing at a very fast pace, with new standards and technologies being introduced every week. Service providers are beginning to deploy wireless devices everywhere—at airports, hotels, train stations, restaurants, cafes, shopping malls, even in public parks. The use of cellular telephones has exploded in the last three decades. Employees in all types of industries are being equipped with smartphones so they can stay in touch through voice and e-mail at all times from anywhere in the world and also so they can access applications and corporate data. Wireless networks and wireless Internet hotspots are becoming commonplace in locations catering to businesspeople and the general public alike. Concerns about security, privacy, and interference, especially in devices that use unlicensed bands, are growing. No matter which type of RF communications you use, some kind of antenna is required.

Antennas play a key role in the successful deployment of any kind of wireless connection. Proper planning and installation of antennas is required to ensure good signal coverage, to permit user mobility, minimize or eliminate interference, and in some cases to enhance security. Cellular service providers spend a great deal of time and effort planning and analyzing utilization and traffic patterns in order to maximize the number of customers that can use the system in a given area and allow for continuous connectivity for both data and voice. In the rush to get wireless networks installed today, many are being deployed with little thought about where the signals originate or how far they reach.

This chapter takes you on an introductory technical tour of antennas—their types, sizes, and applications as well as some of the implementation issues. First, you learn about power gain and loss, then about the physical aspects of antennas. Mostly, this chapter discusses antennas used in a limited range of wireless communications technologies. However, the basic concepts cross over to other RF communications technologies, and the information provided here can be easily extended to other types of antenna system implementation.

Gain and Loss

Understanding RF signal transmission involves knowing:

- The strength or the power with which the transmitter is sending the signal
- The amount of reduction in signal strength caused by cables, connectors, and other components
- The transmission medium (atmosphere or free-space)
- The minimum strength of the signal required by the receiver to be able to properly recover the data sent by the transmitter

These requirements mean that we need to know how much power the signal loses or gains at various points. For example, an analysis of the signal would determine the power level that was fed into the antenna and how much signal strength was lost in transit from the transmitter to the receiver, due to obstacles and other impediments.

Consider a wireless cable/DSL router for home networking, which typically sends out a signal with approximately 32 milliwatts (0.032 watts) of power. The router is on the lower level of the house, and by the time the signal reaches the wireless NIC in a notebook computer in the second floor bedroom, it may only have a strength of about 0.000000001 (10^{-9}) watts, or 1 nanowatt. With received signals being sometimes several million times smaller than the signals that were transmitted, performing calculations is challenging, and it is easy to make a mistake reading, writing, or typing these long numbers, even with a calculator. Fortunately, engineers have had the same kind of difficulty with very large or very small numbers, which is why Bell Labs, in the 1920s, came up with a system to simplify these calculations.

You will recall from the previous chapter that an amplifier boosts the power of a signal; when this happens, the effect is called a **gain**. Conversely, cables and connectors offer a resistance to the flow of electricity and therefore tend to decrease the power of a signal—that is, the medium itself causes a reduction in the amount of energy that an electromagnetic signal has. This effect is called a **loss**. Knowing how much gain or loss occurs in an RF system composed of radio transmitters, receivers, cables, connectors, and antennas is necessary to assist RF engineers and technicians in selecting the appropriate components and properly installing them for reliable signal transmission and reception.

A signal's power does not usually change in linear fashion. Instead, it changes *logarithmically*. Figure 4-1 shows an example of two values: one that changes in linear fashion and one that changes in logarithmic fashion.

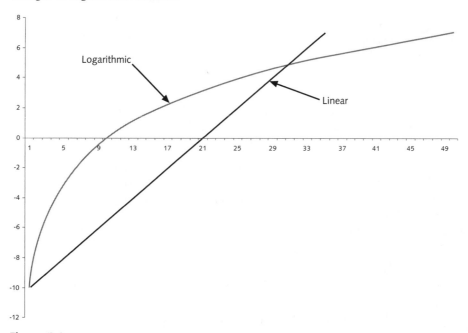

Figure 4-1 Linear vs. logarithmic

© *Cengage Learning 2014*

Gain and loss are relative concepts, which means that you need to know the power level of the signal at two different points, such as at the transmitting antenna and at the receiving antenna. Relative concepts are best quantified with relative measurements, such as percentages. To calculate the signal loss, using percentages, for the wireless cable/DSL router used in the home network, you would still have to deal with numbers that are difficult to read, write, or type. Let's take a look at a much easier way to work with gain and loss, without using long numbers.

Decibel

Decibel (dB) is a ratio between two signal levels—a relative measurement (i.e., one in which a value is dependent on another value) that makes it much simpler to express and calculate power gain or loss. We will now discuss how it's done.

The decibel is named in honor of Alexander Graham Bell, the inventor of the telephone. That is why the "B" in "dB" is written as a capital letter.

To calculate gain, all you need to remember, in practically all cases, is that:

- A gain of 3 dB (+3 dB) means the signal is two times bigger (twice the power).
- A gain of 10 dB (+10 dB) means the signal is 10 times bigger (10 times the power).

What about loss? It is the opposite of gain:

- A loss of 3 dB (−3 dB) means the signal is two times smaller (half the power).
- A loss of 10 dB (−10 dB) means the signal is 10 times smaller (1/10$^\text{th}$ the power).

To say "a loss of minus 3 dB" (−3 dB) is incorrect. The correct form is to say "a loss of 3 dB."

These rules are known as the "*tens and threes of RF mathematics.*" As you will see in the examples that follow, you can easily and quickly calculate the gain or loss with a fair amount of accuracy, without using a calculator, just by following these simple rules.

Using dB to represent gains and losses means that the only types of calculations required are simple additions and subtractions. There is no need for multiplication, division, or any kind of complex calculation to convert the values to the same unit in order to get a meaningful result. For example, if a transmitter is connected to a cable that has a loss of 4 dB and each connector—one on the transmitter end of the cable and one on the antenna end of the cable—has a loss of 1 dB, you can simply add the losses together like this: (−4 dB) + (−1 dB) + (−1 dB) = −6 dB, for a total loss of 6 dB.

Although dB is a relative measurement, at some point we have to make a connection between dB and a linear, absolute measurement. One example of this is **dBm**, which is a relative way to indicate an absolute power level in the linear watt scale:

1 mW = 0 dBm

You can add or subtract any value represented in dB (dBm, etc.) using the "tens and threes" rule; you can also convert a dBm value directly to milliwatts of power. Let's look at some examples:

- +3 dB (3 dB of gain) will double the power: 10 mW + 3 dB = approximately 20 mW
- −3 dB (3 dB of loss) will halve the power: 10 mW − 3 dB = approximately 5 mW
- +10 dB will increase the power 10 times: 10 mW + 10 dB = approximately 100 mW
- −10 dB will decrease the power 10 times: 10 mW − 10 dB = approximately 1 mW

NOTE Converting to mW does not change the relative measurement characteristic of decibel. It simply means that you have a reference point for the values used in the calculations; you can still add or subtract any dB values as if they were all represented in the same units.

Therefore, if you want to know the absolute power level of a particular signal that is supplied by a transmitter and you know from the specifications for this particular unit that the strength of the output signal is +36 dBm, you can calculate the absolute power by breaking down this number like this:

36 dBm = +10 dBm +10 dBm +10 dBm +3 dBm +3 dBm

Because 0 dBm is equal to 1 mW, it follows that:

- Adding 10 dB makes the signal power 10 mW or 1 mW multiplied by 10.
- Adding another 10 dB multiplies the signal power by 10, making it 100 mW.
- Adding another 10 dB multiplies the signal power by 10 again, making it 1000 mW or 1 W.
- Adding another 3 dB doubles the signal power, making it 2 W.
- Adding another 3 dB doubles the signal power again, making it 4 W.

NOTE In the rare instances in which using the "tens and threes" rule does not work, the formula for converting milliwatts (mW) to dBm is $P_{dBm} = 10\log P_{mW}$. Therefore, the formula for converting dBm to mW is: $P_{mW} = \log^{-1}(P_{dBm}/10) = 10$ dBm. P_{mW} is power in milliwatts, and P_{dBm} is the equivalent figure in dB. These formulas are provided here for your reference only.

When assigning a dB factor to the gain of an antenna, the measurement must relate to some absolute value. The most perfect radiator of electromagnetic waves is an **isotropic radiator**, a theoretically perfect sphere that radiates energy equally in all directions. It is not possible to build a real isotropic radiator because it would need a power or signal cable connected to it at some point on the surface of the sphere. The cable connection means that the sphere would no longer be perfect and would not be able to radiate with equal intensity in all directions. However, an isotropic radiator provides a reference point for representing the gain of an antenna, which is usually expressed using **dB isotropic (dBi)**, a unit of measurement for the gain an antenna has, compared to the gain an isotropic radiator would have.

NOTE The closest thing to an isotropic radiator is the sun. However, even the sun is not perfect because of a phenomenon called sunspots, which are dark areas on the surface of the star that change periodically and radiate energy levels different from the rest of the surface.

For microwave and higher frequency antennas, the gain is usually expressed in **dB dipole (dBd)**. A **dipole** is the smallest, simplest, most practical type of antenna that can be made, which therefore exhibits the least amount of gain. A dipole has a fixed gain of 2.15 dB over that of an isotropic radiator. Therefore, if the gain of an antenna is 5 dBd, to convert to dBi, you simply add 2.15 to the 5 and get 7.15 dBi. Table 4-1 shows a summary of the decibel values used in RF communications.

Nomenclature	Description	Refers To:
dBm	dB milliwatts	0 dB = 1 mW of power
dBd	dB dipole	The gain an antenna has over a dipole antenna at the same frequency
dBi	dB isotropic	The gain an antenna has over a theoretical isotropic (point source) radiator

Table 4-1 Decibel values and references

© Cengage Learning 2014

Antenna Characteristics

Now that you have an understanding of gain and loss, it is time to get acquainted with antenna types, sizes, and shapes.

NOTE Antennas are reciprocal devices, which means that an antenna that works well for transmitting a signal on a particular range of frequencies is also effective at receiving signals in the same range of frequencies.

Antenna Types

Antennas used in wireless communications can be characterized as either passive or active. Each type of antenna can be constructed as either passive or active; however, most antennas are passive.

Passive Antennas Passive antennas are the most common type and are constructed of a piece of metal, wire, or similar conductive material. A passive antenna does not amplify the signal in any way; it can only radiate a signal with the same amount of energy that appears at the antenna connector, after any cable and connector losses. However, as you will learn, certain shapes of passive antennas radiate the RF energy supplied by the transmitter in one direction and consequently exhibit an effective gain that is similar to amplification of the signal and is called **directional gain**. This is equivalent to using a flashlight that allows you to focus the beam by moving the reflector with respect to the light bulb. The more focused and narrow the beam is, the farther the light will reach. If you adjust it to spread the beam, you can illuminate a wider area, but as the light disperses over a wider area, less light reaches any point at the target, which makes it less effective as the distance increases (see Figure 4-2).

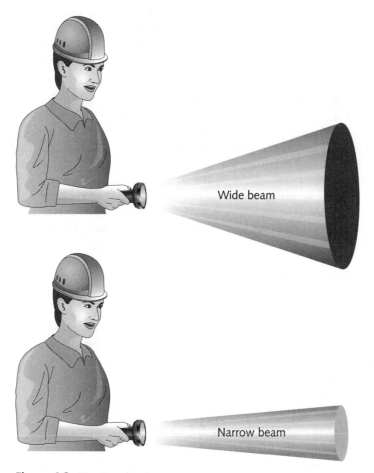

Figure 4-2 Directional gain

© *Cengage Learning 2014*

Active Antennas Active antennas are essentially passive antennas with built-in amplifiers. The amplifier is connected directly to the piece of metal that forms the antenna itself. Most active antennas have only one electrical connection. The RF signal and the power for the amplifier are supplied on the same conductor. This is intended to reduce the cost and make active antennas easier to install.

Antenna Sizes and Shapes

Antennas come in many sizes and shapes, depending on the following three characteristics:

- The frequency that the antenna is designed to transmit and receive

- The direction of the radiated electromagnetic wave
- The power with which the antenna must transmit or how sensitive it needs to be to receive very weak signals

The size of an antenna is inversely proportional to the wavelength of the signal it is designed to transmit or receive. Lower frequency signals require larger antennas. Conversely, higher frequency signals require shorter antennas. For example, the antenna for an AM radio station transmitting at the frequency of 530 KHz (530,000 Hz) is 566 feet (172.5 meters) long, whereas that of a cellular telephone operating at a frequency of 900 MHz (900,000,000 Hz) is just over 13 inches (33.33 cm) long. Antenna shapes vary according to their specific applications.

Omnidirectional Antennas Omnidirectional antennas are used to transmit and receive signals from all directions with relatively equal intensity. Figure 4-3 shows two examples of omnidirectional antennas for use in IEEE 802.11 wireless networks. On the left is a magnetic mount antenna, with an integrated cable designed for use in WLAN applications. These antennas are useful for improving signal reception over antennas that are built inside notebook computers or permanently attached to a wireless NIC. Magnetic mount antennas can be used in office environments, where they can be easily attached to any metal surface, or they can be attached to car and truck roofs for mobile applications. On the right of Figure 4-3 is a "blister"-type ceiling mount antenna. Blister antennas are typically used to hide the antenna or to make it blend with the decor.

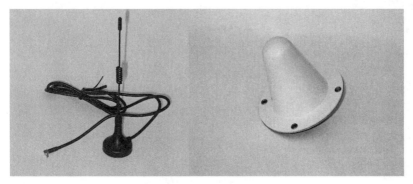

Figure 4-3 Magnetic mount and blister-type omnidirectional antennas

© Cengage Learning 2014

Longer omnidirectional antennas usually have higher gain but are more difficult to mount and hide. Later in this text, you will learn how the size of an antenna can affect its gain. Figure 4-4 shows an example of a high-gain antenna of this type.

Omnidirectional antennas have a gain because they emit a signal in two dimensions only, not in three dimensions, which an isotropic radiator would emit in—if one could be built, that is. When visualized from the side of an omnidirectional antenna, the RF waves form a doughnut-shaped pattern with a stick (the antenna) through the center. This means that the energy leaving the antenna is somewhat focused.

Figure 4-4 High-gain omnidirectional antenna

© Cengage Learning 2014

Directional Antennas

Directional Antennas The intended direction of the radiated RF wave also affects the shape of antennas. A **directional antenna** is used to transmit a signal in one direction only. Although this may sound obvious, it represents an important distinction from omnidirectional antennas. Directional antennas, by focusing the RF waves mostly in one direction, concentrate the energy in (or receive more energy from) a particular direction and therefore have a higher effective gain than omnidirectional antennas.

Some types of directional antennas focus the RF energy more or less than others. A **yagi antenna** emits a wider, less-focused RF energy beam, whereas a **parabolic dish antenna** emits a narrow, more concentrated beam of RF energy. Yagi antennas are used for outdoor applications at distances up to about 16 miles (25 kilometers), and dish antennas are used for outdoor links at distances over 16 miles (25 kilometers). One common application of a dish antenna is to receive satellite signals. Figure 4-5 shows two different models of yagi antennas. The encased model on the left is a 2.4 GHz WLAN antenna, and the open type on the right is used for paging systems. Figure 4-6 shows a typical parabolic dish antenna. In a dish antenna, the parabolic surface of the dish is used to reflect the received signal onto the antenna element. During transmission, the signal leaving the antenna element is reflected by the dish and leaves the antenna in one direction only.

Patch antennas emit an RF energy beam that is horizontally wide but vertically taller than that of a yagi antenna. Considered a semi-directional antenna, it is often used to send RF

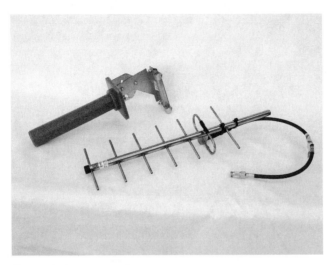

Figure 4-5 Yagi antennas

© Cengage Learning 2014

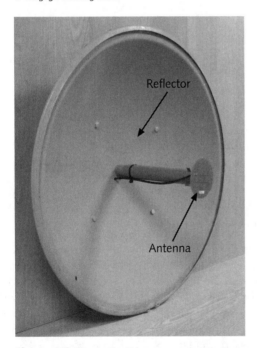

Figure 4-6 Parabolic dish antenna (protective weather dome removed)

© Cengage Learning 2014

energy down a long corridor, although some varieties are designed for installation on the walls of buildings—for example, to send an RF signal in one direction away from the structure. Cellular telephony antennas are also designed to emit signals away from the structure where they are mounted. Figure 4-7 illustrates an example of antennas used in a cellular telephone tower, and Figure 4-8 shows a small patch antenna for use indoors.

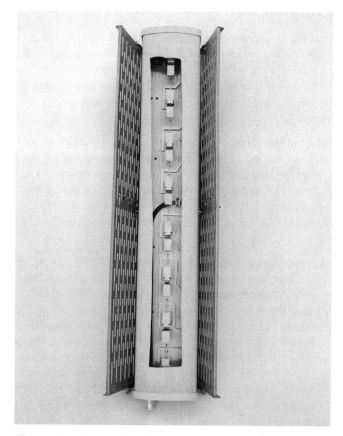

Figure 4-7 Cellular antenna with cutout to show internal construction

© *Cengage Learning 2014*

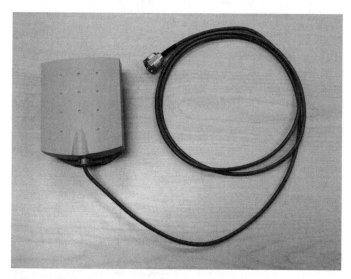

Figure 4-8 Indoor patch antenna

© *Cengage Learning 2014*

Signal Strength and Direction

The distance between the transmitter and receiver determines the strength of the signal you need to send, which in turn determines what size and shape of antenna you need for your application. Recall that most antennas are of the passive type and that transmitters can only produce finite amounts of RF energy. For most applications, active antennas can be extremely expensive, and frequency-licensing restrictions limit the amount of power with which signals may be transmitted.

What is the best solution? An omnidirectional antenna installed high and in a central location works well for sending a signal in all directions, but the strength of the signal is divided more or less equally in a 360-degree circle around the antenna. A directional antenna, on the other hand, sends all the energy in the direction the antenna is pointed; therefore, the RF wave travels farther than a signal sent from an omnidirectional antenna because the power is concentrated in one direction, an effect similar to the flashlight example described earlier.

Signals also lose energy as the electromagnetic wave travels away from the antenna. This behavior is primarily the result of free space loss. In **free space loss**, RF waves tend to spread away from the source of the signal (the antenna) similar to a circular wave created by throwing a stone in a pond. The farther the waves move away from the stone's impact point, the smaller they get because the amount of energy the wave originally had when the stone hit the water is distributed over an ever-wider area. Eventually the wave fades to the point that you can no longer see any movement on the surface of the water. If you place two floating objects on the water's surface—one near the point where the stone hits the water and another farther away—the one closer to the center point will move more than the one farther away because less of the wave's energy reaches the farther object. This energy loss is the same thing that happens with a receiver antenna that is located farther away from a transmitter. It receives less of the energy sent by the transmitter because the RF wave is spreading its energy out in all directions. However, if you experiment with dropping a stone into water in a confined space, such as a bathtub, the movement of the wave is contained by the sidewalls of the tub, and the waves will travel back and forth within the confines of the tub several times before they fade.

Free space loss can be calculated based on the strength of the signal coming out of the transmitter, the loss caused by cables and connectors, the gain of the antenna, and the medium in which the signal is being transmitted, which is most often the atmosphere. You can find many free space loss calculator tools on the Internet by using your favorite search engine to look for "free space loss calculator."

Remember that antenna gain, when referring to passive antennas, is directional gain (not power gain) due to focusing of the energy in one direction.

Radio stations transmit their signals in all directions to reach the largest number of listeners. Although they transmit with a lot of power, as you travel away from the city where the station is located, the signal gets weaker and weaker until your receiver can no longer detect it and all you may be able to hear are intermittent fragments of the transmission interspersed with noise.

Some AM stations in the United States transmit with as much as 50,000 watts of power, and FM stations may send a signal with as much as 150,000 watts of power. Higher-frequency signals need more power to reach the same distance. In comparison, an average IEEE 802.11 WLAN AP sends out a signal with only 100 milliwatts (0.1 watts) of power.

How Antennas Work

Designing antennas and understanding how they perform the magic of sending RF signals out into air or space requires in-depth knowledge of physics, mathematics, and electronics. The details of the science behind how antennas work are beyond the scope of this book and are probably best left to university courses in electronics engineering. However, some general coverage of basic antenna functionality should help you develop a better appreciation of the science of antennas. This section explains how antennas work as transmitters (radiators) and receivers of radio frequency signals.

Wavelength

The length of a single RF sine wave, known as the **wavelength**, is what determines the size of an antenna. An antenna transmits and receives a signal most efficiently at a specific frequency when it is as long as the full length of the wave; this is called a **full-wave antenna**. In most cases, this is not practical. For example, a full-wave antenna for an AM station would be about 1,857 feet (over 566 meters) long, while a typical cellular telephone antenna would have to be just over 13 inches (33.33 centimeters) long. For practical reasons, antennas are more commonly designed to be as long as an exact fraction of the wavelength, and these are called **half-wave antennas, quarter-wave antennas**, and **eighth-wave antennas**. Though not as efficient as full-wave antennas, these smaller antennas work reasonably well. The AM station antenna, for example, could be built as a quarter-wave antenna at about 464 feet (141 meters), which is still quite large, and the cellular antenna, using the same ratio, would only be about 3.25 inches (8.25 centimeters) long.

When antennas with a higher gain are required, you can increase the size of the antenna to the next bigger fraction. A larger antenna exhibits a higher gain than a shorter antenna. Almost any metallic object or any object that conducts electricity will act as an antenna, but if you use an antenna that is much shorter than the wavelength for a frequency, it will not radiate any significant amount of RF. Alternatively, if the antenna is much longer than the wavelength, it will send out some RF energy, just not very efficiently, and this may affect the reliability of the transmitter circuits.

The wavelength of an RF signal is usually given in metric values. The formula for calculating the length of the wave, given that RF waves travel through air or space at the average speed of light (300,000 kilometers per second), is: *wavelength = speed of light/frequency*. Using a value in feet-per-second or inches-per-second for the speed of light will yield a result in feet or inches, respectively, for the wavelength. The average speed of light in miles-per-second is 186,000.

Antenna Performance

Antenna performance is a measure of how efficiently an antenna can radiate an RF signal. The design, installation, size, and type of antenna can affect its performance.

Radiation Patterns

In antenna design, certain items such as fasteners, brackets, and support structures can affect the way the antenna emits RF waves. During the testing phase of an antenna, engineers develop a graphic called an **antenna pattern** by measuring the signal radiating from the antenna. The antenna pattern indicates the direction, width, and shape of the RF signal beam coming from the antenna. An antenna pattern is usually drawn as if you were looking at it from the top. In the case of directional antennas, sometimes you will see an arrow indicating the direction in which the RF signal is being emitted. Figure 4-9 shows examples of antenna patterns.

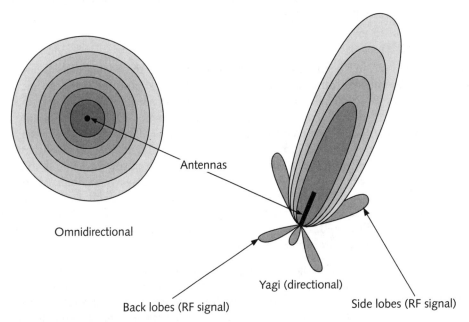

Figure 4-9 Antenna patterns viewed from above

© Cengage Learning 2014

Recall that antennas emit signals in two dimensions: horizontally and vertically. Antenna specifications almost always include the vertical beam angle that a particular antenna emits. Figure 4-10 illustrates the shape of RF waves emitted by an omnidirectional antenna, as viewed from the side.

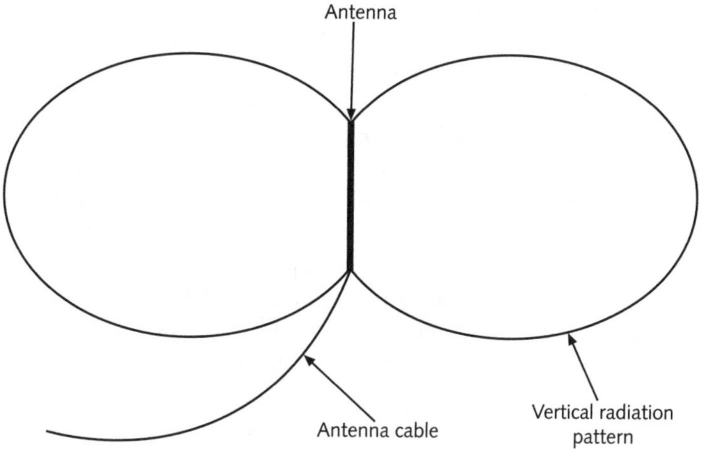

Antenna

Antenna cable

Vertical radiation
pattern

Figure 4-10 Vertical antenna pattern (side view of omnidirectional antenna pattern)

© *Cengage Learning 2014*

Antenna Polarization

When a signal leaves an antenna, the sine waves have a particular orientation; in other words, they oscillate either horizontally or vertically. The orientation of the wave leaving the antenna is called **antenna polarization**. If you hold a portable cellular phone straight up in your hand, the antenna is positioned vertically. The signal leaving the antenna will be vertically polarized, meaning that the sine waves will travel up and down when leaving the antenna. If you are lying down when talking on the cellular phone, the signal is horizontally polarized, which is to say that the sine waves travel from side to side on a horizontal plane. Cellular base station (tower) antennas are mounted vertically and send out signals that are also vertically polarized. Antenna polarization is important because the most efficient signal transmission and reception is experienced when the sending and receiving antennas are equally polarized—that is, they are both either vertically or horizontally polarized. Figure 4-11 illustrates this concept.

Vertically polarized antenna

Horizontally polarized antenna

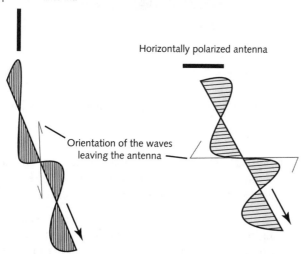

Orientation of the waves
leaving the antenna

Figure 4-11 Antenna polarization

© *Cengage Learning 2014*

Most add-on wireless NICs used in notebook computers have antennas that stick out the side of the computers and are horizontally polarized (provided that the notebook computer is used under normal conditions, such as on top of a desk or on your lap). The devices that the notebook wireless NIC is transmitting to or receiving from usually have their antennas mounted in a vertical position, which means that the signal is not polarized the same way as the signals emitted or received by the notebook computer. Different polarization between devices can cause poor communication between them. The utility software supplied with wireless NICs can show the strength of the signal. If you experience poor reception, try placing the computer on its side (carefully, of course) while monitoring the strength of the signal. You will most likely see a small increase in signal strength due to the antennas having the same polarization. Figure 4-12 shows a notebook computer with an add-on NIC (horizontally mounted antenna) and an AP with the antennas mounted vertically.

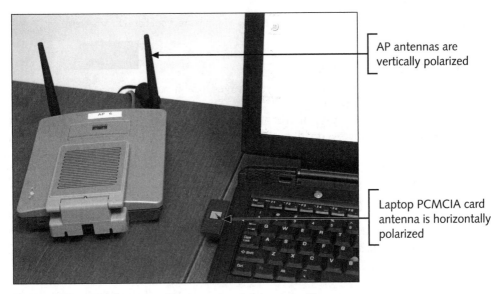

AP antennas are vertically polarized

Laptop PCMCIA card antenna is horizontally polarized

Figure 4-12 Mixed vertical and horizontal antenna polarizations

© Cengage Learning 2014

Antenna Dimensions

The design and construction of an antenna dictates whether it is one-dimensional or two-dimensional in structure.

One-Dimensional Antennas One-dimensional antennas are basically a length of wire or metal. They can be built as a straight piece or bent in some shape, such as the old "rabbit ear" antennas that used to be placed on top of television sets.

A **monopole antenna** is basically a straight piece of wire or metal, usually a quarter of the wavelength, with no reflecting or ground element. As you learned earlier, dipole is the smallest, simplest, most practical type of antenna. Dipoles are commonly built as two monopoles mounted together at the base (the place where the cable(s) connect(s) to the antenna) and laid out in a straight line, with the two ends facing away from each other. Figure 4-13 shows an example of a dipole antenna.

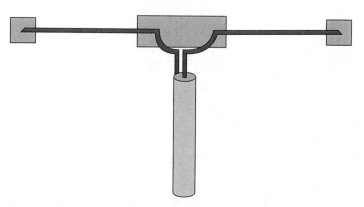

Figure 4-13 Common dipole antenna

© *Cengage Learning 2014*

A monopole antenna is less efficient than a dipole. Dipoles can be built larger because they are usually laid out horizontally. To work properly, monopole antennas are mounted in such a way that they are practically sticking out of the ground (or very close to it) or some other type of large structure that conducts electrical energy. Because the ground is a conductor, it acts as a reflector, and this makes the monopole antenna behave like a dipole, rendering it more efficient. Alternatively, a monopole can be equipped with a large metal base called a **ground-plane** to simulate the signal-reflecting effect of the ground. The most common application of ground-planes is on boats that have fiberglass hulls. Fiberglass is nonconducting; therefore, antennas for nautical radios usually have either a horizontal metal plate near the base or, alternatively, four lengths of wire sticking out horizontally from the base, to act as the ground-plane.

Two-Dimensional Antennas Antennas organized in a two-dimensional pattern, with both height and width, are known as **two-dimensional antennas**. Examples include patch and satellite dish antennas. A satellite dish works like a signal collector, scooping up any signal that comes in a straight line with the center axis of the antenna. A patch antenna is usually a flat piece of metal, with different heights and widths, depending on the desired vertical and horizontal radiation angles. Another type of two-dimensional directional antenna is a **horn antenna**, such as the one shown in Figure 4-14, which resembles a large horn with the wide end bent to one side. These antennas are common in telephone networks and are used to transmit high-power microwave signals between two distant towers.

Figure 4-14 Telephone transmission tower showing two horn antennas

© *Cengage Learning 2014*

Smart Antennas

A recent development in antenna technology is the smart antenna. Used primarily in cellular telephony and WiMAX, **smart antennas**, using the strength of the signal coming from a mobile device, "learn" where it is located, track it, and focus the RF energy in the device's direction to avoid wasting energy and to prevent interference with other antennas. Instead of sending signals with wide beams, smart antennas send narrow beams of energy toward the receiver. Figure 4-15 illustrates this concept. The illustration on the left shows a regular directional antenna. The one on the right shows a smart antenna tracking a mobile receiver.

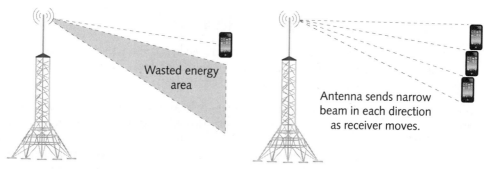

Figure 4-15 Directional antenna vs. smart antenna

© *Cengage Learning 2014*

There are two classes of smart antennas:

- A switched beam antenna uses several narrow beam antennas pointing in different directions and turns each one on or off as the receiver moves across the path of the beams.

- An adaptive or phased array antenna is similar to a patch antenna but, instead of being just a single piece of metal, is divided into a matrix of radiating elements. A computer-based signal processor controls circuits in the antenna system, turning elements of the matrix on or off as well as adjusting the phase of the transmission signal supplied to each one as the mobile user moves across the front of the antenna. This has the effect of sending the energy beam in a particular direction and is generally called "beam forming." The signal processor is used to detect which elements receive a stronger signal; this determines the position of the mobile user.

Phased array antennas are used extensively in ultramodern radar systems. For example, you may have noticed that newer warships have fewer rotating radar antennas than older ones. These antennas are beginning to appear in other applications as well, such as cellular mobile telephony and mobile WiMAX. Figure 4-16 shows an example of a phased array antenna. Note the multiple antenna elements that make up the array.

Figure 4-16 Phased array antenna showing a matrix of transmission elements (small squares)

Source: Courtesy of SSGT Lono Kollars, DoD, USAF

Antenna System Implementation

The proper installation of antennas requires knowledge of the user's requirements as well as an ability to deal with various challenges, including physical obstacles, municipal building codes, and other regulatory restrictions.

As mentioned at the beginning of this chapter, cellular providers spend a great deal of time and effort designing and testing their antenna networks in order to provide the best signal coverage and, hence, the best service to their customers. They also need to know what the user traffic patterns are in a given area. And they need to know how to obtain the proper permissions. In North America, obtaining permits from the government or from private land or building owners takes longer and is more expensive than in other countries around the world. As a result, cellular providers also need to be smarter and more thorough at both maximizing coverage and minimizing interference.

The purpose of a single RF antenna or a system consisting of multiple antennas is to allow a group of users to communicate reliably without wires. The system's performance and reliability are major concerns for the RF technician, and so is security. This is especially true today, when unlicensed frequencies are often accompanied by maximum signal power restrictions, a lack of support from regulatory agencies in case of conflict or interference, and easy access to a wide range of equipment by untrained and inexperienced users and hackers.

When implementing wireless communications—such as when setting up a wireless LAN—using the antennas supplied with the wireless devices limits you to placing the transmitters and receivers where you can achieve a good connection. If you need to go beyond the standard setup, however—if you, say, purchase several different external antennas to ensure good signal reception in a difficult area or to create a long-distance outdoor link—there are a few additional points to consider. We will now provide an overview of these.

You should not attempt to install towers or antennas outdoors without proper training. Instead, you should always hire a professional, bonded installer for outdoor antennas, whether you are installing them in towers, on the sides of buildings or on the roofs.

Antenna Cables

Most antennas are connected to the transmitter or receiver using coaxial cable. This type of cable is built in layers of wires (conducting) and insulators (nonconducting). Figure 4-17 illustrates the construction of a coaxial cable.

Coaxial cable is also used in audio, cable television, and a variety of other applications. It is very important to use the cable with the right specifications for the intended application in order to avoid problems that are difficult to troubleshoot.

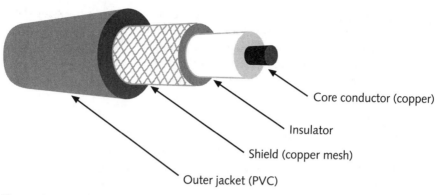

Core conductor (copper)

Insulator

Shield (copper mesh)

Outer jacket (PVC)

Figure 4-17 Coaxial cable construction

© *Cengage Learning 2014*

Coaxial cables come in many sizes (thicknesses) and specifications. In an RF system, it is very important to use the correct type of cable, per the equipment and antenna manufacturer specifications. Among the specifications is the **impedance** of the cable, which is the opposition to the flow of alternating current in a circuit. Represented by the letter "Z" and measured in ohms, impedance is the combination of the circuit's resistance, inductance, and capacitance. The cable's impedance must match that of the transmitter circuit as well as that of the antenna. When you need to connect an external antenna and it is not possible to attach it directly to the transmitter output, you must consider the signal loss caused by the connectors and by the cable itself. Almost all conducting materials offer a resistance to the flow of electricity on a wire. This is particularly important in antenna cables and more so in equipment that transmits at very low power—such as those used in IEEE 802.11 WLANs.

Cable loss is measured in relation to the length of the cable. The longer the cable, the more loss occurs. However, you can use special low-loss antenna cables to minimize signal loss. Table 4-2 lists LMR low-loss cables of varying thicknesses along with the losses that occur at 2.4 GHz for every 100 feet of cable.

Part Number	Diameter	Loss at 2.4 GHz (per 100 ft.)
LMR-100	$^1/_{10}$"	−38.9 dB
LMR-240	$^3/_{16}$"	−12.7 dB
LMR-400	$^3/_8$"	−6.6 dB
LMR-600	$^1/_2$"	−4.4 dB

Table 4-2 Low-loss LMR cables

© *Cengage Learning 2014*

To calculate the total cable loss, divide the loss per 100 feet by 100 and multiply by the required length of your cable. For example, if you needed to install the antenna about 10 feet (3 meters) away from the transmitter, LMR-100 cable will introduce a loss of 3.9 dB (39 dB/100 = 0.39 dB per foot, times 10 = 3.9 dB), which means that significantly more than half of the energy produced at the transmitter output is lost, and that is before adding the connector losses! Using LMR-400, the loss introduced by the cable will be only about 0.7 dB.

To keep loss at a minimum, you may have to use a cable that is too thick for the connector type used in your transmitter, antenna, or both. Therefore, the first consideration when deciding to change the manufacturer-provided or equipment-mounted antennas should be the locations of the transmitter and antenna(s). In addition, be aware that LMR cable is significantly more expensive than regular coaxial cable.

RF Propagation

The way that radio waves propagate, or move, between the transmitter and the receiver through the atmosphere of our planet depends on the frequency of the signal. RF waves are classified in three groups, as shown in Table 4-3. Ground waves follow the curvature of the Earth. Sky waves bounce between the ionosphere and the surface of the Earth. RF waves transmitted in frequencies between 30 MHz and 300 GHz require a line-of-sight path between the transmitter and the receiver antennas.

Group	Frequency Range
Ground waves	3 KHz to 2 MHz
Sky waves	2 MHz to 30 MHz
Line-of-sight waves	30 MHz to 300 GHz

Table 4-3 **RF wave propagation groups**

© *Cengage Learning 2014*

Figure 4-18 illustrates how these different waves propagate through Earth's atmosphere and, consequently, how this affects the implementation of antenna systems.

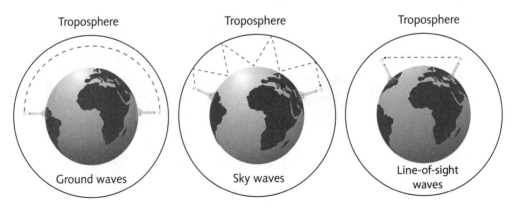

Figure 4-18 How radio waves propagate

© *Cengage Learning 2014*

Point-to-Multipoint Links

In most wireless communications applications, one transmitter communicates with several mobile clients. This is called a **point-to-multipoint wireless link**. If the receiver is installed in a fixed location, as in the case of a central building in a campus with wireless links to other buildings, it is possible to maximize the signal distance by using an omnidirectional antenna at the central location and directional, higher-gain antennas at the remote locations. Figure 4-19 illustrates this type of application.

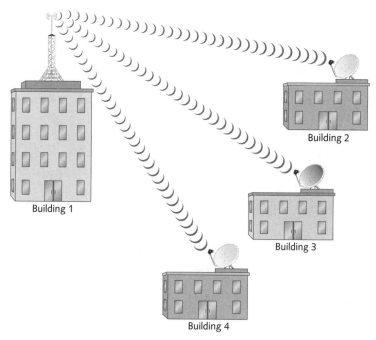

Figure 4-19 Point-to-multipoint links using a combination of omnidirectional and directional antennas

© *Cengage Learning 2014*

Point-to-Point Links

Two computer networks in different buildings can be connected by a **point-to-point** wireless link. In this case, directional antennas provide the most reliable method of transmitting RF waves. Their narrow beams and high gain ensure that most of the energy of the RF wave will be used between the two antennas. The cost is often much lower and the performance comparable to or higher than that of a digital telephone company line. Telephone companies make extensive use of point-to-point microwave links, instead of cables, for long-distance voice and data communications. Although repeater towers are required, the cost of maintaining a wireless link is usually much lower than the cost of installing and maintaining cables, which can be easily damaged and are harder to troubleshoot. Figure 4-20 shows an example of a point-to-point link.

Figure 4-20 Point-to-point link using directional antennas

© *Cengage Learning 2014*

Fresnel Zone

Although the transmission path for point-to-point links is usually represented by a straight line, recall that RF waves have a tendency to spread out. This means that the space between the two antennas would be more accurately represented by something similar to an ellipse (see Figure 4-21). This elliptical region is called the **Fresnel zone**, and its shape is an important consideration in wireless links. When planning a wireless link, at least 60 percent of the Fresnel zone must be kept clear of obstructions, which may affect the height of the antenna tower.

The name "Fresnel" (pronounced Fray-nel) comes from the French physicist Augustin-Jean Fresnel, who studied the polarization of light waves.

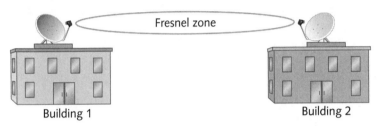

Figure 4-21 Fresnel zone

© *Cengage Learning 2014*

Link Budgets

Once you have considered the cables, propagation method, link type, and Fresnel zone of your transmission, you still need to calculate whether you will have enough signal strength to meet the receiver's minimum requirements. This calculation is called a **link budget** and is used in every type of outdoor wireless link, whether across the road or between a satellite and an earth station.

The process involves all the variables that you have read about in this chapter. The calculations are not overly complex, but there are nevertheless many link budgeting tools available on the Internet. To calculate your link budget, you will need information from the equipment specifications, including the gain of the antennas, cable and connector losses for the receiver and the transmitter, receiver sensitivity, and the free space loss figure.

Antenna Alignment

One of the challenges of implementing a point-to-point link is to position the antennas at the same height and point them toward one another to maximize the strength of the signal. Recall that you must ensure that a minimum of 60 percent of the Fresnel zone is not blocked by obstructions. The height at which the antenna will be mounted can be affected by trees, buildings, and the curvature of the planet surface. Some transmitters and receivers are equipped with tools designed to assist the installers in aligning the two antennas. Others may require the rental or purchase of additional tools to ensure perfect alignment. Some basic tools are essential, such as:

- A compass to position the antenna in the correct direction
- A spotting scope or binoculars, if the other antenna site is within visible range

- A means of communication, such as a walkie-talkie or a cellular phone
- A light source such as a flashlight or laser pointer, if the distance is reasonably short

Technicians who often perform long-distance link installations and who need to align antennas with a great degree of accuracy to ensure maximum reliability (as is the case with dish antennas) are usually equipped with a spectrum analyzer, such as the one shown in Figure 4-22. This tool displays the signal amplitude and frequency and can also detect interference in a particular frequency channel. Spectrum analyzers have varying capabilities and are expensive, ranging in price from about $10,000 to over $100,000, depending on usable frequency range and other features.

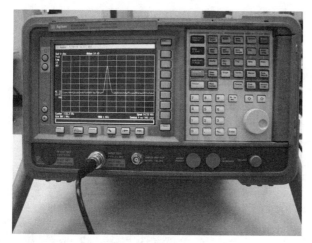

Figure 4-22 Spectrum analyzer

© Cengage Learning 2014

Antenna system implementation, including alignment and troubleshooting, demands hours of practical training. Although it is beyond the scope of this book, it is included here to give you a sense of the complex issues involved. Before moving on to other more practical aspects of wireless communications, we will discuss some of the other challenges that affect implementation, particularly of outdoor links.

Other Challenges of Outdoor Links

Recall that radio waves can reflect off, diffract, or be absorbed by various materials. Weather phenomena (such as heavy fog, rain, dust, or snowstorms), air disturbances (such as air masses rising quickly from the ground because of the sun heating up the surface in deserts and other very hot areas), significant drops in temperature that occur in deep valleys during the course of a day—all can affect the performance and reliability of wireless links. Seasonal changes can also impact a wireless link. For example, say it was set up in the winter, when there were no leaves on the trees; when spring comes, the leaves can block more than 40 percent of the Fresnel zone, absorbing most of the RF waves.

While planning an outdoor link, you should always consider the possibility that the link performance will be seriously affected or the link will go down completely as a result of one or more of the environmental conditions described. Check the history of the region's weather. Contact the municipal planning, parks, and building permit departments to identify short- and long-term plans that may interfere with your intended link. And always take into account how the positioning of an antenna may be affected by vegetation growth in the spring.

The possibility of another company or person setting up a link in which the RF wave beam interferes with the one you set up is an additional concern. If you are using unlicensed frequencies, such as the ISM or U-NII bands, you cannot count on assistance from regulatory agencies or authorities. Of course, you should always be a good citizen and make sure you are not interfering with anyone else's signal before you set up an outdoor link.

Chapter Summary

- By the time an RF signal reaches the receiver, it can be a billion times smaller than when it left the transmitter. Cables, connectors, antennas, and the distance between the transmitter and receiver are all factors that affect how much energy a signal has when it is transmitted and when it is received. A gain occurs when a signal power is increased—for example, when most of the signal's energy is focused in one direction or when it is put through an amplifier before being routed to the antenna. A loss occurs when the energy of a signal is decreased.

- The decibel (dB) is a relative measurement used by engineers and technicians to simplify the calculations of gain and loss as well as to indicate the strength of a signal. A gain of 3 dB doubles the signal's power. A loss of 3 dB halves the signal's power. A gain of 10 dB increases the signal strength 10 times, and a loss of 10 dB decreases the signal strength 10 times. Gains and losses expressed in dB can simply be added or subtracted together.

- An isotropic radiator is a theoretically perfect sphere that radiates power equally in all directions. The two most basic types of antennas are the theoretical isotropic radiator, which is only used as a reference (given that it is not possible to build a working one), and the dipole.

- The most common type of antenna is a passive antenna, which is basically a piece of wire or metal that can only radiate a signal with as much power as is provided by the transmitter. An active antenna has a built-in amplifier to boost the signal power and compensate for the losses caused by cables and connectors.

- The size of an antenna depends primarily on the frequency or range of frequencies that it is designed to transmit or receive, and this is directly proportional to the wavelength of the signal and inversely proportional to the frequency—that is, a longer antenna is required for lower frequencies, and a shorter antenna is used for higher frequencies. To keep antennas at a manageable size, most are built as half-wave (half the wavelength), quarter-wave (a quarter of the wavelength), or eighth-wave (an eighth of the wavelength).

- Omnidirectional antennas transmit and receive signals from all directions. Directional antennas focus the signal energy in one direction only, which has an effect (called directional gain) in passive antennas that is similar to the gain provided by an amplifier, only without adding any additional electrical power.

- Yagi, patch, and dish are different types of directional antennas.

- Free space loss is caused by the natural tendency of RF waves to spread out and is a measure of the amount of loss of signal strength between the transmitter antenna and the receiver antenna.

- Larger antennas have a higher gain; conversely, smaller antennas have lower gain.

- Antennas have a horizontal and a vertical radiation pattern. Antennas also emit a signal that is either vertically polarized or horizontally polarized. The most efficient communications link is when the transmitter and the receiver antennas have the same polarization.

- There are two basic types of one-dimensional antennas: monopole and dipole. The dipole antenna is more efficient than the monopole antenna. Monopoles that are not mounted at or near the ground can make use of an artificial ground-plane. Patch, phased array, and dish antennas are examples of two-dimensional antennas.

- Smart antennas, used mostly in cellular telephone applications, can track a mobile user and send a narrower, more efficient beam of RF energy directed at the user, which also prevents interference with other transmitter antennas. A switched beam antenna uses several narrow beam antennas pointing in different directions. An adaptive array (or phased array) antenna has a matrix of radiating elements and uses a signal processor to enable or disable elements in order to send a focused beam of RF energy in the direction of the mobile user.

- Special LMR antenna cables are used to reduce the signal loss between the transmitter and the antenna.

- RF waves propagate differently depending on the frequency of the signal. Ground waves follow the curvature of the Earth. Sky waves bounce between the ionosphere and the surface of the Earth. RF waves transmitted in frequencies between 30 MHz and 300 GHz require line-of-sight path between the transmitter and the receiver antennas.

- Directional antennas build point-to-point links that connect two buildings using a wireless link; they are also used by telephone carriers for long-distance microwave communication links. Point-to-multipoint links can also be set up using an omnidirectional antenna and multiple directional antennas.

- A Fresnel zone is an elliptical area between two directional antennas. When setting up a wireless link in this way, maintaining a reliable connection requires that no more than 40 percent of the Fresnel zone be blocked by obstructions.

- Directional antennas must be aligned with each other to maximize the strength of the signal between the two. Although some wireless equipment manufacturers include built-in tools to facilitate the alignment of antennas, technicians also use spectrum analyzers to ensure high reliability, accuracy, and for troubleshooting wireless links.

- RF waves can be blocked, partially or completely, by weather phenomena and conditions such as heavy rain, dust, or snowstorms. When designing a long-distance wireless link, you should always check with the local authorities to make sure no buildings or trees are planned for the area, because that could interfere with your connection.

Key Terms

active antenna   A passive antenna with an amplifier built-in.

antenna pattern   A graphic that shows how a signal radiates out of an antenna.

antenna polarization   An indication of the horizontal or vertical orientation of the sine waves leaving an antenna.

dB dipole (dBd)   The relative measurement of the gain of an antenna when compared to a dipole antenna.

dB isotropic (dBi)   The relative measurement of the gain of an antenna when compared to a theoretical isotropic radiator.

dBm   A relative way to indicate an absolute power level in the linear watt scale.

decibel (dB)   A ratio between two signal levels.

dipole   An antenna that has a fixed amount of gain over that of an isotropic radiator.

directional antenna   An antenna that focuses RF energy, sending the signal in one direction.

directional gain   The effective gain that a directional antenna achieves by focusing RF energy in one direction.

eighth-wave antenna   An antenna that is one-eighth of the wavelength of the signal it is designed to transmit or receive.

free space loss   The signal loss that occurs as a result of the tendency of RF waves to spread, resulting in less energy at any given point, as the signal moves away from the transmitting antenna.

Fresnel zone   An elliptical region spanning the distance between two directional antennas that must not be blocked more than 40 percent to prevent interference with the RF signal.

full-wave antenna   An antenna that is as long as the length of the wave it is designed to transmit or receive.

gain   A relative measure of increase in a signal's power level.

ground-plane   A metal disc or two straight wires assembled at 90 degrees, used to provide a reflection point for monopole antennas that are not mounted on or near the surface of the ground.

half-wave antenna   An antenna that is half as long as the wavelength of the signal it is designed to transmit or receive.

horn antenna   A two-dimensional directional antenna typically used for microwave transmission; it resembles a large horn with the wide end bent to one side.

impedance   The opposition to the flow of alternating current in a circuit. Represented by the letter "Z" and measured in ohms, impedance is the combination of a circuit's resistance, inductance, and capacitance.

isotropic radiator   A theoretically perfect sphere that radiates power equally in all directions; it is impossible to construct one.

link budget   The process of calculating the signal strength between the transmitter and receiver antennas to ensure that the link can meet the receiver's minimum signal strength requirements.

loss   A relative measure of decrease in a signal's power level.

monopole antenna   An antenna built of a straight piece of wire, usually a quarter of the wavelength with no ground point or reflecting element.

omnidirectional antenna   An antenna that sends out the signal in a uniform pattern in all directions.

one-dimensional antenna   A straight length of wire or metal connected to a transmitter at one end.

parabolic dish antenna   A high-gain directional antenna that emits a narrow, focused beam of energy and is used for long-distance outdoor links.

passive antenna   The most common type of antenna. Passive antennas can only radiate a signal with the same amount of energy that appears at the antenna connector.

patch antenna   A semi-directional antenna that emits a wide horizontal beam and an even wider vertical beam.

point-to-multipoint wireless link   A link in which one central site uses an omnidirectional antenna to transmit to multiple remote sites, which may use omnidirectional antennas or directional antennas to maximize the distance and the quality of the signal.

point-to-point   The most reliable link between two antenna sites using directional antennas to maximize the distance and the signal quality.

quarter-wave antenna   An antenna that is one quarter of the wavelength of the signal it is designed to transmit or receive.

smart antennas   A new type of antenna that uses a signal processor and an array of narrow beam elements to track the user and send most of the RF energy in the direction of the mobile receiver in order to prevent interference and avoid wasting RF energy.

two-dimensional antenna   An antenna, such as a dish or patch, that has both height and width. In omnidirectional antennas, the thickness of the pole or wire is not considered a second dimension.

wavelength   The length of a single RF wave, measured from the starting point of the sine wave to the starting point of the next sine wave or from any point in a wave (usually the peak) to the same point on the next wave.

yagi antenna   A directional antenna that emits a wide, less-focused beam and is used for medium-distance outdoor applications.

Review Questions

1. One of the purposes of a(n) _____ is to emit an electromagnetic signal into air or space.

   a.   antenna

   b.   modulator

   c.   filter

   d.   mixer

2. Decibel is a relative measurement that requires a(n) _____.

   a. distance

   b. antenna

   c. power level

   d. comparison

   e. gain

3. A gain of 6 dB means that the signal level or strength _____.

   a. increases very little

   b. doubles

   c. doubles twice

   d. does not increase at all

4. A transmitter generates a 15 dBm signal and is connected to an antenna using a cable that induces a 3 dB loss. The cable has two connectors that induce a loss of 2 dB each. What is the signal level at the input of the antenna?

   a. 8 dBm

   b. 10 dB

   c. 22 dBm

   d. 3 db

5. The simplest and most practical type of antenna is a _____ antenna.

   a. straight wire

   b. dipole

   c. yagi

   d. monopole

   e. passive

6. A(n) _____ antenna transmits a signal in all directions with relatively equal intensity.

   a. multidirectional

   b. phased array

   c. directional

   d. omnidirectional

   e. smart

7. Between the transmitting antenna and the receiving antenna, a signal will always be subject to _____.

   a. gain

   b. amplification

   c. free space loss

   d. reflection

   e. diffraction

8. For the best performance between transmitter and receiver, the two antennas should have the same _____.

   a. size

   b. angle

   c. gain

   d. polarization

9. In a direct, point-to-point link, the Fresnel zone should never be obstructed more than _____.

   a. 40 percent

   b. 60 percent

   c. 30 percent

   d. 50 percent

10. To work as efficiently as a dipole, a monopole antenna requires a(n) _____.

    a. LMR cable

    b. longer length

    c. ground plane

    d. amplifier

11. A lower frequency signal uses a _____ antenna, whereas a higher frequency signal uses a _____ antenna.

    a. shorter, longer

    b. longer, shorter

    c. higher, lower

    d. lower, higher

12. The gain of an antenna is the measure of how _____ the direction of an antenna pattern is.

    a. focused

    b. wide

    c. large

    d. low

13. A directional antenna typically has a low gain. True or False?

14. Passive antennas can be designed in a way that effectively increases the strength of a signal in a particular direction. True or False?

15. The _____ of an antenna depends upon the frequency of the RF signal and the gain.

    a. length

    b. amplification

    c. width

    d. height

16. When planning a wireless link, you should always prepare a _____ to ensure that the signal that reaches the receiver meets the minimum signal strength requirements.

    a. free space loss

    b. proposal

    c. link budget

    d. specification

17. List two types of directional antennas.

18. How do smart antennas function?

19. How do sky waves propagate?

20. What happens if someone sets up a pair of antennas that interfere with your point-to-point link between two buildings that uses an unlicensed frequency?

Hands-On Projects

Project 4-1

Using the Internet and other sources, write a one-page paper on adaptive array or phased array antenna systems. Other than for cellular telephony and military radar, what applications is this type of antenna being used for? What are its advantages and disadvantages?

Project 4-2

Write a one-page paper that recommends the type of antenna and the gain that would be required to transmit a signal with 4 watts of power from a transmitter that generates a 36 dBm signal to a building across the street. The transmitter will be installed indoors, and the antenna will be installed on the roof. The cable provided is 50 feet of LMR-400, which is about 10 feet longer than what you need to connect the antenna and transmitter. Show all the steps you went through to arrive at your answer.

Project 4-3

Using specifications that came with the antenna or antenna specifications found on the Internet, draw a diagram that shows the typical horizontal and vertical patterns for the following types of antennas: blister, yagi, dish, and high-gain omnidirectional.

Project 4-4

Using the Internet, research home-built antennas for IEEE 802.11 wireless networks, such as the Pringles can antenna or the wave-guide antenna. Then, using a DSL/cable router or an access point equipped with a removable antenna, build and test one of these low-cost antennas. Test your setup with a laptop or other mobile device that can display the signal strength and record the results. Write a one-page report showing how much farther you were able to extend your wireless connection using one of these home-built wireless antennas compared to using only the regular antenna provided with the router or access point.

Real-World Exercise

Exercise 4-1

The Baypoint Group (TBG), a company of 50 consultants who assist organizations and businesses with issues involving network planning and design, has again requested your services as a consultant.

Triangle Farms is a cooperative that grows vegetables and has two greenhouse locations within six miles of each other on the outskirts of Bennington, Vermont. It wants to install a wireless network in both locations but also wants to interconnect the two facilities. The local telephone company has proposed to install a dedicated digital line to link Triangle's two locations and has argued that wireless links are not reliable and that they will end up costing more than the $1,500 per month that the dedicated line will cost. Triangle has asked TBG for an opinion. TBG has asked you to become involved because you are the expert they always call upon to discuss and recommend antenna systems for wireless links.

TBG is providing the network design and implementation, along with all the wireless networking equipment required for the connection, except for the antennas linking the two sites. The location of the warehouses allows for line-of-sight access to each other, and the building codes do not allow tall buildings in the area, as they are near an airport.

Each Triangle location has an office with about 10 staff members. The office area is large and fairly open. Each of the greenhouses has two 500-foot corridors that require wireless access because staff members perform periodic checks on the planting beds. The staff members would like to be able to upload the updates and harvest predictions directly to the central server using the wireless network.

Create a PowerPoint presentation that outlines the different types of connections and antennas and the advantages and disadvantages of each. Include examples in the form of pictures and stories about similar successful wireless links. TBG has asked you to be very persuasive in your presentation, because Triangle is on the verge of signing the contract with the phone company. You are told that presenting the facts is not enough at this point; you must convince them why they should select a wireless link.

After your presentation, TBG asks you to prepare a presentation regarding the advantages of unregulated bands. Because an engineer who sits on Triangle's board will be there, this PowerPoint presentation should be detailed and technical in its scope.

Challenge Case Project

A local engineering user's group has contacted The Baypoint Group requesting a speaker to discuss the merits of different antennas, such as dish, yagi, and horn antennas. Form a team of two or three consultants and research these technologies in detail. Pay specific attention to how they are used as well as their strengths and weaknesses. Provide an opinion regarding which antenna types will become the dominant players in the future of medium- and long-distance wireless links.

chapter 5

Wireless Personal Area Networks

After reading this chapter and completing the exercises, you will be able to:

- Describe a wireless personal area network (WPAN)
- List the different WPAN standards and their applications
- Explain how Bluetooth and ZigBee work
- Describe the security features of low-rate WPAN technology

For many years, there were few options for connecting and synchronizing your PDA, cellular phone, or smartphone with your laptop or desktop computer without carrying around a collection of cables. A new type of peripheral device usually required consumers to use a different type of cable. One of the first wireless technologies that appeared on the market used infrared light (IR). Although infrared interfaces had been available for quite a long time, IR's maximum speed of 115,200 bps limited the ability to synchronize portable wireless devices. The IR specification was later enhanced, and speeds of up to 16 Mbps were reached—comparable to Fast Ethernet. Despite being secure and extremely easy to use, however, IR required close-range, point-to-point connectivity, and the lack of mobility eventually forced manufacturers to abandon an interface technology that had dominated the world of portable devices for a couple of decades.

Since the late-1990s, many alternative technologies have appeared on the market, with the primary goal of eliminating cables and allowing data devices and peripherals to communicate without wires. This chapter discusses the now-popular Bluetooth, which is available on computers, cellular phones, PDAs, and other products. It also discusses some of the latest developments in short-range, personal area networking, especially those products that are designed to eliminate some of the wires necessary in homes and buildings for lighting, environmental controls, and so forth.

What Is a WPAN?

A **wireless personal area network** (**WPAN**) is a group of technologies used for short-range communications—from a few inches to about 33 feet (10 meters), and occasionally up to 100 feet (30 meters). Most of these technologies were designed to eliminate the need for the large number of wires and cables to interconnect devices such as computers, PDAs, and even room lights and security systems. The WPAN technologies discussed in this chapter are typically designed to support applications in which high-speed data transmission is not required. A large number of Bluetooth devices support a maximum data rate of only 723.5 Kbps, for example. This is sufficient to handle up to three simultaneous voice channels, but it is not enough to handle applications such as high-definition video.

Current and future applications for WPAN technology with low data rates include:

- Home control systems (smart home)
- Connecting headsets to computers, cellular phones and smartphones, and other audio and video devices for voice communications or listening
- Portable device data exchange
- Industrial control systems
- Real-Time Location Services—smart tags used to locate people around the home or office
- Security systems
- Interactive toys
- Asset and inventory tracking

In addition to helping eliminate wires and cables, WPANs offer two key advantages. First, because they are designed to communicate at short ranges, they use very little power; therefore, the batteries that power some of the devices usually last a long time. Second, their short range also helps ensure security and privacy, which has long been a concern with other wireless technologies.

Existing and Future Standards

The Institute of Electrical and Electronics Engineers (IEEE) has developed several standards for WPANs. These cover the two lower protocol layers of Bluetooth, ZigBee, and most of the other technologies discussed in this book. Above layer 2 of the OSI protocol model, the specifications for WPANs are developed by their respective industry alliances. In this chapter, you will learn about the standards for two technologies: IEEE 802.15.1 for Bluetooth and 802.15.4 for ZigBee. These two technologies use wireless connectivity for very different purposes.

The IEEE 802.15.x standard covers all the different Working Groups for WPANs. The last digit in the standard (indicated by the "x" above) identifies a specific working group, such as "1" for Bluetooth, "4" for ZigBee, and "3" for High Rate WPANs.

NOTE

The IEEE creates standards that apply to both the **physical layer (PHY)** of the OSI, which is responsible for converting the data bits into an electromagnetic signal and transmitting it on the medium, and to all or part of the **data link layer**, which is responsible for the transfer of data between nodes in the same network segment and also provides error detection.

Although the OSI model is most often associated with local area networks, it is actually used as a model for most types of data communications protocols.

NOTE

Relationship Between the OSI Model and IEEE Project 802

At about the same time the International Organization for Standardization (ISO) was creating the Open Systems Interconnection (OSI) model, the IEEE started working on Project 802, which would ensure interoperability among data networking products at the two lower layers of the OSI. OSI is a theoretical model of how communication networks function, whereas IEEE 802 sets actual standards for the implementation of hardware and software drivers. The IEEE used the OSI model as a framework for its Project 802 specifications, but with some important differences (see Figure 5-1).

IEEE 802 divides the data link layer of the OSI model into two sublayers: the **Logical Link Control (LLC)**, which is responsible for establishing and maintaining connectivity to the local network, and the **Media Access Control (MAC)**, which is responsible for hardware addressing and error detection and correction.

The PHY layer in IEEE 802 is also divided into two sublayers: the Physical Layer Convergence Procedure (PLCP) and the Physical Medium Dependent (PMD). The PLCP formats the data received from the MAC for transmission by adding a header and a trailer, creating what is called a **frame**—the same way an envelope "frames" a letter. A frame, therefore, is a data link layer packet that includes the header and trailer required by the physical medium for transmission by the PMD. It is at the PMD that the precise method for transmitting and receiving data—in the case of wireless networks, that means Radio Frequency—is defined.

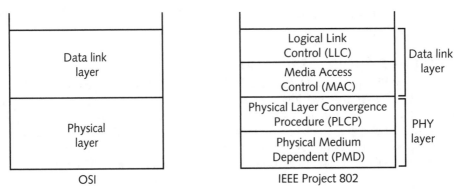

Figure 5-1 OSI model versus IEEE 802

© *Cengage Learning 2014*

RF WPANs

The remainder of this chapter discusses the standards for RF WPANs, beginning with 802.15.1 and Bluetooth and concluding with 802.15.4 and ZigBee.

IEEE 802.15.1 and Bluetooth

Bluetooth is an industry specification that defines small-form-factor, low-cost, short-range wireless radio communications operating primarily in the 2.4 GHz ISM band. As of 2012, more than 14,000 members, including hardware and software manufacturers, participate in the Bluetooth Special Interest Group (SIG).

To ensure that Bluetooth networks can operate in the same areas as 802.11 Wi-Fi networks with a minimum of interference (since they both use the 2.4 GHz frequency band), the IEEE used a portion of the Bluetooth specifications as the base material for 802.15.1. This new standard received final approval on March 2, 2002, and was then incorporated into version 1.2 of the Bluetooth specification. You can find out more about this WPAN technology by visiting *www.bluetooth.org* and *http://ieee802.org/15*.

Most smartphones and cellular phones being sold today are Bluetooth compatible, which means they enable the use of wireless headsets, the synchronization of the device's phone books with computers, and the downloading of pictures from a camera-equipped phone. You can also find printers, print servers, GPS devices, computer keyboards, computer mouse devices, medical equipment, PDAs, and even microwave ovens that are compatible with Bluetooth, and many other devices will likely incorporate this technology in the future. Most current notebook computer models already include Bluetooth interfaces, and even if they don't, adding Bluetooth capability is as easy as plugging in a tiny, low-power USB adapter and installing a small amount of software.

To find out about more products that are Bluetooth enabled, visit *www.bluetooth.com* or *www.palowireless.com/bluetooth/products.asp*.

Bluetooth Protocol Stack

To help you learn how Bluetooth works, let's begin with a tour of its protocol stack. As you know, every wireless networking technology is based on a multilayer protocol model. This simplifies any changes that will need to be made—for example, if the designers need to change only the frequency band used for transmission, in which case the only layer that needs to change is the PHY.

The functions of the lower layers of the Bluetooth stack are typically implemented in the hardware, whereas the functions of the upper layers of the stack are implemented in software. These functions are discussed in the sections that follow. Figure 5-2 illustrates the Bluetooth protocol stack and compares it to the OSI protocol model, for your reference.

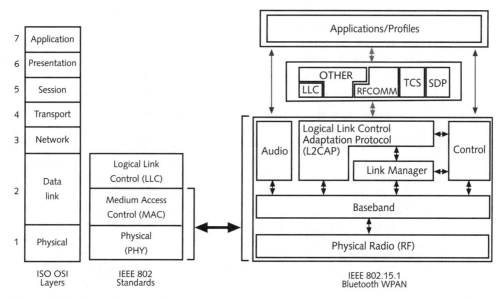

Figure 5-2 Bluetooth protocol stack compared to the OSI protocol model

© Cengage Learning 2014

Bluetooth RF Layer At the lowest level of the Bluetooth protocol stack is the RF layer. It defines how the basic hardware that controls the radio transmissions functions. At this level, the data bits (0 and 1) are converted into radio signals and transmitted. As shown in Figure 5-2, this layer is equivalent to the OSI PHY layer.

Radio Module At the heart of the Bluetooth RF layer is a single radio transmitter/receiver (transceiver) called a **Bluetooth radio module**. (See Figure 5-3 for a sense of its size.) This device includes a tiny Bluetooth chip, which houses the radio module; except for the antenna, this is the only hardware required for Bluetooth to function. The device in Figure 5-3 also includes a USB interface and a blue LED. Bluetooth was designed so that the transceivers that perform all the MAC and PHY functions would fit in a single chip, be as generic or "mainstream" as possible, be low cost, and require a minimum of supporting off-chip components.

Figure 5-3 Bluetooth transceiver (transmitter/receiver)

© Cengage Learning 2014

Putting all the Bluetooth hardware on a single chip has had a significant impact. Instead of needing expensive external devices, such as PC cards, to give a device Bluetooth functionality, the functionality is built into the product itself during the manufacturing process. Because a device with a Bluetooth chip in it has a Bluetooth transceiver (and, usually, an omnidirectional antenna), it is ready to send and receive Bluetooth transmissions the moment it is powered on.

Bluetooth can transmit at a speed of up to 1 Mbps under Bluetooth specification versions 1.1 and 1.2. Most devices list their maximum data rate as 723 Kbps, given that transmission occurs in both directions, with some time slots being used for transmission in one direction and some being used for transmission in the other direction. Version 2.1 adds two modulations that help Bluetooth devices achieve data rates of 2.1 or 3 Mbps while maintaining full backward compatibility with versions 1.1 and 1.2 at 1 Mbps. This feature is called **enhanced data rate** (EDR). Version 3.0 increases the data transmission rate to a maximum of 24 Mbps. Version 4.0 adds low-energy (LE) capabilities to extend battery life at the cost of lower data rates, while maintaining backward compatibility all the way down to 1 Mbps.

Bluetooth Power Classes and Range Bluetooth has three power classes that determine the communication range between devices; the classes are summarized in Table 5-1. Keep in mind that because Bluetooth is based on RF transmission, objects such as walls as well as interference from other RF signal sources (such as Wi-Fi networks) can affect the range of transmission.

Name	Power Level	Distance
Power Class 1	100 mW	330 feet (100 meters)
Power Class 2	2.5 mW	33 feet (10 meters)
Power Class 3	1 mW	3 feet (1 meter)

Table 5-1 **Bluetooth power classes**

© Cengage Learning 2014

Modulation Techniques Versions 1.x of Bluetooth use a variation of frequency shift keying (FSK), which is a binary modulation technique that changes the frequency of the carrier signal. (You learned about FSK in Chapter 2.) Bits transmitted at the higher frequency have a value of 1, and those sent at the lower frequency have a value of 0. The variation of FSK used by Bluetooth is known as **two-level Gaussian frequency shift keying** (2-GFSK).

The amount that the frequency varies between high and low, called the **modulation index**, is between 280 KHz and 350 KHz. This is illustrated in Figure 5-4.

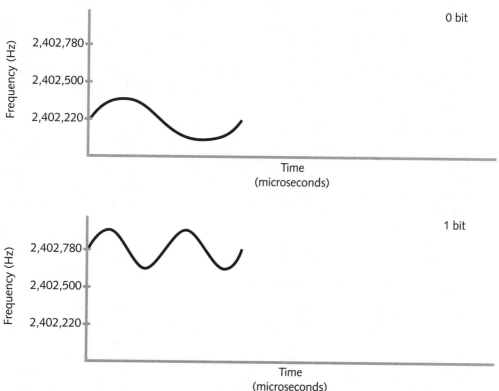

Figure 5-4 Two-level Gaussian frequency shift keying (2-GFSK)

© Cengage Learning 2014

Version 2.x added two modulations: **pi/4-DQPSK** (for 2 Mbps transmission) and **8-DPSK** (for 3 Mbps transmission). Figure 5-5 shows a pi/4-DQPSK waveform. As for 8-DPSK, it can only be used when the signal between two devices is robust—in other words, when there is very little or no interference. In fact, it may only be possible to achieve 3 Mbps when there are no other piconets or Wi-Fi networks nearby.

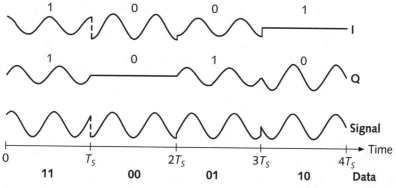

Figure 5-5 pi/4-DQPSK waveform (signal)

© Cengage Learning 2014

Version 3.0 added less power-hungry modes of operation to allow batteries to last longer, and version 3.0+HS added an **alternate MAC/PHY (AMP)**. AMP uses a separate radio module that transmits using the same methods as IEEE 802.11 (discussed in Chapters 7 and 8). All versions of Bluetooth maintain backward compatibility with versions 1.x and 2.x by using the RF layer first, to establish communications. If both devices support AMP, then they can switch to the alternative radio module for data transfers. Due to the simpler Bluetooth protocol stack, it may be possible to achieve data rates as high as 24 Mbps. In this case, all control communications continue to be handled by the RF layer that is compatible with Bluetooth version 1.x.

Bluetooth version 4.0, ratified on June 30, 2010, introduced Bluetooth low energy (BLE), which is also known as ultra low power (ULP). BLE was based on Nokia's Wibree, which was developed in 2001, and BLE-capable devices are designed to transmit at a maximum of 200 Kbps (typically 128 Kbps), which effectively increases the transmission range to approximately 50 feet (15 meters) while reducing power consumption from tens of milliamps to an average of a few microamps. As a comparison with current Bluetooth devices, this would make a button-sized battery last up to one year before needing to be replaced. The technology was originally aimed at competing with near-field communications (NFC) and can be implemented by simply enhancing existing Bluetooth radio designs, thus avoiding costly design and deployment of additional devices to support NFC. BLE can also compete with ZigBee (discussed later in this chapter).

A new generation of cellular phones and tablet computers already supports Bluetooth Smart Ready, which makes use of BLE. For example, the Apple iPhone 4S and the iPad 2, released in March of 2011, already support Bluetooth 4.0 and are compatible with a number of devices—heart monitors for runners and cyclists, devices for locating your car in a large parking lot, smart watches that display caller ID information, and several others yet to be released. Needless to say, it will be very interesting to watch how the industry develops over the next few years and what new applications are made available.

Bluetooth Baseband Layer The Baseband layer lies on top of the RF layer in the Bluetooth stack. This layer manages physical channels and links, handles packets, and does paging and inquiry to locate other Bluetooth devices in the area.

Radio Frequency The part of the spectrum in which Bluetooth operates is the 2.4 GHz Industrial, Scientific, and Medical (ISM) band. Bluetooth divides the 2.4 GHz frequency into 79 frequencies spaced 1 MHz apart and uses the frequency hopping spread spectrum (FHSS) technique to transmit data. The specific sequence of frequencies used—the hopping sequence—is called a **channel**. In other words, the frequency used for transmitting data could be said to hop (i.e., change rapidly) through the 79 different frequencies during transmission. The FHSS technique is shown in Figure 5-6. In just one second of Bluetooth transmission, the frequency changes 1,600 times, or once every 625 microseconds.

Normally, the term *channel* would refer to a frequency. In FHSS, the term is also used to refer to a group of 79 frequencies that form the hopping sequence.

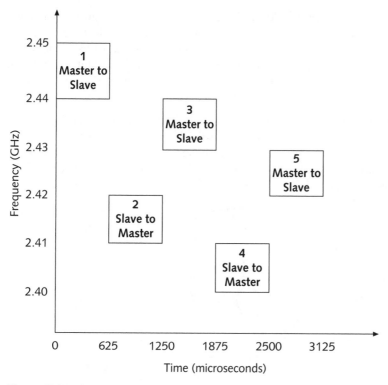

Figure 5-6 Bluetooth FHSS

© Cengage Learning 2014

The Bluetooth hopping sequence is significantly faster than that of most residential cordless telephones that also work in the 2.4 GHz band and that usually switch frequencies approximately 100 times per second. The interference to a Bluetooth transmission that is caused by cordless phones can result in data errors or significant breakups in the voice stream. This interference has a much greater range than the Bluetooth transmission itself.

Because they use the same frequency band as IEEE 802.11b/g/n WLANs, Bluetooth transmissions can interfere with 802.11 WLANs and vice versa. However, after the ratification of IEEE 802.15.1 and subsequent inclusion of this standard in Bluetooth version 1.2 specification, Bluetooth networks coexist with 802.11 WLANs with a minimum of interference and disruption. That is because version 1.2 added a feature called **adaptive frequency hopping (AFH)**, which greatly enhances compatibility with 802.11 WLANs operating in the 2.4 GHz band. Bluetooth accomplishes this by allowing the master device in a Bluetooth network to change the hopping sequence so that devices will not transmit in the frequency occupied by 802.11 in the piconet area.

Coexistence with other wireless devices operating in unlicensed frequency bands is covered under the IEEE 802.15.2 standard. For more information, see *http://standards.ieee.org/getieee802/index.html*.

Bluetooth Network Topologies A Bluetooth device can scan the wireless medium, discovering and connecting to devices in its transmission range, which varies depending on the class of device used (more on this later). A Bluetooth network, called a **piconet**, can have up to seven slave devices connected to one master. The master device initiates the discovery of slave devices within RF range and controls all communications in the piconet. Piconets can sometimes be linked to other piconets; in this case, a Bluetooth network is called a **scatternet**.

When two Bluetooth devices come within range of each other, they can automatically connect with one another. One device, the **master**, controls all the wireless traffic. The other devices, the **slaves**, take commands from the master. A Bluetooth network that contains one master and at least one slave and that uses the same FHSS channel forms a piconet. Examples of piconets are shown in Figure 5-7.

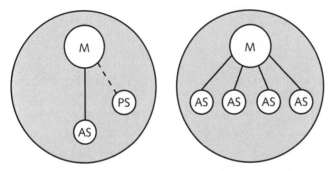

M = Master
AS = Active slave
PS = Parked slave

Figure 5-7 Bluetooth piconets

© Cengage Learning 2014

Each Bluetooth device is preconfigured with an address that is needed when participating or not participating in the piconet. The different addresses used in a Bluetooth piconet are described in Table 5-2.

Name	Description
Bluetooth device address	Unique 48-bit number (IEEE 802 hardware or MAC address), which is preconfigured in the hardware
Active member address	3-bit number valid only as long as device is an active slave in a piconet
Parked member address	8-bit number valid only as long as device is a parked slave; a parked device does not retain the 3-bit active member address

Table 5-2 Piconet radio module addresses

© Cengage Learning 2014

All devices in a piconet must change frequencies at the same time and in the same sequence in order for communication to take place. The timing (called the phase) in the hopping sequence is determined by the clock of the Bluetooth master. Each active slave is synchronized with the master's clock. The hopping sequence is unique for each piconet and is determined by the Bluetooth device address of the master.

In a piconet, the master and slave alternately transmit. The master starts its transmission in even-numbered time slots only, and the slave starts its transmission in odd-numbered time slots only.

Bluetooth Connection Procedure The initial connection between Bluetooth devices, known as a **pairing**, is a two-step process. The first step, known as the **inquiry procedure**, enables a device to discover which devices are in range and then determine the addresses and clocks for those devices. When a Bluetooth device enters the range of other devices, it first attempts to find other Bluetooth devices in the area. During the second step, the **paging procedure**, an actual Bluetooth connection can be established. Once a Bluetooth device is paired with another and has a 3-bit active member address, the inquiry procedure is no longer needed. The master periodically sends out a page in an attempt to establish a connection with known or paired devices. The device that carries out a paging procedure and establishes a connection will automatically become the master of the connection.

Multiple piconets can cover the same area, and each can contain up to seven slaves. Because each piconet has a different master and hop sequence, the risk of collisions (two devices attempting to send at the same time on the same frequency) is slim. However, if many more piconets are added, the probability of collisions increases. The occurrence of collisions diminishes the performance and throughput of the network.

If multiple piconets cover the same area, a Bluetooth device can be a member of two or more overlapping piconets, or a scatternet (see Figure 5-8). To communicate in each piconet, the device must use the master device address and clock of that specific piconet; these are supplied by the master of that piconet.

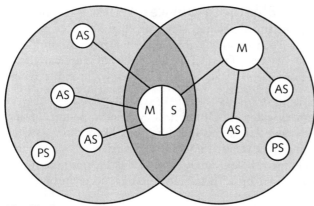

M = Master
AS = Active slave
PS = Parked slave

Figure 5-8 Bluetooth scatternet

© *Cengage Learning 2014*

A Bluetooth device can be a slave in several piconets, but it can be a master in only one piconet. A master and slave can switch roles, however.

Bluetooth Frames Because Bluetooth transmissions are limited to very small networks, it uses a very simple frame structure. The PHY frame for a Bluetooth transmission is shown in Figure 5-9. Each frame consists of three parts:

- Access code (72 bits)—Used for timing synchronization, paging, and inquiry
- Header (54 bits)—Used for packet acknowledgment, packet numbering, slave address, type of payload, and error checking
- Payload (0–2745 bits)—Can contain data, voice, or both

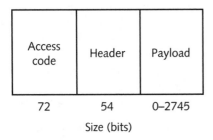

Figure 5-9 Bluetooth PHY frame

© *Cengage Learning 2014*

Bluetooth Link Manager Layer

The Link Manager layer of the Bluetooth stack can be divided into two broad functions: managing the piconet and performing security. The functions of the Link Manager layer are discussed below.

Managing Links Between Bluetooth Devices Managing the piconet involves regulating the steps for attaching and detaching slaves from the master as well as overseeing the master-slave switch. To accomplish this, different types of links have to be established between Bluetooth devices. There are two types of physical links between devices: synchronous connection-oriented (SCO) links and asynchronous connectionless (ACL) links.

- A **synchronous connection-oriented (SCO) link** is a symmetric point-to-point link between a master and a single slave. This link functions like a circuit-switched link by using reserved time slots at fixed intervals. A master and slave can each support up to three simultaneous SCO links. A SCO link carries mainly voice transmissions at a speed of 64 Kbps. These transmissions occur in both directions, as described before.
- An **asynchronous connectionless (ACL) link** is a packet-switched link used for data transmissions. Sometimes called a point-to-multipoint link, the ACL link is from one master to all the slaves participating on the piconet. A piconet can support only a single ACL link between one master and up to seven slaves. In the time slots not reserved for the SCO links, the master can establish an ACL and transfer data to any slave. A slave already engaged in an SCO link can also have an ACL link.

Table 5-3 presents the types of ACL link configurations for a piconet. SCO links are also shown.

Configuration Options	Maximum Transmission Rate Upstream	Maximum Transmission Rate Downstream
3 simultaneous voice channels (SCO)	64 Kbps × 3 channels	64 Kbps × 3 channels
Symmetric data (SCO)	433.9 Kbps	433.9 Kbps
Asymmetric data (ACL)	723.2 Kbps	57.6 Kbps
Asymmetric data (ACL)	57.6 Kbps	723.2 Kbps

Table 5-3 Supported Bluetooth link configurations

© Cengage Learning 2014

If an error occurs on an ACL packet, that packet is retransmitted. A SCO packet is never retransmitted.

Error Correction Another management function of the Link Manager layer is error correction. There are three kinds of error-correction schemes used in the Bluetooth protocol:

- **1/3 rate Forward Error Correction (FEC)**—Repeats every bit three times for redundancy. The maximum data rate is effectively divided by 3, hence "1/3 rate."

- **2/3 rate Forward Error Correction (FEC)**—Adds extra bits that are examined by the receiving device to determine if an error took place in the transmission. For example, if 8 bits of data were sent, they would have been expanded to 11 bits, which includes the error-correction data. The extra bits reduce the maximum data rate that can be achieved for a transmission but allows the receiver to detect multiple bit errors and correct single bit errors, avoiding the need to retransmit the data.

- **Automatic retransmission request (ARQ)**—Continuously retransmits the data fields of a data-only or data-voice packet until an acknowledgment is received or a timeout value is exceeded.

Bluetooth Power Usage Because most Bluetooth devices are designed to be mobile and because they require battery power from a laptop computer, PDA, or similar device, conserving power is essential. The power consumption of Bluetooth devices varies depending on their connection modes. Voice transmissions through a headset use only 10 milliamps (mA). At this rate, a typical battery can last for up to 75 hours of use. Data transmissions use only 6 mA, which means the battery can last up to 120 hours before needing to be recharged. While not transmitting, Bluetooth uses only 0.3 milliamps, which means the battery can last three months if there are no transmissions. Battery life varies, of course, and depending on the type and physical size of devices, this can affect the maximum talk times and data transmission times. The only way to know for sure is to consult the manual for a specific Bluetooth device.

Although amps and watts can be confusing, think of watts as a measure of the actual power used to push the radio signal out, and think of amps as a measure of the power that is needed to make that push.

Once connected to a piconet, a Bluetooth device can be in one of four power modes:

- Active—In **active mode**, the Bluetooth unit actively participates on the channel and consumes an amount of power that corresponds to the type of data being transmitted. Over a period of time, this averages out to 2.5 mW in a Power Class 2 device.

- Sniff—In **sniff mode**, a slave device listens to the piconet master at a reduced rate so that it uses less power. The interval is programmable and depends on the application. It is the least efficient of the power-saving modes.

- Hold—The master device can put slave devices into **hold mode**, in which only the slave's internal timer is running. Slave devices can also demand to be put into hold mode. Data transfer instantly restarts when the slave moves from hold mode back to active mode, but power consumption is kept to a minimum while it is not transmitting.

- Park—In **park mode**, the most efficient of the power-saving modes, a device is still synchronized to the piconet but does not participate in any traffic. These slaves occasionally listen to the traffic of their master in order to resynchronize and check on broadcast messages. Power consumption in this mode is a mere 0.3 mA.

Other Bluetooth Layers and Their Functions

This section provides an overview of the Bluetooth protocol stack's remaining layers (see Figure 5-2). The Logical Link Control Adaptation Protocol (L2CAP) is the layer responsible for segmenting and reassembling data packets, which are then sent through standard data protocols such as TCP/IP for transmission. The Radio Frequency Virtual Communications Port Emulation (RFCOMM) protocol layer provides serial port emulation for Bluetooth data. This layer packages the data so it appears as if it were sent through the computer's standard serial port, which is another feature of Bluetooth.

Control information is also transmitted between devices, such as an instruction for a device to switch from master to slave. This control information comes through the **Link Manager** layer but then bypasses the L2CAP layer, which is only used when transmitting data streams.

Bluetooth Profiles The ability of a device to perform certain types of functions is determined by the profiles that are located at the Application layer of the Bluetooth protocol stack and is implemented in the software driver used with Bluetooth devices. In order for a Bluetooth device to operate as a remote control—to control a slide show using Microsoft PowerPoint, for example—it must support the AVRCP (Audio/Video Remote Control) profile. A headset, on the other hand, would typically implement the Advanced Audio Distribution Profile (A2DP). A comprehensive list of Bluetooth profiles currently adopted by the SIG can be found on the Bluetooth developer's Web site at *http://developer.bluetooth.org/KnowledgeCenter/TechnologyOverview/Pages/Profiles.aspx.*

IEEE 802.15.4 and ZigBee

Another WPAN technology designed to replace cables and wires is ZigBee. Based on the IEEE 802.15.4 standard, ZigBee is primarily aimed at providing wireless connectivity between simple stationary devices or mobile devices—such as remote controls—that require very low data rates (between 20 Kbps and 250 Kbps), consume minimal amounts of power, and connect at distances from 33 feet (10 meters) to 150 feet (50 meters). Although there are several other specifications designed to perform similar functions, ZigBee is the only true global standard.

The **ZigBee Alliance**, formed in 2002, created a set of specifications for monitoring and controlling wirelessly networked products. At the time, there was no global, open standard that enabled manufacturers to build low-cost devices that could interoperate with those of other countries. The requirements for monitoring sensors, sometimes called motes, and for control systems are different from those for wireless computer networks. Although manufacturers could implement devices designed for control and monitoring functions using IEEE 802.11 or Bluetooth, these last two technologies are far more complex and were originally designed for the transmission of either large amounts of data or for cable replacement or for voice and video. In addition, Bluetooth and IEEE 802.11 were not originally designed to support mesh networking, unlike ZigBee. The ZigBee specification is also far more open and relaxed; this helps reduce the implementation costs by simplifying the communications protocols.

The ZigBee specification uses the 802.15.4 standard for the PHY and MAC layers. Both IEEE 802.15.4 and ZigBee designations are used interchangeably throughout this section. You should keep in mind, however, that the ZigBee Alliance and the IEEE are two completely different organizations and that the ZigBee specification goes beyond the IEEE 802.15.4 standards definitions. You can access the ZigBee specifications at *www.zigbee.org*. The IEEE 802.15.4 standard is located at *http://standards.ieee.org/getieee802/index.html*.

Today, the ZigBee Alliance has expanded its specifications to include several industry-specific sets of interoperable standards, including ZigBee Health Care, ZigBee Home Automation, ZigBee Smart Energy, ZigBee Telecom Services, and the ZigBee Building Automation and ZigBee Retail Services specifications.

ZigBee and IEEE 802.15.4 operate in the 868 MHz, 915 MHz, and 2.4 GHz frequencies that are part of the ISM band. Applications for ZigBee-compliant devices include:

- Lighting controls
- Automatic meter readers for natural gas, electricity, water, and similar systems
- Wireless smoke and carbon monoxide detectors
- Home security sensors for doors and windows
- Environmental controls for heating and air-conditioning systems
- Controls for window blinds, draperies, and shades
- Equipment for wireless patient monitoring, such as heart-rate and blood pressure
- Universal remote control for a television set-top box, including home control functions—such as lighting, temperature, etc.
- Industrial and building automation controls for remote machine monitoring

ZigBee Overview The ZigBee specification is based on the relatively low-level performance requirements of sensors and control systems. ZigBee-compliant devices are designed to remain quiescent (without communicating) for long periods of time.

When a ZigBee device is connected to the network but is no longer needed, it can turn itself off, thereby consuming much less power. As a result, ZigBee battery-powered devices are capable of operating for several years before their batteries need to be replaced. Devices can wake up any time they need to communicate, follow the network access protocol, and then transmit on the specific network's channel, which is already known (from when the device first connected to the network). Once they have performed their functions, they can return to sleep mode by turning themselves off again. Their average duty cycle (the percentage of time they will transmit or receive data) is between 0.1 percent and 2 percent of the time, which means that ZigBee-compliant devices use very little power. For example, if a ZigBee device wakes up every 60 seconds and turns on its radio for about 60 ms while it communicates on the PAN, its batteries will last for several years.

Although ZigBee transmissions are designed to be short in range, the specification includes full mesh networking. This means that some ZigBee devices can route packets to other devices, which allows them to reach beyond their radio ranges. In fact, given that each network can simultaneously support 64,000 nodes, a ZigBee network can cover a large area, such as an entire house, conference center, office building, or manufacturing plant. This makes ZigBee technology ideal for sensors and control applications in large buildings such as factories, warehouses, and even tall office buildings.

Mesh networking is supported, but not included, as part of the IEEE 802.15.4 standard. This means that other technologies that use IEEE 802.15.4 may or may not support mesh networking. However, mesh networking is an integral and important part of the ZigBee specification.

There are three basic classes of devices in a ZigBee network:

- **Full-function device (FFD)**—A full-function device can connect to other full-function devices and route frames to other devices in addition to connecting to endpoint devices in a parent-child relationship. It can maintain connections to multiple devices.

- **PAN coordinator**—The first full-function device that is turned on in an area becomes the PAN coordinator, which starts and maintains the network. Coordinators are always plugged in to the main power and never turn themselves off, which allows the ZigBee network to remain available to all other devices.

- **Reduced-function device (RFD)**—This is an endpoint device—such as a light switch or a lamp—that can only connect to one full-function device on the network and can only join the network as a child device. Child devices do not connect to other child devices.

ZigBee Protocol Stack The ZigBee protocol stack is based on the OSI seven-layer model but defines only those layers that are relevant to achieving the specific functions required in the ZigBee specifications. Shown in Figure 5-10, the ZigBee protocol stack has the following characteristics:

- Its two PHY layers operate in separate frequency ranges. The lower-frequency PHY layer covers both the 868 MHz band used in Europe and the 915 MHz band used in countries such as the United States and Australia. The higher-frequency PHY layer covers the 2.4 GHz band; it is used worldwide.

- The MAC sublayer controls access to the radio channel. Its responsibilities include synchronization and providing a reliable transmission mechanism (error checking).

- The Logical Link Control (LLC) sublayer complies with the IEEE 802.2 LLC and is responsible for managing the data-link communication, link addressing, defining service access points, and frame sequencing. A second LLC sublayer is included in the specification to support other protocols and functionality.

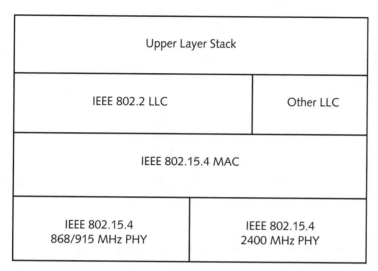

Figure 5-10 ZigBee protocol stack

© Cengage Learning 2014

The upper layers of the ZigBee protocol stack include specific procedures that devices use to join a network (called an **association**), leave a network (called a **disassociation**), apply security to frames, and perform routing. These layers are also responsible for device discovery, maintaining routing tables, and storing information about neighbor devices.

The PHY layer in a ZigBee device is responsible for turning the radio transceiver on and off, detecting the presence of an RF signal in the currently selected channel, analyzing and reporting link quality for received packets, assessing whether the channel is clear before initiating a transmission, selecting a frequency channel for operation, and transmitting and receiving data.

Altogether, there are 27 channels across the various frequency bands that can be used in IEEE 802.15.4. A single channel that's 600 KHz wide is available in the 868 MHz band; 10 channels that are 2 MHz wide are in the 915 MHz band; and 16 channels that are 5 MHz wide are in the 2.40 GHz band. Table 5-4 presents the frequency bands and data rates for 802.15.4 WPANs.

PHY Layer (MHz)	Frequency Range (MHz)	Chip Rate (kchips/second)	Modulation	Bit Rate (Kbps)
868/915	868–868.6	300	BPSK	20
	902–928	600	BPSK	40
2,450	2,400–2,483.5	2000	O-QPSK	250

Table 5-4 802.15.4 frequency bands and data rates

© Cengage Learning 2014

You may recall from Chapter 2 that binary phase shift keying (BPSK) modulation uses two different starting points of an analog wave—typically at 0 degrees and 180 degrees—to encode a digital signal onto an analog wave. However, since DSSS transmission spreads the signal over the bandwidth of the channel, the carrier is modulated with a sequence of 15 chips, instead of the data bits themselves, in both the 868 and 915 MHz bands. To send a binary 1, the sequence 000010100110111 is transmitted at the chip rates indicated in Table 5-4; to send a binary 0, the sequence 111101011001000 is transmitted.

In the 2.4 GHz band, the technique employs 16 different 32-chip sequences called **symbols**, which are data units that represent single bits or a combination of bits. In this case, each of the 16 different 32-chip sequences in this band transmits a different combination of 4 bits.

These 32-chip sequences are then modulated using a technique called **offset quadrature phase shift keying (O-QPSK)**, which uses two carrier waves, at different frequencies, that are exactly 90 degrees out of phase and therefore do not interfere with each other. It modulates some of the chips on one carrier and some on the other. Finally, the two signals are combined and transmitted. Figure 5-11 illustrates the modulation of each signal separately; one is called I-Phase, for "in-phase," and the other is called Q-Phase, for "quadrature signal." The resulting waveform, after combining the two carriers, is similar to QPSK, discussed in Chapter 2.

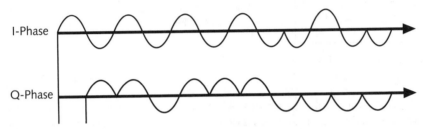

Figure 5-11 Offset quadrature phase shift keying (O-QPSK)

© Cengage Learning 2014

IEEE 802.15.4 PHY Frame Format The PHY frame for IEEE 802.15.4, shown in Figure 5-12, has the following format:

- Preamble (32 binary 0s)—Used for synchronization.
- SFD (8 bits)—A fixed pattern of bits that indicates the end of the preamble and the start of the data (SFD).
- Frame length (8 bits)—The first seven bits indicate the length of the payload, which can be from one to 127 octets; the additional reserved bit makes this field one octet long.
- Payload field (variable)—This field is either five octets long (containing an ACK) or 8 to 127 octets long. Frame lengths of zero to four, six, or seven octets are reserved by the standard.

4 octets	1 octet	7 bits	1 bit	Variable
Preamble	SFD	Frame Length	Reserved	Payload

Figure 5-12 ZigBee PHY frame format

© Cengage Learning 2014

802.15.4 MAC Layer The MAC layer in 802.15.4 handles all access from the upper layers to the physical radio channel and is responsible for:

- Generating time synchronization frames if the device is a PAN coordinator
- Synchronizing to the time synchronization frames (described below)
- Association and disassociation
- Device security and support of security mechanisms implemented by the upper layers
- Managing channel access
- Giving priority for certain devices to transmit at specific times
- Maintaining a reliable link (error detection); 802.15.4 uses a 16-bit ITU cyclic redundancy check for validating the data

Access to the wireless medium is contention based, which means that all devices, before transmitting, listen to the medium to determine if the frequency channel is free. This is called **carrier sense multiple access with collision avoidance (CSMA/CA)**. Because a collision during a wireless transmission can only be detected if a packet is not understood by the intended receiver and therefore not acknowledged, wireless transmissions can avoid, but not actually detect, collisions.

In Ethernet, collisions are detected by using a voltage sensor on the cable, but in wireless there is no way to know what the amplitude of the signal will be, at either the transmitter or the receiver end, due to the variance in attenuation. Wireless devices using a single radio typically assume that there must have been a collision—or some other phenomenon that destroyed the frame—if they do not receive an ACK from the intended receiver.

ZigBee and IEEE Communication Basics

When a ZigBee device needs to determine if a channel is clear, it can do it in one of two ways. The first way is by enabling the receiver to detect and estimate the amount of signal energy in the medium. In this case, the devices do not attempt to receive or decode any data—that is, they do not look for an IEEE 802.15.4 transmission; they only try to estimate the energy level in the wireless medium, which would indicate that another device is transmitting in the same frequency channel. (Note that in energy detection this could be any other type of device transmitting in the same frequency range—such as a laptop computer—and not necessarily another ZigBee device). This procedure is called *energy detection* or *ED*.

The second way for a ZigBee device to decide if a channel is clear is to perform a carrier sense. In this case, the device looks for a specific 802.15.4 signal, and it attempts to decode the data transmission before deciding that the channel is busy. If the channel is not clear of transmissions, the device backs off—does not transmit—for a random amount of time. The process is repeated until the frequency channel is clear of other 802.15.4 transmissions.

Beacon-Enabled vs. Non-Beacon Communications

There are two types of network access used in IEEE 802.15.4: contention-based network access and contention-free network access. In contention-based communications, all devices that want to transmit in a particular frequency use CSMA/CA to determine if a channel is busy. In contention-free communications, the PAN coordinator allocates time slots for specific devices to transmit in. These are called **guaranteed time slots (GTS)**.

In beacon-enabled networks, the PAN coordinator can transmit control information about which devices are allowed to transmit and when, and it may include timing periods in which the other devices contend for access to the medium. The beacons are transmitted at fixed intervals.

In beacon-enabled networks, IEEE 802.15.4 has the option of employing a superframe concept. The **superframe** is a mechanism for managing transmission time in a piconet. It consists of a continuously repeating frame containing contention access periods, but it may also contain GTSs for critical devices to transmit priority data between two beacons. A superframe always begins with a beacon. A **beacon** signals the beginning of a superframe and contains information about the type and number of time slots contained in the time periods between beacons. The beacon is also the time synchronization frame for the network and is required for association when the network is using superframes. The ZigBee coordinator allocates GTSs but always leaves time slots available for use as contention access periods between two beacons. Each time slot consists of a complete PHY frame, which in turn includes a MAC frame. Figure 5-13 shows an example of an 802.15.4 superframe.

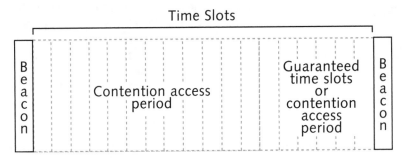

Figure 5-13 802.15.4 superframe

© Cengage Learning 2014

Beacon frames are not required for device-to-device communications. In non-beacon enabled networks, the PAN coordinator will send beacons periodically because they contain addresses and timing information required for new devices to associate with the network.

In 802.15.4, all the procedures for associating with and joining a network, routing, and so on are embedded in the hardware instead of being dependent on client software and a driver that may require configuration. This means that, in most cases, troubleshooting a ZigBee network is limited to configuring which switch turns on a particular light or group of lights. The only other field troubleshooting function in ZigBee networks is determining whether the RF signal from one device is reaching another device so that they can communicate reliably.

ZigBee devices are designed to automatically associate with and join a network once they are powered on. The network topology is defined during initial installation, depending on the specific needs of the system. When a ZigBee device is powered on for the first time, it will listen for traffic on the network and scan the medium in an attempt to identify which RF channel is being used. Only then will it send a request to join the network.

ZigBee devices can query other devices to identify the number of devices that are connected to the network and their locations in a process called **device discovery**. Once the devices are associated with the network, they have the option of performing a **service discovery** to identify the capabilities of specific devices of interest that may be members of the WPAN.

Coexistence with Other Standards Relatively wideband interference, such as that generated by IEEE 802.11b networks, appears like white noise to an IEEE 802.15.4 receiver because only a fraction of the 802.11b power falls within the 802.15.4 receiver bandwidth. Likewise, the impact of interference from Bluetooth (802.15.1) devices should be minimal due to the much smaller bandwidth of each of its frequency channels.

802.15.4 devices should only interfere with approximately three out of the 79 hops of a Bluetooth transmission, or approximately 4 percent. To an IEEE 802.11b receiver, the signal from an 802.15.4 transmitter looks like narrowband interference. The low duty cycles—the result of few transmissions and short, simple frames, which is typical of ZigBee devices—further reduce the impact of interference.

Network Addressing The ZigBee specification defines four levels of addresses for identifying devices within a PAN: IEEE address, network (PAN) address, node address, and endpoint address. The IEEE address, also called an extended address, is a 64-bit static hardware address that is embedded in every radio transmitter. The PAN address is a unique 16-bit identifier for each PAN in an area. It is assigned by the PAN coordinator and is only used for a single network or cluster. The node address is a 16-bit address assigned by the PAN coordinator or parent device; this address comes from a group of addresses distributed by the coordinator and is unique for each radio on the network. The node address is used for the purpose of increasing the efficiency of ZigBee transmissons, given that the IEEE address is 64 bits long. The endpoint address uniquely identifies each endpoint device or service controlled by a single radio—a light bulb, for example.

To understand multiple levels of addressing, see Figure 5-14, in which two switches that control three lights on a single lamp are themselves controlled by a single radio transmitter. Switch A, on the left, controls the bottom light. Switch B, on the right, controls the two top lights. The ZigBee module controlling the switches can be physically located far from the lamp. In this case, for either switch to send a command to the lamp, it needs the PAN address (because it can vary), the node address (to identify the radio module in the lamp), and the endpoint address (to identify the individual light bulbs). The process of creating a relationship between a light and a switch is called **binding**; this needs to be performed only when the WPAN is being set up or reconfigured.

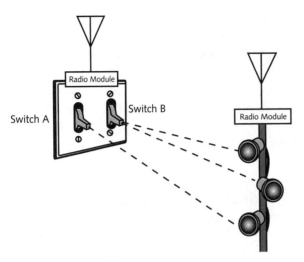

Figure 5-14 Multiple endpoints controlled by a single radio transmitter

© *Cengage Learning 2014*

Note that not all addresses are used in every frame; which address is used depends on which two devices are communicating in the piconet. Although the example in the figure is extremely simple, imagine the same process applied to endpoint devices in a tall office building or a large factory. With ZigBee, if the office layout changes, it is possible to reconfigure all the light switches. As a comparison, in a traditional installation, this would require a significant amount of rewiring, which is often prohibitively expensive.

ZigBee Network Topologies As shown in Figure 5-15, there are three basic topologies for ZigBee networks: star, tree, and mesh.

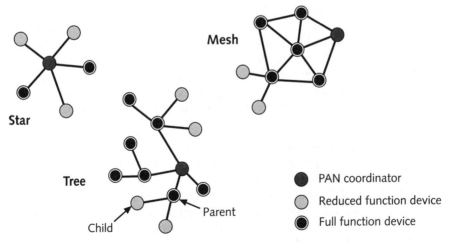

Figure 5-15 Topologies supported in ZigBee networks

© *Cengage Learning 2014*

In both tree and mesh topologies, alternate paths may be available for packets, even if a nearby device is turned off or disconnected from the network. However, in tree and cluster tree networks, alternate paths may only be available to a child or to an FFD if another FFD is within its radio range. If a child device loses the connection with its FFD, it becomes an orphan. An orphan can rejoin the network by becoming a child of another FFD that is within range. If a full-function routing device loses the connection to another full-function device, it will automatically use one of its alternate connections, if available, so that it retains its routing capability. These are important considerations when installing a ZigBee network.

 The IEEE 802.15.4 standard only defines two topologies: star and peer-to-peer, given that a cluster tree network essentially consists of multiple star topology networks.

Figure 5-16 shows multiple paths for packets that are routed in a ZigBee mesh network. Note that the mesh network itself is made up of full-function devices connected in a peer-to-peer fashion, although each of these can have other RFD child devices connected to them. Provided that all full-function routing devices are able to connect to one another, forming a mesh-like topology, packets can be routed across the entire network.

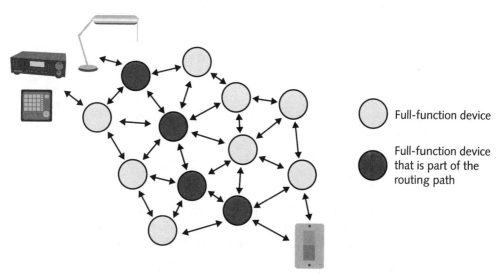

Figure 5-16 Routing of data packets in a ZigBee mesh network

© Cengage Learning 2014

In a star topology, a single device, the PAN coordinator, controls the network. All other devices are known as end-nodes, regardless of whether they have additional capabilities. Because most devices are connected to a coordinator, they only communicate directly with the coordinator.

Cluster tree topologies are made up of two or more tree topology networks that are inter-connected by FFDs. Cluster tree networks have a slight advantage over mesh networks. In a mesh network, performance is diminished because each full-function node must maintain a complete routing table and make decisions on the best route to use when forwarding the packets. However, the reliability of a cluster tree network is not as high as that of a mesh network, because the failure of an interconnecting device can prevent an entire tree from communicating with other trees and other devices on the network, perhaps preventing a light switch from turning on a lamp located at the other end of the office or building.

Figure 5-17 shows an example of a larger cluster tree network. Notice the connections between trees; also notice that each cluster tree uses a different channel to communicate between devices. Each ZigBee router (FFD) must be able to communicate on both channels in order to act as an interface between two trees of a cluster tree topology.

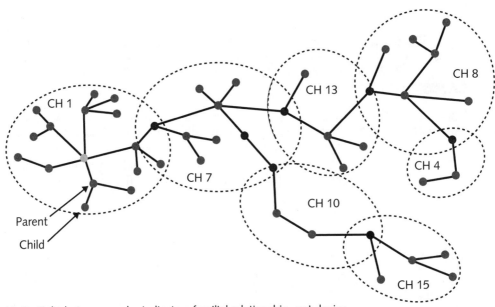

Note: Links between nodes indicate a familial relationship, not device or communications capability.

Figure 5-17 ZigBee cluster tree network

© Cengage Learning 2014

Power Management in ZigBee Networks Packet routing requires a lot of processing overhead and some additional traffic, which diminishes the power-saving effect of ZigBee devices and also reduces the data throughput. In addition, ZigBee devices are designed to be very small—such as a light switch—and for this reason they are more likely to be equipped with low-speed, power-efficient CPUs. In a ZigBee PAN, only the devices that perform routing or are coordinators incur overhead and, consequently, consume more power. The 802.15.4 standard favors battery-powered devices but does not prevent devices from being connected to another power source, such as an electrical outlet. There is also no limitation on devices having additional data-processing power. Most FFDs, which are routing-capable ZigBee devices, typically connect to external power sources, although they can run on battery power during outages. One example is an FFD that includes a temperature sensor and is configured to transmit every 30 seconds, such as those monitoring critical machinery.

The ZigBee specification includes a number of parameters that must be maintained by devices in case of localized or network-wide power failures or resets. These include the PAN ID, the network address, the address of every associated child device, and the channel in use. Availability of the address information enables a ZigBee network to recover without user intervention. This kind of functionality is also crucial for the reliability of ZigBee devices.

Other Technologies Using IEEE 802.15.4

There are two other technologies that take advantage of the IEEE 802.15.4 MAC and PHY: 6LoWPAN and WirelessHART.

6LoWPAN 6LoWPAN, a protocol that implements IPv6 on WPANs, makes interfacing a WPAN to the Internet much simpler because it uses an adaptation layer between the MAC and Network layers of IPv6 to translate the IP information to a format that can be transmitted using the MAC frame format of 802.15.4-compliant hardware.

6LoWPAN supports mesh networking and is designed to be used in nodes that have limited memory space and processing capabilities and, like ZigBee, the Adaptation layer uses a compression algorithm to reduce the size of the 40-octet IPv6 header and employs fragmentation to allow the minimal-size IPv6 packets (1280 octets) to be transmitted in a 802.15.4 payload, which has a maximum size of 127 octets. This makes it possible to access and manage a network node just like any other IP device.

WirelessHART The Highway Addressable Remote Transducer (HART) protocol was designed for industrial-automation applications in wired networks—process control, equipment and process monitoring, and advanced diagnostics, for example. HART supports both a bus topology, in which several instruments are attached to the same cable, and a point-to-point connection that allows both digital and analog signals to be sent on the same cable. In 2007, the HART Communications Foundation (HCF) approved **WirelessHART** to protect manufacturing companies' investment in the over 30 million HART devices installed while permitting their use over a wireless link.

Low Rate WPAN Security

Although security shouldn't be a concern with WPANs, given that most of the transmissions are restricted to a short physical range, there is still the danger that hackers will try to break into devices and networks. In this section, you will learn about the security models for each of the WPAN technologies discussed in this chapter.

One of the most serious concerns—one that is frequently ignored by end-users—is social engineering. Hackers can target a company without anyone knowing it is happening. Therefore, staff members should be constantly on the lookout for situations that might cause a security risk. For example, equipment used outside the office should be configured to reject any kind of file transfer unless there is specific user authorization, even if security is being used. Stolen or borrowed equipment can also compromise security because authorized users may intentionally or unintentionally provide a password or security code to someone else, or they can change configuration parameters, thereby exposing equipment to unauthorized data transfers. If this happens, the security keys must be immediately changed throughout the organization.

Designing security for WPANs can be much more difficult than for other networking technologies. A single solution is not likely to meet all the security requirements, for one thing. Users like to roam free while remaining connected, but they do not want anyone to eavesdrop on their telephone conversations, access their private information, steal the signal, or interfere in any way with their systems. Also, small devices tend to have limited processing capabilities and small amounts of power; they therefore do not lend themselves to the implementation of complex security measures.

Banking and electronic funds transactions present even more difficulties for WPANs. To keep the transactions secure, both the user's identity and the transaction itself have to be verified. This is done using public key infrastructure and a certificate authority. **Public key infrastructure (PKI)** uses a unique security code, or key, provided by a certificate authority, whereas a **certificate authority** is a private company that verifies the authenticity of each user in order to discourage fraud. This kind of authentication will have to be in widespread use before financial institutions will adopt WPAN technology.

The data transmission must also be protected to prevent tampering; otherwise, hackers can intercept a packet, make changes to it, and then forward the same packet with the changes. This is called a man-in-the-middle attack, and the process to prevent it uses both sequential packet freshness information as well as message integrity check (or message integrity code). Both of these security mechanisms are discussed later in this chapter.

Security is an extensive and complex topic that is largely beyond the scope of this book, which nevertheless provides, on a chapter-by-chapter basis, a list of the security options that are available for each technology as well as a brief discussion of the security issues faced by each technology.

Security in Bluetooth WPANs

Bluetooth provides security through authentication or encryption. **Authentication** is based on identifying the device itself, not who is using the device. To accomplish that, Bluetooth uses a **challenge-response strategy** to determine whether the new device knows a secret key. If it does, it is allowed to join the piconet.

Encryption services are also available for Bluetooth networks, but because Bluetooth devices tend to be battery powered and have slower CPUs, encryption is seldom a good idea, except in government or military applications, where it often cannot be avoided.

Encryption is the process of scrambling the data using mathematical algorithms so that the transmission, if intercepted, still has to be decoded into the original data, which discourages many hackers. The Bluetooth specification supports three encryption modes:

- Encryption Mode 1—Nothing is encrypted.
- Encryption Mode 2—Traffic from the master to one slave is encrypted, but traffic from the master to multiple slaves (broadcasts) is not encrypted.
- Encryption Mode 3—All traffic is encrypted.

The authentication key and the encryption key are two different keys. The reason for separating them is to allow the use of a shorter encryption key without weakening the strength of the authentication key.

There are three levels of Bluetooth security:

- Level 1: No security—A Bluetooth device does not initiate any security steps.
- Level 2: Service-level security—Security is established at the higher levels of the protocol stack after a connection is made.

- Level 3: Link-level security—Security is established at the lower levels of the protocol stack before a connection is made.

Note that very few manufacturers implement security beyond the pairing key in Bluetooth. When transferring data other than voice or video, another option that Bluetooth users have is to encrypt the data before it is transmitted. However, you should consider that encryption usually increases the byte count significantly and therefore reduces the speed and efficiency of the piconet.

Security in ZigBee and IEEE 802.15.4 WPANs

ZigBee WPANs use a process called symmetric key for both authentication and encryption. A symmetric key is a sequence of numbers and letters, much like a password, that must be entered by the authorized user on all devices. No automatic key distribution or key rotation is included in the standard, although these options can be implemented at the higher protocol layers. The length of the key can be 4, 6, 8, 12, 14, or 16 octets, with longer keys providing more security than shorter ones.

In addition to symmetric key security, the IEEE 802.15.4 standard provides frame integrity, access control, and security services. Frame integrity is a technique that uses a **message integrity code (MIC)**, a sequence of bits based on a subset of the data itself, the length field, and the symmetric key. This code is used by the receiving device to verify that the data has not been tampered with during transmission from the sender to the receiver. In access control, a device maintains a list of other devices with which it is permitted to communicate. This list is called an **access control list (ACL)**. This technique allows ZigBee devices in a large building, for example, to communicate only with devices belonging to their own network and not with devices in other networks. **Sequential freshness** is a security service used by the receiving device that ensures that the same frames will not be transmitted more than once. The network maintains a sequential number that is continually incremented and tracked by the devices to verify that the arriving data is newer than the last data transmitted. This prevents a frame from being captured and replayed on the network by a hacker who does not have access to the encryption key.

There are three security modes in the 802.15.4 standard: unsecured mode, ACL mode (which uses access control), and secured mode (which uses full authentication and encryption). In secured mode, the MAC layer may optionally provide frame integrity and sequential freshness.

Chapter Summary

- Computer networks require all the network components to follow certain rules if the network is to function properly. A network protocol is the set of rules that specifies the format and order of the messages exchanged between two or more communication devices. Network protocols are organized into layers. When a set of network protocols is viewed as a whole, the group is called a network protocol stack.

- Bluetooth is a wireless technology that uses short-range radio frequency (RF) transmissions, enabling users to connect to a wide range of devices without using cables. Bluetooth can also be used to create a small network.

- Bluetooth is supported by over 2,500 hardware and software vendors who make up the Bluetooth Special Interest Group (SIG). The IEEE used a portion of the Bluetooth specifications as the base material for its 802.15.1 standard. The standard is fully compatible with Bluetooth version 1.2 and higher.

- The Bluetooth protocol stack's functions can be divided into two parts based on how they are implemented: the lower levels and the upper levels. The lower-level functions are implemented in hardware, whereas the upper-level functions are implemented in software. At the lowest level of the Bluetooth protocol stack is the RF layer. It defines how the basic hardware that controls the radio transmissions functions. At the heart of Bluetooth is a single radio transmitter/receiver (transceiver) that performs all the necessary functions. Bluetooth can transmit at a speed of 1 Mbps and has three different power classes for transmitting.

- Up to version 1.2, Bluetooth uses two-level Gaussian frequency shift keying (2-GFSK) modulation and operates in the 2.4 GHz Industrial, Scientific, and Medical (ISM) band. Bluetooth uses the frequency hopping spread spectrum (FHSS) technique to send a transmission. Version 2 of Bluetooth added two modulation methods that help it achieve speeds of 2 Mbps and 3 Mbps. Version 3 added power-saving modes of operation, an alternative MAC, and PHY layers that use a second radio and Wi-Fi, all of which help it achieve transmission rates as high as 24 Mbps.

- When two Bluetooth devices come within range of each other, they automatically connect with one another. One device is the master and the other device is a slave. A Bluetooth network that contains one master and at least one slave using the same channel forms a piconet. A Bluetooth device can be a member of two or more piconets in the same area. A group of piconets in which connections exist between different piconets is called a scatternet.

- There are three kinds of error-correction schemes used in the Bluetooth protocol: 1/3 rate Forward Error Correction (FEC), 2/3 rate FEC, and the automatic retransmission request (ARQ).

- Devices in a piconet can be in active, hold, sniff, or park modes; device activity is lowered during the power-saving modes.

- ZigBee, created by the Zigbee Alliance, is a specification for low-rate WPANs. It offers a global standard for monitoring and controlling small, low-power, cost-effective, wirelessly networked products.

- ZigBee technology is geared toward devices such as lighting controls, wireless smoke and carbon monoxide detectors, thermostats and other environmental controls, medical sensors, remote controls, and industrial and building automation.

- The ZigBee specification includes full mesh networking to allow networks to encompass large buildings. Full-function devices can route frames across the network to remote devices. Reduced function devices are an endpoint device, such as a light switch or lamp.

- There are three ZigBee network topologies: star, tree, and mesh.

- The IEEE 802.15.4 standard defines three frequency bands: 868 MHz, 915 MHz, and the 2.4 GHz ISM band. The protocol stack has two PHY layers. One supports 868/915 MHz, and the other supports 2.4 GHz. There are 27 channels across the three bands. Modulation is BPSK for 868/915 MHz. For 2.4 GHz, it uses O-QPSK modulation with a fixed set of 16 chipping codes, each representing a 4-bit data pattern (also called a symbol).

- 802.15.4 is designed to coexist easily with other WPAN and WLAN technologies transmitting in the same frequency range. Access to the medium is contention based, but support for guaranteed time slots is also provided through the use of superframes.

- Security in Bluetooth supports only device authentication and limited encryption. Secure key distribution is not provided in the standard. ZigBee supports message integrity at the MAC layer and can also check for the freshness of the message to ensure that the same frame will not be transmitted more than once in a piconet.

Key Terms

1/3 rate Forward Error Correction (FEC)   An error correction scheme that repeats each bit three times for redundancy.

2/3 rate Forward Error Correction (FEC)   An error correction scheme that uses a mathematical formula to add extra error correction bits to the data sent.

6LoWPAN   The protocol that implements IPv6 on WPANs. Also the name of an IETF working group that defines how the Internet protocols—IPv6, in particular—are applied to the smallest devices so that they can participate in the "Internet of Things."

8-DPSK   A simple method of phase shift keying that uses eight degrees of phase to encode tribits. This method of modulation is very sensitive to co-channel and inter-symbol interference.

access control list (ACL)   A list of addresses of other devices from which the device that maintains the list expects to receive frames.

active mode   A state in which the Bluetooth device actively participates on the channel.

adaptive frequency hopping (AFH)   A feature added by Bluetooth version 1.2 that further improves compatibility with 802.11b by allowing the master in a piconet to change the hopping sequence so that it will not use the frequency channel occupied by 802.11b in the piconet area.

alternate MAC/PHY (AMP)   A feature added in version 3 of the Bluetooth specification that makes it possible for Bluetooth radio manufacturers to add a second radio that uses 802.11 to transmit data at speeds of up to 24 Mbps. Compatible Bluetooth devices use FHSS to establish communications with each other and exchange commands and control information, while using the secondary radio for data transfers only.

association   A procedure for a device to join a network.

asynchronous connectionless (ACL) link   A packet-switched link that is used for data transmissions.

authentication   The process of verifying that the device asking to join the piconet should be allowed to join.

automatic retransmission request (ARQ)   An error-correction scheme that continuously retransmits until an acknowledgment is received or a timeout value is exceeded.

beacon   A frame that signals the beginning of a superframe and contains information about the type and number of time slots contained in the superframe.

binding   The process of establishing a relationship between endpoints in a ZigBee network.

Bluetooth radio module   A single radio transmitter/receiver (transceiver) that performs all the necessary transmission functions.

carrier sense multiple access with collision avoidance (CSMA/CA) A device-access mechanism in which, before transmitting, a device must listen to the medium to determine if the channel is free.

certificate authority An organization that supplies security keys and authenticates users.

challenge-response strategy A process used to check if the other device knows a shared identical secret key.

channel The frequency or range of frequencies used by a particular technology to transmit and receive data. In Bluetooth, a channel consists of all the frequencies in a hop sequence.

data link layer The layer responsible for the transfer of data between nodes in the same network segment; it also provides for error detection.

device discovery The process of querying other devices on the network to identify their locations and how many of them there are.

disassociation A procedure used by devices to leave (i.e., disconnect from) a network.

encryption The process of encoding communications to ensure that the transmission, if intercepted, cannot be easily decoded, which discourages many hackers.

enhanced data rate (EDR) A feature of the Bluetooth version 2.0 specification that allows it to support data rates of 2 Mbps and 3 Mbps (by adding two modulations) while remaining fully backward compatible with Bluetooth versions 1.1 and 1.2.

frame A data link layer packet that contains the header and trailer required by the physical medium.

full-function device A device used in 802.15.4 (ZigBee) networks that can connect to other full-function devices and has the capability of routing frames to other devices in a ZigBee network. It can also connect to endpoint or child devices. Full-function devices can maintain a connection to multiple devices and can become coordinators.

guaranteed time slot (GTS) A reserved period for critical devices to transmit priority data.

hold mode A state in which the Bluetooth device can put slave units into a mode in which only the slave's internal timer is running.

inquiry procedure A process that enables a device to discover which devices are in range and determine the addresses and clocks for the devices.

Link Manager The Bluetooth layer responsible for establishing and maintaining connections on the piconet.

Logical Link Control (LLC) One of the two sublayers of the IEEE Project 802 data link layer.

master A device on a Bluetooth piconet that controls all the wireless traffic.

Media Access Control (MAC) One of the two sublayers of the IEEE Project 802 data link layer.

message integrity code (MIC) A code composed of a subset of the data, the length of the data, and the symmetric key; used by the receiving device to verify that the data has not been tampered with during transmission.

modulation index The amount that the frequency varies.

offset quadrature phase shift keying (O-QPSK) A transmission technique in 802.15.4 that uses two carrier waves of the same frequency but with a phase difference of 90 degrees between them. This technique modulates even-numbered chips in the in-phase wave and odd-numbered chips in the other phase (Q-Phase), using quadrature amplitude modulation, before combining the waves for transmission.

paging procedure   A process that enables a device to make an actual connection to a piconet.

pairing   A two-step process for establishing a connection between a Bluetooth master and slave devices.

PAN coordinator   The 802.15.4 device that controls access to the piconet and optionally the timing as well.

park mode   A state in which the Bluetooth device is still synchronized to the piconet but does not participate in the traffic.

physical layer (PHY)   The layer that is responsible for converting the data bits into an electromagnetic signal and transmitting it on the medium.

piconet   A Bluetooth network that contains one master and at least one slave that use the same channel.

pi/4-DQPSK   A method of modulation that uses two different frequencies exactly 90 degrees apart and that therefore do not interfere with each other.

public key infrastructure (PKI)   A unique security code that can verify the authenticity of a user.

reduced-function device (RFD)   In ZigBee networks, a device (such as a light switch or lamp) that can only connect to one full-function device at a time and can only join the network as a child device.

scatternet   A group of piconets in which connections exist between different piconets.

sequential freshness   A security service available in 802.15.4 and used by the receiving device; it ensures that the same frames will not be transmitted more than once.

service discovery   The process of sending a query to other devices on the network to identify their capabilities.

slaves   Devices on a Bluetooth piconet that take commands from the master.

sniff mode   A state in which the Bluetooth device listens to the piconet master at a reduced rate so that it uses less power.

superframe   A mechanism for managing transmissions in a piconet. The superframe is a continually repeating frame containing a beacon, contention access periods, channel time allocation periods, and management time allocation periods. Using the superframe is optional in 802.15.4 WPANs.

symbol   A data unit that can represent one or more bits.

synchronous connection-oriented (SCO) link   A symmetric point-to-point link between a master and a single slave in the piconet; it functions like a circuit-switched link by using reserved slots at regular intervals.

two-level Gaussian frequency shift keying (2-GFSK)   A binary signaling technique that uses two different frequencies to indicate whether a 1 or a 0 is being transmitted.

WirelessHART   A wireless sensor network protocol based on the highway addressable remote transducer protocol (HART), designed for interfacing manufacturing equipment and machines.

wireless personal area network (WPAN)   A group of technologies that are designed for short-range communications, from a few inches to about 33 feet (10 meters).

ZigBee Alliance   An association of manufacturers and interested organizations formed to promote the creation of a global standard for wireless devices used in monitoring and control applications.

Review Questions

1. A Bluetooth channel consists of _____.

   a. a specific frequency channel

   b. an IEEE 802.15.1 channel

   c. a hopping sequence including up to 79 frequencies

   d. a frequency range that the signal spreads across

2. Which of the following is not an example of a Bluetooth communication?

   a. cellular phone to PDA

   b. notebook computer to PDA

   c. hard drive to memory

   d. notebook computer to GPS

3. Which of the following is not a feature of Bluetooth?

   a. power-saving

   b. master and slave changing roles

   c. slave authenticates master

   d. asymmetric transmission

4. What is the name of the organization that develops and promotes Bluetooth products and consists of over 2,500 hardware and software vendors?

   a. Bluetooth SIG

   b. IEEE 802.15.1 Task Group

   c. Bluetooth TIA

   d. Bluetooth Standards Organization

5. The lower levels of the WPAN protocol stack are implemented in the _____.

   a. software

   b. hardware

   c. IR

   d. data link layer

6. At the lowest level of the Bluetooth protocol stack is the _____ layer.

   a. RF

   b. LMP

   c. TCP/IP

   d. IR

7. Which of the following is a feature of WPAN devices?

    a. They can transmit signals at a great distance.

    b. They are small and can operate on batteries.

    c. They transmit signals that do not penetrate walls.

    d. Their users cannot roam.

8. The _____ period is when ZigBee devices have time reserved for priority transmissions.

    a. contention access

    b. guaranteed time slot

    c. beacon

    d. time synchronization

9. Which method of Bluetooth transmission uses two different frequencies to indicate whether the bit is a 1 or a 0?

    a. DSSS

    b. FHSS

    c. GFSK

    d. DPSK

10. The amount that the Bluetooth frequency varies, which is between 280 KHz and 350 KHz, is called the _____.

    a. direct sequence

    b. modulation index

    c. hopping sequence

    d. i-phase

11. Bluetooth divides the 2.4 GHz frequency into 79 frequencies that are spaced how far apart?

    a. 5 MHz

    b. 22 MHz

    c. 11 MHz

    d. 1 MHz

12. A ZigBee coordinator cannot allocate guaranteed time slots for devices to transmit data. True or False?

13. Bluetooth has seven power classes for transmitting. True or False?

14. Objects (such as walls) and interference from other sources do not affect the range of Bluetooth transmissions. True or False?

15. Bluetooth devices are usually small and mobile, so conserving power is necessary. True or False?

16. What is the maximum data-transmission rate for ZigBee?

    a. 2 Mbps

    b. 723.5 Kbps

    c. 250 Kbps

    d. 40 Kbps

17. Which frequency band(s) can ZigBee networks utilize?

    a. ISM

    b. U-NII

    c. 3.1 GHz

    d. 60 GHz

    e. All of the above

18. Which of the following topologies are supported by ZigBee?

    a. scatternet and SCO

    b. tree, star, and mesh

    c. inverted tree and ACL

    d. piconet and master/slave

19. Which of the following topologies are supported by Bluetooth?

    a. scatternet and piconet

    b. ACL and SCO

    c. WMAN and WLAN

    d. star and cluster tree

20. What type of security is provided for in the ZigBee specification?

    a. encryption

    b. MIC

    c. short-range communications

    d. ACLs

    e. All of the above

Hands-On Project

Project 5-1

Different Bluetooth interfaces may have different software and procedures. For this project, you will need two computers equipped with Bluetooth interface adapters. The project instructions and illustrations below are based on a Dell laptop with Windows 7 that uses a built-in Dell 365 Bluetooth module. If you are not using a Dell laptop or are using an external Bluetooth adapter, you may need to adjust the specific steps to fit your hardware.

 If you are using Windows XP and installing an external USB Bluetooth adapter, you may need to uninstall the Microsoft drivers and reinstall the vendor software. Go to *http://support.microsoft.com/kb/889814/en-us* and follow the instructions.

1. First, you need to make at least one of the computers discoverable. In Windows 7, if you don't see the Bluetooth icon in the system tray, click the up arrow at the bottom right-hand corner of the screen to show the hidden icons. Now, click the Bluetooth icon, then click **Open Settings**. You will see the arrows shown in Figure 5-18.

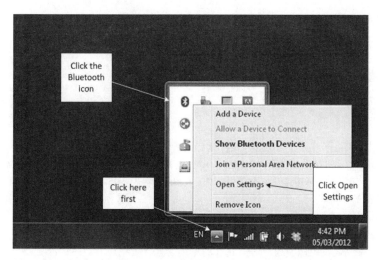

Figure 5-18 Opening Bluetooth settings from the Windows system tray

Source: Microsoft Windows 7

2. In the Bluetooth Settings dialog box, click the **Options** tab and ensure that all the options in this dialog box are checked by clicking the boxes next to them. Your configuration dialog should look like what is shown in Figure 5-19. Click **OK** to set the configuration and close the page.

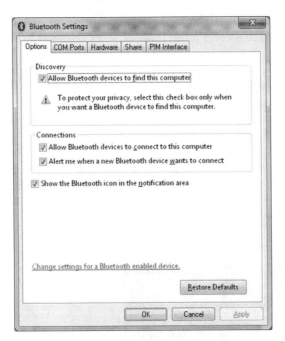

Figure 5-19 Configuring Bluetooth settings

Source: Microsoft Windows 7

3. Next, you need to pair the two computers. Once you have made the first one discoverable, click the up arrow in the system tray of the second computer and then click **Add a device**. Windows will now search for devices and display the ones that it discovers (see Figure 5-20).

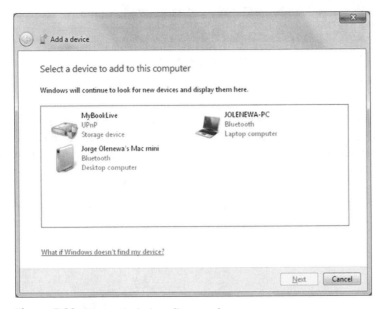

Figure 5-20 Bluetooth devices discovered

Source: Microsoft Windows 7

4. Once an icon for the other computer appears in the Window, click it once to select it, then click **Next**. Remember that the two Bluetooth devices must be placed within a maximum of 33 feet (10 meters) of each other. Windows will now display a dialog page containing an automatically generated number. On the other computer, an information bubble will appear at the bottom right-hand side of the screen. Click the bubble to open a dialog box (see Figure 5-21) that asks you to verify that the pairing code is the same. Click **Next** to accept it. After Windows installs the necessary drivers, it will display a message indicating that the pairing was successful. If not, you may need to turn the Bluetooth device off and on again before attempting to pair.

Figure 5-21 Bluetooth pairing

Source: Microsoft Windows 7

5. Open the Windows system tray on the second computer and click the Bluetooth icon. In the context menu, click **Show Bluetooth Devices**. You should see the other computer identified by name. Double-click it to open the dialog box shown in Figure 5-22.

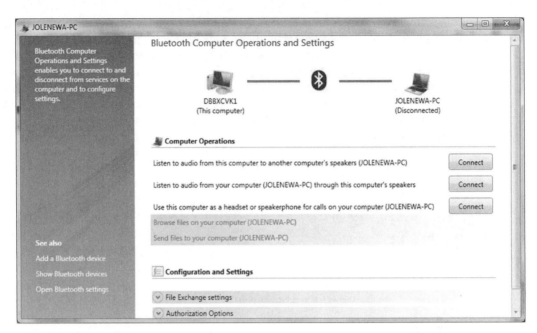

Figure 5-22 Bluetooth Operations

Source: Microsoft Windows 7

6. Click **Send files to your computer** <*Name of the other Computer*>. Windows will open a dialog page that allows you to select the files to send. Click the **Browse Files** button on this page and select a sample picture from the Windows Pictures folder. Click **Open** and then click **Next**.

7. Windows will open a dialog page that asks you to **Select the destination folder** and shows the other computer's name. Click **Send**. On the other computer, Windows will display a bubble confirming that the connection was successful and another bubble requesting authorization for the sending computer to copy a file over Bluetooth. Click the bubble to open the Bluetooth Image Push Service Access Authorization dialog page, and then ensure that **Allow access for the current request only** is checked. Then click **OK**.

8. Windows will now transfer the image using the image push profile mentioned in Step 7. Once the file has been transferred, the receiving computer will display another bubble for File Transfer notification. Click the bubble to open the containing folder and verify that the file was transferred correctly.

9. Experiment with Bluetooth by transferring other images and other types of files. Bluetooth networking is somewhat complex and also sometimes clumsy. Devices must be able to support the right Bluetooth profiles; otherwise, you may not be able to transfer some types of files.

10. To verify which profiles are supported by your Bluetooth hardware and drivers, go to the **Show Bluetooth devices** page again, right-click the icon for the other computer or device with which you are trying to communicate, and click **Properties**. Click **Services** and check the list of Bluetooth services offered by the other device. If some of the options are not checked and you had problems transferring a file, click all the services offered, click **OK**, and then attempt your file transfer again.

If you have an older laptop equipped with an infrared port (IrDA), you may wish to attempt a file transfer using this technology and compare the steps required with performing the same action on Bluetooth. In spite of its distance limitations and the requirement to have the computers' IrDA ports pointed at each other, the technology is much simpler to use and allows all types of data transfer between computers, usually at 4 Mbps.

Real-World Exercises

The Baypoint Group (TBG) has once again requested your services as a consultant. One of its clients, DeLuxe Builders, is interested in making sure that all their future construction projects include wireless control systems for lighting, heating and cooling, and energy management that are based on standards. DeLuxe Builders is aware that ZigBee is a global standard and would like TBG to advise them on how to proceed.

TBG will be in charge of evaluating the right type of technology and making recommendations to DeLuxe.

Exercise 5-1

Create a PowerPoint slide presentation that outlines how ZigBee technology works. Be sure to include information about the standards used, the advantages and disadvantages, and why ZigBee would be the best solution for DeLuxe.

Exercise 5-2

Your presentation convinced DeLuxe's management that using ZigBee would be a good solution. However, DeLuxe's management is concerned about the reliability of the system because it transmits using 2.4 GHz and this frequency band is also used by Wi-Fi and cordless phones. TBG has asked you to be involved in a demonstration to the client of both these technologies. Prepare a three-page paper discussing how ZigBee can coexist with other systems using the same frequency band and how ZigBee devices can also make use of other frequency bands.

Challenge Case Project

Microsoft has included Bluetooth support in Windows XP Service Pack 2 as well and in Windows 7. Most devices today are directly supported using Microsoft drivers.

Manufacturers of Bluetooth devices usually list the capabilities of their hardware but seldom tell you exactly which profiles are supported. If you have many Bluetooth devices or need specific information about your devices and you cannot locate this information on the Internet, sometimes it is useful to be able to obtain this type of information from your devices.

Several sites on the Internet allow you to download a free unsupported utility, originally created by AirMagnet, a company owned by Fluke Networks, which creates and sells a variety of software designed to help you design, deploy, and troubleshoot Wi-Fi LANs. This utility, called BlueSweep, helps you identify nearby Bluetooth devices and the services they offer or profiles that they support.

Download and install BlueSweep on a computer equipped with a Bluetooth adapter using the Microsoft drivers. Most Bluetooth devices that are compatible with this driver will work. Now turn your Bluetooth devices on and let BlueSweep run for a few minutes to identify all the nearby devices and the Bluetooth services they are providing. You should be able to identify cellular phones, PDAs, headsets, and so forth. (Note that the Apple iPhone does not report its capabilities.) Save the file and produce a report listing the devices and Bluetooth services you were able to identify.

BlueSweep may prove useful in a field technical support situation. Be sure to consult the documentation, which is provided with BlueSweep. Write a one-page report outlining how you could use BlueSweep to assist you in the field in solving a connectivity or service availability problem for a customer.

chapter 6

High-Rate Wireless Personal Area Networks

After reading this chapter and completing the exercises, you will be able to:

- Define a high-rate wireless personal area network (HR WPAN)
- List the different HR WPAN standards and their applications
- Explain how WHDI, WiGig, WirelessHD, and UWB work
- Outline the issues facing WPAN technologies
- Describe the security features of each HR WPAN technology

In Chapter 5, you learned about two low-rate wireless personal area network (WPAN) technologies—Bluetooth and ZigBee—that meet the market need for relatively low-speed communications. In this chapter, you learn about standards and technologies (some of which are still under development) that make it possible for businesses and home users to deploy entertainment systems that deliver wireless video, voice, and music throughout an office or home. These high-rate (meaning high data rate or HR) networks are capable of transferring data between computers and peripherals at speeds ranging from 1 to 28 Gbps, which makes them ideal to handle multiple instances of audio, video, and data. This means that, over an HR WPAN, two people can be watching different movies while another listens to high-quality music and yet another accesses the Internet.

The success of these HR wireless technologies depends on which and how many manufacturers adopt them. Currently, consumer electronic equipment (digital and high-definition television, game consoles, and surround sound systems) is leading the way. The first HR wireless devices became available in 2010, but the competition among the various specifications, the development of 802.11n, and the upcoming Gigabit wireless standards from the IEEE, coupled with delays by licensing authorities in some countries releasing parts of the RF spectrum required to support these technologies, have affected the speed of development.

High-Rate WPAN Standards

The IEEE had discontinued work on the original 802.15.3 standard for HR WPANs due to lack of agreement on which modulation and coding system to use. In 2005, it ratified 802.15.3b; in 2009, it released the 802.15.3c amendment as well as the 802.15.5 standard for mesh networking.

The IEEE Project 802.15 covers all the different Working Groups for Wireless Personal Area Networks (WPANs), including the 802.15.1 Bluetooth and 802.15.4 PHY and MAC layers.

IEEE 802.15.3c enables multimedia connectivity between mobile and fixed consumer devices within the home. More than 200 wireless devices compatible with this standard can be linked using low-cost and low-power radio modules. One organization, the WirelessHD Consortium, created a specification based on IEEE 802.15.3c for a wireless digital interface that can combine the transmission of HD video, multichannel audio, and data for the purpose of multimedia streaming in the 60 GHz frequency band. The consortium's specification also supports intelligent formatting of the multimedia streams as well as content protection that is approved by the media producers. Two other specifications have been introduced for HR WPANs that do not use 802.15.3c:

- WirelessHD from the WHDI (Wireless Home Digital Interface) Consortium. This consortium was founded by AMIMON (an integrated circuit design company), Hitachi, Motorola, Samsung, Sharp, Sony, and LG.

- The WiGig specification (developed by the Wireless Gigabit Alliance), which is designed to work with the 802.11ac (Gigabit WLANs) standard and can use the

2.4 and 5 GHz frequency bands as well as 802.11ad (multi-gigabit WLANs) in the 60 GHz frequency band.

You have already learned about Bluetooth and ZigBee WPANs. Why is there yet another WPAN technology? The answer is simple: Although 802.11 and Bluetooth include MAC and PHY layer optimizations for transmitting multimedia signals, no previous wireless standard has been developed exclusively for multimedia to allow the delivery of uncompressed video and audio data, resulting in a better experience for the users. Most of today's technologies support the transmission of this type of digitized and compressed data, which means that the receiving device must be able to expand the data before displaying it on a screen or playing the audio through the speakers in a stereo system. MP3 (Moving Picture Experts Group Audio Layer III), which was made popular by the introduction of music players like the iPod, is a good example of a device that decodes and expands (decompresses) the digital audio files and attempts to reproduce the sound. It is important to consider that whenever video and audio is compressed in any way, the process introduces losses that reduce the quality of the movie or sound. This is the main reason why the three just-mentioned organizations created specifications for wireless transmission of uncompressed data, which requires a lot more band-width than any other types of digital data and helps reduce (or completely eliminates) the need for cables while maintaining exceptional multimedia reproduction quality.

Potential HR WPAN applications include:

- Connecting digital cameras to printers and kiosks
- Connecting laptop computers to multimedia projectors and sound systems
- Connecting camera-equipped cellular phones and PDAs to laptops and printers
- Connecting speakers in a surround sound system to amplifiers and FM receivers
- Linking multiple display monitors (including tablets, computers, and TVs) for simultaneous video distribution
- Distributing video signals from a cable, satellite, or IP over phone line receivers to television sets throughout the house
- Sending high-quality sound to wireless headphones or speakers from CD or MP3 players
- Photographing yourself with mobile remote viewfinders for video or digital still cameras

These applications, whether for consumer electronics or for professional use, all share a set of common requirements:

- High throughput, typically a minimum of 20 Mbps, to support video and multichannel, high-quality audio
- Low-power transceivers so they can be used in handheld, mobile, battery-powered devices
- Low cost to allow manufacturers to implement wireless communications features without a significant increase in the end-user price of the devices
- **Quality-of-service (QoS)** capabilities, which allow devices to request more channel access time in order to prioritize high-volume, time-sensitive traffic, such as voice streams

- Simple and automatic connections, eliminating the need for technical knowledge to set up the systems
- Ability to connect to multiple other devices without the need for additional installation or configuration—in other words, able to inform other devices about their capabilities and performance and therefore connect automatically for the specified purposes
- Security features included to prevent intrusion
- Data access, which enables devices to be connected to the Internet and, for example, allows the use of digital televisions as wireless computer displays

Networking Audio, Video, and Other I/O Devices

Each of the three organizations working on protocols for audio and video distribution has defined different network and RF architectures. Manufacturers of both consumer electronic devices and computers currently support most (if not all) of these three standards, and some have already introduced products that incorporate these specifications.

You can find additional information about these three organizations, the manufacturers that support them, and the available products by visiting their Web sites (*www.wirelesshd.org*, *www.wigig.org*, or *www.whdi.org*) and clicking the News or Products links.

Wireless Home Digital Interface (WHDI) The WHDI Consortium developed the WHDI specification primarily for the delivery of uncompressed video and audio with the same high resolution obtainable with a cable connection. The specification is designed to simply and effectively mirror the screens of multiple devices to the TV screen without the use of cables. This mirroring of screens means that video can be displayed on the small screen of a mobile device, for example, while simultaneously displaying on an HD television screen at full resolution. This is in addition to being able to display a video stream from a Blu-ray player on both a mobile device as well as on the HD television set, all without using a single piece of wire to interconnect the devices. Audio is, of course, an important part of this equation. WHDI works in the 5 GHz frequency band and is designed to coexist with 802.11a and 802.11n, as well as 5.8 GHz cordless phones, without causing interference. The 5 GHz frequency band also allows WHDI to have a maximum range of approximately 100 ft. (30 meters) and to penetrate walls.

What this means is that WHDI can deliver media to a TV screen from a Blu-ray disk player directly, or video stored and delivered from a computer or similar data device that usually requires the use of compression decoding software (CODEC). Using Internet streaming services like Netflix, Hulu, or YouTube, for example, typically requires specialized software (YouTube requires Adobe Flash Player) that can decompress the video stream files.

Although some current television sets are equipped with Wi-Fi interfaces and can already display multiple types of media, they often demand regular software updates, because of the wide variety of video-encoding methods, which can add another level of complexity for end-users. One alternative is to use specialized hardware devices (such as Western Digital WDTV Live) that can decode many different types of video streams; however, this means that additional devices and cables need to be connected to each television set, and software updates are also still required.

WHDI aims to eliminate these complexities by using the TV set as a display-only device, freeing the user to display any content he wishes on his TV set. In this case, the computer, tablet, mobile phone, or any other device capable of playing video decodes the files, which also reduces or completely eliminates the need for multiple cable connections. The responsibility for handling different video or audio compression methods remains with the device that is playing the files, minimizing complexity and compatibility issues with the TV set or stereo system.

WHDI interfaces do not require specialized software drivers installed on the data devices. External adapters can be plugged into virtually any data device with an HDMI interface or a USB-to-HDMI adapter. If the manufacturers of data devices incorporate WHDI interfaces directly into their products, these devices will be able to interface directly with compatible TV sets, and older sets can be upgraded with an external WHDI receiver to support multiple input devices.

WHDI makes use of dedicated integrated circuits and proprietary technology designed by AMIMON and supports the latest versions of the HDMI specification, including copy-protection schemes. The proprietary nature of these interfaces and their communication protocol means that typically very little wireless troubleshooting can or needs to be done. Detailed information about this is typically only available to members of the WHDI Consortium, such as TV and interface manufacturers. The fact that WHDI is not an open standard may result in limited options for users, but the concept appears to be both valid and sound.

External HDMI interfaces are available and can be connected to virtually any data device equipped with a USB 2.0 interface. HDMI adapters are also available for Apple iPhone, Samsung Galaxy, and other brands of smartphones, which makes it easy to interface these with a WHDI-equipped TV set.

A discussion of HDMI is beyond the scope of this book. For more information, visit the HDMI Forum at *www.hdmi.org*.

Wireless Gigabit (WiGig) Architecture

The WiGig specification is unique in the sense that it is designed to be compatible with the IEEE 802.11n standard as well as the 802.11ac standard. It will also support 802.11ad in the 60 GHz band, in which there is far more spectrum available than in the other two bands, although the amount of available spectrum varies depending on the country. The specification calls for WiGig to be able to switch seamlessly between the different frequency bands used by each of the IEEE standards as well.

WiGig also defines **protocol adaptation layers (PALs)** that enable it to directly support audiovisual (A/V) display standards such as HDMI and I/O (USB and PCIe) at the PHY and MAC layers, bypassing higher-layer WLAN protocols such as TCP and IP. Figure 6-1 shows a simplified diagram of the WiGig protocol stack.

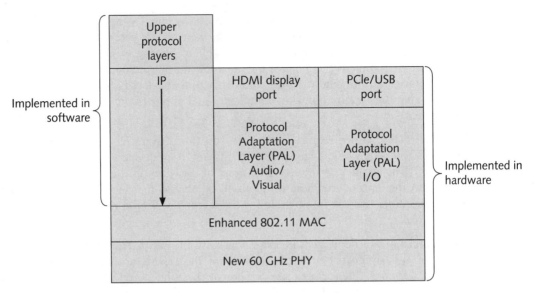

Figure 6-1 WiGig protocol stack

© Cengage Learning 2014

The WiGig Alliance recently announced that the IEEE intends to include the MAC and PHY enhancement layers in the 802.11ad standard. This will allow these layers to be implemented in hardware, enabling peer-to-peer connections between data and display devices when using WiGig for A/V, thereby reducing complexity for end-users. Keep in mind that the 60 GHz band is only suitable for short-range connections—up to a maximum of 33 ft. (10 meters)—due to the signal attenuation at the high frequencies, where even oxygen molecules in the air can significantly decrease RF signal strength.

To maintain reliable connections at the higher frequencies, WiGig makes extensive use of **beamforming**, a technique that enables the transmitting device to use multiple radios and multiple antennas to maximize the signal amplitude at the receiver location. Beamforming is discussed in more detail later in this chapter.

In addition to supporting the existing Wi-Fi modulation schemes in the lower frequency bands, WiGig supports two types of modulation and coding schemes that offer high-transmission speeds in the 60 GHZ frequency band:

- Single-carrier modulation, which is similar to 802.11b. It uses less power, so it is more suitable for mobile devices; it can also achieve speeds of up to 4.6 Gbps.

- Orthogonal frequency-division multiplexing (OFDM), which supports longer distances due to its ability to handle signal reflections and use obstacles such as walls as signal reflectors to help keep devices connected. Using OFDM, WiGig can achieve transmission speeds of up to 7 Gbps.

WiGig also specifies support for advanced security that can be implemented directly in hardware using a highly efficient protocol. This is particularly important in business networks where WiGig can use standard enterprise security mechanisms and still maintain strong security at very high speeds in peer-to-peer A/V connections. A new scheduled access mode allows devices to save power by using it based on the amount of traffic they handle.

WirelessHD and IEEE 802.15.3c As mentioned before, the WirelessHD Consortium is currently the only organization that has adopted the 802.15.3c amendment to the IEEE standard for multimedia distribution. This is also the only standard for which reasonably full documentation is publicly available at the moment, both from the IEEE as well as from the consortium. Access to the other two specifications previously discussed is restricted to individual members of the consortium and member companies. As with WHDI, consumer products that incorporate WirelessHD technology are already available from leading manufacturers. It is best to check the WHDI Web site for additional information regarding these products, because availability can change frequently as manufacturers decide to incorporate WHDI. Visit *www.wirelesshd.org* and click on the Consumers/Product Listing link.

Keep in mind that the 803.15.3c amendment refers only to implementation in the 60 GHz band, and even though the original 802.15.3 standard includes support for the ISM band, WirelessHD does not support transmission in the lower frequency bands. However, it does support devices transmitting at many different speeds in order to allow battery-powered devices—such as mobile phones and tablets—to conserve power.

Table 6-1 shows the range of transmission speeds and typical applications supported by WirelessHD. Note that Table 6-1 shows only a small subsection of the supported combinations of data rates.

Source	Sink	Data Rate(s)	Number of Streams Transmitted
HD A/V	HD A/V	3.0 Gbps	1
HD A/V	HD Video Audio	3.0 Gbps 40 Mbps	2
HD A/V Compressed A/V	HD A/V Compressed A/V	3.0 Gbps 24 Mbps	2
HD A/V HD A/V	HD A/V HD A/V	1.5 Gbps 1.5 Gbps	2
HD A/V Compressed A/V	HD Video Compressed A/V Audio	1.5 Gbps 24 Mbps 40 Mbps	3
Audio	Audio	30 Mbps	1
HD A/V	HD A/V HD A/V	1.5 Gbps 1.5 Gbps	2
Data Source	Data Sink	1.0 Gbps	1
HD A/V HD A/V	HD A/V HD A/V Audio	0.5 Gbps 0.5 Gbps 40 Mbps	3
HD A/V HD A/V	HD A/V Audio Audio	1.5 Gbps 40 Mbps 40 Mbps	3
HD A/V Audio	HD A/V Audio	3.0 Gbps 40 Mbps	2

Table 6-1 Speeds supported in WirelessHD

© Cengage Learning 2014

A source device is the one that transmits the A/V or data, whereas a sink device is the receiver. The receiver may not necessarily be a display or audio device; it may be a recording device instead. The table shows cases in which either the video or audio stream is compressed before transmission, as well as cases where the video stream is compressed but not the audio stream. In addition, consider that some video streams contain embedded audio, whereas others do not.

WirelessHD supports the following video resolutions and transmission speeds:

- Uncompressed video at 2560 × 1440 resolution and a transmission speed of 8.0 Gbps
- Uncompressed 3-D video at 720p (1280 × 1440) at 4.0 Gbps
- Uncompressed 1080p video at 1080p (1920 × 1080) at 7.5 Gbps
- File transfers at speeds greater than 1.0 Gbps
- Several other combinations of compressed and uncompressed audio and video transmissions

The WirelessHD specification divides the PHY layer into three sections:

- Low-Rate PHY (LRP)—supports data rates of 2.5 to 40 Mbps
- High-Rate PHY (HRP)—supports data rates of up to 7 Gbps and over 25 Gbps when using **spatial multiplexing,** which is a technique that divides the data frame into multiple parts and transmits each part of the same data frame using a separate radio and antenna, effectively increasing the transmission rate by sending the data in parallel.
- High-or-Medium-Rate PHY (HMRP)—supports data rates of 476 Mbps to 2 Gbps

WirelessHD simultaneously supports USB version 2.0 or 3.0 links with multiple devices connected to a hub, as well as HDMI, enabling wireless connection of a large variety of existing computer and other mobile devices and peripherals.

Mobile devices like smartphones and tablets can process, decode, and display some compressed video and audio streams but do not currently support HRP, primarily because they need to conserve battery power. This is why WirelessHD-compatible devices need to be capable of supporting multiple data rates for different devices simultaneously. In addition, WirelessHD is able to support devices that have multiple radios and antennas and can make use of beamforming to provide both line-of-sight and non-line-of-sight transmissions.

 Coverage of video resolution is beyond the scope of this book. The information provided here is intended to show the capabilities of WirelessHD and 802.15.3c in the 60 GHz frequency band. More details are available in the WirelessHD overview document available from the WirelessHD Consortium Web site at *www.wirelessHD.org*.

Beamforming uses multiple radios and antennas to steer a signal in the direction of the receiver. If an object blocks the direct signal between the transmitter and receiver so that they can no longer communicate, the transmitter can steer the beam in a different direction so that the signal reflects and still reaches the receiver with enough strength to be decoded correctly. Beamforming takes advantage of multipath reflections—instead of allowing multipath to degrade the quality of the signal—to create what is called constructive interference. By varying the phase and amplitude of the same signal sent via multiple radios, the transmitter is able to create an effective amplitude increase at the location of the intended receiver. The concept is similar to how a phased-array antenna directs the signal, but in this case it requires the transmitter to track the location of the intended receiver. Figure 6-2 shows a simplified example of beamforming. Figure 6-3 shows the recommended protocol-layer implementation for WirelessHD, which will be discussed in the following sections.

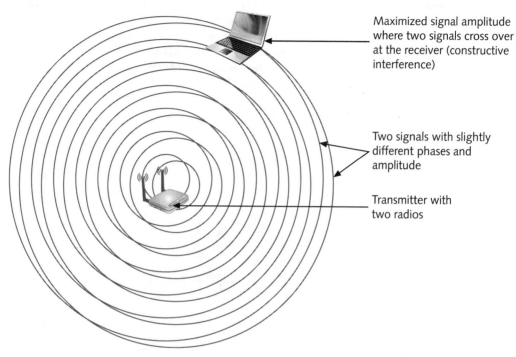

Figure 6-2 Beamforming

© *Cengage Learning 2014*

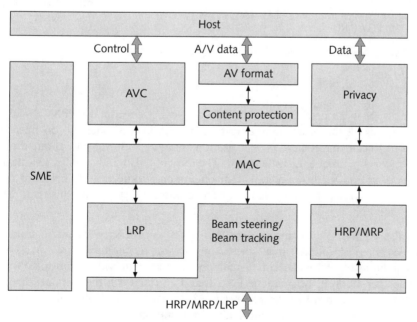

Figure 6-3 Recommended WirelessHD protocol-layer implementation

© *Cengage Learning 2014*

WirelessHD and 802.15.3 MAC layer Devices connect to a WirelessHD network by first associating with the piconet coordinator. PNCs are usually an audio or video sink device—such as an HD television—but can also be a personal video recorder. The coordinator also acts as a station on what the specification calls the **wireless video area network (WVAN)**. Mobile devices are not able to become coordinators in a WPAN, let alone a WVAN, because they may move out of the area and also because, being powered by batteries, they may be turned off or go into power-save mode frequently. The piconet coordinator should be a device that is plugged into an electric outlet. Figure 6-4 shows an example of a WVAN topology.

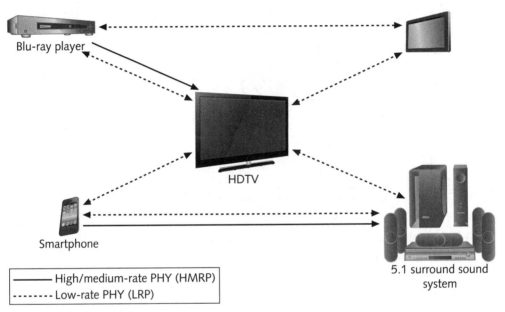

Blu-ray player

HDTV

Smartphone

5.1 surround sound system

————— High/medium-rate PHY (HMRP)
- - - - - - - Low-rate PHY (LRP)

Figure 6-4 Wireless video area network (WVAN) topology example

© *Cengage Learning 2014*

The first sink device in an area assumes the role of **piconet coordinator (PNC)**, which is the device that provides all the basic communications timing in a piconet. To do this, the PNC sends a beacon. Recall that a beacon is a frame containing information about the piconet, such as the piconet's unique identification. The beacon also indicates when devices are allowed to transmit and for how long. The piconet is peer-to-peer, and devices can transmit data directly to each other, but they can only do so based on the timing instructions sent in the beacon by the PNC.

The PNC is also responsible for managing QoS, which is necessary for audio transmissions because breaks or interruptions in a voice conversation or in music are unacceptable to users. A small number of breaks can usually be tolerated in video transmissions (a few dropped frames per second). Because the PNC may be turned off, the standard provides for the PNC to hand over control of the piconet to another device, which will become the new PNC. Remember that the PNC is almost always a stationary device, such as a TV or a Blu-ray player. Figure 6-5 shows an 802.15.3 topology with the PNC sending the beacons.

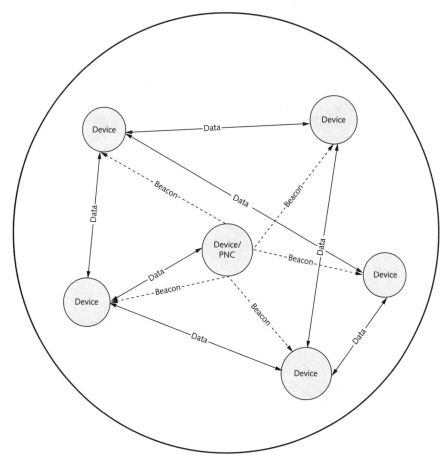

Figure 6-5 802.15.3 piconet topology

© Cengage Learning 2014

There are two other kinds of piconets that can be formed in the 802.15.3c standard. These are called dependent piconets because they are dependent on the PNC of the original or parent piconet:

- A **child piconet** is a piconet that is separate from the original piconet. A child piconet has its own piconet ID, but the child PNC is a member of the original or parent piconet. The child piconet's PNC can exchange data with any member of the parent or child piconet.

- A **neighbor piconet** is a separate piconet that has its own PNC but depends on the original piconet's PNC to allocate a private block of time when its devices are allowed to transmit. This is done in order to share the frequency spectrum between one or more piconets when there are no other available channels for communication.

Both child and neighbor piconets are useful for extending the coverage of a piconet or for shifting some processing or storage requirements to another device. A piconet can have one or more child piconets. A device in the parent piconet can reach a device in the child piconet by using the child PNC to retransmit the frames directed at the device in the child piconet. A child piconet can also share the same frequency channel as the parent PNC but use a different security key. This situation may happen when a friend comes to visit you and brings along her own gaming or music devices that both of you want to use but you want to keep your own piconet's security key private. This may also happen when you purchase and install a new music system that comes preconfigured as a network consisting of the speakers and the player; these new devices may use their own preconfigured security key.

Neighbor piconets exist mainly to allow coexistence with other piconets in the same area. The parent piconet will only allow the formation of a neighbor piconet if there is sufficient free channel time available. If a set of devices cannot use the security features of the parent piconet, these devices can still function in the same area and share the same frequency channel without causing collisions, by becoming a neighbor piconet. Figure 6-6 illustrates the concept of a child piconet, and Figure 6-7 shows a neighbor piconet.

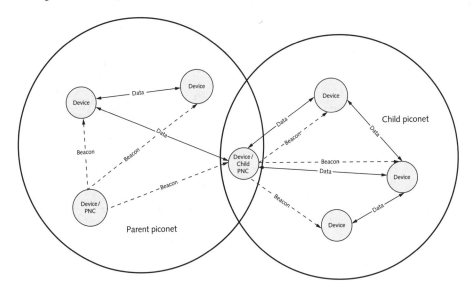

Figure 6-6 Child piconet

© Cengage Learning 2014

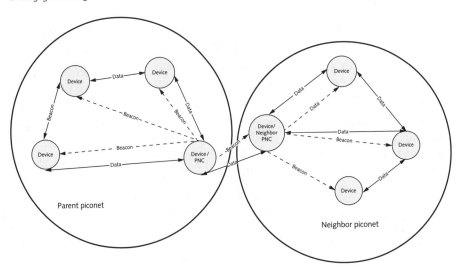

Figure 6-7 Neighbor piconet

© Cengage Learning 2014

Additional 802.15.3 MAC Layer Functionality

The IEEE 802.15.3 MAC layer is designed to support the following HR WPAN features:

- Connection time (association) is fast, with no complicated setup.

- Devices associated with the piconet can use a short, one-octet device ID to ensure fast connection and access times.

- Devices can obtain information about the capabilities of other devices either during the association process, through broadcasts made by the PNC, or by querying the PNC about another device. Devices can also advertise their own capabilities to the PNC. The simplicity of this process is what guarantees fast connection times.

- Peer-to-peer (ad hoc) networking allows all devices to communicate directly with each other.

- Data transport with QoS enables the implementation of voice, music, and video.

- Security (covered in the last section of this chapter) is included to ensure privacy.

- Efficient data transfer allows multiple devices to communicate on the same network.

In 802.15.3 networks, efficient data transfer is accomplished using **superframes**, which function differently than those used in ZigBee networks, as shown in Figure 6-8.

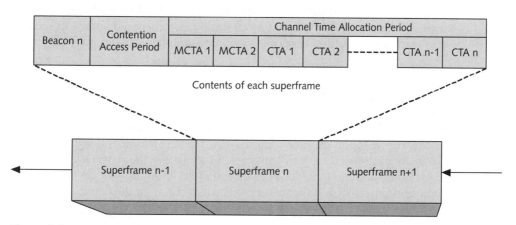

Figure 6-8 802.15.3 superframe

© *Cengage Learning 2014*

Each 802.15.3 superframe is composed of three parts:

- A beacon, which is used to set time allocations for the devices in the piconet and to communicate management information for the piconet.

- An optional **contention access period (CAP)**, which is used for association, for command communication, or for any asynchronous data that may be present in the superframe.

- The **channel time allocation period (CTAP)**. The CTAP includes **channel time allocations (CTAs)**, which are time slots that the PNC allocates to individual devices and which can be used to send commands or data. The CTAP may also include management channel time allocation (MCTA) periods, used for communications between the PNC and devices that don't have CTAs allocated in the current superframe.

Communication in an 802.15.3 piconet is generally accomplished as follows:

- The beacon frame sent by the PNC includes a variable indicating the end of the CAP. No device—not even the PNC—is allowed to transmit data that can extend past the end of the CAP, into the CTAP. This procedure ensures that all devices have an opportunity to communicate, and it prevents collisions.

- Devices send asynchronous data during the CAP, if it exists in the current superframe. The CAP is not allocated, so devices contend for the time using CSMA/CA (refer to Chapter 5). In addition, during the CAP, each device is only allowed to transmit one frame.

- Devices request channel time on a regular basis (such as every superframe or every two or four superframes) in the CTAP from the PNC. The amount of channel time a device requests depends on the type of data the device wants to transmit. The requested channel time is called **isochronous** time, which means a time-dependent or synchronous transmission that must be made every frame or every so many frames to maintain the quality of the connection. Voice and music demand more channel time than video. Video demands more channel time than data files.

- Devices also request channel time for asynchronous communications in the CTAP from the PNC. Asynchronous communications are used to send large data files. Unlike with voice streams, delays or interruptions do not affect the quality of data file transmissions; therefore, large blocks of data are sent asynchronously.

- During the CTAP, communications use a time division multiple access (TDMA) scheme, in which each device gets a window of time to transmit data or commands. Time in a piconet is allocated in units of 1 microsecond. The minimum superframe duration is 1000 microseconds or 1 millisecond, and the maximum duration is 65,535 microseconds or 65.5 milliseconds. The PNC may allocate CTAs of any size to a device, provided the maximum duration of the superframe is not exceeded. Recall that CAPs are optional, so a device may get an allocation that is very large, allowing for the transmission of large blocks of information. In addition, a device may request a change in time allocation from the PNC at any time, or give up its time allocation when it no longer needs to transmit.

Child and neighbor piconets operate in the same frequency channel and must follow the same timing parameters established by the PNC. The WirelessHD specification extends the capabilities of 802.15.3 by allowing the formation of a drone WVAN (**D-WVAN**). A D-WVAN is temporarily established in a different frequency channel, and its purpose is to accommodate more connections that are possible in a WVAN when there are no more CTAPs available in the parent or home WVAN (**H-WVAN**). The D-WVAN functions as an autonomous WVAN, except that the D-WVAN coordinator must maintain a connection to the H-WVAN PNC. D-WVANs use a different connection ID between devices that indicates the piconet is not the H-WVAN. The process of establishing a D-WVAN is as follows:

- An originator device sends a request to a target to form a D-WVAN.

- If the request is accepted, the target device must send a request to the H-WVAN coordinator.

- If the request is granted, the D-WVAN PNC notifies the H-WVAN PCN that it will enter into a power-save mode (discussed in the next section) and then begins searching for an available frequency channel.

- If an available channel is found, the target device sends a request to enter into drone mode to the H-WVAN PNC.

- Once the request is granted, the D-WVAN PNC switches to the new frequency channel and begins sending beacons as the D-WVAN coordinator.

- When the originator device detects that the target has switched to drone mode—when the H-WVAN coordinator grants the request—it may switch to the same channel as the D-WVAN PNC and attempt to associate with it.

General 802.15.3 MAC Frame Format This section presents an overview of the MAC frame format. All MAC frames include a set of fields that are present in the same order in every frame. These are shown in Figure 6-9.

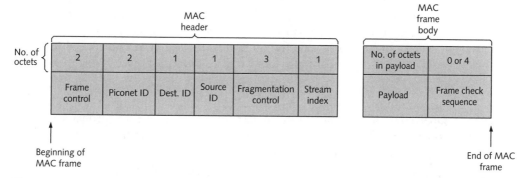

Figure 6-9 General MAC frame format

© Cengage Learning 2014

In any device, the MAC layer must be able to verify that the data was received without error. The frame check sequence (FCS) field that is present in every MAC frame is responsible for this validation. However, before the PHY passes the frame to the MAC, it checks to make sure the MAC header was received without errors by using the header check sequence (HCS) field.

The frame control field contains information about the protocol version, type of frame, whether it is encrypted, how the receiving device should acknowledge it, whether this is a retransmission of a previously sent frame, and whether the data ends with this frame or more data is to follow. The piconet ID (PNID) field contains a unique identifier for each piconet and confirms that the frames were sent by devices belonging to a specific piconet. The destination and source ID fields contain the unique piconet device identifiers for the sender and receiver. The fragmentation control field is used to assist in the fragmentation and reassembly, in the correct sequence, of parts of a large block of data, such as an MP3 file. It contains the number of the current fragment, the number of the last fragment for this data stream, and a frame number. If a frame is lost, the receiving device can request that the transmitting device resend the fragment so that it will be able to reassemble the complete file. The stream index field is used for managing and uniquely identifying different asynchronous and isochronous streams.

The MAC frame payload is a variable length field that carries the actual information to be transferred between two devices or between one device and a group of devices (multicast or broadcast). The frame check sequence (FCS) is a 32-bit **cyclic redundancy check (CRC)** field, a common technique for detecting transmission errors.

The general MAC frame format can vary, but the MAC header is standard for all transmissions. The frame body changes to accommodate the different types of payload and the information required in each one. Unlike Bluetooth and 802.11 WLANs, the MAC is implemented in the hardware of the radio module. This minimizes or eliminates most aspects of configuration of the equipment by consumers.

Power Management

One of the best methods for enabling 802.15.3 devices to user power efficiently is to allow the devices to turn off completely or at least reduce power consumption for long periods of time, but without losing their association with the piconet. Doing so for a period equal to the duration of one or more superframes results in a significant power reduction for WPAN devices. The 802.15.3 standard provides for three different power-saving methods:

- Device synchronized power save (DSPS)—This mode allows devices to sleep for the duration of several superframes but allows them to wake up in the middle of a superframe to transmit or receive data. Other devices in the piconet are informed about which devices in a group (called a DSPS set) are in this mode and when they will awake and be able to receive or transmit data.

- Piconet synchronized power save (PSPS)—This mode allows devices to sleep during intervals defined by the PNC. The PNC selects beacons to serve as system-wide wake beacons and indicates the next one to occur in the beacon fields. All devices in PSPS mode are required to wake up and listen to the wake beacons.

- Asynchronous power save (APS)—This mode allows the devices to sleep for long periods of time until they choose to wake up and listen to a beacon. A device in APS mode must communicate with the PNC before the end of its association time-out period (ATP) in order to maintain its membership in the piconet.

The PNC will always allocate asynchronous CTAs to destination devices that will be in DSPS or PSPS mode in the **wake superframe**. The wake superframe is the superframe designated by the PNC in which devices that are in power-saving mode wake up and listen for frames addressed to them. Of course, a device that does not rely on battery power, such as a DVD player or sound amplifier, can remain in active mode all the time. Regardless of which power-saving mode a device is in, all devices are allowed to power down during the parts of the superframe when they are not scheduled to transmit or receive. Figure 6-10 illustrates the wake beacons.

Two additional methods can help devices save power. In the first method, the PNC can set a maximum transmit power level for associated devices (this feature is not mandatory in the standard, so not all devices may implement it). This method also allows the PNC to save power because the quality of the link between the PNC and other devices defines the coverage area of the

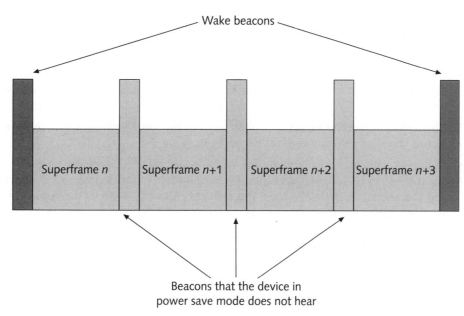

Figure 6-10 Wake beacons

© Cengage Learning 2014

piconet. The second method allows devices to request a reduction or an increase in their own transmit power, as long as the device knows that it can maintain a good link with another device.

802.15.3c PHY Layer

As you know, the PHY layer is responsible for converting data bits into the modulated RF signal that is transmitted over electromagnetic waves. IEEE 802.15.3c is the only standard defined in the WirelessHD specification. It is an extremely complex standard that could justify an entire textbook on its own. This textbook covers only the basics of this standard. If you wish to learn more about 802.15.3c, you can download a copy of the standard from *http://standards.ieee.org/about/get/802/802.15.html*. The 802.15.3c standard uses the 60 GHz band and supports the channel plan, as shown in Table 6-2.

Channel ID	Start Frequency GHz	Center Frequency GHz	Stop Frequency GHz
1	57.240	58.320	59.400
2	59.400	60.480	61.560
3	61.560	62.640	63.720
4	63.720	64.800	65.880

Table 6-2 802.15.3c channel plan

© Cengage Learning 2014

Note that there are only four channels and that each is approximately 2 GHz wide. Not all countries permit the entire 60 GHz band to be utilized, which may reduce the number of channels available in some parts of the world, but the center portion of the band contains sufficient overlap of frequencies to allow at least two or three channels. Channel aggregation—combining multiple adjacent channels—in order to transmit data faster is also covered in the standard; in combination with spatial multiplexing, it is what enables transmission at data rates that exceed 25 Mbps. The PHY layer in 802.15.3c includes a number of enhancements, some of which are optional:

- Passive scanning—Each device scans the channels to detect an existing piconet before joining or starting a new one. The first device to be turned on in an area scans the frequencies to find a channel that is not being used.

- Channel energy detection—This allows stations to detect frequency and signal strength before joining a piconet, without decoding the data.

- Ability to request channel quality information—An 802.15.3 device can probe the channel or request channel quality information from other devices and then make a decision about which modulation and channel coding to use for communicating with another device. If remote devices cannot use the current modulation (because of interference, for example), the controlling device can change the modulation and coding to ensure reliable communications.

- Link quality and received signal strength indication—An 802.15.3c device can request link quality information between itself and other devices. It also monitors the strength of the received signal from other devices, which is important for power management.

- Transmit power control—Upon receiving information about the channel quality and link quality, devices may be able to decrease or increase the transmit power to improve the quality of the link and the received signal.

- Neighbor and child piconet capability—The 802.15.3 standard allows the formation of dependent piconets in the same area; these piconets rely on the device that controls the original piconet to allocate channel time for communications. This feature permits multiple piconets to exist in the same area.

- Two modes of superframe transmission—When using omnidirectional transmission, the superframe is sent only once to all stations. When using beamforming, the superframe is transmitted multiple times in the direction of each station, in a round-robin fashion.

- Maximum data frame length of 8,388,608 octets—This helps maximize throughput.

The 802.15.3 standard defines multiple data rates that are dependent on the modulation and coding scheme employed, the spreading factor (dependent on the length of the chipping code), and the forward error correction (FEC) method. FEC saves time because it avoids retransmission of the data when errors occur. FEC can correct single-bit errors in a group of data bits.

There is always a trade-off between FEC and speed of transmission. The more reliable the FEC technique, the more bits that need to be transmitted and the slower the resulting data rate. Coverage of FEC is an advanced topic that is outside of the scope of this textbook.

Modulation The RF modulation techniques used for each data rate in 802.15.3c are variations of BPSK and QPSK modulation techniques that you learned about in Chapter 2. All devices are required to transmit the headers using LRP. The WirelessHD specification requires that all devices support LRP but not necessarily HRP or MRP. Once the devices associate with the coordinator, they will inform other devices on the WVAN which other data rates and modulations they can support. Devices will also suggest to the transmitter which parameters—such as modulation and data rate—to use for subsequent transmissions, depending on the quality of the signal received.

IEEE 802.15.3c operates in the 57–66 GHz unlicensed band—generally called the 60 GHz band—where there is far more bandwidth available than in all the other unlicensed bands combined. This should enable WirelessHD to coexist with other systems using the same band while minimizing or eliminating the possibility of interference. The 802.15.3c standard covers the use of single carrier for LRP, and it covers the use of OFDM encoding for HRP and MRP.

Table 6-3 provides a summary of all the functional characteristics of a WirelessHD device, as published in WirelessHD specification version 1.1.

Higher Protocol Layers
Video format selection: resolution, color depth, etc.
Clock synchronization
Audio/video control message encoding/decoding
Service discovery
Video and audio encoding and decoding
MAC Sublayer
Cryptographic authentication and key generation
Monitoring of channel characteristics, tracking link quality and informing higher layers
PHY channel selection
Schedule beamforming
Sending and receiving digital data to/from PHY layer
Device discovery
Bandwidth reservation (CTAP) and scheduling
Shutdown and sleep
Connection start and stop
AVC data delivery
Checking for errors in data delivery
PHY Layer
Antenna control
Detecting higher data rate option from received frames
Analog link quality assessment
Passing channel assessment to MAC layer
Verifying header information
FEC, modulation, etc.
Sending and receiving RF data on the wireless medium

Table 6-3 **Functional characteristics of a WirelessHD device**

Mesh Networking (802.15.5)

IEEE 802.15.5 is a standard for **mesh networking**, in which each device connects to all other devices within range, effectively creating multiple paths for transmission. Recall that the concept of mesh networking is integrated into the 802.15.4 (ZigBee) standard. IEEE 802.15.5 is a separate standard that applies to 802.15.3, although the idea is basically the same. Mesh networking can enable WPANs to cover an entire building. Figure 6-11 shows an example of a network using mesh technology.

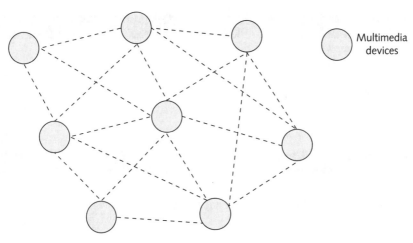

Multimedia devices

Figure 6-11 Mesh network

© Cengage Learning 2014

Ultra Wide Band (UWB)

Ultra wide band (UWB) offers a promising solution to the shortage of available frequencies in the RF spectrum; it allows new transmission techniques based on UWB to coexist with other RF systems, with minimal or no interference. UWB is not really a new technology. It has been used in radar since the 1960s and is a very established technology for ground-penetrating radar. Ground-penetrating radar is used to locate pipes, wires, and objects buried under roads and fields, among other applications.

What is new in UWB is its application to wireless data transmission. Because of its ability to achieve very high data rates, UWB is capable of handling multiple streams, including high-definition and 3-D television, with a quality level equivalent to that of a wired system, albeit at short ranges. It may start out as a wireless PAN solution, but industry experts and analysts have been predicting that, with the addition of mesh networking, UWB can expand to full home and business networking use as well.

The FCC currently allows UWB transmitters to operate in the 3.1–10.6 GHz range at limited power levels of –41 dBm/MHz (approximately 75 nanowatts of power for each MHz of bandwidth), which minimizes interference.

For data applications, UWB has the following characteristics:

- Unlike ground-penetrating radar, it transmits low-power, short-range signals within an enclosed area such as a home or office.

- It transmits using extremely short low-power pulses lasting only about 1 nanosecond or even shorter. These pulses cannot be easily detected by other analog RF equipment; therefore, UWB transmissions do not cause significant interference to other signals.

- UWB transmits over a band that is at least 500 MHz wide, as required by the FCC; such a band helps prevent interference with other RF transmission technologies in current use.

How UWB Works

This section discusses the core UWB RF transmission technique. Note that there is no discussion of the MAC layer. That is because changing the RF layer does not require changes to any other layers, so the MAC layer and all other higher-layer protocols can remain the same.

UWB PHY Layer In Chapter 2, you learned that in traditional RF data transmission, a digital signal is modulated over an analog signal using amplitude, frequency, phase, or a combination of amplitude and phase (for example, 64-QAM). In addition, recall that in order to spread the signal over a wide band and allow for better error detection and correction, digital signals are transmitted using a technique such as frequency hopping spread spectrum (FHSS) or direct sequence spread spectrum (DSSS). In FHSS, signals are transmitted in each of several frequencies for very short periods of time (625 microseconds for Bluetooth). In DSSS, the spreading also has the effect of dividing the signal amplitude across the frequency band, which helps reduce interference.

UWB, on the other hand, is a digital transmission technology. It uses short analog pulses for signaling and does not have to rely on traditional modulation methods. In UWB, this technique is called **impulse modulation**, in which the amplitude, the polarity, or the position of an analog pulse represents either a 1 or a 0. Figure 6-12 illustrates the concept of impulse modulation and compares it with frequency shift keying (FSK) modulation.

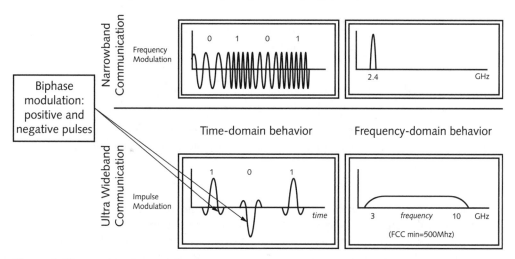

Figure 6-12 UWB impulse modulation

© Cengage Learning 2014

UWB signals can be transmitted using fairly simple techniques by very simple transmitter circuits. Several different types of modulation can be used in UWB, but the most common is **biphase modulation**, which uses a half-cycle positive analog pulse to represent a 1 and a half-cycle negative analog pulse to represent a 0. This kind of modulation is virtually immune to background RF noise and does not cause interference. Biphase modulation requires circuits with two separate transmitter circuits (one to generate positive pulses and one for negative pulses), which makes it more expensive. The concept of biphase modulation is shown in the lower-left part of Figure 6-12.

In addition to the modulation schemes just mentioned, several UWB transmission techniques have been proposed to the IEEE using both direct sequence and multiband orthogonal frequency division multiplexing. Direct-sequence UWB (DS-UWB) takes advantage of the fact that one of the effects of transmitting pulses a nanosecond long—or even shorter—is that the signal naturally spreads over a very wide frequency band without using any spreading codes. In the UWB case, the signal spreads over a band that is at least 500 MHz wide in the high-frequency bands used for this technology. This also spreads the amplitude of the signal across the entire band; as a result, the entire pulse falls below the level of the background noise. Figure 6-13 shows an example of what happens in the frequency domain when a 1-nanosecond pulse is transmitted.

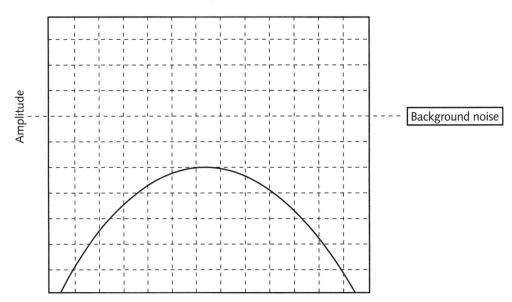

Figure 6-13 Effect of a direct-sequence 1-nanosecond pulse (frequency domain)

© Cengage Learning 2014

The other method proposed to the IEEE, **multiband orthogonal frequency division multiplexing (MB-OFDM)**, is based on the technique used for 802.11g and 802.11a WLAN transmissions (you will learn more about these in Chapter 8). In MB-OFDM, the total bandwidth available is divided into five groups containing a total of 14 frequency bands, as shown in Table 6-4.

Band Group	Band ID	Center Frequency (MHz)
1	1	3,432
	2	3,960
	3	4,488
2	4	5,016
	5	5,544
	6	6,072
3	7	6,600
	8	7,128
	9	7,656
4	10	8,184
	11	8,712
	12	9,240
5	13	9,768
	14	10,296

Table 6-4 MB-OFDM frequency band allocations

© Cengage Learning 2014

Each frequency band is 528 MHz wide, which meets FCC requirements, and is further divided into 128 frequency channels. These channels are orthogonal, meaning that they do not interfere with one another. Several data bits are then sent simultaneously (in parallel), one bit over each of these sub-channels, at a low bit rate per channel. Only 122 out of the 128 channels are used for MB-OFDM transmission. Because several data bits are being sent at the same time, each on a different frequency, OFDM can still achieve high data rates by sending the data bits at a slower rate. This technique is comparable to a parallel printer cable that uses one wire for each bit sent to the printer and therefore transfers one byte at a time. MB-OFDM transmits using pulses that are slightly longer than DS-UWB, at 312 nanoseconds long. Although these longer pulses are easier to generate with electronic circuits, critics claim that MB-OFDM makes the transmitters very complex.

Although UWB offers many advantages, several manufacturers have all but abandoned plans to implement UWB, primarily because of the strong interest in the 60 GHz band. So far, wireless USB is the only technology that has been implemented using UWB, and it has not enjoyed great success. The cost of wireless USB has yet to drop to a level where it would be justifiable, except for aesthetic reasons, to replace a 6-ft. (1.8 meters) cable priced at less than $10.00 with a wireless USB connection currently still costing around $200.00. In addition, the advent of USB version 3.0, which can reach speeds of up to 5 Gbps, and Thunderbolt, developed by Intel and introduced by Apple under a technical collaboration agreement, has further reduced interest from manufacturers in pursuing UWB.

WPAN Challenges

Now that you have explored several WPAN technologies, we will discuss some of the challenges faced by WPAN technologies. Because the ZigBee specification is specifically designed to support devices that only transmit very small amounts of data, at low data rates, most of this section will compare HR WPANs with Blueooth.

Competition Among WPAN Standards

For computer-to-computer and computer-to-handheld devices, you have learned about 802.15.1 Bluetooth and 802.15.3 standards and also how UWB may impact these technologies. Bluetooth products have become far more popular and are being used for many different applications, but the technology is facing serious threats.

The technologies discussed in this chapter are positioned to compete with Bluetooth for market share because HR WPANs are designed for higher data rates as well as for carrying other types of traffic, such as HDMI and USB. Although it will take a few years before these products begin to ship in significant volume, WirelessHD, WiGig, and WHDI have the potential to quickly outpace Bluetooth as a cable-replacement technology. If this happens, Bluetooth may wind up only being used for connecting cellular phone headsets, keyboards, and mouse devices, even though the Bluetooth SIG has released version 4.0 of its specifications, which can achieve speeds of up to 24 Mbps and improved audio connections. For Bluetooth to compete effectively, it will be necessary for manufacturers to incorporate the additional radio required to support the higher rate. This fact alone may increase the cost of high-rate Bluetooth above that of the other three technologies. It is not wise to try to predict which technology will ultimately win this race, but it will be interesting to watch the developments in the industry over the next few years.

WPAN Security

Although security should be less of an issue with WPANs than with traditional wired networks, given that most of the transmissions are restricted to a short range, hackers will go to almost any length to break into devices and networks. This section discusses the security models for Bluetooth, ZigBee, and 802.15.3c. WPAN technologies were discussed in the last two chapters.

Security for Bluetooth
Hackers are already using Bluetooth to attack mobile devices, and Bluetooth security is becoming an issue. In bluejacking, hackers exploit a Bluetooth device's ability to discover nearby devices and send unsolicited messages. Another type of attack is Bluesnarfing, which uses the same discovery ability to access contact lists and other information without the user's knowledge, provided the user has enabled the server functions on his device. **Denial-of-service (DoS)** attacks, which flood a Bluetooth device with so many frames that it is unable to communicate, are another problem. In addition, some Bluetooth devices may be vulnerable to Trojans, viruses, and worms.

These security risks extend well past PDAs and smartphones. Some laptops are shipped with Bluetooth technology, potentially creating a backdoor into a company's network when the computer is connected to a LAN using Ethernet or an 802.11 WLAN. It is both easy and inexpensive for a hacker to surreptitiously add a Bluetooth device to the network, thereby taking advantage of an unsuspecting user's devices. Because of their short-range, low-power signal, devices can remain undetectable for a long period of time, especially when hidden inside a case.

On the other hand, Bluetooth transmissions are not easy to capture and decode. Many hackers are currently trying to develop a system to sniff Bluetooth packets and decode the information, but so far this is proving to be a difficult challenge.

Security for ZigBee WPANs A system that is controlling the lighting and environmental parameters for a building or home still requires some measure of security to prevent intentional or unintentional changes in the settings. The ZigBee specification uses the concept of a trust center, with the PNC (the trust center) being responsible for issuing the encryption keys to all devices on the piconet. ZigBee uses a **symmetric encryption key** for network-wide communications. A symmetric encryption key is a string of characters, numbers, or both that is used to encrypt the data within a frame. When all the devices in a single network use the same key, it is called "symmetric." There are two types of symmetric keys used in ZigBee:

- The network key is normally preprogrammed on each ZigBee node via any type of available direct cable connection to the devices, which is more secure. It is also possible to configure the devices so that only the PNC has this key preconfigured, distributing the key over the wireless medium at installation time in plain text. This means that there may be a temporary vulnerability in a ZigBee piconet until the key is distributed to the devices. This also happens when a new device needs to join the piconet. After all devices in the piconet have received the shared key from the PNC, all subsequent communications between the PNC and devices will be encrypted using the network key.

- Any two devices on the piconet can request a link key from the PNC to set up a secure communications connection between them. The link key is based on the network key and is generated and encrypted with the network key by the PNC before it is distributed to the devices.

ZigBee link and network keys only apply to the application layer of the ZigBee protocol stack. Potential ZigBee users have expressed serious concerns about the temporary vulnerability just described, which can be easily exploited by attackers wishing to break into a ZigBee piconet, perhaps just to prove that they can do it, perhaps to cause problems by changing settings, or perhaps to collect information from ZigBee-based systems such as smart power and gas meters. Utility companies in many countries now consider smart meters a more effective way of collecting usage data and providing their customers with information that enables them to better manage their energy usage.

In addition to symmetric encryption keys, ZigBee uses **message integrity check** and **sequential freshness** to enhance the security of piconets. Message integrity check is a process used to prevent an attacker from modifying a message and resending it on a network. Message integrity makes use of a check number that is generated and included in each frame by the sender. At the receiver end, the number is generated again and compared with the one received in the message. If the two numbers match, the message has not been tampered with. Sequential freshness is the process of assigning a sequential number to each frame to ensure that it is not transmitted more than once in the same piconet within a significant period of time.

Without the use of these two security features, an attacker could perform a **man-in-the-middle** attack by capturing frames, modifying them, and then retransmitting them on the same piconet. When the target ZigBee devices respond to frames that they interpret as valid and coming from an authorized device on the piconet, the attacker may be able to capture enough information to help him decrypt the network, link keys, or both, thereby compromising the security of the piconet. However, remember that the maximum size of a ZigBee frame is 127 octets. This means that it would require a significant amount of frames as well as a long period of time to capture enough frames to be able to crack the security key(s). In addition, ZigBee devices use small, slow processors, which means that when ZigBee devices are encrypting information before transmitting, the process of capturing enough frames would take even longer.

Security for IEEE 802.15.3 HR WPANs Security for this standard is based on the **Advanced Encryption Standard (AES)**, a symmetric key encryption mechanism introduced by the National Institute of Standards and Technology (NIST) in the United States. In 802.15.3, AES uses a 128-bit key. Its two security modes are:

- Mode 0—Does not encrypt or protect the data in any way
- Mode 1—Employs strong cryptography based on AES and supports the protection of commands, beacons, and data frames as well as secure key distribution for command and data frame protection

The standard defines how any two devices can establish a secure communications session to protect both the information as well as the integrity of communications at the MAC and PHY layers. The security key can be shared by all the devices in a piconet or by any two devices. In 802.15.3, the key is 13 octets long and is based on a number of parameters, such as the source and destination address, the current time token on the network, the frame counter to ensure message integrity, and the value of the fragmentation control field. This ensures that the key will be unique for each transaction, which makes it almost impossible for a hacker to break. In addition, this standard provides a mechanism for changing or rotating the symmetric key on a periodic basis. The new key is based on the one that was initially entered by the user. Changing keys periodically makes it far more difficult for a hacker to break the key and be able to decode the data.

The authentication key for the piconet is also changed periodically, or every time a device leaves the piconet or stops responding to beacon frames. This new security implementation is far superior to any of the previous methods employed by Bluetooth and 802.11 WLANs.

802.15.3 also supports message integrity check at the MAC layer. Message integrity check adds certain encrypted random data to each communications session, in addition to a frame counter, so that the receiver can verify that the message has not been tampered with during transit or repeated. Without message integrity check, a would-be hacker could more easily launch a man-in-the-middle attack against the piconet by capturing frames, altering them, and retransmitting them to the intended receiver.

Cost of WPAN Components

Today, Bluetooth supports more devices than other WPAN technologies, but historically it has suffered from the problem of component cost. Bluetooth radio modules originally cost in excess of $75, however, the cost has decreased to around $5 in large quantities, which is the reason behind the increased availability of Bluetooth in many different devices.

However, when you consider Bluetooth's low transmission speed, it still does not make much economic sense to use a chip that costs $5 to replace a cable that costs less than $10 but can achieve much higher data rates. So far, the only advantage that Bluetooth has enjoyed is the widespread availability of devices. The main challenge facing manufacturers of 802.15.3-compatible devices will be to ensure that the technology is incorporated into their products without significantly increasing the cost for consumers and businesses.

Industry Support for WPAN Technologies

Industry experts predict that new technologies such as WirelessHD and ZigBee will be more quickly embraced by manufacturers. ZigBee support is likely to come initially from qualified installation technicians, which means that these devices will not likely suffer from the problems that have affected Bluetooth from its early days.

Protocol Functionality Limitations

One of the major limitations of the Bluetooth protocol is that slave devices are not designed to move from one piconet to another without losing the connection to the master of the original piconet. If a Bluetooth device moves beyond the communications range of each device that controls the communications, it will disconnect from the piconet. Even if a Bluetooth device immediately moves into the range of another piconet, and even if it is paired to both masters, it will lose the connection to the first piconet. In cellular technology, for example, the handsets are designed to switch from one cell or base station to the next as the user drives down the road, without losing the connection to the cellular phone network. Devices supporting multimedia technologies such as WirelessHD are able to remain connected to the piconet provided that another device (or devices) can route (i.e., forward) frames across the network. This allows a device to remain connected to the PNC and to other devices even when they are not within RF direct communications range of the destination device. The inability of most Bluetooth devices to route frames may prevent Bluetooth from being adopted as a technology for cordless phones that need to roam throughout a house or office, out of range of the piconet master.

Although Bluetooth devices can discover other Bluetooth devices in the area, they cannot (at present) automatically determine how the functions of other devices can be used in a cooperative setting. You may remember that Bluetooth devices only communicate with the piconet master and cannot communicate directly with other slave devices. Messages in a scatternet, for example, must be sent via the piconet masters and from there to the slave devices. This implies that all devices in a piconet must remain within RF range of a master at all times and that, in a scatternet, the two masters must be within RF communications range of each other. These are concerns that Bluetooth needs to address if it is to compete with ZigBee and WirelessHD, but this would mean a monumental change to the Bluetooth specification. Here again, all the other technologies discussed in this chapter (and ZigBee) have a built-in advantage because they can automatically identify the services and capabilities offered by other devices in the piconet, even if these other devices are out of range of the piconet coordinator. In addition, ZigBee and 802.15.3 devices can indeed communicate directly with each other.

Although there is no other major protocol limitation with any of the technologies discussed in this chapter, it is important to realize that the drive in the industry is toward standardizing the protocols as much as possible. In most cases, this will mean using TCP/IP at higher layers and using one of the MAC and PHY protocols in lower layers.

Spectrum Conflict

Of all of the issues with WPANs, spectrum conflict is the one that will potentially affect their success in the market. **Spectrum conflict** is the potential for technologies using the same frequency bands to interfere with one another to the extent that they sometimes perform poorly when used within close range of one another. Applying UWB technology or using the 60 GHz band can significantly reduce or eliminate this issue, unlike what happens with the limited bandwidth available for Wi-Fi networks.

For example, today's 802.11b/g WLANs perform poorly in environments where a 2.4 GHz cordless phone is also in use. This issue affects all the technologies that use FHSS and DSSS in the same frequency band. To make their products more attractive and to avoid the technical support issues related to spectrum conflict, manufacturers of cordless phones have been introducing models that transmit at 1.6 GHz instead, using the newer DECT 6.0 specification.

As noted previously, because Bluetooth uses the ISM 2.4 GHz band for its transmissions, it can conflict with other technologies that use the same frequency band. One of the major conflicts comes with IEEE 802.11b and 802.11g WLANs. Older Bluetooth devices are almost unusable in these situations. Most vendors have already implemented the recommendations of the IEEE 802.15.1 standard, which lets Bluetooth and 802.11b/g WLANs share the spectrum by first checking to see if the airwaves are clear for transmission and also by avoiding frequencies that interfere with Wi-Fi networks. UWB can interfere with 802.11a networks, depending on the frequency range used. Extensive tests run by the IEEE indicate that both ZigBee products should be able to coexist with 802.11b/g without any serious problems. However, experience with RF waves suggests that we will not know how well they actually perform until these products have been deployed in large volume and in many different environments.

Chapter Summary

- HR WPANs are technologies optimized for the transmission of multimedia digital-format sound and video files. There are three technologies currently competing to become the accepted standard: WHDI, WiGig, and WirelessHD, each promoted by a different organization.

- WHDI, founded by AMIMON Inc., defines wireless connectivity using the 5 GHz band for distribution of high-quality video and audio signals to display devices such as TVs and stereo sound systems. WHDI has a range of 100 ft. (30 meters) and is able to penetrate walls. It eliminates the complexities of networking and delivering digital format files by using the display devices or sound systems for what they were originally designed to do, which is to simply work as display or sound reproduction devices. WHDI is also designed to coexist with 802.11a and 802.11n networks operating in the same frequency band. It uses proprietary chip technology designed by AMIMON. WHDI can directly support USB and HDMI connections, making them work over the same wireless connection as video and sound.

- The Wireless Gigabit Alliance defined a set of specifications that include protocol adaptation layers to support wireless HDMI, USB, PCIe, data, video, and audio transmissions using the IEEE 802.11ac gigabit wireless connections in the ISM and U-NII bands. The specifications will also work in the 60 GHz band using the IEEE 802.11ad standard.

- The 60 GHz band can only support short-range connections up to 33 ft. (10 meters) due to the increased attenuation at high-frequency bands, and it does not penetrate walls. To get around some of the line-of-sight limitations of the 60 GHz band, transmitters use beamforming to maximize the signal strength at the receiving device location and to deal with moving obstacles, such as a person walking between the receiver and the transmitter.

- WiGig supports the same modulation and coding schemes in the ISM and U-NII bands as 802.11 but defines two new modulations for the 60 GHz band: single carrier for speeds up to 4.6 Gbps and OFDM for speeds up to 7 Gbps. OFDM provides better handling of signal reflections. Using MIMO and beamforming WiGig can also use obstacles as reflectors to help it maintain connections between devices.

- WirelessHD is the only specification that uses the IEEE 802.15.3c standard. This IEEE standard specifies operation in the 60 GHz band only. WirelessHD supports many different transmission speeds as well as the use of several different kinds of mobile and stationary devices transmitting video, sound, or data on the piconet. A source device is the one that transmits the video or audio data, whereas a sink device is either a video display, such as a TV set, or a stereo sound system.

- WirelessHD defines three PHY layers: LRP for data dates up to 10 Mbps, HRP for data rates up to 7 Gbps (and over 26 Gbps when using spatial multiplexing), and MRP for data rates ranging from 476 Mbps to 2 Gbps. WirelessHD can also support USB up to version 3.0 and can carry HDMI connections over the wireless link. A WirelessHD piconet is also called a WVAN.

- WiGig and WirelessHD both support beamforming, which enables a device with multiple radios to virtually steer the beam in the direction of the intended receiver. Beamforming can use multipath reflections to create constructive interference, effectively increasing the signal amplitude at the receiver end.

- 802.15.3c supports peer-to-peer networking, but the timing of transmissions on the piconet is always controlled by the PNC. The PNC accomplishes this by sending a periodic beacon containing information about the piconet, such as its unique ID and the time when devices are allowed to transmit. Devices can communicate directly to other devices but can only transmit during the contention access period (CAP) or during the times that the PNC allocates for each device. The PNC is responsible for QoS and allocates reserved time periods, called CTAPs. Devices can request additional channel time from the PNC. If the PNC leaves the piconet, it can hand over control to another device.

- 802.15.3 piconets support child and neighbor piconets. The PNC in child piconets is a member of the original piconet. The PNC in a neighbor piconet is not a member of the original piconet but depends on the original piconet's PNC to allocate a private block of time for all devices belonging to the neighbor piconet to transmit. The two piconets share the same frequency channel. Child piconets are useful for extending the coverage of a piconet or for shifting processing or storage requirements to another device. The WirelessHD specification extends this concept by supporting drone WVANs using a different frequency channel when there are no longer any CTAPs available for use by all the piconet devices.

- The process of association with the piconet is implemented in hardware to simplify installation, use, and maintenance. The PNC maintains a table of all devices in the piconet. It also broadcasts information about the piconet to all devices. It will only send information about the availability of services when requested by a device.

■ Efficient data transmission is accomplished by use of a superframe, which is the mechanism the PNC uses to allocate CAP, CTAP (which includes MCTAs), and CTAs. For communications during the CAP, devices must use the CSMA/CA mechanism to avoid collisions. Devices listen to the medium for traffic. If the medium is busy, devices must wait before transmitting. This wait period is never applied to the transmission of beacons. During the CTAP communications period, the piconet uses a TDMA scheme for transmission.

■ Devices can send asynchronous data in the CAP or can request channel time for asynchronous communications during the CTAP. Normal communications during the CTAP are isochronous or synchronous communications.

■ In 802.15.3, devices can be in one of several power-saving modes. DSPS allows devices to sleep for several superframes but wake up in the middle to transmit or send data. The PNC informs all devices which one will be the wake superframe for each device. In PSPS mode, devices can sleep during intervals defined by the PNC, but all devices must wake up at the same time to listen to system-wide wake beacons. In asynchronous power save mode, devices can sleep for long periods of time and decide when to wake up and listen to a beacon. The PNC can also set a maximum transmit power level for capable devices during the CAP, beacon, and MCTA time periods. This method also allows the PNC to save power.

■ Ultra wide band (UWB) is a digital transmission technology that supports very-high-speed transmissions—up to 2 Gbps. Only the PHY layer needs to change in UWB; the MAC layer remains the same one that is used with the other RF methods of transmission. Currently, UWB is only implemented to support wireless USB. These wireless interfaces transmit at 480 Mbps.

■ UWB transmissions occupy a bandwidth of at least 500 MHz and transmit using very short pulses. UWB uses an extremely simple modulation scheme called impulse modulation, but it can also use multiband OFDM.

■ Challenges for WPANs include speed, security, cost, industry support, interference, and protocol limitations. Bluetooth suffers from these limitations more than its competing standards do. 802.15.3 has a number of advantages over Bluetooth, including enhanced security and the ability to extend the network through communications with neighbor and child piconets.

■ WPAN devices that are designed to be small and consume very little power have limited processing capabilities and storage. This makes it difficult to implement sophisticated security mechanisms, a source of concern when using WPANs.

Key Terms

Advanced Encryption Standard (AES) A symmetric key encryption mechanism introduced by the U.S. National Institute of Standards and Technology.

beamforming A technique that enables the transmitting device to use multiple radios and multiple antennas to maximize the signal amplitude at the receiver location.

biphase modulation   Modulation that uses a half-cycle positive analog pulse to represent a 1 and a half-cycle negative analog pulse to represent a 0.

channel time allocation (CTA)   Periods of time allocated by the PNC to a specific device for prioritizing communications in a WPAN. *See also* management channel time allocation (MCTA).

channel time allocation period (CTAP)   The component of a superframe used for communications between the PNC and other devices.

child piconets   Separate piconets with their own ID; the child PNC is a member of the original or parent piconet.

contention access period (CAP)   A mechanism used to communicate commands or any asynchronous data that may be present in a superframe. The CAP is also used to allow devices that are not yet part of a piconet to send a request to the PNC to join the piconet.

cyclic redundancy check (CRC)   A common technique for detecting data transmission errors.

denial-of-service (DoS)   A type of security attack on a networked device in which the attacker sends so many frames to a single device that the device is unable to communicate with other devices.

D-WVAN   A secondary wireless video area network that operates in a different frequency channel and is formed when two devices require additional bandwidth but there is no bandwidth available in the current frequency channel.

H-WVAN   The home or parent WVAN of a D-WVAN. *See* WVAN.

impulse modulation   A digital transmission technique employed by UWB in which the polarity of a single analog pulse (one-half of a sine wave) represents a binary digit 1 or 0.

Isochronous   A time-dependent transmission that must occur every frame or every so many frames to maintain the quality of the connection.

management channel time allocation (MCTA)   Time periods used for communication between the devices and the PNC.

man-in-the-middle   A type of security attack in which a hacker captures frames, alters them, and then retransmits them to the intended receiver or another device on the network.

mesh networking   A network topography in which each device connects to all other devices within range.

message integrity check   A process of adding certain encrypted random data to each communications session so that the receiver can verify that the message has not been tampered with after being transmitted.

multiband orthogonal frequency division multiplexing (MB-OFDM)   A transmission technique in which the frequency band is divided into a number of frequencies (called sub-frequencies or channels) that do not interfere with one another.

neighbor piconets   Separate piconets that have their own PNC but that depend on the original piconet's PNC to allocate a private block of time when their devices are allowed to transmit.

piconet coordinator (PNC)   A device that provides all the basic communications timing in an 802.15.3 piconet.

protocol adaptation layers (PALs)   A set of protocol implementation rules based on the 802.15.3 standard that enables, among other possible protocols, wireless USB at 480 Mbps.

quality of service (QoS) A feature of some PANs that allows devices to request more channel access time in order to prioritize high-volume, time-sensitive traffic, such as a voice stream.

sequential freshness The process of assigning a sequential number to each frame to ensure that it is not transmitted on the same network more than once.

spatial multiplexing A technique that uses multiple radios and multiple antennas to transmit and receive different parts of the same PHY frame.

spectrum conflict The potential for technologies using the same frequency bands to interfere with one another to the extent that they sometimes perform poorly when used within close range of one another.

superframe A mechanism for managing transmissions in a piconet. The superframe is a continually repeating frame containing a beacon, contention access periods, channel time allocation periods, and management time allocation periods.

symmetric encryption key A string of characters, numbers, or both used to encrypt the data within a frame. When all devices in a single network use the same encryption key, they are called "symmetric."

wake superframe The superframe designated by the PNC in which devices that are in power-saving mode wake up and listen for frames addressed to them.

wireless video area network (WVAN) The name given to a network in WirelessHD that is dedicated to transmitting multimedia files, usually in an uncompressed format, to a television or similar type of display device. WVANs may also include audio-only devices, such as stereo systems.

Review Questions

1. In a piconet, the 802.15.3 PNC is primarily responsible for _____.

   a. timing

   b. acting as the router

   c. switching

   d. Internet connections

2. The 802.15.3 standard was developed to _____.

   a. compete with Bluetooth technology

   b. provide short-range PC networking

   c. support multimedia

   d. all of the above

3. In 802.15.3, the lower levels of the protocol stack are implemented in the _____.

   a. software

   b. hardware

   c. infrared

   d. data link layer

4. In WPANs, the _____ layer of the protocol stack handles the different types of traffic.

   a. radio frequency

   b. video

   c. IP

   d. adaptation

5. How many RF channels are available in 802.15.3c?

   a. 2

   b. 14

   c. 4

   d. 11

6. In 802.15.3, frame collisions can only happen during the _____.

   a. CTAP

   b. MCTA

   c. CTA

   d. CAP

7. In 802.15.3c, using _____ prevents collisions.

   a. CAP

   b. CTAP

   c. CSMA/CA

   d. CSMA/CD

8. Which of the following technologies uses an RF frequency band in which signals can still get through walls?

   a. WirelessHD

   b. WHDI

   c. WiGig

   d. none of the above

9. In the _____ power-saving mode, 802.15.3c devices must listen to the system-wide wake beacons.

   a. SPSS

   b. DSPS

   c. PSPS

   d. APS

10. In the 60 GHz band used in 802.15.3c, RF channels have approximately how much bandwidth?

   a. 2 MHz

   b. 500 MHz

   c. 2 GHz

   d. 5 MHz

11. The frequencies between approximately _____ and _____ form the entire range approved by the FCC for use with UWB technology.

   a. 3.4 GHz; 4.5 GHz

   b. 5.0 GHz; 9.2 GHz

   c. 3.4 GHz; 10.3 GHz

   d. 6.6 GHz; 9.2 GHz

12. The maximum data rate of WiGig is _____ Gbps.

   a. 1

   b. 2

   c. 7

   d. 4.9

13. In WirelessHD, the PNC is usually a video source. True or False?

14. The name of the process used in ZigBee to ensure that the same frame is not transmitted more than once is _____.

   a. symmetric key

   b. sequential freshness

   c. man-in-the-middle

   d. message integrity check

15. The beacon carries timing information for the piconet. True or False?

16. Devices in an 802.15.3c piconet can only communicate through the PNC. True or False?

17. CAPs are optional. True or False?

18. A WiMedia device cannot request more channel time from the PNC. True or False?

19. UWB can cause interference with the frequency band used in _____.

   a. ISM

   b. 802.11a

   c. 60 GHz

   d. WirelessHD

20. What is the generic name of the error-correction mechanism that is used to ensure the reliability of transmissions in HR WPANs?

    a. FEC

    b. CRC

    c. parity

    d. HRC

Real-World Exercises

The Bay Area Cable TV Corporation installs home entertainment systems throughout California. About 10,000 systems are installed, expanded, or upgraded on a yearly basis. Many customers are upgrading their equipment to multiple television sets and high-definition TV. Each time the company sends a technician or contractor to a customer's home or business, it's an additional $150 and $200 in labor costs to install the cable for additional set-top boxes in different rooms of a house or office.

The company's management has heard about a new way to deliver this service using wireless networks, which would dramatically reduce installation costs. Customers also want to be able to send multiple media streams, either movies or music, to different rooms or offices simultaneously. They have hired you as a networking expert to help them plan for the expansion of their services over the next five to 10 years.

Exercise 6-1: Explaining HR WPAN Advantages

Create a PowerPoint slide presentation to demonstrate the advantages of HR WPANs for the Bay Area Cable TV Corporation. Your presentation should cover any existing technology but should also include some recommendations based on some of the developments you learned about in this chapter. Bay Area is not asking you to guess which of the HR WPAN technologies will be chosen, but they would like to hear your expert review of the future of multimedia distribution in homes as well as the potential applications for businesses.

Exercise 6-2: Comparing HR WPAN Technologies

Although Bay Area's management is thinking progressively, the board of directors is still not sure whether to direct management to continue with wired technologies or begin to explore wireless right away. They would like you to draw a comparison between the different HR WPAN technologies and Wi-Fi. Therefore, create a PowerPoint slide presentation that explains the advantages and disadvantages of the various HR WPAN alternatives and what can be done with Wi-Fi today and in the near future.

Challenge Case Project

Microsoft, Hewlett Packard, and many other companies have released hardware that supports the Windows 7 Media Center Edition, a special version of Microsoft Windows that enables the distribution of multimedia throughout the home.

Develop a group report that discusses how you could use one of the HR WPAN technologies discussed in this chapter instead of Windows 7 Media Center Edition. Your report should cover the delivery of audio, video, and gaming to multiple appliances like television, MP3 players, tablets, and PCs throughout the home, and it should explain the advantages of adopting a design that addresses not only media distribution but also the transfer of files as well as Internet access throughout the home. Research the features of Windows 7 Media Center Edition and HR WPANs and provide an assessment of the issues related to range and interference.

chapter 7

Low-Speed Wireless Local Area Networks

After reading this chapter and completing the exercises, you will be able to:

- Describe how WLANs are used
- List the components and modes of a WLAN
- Describe how an RF WLAN works
- Explain the differences between IR, IEEE 802.11, and IEEE 802.11b WLANs
- Outline the user mobility features offered by IEEE 802.11 networks

WLANs are probably the technology that has attracted the most attention since the introduction of personal computers to the consumer market. The explosive growth of wireless networks all over the world has been driven by home and small-office sales, but after the ratification of the latest wireless networking standard—IEEE 802.11n, in 2009—more companies have started deploying wireless networks than ever before. And growth is expected to continue with the introduction of gigabit wireless. The Wireless Broadband Alliance (*www.wballiance.com*) predicts that global public access (hotspots) deployments alone will increase 350 percent (to 5.8 million) by 2015 as a result of mobile phone carriers recognizing the importance of this technology and offloading some of the data traffic from their networks. Total mobile data traffic is forecast to reach 16.84 million terabytes (that is 16,840,000,000,000,000,000 bytes) in 2014. This figure includes both smartphones and WLANs.

As you have learned in previous chapters, WLAN technology supports a very broad spectrum of applications. Practically all laptop computers, netbooks, tablets, and smartphones are shipped with WLAN interfaces today. Many of the most popular coffee shops and fast-food outlets, most hotels anywhere in the world, and even some airlines offer wireless Internet access today. Public transit buses in the city of Markham, Ontario, offer wireless Internet access to their passengers in a bid to prompt residents to use public transportation.

This chapter begins by reviewing ways in which WLANs are used, focusing on low-speed WLANs (up to 11 Mbps). This background will help you understand the higher-speed technologies and new standards covered in Chapter 8. So far, you have learned about various technologies that do not always carry data that must remain private. The open nature of the WLAN medium, which makes the signals available virtually everywhere, means not only that these networks need to be made more secure but that working in this field requires a more in-depth understanding of how WLANs work.

WLAN Applications

Wireless networks are increasing in popularity, especially in North America, as computer users seek the freedom to use their mobile devices in various locations throughout their homes or office environments. Installing cabling is inconvenient and very expensive, especially after the building is already finished. Also, the locations available for connecting a high-speed cable modem or digital subscriber line (DSL) modem may not be ideal for working or studying. Wireless networks solve these problems. Additionally, with a wireless network, multiple users can easily share a single Internet connection. Some wireless network devices also allow Internet and printer sharing. An example of this is a **wireless residential gateway**, a device that combines a router, Ethernet switch, wireless access point, and in some cases the cable or DSL modem. Wireless residential gateways provide better security than connecting a computer directly to the Internet because most of them include a security firewall that prevents some kind of security attacks on your network devices.

Wireless LAN applications today are so widespread that we could spend most of the chapter listing different uses and applications. The Internet is packed with information in the form of press releases and white papers about wireless LAN applications.

WLAN Components

The hardware needed for a WLAN is surprisingly minimal. In addition to a computer and an Internet service provider for Internet access, only wireless network interface cards (NICs) and access points (APs) are needed for communication to take place.

Wireless Network Interface Card

The hardware that allows a computer to be connected to a wired network is called a network interface card (NIC) or a network adapter. A NIC is the device that connects the computer to the network so that it can send and receive data to other devices, either locally or via the Internet. A wired NIC has a port for a cable connection. The cable connects the NIC to the network, thus establishing the link between the computer and the network.

A wireless NIC performs the same functions as a wired NIC, with one major exception: There is no port for a wire connection to the network. In its place is an antenna to send and receive RF signals. Specifically, when wireless NICs transmit, they:

- Change the computer's internal data from parallel to serial prior to transmission
- Divide the data into packets (smaller blocks of data) and attach the sending and receiving computers' addresses
- Determine when to send the packet
- Transmit the packet

A wireless NIC is most often a separate card that is inserted into one of the desktop computer's internal expansion slots. For desktop computers, wireless NICs are available for a peripheral component interface (PCI) expansion slot. Another option is an external wireless adapter that can be connected to a computer's Universal Serial Bus (USB) port. Examples of these devices were shown in Figure 1-8.

For notebook and laptop computers, wireless NICs are available in two different formats. The first is a standard PC Card Type II slot, as seen in Figure 1-8. Another format is known as the **Mini PCI**. A Mini PCI is a small card that is functionally equivalent to a standard PCI expansion card. It was specifically developed for integrating communications peripherals, such as modems and NICs, onto a notebook computer. When a notebook computer is equipped with a Mini PCI NIC, the antenna is usually embedded in the part of the notebook that surrounds the screen. Figure 7-1 shows a Mini PCI card installed on the underside of a notebook computer.

Figure 7-1 A Mini PCI wireless NIC

Smaller devices such as smartphones already include a wireless radio chip and an antenna to connect to a WLAN. These small radios are the result of the development of very low-power chips.

WLANs are so popular that separate wireless NICs are quickly becoming a thing of the past. Intel has integrated all the functions of a wireless interface into the set of chips (called a chipset) that is builtin to laptop computers. The chips in the set are mounted directly on the motherboard, reducing the physical space requirements. Most notebook computer manufacturers ship all their models with integrated wireless LAN capabilities, whether using the Intel Centrino chipset or a Mini PCI card.

The software that interfaces the wireless NIC with the computer can either be part of the operating system or a separate program. Beginning with Microsoft Windows XP, all Microsoft desktop operating systems recognize a wireless NIC without the need for additional software drivers; previous versions of Windows required specialized driver programs. Incorporating the software into the operating system eases installation and also provides additional features, such as the ability to create multiple wireless profiles that enable devices to automatically connect to different WLANs as the user roams, instead of manually configuring the settings. Some wireless NIC vendors include software drivers for other operating systems—such as Linux—as well as for some dedicated devices that do not rely on industry-standard software.

Access Points

As you learned in Chapter 1, an access point (AP), as its name implies, provides wireless LAN devices with a point of access into a wired network. APs consist of three major parts: (1) a radio transmitter/receiver to generate the signals that are used to send and receive wireless data; (2) an antenna to radiate these signals; and (3) an RJ-45 wired network interface port that uses a cable to connect the AP to a standard wired network.

 **NOTE** It is possible to use a standard PC as an AP by installing a wireless NIC (which functions as the transmitter/receiver), a standard NIC (which serves as the wired network interface), and special software that allows the PC to serve as an AP as well as a security firewall. You can find free public domain versions of this kind of software at the following links: *www.microtik.com* and *www.m0n0.ch*. (The "0s" in "m0n0" are the digit zero, not the letter "O").

An AP has two basic functions:

- It acts as the wireless communications base station for the wireless network. All the devices that have a wireless NIC transmit to the AP, which in turn redirects the signal to the other wireless devices.

- It acts as a bridge between the wireless and wired networks. The AP is connected to the wired LAN by a network cable, allowing the wireless devices to access the wired network through it, as shown in Figure 7-2.

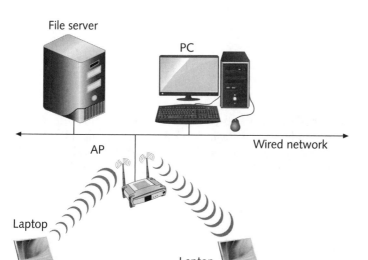

Figure 7-2 The AP as the point of access into a wired network

© *Cengage Learning 2014*

The range of an AP acting as the base station is approximately a maximum of 375 feet (115 meters) in an unobstructed office environment, in which there is little interference. However, the data rate will drop as the signal strength, quality (affected by interference), or both begin to fade. The exact point at which the data rate begins to drop depends on the specific environment, the type and number of obstructions, and any sources of interference. The AP will automatically select the highest possible data rate for transmission, depending on the strength and quality of the signal. This process is called **dynamic rate selection**, and it makes testing the signal before implementation of a WLAN an extremely important part of the deployment. You will learn more about testing the WLAN signal in Chapter 12.

The largest number of connected devices that a single AP can support varies but is usually over 100. However, because the radio frequency (RF) network signal is shared among users, most vendors recommend one AP per maximum of 50 users if the network is lightly used—that is, for e-mail, occasional Web surfing, and occasional transferring of medium-sized files. On the other hand, if the users are mainly transferring large files—such as digital pictures, video, or voice—the maximum number of users should be kept to between 20 and 25 per AP.

When the antennas are directly attached to the AP, the AP is typically mounted near the ceiling or in a similar area high off the ground to ensure the clearest possible path for the RF signal. However, electrical power outlets are generally not found in these locations and, due to building code restrictions, these outlets can be very expensive to install near the ceiling. The IEEE has published two enhancements to the 802.3 Ethernet standard for wired networks—namely, 802.3af and 802.3at—that define how manufacturers may implement the distribution of **power over Ethernet (PoE)** media. Instead of receiving power directly from an AC outlet, DC power is delivered to the AP through the same wires that are used for data in unshielded twisted pair (UTP) Ethernet cables that connect the AP to the wired network. This eliminates the need for expensive electrical wiring to be installed in or near the ceiling and makes the mounting of APs more flexible.

WLAN Modes

In an RF WLAN, data can be sent in one of two connection modes: ad hoc mode and infrastructure mode.

Ad Hoc Mode **Ad hoc mode** is also known as **peer-to-peer mode**, although its formal name in the 802.11 standard is **Independent Basic Service Set (IBSS)**. In ad hoc mode, wireless clients communicate directly among themselves without using an AP, as shown in Figure 7-3. This mode is useful for a quick and easy setup of a wireless network anywhere that a network

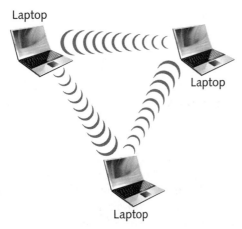

Figure 7-3 Ad hoc mode

© Cengage Learning 2014

infrastructure does not already exist or is not permanently required. Examples of locations that use ad hoc mode WLANs include hotel meeting rooms or convention centers. The drawback is that the wireless clients can only communicate among themselves; there is no access to a wired network.

Infrastructure Mode The second wireless network mode is the **infrastructure mode**, also known as the **Basic Service Set (BSS)**. Infrastructure mode consists of at least one wireless client connected to a single AP. If more users need to be added to the WLAN or the RF coverage area needs to be increased, more APs can be added. When an infrastructure WLAN has more than one AP using the same **Service Set IDentifier (SSID)**, this is called an **Extended Service Set (ESS)**. An ESS is simply two or more BSS wireless networks installed within the same area, providing users with uninterrupted mobile access to the network, as shown in Figure 7-4. The SSID is an alphanumeric character string that uniquely identifies each WLAN. In an ESS, each AP is tuned to a different frequency channel, but all APs are connected to the same wired LAN, creating a virtually seamless wireless connection. In an IEEE 802.11 WLAN, the MAC address of each AP is called the basic service set identifier or **BSSID**, and in the case of an ESS, where the alphanumeric SSID is the same for several different APs, the client device uses the BSSID to identify which AP it is connected to.

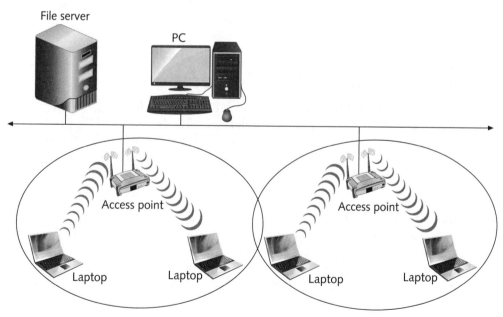

Figure 7-4 Extended Service Set (ESS)

© Cengage Learning 2014

When multiple APs are used, they create areas of coverage, much like the individual cells in a beehive. However, unlike a beehive, these cells overlap to facilitate roaming. When a mobile user carrying a wireless device enters into the range of more than one AP, his wireless device chooses an AP with which to associate, usually based on signal strength. Once the AP accepts the connection from that device, the client device changes to the radio frequency used by that particular AP.

Whenever a wireless client is not communicating on the WLAN, it will monitor all the radio frequency channels on the network to determine if a different AP can provide a better-quality or stronger signal. If the client finds one (perhaps because the user has moved), it then associates with the new AP, changing to the radio frequency that the AP is set to. In an ESS, this transition is called a **handoff**. To the user, a handoff is seamless, because the connection between the wireless device and the wired network is never interrupted. The client device remains connected to the same WLAN.

A drawback of ESS WLANs is that all wireless clients and APs must be part of the same network for users to be able to roam freely between one AP and the other. Sometimes, it is difficult to manage one large network. Performance and security may also be adversely affected. Because of this, network managers usually subdivide large networks into units known as **subnets** that contain fewer computers. In an ESS divided into subnets, a mobile user might not be able to freely roam between APs and would need to reconnect each time he moves between subnets, because an IP address belonging to one subnet would not allow him to communicate in another. Some of the business-class network devices that connect these subnets are equipped with special software that allows the wireless device to be accepted in other subnets without changing IP addresses and to maintain the connection. In these cases, the wired switches and routers across the network allow packets to be forwarded transparently to the user's own subnet.

Wireless LAN Standards and Operation

In this section, you will learn about the first IEEE standards for wireless LANS. Most WLANs are based on these initial IEEE 802.11 standards. 802.11a and 802.11g, which are covered in Chapter 8, follow the same basic principles, albeit with a number of enhancements. Each of these standards implements specific transmission technologies based on the differences in the PHY and MAC layers.

IEEE 802.11 Standards

The original IEEE **802.11 standard**, ratified in 1997, defines a local area network that provides cable-free data access for clients that are either mobile or in a fixed location, at a rate of either 1 or 2 Mbps using either diffused infrared or RF transmission. In addition, when using RF technology, this standard defines the implementation of WLANs using FHSS or DSSS.

The standard specifies that the features of a WLAN be transparent to the upper layers of the TCP/IP protocol stack or the OSI protocol model. That is, the functions of the PHY and MAC layers provide full implementation of all the WLAN features so that no modifications are needed at any other layers, as shown in Figure 7-5. Because all the WLAN features are isolated in the PHY and MAC layers, any network operating system or LAN application will run on a WLAN without any modification necessary. In order to accomplish this, some features that are usually associated with higher layers are now performed at the MAC layer.

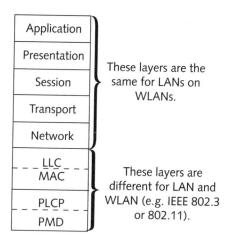

| Application |
| Presentation |
| Session |
| Transport |
| Network |

These layers are the same for LANs on WLANs.

| LLC |
| MAC |
| PLCP |
| PMD |

These layers are different for LAN and WLAN (e.g. IEEE 802.3 or 802.11).

Figure 7-5 WLAN features restricted to the PHY and MAC layers

© Cengage Learning 2014

Because no IEEE 802.11 equipment has ever been introduced in the consumer market using IR and FHSS, this book does not cover these technologies. Instead, this chapter focuses on the basics of 802.11, which is applied across the products available on the market.

The slow maximum bandwidth of only 2 Mbps for the original 802.11 standard is not sufficient for most network applications. As a result, the IEEE body revisited the 802.11 standard shortly after it was released to determine what changes could be made to increase the speed. In 1999, the 802.11b and 802.11a standards were published, increasing the speeds to 11 Mbps and 54 Mbps in the ISM and U-NII bands, respectively. Due to user demand, the IEEE published the 802.11g standard in 2003, raising the speed of 802.11b-compatible networks to a maximum of 54 Mbps. This drive for more speed has not subsided yet. New standards are in the works to increase the speeds even beyond the current maximum of 300 Mbps to 600 Mbps possible with IEEE 802.11n.

It is important to remember that the most current version of the IEEE 802.11 standard is still backwards compatible with the original maximum data rates from 1997 of 1 Mbps or 2 Mbps. This backwards compatibility has the effect of making it easier for clients to initially establish connectivity to the WLAN, as will be explained later. The techniques used to achieve the slower data rates will be discussed, where applicable, in the remainder of this chapter.

IEEE 802.11b Standard

The **IEEE 802.11b** amendment, ratified in 1999, was dubbed Higher Speed Physical Layer Extension in the 2.4 GHz band by the IEEE. It added two higher speeds to the 1997 standard, 5.5 Mbps and 11 Mbps, and specified RF and direct sequence spread spectrum (DSSS) as the only transmission technologies. 802.11b also became known as **Wi-Fi** shortly after the establishment of the Wi-Fi Alliance.

Physical Layer Remember that the basic purpose of the IEEE PHY layer is to send signals to and receive signals from the network. The 802.11b PHY layer is also divided into two parts, as shown in Figure 7-5: the physical medium dependent (PMD) sublayer and the physical layer convergence procedure (PLCP) sublayer. The 802.11b standard made changes only to the PHY layer of the original 802.11 standard.

Physical Layer Convergence Procedure PLCP standards for 802.11b are based on direct sequence spread spectrum (DSSS). The PLCP must reformat the data received from the MAC layer (when transmitting) into a frame that the PMD sublayer can transmit. An example of a PLCP frame is shown in Figure 7-6.

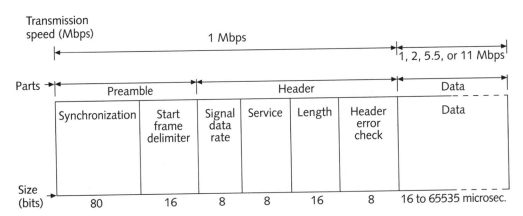

Figure 7-6 802.11b PLCP frame

© *Cengage Learning 2014*

The PLCP frame is made up of three parts: the preamble, the header, and the data. The preamble allows the receiving device to prepare for the rest of the frame. The header provides information about the frame itself. The data portion of the PLCP frame is the information to be transmitted. The fields of the PLCP frame are:

- Synchronization—Consists of alternating 0s and 1s to alert the receiver that a message may be on its way; the receiving device then synchronizes with the incoming signal.

- Start Frame Delimiter—Always the same bit pattern (1111001110100000); it defines the beginning of a frame.

- Signal Data Rate—Indicates how fast the data is being sent.

- Service—Most of the bits in this field are reserved for future use and must be set to 0. Bits 2, 3, and 7 are used in combination with the Length field for data rates higher than 8 Mbps.

- Length—Indicates how long, in microseconds, the data portion of the frame (the MAC frame) is. The value of the Data field ranges from 16 to 65535. Approximately two pages of the 802.11b standard are devoted to calculating the length of the data. The details are beyond the scope of this book.

- Header Error Check—Contains a value that the receiving device can use to determine if the data was received correctly.

- Data—Can be up to 4095 bytes (the maximum length of an IEEE 802.11 MAC frame).

The 802.11b PLCP frame preamble and header are always transmitted at 1 Mbps to allow for communication between slower and faster devices. The slow PLCP preamble and header transmission speed permits a slower transmission to cover a larger area than a faster one. The disadvantage of using the lowest common denominator speed is that faster devices must still fall back to the 1 Mbps transmission rate for the preamble and header, and this affects the overall performance of the WLAN. However, the data portion of the frames can be sent at the faster rates, if supported by the client devices.

Physical Medium Dependent Standards Once the PLCP has formatted the frame, it then passes the frame to the PMD sublayer of the PHY layer. Again, the job of the PMD is to translate the binary 1s and 0s of the frame into radio signals that can be used for transmission.

The 802.11b standard uses the Industrial, Scientific, and Medical (ISM) band (an unregulated band that you learned about in Chapter 3) for its transmissions. For use in 802.11b, the standard specifies 14 available frequencies, beginning at 2.412 GHz and incrementing by .005 GHz (or 5 MHz of bandwidth per channel), except for Channel 14. The frequencies for each channel are listed in Table 7-1.

Channel Number	Frequency (GHz)
1	2.412
2	2.417
3	2.422
4	2.427
5	2.432
6	2.437
7	2.442
8	2.447
9	2.452
10	2.457
11	2.462
12	2.467
13	2.472
14	2.484

Table 7-1 802.11b ISM channels

© *Cengage Learning 2014*

The United States and Canada use channels 1–11; Europe permits channels 1–13, with the maximum power limited at 10 mW between 2454 and 2483 MHz; and Japan permits the use of all 14 channels but limits the use of channel 14 to 802.11b only.

The PMD can transmit data at 11, 5.5, 2, or 1 Mbps. By employing dynamic rate selection, the transmission rate will adjust automatically from 1 Mbps to 2 Mbps, 5.5 Mbps, or 11 Mbps and down again depending on the signal strength and quality. For transmissions at 1 Mbps, two-level differential binary phase shift keying (DBPSK) is specified as the modulation technique. The phase angle change for a DBPSK 0 bit is 0 degrees; for a 1 bit, it is 180 degrees. Transmissions at 2, 5.5, and 11 Mbps use differential quadrature phase shift keying, similar to QPSK (covered in Chapter 2), which means a four-level phase/amplitude change is used. Instead of having only two variations in phases for 0 and 1, the four-level phase change has four variations in phase for the dibits 00, 01, 10, and 11.

You may remember that DSSS uses an expanded redundant code, called the Barker code, to transmit each data bit. The Barker code is used when 802.11b is transmitting at 1 Mbps or 2 Mbps. However, to transmit at rates above 2 Mbps, **Complementary Code Keying (CCK)**, a table containing 64 8-bit code words, is used instead. As a set, these code words have unique, mathematically calculated properties that allow them to be correctly distinguished from one another by a receiver. The 5.5 Mbps rate uses CCK to encode 4 bits per signal unit, whereas the 11 Mbps rate encodes 8 bits per signal unit.

The maximum transmission rate of 802.11b networks is 11 Mbps, but because all 802.11 transmissions use a single frequency, they are half-duplex, which means that the maximum throughput achievable in an 802.11b network is only between 5 and 6 Mbps.

Media Access Control Layer   The 802.11b Data Link layer consists of two sublayers: Logical Link Control (LLC) and Media Access Control (MAC). The 802.11b standard specifies no changes to the LLC sublayer (the LLC remains the same as for IEEE 802.3 wired networks), therefore all the changes for 802.11b WLANs are confined to the MAC layer.

Coordinating Transmissions in the Shared Wireless Medium

Because all devices in the same 802.11 WLAN must share the medium by transmitting in the same frequency, if two computers start sending messages at the same time, a **collision** results and the data becomes scrambled. Figure 7-7 shows an example of a collision in a wired network. To prevent this, wireless network devices must use a variety of **channel access**

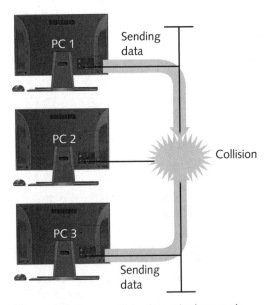

Figure 7-7   Frame collision in a wired network

methods. One way to prevent network collisions, for example, is for each device to listen to the medium first, to make sure no other device is transmitting. In addition, after a device transmits a frame, it must wait to receive an acknowledgment from the receiving device. If it does not receive an ACK, it assumes there has been a collision. This process is called **distributed coordination function (DCF)**.

In Chapter 5, you learned about a channel access method called carrier sense, multiple access with collision avoidance (CSMA/CA). In this chapter, we will further explore CSMA/CA and how it works in 802.11. This method of detecting collisions is based on the one used in IEEE 802.3 Ethernet. When Ethernet devices are connected using a shared medium, such as a coaxial cable, or when they operate in half-duplex mode using hubs and only two wires to communicate, they use a contention access method called carrier sense, multiple access with collision detection (CSMA/CD). CSMA/CD specifies that before a computer starts to send a message it should listen on the cable to see if any other computer is transmitting. If it hears traffic, it should wait until that traffic is finished. If it hears no traffic, then the computer can send a packet. However, what if two computers simultaneously listen for traffic and hear nothing on the cable and then both start to send at exactly the same time? A collision would still result. CSMA/CD also specifies that each computer must continue to listen while sending its message. If it detects a collision, each computer stops sending data and broadcasts a jam signal over the network, which tells all other computers not to send any messages for a random period of time (the backoff interval) before attempting to resend.

CSMA/CD in Ethernet uses voltage sensors on the NIC. Whenever they detect a voltage higher than 5 volts, this means that more than one device is transmitting at the same time. The same method of detecting a collision cannot be used in a wireless system. Collision detection is virtually impossible with wireless transmissions when the signals are transmitted and received in the same frequency. The RF signal from a transmitter is so strong when it gets to the antenna that it will overpower that same antenna's ability to receive a signal simultaneously. In short, while it is transmitting, a device drowns out its own ability to detect a collision. In addition, the amount of attenuation of a signal sent by another device cannot be effectively predicted in a wireless system, therefore measuring the strength of voltage of an RF signal is not practical.

The shared medium of Ethernet networks is limited in maximum length, and this, together with tight cable specifications, makes the maximum signal attenuation predictable. In a WLAN, the signal may be affected by unknown obstacles in the environment as well as by signal reflections, which makes attenuation impossible to predict.

The entire family of 802.11 standards primarily uses DCF to avoid collisions. DCF specifies that a modified procedure—CSMA/CA—be used. Whereas CSMA/CD is designed to handle collisions when they occur, CSMA/CA attempts to avoid collisions altogether.

When using a contention-based channel access method, the time at which the most collisions occur is immediately after a device completes its transmission. This is because all other devices wanting to transmit have been waiting for the medium to clear so they can send their messages. Once the medium is clear, they may all try to transmit at the same time, resulting in collisions.

CSMA/CA in DCF handles the situation by making all devices wait a random amount of time (the backoff interval) after the medium is clear, which significantly reduces the occurrence of collisions. The amount of time that a device must wait after the medium is clear is measured in **time slots**. Each client must wait a random number of time slots as its backoff interval. The time slot for a DSSS 802.11b WLAN is 20 microseconds. If a wireless client's backoff interval is three time slots, then it must wait 60 microseconds (20 microseconds times three time slots) before attempting to transmit.

 The time slot for an 802.3 Ethernet 10 Mbps transmission is 51.2 microseconds; for 100 Mbps Ethernet, it is 5.12 microseconds.

CSMA/CA also reduces collisions by using an explicit **acknowledgment (ACK)**. An acknowledgment frame is sent by the receiving device back to the sending device to confirm that each data frame arrived intact. If the sending device does not receive the ACK frame, either the original data packet was not received or the ACK was not received intact. In either case, the sending device assumes that a problem has occurred and retransmits the data frame after waiting for a time-out period. This explicit ACK mechanism can also handle interference and other radio-related problems, such as one client device being able to hear the transmission from an AP but not being able to hear another client that is too far away. CSMA/CA and ACK are shown in Figure 7-8.

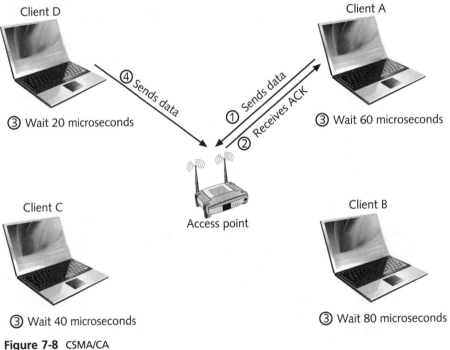

Figure 7-8 CSMA/CA

© Cengage Learning 2014

CSMA/CA reduces potential collisions, but it does not eliminate them altogether. The 802.11b standard provides two additional mechanisms to reduce collisions. The first is known as the **request–to-send/clear–to-send (RTS/CTS)** protocol (also called *virtual carrier sensing*). RTS/CTS is shown in Figure 7-9. The client wishing to transmit sends a request-to-send (RTS) frame to the AP. This frame contains a Duration field that defines the length of time needed for both the transmission and the returning ACK frame. The AP then alerts all other wireless clients that Client B needs to reserve the medium for a specific number of time slots by responding back to the client with a clear-to-send (CTS) frame that also tells all clients that the medium is now being reserved and that they should therefore suspend any transmissions. Once the client that sent the RTS to the AP receives the CTS frame, it can proceed with transmitting its message.

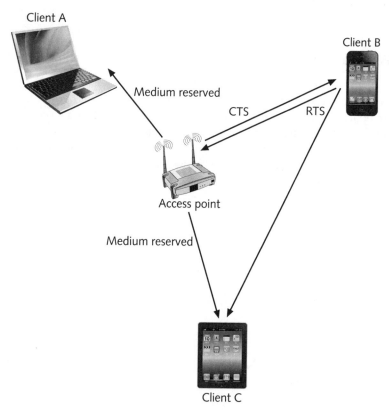

Figure 7-9 RTS/CTS

© Cengage Learning 2014

The RTS/CTS protocol imposes additional overhead and is not used unless there is poor network performance due to excessive collisions. The second option to reduce collisions is packet **fragmentation**. Fragmentation involves dividing the data to be transmitted from one large frame into several smaller ones. Sending many smaller frames instead of one large frame reduces the amount of time that the wireless medium is being used to transmit each frame, and because of this it can also reduce the probability of collisions.

In fragmentation, if the length of a data frame to be transmitted exceeds a specific value, the MAC layer will divide, or fragment, that frame into several smaller frames. Each fragmented frame is given a fragment number (the first fragmented frame is 0, the next frame is 1, and so on). The frames are then transmitted to the receiving client. The receiving client sends back an ACK and then is ready to receive the next fragment. After all the fragments are received at their destination, they are reassembled, based on their fragment numbers, back into the original frame by the MAC layer of IEEE 802.11.

Fragmentation can reduce the probability of collisions and is an alternative to RTS/CTS; however, it does create additional overhead in two ways. First, additional frames imply additional MAC and PLCP headers. Second, the receiving device must send a separate ACK for each smaller fragment received. Fragmentation does not always have to be used separately from RTS/CTS; in a busy WLAN, they may have to be combined to reduce collisions. The standard allows both methods to be used simultaneously.

Point Coordination Function

Another type of channel access method is **polling**. With this method, each computer is sequentially "asked" if it wants to transmit. After associating with the AP, client devices cannot transmit unless they are polled. If the client has something to transmit, it will send a positive response to the AP. The AP then gives permission for the client to transmit while all other devices must wait. If the client does not have anything else to transmit, it will send a **null data frame** to the AP, and then the next device in sequence will be polled. It is a very orderly way of allowing each device to send a message. Each device is given a turn, as shown in Figure 7-10. Polling

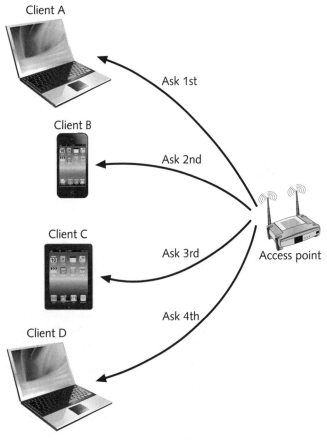

Figure 7-10 Polling in PCF

© Cengage Learning 2014

effectively eliminates collisions because every device must wait until it receives permission from the AP before it can transmit.

This optional polling method is known as **point coordination function (PCF)**. With PCF, the AP serves as the polling device. When using PCF, the AP (the point coordinator) first listens for wireless traffic. This is because in order to allow other clients to associate with the AP and join the WLAN, PCF must still allow some time slots for contention access, in which case the WLAN is using DCF. If the AP hears no traffic on the wireless medium, it sends out a beacon frame to all clients. One field of this frame contains a value that indicates the number of time slots that will be used for PCF (polling) as well as the number of time slots that will be used for DCF (contention). After the associated clients receive this beacon frame, they must cease transmitting for the duration of PCF. Clients that are not yet associated will take advantage of the DCF period to contact the AP and join the WLAN.

PCF is designed for WLANs that transmit time-sensitive frames. These types of transmissions—often voice or video—depend on each frame arriving in an orderly sequence very quickly, one after the other. Delays in transmission can result in a video that freezes on the screen or a voice conversation that has gaps of dead space. Data transmissions, on the other hand, are not as sensitive to timely data delivery. DCF cannot distinguish between voice, video, and data frames. Using PCF or a combination of DCF and PCF allows for the smooth transmission of these time-sensitive frames.

Although PCF was never implemented in any commercial-grade 802.11 APs or wireless residential gateways, a hybrid of this method and DCF is used in later amendments to the standard, so it is still important to understand the basics of how PCF functions.

Association and Reassociation

The MAC layer of the 802.11b standard provides the functionality for a client to join a WLAN and stay connected. The processes of joining and staying connected to a WLAN are known as **association** and **reassociation**. Remember that there are two different modes in RF WLANs: ad hoc and infrastructure. Regardless of which mode is being used, a client must first go through a process of communicating with the other wireless clients or the AP in order to become accepted as part of the network. This acceptance process is known as association.

The process of association begins with the client scanning the wireless medium to discover all the APs from which it can detect a RF signal. The client that wants to connect to the wireless network must first listen to the medium for the information that it needs to begin the association process. There are two types of scanning: passive and active. **Passive scanning** involves a client listening to each available channel for a set period of time (usually 10 seconds). The client listens for a beacon frame transmitted from all available APs. The information contained within most beacon frames includes how often beacon frames are sent, the supported transmission rates of the network, and the AP's SSID and BSSID. The transmission of the SSID can be disabled on the AP to attempt to "hide" the network from some clients. This hiding of the SSID will be discussed in Chapter 8.

SSIDs are case sensitive. For example, if you set the SSID on an AP as "AP1" and set the SSID on the client devices as "ap1," the client devices will not be able to associate with the AP using this configuration. The same is true for ad hoc networks. All devices must use the same SSID.

The second type of scanning, **active scanning**, involves the client first sending out a special frame, called a **probe** frame, on each available channel. It then waits for an answer, the **probe response** frame, from all available APs. Like the beacon frame, the probe response frame contains information the client needs to begin a dialogue with the AP. According to the IEEE 802.11 standard, the probe response frame must always include the SSID, regardless of whether the AP is configured to transmit it in the beacon or not. Client devices do not normally perform active scans of the wireless medium, but the client's wireless NIC is capable of sending probe frames. Some WLAN software tools, such as inSSIDer from Metageek (*www.metageek.net*), can use the client's wireless NIC to perform active scans by sending probe frames.

Once the client scans and receives the connection information in the beacon from the AP, it can begin to negotiate a WLAN connection with the AP. To join the WLAN, the client sends an **associate request frame** to the AP that includes the client's own capabilities and supported rates. The AP then returns an **associate response frame**, containing a status code and client ID number that will be used as long as this client is connected to the same AP. At this point, the client becomes part of the WLAN and can begin communicating.

If the WLAN includes multiple APs, the client may need to choose from many different APs. The decision can be based on several criteria. A client can be preconfigured to connect only to a specific AP. In this case, the client already contains the SSID of the AP with which it needs to connect. Likewise, some APs can be configured to accept or reject a connection from certain clients, usually based on the MAC address. As it receives beacon frames from the different APs, the client compares its preconfigured profile's SSIDs to the SSID of the preferred AP. The client will not attempt to connect to APs until it finds a match, at which time it will send an associate request frame to that AP. If a client has not been preconfigured to connect with a specific AP, it will attempt to connect with the AP from which it has received the strongest radio signal.

Connecting with one AP does not restrict a client from associating with other APs, except that clients can only be associated with one AP at a time. A client may disconnect from one AP and reestablish a connection with another AP. This is known as reassociation. Reassociation may be necessary when mobile clients roam beyond the coverage area of one AP in an ESS and are receiving a stronger signal from a different AP in the same ESS, in which case the client reassociates with the new AP. Reassociation can also occur when the signal from one AP weakens because of interference.

When a client determines that the link to its current AP is poor because it has been scanning the medium and saving information related to the various APs in an ESS, it will pick the AP with the strongest signal and send a **reassociate request frame**. If the new AP accepts the reassociation request, it will send a **reassociate response frame** to the client. The new AP will then send a **disassociate frame** to the previous AP that the client was connected to, via the wired network, terminating the old AP's association with the client. This process is shown in Figure 7-11.

Disassociate frame sent
between APs over wired
network

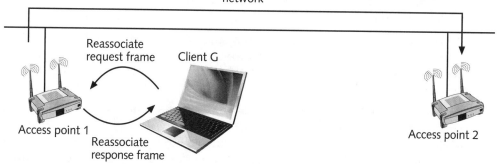

Reassociate
request frame

Client G

Reassociate
response frame

Access point 1

Access point 2

Figure 7-11 Reassociation process

© *Cengage Learning 2014*

In the 802.11 and 802.11a/b/g standards, multiple APs can only communicate with one another over the network cabling. In other words, they cannot communicate over a wireless connection. As you will learn in the next chapter, there are two separate enhancements to the 802.11 standards that permit APs to communicate with each other over the wireless medium, when necessary.

Power Management

Most clients in a WLAN are portable computers, smartphones, or tablets, giving the users the freedom to roam without being tethered to the network by wires. When these devices are mobile (and consequently not connected to a power outlet), they depend on batteries as their primary power source. To conserve battery power, wireless devices can go into **sleep mode** after a period of inactivity, when particular functions (such as hard drive, display, and so on) are temporarily powered down by the computer's operating system.

Note that Microsoft Windows hibernate mode, which literally shuts down the computer, is not the same as sleep mode or standby mode; however, it is similar to sleep mode. As defined in 802.11, a computer in sleep mode must remain powered up, although the hard drive and display may be temporarily shut down by the notebook's power save mode. In both hibernate and standby modes, the NIC also shuts down completely. To learn more about these features of Microsoft Windows, refer to Windows documentation or your operating system's Windows Help feature.

When a client is part of a WLAN, it must remain fully powered up to receive network transmissions. Missing transmissions because it is in sleep or hibernate mode may cause an application running on the device to lose connection with a server application running elsewhere on the network. The answer to the issue of a battery-powered client being able to shut down its radios to save energy is known as **power management**. In the 802.11 standard, power management allows the mobile client's NIC to be off as much as possible to conserve battery life but still not miss out on data transmissions. Power management in 802.11 is transparent to all protocols and applications so that it does not interfere with normal network functions. The 802.11b power management function can only be used when connecting in infrastructure mode.

The key to power management is synchronization. Every client on a WLAN has its own local timer. At regular intervals, the AP sends out a beacon signal to all clients that contains a timestamp. When the clients receive this frame from the AP, they synchronize their local timers with that of the AP.

When a mobile 802.11 client goes into sleep mode, it first informs the AP of the change in its status. The AP keeps a record of those clients that are awake and those that are sleeping (with the client's wireless NIC receiver and transmitter powered down). As the AP receives transmissions, it first checks whether the client's NIC is in sleep mode. The AP temporarily stores the frames that are destined to the clients that are sleeping (this function is called **buffering**).

At predetermined times, the AP sends out a beacon frame to all clients. This frame contains a list—known as the **traffic indication map** (**TIM**)—of the network IDs of the clients that have buffered frames waiting at the AP. At that same set time, all clients that have been sleeping must awaken (by turning on their wireless NICs) and go into an active listening mode. If a client learns that it has buffered frames waiting, that client will send a request to the AP for those frames. If TIM does not include the network ID of a client, signaling that it has no buffered frames, the client can return to sleep mode. This process is shown in Figure 7-12. Note that clients that are in hibernation mode will effectively be disconnected from the WLAN and cannot awaken to receive frames.

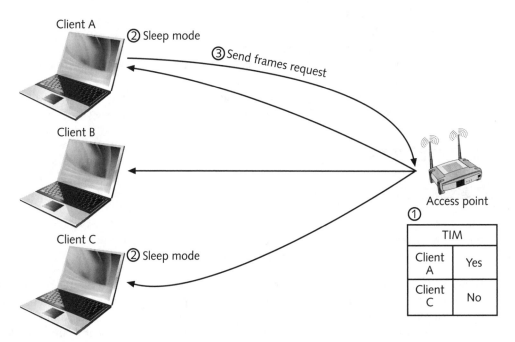

Figure 7-12 Power management in 802.11

© *Cengage Learning 2014*

The maximum amount of sleep time for a mobile client is generally set to 100 milliseconds. This means that every client in sleep mode must awaken and listen for the TIM every 100 milliseconds.

MAC Frame Formats

The 802.11b standard specifies three types of MAC frame formats. The first are known as **management frames**. These are used to set up the initial communications between a client and the AP. The reassociation request frame, the reassociation response frame, and the disassociation frame are all types of management frames.

The format of a management frame is shown in Figure 7-13. The Frame Control field indicates the current version number of the standard and whether encryption is being used. The Duration field contains the number of microseconds needed to transmit. This value will differ depending on whether the point coordination function or distributed coordination function mode is being used. Sequence control is the sequence number for the frame and, if necessary, the fragment number.

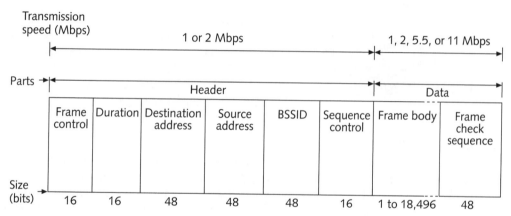

Figure 7-13 Structure of a management frame

© Cengage Learning 2014

Control frames are the second type of MAC frames. After association and authentication between the clients and the APs are established, the control frames provide assistance in delivering the frames that contain the data. A request-to-send (RTS) frame is a control frame and is shown in Figure 7-14.

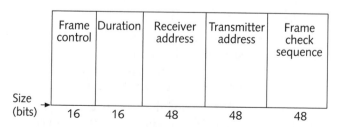

Figure 7-14 RTS (control) frame

© Cengage Learning 2014

Data frames are the third type of MAC frames. They carry the information to be transmitted to the destination client. The format of a data frame is shown in Figure 7-15. The fields Address 1 through Address 4 contain the SSID, the destination address, the source address, and the transmitter address and the receiver address, depending on how the network is configured. Not all address fields are present in every type of MAC data frame. The content of the address fields varies depending on the type of frame transmitted.

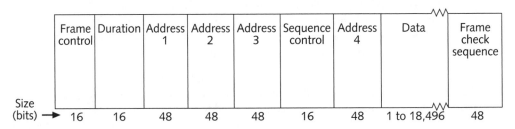

Frame control	Duration	Address 1	Address 2	Address 3	Sequence control	Address 4	Data	Frame check sequence
16	16	48	48	48	16	48	1 to 18,496	48

Size (bits) →

Figure 7-15 Data frame

© Cengage Learning 2014

A full discussion of the use of the address fields is beyond the scope of this book. For additional information regarding the content of the address fields, see the 802.11-1999 standard. You can find it at *http://standards.ieee.org/about/get*. Copies are usually available at no cost six months after the publication of a standard's latest version.

Interframe Spaces

To understand the message exchange process, you need to understand the collision avoidance mechanism in DCF that is used by an AP and a client to communicate. For CSMA/CA to work properly in DCF, the 802.11 standard defines a number of **interframe spaces** (IFS), or time gaps. These are designed to handle the contention for the medium among several devices attempting to communicate.

To keep this explanation as simple as possible, we will only review the procedure and rules associated with using the DCF. We will not look at the procedure or rules associated with RTS/CTS or PCF. For additional information, you can download the 802.11-1999 standard from the address provided in an earlier note.

In 802.11, interframe spaces perform various critical functions, depending on what type they are:

- The **Short Interframe Space (SIFS)** is a time period used to allow all transmitted signals to arrive and be decoded at the receiving device. An SIFS occurs immediately after the transmission of any frames. No device is allowed to transmit during the SIFS. If a frame has been transmitted to one specific device, and provided there were no errors, the receiving device will send an ACK immediately after the SIFS time.

- The **DCF Interframe Space (DIFS)** is a time period during which all devices must wait between transmissions of data frames. The DIFS occurs after the transmission of an ACK or after the SIFS if the frame transmitted was a broadcast. Devices remain idle during the DIFS.

The times of these space intervals are measured in microseconds, as shown in Table 7-2.

DSSS Interframe Space	Duration in Microseconds
SIFS	10
DIFS	50

Table 7-2 Interframe space duration

© Cengage Learning 2014

The basic rules of communication in an 802.11 network are as follows (see Figure 7-16):

- A device that wants to transmit begins listening for an RF signal (carrier sensing), which indicates the presence of frame traffic on the network, during the DIFS.

- If no RF signal is detected at the end of the DIFS and the device's backoff interval has counted down to 0, it can begin transmitting a data or management frame.

- The size of a frame includes both the length of time necessary to send the data and the SIFS time. When the transmission is over, the sending device begins listening for an acknowledgment (ACK) from the receiving device.

- The receiving device must send the ACK immediately after the SIFS. After receiving an ACK, the transmitting client begins to wait a random backoff interval.

- If the transmitting device does not receive an ACK after the SIFS, it is allowed to maintain control of the medium and begin retransmitting the frame that was not acknowledged immediately after the DIFS time.

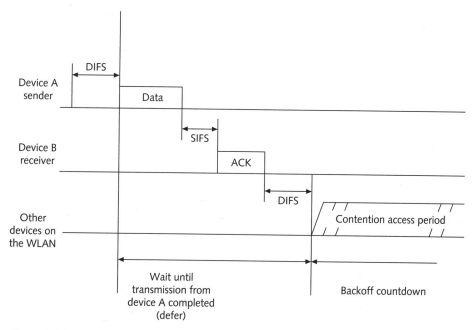

Figure 7-16 Single device transmitting

© Cengage Learning 2014

- If the frame was acknowledged correctly, the transmitting device listens to the medium while waiting its backoff interval, but not during the SIFS or DIFS. Once the interval ends, the device checks for traffic at the end of the next DIFS and the process repeats itself from the first point above.

In the case of two devices having frames to transmit, the process works as follows (see Figure 7-17):

- Client A has a frame to transmit. Its backoff period counter is 0. It senses the carrier after the last DIFS (the one on the left in Figure 7-17) and finds no traffic on the medium, so it transmits the frame.
- Client B had two time slots left to count down, but it can only count during a contention access period.
- After Client A finishes the transmission of its data frame, it sets its random backoff counter to 3.
- The network enters a contention access period, and both Client A and Client B begin counting down backoff time slots.
- After two time slots, Client B's counter reaches 0 and it has something to transmit. Client B finds the medium free and transmits its data frame.
- Like Client B before, Client A does nothing while Client B's data frame transmission is going on. Once Client B has received an ACK for its most recent transmission, the process continues.

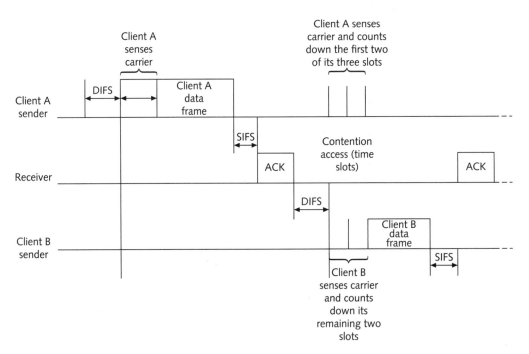

Figure 7-17 CSMA/CA with two clients transmitting

© Cengage Learning 2014

The process just described is a simplified version of what actually occurs, but it is the essence of collision avoidance in IEEE 802.11 WLANs. In Chapter 8, we will briefly explore some additional types of interframe spaces that are used in other amendments to the standard.

Chapter Summary

- The wireless technology that attracts the most attention today is wireless local area networks (WLANs). WLAN deployments are growing, and usage is increasing at a dramatic pace, all because WLANs allow users to access networks such as the Internet from a wider range of locations than was ever possible before.

- A wireless NIC performs the same functions as a wired NIC, except instead of a port for a cable connection to the network, the wireless NIC uses an antenna to send and receive RF signals. Wireless NICs are usually a separate card that is inserted into one of the computer's expansion slots.

- An AP's main function is to interconnect the wired network and the WLAN. The AP acts as the base station for the wireless network and also serves as a bridge between the two networks. An AP consists of three major parts: an antenna, a radio transmitter/receiver, and an RJ-45 wired network interface that allows it to connect by cable to a standard wired network.

- Data can be sent and received in an RF WLAN either in ad hoc or infrastructure mode. In ad hoc (or peer-to-peer) mode, the wireless clients communicate directly with each other without using an AP. Ad hoc mode is known in the 802.11 standard as an IBSS. Infrastructure mode, also known as the Basic Service Set (BSS), consists of wireless clients and an AP. If more users need to be added to the WLAN or the range of coverage needs to be increased, more APs can be added using the same network name, or SSID. This creates an Extended Service Set (ESS), which consists of two or more BSSs.

- The IEEE 802.11 standard defines a local area network that provides cable-free data access at a rate of up to 2 Mbps for clients that are either mobile or in a fixed location. The 802.11 standard also specifies that the features of a WLAN be transparent to the upper levels of the OSI protocol model. However, the slow bandwidth of only 2 Mbps for the 802.11 standard proved insufficient for most network applications.

- The 802.11 standard uses an access method known as the distributed coordination function (DCF). The DCF specifies that a modified procedure known as carrier sense, multiple access with collision avoidance (CSMA/CA) be used. CSMA/CA attempts to avoid collisions. The CSMA/CA process ensures that all clients wait a random number of time slots after the medium is clear. CSMA/CA also reduces collisions by using explicit packet acknowledgment (ACK). Although CSMA/CA dramatically reduces the potential for collisions, it does not eliminate them altogether. The 802.11 standard provides two options that may be used to reduce collisions. The first is known as the request-to-send/clear-to-send (RTS/CTS) protocol. RTS/CTS reserves the medium for a single client to transmit. The second option to reduce collisions is fragmentation. Fragmentation involves dividing the data to be transmitted from one large frame into several smaller ones.

- The 802.11 standard provides for an optional polling function known as point coordination function (PCF). With PCF, the AP serves as the polling device and queries each client to determine if the client needs to transmit. The MAC layer of the 802.11 standard provides the functionality for a client to join a WLAN and stay connected. This is known as association and reassociation. Association is the process of communicating with the other wireless clients in ad hoc WLANs or with the AP in order to become accepted as part of the network. To associate with a WLAN, the client first scans the wireless medium and listens for beacons from the APs. There are two types of scanning: passive scanning and active scanning. A client may drop the connection with one AP and reestablish the connection with another, which is known as reassociation.

- Mobile WLAN devices often depend on batteries as their primary power source. To conserve battery power, they can go into sleep mode after a period of time. Power management, as defined by the 802.11 standard, allows the mobile client to be off as much as possible to conserve battery life but still not miss out on data transmissions by waking up and listening to beacons. The beacon may contain a Traffic Information Map (TIM) that indicates whether there is data waiting at the AP to be transmitted to the client. If so, the station will then remain awake and request the data from the AP.

- The 802.11 standard specifies three different types of MAC frame formats. Management frames, the first type, are used to set up the initial communications between a client and the AP. Control frames, the second type, provide assistance in delivering the frames that contain the data. Data frames, the third type, carry the information to be transmitted. The 802.11 standard also defines two different types of interframe spaces (IFS), or time gaps, which are standard spacing intervals between the transmissions of frames. Instead of being just dead space, these time gaps are used to allow enough time for a device to finish receiving transmissions, checking for errors, and sending an ACK.

- In 1999, IEEE approved two new standards: 802.11b and 802.11a. The IEEE 802.11b standard added two higher speeds, 5.5 Mbps and 11 Mbps, to the original 802.11 standard. With the faster data rates, the 802.11b quickly became the standard for WLANs.

- The physical layer convergence procedure (PLCP) for 802.11b is exclusively based on direct sequence spread spectrum (DSSS). The PLCP must reformat the data received from the MAC layer (when transmitting) into a frame that the PMD sublayer can transmit. The frame is made up of three parts, which are the preamble, the header, and the data. The 802.11b standard uses the 2.4 GHz Industrial, Scientific, and Medical (ISM) band for its transmissions and can transmit data at 11, 5.5, 2, or 1 Mbps.

Key Terms

802.11 standard   An IEEE standard released in 1997 that defines wireless local area networks at a rate of either 1 Mbps or 2 Mbps. All WLAN features are confined to the PHY and MAC layers.

acknowledgment (ACK)   A procedure used to reduce collisions by requiring the receiving station to send an explicit packet back to the sending station, provided that the received transmission had no errors.

active scanning   The process of sending frames to gather information.

ad hoc mode   A WLAN mode in which wireless clients communicate directly among themselves without going through an AP.

associate request frame   A frame sent by a client to an AP that contains the client's capabilities and supported rates.

associate response frame   A frame returned to a client from the AP that contains a status code and client ID number.

association   The process for a client device to join a BSS. *See also* Basic Service Set.

Basic Service Set (BSS)   A WLAN mode that consists of at least one wireless client and one AP.

BSSID   In an infrastructure WLAN, the BSSID is the MAC address of the AP. In a peer-to-peer network, the BSSID is the MAC address of the first station to be turned on and configured to establish the ad hoc WLAN.

buffering   The process that the AP uses to temporarily store frames for clients that are in sleep mode.

channel access methods   The different ways of sharing resources in a network environment.

collision   The scrambling of data that occurs when two computers start sending messages at the same time in a shared medium.

Complementary Code Keying (CCK)   A table containing 64 8-bit code words used for transmitting at speeds above 2 Mbps. This table of codes is used instead of the process of adding a Barker code to the bit to be transmitted.

control frames   MAC frames that assist in delivering the frames that contain data.

data frames   MAC frames that carry the user information to be transmitted to a device.

disassociate frame   A frame sent by the new AP to the old AP in an ESS to terminate the old AP's association with a client. Disassociation frames are transmitted from one AP to another over the wired network only, not via the wireless medium.

distributed coordination function (DCF)   The default channel access method in IEEE 802.11 WLANs, designed to avoid collisions and grant all devices on the WLAN a reasonably equal chance to transmit on the selected channel.

DCF Interframe Space (DIFS)   The standard interval between the transmission of data frames.

dynamic rate selection   A function of an AP that allows it to automatically select the highest transmission speed based on the strength and quality of the signal received from a client NIC.

Extended Service Set (ESS)   A WLAN mode that consists of wireless clients and multiple APs using the same SSID, extending a WLAN seamlessly beyond the maximum range of an 802.11 transmission.

fragmentation   The division of data to be transmitted from one large frame into several smaller frames.

handoff   In an ESS, when a WLAN device reassociates with an AP on the network and disassociates with the one to which it was previously connected.

IBSS   *See* ad hoc mode.

IEEE 802.11b   An amendment to the IEEE 802.11 standard for WLANs that added two higher speeds, 5.5 Mbps and 11 Mbps, and is also known as Wi-Fi, a name given by the

Wi-Fi Alliance to technology that has been certified for interoperability with equipment from different manufacturers.

Independent Basic Service Set (IBSS) A WLAN mode in which wireless clients communicate directly among themselves without using an AP. *See also* ad hoc and peer-to-peer.

infrastructure mode *See* Basic Service Set.

interframe spaces (IFS) Time gaps used in CSMA/CA to allow devices to finish receiving a transmission and checking for errors before any other device is allowed to transmit.

management frames MAC frames that are used, for example, to set up the initial communications between a client and the AP.

Mini PCI A small card that is functionally equivalent to a standard PCI expansion card used for integrating communications peripherals onto a notebook computer but that is much smaller.

null data frame The response that a client sends back to the AP to indicate that the client has no transmissions to make in PCF.

passive scanning The process of listening to each available channel for a set period of time.

peer-to-peer mode *See* ad hoc mode.

point coordination function (PCF) The 802.11 optional polling function.

polling A channel access method in which each computer is asked in sequence whether it wants to transmit.

power management An 802.11 standard that allows the mobile client to be off as much as possible to conserve battery life but still not miss out on data transmissions.

power over Ethernet (PoE) A technology that provides power over an Ethernet cable.

probe A frame sent by a client when performing active scanning.

probe response A frame sent by an AP when responding to a client's active scanning probe.

reassociation The process of a client disconnecting from one AP and reestablishing a connection with another AP.

reassociate request frame A frame sent from a client to a new AP asking whether it can associate with the AP.

reassociate response frame A frame sent by an AP to a station indicating that it will accept its reassociation with that AP.

request-to-send/clear-to-send (RTS/CTS) An 802.11 protocol option that allows a station to reserve the network for transmissions.

Service Set IDentifier (SSID) A unique network identifier assigned to an AP during configuration. In an ESS, all APs will be configured with the same SSID.

Short Interframe Space (SIFS) A time period used to allow a receiving station to finish receiving all signals, decode them, and check for errors.

sleep mode A power-conserving mode used by portable, battery-powered devices in a WLAN.

subnets Subsets of a large network that use a different group of IP addresses belonging to the same domain IP address. Subnets are separated from other subnets by routers.

time slots The measurement unit in a PLCP frame.

traffic indication map (TIM)   A list of the stations that have buffered frames waiting at the AP. The TIM is sent in the beacons by the AP.

Wi-Fi   A trademark of the Wi-Fi Alliance, used to refer to 802.11b WLANs that pass the organization's interoperability tests.

wireless residential gateway   A combination of several technologies that permit home users to have wireless capabilities and also allow Internet and printer sharing and provide better security than connecting a computer directly to the Internet.

Review Questions

1. A wireless NIC performs the same functions as a wired NIC except that it _____.
   a. does not transmit the packet
   b. uses an antenna instead of a wired connection
   c. contains special memory
   d. does not use parallel transmission

2. Some vendors have already integrated the components of a wireless NIC directly onto the notebook's _____.
   a. motherboard's chipset
   b. floppy drive
   c. hard drive
   d. CD-ROM drive

3. Which of the following is not a function of an AP?
   a. sends and receives RF signals
   b. connects to the wired network
   c. serves as a router
   d. acts as a bridge between the wired and wireless networks

4. The range of an AP acting as the base station is approximately _____.
   a. 573 feet
   b. 375 feet
   c. 750 feet
   d. 735 feet

5. The highest data rate for an 802.11 RF WLAN is about _____ Mbps.
   a. 22
   b. 1
   c. 2
   d. 54

6. The IEEE 802.11b standard that outlines the specifications for RF WLANs is based on _____.

   a. FHSS

   b. DSSS

   c. infrared

   d. OFDM

7. Power over Ethernet delivers power to an AP through the same wires used for data in a standard unshielded twisted pair (UTP) Ethernet cable. True or False?

8. In ad hoc mode, the wireless clients communicate directly with the AP. True or False?

9. An Extended Service Set (ESS) consists of two or more BSSs. True or False?

10. On a regular basis, wireless clients will scan all the radio frequencies to determine if a different AP can provide better service. True or False?

11. Network managers like to subdivide large networks into smaller units known as subnets because this makes it easier to manage the entire network. True or False?

12. The IEEE _____ standard defines a local area network that provides cable-free data access at a rate of up to 2 Mbps for clients that are either mobile or in a fixed location.

    a. 802.3

    b. 802.21

    c. 802.11

    d. 802.3.1

13. Because all the IEEE WLAN features are isolated in the PHY and _____ layers, any network operating system or LAN application will run on a WLAN without any modification.

    a. MAC

    b. network

    c. PLCP

    d. PMD

14. The Physical Layer Convergence Procedure (PLCP) standards for 802.11b are based only on _____ spread spectrum.

    a. frequency hopping

    b. QAM

    c. direct sequence

    d. BPSK

15. A PLCP frame is made up of three parts, which are the preamble, the header, and the _____.

    a. error correction

    b. CRC

    c. SIFS

    d. data

16. The PLCP frame preamble and header are always transmitted at _____ Mbps.

    a. 2

    b. 5.5

    c. 1

    d. 11

17. The method used in 802.11 to implement CSMA/CA is based on _____.

    a. DSSS

    b. DCF

    c. FHSS

    d. PCF

18. IEEE 802.11 operates in _____ mode, and each frame must be acknowledged.

    a. ACK

    b. FDMA

    c. half-duplex

    d. full-duplex

19. If the AP does not send the SSID of the WLAN in the beacon, client devices can still obtain the SSID by _____.

    a. sending an associate request frame

    b. transmitting an SSID request frame

    c. sending a probe frame

    d. transmitting a special data frame

20. In PCF, the client devices cannot transmit unless _____.

    a. the WLAN is operating in peer-to-peer mode

    b. the AP sends an ACK frame

    c. the AP sends data first

    d. the client is "polled" by the AP

Hands-On Projects

HANDS-ON PROJECTS

Project 7-1

In this project, you will configure a wireless network connection in Microsoft Windows 7. As usual, there is more than one way to accomplish this task. Windows 7 provides a built-in tool called "WLAN AutoConfig," which is designed to make it much simpler for the average computer user to connect to a wireless network. WLAN AutoConfig can be used to connect to WLANs in most homes, offices, hotspots, as well as hotels. The procedure presented in this project is generic and can be used regardless of the type or make of computer you have, provided that you are running the Windows 7 operating system. Setting up a connection to an Enterprise network, which typically uses a separate authentication server, is more complex and will not be covered in this exercise.

Manufacturers almost always provide WLAN utilities with their hardware, and in Windows you can choose to configure a WLAN with either the WLAN AutoConfig tool or the WLAN NIC manufacturer's utility. The manufacturer's utility often has additional features, but it can be more complex to use. For this project, you will be configuring an ad hoc WLAN. You will need two computers equipped with wireless NICs.

1. Log in to both computers as administrator or to an account with administrator privileges. Windows will not allow you to complete any of the following steps unless you are the system administrator or your account has administrator privileges.

2. Click the **Windows Start** button on the lower-left corner of the Windows taskbar, and then click **Control Panel** on the right-hand side of the Start menu.

3. In Control Panel, search for and click **Network and Sharing Center**.

4. When you set up an ad hoc network, your computer is not connected to a router or DHCP server that can provide you with an IP address. Because of this, you will need to configure a static IP address. You will also not have access to the Internet, only to shared files on the other computer(s) connected to the same ad hoc WLAN.

5. Once you have configured unique IP addresses on the WLAN NIC of each computer, return to the Network and Sharing Center window. Click **Manage wireless networks** on the menu in the left column of the window. If you have WLAN connections already configured and your NIC is enabled, you will see a list like the one shown in Figure 7-18.

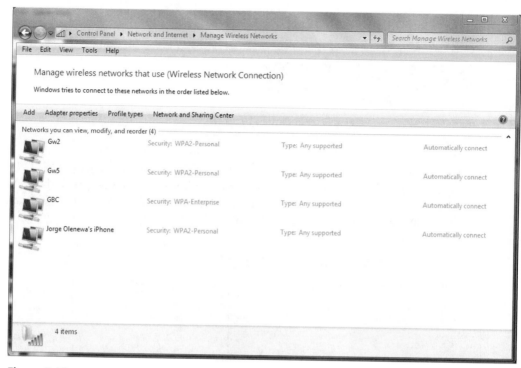

Figure 7-18 Managing wireless networks in Windows 7

Source: Microsoft Windows 7

6. Click **Add** in the toolbar above the network list area, then click **Create** and **ad hoc network** on the pop-up window.

7. Read the information on the "Setup a wireless ad hoc network" window that opens, then click **Next**. Type a unique name for this network, one that is not being used by any other students working on this project at the same time. Remember that the network name is the SSID of the network and is case sensitive.

8. Under "Security type," click the drop-down box and select **No authentication (Open)**.

9. Click the checkbox next to "Save this network," then click **Next**. Check the parameters of your network, then click the **Close** button. You should now see your network at the top of the list in the "Manage wireless networks" window. On the right-hand side of the ad hoc network entry you just created, you will see that the network is configured to "Manually connect." Perform the same steps on the other computer(s) you want to connect to your ad hoc WLAN.

10. If your ad hoc WLAN appeared at the top of the list in Step 9, once you finish configuring the second computer, they should connect automatically. To check this, click the Windows network icon located on the far right-hand side of your Windows taskbar. (If your taskbar is located at either side of your computer screen, the icon will appear at the bottom.) This is shown in Figure 7-19.

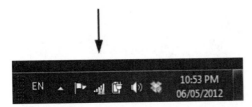

Figure 7-19 Windows network icon (indicated by arrow)

Source: Microsoft Windows 7

11. You will see a list of the networks available. Your ad hoc network name should be at the top of the list, and it should say "Connected." If it is not connected, click the ad hoc network entry and click the **Connect** button. The connected ad hoc network should look similar to the one highlighted by the ellipse in Figure 7-20, but with your own SSID.

Figure 7-20 Network connections list

Source: Microsoft Windows 7

12. To test the connection to the other computer, click the **Windows Start** button on the left-hand side of the Start bar and type **cmd** in the "Search programs and files" text box to open a command window. At the command prompt, type **ping** and the IP address of the WLAN NIC of the other computer you are using for this project, then

press Enter. You should receive three or four successful ping replies from the other computer, as shown in Figure 7-21. (Remember that your IP addresses must be unique and may be different than the one shown in the figure.)

```
C:\Users\jolenewa>ping 192.168.1.12

Pinging 192.168.1.12 with 32 bytes of data:
Reply from 192.168.1.12: bytes=32 time=1ms TTL=64
Reply from 192.168.1.12: bytes=32 time=1ms TTL=64
Reply from 192.168.1.12: bytes=32 time=1ms TTL=64
Reply from 192.168.1.12: bytes=32 time=3ms TTL=64

Ping statistics for 192.168.1.12:
    Packets: Sent = 4, Received = 4, Lost = 0 (0% loss),
Approximate round trip times in milli-seconds:
    Minimum = 1ms, Maximum = 3ms, Average = 1ms
```

Figure 7-21 Ping replies

Source: Microsoft Windows 7

13. Be sure to return the IP address settings to **Obtain an IP address automatically** and delete the ad hoc entry you just created from the "Manage wireless networks" window.

HANDS-ON PROJECTS

Project 7-2

In this project, you will manually configure a wireless residential gateway, which is more commonly known as a wireless router or broadband router, to create a WLAN. The device used in this project is a Linksys WRT54G, but you can use any model available to you and adapt the following instructions. The settings you will configure are very similar among different manufacturers' products, and even when different names are used for the parameters, they are usually easy to figure out. Remember that a wireless residential gateway includes an AP, a router, firewall, and a network switch, and in some cases it also includes a built-in DSL or cable modem.

1. Obtain a wireless residential gateway from your instructor, or you can use your own.

2. If the device has external antennas, make sure they are positioned vertically; and if they use a screw-in connector, make sure the antennas are finger-tight and do not fall to the horizontal position again. Never turn on a wireless device equipped with external antennas without first having them connected and tightened up. The absence of a proper load at the output of the transmitter can damage the circuit. In addition, despite the very low power levels of most WLAN devices, you are strongly advised to never touch the antennas when the device is turned on as this may represent a health risk.

3. Connect an RJ-45 Ethernet crossover patch cable to one of the switch ports in the back of the device. Note that one port is separated from the others and is usually marked "WAN." Do not connect anything to the WAN port. Plug the other end of the cable into an Ethernet port on your computer.

4. Plug in the power adapter and connect it to the back of your AP or broadband router.

5. Make sure the Ethernet adapter on your computer is configured to obtain an IP address automatically.

6. Open a Web browser. In the address line, type `http://192.168.1.1` for a Linksys device. Other manufacturers' devices may use a different address. Consult the manual or download it from the Internet for the device you have.

7. At the login prompt, leave the user name blank and type `admin` in the password field. The Linksys setup page will appear. For this project, you will not use an Internet connection. You can leave all the fields in the main Setup page in their default settings (see Figure 7-22).

Figure 7-22 Linksys WRT54G main Setup page

Source: Linksys

8. Click the **Wireless** tab to display the wireless setup page.

If you are setting up more than one Linksys AP or broadband router in the same or an adjacent lab or classroom, make sure you select a different channel for each of the devices. Recall that to avoid interference, you can only use channels 1, 6, and 11.

9. Leave "Mode" as Mixed. Change the SSID to the same one you used in Project 7-1. Click **Save Settings**. A page should appear indicating that your settings are

successful. Click **Continue** and you will be returned to the Wireless setup page (see Figure 7-23).

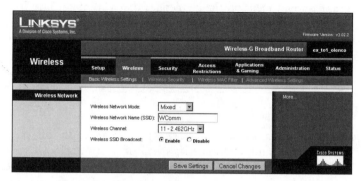

Figure 7-23 Wireless Setup page on the Linksys WRT54G

Source: Linksys

10. On the computer, click the network icon on the right-hand side of the Start bar to view the wireless networks detected.

11. Click the SSID you set up on the gateway and then click the **Connect** button. Windows may display an information dialog box stating that you are connecting to an unsecured network. If so, click **Connect Anyway**. Windows will display a dialog box with a progress bar and the text "Connecting to *<your SSID>*." If the connection is successful, Windows 7 will close the dialog box and not give you any additional indication other than a tiny icon on the Start bar that shows five bars.

12. You can verify the connection using the same procedures described in Steps 11 and 12 of Project 7-1.

Real-World Exercises

Exercise 7-1

A hotspot is a public place—such as a train, bus station, coffee shop, or restaurant—that offers (usually) free Internet access to its customers. Using the Internet, search for hotspots by accessing the Web sites for various nationwide cellular phone companies, such as AT&T or Sprint. Alternatively, you can search the local media Web sites and local Internet service provider (ISP) sites. If you have access to a notebook computer, wireless-enabled smartphone, or tablet computer and it is equipped with a WLAN interface, once you locate a hotspot, try to visit the site and get a connection to the Internet. If you do not have access to the Internet but you can either telephone the provider or visit the hotspot location, interview the staff at the location and write a one-page report describing how the wireless access is provided. What steps did you have to go through to get a connection? For how long was the connection available? Was there a cost associated with accessing the Internet? How many people use the service daily? Were there any limitations? Who provides technical support for the site?

Exercise 7-2

Using the Internet, research wireless LAN applications. Compile a list of at least five WLAN applications that you had not thought about before, and write a one-paragraph description for each one. The paragraph should mention the challenges that you might face if you were asked to provide support for such an implementation. If possible, contact users of the new application and ask them about their particular experiences with the WLAN implementation. Add this information to your report.

Challenge Case Project

CASE PROJECTS

How do you measure a wireless network's performance? In this project, you will test your network and determine its speed of data transfer. Keep in mind, though, that most wireless networks communicate in half-duplex mode, so the data rate reported by the operating system does not reflect the maximum data rate the network is capable of.

There are many network performance-testing tools available on the Web. Begin by opening your favorite browser and, using the search engine of your choice, typing in the question "How do you measure a wireless network's performance?" Browse the results that appear, then download and install a free or trial version of one or more network-testing tools. Run as many of the following tests as possible, using Wi-Fi-enabled devices that are available to you, while copying a large file (over 10 MB) from one device to another:

- Create and test an ad hoc link between two devices.
- Test from a wired to a wireless device, and vice-versa.
- Test with more than one pair of devices transmitting via the same AP.
- Run the tests in both directions.
- Try to test with both a clear channel and one that is already in use in the same area. Use inSSIDer from *metageek.net* to view available channels and signal strength.

Carefully record your results for each test, then write a one-page report detailing each of the results, the tools and devices you used, and your conclusions.

chapter 8

High-Speed WLANs and WLAN Security

After reading this chapter and completing the exercises, you will be able to:

- Describe how IEEE 802.11a networks function and how they differ from 802.11 networks
- Explain how 802.11g enhances 802.11b networks
- Discuss the 802.11n, 802.11ac, and 802.11ad amendments to the standard
- Explain how the use of wireless bridges and wireless switches expands the functionality and management of WLANs
- List the security features and issues with IEEE 802.11 networks

Higher data rates and lower costs have made 802.11 WLANs very competitive with wired networks, and corporations continue to deploy WLANs as a viable alternative. In terms of speed, WLANs have come a long way since the original IEEE 802.11 WLAN standard, established in 1997, offered speeds of only 1 and 2 Mbps. Today's WLANs can operate at data rates of 1 Gbps and above.

In 1999, the IEEE approved the 802.11b standard, which added two higher speeds—5.5 Mbps and 11 Mbps—to the 802.11 standard. At that time, IEEE also issued the **IEEE 802.11a** standard, which offered even higher speeds. IEEE 802.11a has a maximum speed of 54 Mbps and also supports transmission at 48 Mbps, 36 Mbps, 24 Mbps, 18 Mbps, 12 Mbps, 9 Mbps, and 6 Mbps. 802.11a WLANs quickly became very attractive to users because the speed of transmission represented a significant increase over that of 802.11b systems. In addition, because of more bandwidth, 802.11a offered an additional five channels, which gave it a clear advantage over 802.11b.

IEEE 802.11a

Although the IEEE ratified 802.11b and 802.11a at the same time (in 1999), 802.11b products started to appear almost immediately, whereas 802.11a products did not arrive until late 2001. 802.11a products came to the market later because of technical issues and, at least initially, the high cost of implementation.

The 802.11a standard maintains the same medium access control (MAC) layer functions as 802.11b WLANs, with practically all differences confined to the Physical layer. It achieves its increase in speed and flexibility over 802.11b through the use of its multiplexing technique and through a more efficient error-correction scheme. These factors are described in detail in the following sections.

This book refers to the amendments to the standards by the lower-case letter appended to the end of the standard number (e.g., IEEE 802.11n) even though the IEEE, when an amendment is ratified, now incorporates the content into the latest revision of the standard documentation and appends the year in which the work was completed (e.g., IEEE 802.11-2009, which includes the 802.11n amendment).

U-NII Frequency Band

Recall that the 802.11b standard uses one part of the unlicensed Industrial, Scientific, and Medical (ISM) band for its transmissions and specifies 14 frequencies that can be used, beginning at 2.412 GHz and increasing by increments of .005 GHz. IEEE 802.11a uses another unlicensed band, the Unlicensed National Information Infrastructure (U-NII). The U-NII band is intended for devices that provide short-range, high-speed wireless digital communications. Table 8-1 compares ISM and U-NII bands available for use in WLANs.

Unlicensed Band	Frequency Bands	WLAN Standard	Total Bandwidth
Industrial, Scientific, and Medical (ISM)	2.4–2.4835 GHz 5.725–5.875 GHz	802.11b, 802.11g, 802.11n 802.11n	83.5 MHz 150 MHz
Unlicensed National Information Infrastructure (U-NII)	5.15–5.25 GHz 5.25–5.35 GHz 5.47–5.725 GHz 5.725–5.825 GHz	802.11a, 802.11n, 802.11ac	100 MHz 100 MHz 255 MHz 100 MHz

Table 8-1 ISM vs. U-NII

© Cengage Learning 2014

The U.S. Federal Communications Commission (FCC) has segmented the total 555 MHz of the U-NII spectrum into four bands. Each band has a maximum power limit. These bands and their maximum power outputs as per the 802.11 standard are shown in Table 8-2.

In 2008, the IEEE ratified the 802.11y amendment, which extended operation of 802.11a to the licensed 3.7 GHz band. This band offers increased power limits, which allows radios to achieve a maximum range of up to 16,400 feet (5,000 meters), but an FCC license is required to operate in this band.

U-NII Band	Frequency (GHz)	Maximum Power Output (mW)
U-NII-1	5.15–5.25	40
U-NII-2	5.25–5.35	200
U-NII-2 Extended	5.47–5.725	200
U-NII-3	5.725–5.825	800

Table 8-2 U-NII bands

© Cengage Learning 2014

The U-NII-3 band is only approved for outdoor use and is deployed most often for building-to-building, point-to-point wireless connections using directional antennas.

Outside the United States, parts of the 5 GHz band are allocated to users and technologies other than WLANs, and the bands may have different widths and power limitations. When you configure computers or APs that will be used during business trips or will be deployed in other countries, it is always wise to check the limitations and ensure that the local regulations will be followed. To automatically adjust power requirements and meet the limitations in other countries, most enterprise-class 802.11 equipment manufacturers require that you select the country in which you are going to install the equipment before it enables the radios. Channel availability as well as the maximum transmission power for different channels are then set automatically.

Although the U-NII band is segmented, the total bandwidth available for IEEE 802.11a WLANs using U-NII is almost seven times that available for 802.11b. The ISM band offers only 83.5 MHz of spectrum in the 2.4 GHz range, whereas the U-NII band offers 555 MHz.

Channel Allocation in 802.11a

A second reason for the higher performance of an 802.11a WLAN is increased channel allocation. Remember that in 802.11b the available frequency spectrum (2.412–2.484 GHz) is divided into 14 channels and that only 11 of those channels are available in North America. The center points of each channel—2.412 GHz, 2.417 GHz, 2.422 GHz, and so on—are the frequencies at which the transmissions actually occur, before spreading. IEEE 802.11 requires a 25 MHz passband, so only three non-overlapping channels are available for simultaneous operation: channels 1, 6, and 11. This is shown in Figure 8-1.

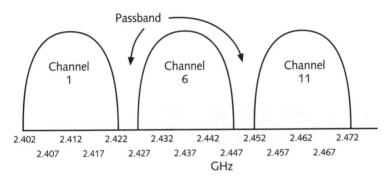

Approximate frequency domain representation of total bandwidth occupied by each 802.11b channel

Figure 8-1 802.11b channels

© Cengage Learning 2014

In 802.11a, eight frequency channels can be used simultaneously in U-NII-1 (5.15–5.25 GHz) and U-NII-2 (5.25–5.35 GHz). When using newer-model equipment that can also transmit in the U-NII-2 Extended band, up to 23 channels are available. Within each frequency channel, there is a 20-MHz-wide channel that is divided into 52 subcarrier frequencies, with each subcarrier being 300 KHz wide. This is shown in Figure 8-2.

The channel numbers in the 5 GHz band are the result of a mathematical formula, whereas in the 2.4 GHz band, channels numbered 1 to 11 are arbitrarily assigned.

With only three channels available in the ISM band, it follows that a maximum of three APs can be installed within a radius of roughly 300 feet. Using 802.11g APs, for example, this would provide a maximum data throughput of only 162 Mbps (54 Mbps × 3) spread evenly across the three APs.

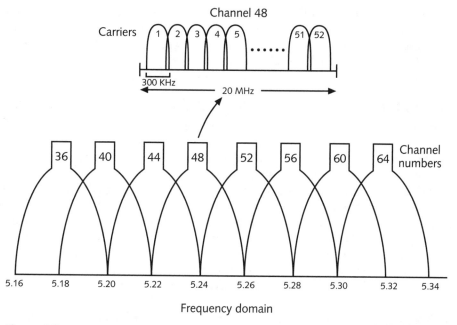

Figure 8-2 802.11a channels

© *Cengage Learning 2014*

Using 802.11a instead of 802.11g, up to 23 channels are available, depending on whether the equipment can transmit in the U-NII-2 Extended band. Because there are more available channels than in the ISM band, additional APs can be added, providing up to 1,242 Mbps (23 × 54 Mbps) of total throughput. A comparison of co-locating three APs in 802.11b versus co-locating eight APs in 802.11a is shown in Figure 8-3.

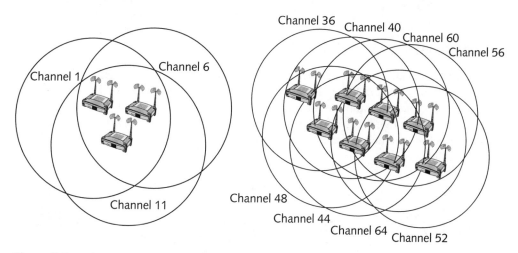

Figure 8-3 Co-locating APs in 802.11b vs. 802.11a

© *Cengage Learning 2014*

When multiple APs are used, you can configure them to allow only certain user's devices to associate. This enables you to support a larger number of users per area. Using technologies such as wireless controllers (discussed later) can offer load-balancing methods to automatically distribute clients across multiple channels so that one AP doesn't get overcrowded when others are available. Another advantage of having more channels available is that if a nearby WLAN is using the same channel as you are, you have more options and can set your AP to use a different channel to eliminate the interference.

Orthogonal Frequency Division Multiplexing

In Chapter 3, you learned about multipath distortion, which occurs when the receiving device gets the same signal from several different directions at different times, due to signal reflections, diffraction, or scattering. Even though the receiving device may have already received the complete transmission, it must still wait until all reflections are received. If the receiver does not wait until all reflections are received, some of the signals that arrive later may spread into the next transmission because the reflected signals traveled a longer path and, as a result, have been delayed. Increasing the data transmission speed through denser and more complex modulation schemes tends to make multipath distortion worse and force the receiver to wait even longer before it gets the reflected signals. The required waiting time effectively puts a limit on the overall speed of the WLAN. With a single carrier modulation radio technology, the maximum data transmission rate falls between 10 and 20 Mbps.

A baseband processor, or equalizer, is required in 802.11b systems to unravel the delayed radio frequency signals as they are received.

IEEE 802.11a solves the multipath distortion problem by using a multiplexing technique called orthogonal frequency-division multiplexing (OFDM). Its primary function is to split a high-speed digital signal into several slower signals running in parallel.

OFDM is also the technology used for consumer-based digital subscriber line (DSL) service, which provides home Internet access over standard telephone lines at speeds ranging from 256 Kbps to 16 Mbps.

Instead of sending one long stream of data across a single channel, OFDM radios transmit the data bits in parallel, at lower speeds, across several narrower frequency channels. The receiving device recombines the signals received in each individual frequency channel and rebuilds the frame. By using these parallel transmission channels, OFDM can combine several lower-speed channels to send data at higher speeds. This is shown in Figure 8-4.

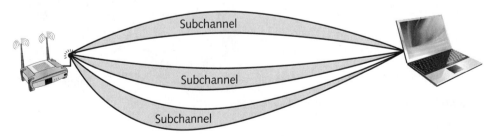

Figure 8-4 Transmitting on multiple subcarriers simultaneously
© Cengage Learning 2014

Although it may seem contradictory, OFDM breaks the 802.11b data-rate limit by transmitting data at a slower bit rate than 802.11b does. OFDM avoids problems caused by multipath distortion by sending the bits slowly enough that any delayed copies (multipath reflections) are late by a much smaller amount of time than those sent in 802.11b transmissions. This means that the network does not have to wait as long for the reflections to arrive at the receiver, thus the total throughput is actually increased. With OFDM, in other words, the total amount of data sent in parallel over a given unit of time is greater and the time spent waiting for reflections to arrive is less than with a single-carrier transmission. A comparison between the two systems is shown in Figure 8-5.

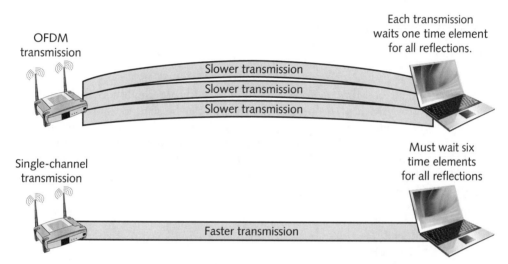

Figure 8-5 Comparison of OFDM and single-channel transmission

© Cengage Learning 2014

In 802.11a, OFDM uses 48 of the 52 subcarriers for data. Data is modulated on to each of these 48 subcarriers using simpler modulation schemes, which are also easier to decode at the receiver. The remaining four subcarriers are used for monitoring the signal quality and correcting timing errors during transmission.

The modulation techniques used to encode the data vary depending on the speed. At 6 Mbps, phase shift keying (PSK) is used (see Chapter 2). The change in the starting point of the cycle varies depending on whether a 0 or a 1 bit is being transmitted. PSK can encode 125 Kbps of data per each of the 48 subcarriers, resulting in a 6,000 Kbps (125 Kbps × 48), or a 6 Mbps data rate. (You may wish to review the waveform shown in Figure 2-29.)

Whereas PSK has only two possible changes in the starting point of a wave, allowing 1 bit to be transmitted at a time, quadrature phase shift keying (QPSK) has four possible changes in the starting point of a wave, allowing it to transmit 2 bits per symbol (see Chapter 2), as shown in Figure 8-6. QPSK can double the amount of data encoded over PSK to 250 Kbps per subcarrier, which produces a 12 Mbps (250 Kbps × 48) data rate.

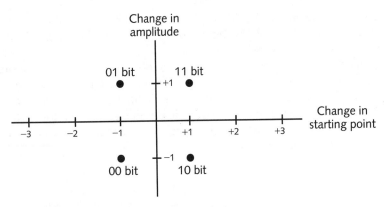

Figure 8-6 Quadrature amplitude modulation

© Cengage Learning 2014

Transmitting at 24 Mbps requires a 16-level quadrature amplitude modulation (16-QAM) technique. 16-QAM has 16 different signals that can be sent, as shown in Figure 8-7. Each group of bits modulated into one signal change in a carrier is called a **symbol**, which is also referred to as a baud. Whereas QPSK transmits 2 bits per symbol, 16-QAM can transmit 4 bits per symbol. For example, to transmit the bits 1110, QPSK would send 11 and then 10 by modifying the phase and amplitude. 16-QAM would only send one signal (1110). 16-QAM can encode 500 Kbps per subcarrier.

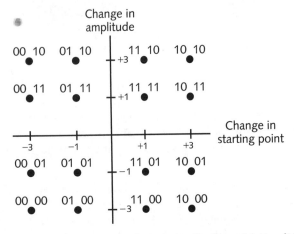

Figure 8-7 16-level quadrature amplitude modulation (16-QAM)

© Cengage Learning 2014

A data rate of 54 Mbps is achieved by using 64-level quadrature amplitude modulation (64-QAM), which can transmit at a rate of 1.125 Mbps over each of the 48 subcarriers (see Figure 8-8).

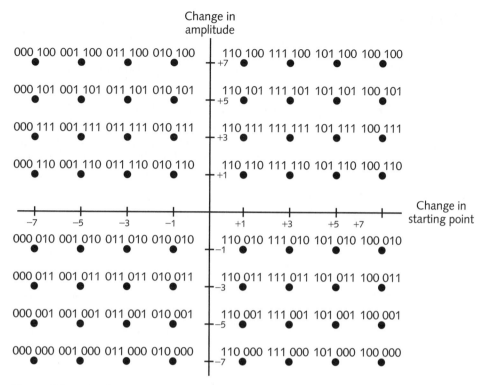

Figure 8-8 64-level quadrature amplitude modulation (64-QAM)

© Cengage Learning 2014

Hardware developers cannot increase the complexity of the modulation on the subcarriers beyond the maximum 54 Mbps rate because of the maximum amount of noise allowed. Transmitting at higher speeds requires additional subcarriers and a wider bandwidth.

Error Correction in 802.11a

IEEE 802.11a also handles errors differently than 802.11b. The number of errors is significantly reduced due to the nature of 802.11a transmissions. Because transmissions are sent over parallel subcarriers, radio interference from outside sources is minimized. Instead of the interference impacting the entire data stream, it generally affects only one subcarrier. IEEE 802.11a uses a technique called forward error correction (FEC), which transmits extra bits per byte of data. These extra bits allow the receiver to recover (through sophisticated algorithms) data bits that may be lost during the transmission. This can eliminate a lot of retransmissions when errors occur, which saves time and increases the total throughput of the WLAN. A full discussion of FEC is beyond the scope of this book, but it is widely employed in many modern digital communications systems.

The extra bits transmitted when using FEC means that transmission overhead is increased, but because of its higher speed, 802.11a can accommodate the FEC overhead with a negligible impact on performance.

802.11a PHY Layer

The 802.11a standard made changes only to the Physical layer (PHY layer) of the original 802.11 and 802.11b standards; the MAC layer remains the same. Recall that the basic purpose of the IEEE PHY layer is to send and receive the signal from the network.

The 802.11a PHY layer is divided into two parts: the Physical Medium Dependent (PMD) sublayer and the Physical Layer Convergence Procedure (PLCP) sublayer. The PMD sublayer defines the characteristics of the wireless medium as well as the method for transmitting and receiving data through that medium. The PLCP sublayer reformats the data received from the MAC layer (for transmission) into a frame that the PMD sublayer can transmit. The PLCP is also the sublayer that determines when the medium is free so that data can be transmitted.

The PLCP for 802.11a is based on OFDM instead of direct sequence spread spectrum (DSSS). An example of a PLCP frame is shown in Figure 8-9.

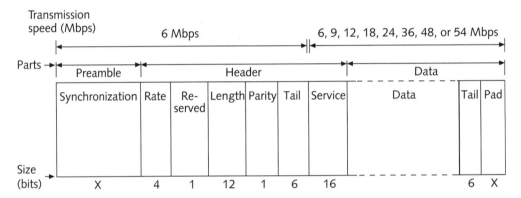

Figure 8-9   802.11a PLCP frame

© Cengage Learning 2014

The frame is made up of three parts: the preamble, the header, and the data. The preamble allows the receiving device to prepare for the rest of the frame. The header provides information about the frame itself—such as the length of the current frame. The data portion of the PLCP frame is the information that is to be actually transmitted, which is essentially the MAC frame. Here are descriptions of the fields in the PLCP frame:

Synchronization—Consists of 10 repetitions of a short training sequence signal and two repetitions of a long training sequence signal. The purpose of these signals is to synchronize the transmitter and receiver in both time and frequency. The Synchronization field is transmitted in 16 microseconds.

Rate—This field, which is 4 bits long, specifies the speed at which the Data field will be transmitted.

Reserved—Kept available by the standard for future use.

Length—Contains the value that indicates the length of the Data field, from 1 to 4095 octets.

Parity—This single bit is used to check for errors in the previous fields.

Tail (header)—Indicates the end of the header. All six bits are set to 0.

Service—The first seven bits are used to initialize part of the transmitter and receiver circuits and are set to 0; the remaining nine bits are reserved for future use and are also set to 0. The Service field is part of the header but is transmitted at the same rate as the Data field.

Data—The actual data to be transmitted is contained in this field. The length of the Data field is from 1 to 4095 octets.

Tail (Data)—Indicates the end of the Data field. All six bits are set to 0.

Pad—The IEEE standard specifies that the number of bits in the Data field must be a multiple of 48, 96, 192, or 288. If necessary, the length of the Data field may need to be extended with padding bits to match this requirement.

802.11a WLANs are being deployed in areas that demand higher transmission speeds, greater throughput, or a larger number of users. The disadvantage of 802.11a networks is that they have a shorter range of coverage due to the higher signal attenuation in the 5 GHz band as well as to the lower power limit of U-NII-1. An 802.11a WLAN has a range of up to approximately 225 feet, compared to up to 375 feet for an 802.11b WLAN. Of course, this depends upon a number of factors, such as walls and other obstacles that can affect the RF transmission.

IEEE 802.11g

The tremendous success of the IEEE 802.11b standard shortly after its release prompted the IEEE to reexamine the 802.11b and 802.11a standards to determine if a third, intermediate standard could be developed. This best-of-both-worlds approach preserves the stable and widely accepted features of 802.11b but increases the data transfer rates to that of 802.11a. The **IEEE 802.11g** standard, which was published in June 2003, specifies that 802.11g operates in the same frequency band as 802.11b and not the higher frequency band used by 802.11a.

802.11g PHY Layer The PHY layer for 802.11g basically follows the specifications for 802.11b, with changes (described next) for data rates between 1 and 11 Mbps. As with 802.11a, no changes were required to the MAC layer of the 802.11g standard. The standard specifies two mandatory transmission modes along with two optional modes.

The first mandatory transmission mode is the one used by 802.11b; it supports data rates of 1 Mbps, 2 Mbps, 5.5 Mbps, and 11 Mbps. The second mandatory transmission mode uses OFDM like 802.11a but in the 2.4 GHz frequency band used by 802.11b. The 802.11g standard divides each of the three usable channels in the ISM band into the same number of subcarriers, as 802.11a does (48 data subcarriers and four pilot subcarriers), and provides the same data rates. However, the number of non-overlapping channels available for 802.11g (i.e., three) is the same as the number available for 802.11b, compared with the 23 channels available for 802.11a.

An additional coordination method is required to allow legacy devices (802.11 and 802.11b) to participate in the WLAN. Using this method, which is called **CTS-to-self**, an 802.11g client transmits a clear-to-send frame before initiating an OFDM transmission. Remember that a clear-to-send frame includes a field containing the number of time slots required to send a frame of data. Because legacy clients do not "understand" OFDM, one or more of them could potentially attempt to initiate a transmission using DSSS (802.11) or CCK (802.11b). By transmitting a clear-to-send using DSSS, an 802.11g device effectively prevents any legacy device from initiating a transmission before the end of the 802.11g device's OFDM transmission.

There are two optional transmission modes. The first mode uses PBCC (Packet Binary Convolutional Coding), can transmit at 22 or 33 Mbps, and is capable of supporting 802.11b. The second, known as DSSS-OFDM, is a combination mode that uses the standard DSSS preamble of 802.11b so that both APs and clients are able to understand the beginning of the transmissions and then remain quiet while a frame is being transmitted, regardless of whether they understand the modulation and coding. The data portion of the frame, in this mode, is transmitted using OFDM. This mode does not require any additional coordination, such as a CTS-to-self, because all devices will be able to receive and decode the full contents of the frame headers and therefore will not initiate a transmission while another device is transmitting using OFDM.

To be fully compliant with 802.11a and 802.11g at the higher data rates, a device must be able to transmit only at 6, 9, 12, and 24 Mbps. Data rates of 36, 48, and 54 Mbps are not required for compliance with the standards.

There are two other important differences among the 802.11g, 802.11a, and 802.11b standards; they are related to signal timing. First, 802.11g specifies that any time a device is transmitting at a higher rate than 802.11b, a 6-microsecond quiet time (no transmission) is included at the end of the data portion of every frame to allow additional processing time for the receiver to decode the data. This requirement accommodates both 802.11b-only devices and devices that can transmit at higher data rates. In 802.11a, this additional time is not required because the standard does not have to maintain backward compatibility with any other standard.

The other difference has to do with short interframe space (SIFS) timing. In Chapter 7, you learned that 802.11b time slots are 20 microseconds and the SIFS time is 10 microseconds. 802.11g maintains the same time slot duration; however, the SIFS duration is affected by the addition of the quiet time. Therefore, when data is being transmitted at rates above 11 Mbps, the SIFS cannot begin until the quiet time is completed, effectively extending the SIFS to 16 microseconds. This change in the SIFS affects the performance of 802.11g, meaning that although it can transmit at 54 Mbps, the overall performance is lower than that of 802.11a. Note that when the network is supporting only 802.11g devices, the standard allows the time slot to be reduced to 9 microseconds instead of 20 microseconds, which removes the performance difference between the 802.11a and 802.11g standards. Figure 8-10 shows the format of an 802.11g PLCP frame.

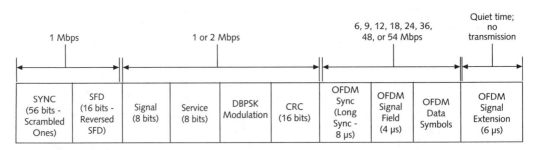

Figure 8-10   802.11g PLCP frame

© Cengage Learning 2014

The PLCP frame formats used in 802.11g are the same as for 802.11b. For transmission at 54 Mbps, the PHY layer follows the same general specifications as for 802.11a. Note, however, that when 802.11b and 802.11g devices share the same network, the standard defines how the frame header is transmitted at 1 or 2 Mbps using DSSS, for compatibility with 802.11b devices. If the communicating device is 802.11g-capable, the transmission changes to OFDM for the data portion of the frame. This is shown in Figure 8-11.

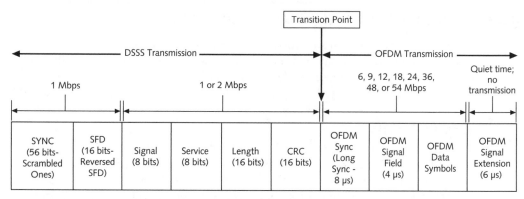

Figure 8-11 802.11b (DSSS) to 802.11g (OFDM) transition after the frame header

© *Cengage Learning 2014*

The optional 22 Mbps rate is achieved by using the PBCC encoding method. PBCC uses a 256-state code (the spreading code) to send 8 bits per transmission symbol. To achieve the data rate of 33 Mbps using PBCC, the 802.11g standard specifies a change in the clock rate used to transmit the chips from 11 MHz to 16.5 MHz. The preamble is transmitted with an 11 MHz clock (at 1 or 2 Mbps), and the change is accomplished in a 1-microsecond-long clock switch section of the PLCP frame, as shown in Figure 8-12.

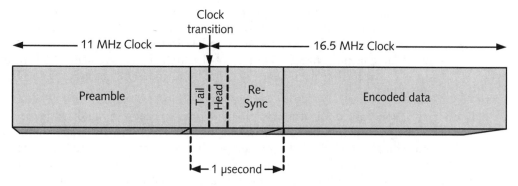

Figure 8-12 Clock switching during transition from 22 Mbps to 33 Mbps

© *Cengage Learning 2014*

The tail is 3 clock cycles at 11 Mchip/s, and the head is 3 clock cycles at 16.5 Msymbols/s (QPSK). The resync is 9 clock cycles at 16.5 Msymbols/s. The total clock switching time (tail, head, and resync) is 1 ms. The tail bits are 1 1 1, the head bits are 0 0 0, and the resync bits are 1 0 0 0 1 1 1 0 1. The modulation used for transmission at 22 or 33 Mbps is binary phase shift keying (BPSK), which is essentially the same modulation as PSK, which you learned about in Chapter 2. Only two phase changes are used to represent either a 1 or a 0. The phase change is always made with reference to the phase of the signal received immediately before the current one.

IEEE 802.11n and Other Amendments

As you have realized by now, work on dynamic standards such as those for WLANs never ends. User demand for faster and more reliable WLANs suggests that the IEEE will continue to enhance these technologies for the foreseeable future. This section covers some of the latest amendments and how they differ from the other WLAN technologies discussed earlier.

IEEE 802.11n

The IEEE began working on the 802.11n amendment in 2004, shortly after the ratification of 802.11g in 2003. Several other amendments were introduced in the 2007 revision of the 802.11 standard, but it was clear that 54 Mbps was not enough for the 802.11 standard to compete effectively with wired networks. The work on 802.11n became the most widely discussed enhancement to this WLAN technology. A few consumer equipment manufacturers began introducing devices based on the first draft of the standard. Before we continue discussing this technology, it is important for you to understand that 802.11n is an extremely complex topic that could easily fill an entire book. This section will provide you with an introduction, but it is not intended to offer complete coverage of 802.11n.

The excitement about this new technology reached a high point when the Wi-Fi Alliance began certifying equipment based on the second draft of the amendment in 2007, roughly two years before the members of the IEEE ratified the standard. Some enterprise-class equipment manufacturers also began shipping compatible equipment and recommending it to their customers while offering guarantees that if any other changes were introduced before ratification, their equipment would require only a software upgrade to meet the standard. Wi-Fi-certified products must also support Wi-Fi multimedia (WMM) capabilities, including quality-of-service (QoS) as well as WPA and WPA2 security mechanisms, all of which are discussed later in this chapter. Draft 2 of the 802.11n amendment—high throughput (HT), as it is called in that document—was finally ratified and released by the IEEE near the end of 2009.

In Chapter 3, you learned about multipath interference and how it can degrade the quality of a signal to the point where the SNR is so low the data can become corrupted and no longer understood by a receiver. HT utilizes a completely new approach to implementing the PHY layer. The 802.11n amendment uses multiple antennas along multiple radios in each device. This allows it to take advantage of multipath interference to actually increase the SNR, which results in an increase in the range and reliability of WLAN transmissions. Additional enhancements to the MAC layer, together with the changes to the PHY layer, help 802.11n achieve data rates that were not possible before.

Although the transmission techniques are somewhat different than those of previous versions of the standard, HT-capable devices are required to maintain backwards compatibility with 802.11b and 802.11g in the 2.4 GHz ISM band. A novel aspect of 802.11n is that it is also designed to work in the 5 GHz band; therefore, it is required to maintain backwards compatibility with 802.11a.

MIMO Technology Multiple-input and multiple-output (MIMO) technology is based on using multiple radios, both transmitters and receivers, as well as multiple antennas. Until its introduction in 802.11n, most devices employed a single radio with two antennas and supported a technique called **antenna diversity**, which increases a signal's range. With antenna diversity, the receiver senses which one of its two antennas is getting the strongest signal from the transmitter, and when it sends a response frame—an ACK, for example—it uses the antenna that received the strongest signal.

Instead of antenna diversity, 802.11n MIMO-capable devices use multiple radios, each with its own antenna, and they employ beamforming to virtually direct a transmission back to the device from which they just received a frame, thus increasing the transmitted signal's range. Multiple radios can also increase the throughput. Instead of transmitting a frame via a single radio, 802.11n MIMO-capable devices breakup a frame into multiple parts and transmit each one via a different radio. This is called **spatial multiplexing**. At the receiver end, the data is reassembled into a full PHY frame before being passed back to the MAC layer. Keep in mind that, for reliability reasons, it is always better, when possible, to have more receivers than transmitters. Figure 8-13 shows a graphical example of this concept.

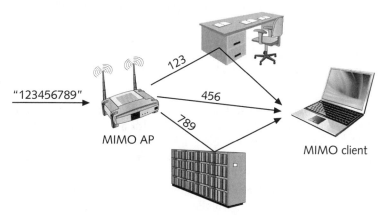

Figure 8-13 Spatial multiplexing sending multiple (spatial) streams of data

Source: Fluke Networks

The 802.11n amendment specifies the different radio configurations of multiple transmitters and receivers, up to a maximum of four transmitters and four receivers, for a maximum transmission speed of 600 Mbps. For example, a 2×3 (two-by-three) device has two transmitters and three receivers, whereas a 3×3 device has three transmitters and three receivers, and so on. Each transmitter sends a different spatial stream of data containing different parts of a frame. Figure 8-14 shows examples of 2×3 and 3×3 MIMO devices. Note that to take advantage of spatial multiplexing, the receiver and the transmitter need to have the same number of radios. The more radios a device has, the higher the cost as well as the higher the power consumption. Because of these two factors, few manufacturers have implemented devices beyond a 3×3 configuration.

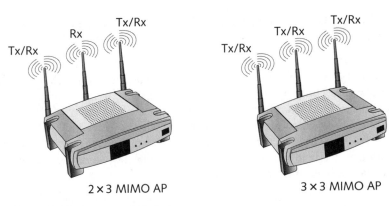

Figure 8-14 802.11n MIMO devices

© Cengage Learning 2014

Spatial multiplexing and beamforming can be combined to increase range and reliability of transmission. Both of these techniques rely on feedback information from the receiver, meaning that any two devices need to be able to evaluate each other's capabilities and wireless medium information—such as signal quality—and inform each other. This can be accomplished by the devices monitoring the medium and following up with an exchange of information within a data frame header or via the exchange of management frames.

Channel Configuration One of the ways 802.11n is able to achieve high data rates is by using more bandwidth in both the 2.4 GHz and 5 GHz bands. IEEE 802.11a and 802.11g each consume 20 MHz of bandwidth to transmit using OFDM; 802.11b uses about 22 MHz of bandwidth.

HT radios can support DSSS and OFDM in the ISM band, which means they can be configured to automatically use 20 MHz or 22 MHz of bandwidth and support communications with 802.11b and 802.11g devices. However, the higher speeds of up to 300 Mbps or 600 Mbps can only be achieved if the radios are configured to utilize 40 MHz of bandwidth. In the ISM 2.4 GHz band, this means that HT uses either channels 1 and 6 or channels 6 and 11, and this can result in excessive interference in channel 6 if more than one AP is in use or if channel 6 is already being used nearby, whether in an office building, a public hotspot network—such as a coffee shop—or a residential neighborhood.

The kind of interference that happens when two devices are using the same channel on a different BSS is called **co-channel interference**. Depending on how close the WLANs or the BSSs are, interference on channel 6 may prevent 802.11n devices from achieving their maximum data rates in the ISM band. The only viable solution in this case is to deploy equipment that works in the 5 GHz U-NII band. Keep in mind that, to conserve power, many different models of mobile devices are not able to make use of the 5 GHZ frequency band.

When communicating with other HT devices, 802.11n radios divide the frequency space into 56 subcarriers for 20 MHz of bandwidth and use four of them as pilot subcarriers. When using 40 MHz-wide channels and communicating with other 802.11n devices that are also capable of using the wider bandwidth, the radios divide the frequency space into 114 subcarriers and use six of them as pilot subcarriers. In essence, HT combines two 802.11 channels in either the 2.4 GHz or 5 GHz frequency band to allow it to carry more data. Figure 8-15 shows a graphical example of the channel bonding in 802.11n. Note how the channels overlap on channel 6 in the 2.4 GHz band when using 40 MHz wide channels.

Note also that both 802.11a and 802.11g use only one 20 MHz channel. In the 2.4 GHz band, there is approximately 5 MHz of frequency space between usable channels—channels 1, 6, and 11—that is left unused. This frequency space between the channels is called a **guard band**, and it helps prevent **adjacent channel interference**, which occurs when signals in two adjacent channels cause interference with each other. When 802.11 uses a 40 MHz channel, there is no need for the 5 MHz guard band. The additional frequency space allows for more subcarriers, and this also helps 802.11n achieve higher data rates in both the ISM and U-NII bands. Figure 8-15 shows a graphical example of channel bonding in 802.11n, which is when two channels are combined into one 40 MHz channel.

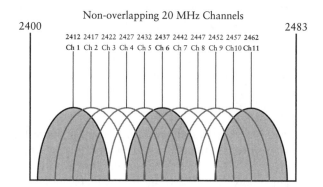

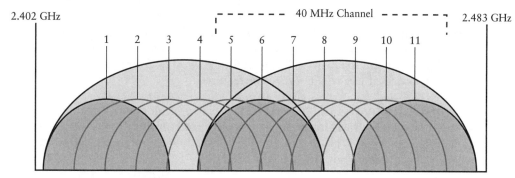

Figure 8-15 Channel bonding in 802.11n

Source: Fluke Networks

Guard Interval As was discussed in the "IEEE 802.11a" section, to transmit digital signals, data is modulated onto a carrier in either single bit streams or groups of bits called symbols. The more bits that are encoded in each symbol, the higher the data rate. In non-HT transmissions (compatible with 802.11a/g), because of multipath, a certain amount of delay is required at the end of every frame to allow all reflected signals to arrive at the receivers. This is called a **guard interval** (**GI**), and it prevents a new symbol from arriving at the receiver before the last multipath signal reaches the receiver's antenna, which can cause data corruption. This kind of data corruption is called **intersymbol interference** (**ISI**). Although it normally takes a maximum of 200 nanoseconds for all the multipath signals to arrive at the receiver's antenna, the GI, in order to prevent data corruption, should always be two to four times larger than that. In 802.11a/g, the GI is set at 800 nanoseconds.

The 802.11n amendment specifies an 800-nanosecond GI for compatibility with 802.11a/g, but it optionally specifies a 400-nanosecond GI to reduce the symbol time and increase data rates by about 10 percent. When using the shorter GI, ISI can still occur, and the resulting data corruption means that frames would have to be retransmitted, which has the effect of reducing throughput.

Modulation and Coding Scheme   Because of the multiple factors involved in determining the data rate in 802.11n—the type of modulation, the number of spatial streams, the GI, the FEC coding, etc.—the amendment now uses combinations of nine different factors to define the data rates. These combinations are referred to as modulation and coding schemes (MCSs). The 802.11-2012 version of the standard lists 77 different definitions that apply to both 20-MHz-wide and 40-MHz-wide channels and specify a different data rate. There are eight mandatory MCSs supporting data rates of up to 72.2 Mbps. All the other rates, up to those for a 4×4 device supporting up to 600 Mbps, are optional. By comparison, 802.11a and 802.11g support only 6, 12, 24, 36, 48, and 54 Mbps, and the only mandatory rates are 6, 12, and 24 Mbps.

HT PHY Layer   The 802.11n HT PHY layer supports three different frame formats. The first frame format is used to transmit in non-HT mode when communicating with 802.11a/g devices. The second frame format is used in mixed environments, with both HT and non-HT (legacy 802.11a/g devices). This allows non-HT devices to decode the beginning of the preamble, which contains information about the duration of the frame, so that legacy devices will not attempt to communicate until the transmission ends, thereby avoiding collisions. The third frame format is used when the WLAN is exclusively supporting 802.11n devices. This mode of operation is called **greenfield** and is not compatible with non-HT devices. Though optional in 802.11n, it is the most efficient way to communicate with other HT devices if legacy support is not required.

HT MAC Sublayer   The 802.11n MAC sublayer includes new enhancements designed to address the increase in throughput and power management. Power management becomes really important in 802.11n because of the optional use of multiple radios. The more radios a device has, the more power it will consume.

One of the new enhancements deals with frame aggregation, a method of combining multiple MAC frames into one PHY frame to reduce the number of MAC headers as well as the overhead caused by random back-off timers during medium contention, which contributes to increased WLAN throughput and reduced collisions.

There are two variations of frame aggregation. The first combines multiple MAC frames into one PHY frame, removing the individual headers. When using this method, all MAC frames must be of the same type, meaning that voice frames cannot be combined with video frames. The aggregated frames must also have a single destination—in other words, they must be unicast frames. As you know, in 802.11 the receiver must acknowledge each transmitted MAC frame, but in this case a single ACK is transmitted for the entire group of aggregated frames, which saves time and overhead, increasing throughput. The disadvantage of this method is that, should an error occur, the entire group of aggregated frames must be retransmitted.

The second method of frame aggregation combines individual MAC frames, including the headers, body, and trailers. Here again, the frames must all be unicast. In this case, the receiver sends an ACK for each individual MAC frame. However, if the receiving device is 802.11e compliant (802.11e is discussed in the next section), then a block ACK frame is transmitted back to the sender acknowledging the multiple MAC frames transmitted. In case of an error, only the frames following the one in which an error was detected must be retransmitted.

Because of the higher power consumption of 802.11n devices with multiple radios, the standard defines two new power management methods. In Spatial Multiplexing Power Save (SMPS) mode, a MIMO device can shut down all but one of its radios, then wake up and listen for a TIM in the beacons sent by the AP. If the TIM indicates that there is data waiting, the device must wake up and inform the AP, which will then transmit the buffered data. In the second new power management method, called Power Save Multi-Poll (PSMP), the devices also turn off all but one radio. When there is data to be transmitted to the device, the AP can wake up the devices by transmitting an RTS frame. The device will then inform the AP when all of its radios are operating again, in preparation for receiving the data using HT.

 The Wi-Fi Alliance Web site offers a variety of resources on the topic of Wireless Multimedia (WMM) power management, especially for mobile devices. For more information, visit *www.wi-fi.org* and use the search feature.

Reduced Interframe Space (RIFS) In greenfield mode, the 802.11n amendment allows for a **Reduced Interframe Space (RIFS)**—a shorter (2-microsecond) interframe space that can be used instead of an SIFS at the end of each transmitted frame, resulting in far less timing overhead and helping further increase the overall throughput of 802.11n. Remember that the SIFS interval in 802.11 is 10 microseconds long; in 802.11g, in order to maintain backward compatibility with 802.11, it is extended by 6 microseconds of quiet time at the end of each frame.

HT Operation Modes To allow 802.11n WLANs to coexist with non-HT devices (both APs and clients) and to allow devices that can only support 20 MHz channels (maximum data rate of 150 Mbps) to participate in the WLAN, 802.11n can operate in one of four different modes, depending on the presence or absence of different types of devices. Here are brief descriptions of these four modes of operation:

- Mode 0, the greenfield mode, supports only HT-capable devices using either 20 MHz or 40 MHz channels but not both in the same WLAN.
- Mode 1 is an HT mode, but if the AP detects stations that are not HT-capable and transmitting in a 20 MHz channel that interferes with either the primary or secondary channel in a 40 MHz channel, the AP will employ protection mechanisms to reduce or eliminate interference.
- Mode 2 supports either 20 or 40 MHz channels. If the AP detects a device that cannot communicate using a 40 MHz channel, it will employ protection mechanisms to allow 20-MHz-only devices to associate and communicate on the network.
- Mode 3, also called non-HT Mixed Mode, is used when one or more non-HT devices are associated with an HT AP. Mode 3 supports HT devices at 20 MHz or 40 MHz and

employs protection mechanisms to allow non-HT devices to participate in the BSS. Of all the modes, it is the one most commonly used and implemented by AP manufacturers, because in the near future most networks will have to support non-HT devices.

IEEE 802.11e

The **IEEE 802.11e** standard was approved for publication in November 2005. It defines enhancements to the MAC layer of 802.11 to expand support for LAN applications that require Quality of Service (QoS), and it provides for improvements in the capabilities and efficiency of the protocol. When combined with other recent enhancements to the PHY layers, it promises to increase overall system performance and expand the application space for 802.11.

Unlike the 802.11a and 802.11g standards, which require that each frame be acknowledged before a transmission can continue, 802.11e allows the receiving device to acknowledge after receiving a burst of frames (i.e., after several frames are transmitted). Figure 8-16 shows a logical diagram comparing the two methods.

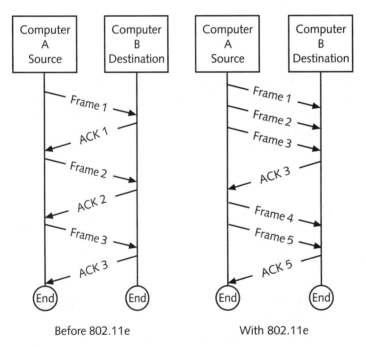

Before 802.11e   With 802.11e

Figure 8-16 802.11e frame acknowledgments

© Cengage Learning 2014

The 802.11e standard enables prioritization of frames in distributed coordination function (DCF), taking advantage of the higher data rates of 802.11a and 802.11g. In addition to delayed or burst acknowledgements, 802.11e implements two new coordination functions: enhanced DCF (EDCF) and hybrid coordination function (HCF).

All APs that comply with the standard must implement both modes, although the network administrator has different levels of control over how these are configured. In addition, both modes include a traffic class (TC) definition. E-mails, for example, would be assigned a low priority, whereas voice communications would be assigned a higher-priority class. In EDCF, a station with higher-priority traffic waits less long to transmit and therefore has a better chance of getting its traffic through.

HCF is a combination of DCF and point coordination function (PCF). The interval between beacon frames is divided into a contention-free period and a contention period. During the contention-free period, the hybrid coordinator (the AP) controls access to the medium and, based on information about the traffic received from a client, allocates more time slots to the station with high-priority traffic—such as voice-over-IP frames. During the contention period, all stations work in EDCF mode.

This prioritization aspect is an important development of the 802.11 standards family. The 802.11e standard enables voice, audio, and video to be transmitted reliably over WLANs by supporting traffic prioritization based on **QoS (quality-of-service)**. QoS is a resource reservation mechanism that allows certain types of network traffic—voice and video, for example—to be transmitted with a higher priority than traffic that is not time sensitive, such as copying a data file. QoS also adds improved security features for both mobile and nomadic applications. A **nomadic user** is one that moves frequently but does not use the equipment while in motion.

IEEE 802.11r

The amount of time required by 802.11 devices to associate with one AP and disassociate from another in an ESS is in the order of hundreds of milliseconds. For 802.11 devices to be able to support mobile phones used for voice calls, the reassociation time cannot exceed 50 milliseconds; otherwise, the human ear will sense a break in the continuity of the voice stream. This will make users unhappy with the quality of the call, and they may stop using the mobile phones. To support **voice over WLAN (VoWLAN)**, which enables organizations to implement and use VoIP in their ESSs, the 802.11 standard needs a way to provide quicker handoffs. A **handoff** in a WLAN happens when a computer or a handset connects with a new access point and disconnects from the previous one. Another issue is that the current 802.11 MAC protocol does not allow a device to find out if the necessary QoS resources, such as the required number of time slots and security features, are available on an AP before a telephone handset associates with it, which can affect the quality and reliability of a voice call.

The 802.11r standard is designed to resolve these issues as well as security concerns regarding the handoff. It does so by refining the MAC protocol and providing a way for the client to communicate with multiple APs on different channels to establish all the necessary parameters, including security, before a handoff occurs. This amendment to the standard is designed to enhance the convergence of wireless mobile voice, data, and video by improving the functionality and performance of WLANs.

IEEE 802.11s

Imagine that you need to deploy a WLAN over the entire downtown area of a medium-sized city and provide seamless connectivity to all city employees for events and functions. Though theoretically possible, connecting each of the APs to a wired network and configuring the system would be a monumentally expensive and complex undertaking because of the need for interconnecting all the different locations. Installing network cabling outdoors is not an option, so the only way to address this would be to lease communications lines from a local utility. Not only would this make the cost prohibitively high, achieving high data rates might also be difficult, depending on the technology available.

The ideal solution would be to connect the wireless APs to each other over the wireless medium. However, as you recall from previous sections of this chapter, 802.11 does not currently provide a way for APs to communicate with each other, much less forward wireless frame traffic, except over the wired interface.

The 802.11s standard provides the solution. Figure 8-17 shows an example of a wireless mesh network. In this figure, AP5 provides the single connection to the Internet to keep the landline connection costs low. The notebook associated with AP3 and the PDA connected to AP7 would be able to access the wired network or the Internet because the APs can communicate with each other over the wireless medium until the frames get to AP5.

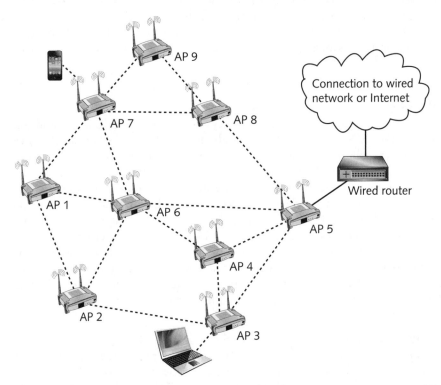

Figure 8-17 Wireless APs connected in a mesh network

© Cengage Learning 2014

802.11ac and 802.11ad As of this writing, 802.11ac and 802.11ad are under development. The 802.11ac amendment achieves data rates ranging from 433 Mbps to nearly 7 Gbps at the cost of using a minimum of from 80 to 160 MHz of bandwidth per channel.

It also allows between two and eight radios to transmit a maximum of eight spatial streams per AP. If all eight radios are present in an AP and not all are being used to communicate with a client device, the additional spatial streams can be used to communicate with other client devices simultaneously. The 802.11ac amendment only works in the 5 GHz U-NII band, given that the ISM 2.4 GHz band has only a total of 83.5 MHz of bandwidth available.

The IEEE 802.11ad standardization effort was spawned by the WiGig Alliance specification, which you learned about in Chapter 6. The goal is to expand the 802.11 standard to work in the 60 GHz band while maintaining backward compatibility with 802.11 in both the ISM and U-NII bands simultaneously.

Expanding WLAN Functionality

Thus far, this book has focused on two primary WLAN hardware components: APs and WLAN interfaces on client devices. In this section, you will learn about other types of devices that expand the functionality of WLANs and improve the ability of IT staff to manage and support WLANs in large companies.

As you know, the signal range of a WLAN is limited to a few hundred feet. An optional component of WLANs, **wireless bridges**, are specifically designed to interconnect two wired networks or to extend the range of a WLAN beyond its maximum range.

Wireless Bridges and Repeaters

Wireless bridges are the ideal solution for connecting such sites as remote campus buildings or temporary office locations, especially when there are such obstacles as roads or railroads, which make using a wired connection impractical or too expensive. For 802.11 bridges, the distance between buildings can be up to 18 miles (29 kilometers) when transmitting at 11 Mbps or up to 25 miles (40 kilometers) when transmitting at 2 Mbps. In point-to-point, 802.11a wireless bridges can transmit at 54 Mbps at distances of up to 8.5 miles (13.5 kilometers) or at 28 Mbps at up to 20 miles (32 kilometers). IEEE 802.11a wireless bridges typically operate in the U-NII High band, between 5.725 and 5.825 GHz, which is only approved for outdoor applications and can use very-high-power transmitters when deployed with directional antennas.

 At 11 Mbps, remote wireless bridges are several times faster and a fraction of the cost of high-speed digital communication lines that are available from telephone carriers.

When used to interconnect two buildings, wireless bridges are typically deployed in a point-to-point configuration, as illustrated in Figure 8-18.

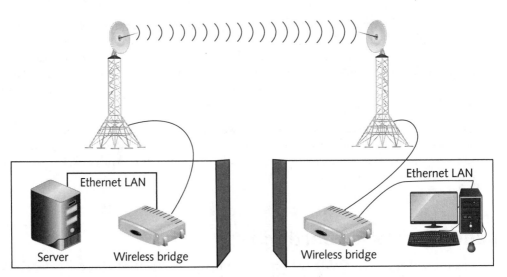

Figure 8-18 Wireless bridging of two LANs

© *Cengage Learning 2014*

For long-distance links, in which the signal may take longer to arrive at the receiver, transmitting wireless bridges can extend the SIFS time, thereby allowing the receiver enough time to acknowledge a frame. (Recall that the ACK is always sent after the SIFS.) Extending the SIFS means that wireless bridges operate without fully conforming to the 802.11 standards. This is only possible in a point-to-point configuration.

WLAN Extension Wireless bridges can also extend the range of a WLAN. A bridge is a device that can also be configured to connect to an AP as a repeater in point-to-multipoint mode. Client devices that are out of the range of the access point can associate with the bridge, which will receive and acknowledge each frame sent by the AP or by the client, then forward the frame to the AP or client, depending on the direction of the transmission. Some manufacturers' APs can also be connected as a repeater or as a bridge. Before purchasing an access point for this purpose, you should carefully check the user manual to make sure it meets your requirements.

One thing that a network designer must keep in mind is the amount of extra delay introduced in WLAN extension applications. Because the device configured as the repeater must receive each frame correctly, acknowledge it, then wait the appropriate number of back-off time slots for its next turn to communicate, certain kinds of applications running on the client may not be able to tolerate the resulting additional transmission delay. In addition, you must consider that this increased delay effectively cuts the throughput in half. This means that in a WLAN operating at 300 Mbps, the maximum throughput is reduced to as little as 75 Mbps.

Wireless Controllers

When a large number of APs are deployed throughout a building or campus, managing these devices remotely can become very difficult. Most configuration settings can be distributed and administered remotely, but physical problems such as network connectivity and hardware failures may demand that a technician be sent to the location—an expensive way to provide support.

In addition, APs often need to be deployed in branch offices, which increases the support delays and cost. The more features an AP has, the more complex it can be to configure and maintain; also, signal coverage and strength are more difficult to monitor remotely.

An alternative way to simplify the management of a wireless network is to use a **wireless controller**. Wireless controllers are devices that incorporate most of the functions of an AP but do not have any radios. They connect to multiple, less-complex APs either via direct cable connection or, for remote locations, via a logical network connection. These simpler APs consist of PHY-layer devices (radios) with some MAC-layer functionality. The wireless controller handles the interface and communications with the wired LAN and most of the MAC-layer functionality.

This way, the management of a WLAN is effectively centralized. The network administrator configures the WLAN on the wireless controller, including the parameters of the radios, and the configuration is then pushed to the APs. If an AP fails, the controller is able to adjust the transmit power on two nearby APs to restore signal coverage to the area previously served by the failed AP. Extra APs can be set up as monitoring devices to detect the presence of unauthorized APs as well as to monitor the quality of the wireless signals.

8

Quality-of-service (QoS) features incorporated into the wireless controllers can make it easier to deploy VoWLAN, which enables users to make calls while roaming in an ESS. Wireless controllers can greatly simplify the deployment and continuous management of large WLANs.

 For additional information on wireless controllers, see *www.aruba networks.com*, *www.cisco.com*, and *www.meraki.com* and search for their wireless products. Meraki is among a few WLAN equipment manufacturers that do not make a hardware-based controller. Instead, its APs are managed via the Internet (i.e., using cloud-based software controllers).

Other WLAN Expansion Hardware

The explosive growth in the WLAN market spawned an entirely new range of devices for the wireless home and office. However, with the introduction of the latest IEEE 802.11 standards, as well as the WMM specification from the Wi-Fi Alliance that is intended to support audio and video, many of the products that were specifically built for distributing media or connecting computers and media projectors for business or classroom use are being discontinued. With the exception of media players like Apple TV, Western Digital's WDTV Live, and others, products that simply take advantage of an existing WLAN in a home or office are replacing most of the dedicated devices today.

WLAN Security

No discussion of WLANs is complete without looking at the topic of security. Broadcasting network traffic over EM waves has created an entirely new set of issues for keeping data transmissions secure. It is no secret to IT professionals that the security provisions in the original IEEE 802.11 were seriously flawed. This section introduces a few types of network attacks and additional measures that have been engineered by the IEEE and Wi-Fi Alliance to improve WLAN security.

It is important to keep in mind that these measures apply equally to wireless networks, regardless of the standards they use. Because the standards define how data is transmitted at the PHY layer, the security implementations are analogous to those in an Ethernet network. However, because the WLAN transmissions utilize a medium that is not contained in any way, a WLAN is far more exposed to intrusion, jamming, and hijacking of the information.

No security setup can prevent all potential breaches. Security must always be viewed as a work-in-progress. Network administrators must check systems and logs regularly to ensure that the security features have not been compromised. For example, a user who often travels with a laptop computer may temporarily reconfigure his system to solve an immediate problem connecting to another network, thereby potentially exposing the corporate WLAN to security attacks and breaches unless specific measures are taken to protect the network.

Attacks Against WLANs

A variety of attacks can be generated against WLANs. Some of the more dangerous are hardware theft, AP impersonation, passive monitoring, and denial of service (DoS) attacks, all discussed in this section.

The theft of a laptop computer is a threat because the device may contain information—for example, the security key and passwords—that can be used to break into a network.

AP impersonation takes advantage of a problem with legacy 802.11 WLANs, which is that clients authenticate themselves with the APs but the APs do not authenticate themselves with clients. When a rogue AP or software installed on a laptop computer impersonates a valid AP, thereby tricking clients into associating with it, information from the clients can be monitored and security keys broken. AP impersonation can also form the basis for other types of security attacks targeted at specific devices on the WLAN, such as using software on a laptop PC to impersonate an AP by spoofing the AP's MAC address and other parameters. This type of attack is called **man-in-the-middle**.

Passive monitoring, in which an attacker simply captures data transmissions, can also be used to acquire information, such as the MAC and IP addresses of APs and wireless clients. Over time, the attacker can build a profile of the WLAN and may be able to use this information to break into the network. An attacker can use a wireless sniffer to capture enough frames to decode the security key. Although this requires capturing perhaps several million frames (depending on the type of security key used) and can consume a huge amount of computer processing power, it can be done, especially if an attacker is targeting a particular company and has plenty of time to spare. Because the frames used to associate with the WLAN are not always encrypted, they can be intercepted and important data collected to help create an attack. An unauthorized user can use this information to flood the network with transmissions directed at one or more devices. This is one example of a DoS attack that can effectively deny other devices access to the WLAN.

DoS attacks and AP impersonation can be easily detected and avoided through the use of special equipment or software such as AirMagnet Enterprise (see *www.airmagnet.com*) or AirCheck (see *www.flukenetworks.com*). Although the equipment and software can cost $2,500 or more, it can prove a worthwhile investment if the company is subject to an attack, which may end up costing a lot more in lost productivity or failure to comply with privacy laws (in cases where information is stolen). Another way to prevent these types of attacks is to deploy an external authentication mechanism such as those outlined in 802.1X and 802.11i, described later in this chapter.

802.11 Security

The IEEE 802.11 standard defines basic security measures along with support for encryption. Authentication in 802.11 is essentially limited to the client devices being authenticated by the AP. However, the clients do not authenticate the AP and therefore do not know whether they are connected to an enterprise or an attacker's computer impersonating one of the company's APs.

Authentication

Authentication is the process of verifying that the client device has permission to access the network. Although authentication is important in wired LANs, it is even more important in WLANs because of the open nature of wireless transmissions.

IEEE 802.11 WLANs provide a very basic means of authenticating potential client devices. Each WLAN client can be given the SSID of the network. This value is transmitted to the AP when the client is negotiating permission to connect to the network. Only those clients that know the SSID are then authenticated as valid users and are allowed to connect to the network.

A wireless client can be given an SSID in one of two ways. First, the SSID can be manually entered into the wireless client device. Once it is entered, anyone who has access to that wireless device can see the SSID and pass this information along to other people. By default, APs freely advertise the SSID to any mobile device that comes within the range of the AP's wireless radio and can decode the beacon frames.

An administrator can configure the APs to not broadcast the SSID. However, keep in mind that when a client transmits a probe frame, the AP is required by the 802.11 standard to send a probe response frame that includes the SSID of the network. An attacker using a simple tool like Metageek's InSSIDer software, which sends probe request frames to all APs it detects, has access to all the information contained in the probe response frames.

Privacy

Privacy is different from authentication. Authentication ensures that the user (or device) has permission to be part of the network. Privacy is a collection of processes that attempts to ensure that unauthorized users cannot understand wireless transmissions. This is accomplished with data encryption, which scrambles the data in a way that it cannot be read and can only be decoded by the intended recipient, who also has access to the encryption key

8

and can decode the message. The strength of encryption rests not only on keeping the keys secret but also with the length of the key itself. The longer the key is, the stronger the encryption, because longer keys are more difficult to break. The trade-off is that stronger encryption increases the number of octets transmitted, which in turn decreases the overall throughput of the WLAN.

Wired Equivalent Privacy

The 802.11-1997 standard provided an optional specification called **Wired Equivalent Privacy (WEP)** that is used to encrypt the data between wireless devices to prevent eavesdropping. WEP encryption comes in two versions: 64-bit encryption and 128-bit encryption. The former uses a 40-bit key (5 bytes or 10 hexadecimal digits) plus a 24-bit initialization vector (IV), which is part of the encryption key sent in clear text, before the encrypted data. Likewise, 128-bit encryption uses a 104-bit key plus a 24-bit IV. Some vendors offered 256-bit encryption in their equipment; however, the equipment uses the same 24-bit IV. Also, with 256-bit encryption, there may be compatibility problems among equipment sold by different manufacturers.

In 2001, researchers at various universities outlined just how an attacker could collect the necessary data for breaking WEP encryption. By late 2001, they were able to decrypt the 128-bit WEP key used in a WLAN transmission in less than two hours. And in 2005, the time was reduced to less than two minutes when the attacker was able to capture around 200,000 frames. WEP uses a weak implementation of the RC4 encryption algorithm that was developed by Ron Rivest for RSA Data Security, Inc.; except in the case of home networks, it is seldom used today.

Wi-Fi Protected Access

Wi-Fi Protected Access (WPA) is a standard for network authentication and encryption introduced by the Wi-Fi Alliance in response to the weaknesses of WEP. WPA uses a 128-bit **pre-shared key (PSK)**, also known as "Personal mode," which needs to be manually added to the configuration of every device that will be connected to the WLAN. Unlike WEP, which only varies the 24-bit IV, WPA-PSK uses a different encryption key for each client device, for each packet, and for each communications session.

WPA-PSK is not suitable for larger companies with many client devices because the passphrase has to be created by the user and manually entered on both the AP and clients. Strong passphrases should be longer than 8 bytes and should include a mixture of letters, numbers, and non-alphanumeric characters. The passphrase is used by the hardware to generate an encryption key. This key is rotated, based on a user-configurable timer that is often set to 300 seconds by manufacturers. This mode does not offer the same level of protection as enterprise class systems that rely on an authentication server installed somewhere else on the network.

WPA employs the **temporal key integrity protocol (TKIP)**, which provides per-packet key-mixing. In addition, TKIP provides **message integrity check (MIC)**, which uses a combination of variable and static data items, such as the current network uptime (not based on current clock time) and other data items, to ensure that the encrypted data has not been tampered with. With WEP, it was possible to tamper with the encrypted data without the possibility of detection. MIC verifies that an attacker has not modified the data sent by the source device.

TKIP uses a 48-bit hashed initialization vector and also changes the key after a user-specified amount of time. WPA includes the mechanism necessary for the AP to change the keys and transmit the new key to all client devices.

WPA2 is the WPA version that the IEEE certified as compatible with IEEE 802.11i, which is described in the next section. It adds support for the advanced encryption standard (AES), which meets U.S. government security requirements. However, because AES requires additional processing power, it may not be supported by older hardware.

The Wi-Fi Alliance also has certification programs for WPA and WPA2. Vendors use these programs to verify that their equipment complies with the standard and to ensure that it will interoperate with equipment from other vendors. Vendors pay the Wi-Fi Alliance and supply equipment for the interoperability tests. In exchange, if the equipment passes all tests, vendors are allowed to add the "Wi-Fi CERTIFIED" logo to their equipment, packaging, brochures, and other promotional material.

IEEE 802.11i and IEEE 802.1X

The 802.11i amendment, ratified in June 2004, was the result of a series of efforts to deal with the security weaknesses of the original WLAN standard. In combination with **IEEE 802.1X**, **IEEE 802.11i** defines a **Robust Security Network Association (RSNA)**, which is a grouping of several security functions that protects data frames by providing mutual authentication between client devices and access points, controlled access to the network, establishment of security keys, and key management. Although full coverage of 802.11i and 802.1X is beyond the scope of this text, you can obtain more information by downloading the 802.1X and 802.11i standards documents from *http://standards.ieee.org/getieee802/index.html*.

802.1X is part of the IEEE 802.1 group of network standards and applies to wired as well as wireless networks. However, 802.1X is not an amendment to any standard; it is a set of recommendations for implementation of RSNA.

In 802.11i, a client device must be authenticated on the network by an external authentication server—such as a Remote Authentication Dial In User Service (RADIUS), a popular method of authenticating users on a network—before associating with an AP. Another option is for the client to be authenticated by an authentication server similar to RADIUS but provided by the AP itself. All communication between the client device and the AP is blocked until the authentication process is completed. After the authentication process is completed, data protection through encryption and MIC are enabled. Only then is the client association with the AP allowed and communication unblocked. Figure 8-19 shows a diagram of a typical network employing an authentication server.

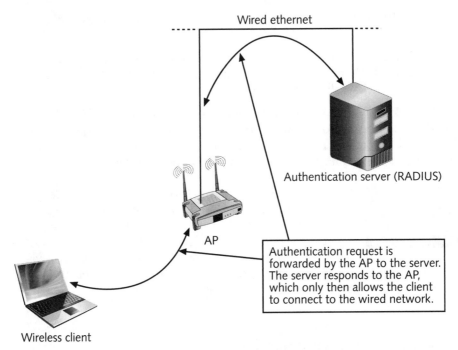

Wired ethernet

Authentication server (RADIUS)

AP

Authentication request is forwarded by the AP to the server. The server responds to the AP, which only then allows the client to connect to the wired network.

Wireless client

Figure 8-19 Securing a wireless network using a RADIUS server

© *Cengage Learning 2014*

NOTE

RADIUS software is available from many different vendors and also in a free version called FreeRADIUS. The "Dial In" portion of the RADIUS acronym is a holdover from the old telephone-line modem days. RADIUS is applicable to wired as well as wireless networks. FreeRADIUS is available for download from many Internet sites and is supported by a variety of networking devices, including APs, routers, and so on.

802.1X uses the **Extensible Authentication Protocol (EAP)** for relaying access requests between a wireless device, the AP, and the RADIUS server. There are several variations of EAP, each supporting a different authentication method and its associated network security policy. For EAP to work, all three devices must support the same authentication method. When EAP is used, the network administrator does not need to configure a WPA passphrase or WEP key in each computer. The RADIUS server provides the key to the wireless device and AP. This saves configuration effort and time both initially and when the key has to be changed for any reason. It also indirectly verifies to the client device that it is communicating with an authorized AP.

Push-Button Wireless Security

Because many home users who install wireless networks fail to set up proper security, leaving their networks exposed to potential attackers, a few vendors have joined forces to create a new method of configuring wireless residential gateways as well as client devices. Although each vendor's method has a different name or acronym, all of them provide an additional button on the front panel of the wireless gateway or in the configuration software that automatically configures the security settings in both the wireless gateway and the client device. Keep in mind that to take advantage of push-button wireless security, both the wireless NIC and the AP or gateway must support the feature. The button needs to be activated once on each device, and for each client, one at a time. The feature transfers the security key to the wireless NIC, then automatically establishes a connection with the wireless device. If you are using wireless NICs and gateways from different vendors, check first to make sure this feature is compatible.

Virtual Private Networks

Virtual private networks (VPNs) use an encrypted connection to create a virtual tunnel between two points across a public or corporate network. VPNs using strong encryption algorithms, such as AES, are the most secure method of implementing a wireless network. Due to the encryption requirements, VPNs consume a large amount of processing resources, thus some time-sensitive client-server applications may not perform acceptably in a VPN environment. In these cases, wireless networks should be secured using one of the techniques described previously in this chapter. However, employees who use wireless-equipped portable computers to access a company network through the Internet from remote locations should do so only through a VPN. Most public wireless networks are not secure, and this can expose corporate data—such as e-mails and even customer names and addresses—to an attacker. In fact, if VPNs are not implemented properly, the entire corporate network can be exposed to attacks from the Internet. Disabling access to the Internet when users log in to the corporate network through a VPN avoids this problem, so most VPNs are set up in this way.

Additional WLAN Security Tactics

In addition to the security strategies discussed in the previous section, you can increase WLAN security by reducing WLAN transmission power. However, keep in mind that an attacker equipped with a high-gain directional antenna would still be able to detect the RF signal. Changing the default security settings on the APs is probably the most important first step. Don't forget antivirus and antispyware software. Mobile wireless clients are exposed to more of these threats when operating outside company offices and can introduce those threats into your wired network.

For highly secure WLANs, you may need to separate WLAN transmissions from wired network traffic by placing a firewall between the WLAN and the wired LAN, although this means that you will need to implement virtual local area networks (VLANs) in order to allow authorized users to access the wired network. This is especially important if you allow guest wireless devices to connect to your WLAN.

Chapter Summary

- Operating in the 2.4 GHz ISM frequency range, 802.11b has a maximum data rate of 11 Mbps and has been widely deployed, though mostly for residential applications. However, the ISM band is crowded and subject to interference from other networking technologies, cordless phones, and Bluetooth.

- The 802.11a standard has a maximum rated speed of 54 Mbps and also supports 48, 36, 24, 18, 12, 9, and 6 Mbps. 802.11a achieves its increase in speed and flexibility over 802.11b through a higher frequency, more transmission channels, and a new multiplexing technique.

- IEEE 802.11a networks use the Unlicensed National Information Infrastructure (U-NII) band. The total bandwidth available for IEEE 802.11a WLANs using U-NII is 555 MHz, almost seven times what is available for 802.11b networks using the ISM band.

- In 802.11a, 23 frequency channels can operate simultaneously. Each frequency channel is 20 MHz wide and supports 52 subcarriers 300 KHz wide. Because there are more available channels, more users can access more bandwidth in an 802.11a WLAN, when managed correctly.

- IEEE 802.11b WLAN reception is slowed down by multipath distortion. The 802.11a standard solves this problem through a new multiplexing technique called orthogonal frequency division multiplexing (OFDM). OFDM transmits several bits at a slower rate, in parallel, across several subcarriers instead of sending a long stream of data across a single channel. This increases the data rate while reducing the multipath problems created by higher speed transmissions in 802.11b.

- OFDM uses 48 of the 52 subcarriers for data, with the remaining four used for monitoring and error correction. The modulation techniques used to encode the data vary depending upon the speed.

- The number of errors in an 802.11a transmission is significantly reduced compared to 802.11b. Error correction is enhanced using forward error correction (FEC). IEEE 802.11a also transmits a secondary, redundant copy of the data, which helps to increase reliability.

- The 802.11a standard made changes only to the Physical layer (PHY layer) of the original 802.11 and 802.11b standard; the MAC layer remains the same. The 802.11a PHY layer is divided into two parts: the Physical Medium Dependent (PMD) sublayer and the Physical Layer Convergence Procedure (PLCP). The PMD covers the characteristics of the wireless medium and defines the method for transmitting and receiving (OFDM) data through that medium. The PLCP reformats the data received from the MAC layer (when transmitting) into a frame that the PMD sublayer can transmit and listens to the medium to determine when the data can be sent.

- IEEE 802.11g preserves the features of 802.11b but increases the data transfer rates to those of 802.11a. The 802.11g amendment operates in the 2.4 GHz ISM frequency band and not the U-NII band used by 802.11a.

- The 802.11e amendment adds QoS to the original 802.11 standard. In addition, it helps improve performance through burst acknowledgements and two new coordination functions: enhanced DCF (EDCF) and hybrid coordination function (HCF).

- The 802.11n amendment increases the data rate up to 600 Mbps using either the 2.4 GHz ISM or the 5 GHz U-NII band. This is accomplished by bonding two frequency channels for up to 40 MHz of bandwidth using OFDM, and transmitting up to four simultaneous data streams using a different radio and a different antenna. To maintain backward compatibility with 802.11a/b/g, 802.11n includes a number of MAC enhancements called protection mechanisms.

- The 802.11r amendment enables fast roaming and reduces the time required for a device to associate with a new AP from hundreds of milliseconds to less than 50 milliseconds. This permits WLANs to effectively support VoWLAN in ESS environments. It also allows a client device, prior to establishing a connection, to obtain information from multiple APs regarding bandwidth availability and security features.

■ The 802.11s amendment enables APs to communicate and pass traffic from one to the other, over a wireless connection, supporting cost-effective deployment of extensive mesh WLANs over a larger geographical area without the need to connect every AP to the wired network.

■ The 802.11ac amendment boosts the speed of WLANs up to nearly 7 Gbps using the U-NII band and between 80 and 160 MHz of bandwidth.

■ The new 802.11ad amendment operates in the 60 GHz band for short-range connections at up to 7 Gbps but remains backward compatible with 802.11a/ac/b/g/n, being able to also transmit in the U-NII and ISM bands.

■ WLANs can suffer a range of security attacks. IEEE WLANs require enhanced security measures. WLAN security has been greatly enhanced through the introduction of Wi-Fi Protected Access (WPA and WPA2).

■ WLANs can be protected against attacks through the use of VPNs, 802.11i authentication, and 802.1X security measures. Authentication is a process for verifying that the user has permission to access the network and ensuring that the client device is communicating with an authorized AP. Privacy is a collection of data-encryption processes for ensuring that unauthorized persons do not read transmissions.

8

Key Terms

adjacent channel interference   When signals from two adjacent channels interfere with each other.

antenna diversity   A technique that uses two antennas to improve the range of 802.11 and transmits a signal through the antenna that received the strongest signal during the last transmission.

authentication   A process that verifies that the client device has permission to access the network.

co-channel interference   Interference between two devices configured to use the same frequency channel.

CTS-to-self   Short for "clear-to-send-to-self," a coordination method used by 802.11g devices that prevents 802.11 and 802.11b devices that do not "understand" OFDM from attempting to initiate a transmission while the 802.11g device is transmitting data.

Extensible Authentication Protocol (EAP)   A collection of protocols used by IEEE 802.1X for network authentication between a wireless device, an AP, and a RADIUS server.

greenfield   A mode of operation of 802.11n in which only HT-capable devices are supported.

guard band   The unused frequency space between two adjacent channels.

guard interval (GI)   An added 800 nanosecond delay at the end of each 802.11 that allows all reflected signals to arrive at the receiver's antennas before another symbol is transmitted.

handoff   The transition that occurs when a client device connects with a new access point and disconnects from the previous one.

IEEE 802.11a   Developed in 1999, a standard for WLAN transmissions at speeds of up to 54 Mbps.

IEEE 802.11e   A standard for WLAN applications that implements QoS for WLANs and provides for improvements in their capabilities and efficiency.

IEEE 802.11g   A standard for WLAN transmissions at speeds of up to 54 Mbps using the ISM band.

IEEE 802.11i   An enhancement to 802.11 that deals with security weaknesses of the original standard and supports the use of network-based authentication servers running software such as RADIUS.

IEEE 802.1X   A set of recommendations for increasing the security of IEEE 802 LANs that is also applicable to 802.11 WLANs.

intersymbol interference (ISI)   Interference caused when the beginning of a symbol arrives at the receiver antenna while multipath reflections from the previous symbol are still reaching the antenna.

man-in-the-middle   A network-security attack in which the attacker uses software installed in a computer to duplicate the behavior of an enterprise AP.

message integrity check (MIC)   A combination of variable and static data items that ensures encrypted data has not been altered during transmission between source and destination devices.

multiple-input and multiple-output (MIMO)   A technology that uses multiple antennas (usually three or four) and reflected signals (multipath reflections) to extend the range of the WLAN by attempting to correctly decode a frame from multiple copies of it received at different times.

nomadic user   A user that moves frequently but does not use the equipment while in motion.

pre-shared key   A 128-bit key used by WPA; it is called "pre-shared" because it is manually configured in each WLAN device before connections can be established.

privacy   Standards that ensure transmissions are not read by unauthorized users.

QoS (quality-of-service)   A resource reservation enhancement to the 802.11 MAC layer that enables prioritization of traffic and is most often used to support delivery of voice, video, and audio frames between WLAN devices.

Reduced Interframe Space (RIFS)   A 2-microsecond interframe space that can be used in 802.11n networks working in greenfield mode to help reduce overhead and increase throughput.

Robust Security Network Association (RSNA)   A grouping of several security functions to protect data frames by providing mutual authentication between client devices and access points, controlled access to the network, establishment of security keys, and key management.

spatial multiplexing   A transmission technique that uses multiple radios and multiple antennas to send different parts of the same message simultaneously, thus increasing the data rate.

symbol   A change in the signal, also known as a baud.

temporal key integrity protocol (TKIP)   A security protocol used in WPA that provides per-packet key-mixing.

virtual private network (VPN)   A secure, encrypted connection between two points over a public or private network.

voice over WLAN (VoWLAN)   A term used to describe the transmission of telephone calls on WLANs.

Wi-Fi Protected Access (WPA) and WPA2   A security enhancement and interoperability certification introduced by the Wi-Fi Alliance in advance of the 802.11i standard to deal with the security flaws in WEP.

Wired Equivalent Privacy (WEP)   The IEEE specification for data encryption between wireless devices to prevent an attacker from eavesdropping.

wireless bridges   A networking component that connects two wired networks or extends the range of a WLAN.

wireless controller   Devices that make it much easier to manage large WLANs by implementing most of the functions of an AP and controlling the operation of local or remotely connected radios.

WPA2   A security specification and interoperability certification introduced by the Wi-Fi Alliance that includes support for AES encryption as well as support for 802.11i and 802.1X.

Review Questions

1. The original IEEE 802.11 standard, established in 1997, was for WLANs operating at what maximum speed?

    a.   1 Mbps

    b.   2 Mbps

    c.   3 Mbps

    d.   4 Mbps

2. The maximum mandatory rate of an IEEE 802.11a WLAN, according to the standard, is _____.

    a.   11 Mbps

    b.   24 Mbps

    c.   54 Mbps

    d.   108 Mbps

3. The most important change made to the MAC layer of 802.11a was _____.

    a.   to make the frames shorter

    b.   to increase security

    c.   to make the frames longer for efficiency

    d.   none of the above

4. IEEE 802.11a achieves its increase in speed and flexibility over 802.11b by each of the following except _____.

    a.   higher frequency

    b.   using less bandwidth

    c.   more transmission channels

    d.   a new multiplexing technique

5. The Unlicensed National Information Infrastructure (U-NII) band operates at the _____ frequency.

   a. 2.4 GHz

   b. 33 GHz

   c. 5 GHz

   d. 16 KHz

6. The Federal Communications Commission (FCC) has segmented the 555 MHz of the original U-NII spectrum into four segments or bands, and each band has a maximum power limit. True or False?

7. All 5 GHz bands are available to WLANs worldwide. True or False?

8. Although such devices as 2.4 GHz cordless phones, microwave ovens, and Bluetooth devices may cause interference problems with 802.11b networks in the 2.4 GHz ISM band, they are not a problem with 802.11a. True or False?

9. Each frequency channel in an 802.11a WLAN is 20 MHz wide and supports _____ subcarrier signals.

   a. 56

   b. 114

   c. 52

   d. 48

10. Although 802.11n can achieve data rates of 300 Mbps when using 40 MHz of bandwidth in the ISM band, one of the main challenges of deploying a WLAN in this frequency range is _____.

    a. intersymbol interference

    b. co-channel interference on channel 6

    c. excessive multipath interference on channels 1 and 11

    d. interference from the U-NII band

11. How many pilot carriers are available in 802.11n in the U-NII band using 40 MHz of bandwidth?

    a. 4

    b. 2

    c. 6

    d. 8

12. One of the reasons that 802.11n achieves a higher bandwidth is that it bonds two ISM or U-NII channels. Another important reason is that it _____.

    a. eliminates multipath interference

    b. uses antenna diversity

    c. can transmit using multiple spatial streams

    d. can transmit in any two frequency channels simultaneously

13. When actively using a network while roaming in an ESS, the process of connecting and disconnecting from the APs in one's path is called _____.

   a. MIMO

   b. handoff

   c. switching

   d. nomadic

14. The change the 802.11e amendment made to the MAC layer to enable WLAN traffic to be prioritized is called _____.

   a. RSNA

   b. QoS

   c. VoWLAN

   d. WPA2

15. Which of the following is one of the most important reasons that companies deploy wireless controllers?

   a. It enables bridging of multiple WLANs.

   b. It enhances security.

   c. It simplifies management of the WLAN.

   d. Wireless controllers support TKIP.

16. Which of the following is the best method for enhancing WLAN security in an enterprise?

   a. using TKIP and WEP

   b. deploying an authentication server on the network

   c. changing frequencies periodically

   d. installing equipment that supports 802.11s

17. Why is WEP considered far inferior to WPA and WPA2?

   a. It transmits an unencrypted 24-bit IV.

   b. The AP cannot properly authenticate the client devices.

   c. It does not support encryption at all.

   d. It is more secure than using RADIUS.

18. Which of the following is a key advantage of WPA2 over WEP?

   a. It uses a much stronger encryption algorithm.

   b. It supports EAP.

   c. It supports TKIP and MIC.

   d. All of the above.

8

19. Which of the following is specifically designed to enhance support for audio and video in 802.11 WLANs?

    a. wireless controllers

    b. WPA2

    c. wireless repeaters

    d. WMM

20. Which of the following is a reason that 802.11a is more efficient than 802.11g when both operate at the same data rate?

    a. 802.11g has a longer SIFS.

    b. 802.11a devices can handle more data.

    c. 802.11a equipment is more sophisticated and expensive.

    d. 802.11a time slots are shorter.

Hands-On Project

Project 8-1

This project covers the basic configuration of an 802.11n-capable residential gateway or AP. You can do this project using any manufacturer's device. The brand of the equipment is not important, because in the real world you will likely be configuring a variety of different equipment makes and models. Although the configuration screens will be different than the ones shown in the figures, the point of the exercise is for you to understand which configuration items to modify and how these will affect the speed and performance of the wireless links.

The devices used to create this exercise are a DLink DIR-825 simultaneous dual-band (2.4 GHz and 5 GHz) wireless residential gateway and a Dell Latitude E4300 Notebook PC, but virtually any type of wireless residential gateway and PC compatible with 802.11n will work. To keep it simple, a wireless residential gateway (hereafter called "gateway") was used to create this project. The project covers only those settings that are relevant and assumes you already know (from Chapter 7) how to perform the basic configuration steps and connect a computer with a wireless NIC to the gateway.

1. Connect your computer to the gateway for configuration purposes. Whenever possible, you should use a wired connection to change settings on a gateway or access point. Some of the settings, such as security, will cause your computer to disconnect until you reconfigure it to use the new settings.

2. Consult the documentation for your gateway on how to configure the wireless settings manually. Even if a configuration wizard is available, it often does not provide you with enough control over the parameter settings, so you will want to follow the procedures for manual configuration. Figure 8-20 shows an example of the settings you need to access to fully configure the 2.4 GHz wireless settings for 802.11n.

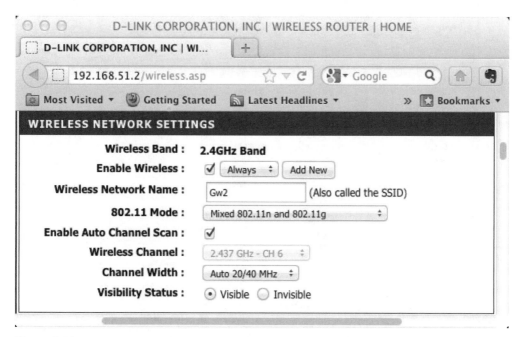

Figure 8-20 802.11n 2.4 GHz wireless network settings (DLink DIR-825)

Source: D-LINK Corporation

3. Configure a unique SSID for your WLAN. Consult with your instructor if there are other devices being used in the same classroom.

4. It is usually better, especially in 802.11n, to allow the gateway to automatically select the channel, but you can select the channel manually, if you prefer, keeping in mind that, with more than two gateways in the same room, there are really only two usable channels, 1 and 6, and that interference will affect the overall performance of your wireless link.

5. To achieve data rates of up to 300 Mbps, you need to configure the gateway to use Auto 20/40MHz. Make sure you turn off any devices in the room—cellular phones, etc.—that only support 802.11g and therefore can only use 20 MHz of bandwidth. Otherwise, you may find that your gateway will only use 20 MHz. This is because every time a broadcast frame is transmitted, the gateway needs to send it in a way that is compatible with non-802.11n devices.

6. You will not need to transfer any files to determine the data rate for the connection. Windows 7 will provide this information in the Wireless Network Connection Status dialog box. To get to this dialog box, click the wireless network icon on the bottom-right-hand side of the screen and click **Open Network and Sharing Center**. On the right-hand side of the window, click **Wireless Network Connection**. Figure 8-21 shows the Wireless Network Connection Status dialog box.

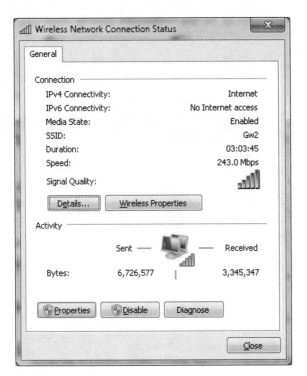

Figure 8-21 Wireless Network Connection Status dialog box

Source: Microsoft Windows 7

7. You will see the data rate beside the label "Speed." If your data rate is showing any-thing less than 300 Mbps, you may need to modify the configuration of the NIC. To do this, click the **Properties** button at the bottom of the Wireless Network Connection Status dialog box (not the Wireless Properties button). This will open the Wireless Net-work Connection Properties dialog box.

8. Click the **Configure ...** button next to the name of your wireless NIC. Click the **Advanced** tab. Note that some NIC manufacturers do not provide you with the abil-ity to configure advanced parameters on the NIC from this dialog box, in which case you may need to use the manufacturer's utility, which should be installed when you install your NIC. There is no industry standard for configuring these parameters, so each manufacturer's adapters may use different parameter names, etc. Figure 8-22 shows an example of the dialog box displayed for the Dell Wireless 1510 WLAN Mini-Card. Make a note of all the current settings for your card before changing any values, and then make sure that it is configured for 802.11n and for 20/40 Mhz. Try changing some of the settings that appear to be related to bandwidth or standard support and observe the results you get when communicat-ing on the WLAN.

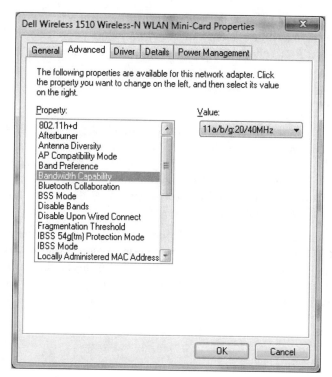

Figure 8-22 Wireless NIC settings

Source: Microsoft Windows 7

8

9. Download and install the free Metageek inSSIDer utility on your computer (see *www. metageek.net*). Start inSSIDer and check for interference from other networks using the same configuration you just completed. If your gateway device supports the 5 GHz band, perform the same configuration steps on the gateway, but configure this band instead. Check the interference with inSSIDer again and compare with the results you obtained for the 2.4 GHz band.

Real-World Exercise

Exercise 8-1

The Baypoint Group (TBG) needs your help to prepare a presentation for Academic Computing Services Inc. (ACS), a nationwide organization that assists colleges and universities with technology issues. ACS would like to learn more about WLAN security so that its staff will be better prepared to explain the options to their customers.

Prepare a PowerPoint presentation that outlines the security strengths and weaknesses of WLANs and makes recommendations about the level of security that ACS should recommend to its customers in a variety of situations, such as when equipment is used in office applications and when wireless notebook computers are used by students. Your presentation should consist of at least 15 slides and should cover encryption and authentication using 802.11i and 802.1X. To assist you in preparing your presentation, read the white paper titled "Wireless LAN Security Best Practices" at *www.phoenixdatacom.com/security-wp.html*.

Challenge Case Project

CASE PROJECTS

ACS found your presentation very useful but would like to know how using encryption would impact the performance of its WLAN. To prepare a report, you can use the same tools you used for the Chapter 7 Challenge Case Project. Alternatively, you can go to *www.openmaniak.com/iperf* and review the tutorial on how to use Iperf tools to measure the bandwidth and quality of a network link. Then download and install Iperf from *sourceforge.net/projects/iperf*.

Using the hardware and configuration you set up for Hands-On Project 8-1, measure the network's performance before configuring security and encryption. Record your results. Next, configure your gateway to use WPA2 with AES encryption and measure the performance again. Then write a one-page report outlining any differences in performance that you encounter. Be sure to calculate and provide a brief comparison of how long it would take to copy a 10 MB or larger file.

chapter 9

Wireless Metropolitan Area Networks

After reading this chapter and completing the exercises, you will be able to:

- Explain why wireless metropolitan area networks (WMANs) are needed
- Describe the components and modes of operation of a WMAN
- Describe several WMAN technologies, including FSO, LMDS, MMDS, and 802.16 (WiMAX)
- Explain how WMANs function
- Outline the security features of WMANs

By now, you understand the tremendous impact that wireless communications has and will continue to have on the world around us. Wireless networks allow users to be connected as they move about, freeing them from cables and phone lines. However, the WPANs and WLANs you have learned about thus far have restricted user mobility to homes, offices, or campuses, allowing them to roam from only a few feet to a few hundred feet from the source of the RF signal. Limits on the strength of these RF signals, mandated by the regulatory authorities and designed to prevent interference in the unlicensed bands, are the main reason for this restriction. Users have also been subject to line-of-sight limitations. Therefore, except for voice communications and data over cellular networks, user mobility has remained largely confined to homes, offices, and hotspots that offer wireless access, which include coffee shops and airports as well as the core downtown areas of a few cities that have deployed Wi-Fi networks.

In small towns and remote areas, the relatively small number of wireless network users may not make it economically viable to implement hotspots and mobile access. In fact, in areas with low user density, the cost of installing wired high-speed communications channels over long distances often prevents telephone companies or small ISPs from offering high-speed Internet access at all.

In this chapter, you will learn about technologies and standards that allow wireless access to expand beyond a few hundred feet—to connect buildings several miles apart, for example, or an entire city. The chapter begins with coverage of infrared (IR)-based short-distance and medium-distance technologies and concludes with standards for medium-distance and long-distance RF-based WMAN technologies.

What Is a WMAN?

Wireless metropolitan area networks (WMANs) are a group of technologies that provide wireless connectivity across a substantial geographical area such as a large city. WMANs have two primary goals:

- To extend the reach of existing wired networks beyond a single location without the expense of deploying and maintaining high-speed wire or optical-cable-based connections.

- To extend user mobility throughout a metropolitan area. An important additional benefit of a WMAN is that it can provide high-speed connections, including Internet, to areas not serviced by any other method of connectivity. Such connectivity can encompass metropolitan areas, expanding to small towns nearby, as well as to remote locations not usually serviced by high-speed communications lines.

Last Mile Wired Connections

A **last mile connection** is typically defined as the link between an end-user and an ISP. Even today, most last mile connections are based on some type of copper wiring; more recently, they are based on optical fiber cables. As of April 2012, only about 19.3 million homes in the United States are directly connected to fiber networks, and only a very small number of office buildings are wired for cable TV. In spite of its exceptional reliability for data communications, fiber optics is slow, inconvenient, and expensive to install; most important of all, it is costly to maintain, especially in regions where the ground freezes and thaws once or twice a year, which can damage buried cables. Figure 9-1 shows an example of an overhead-wire last mile connection.

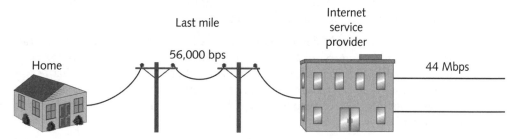

Figure 9-1 Last mile connection

© Cengage Learning 2014

Today, home users in large metropolitan areas can take advantage of both DSL at up to 16 Mbps and cable-TV connections at up to 105 Mbps. However, these types of connections are usually not available in small, remote communities. Business users do have a few other options beyond basic copper wiring, however. As you have learned, ISDN, T1, and DSL technologies offer higher data rates, are widely available, and are wire based. Similar to T1 is T3, which is a faster but more expensive digital line. Table 9-1 summarizes some of the connection options and speeds for homes, office buildings, and Internet service providers.

Connection Type	Speed (or Range)	Typical Use	Approximate Cost Per Month	Approximate Time to Download Full Content of a 680 MB CD-ROM (Hours:Minutes)
Dial-up modem	56 Kbps	Home	Free and up	26:53
ISDN (1 or 2 channels)	64 or 128 Kbps	Home or business	Residential: $50 setup + $29.95 Business: $49.95	24:10 or 12:50
Cable modem	1.5–105 Mbps	Home	$30–$199	0:58 to less than 0:01
ADSL	6–16 Mbps	Home	$15–$140	0:15–0:06
T1	1.544 Mbps	Office	$400 and up	0:58
T3	44.736 Mbps	Office, ISP	$2,500–$5,000	0:02
OC-3 (optical fiber)	155 Mbps	ISP	$10,000–$30,000	32 seconds
OC-12 (optical fiber)	622.08 Mbps	ISP	Varies greatly	8 seconds
OC-192 (optical fiber)	9.6 Gbps	Large ISP	Varies greatly	Less than 1 second

Table 9-1 Wired connection options

© Cengage Learning 2014

For long-distance connections between cities and states, copper-based digital communications lines, such as T1, require the signal to be regenerated every 6,000 feet (1.8 kilometers). In addition to the challenges of cable installation and maintenance, regenerating the signal requires electrical power at each repeater location. Maintenance costs for this type of connection are extremely high, especially where the geography or the environmental conditions (e.g., mountainous or desert areas) are challenging.

Last mile delivery of telephone and data lines has long been a problem for the **carriers** (i.e., the providers and operators) of the networks, who must be able to justify the cost of installing wired connections in remote areas. In previous chapters, you learned that "carrier" refers to the RF signal that carries data. The term also refers to telephone, cable TV, and other communications-provider companies that own the wires and transmission towers that carry voice and data traffic.

Since the early 1980s, fiber-optic technology has largely replaced all other technologies for connections between major metropolitan centers, mainly because it has a higher capacity for carrying voice and data transmissions, lower maintenance requirements, and is much more reliable than copper wiring. However, the higher costs of the fiber-optic medium and in-ground installation often preclude its use in remote and less-populated areas. Fiber-optic cables are also used to carry voice and data traffic across the world's oceans. Submarine fiber-optic cables span practically the entire globe and are laid and maintained by specialized ships and crews. The cost of deploying and maintaining these cables is extremely high, but today the world is heavily dependent on them. For more information, search for "submarine cable" on the Internet.

Last Mile Wireless Connections

Most of the technologies used in WMANs and last mile wireless connections are based on microwave signals, but they also include infrared light. **Microwaves** are higher frequency RF waves with transmission taking place in the 3–30 GHz range of the electromagnetic spectrum, which is known as the **super high frequency (SHF)** band. Microwaves were introduced in the early 1950s by AT&T and brought about a new era in communications. Originally, they were used to transmit data in a point-to-point fashion, using the lower and middle portions of the SHF band. The conventional thinking in the early days was that the lower-frequency, high-powered approach was the only way in which microwaves could be used for communication. High-frequency microwave technology was ignored for many years, and the section of the RF spectrum between 27.5 and 29.5 GHz went virtually unused.

Microwave towers are installed roughly 35 miles (56 kilometers) apart from each other, and a link operating at 4 GHz carries about 1,800 voice calls simultaneously. In comparison, a T1 link can carry only 24 simultaneous voice calls. Improvements in microwave technology have reduced the cost of the equipment and have made telephone and data communications services available in many remote locations across the United States that were previously out of range of high-capacity connections.

The first transcontinental microwave link was completed in 1951, connecting New York and San Francisco. It used 107 towers spaced about 30 miles (48 kilometers) apart, covering a distance of about 3,200 miles (5,140 kilometers). The same link using T1 digital copper-based lines requires over 2,850 repeaters to regenerate the signal.

The options for WMANs and last mile connections include Free Space Optics, RF-based (microwave) local multipoint distribution service, and multichannel multipoint distribution service as well as WiMAX, and they are discussed in the remainder of this chapter. The advantages of these types of wireless connections are that they can cost less, can be installed relatively quickly, offer greater flexibility, and have better long-term reliability. Using wireless as the last mile connection for buildings is called **fixed wireless** because buildings are fixed in one location.

Fixed wireless networks have been used for several years for both voice and data communications, generally in backhaul networks operated by telephone companies, cable TV companies, utilities, railways, paging companies, and government agencies. A **backhaul** connection is a company's internal infrastructure connection. For example, a phone company's backhaul network may be a connection from one telephone company central office to another. Cellular telephone towers along highways are often interconnected using a microwave backhaul link.

Fixed wireless systems can be used to transmit the same type of data that is sent over a wired cable system. However, point-to-point long-distance microwave links, such as those employed by telephone carriers, use high-power signals that are not suitable or safe for use in crowded city skylines. In addition, microwaves require licensed frequencies, which carry a high cost, and spectrum availability may be very limited in busy metropolitan areas.

In Chapter 8, you learned that WLAN equipment such as 802.11 wireless bridges can be set up to connect two buildings provided the installation does not interfere with other wireless links using the same unlicensed RF bands. Installation of longer-distance connections with this technology—beyond the range of Wi-Fi (375 feet)—is possible but can be a lot more complicated. In addition to loss of speed as the distance increases, 802.11 technologies are designed to support only a single repeater link, which means that a maximum of three bridges can be used between two destination points. Achieving line of sight between two directional antennas is difficult or may not be possible due to tower height limitations in metropolitan areas. Additionally, the throughput of a single 802.11 frequency channel is typically only enough to carry a limited amount of data, such as e-mail, Web browsing, and moderate file transfers, mainly due to the half-duplex characteristic of wireless bridges. Although using multiple bridge links to increase bandwidth can alleviate the problem, it tends to make antenna installation far more complicated because you would have to align multiple pairs of directional antennas instead of just one.

Baseband vs. Broadband

Another point to consider when designing wireless links is that there are two ways in which digital signals can be transmitted over a wireless medium. The first is called **broadband** transmission, in which multiple signals are simultaneously sent over the medium at different frequencies. An example of broadband transmission is cable TV, in which multiple entertainment channels are sent on a single cable. When you pick a channel to watch, the TV set filters out all other frequencies and decodes and displays a single channel.

The second technique is called **baseband** transmission. Baseband treats the entire transmission medium as if it were only one channel and transmits only one data signal at a time over a single frequency. An example of baseband transmission is Ethernet, in which digital signals are sent over a cable. Ethernet 100BaseT, for example, means 100 Mbps, baseband signaling using twisted pair cabling. As you learned in Chapter 2, digital signals use a change in voltage to represent a 1 or a 0. You can change the voltage differential between two wires on a cable, but you cannot transmit this change over an analog medium such as an EM wave, which is an analog medium. To transmit digital signals over an analog medium, you need to modulate a carrier wave to represent a change between a 1 and a 0.

The examples just given describe the differences between broadband and baseband transmissions over a cable, but keep in mind that transmissions over an analog medium (such as EM waves) can be sent as broadband or baseband. Purely digital signals can only be transmitted over a wire as baseband, because mixing multiple voltage changes on a cable would create different bit patterns and corrupt the data, given that there is no way to separate one signal from the other. However, if you modulate multiple digital signals over different carrier frequencies, they can be transmitted over any analog medium. The receiver can then separate each frequency using filters and decode each of the digital signals individually.

Note also that there is no predefined frequency bandwidth separating baseband from broadband. For example, the wider the bandwidth, the more frequencies are available to transmit separate channels of data using frequency division multiplexing. Alternatively, broadband transmissions can be made using time division multiplexing. Both methods can be considered broadband transmission. In comparison, a baseband transmission consists of only one data channel.

Figure 9-2 shows a rough visual comparison between baseband and broadband transmissions.

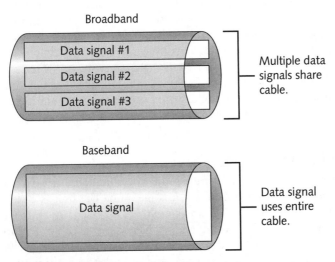

Figure 9-2 Baseband vs. broadband transmissions

Land-Based Fixed Broadband Wireless

The data communications industry has developed a few different solutions for last mile connections over the past few decades. Some have proven too costly and were hard to justify. Others have proved to be less than 100 percent reliable for implementation in all locations, as explained later in this chapter. Most are proprietary solutions or RF-based equipment that require licensed frequency bands. Until 2001, RF-based fixed broadband systems operated at frequencies and with modulation techniques that limited implementation to line of sight only. In addition, most fixed broadband systems could only send from one site to another—in other words, they are set up in point-to-point fashion. As a comparison, in cellular telephone systems, a single base station can communicate with several mobile devices simultaneously. However, cellular technology was originally designed to carry multiple voice conversations and not for high-capacity data transmissions, although this is changing today.

Faced with having to rely on land-based lines from telephone and cable TV carriers, many companies have deployed their own building-to-building connectivity solutions. This section begins with an IR-based solution called Free Space Optics. We look briefly at two types of legacy proprietary last mile microwave connection technologies: local multipoint distribution service and multichannel multipoint distribution service. Later in the chapter, you will learn about the IEEE 802.16 group of wireless standards, which is already in use in many fixed business wireless networks and for Internet connectivity applications. Recent enhancements to the 802.16 standards also promise to help solve the challenges of user mobility and compete with DSL, cable TV, and even local telephone carriers.

9

Free Space Optics

Free Space Optics (FSO) is an optical, wireless, point-to-point, line-of-sight broadband technology. Although it was originally developed over 30 years ago by the military, FSO has become an excellent alternative to high-speed fiber-optic cable. Currently, FSO can transmit at speeds comparable to fiber-optic transmissions, reaching up to 1.25 Gbps at a distance of 4 miles (6.4 kilometers) in full-duplex mode. Future improvements in the technology will likely push the top speed to 10 Gbps and possibly beyond.

FSO uses infrared (IR) transmission instead of RF. The technology is similar to that used with a fiber-optic cable system. A fiber-optic cable contains a very thin strand of glass called the core, which is as thick as a human hair. Instead of transmitting electrical signals, fiber-optic cables use light impulses. A light source, usually created by a laser or light-emitting diodes (LEDs), flashes a light at one end of the cable that is detected at the receiving end. Light travels at 186,000 miles (300,000 kilometers) per second, so fiber-optic cable systems can transmit large amounts of data at high speeds. In addition, these transmissions are immune to electromagnetic interference and cannot be easily intercepted.

FSO is an alternative to fiber-optic cables. Sometimes called "fiberless optical," FSO does not use a medium, like a fiber-optic cable, to send and receive signals. Instead, low-powered invisible infrared beams carry the data. These beams, which do not harm the human eye, are transmitted by transceivers, as shown in Figure 9-3. Because FSO is a line-of-sight technology, the transceivers are mounted in the middle or upper floors of office buildings to provide a clear transmission path. However, unlike other technologies that require the units to be located on an open roof (which sometimes requires leasing roof space from the building's owner), FSO transceivers can be mounted behind a window in an existing office.

Figure 9-3 FSO transceiver (transmitter/receiver)

Source: Courtesy of fSONA Networks Corp

 Under perfect conditions, such as environments free of fog, dust, and high heat and humidity, FSO can transmit at distances of up to 6.2 miles (10 kilometers).

Recall that the lower-frequency portion of the electromagnetic spectrum is the area in which RF EM waves travel. The spectrum above 300 GHz is the area in which IR waves move. FSO also uses this part of the spectrum. This higher frequency is unlicensed worldwide, so it can be freely used. The only limitation on its use is that the radiated power must not exceed specific limits in order to avoid harming the human eye.

 FSO equipment works at either of two wavelengths. A single worldwide wavelength will likely be standardized for these devices.

Advantages of FSO The advantages of FSO include cost, speed of installation, transmission rate, and security.

FSO installations cost significantly less than installing new fiber-optic cables or even leasing lines from a local carrier. One recent project compared the costs of installing fiber-optic cables to FSO in three buildings. The cost to install the fiber-optic cables was almost $400,000, compared to less than $60,000 for FSO.

FSO can be installed in days, compared to months—or sometimes years—for fiber-optic cables, which require a series of permits from city authorities, whether installed underground or strung along lampposts. In some instances, installers can set up FSO systems over a weekend without disrupting the users.

The transmission speed for FSO can be scaled to meet users' needs—anywhere from 10 Mbps to 1.25 Gbps. If high speeds are not required, the user does not have to pay a premium for unused capacity.

Security is a key advantage in an FSO system. IR transmissions cannot be as easily intercepted and decoded as some RF transmissions.

Disadvantages of FSO The primary disadvantage of FSO is that atmospheric conditions can have an impact on FSO transmissions. **Scintillation** is the temporal and spatial variations in light intensity caused by atmospheric turbulence. Turbulence caused by wind and temperature variations can create pockets of air with rapidly changing densities. These air pockets can act like prisms and lenses that distort an FSO signal. Inclement weather is also a threat. Although rain and snow can distort a signal, fog does the most damage to light-based transmissions. Fog is composed of extremely small moisture particles that act like prisms, scattering and breaking up the light beams.

Scintillation is readily observed in the twinkling of stars in the night sky and the shimmering of the horizon on a hot sunny day.

FSO overcomes scintillation by sending the data in parallel streams from several separate laser transmitters. These transmitters are all mounted in the same transceiver but are separated from one another by distances of about 7.8 inches (200 mm). It is unlikely that, while traveling to the receiver, all the parallel beams will encounter the same pocket of turbulence, given that scintillation pockets are usually quite small. At least one of the beams will arrive at the target node with adequate strength to be properly received. This solution is called **spatial diversity** because it exploits multiple regions of air space. An example of spatial diversity is shown in Figure 9-4, with parallel light beams coming from an FSO transmitter.

In dealing with fog, there are several potential solutions. One solution is simply to increase the transmit power of the signal (the intensity of the light). In regions of heavy and frequent fog, it may be necessary to choose FSO systems that transmit at the highest available frequency because these devices can also emit light at higher power levels. Several vendors also claim to customize their distance and product recommendations based on weather statistics for particular cities. Other FSO vendors use a backup (wired) connection along with FSO to ensure that transmissions go through in foggy weather.

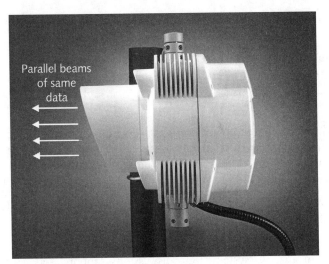

Parallel beams of same data

Transceiver

Figure 9-4 Spatial diversity

Source: Courtesy of fSONA Networks Corp

In order to prove that FSO can send transmissions through fog, one vendor ran trials in some of the foggiest cities in the United States. In San Francisco, one of the worst cities in the country for fog, one vendor has proven that FSO can maintain carrier-class transmission speeds (1.25 Gbps) over 90 percent of the time.

Some experts recommend that the distance between FSO transceivers in regions of heavy and frequent fog should be limited to 650 to 1,640 feet (200 to 500 meters).

Signal interference can also be a problem for FSO, such as when birds fly through the IR beam and block it. If the signal is temporarily blocked, the beam automatically reduces its power, then raises itself to full power when the obstruction clears the beam's path.

Another potential problem is that storms and earthquakes can cause tall buildings to move enough to affect the aim of the beam. This problem can be handled in two ways. In the first method, known as "beam divergence," the transmitted beam is purposely allowed to spread, or diverge, so that by the time it arrives at the receiving device it forms a fairly large optical cone. If the receiver is initially positioned at the center of the beam, divergence can compensate for any movement of the building. The second method, known as "active tracking," is based on movable mirrors that are controlled by gyroscopes that, in turn, control the direction in which the beams are sent. A feedback mechanism continuously adjusts the mirrors so that the beams stay on target.

FSO Applications There is a variety of applications for FSO. More common ones include:

- Last mile connection—FSO can be used in high-speed links that connect end-users with Internet service providers or other networks.

- LAN connections—FSO devices are easily installed, making them a natural solution for interconnecting LAN segments that are housed in buildings separated by public streets or other obstacles, such as in a university campus spanning several city blocks.

- Fiber-optic backup—FSO can be deployed in redundant links to back up fiber-optic cables in case of a break in the cable.

- Backhaul—FSO can be used to carry cellular telephone traffic from antenna towers back to facilities wired to carrier-provided high-speed communications lines.

Most experts agree that FSO holds great potential for fixed wireless communications as well as for other wireless applications. In spite of all the other technology developments, FSO has remained a stable player in the wireless field.

Local Multipoint Distribution Service (LMDS)

Local Multipoint Distribution Service (LMDS) is a fixed broadband microwave, line-of-sight technology that can provide a wide variety of wireless services. LMDS has often been called "wireless cable" for its ability to compete with cable TV networks in localized areas. The services that can be provided with LMDS technology include high-speed Internet access, real-time multimedia file transfer, remote access to local area networks, interactive video, video-on-demand, video conferencing, and telephone service. LMDS can transmit anywhere from 51 to 155 Mbps downstream and 1.54 Mbps upstream over a distance of up to about 5 miles (8 kilometers).

One of the best ways to explain LMDS is by examining each of the words that make up its name:

- Local (L)—Refers to the area of coverage of LMDS systems. Because they use high-frequency, low-powered RF waves, these systems have a limited range. The coverage area for LMDS is only 2–5 miles (3.2–8.0 kilometers).

- Multipoint (M)—Indicates that signals are transmitted to the remote stations in a point-to-multipoint fashion from a base station omnidirectional antenna. The signals that are transmitted back from the remote stations to the base station are point-to-point transmissions from directional antennas.

- Distribution (D)—Refers to the distribution of the various types of information that can be transmitted. These types include voice, data, Internet, and video traffic.

- Service (S)—Indicates that there is a variety of services available. However, the local carrier determines which services are offered. This means that all the services that can be offered—voice, data, Internet, and video traffic—may not be available to the LMDS users in each location.

Figure 9-5 shows examples of point-to-point and point-to-multipoint LMDS transmissions.

The U.S. Federal Communications Commission (FCC) grants LMDS frequency band licenses to carriers for a specific area. This way, the same frequencies can be licensed to other carriers in different areas.

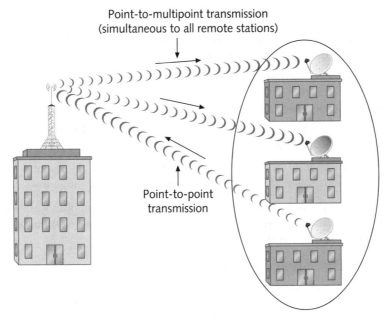

Point-to-multipoint transmission
(simultaneous to all remote stations)

Point-to-point
transmission

Figure 9-5 LMDS transmissions

© *Cengage Learning 2014*

Frequency Bands In 1996, the FCC began making frequency spectrum allocations for LMDS. In 1998, the U.S. government auctioned the frequency spectrum in two blocks: Block A, consisting of frequencies in the 27.5–28.35 GHz range, the 29.1–29.25 GHz range, and the 31.075–31.225 GHz range, for a total of 1,150 MHz; and Block B, another 150 MHz of frequency spectrum, this in the 31–31.075 GHz range and the 31.225–31.3 GHz range. These were all allocated to LMDS on a co-primary (shared) basis.

LMDS Network Architecture Because an LMDS signal can only travel up to 5 miles (8 kilometers), an LMDS network is composed of cells similar to a cellular telephone system. Unlike a cellular telephone network, however, LMDS radios transmit only to fixed buildings within the cell. There is a variety of factors that can affect the size of the LMDS cell. The main factors that determine the cell size are line of sight, antenna height, overlapping cells, and rainfall. An example of an LMDS cell setup is shown in Figure 9-6.

Because of the line-of-sight requirement, if the transmitting and receiving antennas can be placed on the rooftops of tall buildings, particularly those buildings that are farthest away from each other, then cells can typically be larger because the number of obstructions is reduced. LMDS cells can also overlap one another to ensure better coverage.

Rainfall also determines the size of an LMDS cell. Because of the higher frequencies in which LMDS works, signals lose strength in the presence of heavy rain or snow. To correct this, LMDS equipment can increase the transmit power of radios to ensure a strong signal that reaches the receivers. Most LMDS cells are sized according to the average local annual rainfall. An LMDS cell, under ideal conditions, can be up to 5 miles (8 kilometers) across.

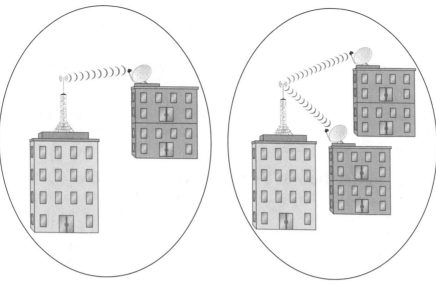

Figure 9-6 LMDS system with multiple cells

© Cengage Learning 2014

However, cells located in areas of heavy rainfall are between 2 and 5 miles (3.2 to 8 kilometers) across.

LMDS signals are broadcast from radio hubs (transmitters) that are deployed throughout the carrier's market, which is the area in which the carrier has a license to use a certain frequency. This area is usually limited to a city or part of a city. Each hub broadcasts signals to buildings within its cell. The hub connects to the service provider's central office, which in turn can connect to other networks, such as the Internet.

At the receiving site, there are three pieces of equipment: a 12–15-inch diameter directional antenna, a digital radio modem, and a network interface unit. The digital radio modem performs digital-to-analog and analog-to-digital conversions. The **Network Interface Unit (NIU)** connects to a local area network as well as to other services provided via a digital wired communications line.

LMDS systems can use either Time Division Multiple Access (TDMA) or Frequency Division Multiple Access (FDMA) to share the frequency spectrum among users. The modulation techniques can also vary among carriers. Most use a form of quadrature phase shift keying (QPSK) or quadrature amplitude modulation (QAM).

Advantages and Disadvantages of LMDS
The advantages of LMDS include cost, service area, and data capacity. LMDS costs less to implement than fiber-optic cables. These costs are low for both the user and the carrier. For the user, the cost is minimal to install the antenna, modem, and NIU compared to the cost of installing fiber-optic cable. For the carrier, LMDS is an attractive last mile solution because it allows a number of concentrated customers that connect to a cell to access the carrier's network at a lower

cost than wired alternatives. LMDS carriers can have as much as 1,300 MHz of spectrum in a local market. This spectrum can simultaneously support 16,000 telephone calls and 200 video channels.

In spite of its relatively low cost and data-carrying capacity, LMDS began to face serious competition in the late 1990s and early 21st century from the rapid development of DSL, cable TV networks, and much-higher-capacity fiber-optics networks. Deployments were limited and today there are only a few manufacturers that still provide this type of equipment. In most cases, today's LMDS systems are being deployed in point-to-point fashion as a backhaul for cellular telephone towers.

Multichannel Multipoint Distribution Service (MMDS)

Multichannel Multipoint Distribution Service (MMDS) is a fixed broadband wireless technology similar to LMDS. A significant difference between the two involves transmission capabilities. MMDS can transmit video, voice, or data signals at 1.5–2 Mbps downstream and 320 Kbps upstream at distances of up to 35 miles (56 kilometers), compared to 155 Mbps downstream and 1.54 Mbps upstream at distances of up to 5 miles for LMDS.

MMDS was designed in the 1960s to provide transmission for 33 one-way analog television channels (simplex transmission). This multiple-channel technology (hence the term "multichannel") was designed to provide long-distance learning for educational institutions. The FCC allocated the 2.5–2.7 GHz part of the frequency band for MMDS, but in other international markets it has been deployed in the 3.5 GHz frequency band. Unlike LMDS, MMDS is a non-line-of-sight technology, and the signals can also penetrate walls better than LMDS signals because of their lower transmission frequency.

 The acronym "MMDS" is sometimes expanded to "Multipoint Microwave Distribution System" or "Multichannel Multipoint Distribution System." All three terms refer to the same technology.

The original vision for MMDS never fully materialized. Private companies later purchased part of this spectrum to compete against wired cable television companies. (MMDS is also sometimes called wireless cable.) Using MMDS, television signals could be wirelessly beamed to homes instead of delivered over a cable system. In the 1980s, new digital technology allowed service providers to increase their capacity from 33 analog channels to 99 digital channels. Later improvements in video compression and modulation techniques increased the capacity of MMDS, enabling the technology to broadcast 300 channels.

A major change to MMDS occurred in 1998. The FCC allowed service providers to use the 200 MHz of bandwidth in the MMDS frequency bands to provide two-way services such as wireless Internet access at the same time as voice and video transmissions. In the home, Internet access using MMDS is an alternative to cable modems and DSL service, particularly in rural areas where cabling is scarce. For businesses, MMDS is an alternative to T1 or expensive fiber-optic connections, but although it can support downstream speeds of up to 1.5 Mbps, the upstream speed is only 300 Kbps, limiting its use in businesses that host their own Web sites and other similar services.

Note that, for Internet access, most of the traffic is downstream. For example, when you are browsing the Web, fewer packets are sent upstream to request the pages from the servers. The amount of data transmitted from the Web servers to the user's computer (downstream), which may include graphics, is much larger. Most home Internet users download far more data than they upload. This is why services such as DSL, cable Internet, and MMDS have a higher bandwidth downstream and a lower bandwidth upstream. This type of communications is known as asymmetric because there are different upstream and downstream data rates.

MMDS Network Architecture An MMDS hub (transmitter) is typically located on a high point, such as a mountain, tower, or building. The hub uses a point-to-multipoint architecture that multiplexes communications to multiple users. The tower has a backhaul connection to the carrier's network, and the carrier network connects with the Internet.

Because they operate at a lower frequency than LMDS signals, MMDS signals can travel longer distances. This means that MMDS can provide service to an entire area with only a few radio transmitters. MMDS uses cells, as LMDS does. However, an MMDS cell can have a radius of up to 35 miles (56 kilometers), which covers 3,800 square miles (9,481 square kilometers) of area. A similar area would require over 100 LMDS cells.

At the receiving location, a directional antenna approximately 13 × 13 inches (33 cm) is aimed at the hub to receive the MMDS signal, as shown in Figure 9-7. This antenna, sometimes called a **pizza box antenna,** is usually installed on the roof of a building so that it has a direct line of sight to a radio transmitter. A cable runs from the antenna to an MMDS wireless modem, which converts the transmitted analog signal to digital. The modem can then connect to a single computer or a LAN, as shown in Figure 9-8.

9

Figure 9-7 Pizza box antenna

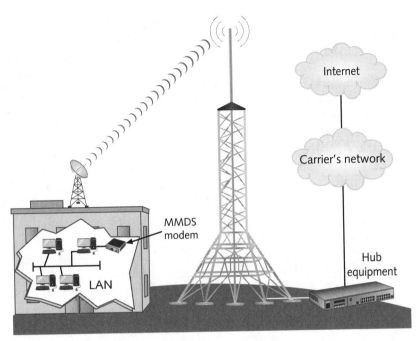

Figure 9-8 MMDS system infrastructure

© Cengage Learning 2014

Advantages and Disadvantages of MMDS Advantages of MMDS include signal strength, large cell size, and cost. Low-frequency MMDS RF signals can travel farther, generally are less susceptible to interference from rain or fog, and are better able to penetrate buildings than high-frequency LMDS RF signals. These characteristics permit MMDS transmitters to cover areas seven times larger than LMDS transmitters. Finally, the cost of electronic equipment is typically linked to the frequency used to transmit: The higher the frequency, the higher the cost of the equipment. Because MMDS uses a lower frequency in comparison to LMDS, MMDS equipment is less expensive.

The disadvantages of MMDS include physical limitations, frequency sharing, security, and availability of the technology. Current-generation MMDS still requires a direct line of sight between the tower and the buildings. This makes installation more difficult and prevents MMDS from being used in a large number of buildings in a given cell because the signals are blocked by taller obstructions. Also, a single MMDS cell might be servicing a larger number of users within its 35-mile (56-kilometer) radius. These users all share the same radio channels; and, as a result, data throughputs and speed decrease as more users are added. Providers of MMDS technology sometimes quote transmission rates of up to 10 Mbps, but because the channels are shared, the actual speed may be closer to 1.5 Mbps.

Carriers do not encrypt the wireless MMDS transmissions. Although only a highly sophisticated user could intercept and read the transmissions, business users should add security enhancements to their transmissions to keep them safe. MMDS is available in only a limited number of areas across the United States at the present time and has not experienced any significant growth, due to competition from other technologies.

IEEE 802.16 (WiMAX)

IEEE 802.16 is an open-standard, broadband MAN technology that can work in either line-of-sight or non-line-of-sight mode, depending on the frequency used, and is designed to support a large variety of fixed or mobile digital data communications services for MANs. The term **WiMAX** stands for "Worldwide Interoperability for Microwave Access." The IEEE introduced 802.16 in 2000, with the goal of standardizing fixed broadband wireless connections as an alternative to wired access networks such as fiber-optic links, cable TV modems, and DSL. IEEE 802.16 supports enhancements and extensions to the MAC protocols so that it is possible for a **base station (BS)** (the transmitter connected to the carrier network or to the Internet) to communicate with another BS as well as directly with **subscriber stations (SS)**, which can be either a laptop computer or a device that attaches to a LAN. LMDS and MMDS do not provide connectivity with mobile devices and are also not designed to work beyond the size of a single cell by allowing one BS to communicate with another. FSO also cannot support mobile communications because of its directional requirements.

Figure 9-9 shows a WiMAX lab setup that includes two BS controllers (top) and four SSs (bottom). Each two SSs in the photo are connected to one of the BS radios (middle, vertical). The flat areas in the front of the SSs are integrated antennas, which in this case are disabled for safety (because of the high-power microwaves); instead, cables are used to interconnect all the devices. The SSs in the photo are normally installed on the outside wall of a house or building that faces the antenna of the nearest BS.

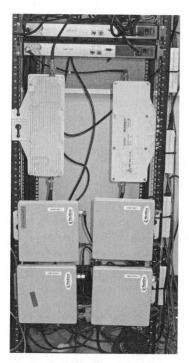

Figure 9-9 WiMAX devices

© *Cengage Learning 2014*

In January 2006, Samsung introduced a notebook computer and mobile telephone handset that were both 802.16-compliant. Several other PC manufacturers followed shortly after by offering built-in WiMAX connectivity options in their portable computer product lines.

FSO, LMDS, and MMDS are not based on an open standard, which means that equipment from different manufacturers may not interoperate. This forces both customers and carriers to purchase all their equipment from a single manufacturer.

A group of manufacturers established the **WiMAX Forum** in June of 2001 to promote the implementation of 802.16 by testing and certifying equipment for compatibility and interoperability. Currently, the Forum's Web site lists approximately 150 member companies.

Many standards become loosely known by the more popular name of the industry organizations, such as "WiMAX" instead of the IEEE designation "802.16." You can find out more about WiMAX by visiting the Forum's Web site at *www.wimaxforum.org*.

The IEEE 802.16 standard offers multiple RF interfaces (PHY layers), depending on the frequencies used and associated regulations for different countries, but they are all based on a common MAC protocol. Next, you will learn about the applications and situations in which WiMAX can be employed.

South Korea was one of the first countries in the world to implement wireless broadband networks based on the nation's WiBro standard. The IEEE subsequently made the 802.16 standard fully compatible with the Korean standard.

WiMAX Applications With data rates of up to 70 Mbps in the 2–11 GHz bands and up to 120 Mbps at short distances (indoors) in the 10–66 GHz bands, WiMAX is suitable for backhaul business applications as well as last mile delivery applications that replace T1, DSL, and cable TV modems for Internet connectivity. WiMAX can support simultaneous voice, video, and data transmission with QoS. This makes it particularly suitable for voice-over-IP (VoIP) connections, which has enabled small companies to enter the telecommunications market and compete with major carriers in providing telephone services to consumers. The convergence of voice, video, and data on IP networks is what the industry calls **triple-play**.

WiMAX enables vendors to create many different types of products, including various configurations of base stations and **customer premises equipment (CPE)**, which are the devices that are installed in a customer's office or home. In addition to supporting the point-to-multipoint applications just mentioned, WiMAX can be deployed as a point-to-point network to provide broadband access to rural and remote areas.

To see other examples of CPE devices and other WiMAX hardware, visit *www.greenpacket.com/devices.html*. For examples of base stations, visit *www.ruggedcom.com/products/ruggedmax/win7200*. You can also search "WiMAX CPE" and "WiMAX base station" to locate other manufacturers' Web sites.

Manufacturers can design and build standards-based equipment that can be employed by wireless operators using licensed frequencies and also by business users using both licensed and unlicensed frequencies. Compared to MMDS and LMDS, the cost for the equipment and service has already dropped significantly. Whereas an LMDS network can cost upwards of $60,000, an 802.16 network can be put together for under $10,000. The cost of CPEs has dropped to as low as $80 each. Some CPE devices can support TV (video), telephone (voice), and data on the same network.

The WiMAX MAC layer includes features designed to make it easy for carriers to deploy the network. Once the BSs are in place, an end-user can connect to a WiMAX network by simply taking the CPE device out of the box, placing the antenna near a window or mounting it on an outside wall, roughly in the direction of the BS, and turning it on. In contrast to configuring a Wi-Fi wireless residential gateway, for example, little or no configuration is required by the customer to install a WiMAX CPE. This process also has the effect of dramatically reducing the installation costs for the service provider, who will no longer have to send a technician to the customer's site. By remotely managing the device, the provider also reduces ongoing maintenance costs.

In December 2005, Nortel deployed the first commercial WiMAX network, which covers 8,000 square miles (20,720 square kilometers) in the southeast region of Alberta, Canada. The network, which began serving both the public and the provincial government in 2006, operates in the 3.5 GHz band and provides Internet access to this large rural area at speeds between 1 and 3 Mbps. The network is easily upgradeable to 802.16e to support mobile WiMAX.

The range of a WiMAX network is measured in miles, unlike Wi-Fi, which is measured in feet. With low costs and interfaces becoming available for laptop computers and other handheld devices, even at slightly lower speeds, WiMAX can offer serious competition to 802.11 networks and hotspots.

Standards Family Overview

IEEE 802.16 covers a wide range of functionality and has a number of variations that address specific applications. It defines the interface specification for fixed, point-to-multipoint broadband wireless metropolitan area networks. The 802.16-2001 standard includes a PHY-layer specification for systems operating in the 10–66 GHz range and forms the basis for all the other standards in the family. IEEE 802.16-2004 is a revised version of the initial standard that adds support for systems operating in the 2–11 GHz range.

The 802.16e standard, ratified in December 2005, is an amendment to the 802.16-2004 standard that defines the specifications for a mobile version of WiMAX. This enhancement can enable data rates of up to 2 Mbps for portable devices that are slow moving or stationary, and speeds of up to 320 Kbps in fast-moving vehicles. IEEE 802.16-2009 is the latest full version of the standard and incorporates all the amendments up to that year. The most recent amendment is 802.16m, which the WiMAX Forum calls "Release 2." It raises the data rate to 100 Mbps and makes it possible to combine MIMO, multiple frequency channels, and spatial multiplexing to achieve rates of up to 1 Gbps.

WiMAX Protocol Stack

As with many of the technologies you have learned about in this book, the PHY and MAC layers are the only ones that change between different networking standards. WiMAX is unique in that, in addition to the PHY layer supporting multiple frequency bands, its PHY layer is able to adapt on the fly. The modulation techniques and access mechanisms can change dynamically from a BS to the remote devices and to other BSs, depending on distance, the existence of any interference, or the requirements of the particular device itself.

Unlike Ethernet and other protocols, the MAC layer for WiMAX is connection oriented and includes service-specific convergence sublayers that interface to the upper OSI layers. Remember that in the OSI protocol model, only the Transport layer (layer 4) is connection oriented. The convergence sublayers of the MAC layer in WiMAX can map a particular service to a connection, which allows WiMAX to offer multiple simultaneous services through the same link and to carry a mix of protocols, such as asynchronous transfer mode (ATM), IPv4, IPv6, Ethernet, VLAN, and others, all in the same network. The MAC layer in WiMAX also includes a privacy sublayer that is used to secure the link (discussed in the security section of this chapter). The 802.16 WiMAX protocol stack is shown in Figure 9-10.

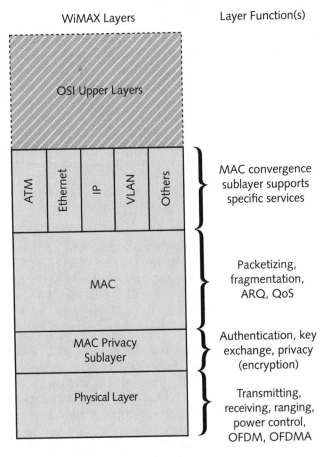

Figure 9-10 802.16 protocol stack

© Cengage Learning 2014

PHY Layer There are several variations of the PHY layer in 802.16. Determining which variation to use for a particular implementation depends on the frequency range and whether it is a point-to-point or point-to-multipoint setup. The first two are based on the modulation of a single carrier signal. Remember that when transmitting on a single frequency, all transmitters have to work in half-duplex mode because they cannot transmit and receive at the same time. In this case, each transmission is divided into fixed duration frames that are 5 milliseconds long. Each frame is subdivided into one uplink subframe and one downlink subframe. The BS transmits to the SSs during the downlink subframe, and the SSs transmit to the BS during the uplink subframe.

The PHY frames can be 0.5 ms, 1 ms, or 2 ms long and are divided into a variable uplink subframe and downlink subframe. The subframes are further divided into a series of time slots. The number of time slots in the uplink and downlink subframe varies, which helps the BS allocate more time slots for the uplink or downlink. The number of uplink or downlink time slots allocated depends on the amount of data being transmitted in either direction. A data transmission to or from a single device is called a **burst** in the 802.16 standard. A burst can also be a broadcast transmission from the BS to all SSs. A transmission also contains commands or network management information that is sent prior to the transmission of the frame's data portion. The BS allocates time slots for specific SSs in both the downlink frame and the uplink frame. The amount of data contained in a burst depends on the number and length of the time slot as well as on the modulation and coding scheme used for that particular burst. This mechanism, called **time division duplexing (TDD)**, is shown in Figure 9-11.

9

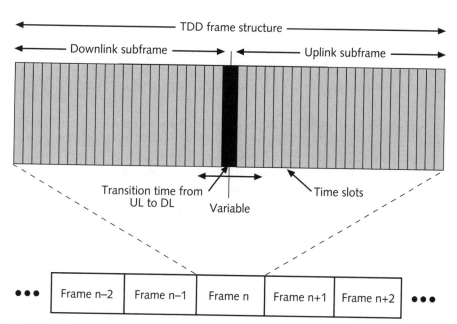

Figure 9-11 WiMAX TDD frame

© Cengage Learning 2014

WiMAX also allows the use of two different frequency channels, in which case one frequency is used for downlink and another for uplink. This mechanism is called **frequency division duplexing (FDD)**. The structure of the frame in FDD is similar to that for TDD, except that one frequency is used exclusively for the downlink and the other is used exclusively for the uplink.

WiMAX can support less-expensive half-duplex equipment that does not transmit and receive simultaneously as well as higher-performance, full-duplex stations that can transmit and receive simultaneously, using different frequencies on the same network and at the same time. The adaptive characteristic of the uplink and downlink, coupled with support of both TDD and FDD, allows 802.16 to use the frequency spectrum more efficiently.

A WiMAX FDD network can support a mixture of full-duplex and half-duplex devices. When half-duplex transmitters are connected to an FDD network, the BS needs to make sure that it does not schedule time for those devices to transmit and receive simultaneously, given that these are half-duplex-only stations.

In a point-to-multipoint architecture, the BS transmits using time division multiplexing (TDM). The SSs are each allocated a time slot in sequence. Note that because only the BS transmits in the downlink direction, it does not have to be concerned with contention and can simply address information in different time slots to different SSs.

Access in the uplink direction (from the SSs to the BS) uses time division multiple access (TDMA), in which one or more time slots are allocated to each SS depending on the requirements of the type of data being transmitted. Some of the time slots are also allocated for contention access, which enables SSs that are not currently members of the network to communicate with the BS for the purpose of establishing a connection to the network.

In the 10–66 GHz licensed bands, 802.16-2009 supports one transmission mode: **WirelessMAN-SC (single carrier)**. It is used for fixed point-to-point connections using either TDD or FDD. At these higher frequencies, line of sight to the transmitter and directional antennas are required.

All the other transmission modes in WiMAX are designed to work in the 2–11 GHz licensed or unlicensed bands. The 802.16 standard also supports non-line-of-sight applications. **Non-line of sight (NLOS)** occurs when the transmitter antenna cannot be seen from the receiver end or vice versa because of the geography of the area or obstructions such as buildings and trees that block the direct path of the signal.

Outdoor, tower-mounted antennas for homes can be expensive to purchase and install, especially in areas subject to high winds or ice accumulation, and significant multipath distortion is likely to occur. Remember that when using directional antennas in line-of-sight applications, multipath distortion is negligible and can be ignored; however, in point-to-multipoint applications, the BS will typically use an omnidirectional antenna. Examples of LOS and NLOS are shown in Figure 9-12.

To support NLOS applications, additional PHY-layer functionality is required. The introduction to WiMAX in this book discusses only the generic functionality because there are far too many options, and to cover all of them would require an additional chapter. For NLOS applications, 802.16 supports three additional PHY-layer transmission modes: WirelessMAN-OFDM, WirelessMAN-OFDMA, and WirelessHUMAN.

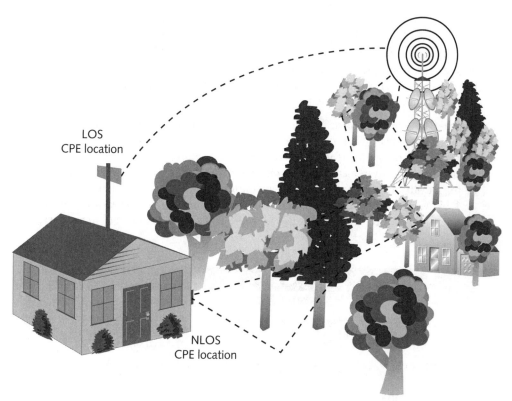

Figure 9-12 Line-of-sight and non-line-of-sight examples

© Cengage Learning 2014

WirelessMAN-OFDM can be used for fixed, mobile, or mesh applications. It uses TDD or FDD in licensed bands below 11 GHz. This mode divides the frequency band into a number of data subcarriers, pilot subcarriers, and null subcarriers to make it resistant to multipath problems. The radio does not transmit during null subcarriers; the null subcarriers are used as guard bands to prevent adjacent channel interference. The number of subcarriers is dependent on the bandwidth of the RF channel. For example, in a 1.25 MHz-wide channel, there can be up to 256 subcarriers, of which 192 are used for data, eight are used as pilot subcarriers, and 55 are used for guard bands. Conversely, for a 20 MHz-wide channel, there can be up to 2048 subcarriers.

WirelessMAN-OFDMA uses **Orthogonal Frequency-Division Multiple Access (OFDMA)**, a technique based on OFDM that divides the available frequency channel into 1536 orthogonal data subcarriers. These subcarriers are then grouped into subchannels and each SS is allocated a subchannel, allowing multiple stations and the BS to communicate in a single transmission. Here again, the number of data subcarriers is dependent on the channel width. OFDMA is also extremely resistant to multipath problems and is used in licensed bands below 11 GHz.

A third transmission mechanism, **Wireless High-Speed Unlicensed Metro Area Network (WirelessHUMAN)**, is also based on OFDM and is specifically designed for use in the unlicensed 5 GHz U-NII band.

In 802.16, OFDMA is also scalable, meaning that the number of subcarriers allocated to an SS for the uplink can vary, depending on the QoS requirements of the transmission, the signal quality, or the distance between the SS and the BS. However, to accommodate channel aggregation (multiple contiguous channels used to increase data rates) in 802.16m, the number of UL and DL frames is fixed and asymmetric, meaning that there are more DL frames than UL frames.

Another key characteristic of the 802.16 PHY is that it supports adaptive modulation. In simple terms, this means that for each SS, 802.16 can dynamically change the modulation, increasing or decreasing the data rate based on signal quality. In addition, in order to meet the regulatory requirements in different countries as well as to optimize the use of the spectrum, the 802.16 standard allows transmitters to use frequency bandwidths of a minimum of 1.25 MHz up to a maximum of 20 MHz. Table 9-2 summarizes the WiMAX specification's nomenclature, frequencies used, applications, and duplexing alternatives.

Designation	Frequencies	Application	Duplexing
WirelessMAN-SC	10–66 GHz licensed bands	Fixed only	TDD, FDD
WirelessMAN-OFDM	Below 11 GHz licensed bands	Fixed, mobile, or mesh	TDD, FDD
WirelessMAN-OFDMA	Below 11 GHz licensed bands	Fixed or mobile	TDD, FDD
WirelessHUMAN	5 GHz U-NII band	Fixed or mesh	TDD only

Table 9-2 WiMAX specifications summary

© Cengage Learning 2014

Modulation and Error Correction
In 802.16, modulation and error correction are directly linked. You may remember that forward error correction (FEC) is a technique that inserts additional bits in the data stream to enable the receiver to detect multiple-bit errors and to correct single-bit errors in groups of bits. In the extreme case, FEC simply sends another copy of the same data bit for each one transmitted.

In addition to FEC, 802.16 uses automatic repeat requests (ARQ) to ensure the reliability of the transmissions. In other words, sometimes it is necessary to resend the frame. IEEE 802.16 was designed to achieve 99.999 percent reliability—"five nines," as this level of reliability is commonly referred to in the data communications industry. FEC improves the chances of receiving the data correctly and thus reduces the number of retransmissions, which increases the performance of the link. However, the additional bits add overhead to the transmissions, increasing the total amount of data and therefore reducing the overall performance of the link. By dynamically changing the modulation, 802.16 can achieve an optimum balance of speed and transmission for a given signal quality.

Table 9-3 lists the types of modulation supported in 802.16 and the associated mandatory FEC coding. The coding rates are listed here for informational purposes only; a full explanation of the FEC coding techniques requires complex mathematical formulas and is beyond the scope of this book. However, it is important to know that the different FEC coding rates are used for increasing the reliability of the transmission.

Modulation	FEC Coding Rates
BPSK	1/2, 3/4
QPSK	1/2, 2/3, 3/4, 5/6, 7/8
16-QAM	1/2, 3/4
64-QAM	2/3, 5/6
256-QAM (optional)	3/4, 7/8

Table 9-3 802.16 modulations and mandatory FEC coding

© Cengage Learning 2014

The ability of 802.16 to dynamically change modulations is also what makes it possible for WiMAX to reduce latency and improve QoS. **Latency** is the amount of time delay it takes a packet to travel from source to destination device. Figure 9-13 shows how WiMAX uses different modulations. Adaptive modulation also helps WiMAX use the channel bandwidth more efficiently.

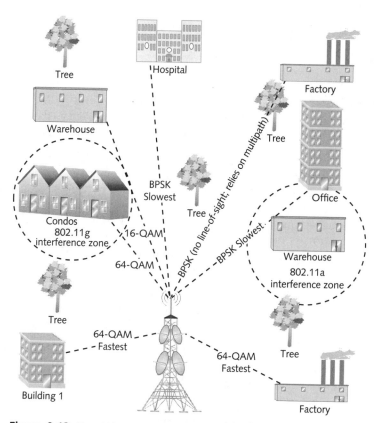

Figure 9-13 How WiMAX can apply different modulations

© Cengage Learning 2014

The BS sends information to the SSs about which modulations it will use for a particular burst and for a particular SS in a downlink map (DL-MAP) in the first few data frames at the beginning of the transmission. The SSs respond by sending an uplink map (UL-MAP) at the beginning of their assigned bursts. The DL-MAP and UL-MAP are parts of the frame that describe the method of transmission as well as the contents of the bursts, time allocations, and other information.

WiMAX Profiles IEEE 802.16 defines certain **profiles**, which are sets of predefined parameters that can include the frequency channel, bandwidth of the channel, and transmission modes (OFDM, OFDMA, etc.). These profiles also help to reduce or eliminate the need for **truck-rolls**, which are support-technician visits to the site, given that they can be changed remotely, when a user signs up for a new type of service. WiMAX also specifies basic profiles: point-to-multipoint (P2MP) and point-to-point (PTP) as well as an optional mesh networking profile. A WiMAX **system profile** is a combination of the basic profile and one of the transmission profiles; it is preset on the equipment by the operator companies (carriers) before it is shipped to an end-user site. **Burst profiles** are negotiated between BSs and SSs for the allocation of time slots required to maintain QoS.

Each truck-roll to install a single broadband network device at an end-user's site can cost a communications operator up to $500.

Range and Throughput The maximum distances achievable in a WiMAX network depend on the frequency band used. Recall that the higher the frequency, the shorter the range of the signal at a given power setting. Conversely, higher frequency signals allow for higher data rates.

In general, higher frequencies are used for metropolitan-area line-of-sight, point-to-point, or multipoint applications at very high data rates for carrier networks using licensed frequencies. Lower licensed frequencies—below 11 GHz—are typically used for private, line-of-sight network connections of up to 10 miles (16 kilometers) as well as for long-distance links of up to 35 miles (56 kilometers). Frequencies below 11 GHz are also used for non-line-of-sight networks with a maximum range of up to 5 miles (8 kilometers).

WiMAX base stations and subscriber stations perform ranging (distance) calculations based on signal quality. This process occurs when a subscriber station initially joins the network and periodically thereafter, and it helps the equipment establish the modulation and FEC coding to use for data transmissions.

As you already learned, the maximum achievable data rates in WiMAX depend on the modulation, channel bandwidth, and FEC coding used. Table 9-4 shows a summary of some of the data-rate combinations that are possible.

Note that a wider channel bandwidth also means that more data can be sent per signal unit (symbol), as you learned in Chapter 2, hence the higher data rates achievable with wider channels. Realistic throughput will be lower than the rates shown in Table 9-4. One reason

Modulation/ FEC Coding	QPSK 1/2	QPSK 3/4	16 QAM 1/2	16 QAM 3/4	64 QAM 2/3	64 QAM 3/4
Channel Bandwidth 1.75 MHz	1.04	2.18	2.91	4.36	5.94	6.55
3.5 MHz	2.08	4.37	5.82	8.73	11.88	13.09
7.0 MHz	4.15	8.73	11.64	17.45	23.75	26.18
10.0 MHz	8.31	12.47	16.63	24.94	33.25	37.40
20.0 MHz	16.62	24.94	33.25	49.87	66.49	74.81

Table 9-4 Sample of WiMAX data rates in Mbps vs. channel bandwidth and FEC

© Cengage Learning 2014

for this is that the WiMAX channel bandwidth is shared, and therefore the number of simultaneous users affects the maximum data rates at any given time. Another reason for the lower throughput is that some of the overhead, such as MAC layer framing, is not included in the rate calculations shown in the table.

MAC Layer WiMAX is typically implemented on a point-to-multipoint basis, with one BS and potentially hundreds of SSs, including mobile users. The 802.16 MAC dynamically allocates bandwidth to individual SSs for the uplink; this is the key to the high data rates possible in WiMAX networks. In addition to supporting a large number of SSs, the MAC convergence sublayers allow WiMAX to be implemented as an efficient transport in point-to-point systems for backhaul applications and support such line protocols as ATM and T1.

A point-to-multipoint WiMAX network usually operates with a central BS that can be equipped with either an omnidirectional or a smart, sector-based antenna, which is also called an **advanced antenna system (AAS)**. An AAS can transmit multiple simultaneous signals in different directions to stations that fall within the range of each of the antennas. It also helps to maximize the amount of RF energy sent in each direction. Remember that, for the uplink, the only stations sending signals are the ones that were scheduled by the BS to transmit. WiMAX can also take advantage of multiple-in and multiple-out (MIMO) antenna systems to reduce interference with other systems (see the next section, on WiMAX coexistence) and the impact of multipath distortion. In addition, 802.16m enables support for multiple radios and spatial multiplexing to increase data rates.

To address a burst to a particular SS, the BS uses a 16-bit number called a connection identifier (CID), which is used to identify both the device and the connection after it connects to the WiMAX network. (Recall that the WiMAX MAC is connection oriented.) Each station also has a 48-bit MAC address, which is only used during connection establishment. When the stations receive a transmission from the BS, they check the CID and keep only the MAC frames that contain data addressed to them.

Stations can request additional dedicated bandwidth (for QoS) if this is required to support a particular service, such as the transmission of telephone calls or a video stream. The BS polls the SSs periodically to identify their bandwidth needs, granting bandwidth as required. Except in the case of connections that require a guaranteed bit rate, such as T1, most data connections cannot tolerate errors but can tolerate latency and **jitter**, which is the maximum delay variation between two consecutive packets over a period of time. Web browsing, transmitting e-mail messages, and downloading files are latency-tolerant and jitter-tolerant activities. Video and voice, on the other hand, can tolerate a certain amount of errors but not latency or jitter.

The WiMAX MAC protocol maintains a consistent bandwidth by using a self-correcting mechanism for granting more bandwidth to SSs. This creates less traffic on the network, given that there is no need for SSs to acknowledge the grant. Instead, if an SS does not receive the bandwidth grant or the BS does not receive the request, the SS will simply request it again. The requests from the SSs are cumulative, but they will also periodically inform the BS of their total bandwidth needs. This mechanism is far more efficient than those used by other networking standards.

 The scheduling services in WiMAX that map the connections in the uplink direction for allocating channel bandwidth to the SSs are based on the scheduling services defined for cable modems in the Data Over Cable Service Interface Specification (DOCSIS) standard. Go to *www.cablemodem.com/specifications* and click "DOCSIS."

A MAC frame includes a fixed-length header, an optional and variable-length payload (data), and an optional cyclic redundancy check (CRC). Header-only MAC frames are used to send commands and requests between the BS and the SSs. The generic MAC frame format is shown in Figure 9-14.

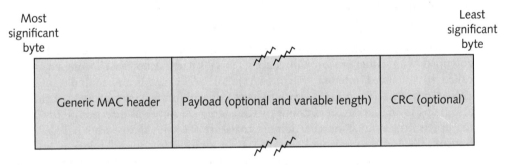

Figure 9-14 802.16 (WiMAX) MAC frame

© Cengage Learning 2014

WiMAX Coexistence

One of the concerns of end-users and carriers when considering wireless data transmission in the unlicensed bands is that as the number of transmitters grows, so does interference. Eventually, interference can make the technology and, consequently, the user's investment worthless. This concern is of particular importance considering the distances achievable with 802.16.

WiMAX is different from technologies such as 802.11 in that it is not limited to the 2.4 GHz band or the 5 GHz band. Although business users are encouraged to develop a sharing agreement when operating in the unlicensed bands (see "IEEE 802.16.2-2004" at *standards.ieee.org/getieee802/index.html*), service providers that expect to sell wireless connectivity to customers should consider a low-cost purchase or lease of a small amount of spectrum in the 2–11 GHz band. FCC policies allow spectrum holders to resell unused spectrum to other operators.

The ISM band offers approximately 80 MHz of bandwidth; however, the U-NII band offers 24 channels and 555 MHz of bandwidth, which users and operators can share. Depending on the distance between transmitters, interference may not be a serious problem because WiMAX signals are limited to between 30 and 35 miles (approximately 48 to 56 kilometers) under ideal, line-of-sight conditions. When adaptive modulations, variable data rates, and FEC are taken into account, testing the performance of a link can dispel any remaining concerns. Most vendors, eager to sell their equipment, would be happy to assist in this process. Power levels can also be adjusted, as long as these adjustments do not exceed the limits mandated by the FCC or the regulatory bodies in other countries. Smart antenna systems are another potential solution to this type of problem.

The European Telecommunications Standards Institute (ETSI), which you learned about in Chapter 3, has published a standard called High Performance Radio Metropolitan Area Network (HIPERMAN). It is based on 802.16 and specifies systems that are based on OFDM and work at frequencies between 2 and 11 GHz only.

WMAN Security

As with other types of networks, security in WMANs is a major concern. Despite using multiple beam technology (which could allow an attacker to attempt to capture information by interrupting a single beam), FSO systems are generally considered secure. Anyone trying to *sniff* information from FSO systems would have difficulty accessing the equipment and blocking only a portion of an invisible beam. In addition, such interference would affect the performance of the network, immediately alerting the user or operator. In LMDS and MMDS systems, a receiver can capture RF signals without blocking the radio signal. Because most of these systems are proprietary and expensive, system manufacturers or operators are typically responsible for designing custom security measures into their equipment. Because most future WMAN installations will likely be based on WiMAX technology, this section will focus on WiMAX security measures.

WiMAX Security

As you learned in the section on the WiMAX protocol stack, the MAC layer includes a privacy sublayer. Unlike 802.11 and Bluetooth, the WiMAX standard was initially designed to include very powerful security measures. These features make it extremely difficult—if not impossible—for a would-be hacker to steal information from WiMAX transmissions.

The privacy sublayer provides a client/server authentication and key management protocol, with the BS controlling the distribution of security keys to the SSs. In addition, the standard encrypts all the data transmitted between the BS and SSs and makes use of **digital certificates**, which are messages digitally signed by a certification authority, as well as public-key infrastructure embedded in the BS, to ensure privacy and protection against information theft. Manufacturers install a unique digital certificate, which includes a serial number in every device. The digital certificates can be verified with the manufacturer as being valid and unique by sending a copy of the certificate encrypted with the manufacturer's public key over the Internet (a connection to the Internet is required). This is a requirement of the 802.16 standard.

The privacy sublayer has two protocol components: the encapsulation protocol and the privacy key management protocol. The encapsulation protocol is used for encrypting packet data and includes a set of cryptographic suites (the encryption and authentication mechanisms) used to apply encryption to the transmitted data. The privacy key management protocol is used for securing key distribution from the BS to the SSs; it is used for synchronizing the security keys between the BS and SSs as well as for preventing unauthorized stations from associating with a WiMAX network.

Once a device is authenticated with the BS using the digital certificate, a **traffic encryption key (TEK)**, which is the security key used to encrypt the data, is exchanged between the BS and SS for each service connection that's being carried over the wireless interface. Remember that the 802.16 MAC is connection oriented and can carry multiple types of service. TEKs expire, and the SS must periodically renew the keys with the BS. The default TEK lifetime is 12 hours. The minimum value is 30 minutes, and the maximum value is seven days.

Only the headers are not encrypted in WiMAX, to allow SSs to associate with the network. Although data can be sent unencrypted, most users are likely to (and should) use encryption. All data sent across the wireless medium is then encrypted using one of the following algorithms:

- 3-DES (Triple-DES)—Data is encrypted three times with a 128-bit key, using the United States **Data Encryption Standard (DES)**.

- RSA with 1024-bit key—**RSA** was developed in 1977 by Ron Rivest, Adi Shamir, and Leonard Adleman. The algorithm uses a large integer, composed of smaller numbers that are multiplied by each other. It is based on the idea that it will be difficult to figure out each of the smaller numbers that are used to arrive at the large integer.

- AES with a 128-bit key—The **Advanced Encryption Standard (AES)**, the latest encryption standard, was developed by the National Institute of Standards and Technology (NIST) to replace DES. It is considered unbreakable and is used to encrypt unclassified U.S. government material.

The security mechanisms designed into WiMAX should be sufficient to allay any concerns that end users may have.

The high reliability and high security of WiMAX, together with its long distance and NLOS characteristics, make it an excellent candidate for use by security companies providing burglar alarms for homes and businesses. WiMAX makes it viable to secure a building or home using a live video link and IP-based security cameras.

Chapter Summary

- WMANs are a group of technologies that provide wireless connectivity throughout an area, such as a city without cable infrastructure. WMANs also extend user mobility throughout a metropolitan area.

- Last mile wired connections are the link between the customer's premises and an ISP. Most last mile connections today are still based on copper wiring.

- Long-distance telephone and data connections between cities have mostly migrated to fiber-optic cable due to its high speed, reliability, and channel capacity.

- There are two ways in which a signal can be sent. The first technique, called broadband, sends multiple data signals at different frequencies. This allows many different signals to be sent simultaneously. The second technique, called baseband, treats the entire transmission medium as if it were only one channel, sending only one stream of data. Until 2001, RF-based fixed broadband systems were limited to connecting with only one other device at a time and could only transmit using a line-of-sight link.

- Free Space Optics (FSO) has been an excellent alternative to costly high-speed fiber-optic connections. FSO transmissions are sent by low-powered infrared beams in point-to-point fashion. Because FSO is a line-of-sight technology, the transceivers must be mounted in high locations to provide a clear transmission path.

- Local Multipoint Distribution Service (LMDS) is a fixed broadband technology that can provide a wide variety of wireless services, including high-speed Internet access, real-time multimedia file transfer, remote access to LANs, interactive video, video-on-demand, video conferencing, and telephone service. LMDS can transmit anywhere from 51 to 155 Mbps downstream and 1.54 Mbps upstream over a distance of up to about 5 miles (8 kilometers).

- Because an LMDS signal can only travel up to 5 miles, an LMDS network is composed of cells much like a cellular telephone system. A transmitter sends signals to the fixed buildings within the cell. LMDS is a fixed technology for buildings. The main factors that determine the LMDS cell size are line of sight, antenna height, overlapping cells, and rainfall.

- Multichannel Multipoint Distribution Service (MMDS) is a fixed broadband wireless technology. MMDS can transmit video, voice, or data signals at distances of up to 35 miles (56 kilometers). Because MMDS operates at a lower frequency, the signals can travel longer distances. These longer distances mean that MMDS requires fewer radio transmitters compared to the equipment required by LMDS to send the same signal. MMDS is used as an option in both home and business settings. MMDS uses the 2.1 GHz and 2.5–2.7 GHz bands to offer two-way service at speeds of up to 1.5 Mbps downstream and 300 Kbps upstream. LMDS and MMDS technology is not based on standards.

- The IEEE 802.16 (WiMAX) standard was introduced in 2000 with the goal of standardizing fixed broadband wireless services and as an alternative to wired access networks. A single WiMAX base station (BS) can communicate with hundreds of subscriber stations (SSs) simultaneously in point-to-multipoint mode, or with another BS in point-to-point. IEEE 802.16 equipment can transmit in either the 10–66 GHz range or in the 2–11 GHz range and can use licensed or unlicensed frequency bands. A BS can also connect directly with a laptop computer equipped with a WiMAX wireless interface.

- WiMAX can transmit at speeds of up to 70 Mbps in the 2–11 GHz bands and can achieve 120 Mbps at short distances in the 10–66 GHz bands. The 802.16m amendment allows the use of multiple radios and spatial multiplexing and can potentially increase the data rates to 1 Gbps when aggregating multiple 20-MHz-wide frequency channels. QoS support makes WiMAX suitable to carry simultaneous voice, video, and data (triple-play) at a much lower cost than LMDS and MMDS networks. WiMAX equipment is relatively easy and inexpensive to install and maintain.

- WiMAX range is measured in miles. Cellular phone operators can overlay WiMAX networks on their existing networks, which will reduce the cost of sending data from handheld cellular phones.

- The 802.16e amendment brings full support of mobile devices to WiMAX technology. Mobile WiMAX can achieve data rates of up to 2 Mbps for portable devices that are slow moving or stationary and up to 320 Kbps in fast-moving vehicles.

- The WiMAX MAC layer is connection oriented and includes convergence sublayers that allow WiMAX to directly support ATM, T1, Ethernet, and VLANs in addition to other services. There are five variations of the 802.16 PHY layer. The first two are based on the modulation of a single carrier signal. All devices work in half-duplex. The PHY frames can be 0.5 ms, 1 ms, or 2 ms long and are divided into a variable uplink subframe and downlink subframe. The subframe is divided into time slots that carry the payload. A single time slot or multiple time slots can be allocated to a specific station. The mechanism is called time division duplexing (TDD). WiMAX also supports the use of two frequency channels, one for the uplink and another for the downlink. This is called frequency division duplexing (FDD).

- The BS can support both half-duplex and full-duplex devices simultaneously on the network and is the only device transmitting on the downlink. The BS transmits using time division multiplexing (TDM). The stations transmit using time division multiple access (TDMA). The BS allocates time slots for contention access in the uplink subframe in order to allow stations to establish a connection and join the network.

- The WiMAX 802.16 standard defines three PHY layers for LOS and NLOS implementations in the 2–11 GHz licensed or unlicensed frequency bands: WirelessMAN-OFDM, WirelessMAN-OFDMA, and WirelessHUMAN, the last which is intended for use in the 5 GHz U-NII band.

- OFDM and OFDMA in 802.16 are scalable, meaning that the number of subcarriers allocated to an SS for the uplink can vary depending on the QoS requirements of the SS, the distance between the SS and BS, and the signal quality. The WiMAX PHY layer uses adaptive modulation. It can dynamically change modulation techniques depending on the distance and signal quality. WiMAX transmitters can transmit using frequency bandwidths from 1.25 MHz up to 20 MHz. Through the use of error-correction techniques and adaptive modulation, WiMAX makes efficient use of the spectrum and achieves high performance.

- WiMAX profiles specify the frequency channel, bandwidth, and transmission mechanism. A basic profile specifies whether the network is point-to-point or point-to-multipoint. A system profile is the combination of a basic profile and transmission profile. The use of profiles helps make WiMAX installations simpler and reduces the cost of implementation for the operators.

■ The MAC layer is the key to the intelligence and security behind WiMAX networks. Efficient bandwidth-saving protocols and QoS help WiMAX reduce latency and jitter and maintain a consistent bandwidth. WiMAX includes a number of features that help operators and end-users reduce interference problems.

■ The security features of WiMAX were designed to offer operators and end-users the peace of mind that other wireless technologies have failed to provide so far. WiMAX uses verifiable digital certificates, the most advanced encryption mechanisms (3-DES, RSA, and AES), and secure key exchange protocols.

Key Terms

advanced antenna system (AAS)   An antenna that can transmit multiple simultaneous signals in different directions to stations that fall within the range of each of the antennas.

Advanced Encryption Standard (AES)   The latest encryption standard, developed by the National Institute of Standards and Technology (NIST) to replace the Data Encryption Standard. *See* Data Encryption Standard.

backhaul   A company's internal infrastructure connection.

baseband   A transmission technique that treats the entire transmission medium as only one channel.

base station (BS)   The transmitter connected to the carrier network or to the Internet.

broadband   A transmission technique that sends multiple signals at different frequencies.

burst   A transmission containing data to or from a single SS or a broadcast transmission from the BS.

burst profiles   A profile negotiated between the BS and the SSs that specifies the number of time slots allocated to the SSs to maintain QoS.

carriers   Telephone, cable TV, and other communication providers that own the wires and transmission towers that carry voice, video, and data traffic.

customer premises equipment (CPE)   The WiMAX devices that are installed in a customer's office or home.

Data Encryption Standard (DES)   The encryption standard used in the United States until the adoption of AES. *See* AES.

digital certificates   A special message signed by a certification authority that is used for security and authentication.

fixed wireless   A wireless last mile connection.

Free Space Optics (FSO)   An optical, wireless, point-to-point, line-of-sight broadband technology.

frequency division duplexing (FDD)   A mechanism that uses one frequency for uplink and another for downlink. *See* time division duplexing.

IEEE 802.16   The IEEE standard for wireless broadband metropolitan area networks.

jitter   The maximum delay variation between two consecutive packets over a period of time.

last mile connection   The link between the customer's premises and the telephone company, cable TV company, or ISP.

latency   The amount of time delay that it takes a packet to travel from source to destination device.

Local Multipoint Distribution Service (LMDS)   A fixed broadband technology that can provide a wide variety of wireless services.

microwaves   The part of the electromagnetic spectrum from 3 to 30 GHz.

Multichannel Multipoint Distribution Service (MMDS)   A fixed broadband wireless technology that transmits at 1.5 Mbps over distances of 35 miles (56 kilometers).

Network Interface Unit (NIU)   A device that connects an LMDS modem to a LAN or telephone system.

non-line of sight (NLOS)   When the transmitter antenna cannot be seen from the receiver end, or vice versa.

Orthogonal Frequency-Division Multiple Access (OFDMA)   A multiple access technique, based on OFDM, that divides the frequency channel into 1536 orthogonal data subcarriers.

pizza box antenna   A small antenna used for MMDS systems.

profiles   Sets of predefined WiMAX connection parameters that include the frequency channel, bandwidth of the channel, and transmission mechanism (OFDM, OFDMA, etc.).

RSA   An encryption algorithm that uses a large integer composed of smaller numbers that are multiplied by each other. It is based on the idea that it will be difficult to figure out each of the smaller numbers that are used to arrive at the large integer.

scintillation   The temporal and spatial variations in light intensity caused by atmospheric turbulence.

spatial diversity   The sending of parallel beams during Free Space optical transmissions.

subscriber station (SS)   In a WiMAX network, either a CPE device that attaches to a LAN or a laptop computer.

super high frequency (SHF)   The part of the frequency spectrum from 3 to 30 GHz.

system profile   A combination of the basic WiMAX profile and one of the transmission profiles.

Time Division Duplexing (TDD)   A mechanism that divides a single transmission into two parts: an uplink part and a downlink part. *See* frequency division duplexing.

traffic encryption key (TEK)   The security key used to encrypt the data in a WiMAX network.

triple-play   The support of transmission of video, voice, and data on the same network.

truck-rolls   Visits to a site by support technicians.

WiMAX   Worldwide interoperability for microwave access.

WiMAX Forum   An industry organization dedicated to promoting the implementation of 802.16 by testing and certifying equipment for compatibility and interoperability.

Wireless High-Speed Unlicensed Metro Area Network (WirelessHUMAN)   A WiMAX specification based on OFDM that is specifically designed for use in the 5 GHz U-NII band.

WirelessMAN-SC (single carrier)   A WiMAX specification that uses a single carrier and is intended for point-to-point connections in the 10–66 GHz bands.

wireless metropolitan area networks (WMANs)   A group of technologies that provide wireless connectivity across a substantial geographical area such as a large city.

Review Questions

1. The term "fixed wireless" is generally used to refer to _____.

   a. buildings

   b. cars

   c. satellites

   d. cell phones

2. What is the common name for connections that begin at a service provider, go through the local neighborhood, and end at the home or office?

   a. 1 mile

   b. last mile

   c. ISP

   d. link

3. Which of the following is not an example of a last mile connection for home users?

   a. satellite

   b. dial-up modem

   c. DSL

   d. baseband

4. A leased special high-speed connection from the local telephone carrier for business users that transmits at 1.544 Mbps is called _____.

   a. T1

   b. T3

   c. DSL

   d. Ethernet

5. The technique that treats the entire transmission medium as if it were only one channel is called _____.

   a. broadband

   b. analog

   c. baseband

   d. line

6. Over short distances, WiMAX can communicate at speeds of up to _____ in the 10–66 GHz bands.

   a. 100 Mbps

   b. 70 Mbps

   c. 120 Mbps

   d. 30 Mbps

9

7. The convergence sublayers in the WiMAX MAC protocol allow it to support _____.

   a. T1

   b. ATM

   c. voice and video

   d. all of the above

8. In the uplink direction, 802.16 transmits using _____.

   a. TDMA

   b. half-duplex only

   c. TDM

   d. the downlink frame

9. LMDS has an advantage over MMDS in that the signals can travel up to 35 miles from the transmitter. True or False?

10. One of the limitations of LMDS and MMDS is that both these systems operate at frequencies that require line of sight. True or False?

11. Devices in a WiMAX network must transmit in half-duplex only. True or False?

12. The WiMAX base station controls all transmissions in a WiMAX network. True or False?

13. Non-line-of-sight transmissions in the 802.16 standard can only be supported in the 2–11 GHz bands. True or False?

14. What system, sometimes called fiberless optical, uses low-powered infrared beams instead of fiber-optic cable?

   a. MMDS

   b. LMDS

   c. FSO

   d. WiMAX

15. The maximum distance for a local multipoint distribution service (LMDS) network is _____ miles.

   a. 2

   b. 5

   c. 8

   d. 35

16. A single WiMAX base station can communicate with _____ of subscriber stations simultaneously.

   a. dozens

   b. thousands

    c.   hundreds

    d.   millions

17. WirelessHUMAN is used in the _____ band.

    a.   U-NII

    b.   2–11 GHz

    c.   10–66 GHz

    d.   none of the above

18. WiMAX network coverage is typically measured in _____.

    a.   miles or kilometers

    b.   feet

    c.   hundreds of feet

    d.   meters only

19. What key factor outlines how WiMAX maximizes the use of the frequency bands?

    a.   better error correction

    b.   more frequency stability

    c.   multiple frequency bands

    d.   adaptive modulation

20. How does the BS send information to the SSs about which modulations will be used for a particular burst or transmission?

    a.   in the header of the frames

    b.   in a burst profile

    c.   in a system profile

    d.   in the MAC frame

Hands-On Projects

Project 9-1

Identify at least two manufacturers of WiMAX equipment. Prepare a report on what type of equipment they supply (such as base stations, CPEs, or adapter cards for laptop computers). Ensure that the manufacturer can supply at least two of the different classes of products noted. Create a one-page or two-page list that includes the frequencies that the equipment is capable of operating on (if available) and at least one other important feature of the equipment.

Project 9-2

By researching news media Web sites, locate one or two places in North America (not mentioned in the chapter) where the local government, a vendor, or a business association is planning to deploy a WiMAX network. Outline the purpose and the extent of the deployment as well as the expectations of the project, such as what types of services are offered (i.e., Internet access, video, and telephone). To help you in your search, try to think of situations for which WiMAX would be an excellent alternative. One example of this is using WiMAX to connect oil-drilling platforms that are located near the coast.

Real-World Exercise

The Baypoint Group (TBG) is once again calling on you, their wireless expert. A customer, Advancomms Inc., plans to deploy smart (advanced) antenna systems for a mobile WiMAX network it wants to install in your area, and you will be locating possible sites for the system. The ideal location would be a building at least eight stories high, which avoids the high cost of erecting towers and supplying power. Another important factor in selecting the site is avoiding, as much as possible, interference from other wireless systems in the area.

Exercise 9-1

Your job is to drive or walk around the downtown area and spot as many wireless antennas as you can, marking on a map the location and positioning of each antenna. Smart antenna systems require several small antennas that point in all directions. If there are antennas already installed on top of the buildings in your area, you will need to consider whether there is enough vertical space to mount the smart antennas. If there are no tall buildings in your area, you should try to identify possible tower locations while ensuring that the antenna signals will not be blocked by any other structures or terrain, such as hills and mountains. If you live in a large city with many tall buildings already filled with antennas, you may need to consider installing the smart antenna system on the side walls, close to the top, if there is space available.

Identify the existing links where two directional antennas are pointed towards each other, and mark these on your map as well. You can use Google Maps to display and print a map of your local downtown area.

Produce a short (5–10 slide) PowerPoint presentation that includes the maps and locations of all the potential sites. Also prepare a one-page report to accompany your slides, indicating any potential problems. Use Google Images or your favorite search engine to identify as many different types of antennas as possible, and include this information in your report. If you have a camera, you may also want to use your own pictures of the potential sites in your presentation.

Challenge Case Project

CASE PROJECTS

Wheeler University's campus is spread over a remote area about the size of three city blocks to the south of Buffalo, New York. Wheeler administrators have contacted The Baypoint Group (TBG) and asked for a proposal for connecting their three student residence buildings to the university's network. The buildings are wired for Ethernet, but students currently do not have access to either the university's network or the Internet because the dorms are in a remote area without DSL or cable TV service, due to the remoteness of the campus. The university considered implementing a satellite-based system or installing fiber optics, but the cost of each option proved prohibitive. The university has access to the Internet through a backhaul MMDS connection to an ISP, but the cost of installing a private MMDS network also is too high. TBG has asked you to become involved, given that you are its wireless networking expert. The residence buildings have line-of-sight access to each other and to the computer center building.

Based on the research you did for Project 9-1, prepare a two-page recommendation and a 10-minute PowerPoint presentation for a specific WiMAX implementation. Make sure you address the features of WiMAX and how it can provide long-term benefits for the university. Include photos and basic specifications for the equipment in your presentation. Also include similar examples that you may have located in Project 9-2.

9

chapter 10

Wireless Wide Area Networks

After reading this chapter and completing the exercises, you will be able to:

- Describe wireless wide area networks (WWANs) and how they are used
- List the types of applications that can be used on a digital cellular phone
- Explain the basic concepts of how cellular telephony functions
- Describe the various generations of cellular telephony
- Discuss satellites and their application in WWANs

A wireless wide area network (WWAN) spans a geographical area as large as an entire country or even the entire world. WWANs can use the cellular phone network to span a country or an entire continent. Where cellular phone networks are not available, satellite technology enables users to make telephone calls or access the Internet from remote areas. These two technologies complement each other in many ways and make it possible for users to connect to corporate networks via the Internet and run business applications from virtually any location on the planet.

Although the browsers on cellular phones often lack the capabilities of PC and MAC browsers, a cellular phone can be connected to a laptop using a cable, and the resulting Internet connection can be used to run applications that would otherwise not work on the cellular phone. Several models of smartphones also include a "hotspot" feature that enables them to act as Wi-Fi APs, which allows users to connect to the Internet using two different wireless technologies simultaneously, thereby increasing productivity while away from the office or home.

From the user's perspective, cellular phone technology is ubiquitous. No matter where you look, people are using cellular phones and smartphones to make and receive calls, send and receive short text messages, send and receive e-mails, access the Web, send faxes, upload pictures and movies, even watch TV and movies. Using a digital cellular phone today is as common as making a landline telephone call; and in many parts of the world, especially where the traditional telephone wire infrastructure is either outdated or nonexistent, cellular phones are making these services available to users who never before had access to a private telephone line, let alone the Internet. In fact, cellular phones are quickly replacing traditional land-based telephone lines for large groups of people.

Cellular phones are literally changing lives. By the time fishermen tie their boats to the dock, the catch is often already sold to the highest bidder. Farmers in remote communities sell their products directly to retailers while on their way to the market. Often, this remote marketplace enables producers and small manufacturers to bypass the middlemen and enjoy higher profits, something that in the end benefits both producers and consumers.

From a technological point of view, there is nothing simple about digital cellular telephony. On the contrary, cellular telephony is probably one of the most complex of all wireless communication technologies, and users expect it to perform as well for data as it does for voice calls. Over the past four decades, developments in cellular phone technology have been driven by the users' demand for high data rates and quality of voice connection. These technologies all have strange acronyms, such as GSM, EDGE, CDMA, HSDPA, HSPA+, and LTE. The cellular phone business, from the manufacturer to the carriers, is one of the most fiercely competitive businesses anywhere in the world. Even governments are taking advantage of the growth of the cellular phone business, auctioning off parts of the wireless spectrum to the highest bidders, thereby earning billions of dollars.

For many years, satellites have provided us with global positioning systems, brought communications to the remotest of areas, and transmitted radio and TV signals that can reach virtually anyone anywhere on the planet in real time. They have also played an important role in WWAN data networks because they can deliver signals to any point on the oceans that cover most of Earth's surface, to the Arctic and Antarctic continents, and to remote and mountainous areas where electricity and cellular phone transmission tower infrastructure does not yet exist. Because of the complexity of launching them into space and placing them in the correct orbit, satellites are one of the most expensive of all wireless communications technologies.

This chapter explores how cellular phones work and looks at some of the complex technology behind digital cellular phone networks. We will also examine what tasks can be achieved using digital cellular phone devices, the various platforms and software that make these enhanced features work, and issues surrounding implementation of digital cellular phone technology. Finally, we will take a look at how satellites are deployed, some of the issues surrounding the use of satellites for data transmission, and how satellites complement cellular telephony to help provide a truly global wireless wide area network.

Cellular Telephone Technology

Cellular phone technology has continued to expand at what can only be described as an alarming rate. The range of applications and features that digital cellular networks provide to mobile users is the main cause of this growth. Today, cellular phone networks are based on digital instead of analog transmission technology. They can transmit at ever-increasing speeds and are no longer limited to voice communications. Digital cellular phones can be used to:

- Browse the Internet
- Send and receive short messages and e-mails
- Participate in videoconferencing
- Receive travel reports, news reports, weather updates, entertainment, and many other types of information
- Connect to corporate networks and run a large variety of business applications
- Watch television or on-demand movies
- Take and transmit pictures and short movies
- Display maps and information about your current location as well as locate vehicles, family members, and employees using GPS
- Scan barcodes, QR codes, and even product labels to get more information or pricing for products
- Play online and offline games
- Access and control servers and workstation console displays remotely

Short Message Services (SMS), which allows for the delivery of short (160 character) messages (70 characters for non-Latin Arabic and Chinese) between cellular phones, remains one of the most widely used cellular phone applications. In 2011, the number of SMS messages sent worldwide exceeded 7 trillion. Unlike text-message services that send messages over the Internet from a central site, such as an answering service that sends a message to a physician's pager, SMS lets users send messages directly from one device to another without using the Internet. The cellular phone carrier's equipment stores the message if the receiver's telephone is out of range or powered off.

SMS can be used in the following ways:

- Person-to-person—This is the most common use of SMS, namely one user sending a text message to another user. It has been called the digital cellular phone equivalent of instant messaging.

10

- Agent-to-person—Automated agents can send notifications whenever an event occurs. The users set the parameters and criteria. For example, an automated agent can send out an SMS message when a stock reaches a certain price or the user has received a voice mail message.

- Information broadcast services—These include news, weather, and sports scores sent on a regular basis or when a breaking story occurs.

- Software configuration—SMS can make some changes to the software running on a cellular phone device; it can also send links for downloading software to smartphones.

- Advertising—Messages containing advertising can be sent to users over SMS.

How Cellular Telephony Works

There are two keys to understanding how cellular telephony works. The first key is that the coverage area is divided into smaller individual sections, called **cells**, as shown in Figure 10-1. A typical cell ranges from a few thousand feet in diameter to approximately 10 square miles (26 square kilometers). At the center of each cell are a transmitter and a receiver with which the mobile devices near that cell communicate, via RF signals. These

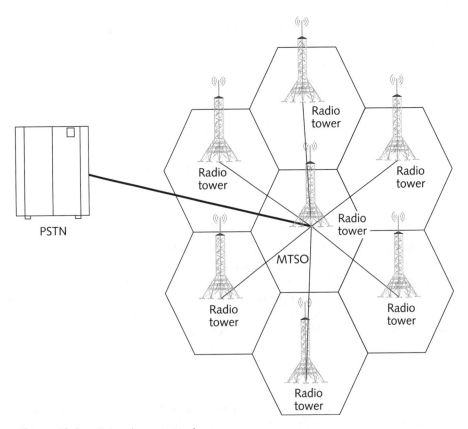

Figure 10-1 Cellular phone network

© Cengage Learning 2014

transmitters are connected to a base station, and each base station is connected to a **mobile telecommunications switching office (MTSO)**. The MTSO is the link between the cellular phone network and the wired telephone world; it controls all transmitters and base stations in the cellular phone network. A large city may have multiple MTSOs, each controlling a group of cells.

Cells are drawn as hexagons simply because it makes it easier to show adjacent cells without the use of overlapping lines, which can be confusing. In reality, a cell's shape is closer to a circle, although buildings and other geographic features can affect the shape.

In 2011, the number of cellular phone subscribers worldwide was approaching 6 billion and growing fast. For more information, see *mobithinking.com/mobile-marketing-tools/latest-mobile-stats*.

The second key to understanding how cellular telephony works is that all of today's digital transmitters and digital cellular phones operate at a low power level. This enables the signal from a single phone to stay confined to the cell and not cause any interference with any other cells. Because the signal at a particular frequency does not go far beyond the cell area, that same frequency can be used in other cells at the same time, though not in adjacent cells. This is called frequency reuse, and it is shown in diagram format in Figure 10-2.

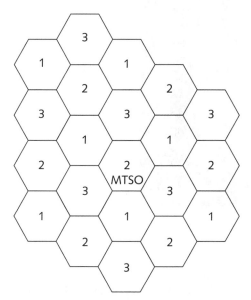

MTSO= Mobile telecommunications
switching office

Figure 10-2 Frequency reuse with three frequencies

Cellular phones have special codes associated with them. These codes are used to identify the phone, the phone's owner, and the carrier or service provider (such as AT&T or Sprint). Some of these codes are preprogrammed when the phone is manufactured, whereas others are associated with the user's account. Some cellular phones require a SIM card to be installed on the phone before they can be used. A **SIM (subscriber identity module) card** is a very small electronic card used to associate the phone with the user's account and with the carrier. Figure 10-3 shows a regular-size SIM card and a micro SIM card—the type used on Apple iPhones and some other cellular phone devices.

Figure 10-3 SIM and micro SIM cards

© Cengage Learning 2014

SIM cards have between 64 KB and 512 KB of ROM, between 1 KB and 8 KB of RAM, and between 64 KB and 512 KB of EEPROM. The user's phone number is stored on the SIM card, and users have a choice of storing contact numbers on the phone's memory or on the SIM. Users can move the card between one phone and another and use different phones without reprogramming. An example of this is when a user is travelling in an area where the frequency bands used are different than those she uses in her home area. She may be able to rent a phone that is compatible with the local cellular phone service but still use her home account simply by moving the SIM to a different phone.

Table 10-1 summarizes the codes used in cellular telephony along with their respective sizes and purposes.

Code Name	Size	Purpose
System Identification Code (SID)	5 digits	A unique number that identifies the carrier
Electronic serial number (ESN)	32 bits	The cellular phone's unique serial number; not used on phones with a SIM card
International Mobile Equipment Identity (IMEI)	15 decimal digits (14 plus a check digit)	A unique number that identifies mobile phones as well as some satellite phones; also acts as the serial number
Mobile identification number (MIN)	10 digits	A unique number generated from the phone's telephone number; not used on phones with a SIM card

Table 10-1 Cellular phone codes

© Cengage Learning 2014

NOTE An ESN or IMEI number is permanently assigned to a specific cellular phone when it is manufactured. The carrier or reseller programs the MIN into the phone at account-activation time. The SID code is programmed into the carrier's system and associated with the SIM card at account-activation time.

When a cellular phone user moves around within a particular cell, the transmitters at the base station for that cell handle all the communications. As the user moves toward the next cell, the cellular phone will automatically associate with the base station of that cell. The process of the new cell taking over the user's call is called a handoff. However, what happens if a cellular phone user moves beyond the coverage area of the entire cellular phone network—for example, if he goes from Nashville to Boston? In this case, the cellular telephone would connect with the cellular phone network in Boston, which then communicates with the network in Nashville to verify that the user has a valid account and can make calls. This connection to a cell outside a user's home area is known as **roaming**. A comparison between handoff and roaming is shown in Figure 10-4.

A cellular phone user's home area is the location where she lives or works and where she has an account with the cellular phone carrier. When connected to the home area, the user pays local, per-minute call rates. When roaming, the per-minute rates tend to be higher, and a roaming fee may apply. Per-minute rates and roaming rates depend on the carrier with which the user has an account.

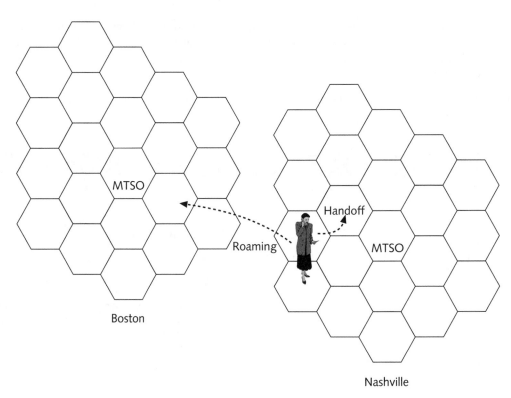

Figure 10-4 Handoff and roaming

© *Cengage Learning 2014*

The steps (shown in Figure 10-5) that a cellular phone uses to receive a call are as follows:

1. When the cellular phone is turned on, it scans the frequencies that it is programmed to use and listens for a broadcast from the nearest base station on a selected frequency known as a **control channel**. This broadcast contains information about the network, the frequencies used in a particular cell, etc. If the phone cannot detect a control channel, it may be out of range of a compatible network, in which case it displays a message to the user such as "No Service."

2. If the cellular phone receives the broadcast information correctly, it compares it with the SID of the carrier that was programmed into the phone or the SIM card. If the information on the phone or the SIM card matches the broadcast, the cellular phone is in a network owned by its carrier. The cellular phone then transmits a registration request number to the base station that the MTSO uses for tracking the cell(s) in which the phone is located.

3. If the SID does not match, then the phone is roaming. The MTSO of the remote network contacts the MTSO of the home network, which confirms that the SID of the phone belongs to a valid account. The MTSO of the remote network then tracks the phone and sends the call information (including length of call and the call's status as a roaming connection) back to the home MTSO.

4. When a call comes in, the MTSO locates the phone through the registration request and then selects a frequency that will be used for communication. The MTSO sends the frequency information to the phone over the control channel. Both the phone and the transmitter switch to that frequency, and the connection is then completed.

5. As the user moves toward the edge of a cell, the base station notes that the phone's signal strength is decreasing while the base station in the next cell determines that the phone's signal strength is increasing. The two base stations coordinate with each other through the MTSO. The cellular phone then gets a message on the control channel to change frequencies as the call is handed off to another cell.

6. The phone and transmitter change frequencies as required.

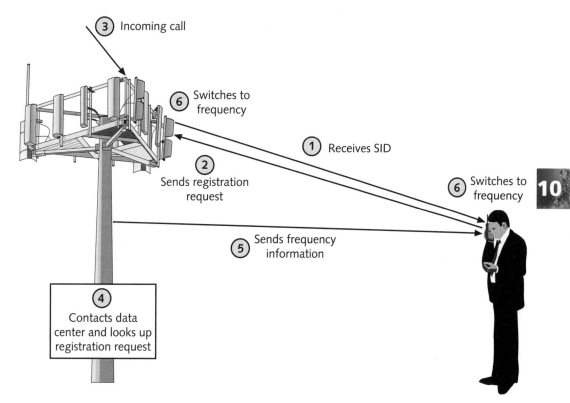

Figure 10-5 Receiving a call on a cellular phone

© Cengage Learning 2014

The process of making an outgoing call is similar to the one for receiving a call.

Although the Telecommunications Act of 1996 makes it illegal to intercept cellular transmissions, callers should remember that their conversations are being broadcast across the public airwaves and may not be as private as calls using the wired telephone network.

Evolution of Cellular Technology

Because cellular technology is available worldwide, it is useful to learn about how it evolved and where it might be going in the future, because you never know where you may travel or where you may end up working some day. Cellular phones have been available since the early 1980s in the United States. Since that time, cellular phone technology has changed dramatically. Most industry experts talk in terms of several generations of cellular telephony, which are discussed next.

First Generation Cellular Telephony The first generation of wireless cellular technology is known, appropriately enough, as **First Generation**, or **1G**. 1G transmissions use analog signals, which are radio frequency (RF) transmissions in which the caller's voice is modulated using basic frequency modulation (FM).

1G technology is based on, and sometimes referred to as, **Advanced Mobile Phone Service (AMPS)**. AMPS operates in the 800–900 MHz frequency spectrum. Each channel is 30 KHz wide, with a 45 KHz passband. There are 832 frequencies available for transmission. Out of those frequencies, 790 are used for voice traffic and the remaining 42 are used for control channels. However, because two frequencies are used for each cellular telephone conversation (one to transmit and one to receive, in full-duplex), there are actually 395 voice channels, 21 of which are used for control channel functions.

Channels that are 30 KHz wide provide voice quality comparable to a standard wired telephone transmission, which is why AMPS channels are 30 KHz.

AMPS uses Frequency Division Multiple Access (FDMA), which you learned about in Chapter 3. Remember that in RF communications systems there are two resources, frequency and time. Division by frequency, so that each caller is allocated part of the spectrum for all of the time, is the basis of FDMA. This is shown in Figure 10-6. FDMA allocates a single cellular channel, with two frequencies to one user at a time. If the channel deteriorates due to interference from other frequencies, the user is switched to another channel, if one is available.

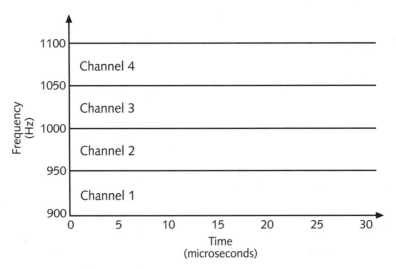

Figure 10-6 FDMA

© Cengage Learning 2014

AMPS was one of the first wireless communications systems to use FDMA. Today, AMPS is not commonly used; however, some older tri-mode mobile phones still support the AMPS system.

1G networks use circuit-switching technology. When a telephone call is made, a dedicated connection is made between the caller and the recipient of the call through the telephone company's switch. While the telephone conversation is taking place, the connection remains open between only these two users. No other calls can be made from that phone while the first conversation is going on, and anyone who calls that phone will receive a busy signal. This direct connection lasts for the duration of the call. At the end of the call, the switch drops the connection and the frequencies are released, so that another caller can use them.

Analog signals, the basis for 1G cellular telephony, are prone to interference, and the connections do not exhibit the same quality as systems that employ digital transmission. In addition, sending data over an analog signal requires a modem or similar device to convert the signals from digital to analog and then back again. A 1G analog cellular telephone can be realistically used only for voice communications. For these reasons, 1G was soon replaced with improved digital technology.

Second Generation Cellular Telephony

The next generation of cellular telephony, known as **Second Generation,** or **2G,** started in the early 1990s and continues to the present but will likely be phased out very soon. 2G networks are capable of transmitting data at between 9.6–14.4 Kbps in the 800 MHz and 1.9 GHz frequency bands. The only major feature that 2G systems share with 1G is that they are circuit-switched networks.

2G systems use digital instead of analog transmissions. Digital transmissions provide several improvements over analog transmissions:

- Digital transmissions use the frequency spectrum more efficiently.

- Over long distances, the quality of the voice transmission does not degrade as it does with analog. This is because analog signals can be amplified, but any noise that appears cannot be removed since there is no way for the receiver to differentiate between the noise and the voice signal.

- Digital transmissions are difficult to decode and consequently offer better security.

- On average, digital transmissions use less power. As a result, they enable smaller and less expensive individual receivers and transmitters.

Another difference between 1G and 2G systems is that the carriers of 2G cellular networks build their cellular networks around various multiple access technologies. Three technologies are used with 2G: time division multiple access (TDMA), code division multiple access (CDMA), and **GSM (Global System for Mobile Communications).**

Whereas FDMA, used with AMPS, divides the available spectrum into several frequency channels, so that each caller is allocated part of the spectrum for all of the time, TDMA divides by time, so that each caller is allocated the entire spectrum for part of the time, as shown in Figure 10-7. TDMA divides a single 30 KHz radio frequency channel into six unique time slots, and each caller uses two time slots (one for transmitting and one for receiving). TDMA can send three times as many calls over a single channel as FDMA can.

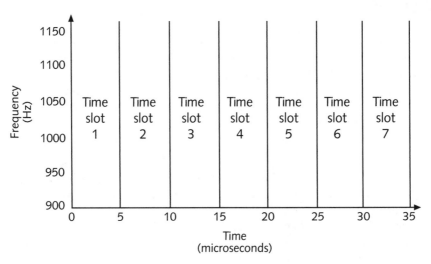

Figure 10-7 TDMA

© Cengage Learning 2014

With CDMA, which was discussed in Chapter 3, every caller is allocated the entire spectrum all of the time, as shown in Figure 10-8. CDMA uses direct sequence spread spectrum (DSSS) and unique digital codes, rather than separate RF frequencies, to differentiate between the different transmissions. A CDMA transmission is spread across the frequency, and the digital codes are applied to the individual transmissions. When the signal is received, the codes are removed from the signal in the way described in Chapter 3.

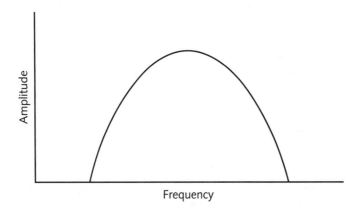

Figure 10-8 CDMA

© Cengage Learning 2014

GSM, which was developed in the 1980s as a European standard for public mobile communications, uses a combination of FDMA and TDMA technologies. It divides a 25 MHz channel into 124 frequencies of 200 KHz each. Each 200 KHz channel is then divided into eight time slots using TDMA. The modulation employed is a variation of FSK called Gaussian minimum shift keying (GMSK), which uses filters to help reduce interference between adjacent channels. GSM systems can transmit data at speeds up to 9.6 Kbps.

In 1989, the Cellular Telecommunications Industry Association (CTIA) chose TDMA over FDMA as the technology of choice for digital cellular networks. However, with the growing technology competition posed by CDMA and the fact that Europe was using GSM for mobile communications, the CTIA reconsidered and decided to let carriers make their own technology choices.

These three technologies—TDMA, CDMA, and GSM—make up the backbone of 2G digital cellular telephony.

2.5 Generation Cellular Telephony

Current digital cellular telephony far surpasses the characteristics of 2G, and the industry's transition to Third Generation proceeded at an accelerated pace. Carriers were making major changes to the infrastructure of their networks, and a completely new generation of mobile cellular devices was on its way. Until the migration to Third Generation technology was completed, an interim step known as **2.5 Generation**, or **2.5G**, cellular systems was being widely deployed throughout North America. 2.5G networks operated at a theoretical maximum data rate of 384 Kbps for data transmissions. They were also widely deployed in many other nations, such as China, Japan, and Korea, along with a few cities in Europe.

The primary difference between 2G and 2.5G networks is that in 2.5G networks data is transmitted over a packet-switched connection instead of a circuit-switched connection. Although circuit switching is ideal for voice communications, it is not efficient for transmitting data because data transmissions normally occur in bursts, with periods of delay in between, when nothing is being transmitted. The delays result in time wasted while a channel is tied up, dedicated to one user.

Packet switching has two major advantages over circuit switching. First, packet switching is much more efficient because it can handle three to five times more transmissions over a given channel. Second, packet switching permits an always-on connection. With a circuit-switched network, a connection between two devices ties up an entire channel that is dedicated only to those devices; it is not practical to keep that connection open when there is little or no traffic. Doing this would be like calling a friend on the telephone and then laying the telephone down but not hanging up just in case you want to talk again later. Tying up the line in this way prevents any other calls from coming in or going out. With packet switching, it becomes practical to keep the data connection up all the time. Each packet is transmitted independently through the network to the destination and only uses the channel for the time required to transmit it. Other devices can use the same packet-switched connection to send and receive data, with each device taking a turn sending packets.

The always-on feature, along with higher transmission speeds, made cable modems and DSL connections more popular than dial-up connections for home use. You can watch TV or talk on the phone and access the Internet at the same time. The computer can remain connected to the Internet, and you don't have to wait for a connection to be reestablished when you want to browse the Web, send or check your e-mails, chat, etc.

There are three 2.5G network technologies. Which one is used depends on which 2G-network technology is being migrated from. For TDMA or GSM 2G networks, the upgrade path is a 2.5G technology known as **general packet radio service (GPRS)**. GPRS uses eight time slots in a 200 KHz spectrum and four different coding techniques, in addition to the modulation used by GSM, to transmit at a top speed of 114 Kbps. The next upgrade step beyond GPRS was **Enhanced Data rates for GSM Evolution (EDGE)**.

EDGE is a booster for GPRS systems and can transmit data at up to 384 Kbps. It is based on a **8-PSK** modulation, in which the phase of the carrier is shifted in 45-degree increments and 4 bits can be transmitted per phase change. EDGE-based networks can coexist with standard GSM networks.

If migrating from a 2G CDMA network, the transition is to **CDMA2000 1xRTT** ("1xRTT" stands for "1-times Radio Transmission Technology"), which operates on a pair of 1.25-MHz-wide frequency channels and is designed to support 144 Kbps packet data transmission and to double the voice capacity of CDMA networks.

Third Generation Cellular Telephony Imagine using your cellular telephone to videoconference with a friend in the United States while you are traveling on a train in Japan. That was the original vision of **Third Generation (3G)**, which was designed to be a uniform and global standard for cellular wireless communication. The International Telecommunications Union (ITU) suggested the following standard data rates for a wireless cellular digital network:

- 144 Kbps for a mobile user
- 386 Kbps for a slowly moving user
- 2 Mbps for a stationary user

As with converting from a 2G network to a 2.5G network, converting from a 2.5G network to a 3G network depends on the 2.5G technology that's being converted from. If the transition is being made from CDMA2000 1xRTT, the transition would be to **CDMA2000 1xEVDO** ("EVDO" is short for "Evolution Data Optimized"). This technology can transmit at 2.4 Mbps. However, EVDO can only send data and must be coupled with 1xRTT to process both voice and data. EVDO transmissions are very similar to those of 1xRTT, but EVDO uses a pair of separate dedicated channels for data, often in new frequency bands being added to the bands available for use with CDMA2000 technologies. EVDO radios measure the signal-to-noise ratio (SNR) in each channel pair every 1.667 milliseconds to determine which cellular phone device to service next. By using dedicated data channels and continually optimizing transmissions to the devices that have the best signal at any given time, EVDO can achieve its higher data rates. The successor to CDMA2000 1xEVDO was to be **CDMA2000 1xEVDV** ("EVDV" is short for "Evolution Data and Voice"), which can send both data and voice transmissions simultaneously over a packet-switched network. EVDV was the next logical upgrade path for this technology. It can reach data transfer speeds of up to 3.09 Mbps. Release D of EVDV supports up to 1.0 Mbps upstream.

In 2005, Verizon Wireless and Sprint Nextel Corporation in the United States as well as Bell Canada and TELUS in Canada initiated nationwide deployment of 1xEVDO. Alaska Communications Systems (ACS) deployed 1xEVDO in Alaska's main population centers.

If a network is transitioning from EDGE 2.5G technology, **Wideband CDMA (W-CDMA)** is the migration path to 3G. W-CDMA adds a packet-switched data channel to a circuit-switched voice channel. It can send at up to 2 Mbps in a fixed position and 384 Kbps when mobile.

Beyond W-CDMA, the upgrade path is to **High-Speed Downlink Packet Access, or HSDPA,** which can transmit at 8–10 Mbps downstream. HSDPA uses a 5 MHz W-CDMA channel along with a variety of adaptive modulation, multiple-input multiple-output (MIMO) antennas, and hybrid automatic repeat request (HARQ) techniques, all grouped together to achieve very high data rates. Several carriers in North America that were supporting GSM moved quickly to update their equipment to HSDPA.

But the changes do not end there. As the number of subscribers increases, carriers are under pressure to support more users with a limited amount of bandwidth. Most, if not all, of the carriers that had deployed CDMA found themselves under pressure to move to a technology that was proposed in 2005 and could support theoretical peak download data rates as high as 300 Mbps and upload rates of 75 Mbps. CDMA carriers needed to match these speeds, which could not be accomplished with EVDV, so they began deploying and testing the immediate successor to HSDPA, which is **HSPA+**. This technical standard, also called Evolved HSPA, provides theoretical data rates of up to 168 Mbps on the downlink (a realistic maximum is around 42 Mbps) and 22 Mbps on the uplink and combines two HSDPA transmitters into one, using MIMO, 64 QAM modulation (downlink; 6 bits per symbol) and 16 QAM modulation (uplink; 4 bits per symbol). The two parallel transmission channels form a spatially multiplexed channel that allows HSPA+ to achieve the higher data rates. Keep in mind that higher data rates are also dependent on the processing capacity of the cellular phones themselves.

HSPA+ allows the carriers to move to an all-IP, packet-only architecture in which the base stations can bypass the legacy infrastructure of cellular networks, connecting directly to a gateway and using IP routing technology to forward packets to and from a mobile user. This means that even voice calls are encapsulated into IP packets (VoIP), and this promotes more efficient use of the available RF spectrum, reduces latency, and can handle up to five times more users per cell on the downlink and twice the number of users on the uplink than previous generation systems. All of this reduces the cost per bit for the carrier, and the savings eventually flow through to the end users.

HSPA+ also provides an upgrade path to the latest-generation technology, which many carriers worldwide are fast moving towards: **LTE (Long Term Evolution)**, also known as "4G LTE." LTE expands the MIMO/Spatial Multiplexing beyond the 2 × 2 radio configuration of HSPA+, utilizes OFDM, and allows the use of wider bandwidth RF transmission channels, up to 20 MHz to achieve data rates up to 100 Mbps on the downlink.

You may be wondering if there is a next step in cellular technology. Yes, there is, and it is called LTE Advanced, which the **3rd Generation Partnership Project (3GPP)** introduced in 2009. The 3GPP (see *www.3gpp.org/Partners*) is a group of six standards organizations from Asia, Europe, and North America that proposed standards for GSM, GPRS/EDGE, HSDPA, HSPA+, and LTE. **LTE Advanced**, its proposed standard for broadband cellular telephony, expands on LTE by allowing carriers to combine up to five 20-MHz-wide frequency channels to raise the maximum downlink data rate possible for mobile cellular devices to 1 Gbps. In addition, LTE Advanced standardizes the use of very small cells, called microcells and femtocells, to further optimize frequency reuse and allow more carriers to share the available frequency space (spectrum).

As competition increases and users demand better service and higher speeds for data, most cellular networks worldwide are being rapidly upgraded to LTE technology. Some challenges remain in a few countries concerning the availability of spectrum, but most governments realize the potential for expansion of connectivity and are working towards making more of the spectrum available. Figure 10-9 summarizes the technology paths to 4G.

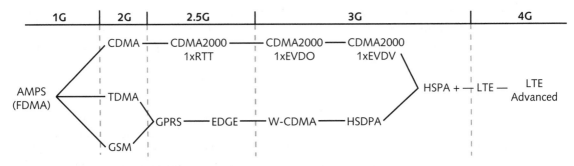

Figure 10-9 Cellular technology migration paths

© Cengage Learning 2014

Table 10-2 summarizes all the cellular technologies we have discussed so far.

Name	Generation	Technology	Maximum Peak Data Rate (Downlink)
AMPS	1G	Analog, circuit switched	9.6 Kbps
GSM	2G	Digital, circuit switched	9.6 Kbps
TDMA	2G	Digital, circuit switched	14.4 Kbps
CDMA	2G	Digital, circuit switched	14.4 Kbps
GPRS	2.5G	Digital, packet switched for data only; circuit switched for voice calls	114 Kbps
CDMA2000 1xRTT	2.5G	Same as GPRS	144 Kbps
EDGE	2.5G	Same as GPRS	384 Kbps
CDMA2000 1xEVDO	3G	Digital, packet switched for both voice and data	2 Mbps
W-CDMA	3G	Digital, packet switched for data; optionally circuit switched or packet switched for voice calls	2 Mbps
CDMA 1xEVDV	3G	Digital, packet switched for data, circuit switched for voice	3.09 Mbps
HSDPA	3G	Same as CDMA2000 1xEVDV	21 Mbps
HSPA+	3G	Digital, packet switched for both voice and data (IP-based)	42 Mbps
LTE	4G	Same as HSPA+	300 Mbps
LTE Advanced	4G	Same as LTE	1 Gbps

Table 10-2 Digital cellular technologies

© Cengage Learning 2014

Figure 10-10 shows a comparison of the data-rate speeds for various cellular technologies.

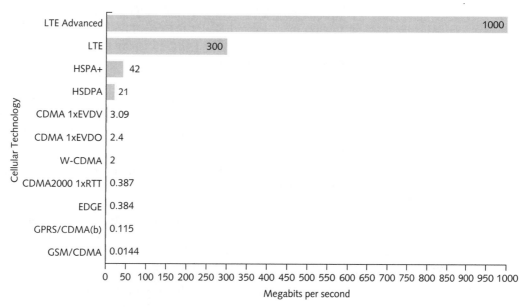

Figure 10-10 Comparison of data-rate speeds for various cellular technologies

© Cengage Learning 2014

Client Software

Features such as Internet surfing and videoconferencing require client software to operate on a wireless digital cellular device. The software provides the functions and interfaces that allow users to display or manipulate the data. In the recent past, the number of cellular-capable handheld devices that could display all the information on a Web page was very limited. This has, of course, changed dramatically with the introduction of Apple iOS and Android operating systems for mobile devices. Today, these devices can display almost all Web page content, with a few exceptions, notably Adobe Flash-based movies or similar animated content.

A few remaining legacy devices may still incorporate client software that is unique to cellular telephones, but this situation is changing rapidly; in the near future, most mobile browsers will support HTML 5 and will be able to display virtually any Web content in addition to running a variety of software applications, including cloud-based applications. In fact, this is the case with the Apple iOS and Android environments for both cellular phones and tablet computers, as well as with some Nokia Symbian phones and the newest Blackberry models.

Historically, four technologies have provided standard ways to display Web content on cellular phones:

- Wireless Application Protocol (WAP)—Developed in 1997, WAP employed a tiny Web browser program that ran on cellular phones and required a gateway computer that translated Web pages into plain text. It was designed for monochrome display screens and did not support color text or pictures. The WAP gateway translated the Web pages using a simplified markup language called Wireless Markup Language (WML).

- Wireless Application Protocol version 2 (WAP2)—WAP2 was based on XHTML and could display text and graphics in color on small cellular phone screens without the need for a gateway computer to translate the Web content.

- Binary Run-Time Environment for Wireless (BREW)—Brew was a tiny software environment that competed with WAP2 and could display a variety of content. It also did not require a gateway to translate Web content for display on a cellular phone.

- i-mode—**i-mode** was a complete carrier-based Internet access system developed and owned by the Japanese corporation NTT DoCoMo. It was based on **compact HTML** (cHTML), a subset of HTML designed for mobile devices, which has its own set of tags and attributes.

In addition to these specialized technologies, manufacturers began including support for the Java programming language in some of the early smartphones. **Java** was developed by Sun Microsystems (now part of the Oracle Corporation) as an object-oriented programming language used for general-purpose business programs as well as for interactive Web sites. Java can run on almost any hardware platform today, notable exceptions being the Apple iPhone and iPad. A subset of Java, **Java 2 Micro Edition (J2ME)**, was specifically developed for programming software applications for wireless devices.

J2ME-enabled cellular telephones have more intelligence than basic digital cellular telephones that run a WAP microbrowser or i-mode. J2ME enables a cellular phone to access remote applications and e-mail as well as run programs on the cellular phone itself. These programs include voice-activated dialing, calendars, and voice recorders. The cellular phone can handle specific tasks, such as automatically turning off the phone's ringer and forwarding calls to voicemail when the user is in a meeting that has been entered into the phone's calendar.

Digital Cellular Challenges and Outlook

Despite strong public skepticism in the late 1990s and early 2000s, cellular telephony did sweep the world and has significantly changed the way people work and communicate. With other options competing for users, such as WiMAX, and with globalization of markets continuing, users stand to benefit the most from digital cellular telephony once the industry settles on a single cellular standard, such as LTE. Having one standard available worldwide will eventually lower costs for carriers, forcing them to deliver more competitive pricing and services; it will also enable consumers to use their phones regardless of where they are in the world.

Limited Spectrum The single largest factor limiting the development of 3G is the availability of spectrum. This problem was especially apparent in the United States, where a shortage of frequencies delayed 3G and 4G implementation. Although both 3G and 4G can operate in almost any part of the spectrum, the various cellular industry associations have tried to designate a particular part of the spectrum for communications all over the world, primarily to benefit users and lower costs for carriers. Currently, the 1.710–1.855 GHz and 2.520–2.670 GHz bands are designated as the spectrum to be used for 3G and 4G worldwide. In North America, the 700 MHz band, formerly used for analog television channels, is also being used for cellular networks; in Europe, the 500–800 MHz part of the spectrum is being used.

For more information on 3G and 4G cellular technologies, visit *www.3gpp.org* and *www.umts-forum.org*.

Cellular equipment manufacturers and carriers are continually looking for ways to maximize the use of the available frequency bands. Overlaying an inexpensive WiMAX network on a cellular network for handling data is one potential way to free up more bandwidth for voice calls and allow for a higher user load for data as well, provided that WiMAX-enabled cellular devices are readily available.

The use of cellular data is growing at such a fast rate that carriers are struggling to keep their networks updated. In fact, many of them are spending large sums of money to acquire more bandwidth and are deploying more Wi-Fi hotspots, both in an attempt to reduce the data load on their cellular networks. Because smartphone users are the largest users of data, and because all smartphones today are equipped with Wi-Fi interfaces, this should not be a problem. However, increased Wi-Fi use will reduce the revenues for the use of data on the cellular networks, so carriers need to strike a balance between the two.

Costs The service fees for data can easily run over $100 per month for 500 megabytes of e-mail, especially for people who travel often and need to roam with their phones. However, this cost pales in comparison to the billions of dollars that carriers have to spend to build and constantly upgrade their cellular networks. Just the cost of buying the necessary spectrum is astronomical. In early 2001, carriers in Germany paid over $46 billion for licenses to use the spectrum. Carriers in other nations face similar costs, and that's just one element in building a modern cellular network. Networks must be deployed, tested, managed, and maintained to keep customers satisfied with the service. In addition, the costs associated with high-volume data connections to the Internet runs into the millions of dollars per month.

Satellite Broadband Wireless

Although the use of satellites for personal wireless communications is fairly recent, satellites have been used for worldwide communications for nearly 50 years. Satellite use falls into three broad categories. The first use is for acquiring scientific data (e.g., measuring the radiation from the sun) and performing research in space (e.g., gathering data from the Hubble Space Telescope). The second use is for looking at Earth from space. This includes weather and mapping satellites as well as military satellites. The third use is as reflectors that bounce or relay signals from one point on Earth to another. This includes communications satellites that reflect telephone and data transmissions, broadcast satellites that reflect television signals, and navigational satellites. The three types of satellites are compared in Figure 10-11.

Wireless communications falls under the third use of satellites: bouncing signals from one point on Earth to another.

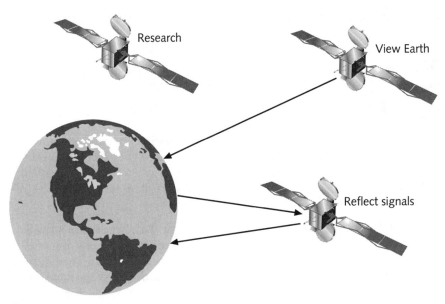

Figure 10-11 Three types of satellites

© *Cengage Learning 2014*

Satellite Transmissions

Satellites generally send and receive on one of four frequency bands, which are known as the L band, the C band, the Ku band, and the Ka band. These bands are summarized in Table 10-3.

Band	Frequency
L band	1.53–2.7 GHz
C band	3.6–7 GHz
Ku band	11.7–12.7 GHz for downlink; 14–17.8 GHz for uplink
Ka band	17.3–31 GHz

Table 10-3 Satellite frequencies

© *Cengage Learning 2014*

As you already know, frequency band affects the size of the antenna. Figure 10-12 compares the typical sizes of antennas used for the four bands.

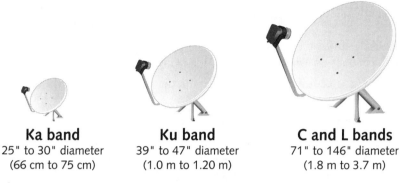

Ka band	**Ku band**	**C and L bands**
25" to 30" diameter	39" to 47" diameter	71" to 146" diameter
(66 cm to 75 cm)	(1.0 m to 1.20 m)	(1.8 m to 3.7 m)

Figure 10-12 Satellite antenna sizes

© Cengage Learning 2014

Class and Type of Service

Satellites provide two classes of service: consumer class and business class. Consumer class service shares the available bandwidth among the users; business class service, the more expensive of the two, offers dedicated channels with dedicated bandwidth.

Satellites that reflect signals back to Earth offer different types of service. They may be designed for point-to-point, point-to-multipoint, or even multipoint-to-multipoint communications. This is shown in Figure 10-13.

10

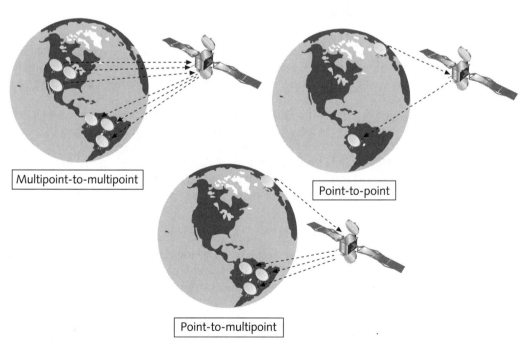

Multipoint-to-multipoint

Point-to-point

Point-to-multipoint

Figure 10-13 Types of satellite service

© Cengage Learning 2014

Modulation Techniques Satellites use a variety of common modulation techniques, most of which were discussed in Chapter 2. Here are brief descriptions of them:

- Binary phase shift keying (BPSK)—Shifts the starting point of a carrier wave by 180 degrees, depending on whether a 1 or a 0 is being transmitted

- Quadrature phase shift keying (QPSK)—Shifts the starting point of the carrier wave by 90 degrees; can transmit 2 bits per symbol

- Eight-phase shift keying (8-PSK)—Can transmit up to 3 bits per symbol

- 16-level quadrature amplitude modulation (16-QAM)—Primarily used for sending data downstream; considered very efficient but is susceptible to interference, so not generally used for upstream transmissions

Multiplexing Techniques Satellite systems employ two common multiplexing techniques, FDMA and TDMA, along with some specialized techniques designed to maximize utilization of these very expensive communications channels. Detailed coverage of these specialized techniques is beyond the scope of this book, but here are brief descriptions of them:

- Permanently Assigned Multiple Access (PAMA)—One of the oldest techniques, in which a frequency channel is permanently assigned to a user

- Single channel per carrier (SCPC)—Assigns a frequency channel to a single source; used for broadcasting radio stations, which are always transmitting

- Multiple channel per carrier (MCPC)—Uses TDM to consolidate traffic from different users on to each carrier frequency; in the European digital video broadcasting standard, typically used in point-to-multipoint applications

- Demand Assigned Multiple Access (DAMA)—Allocates bandwidth on a per-call or per-transmission session between two or more Earth stations; can efficiently share the pool of available frequency and time resources and permits full mesh routing, similar to how a telephone company's switch works, but requires more complex and costly hardware

For TV broadcasting directly to the user (satellite TV), the set-top box at the user's home or office includes a utility that enables the installation technician to align the dish antenna with the satellite antenna. The antenna needs to be initially positioned in a certain direction and at a certain angle, then the technician uses the TV set and set-top box and fine-tunes the antenna position until the strongest possible signal is achieved.

Satellite Classification

Satellite systems are classified according to the type of orbit they use. The three orbits are low earth orbit (LEO), medium earth orbit (MEO), and high earth orbit (HEO). Most HEO satellites fall into a subclass called geosynchronous earth orbit (GEO).

Low Earth Orbit (LEO) Low earth orbit (LEO) satellites circle the Earth at altitudes between 200 and 900 miles (321 and 1,448 kilometers). Because they orbit so close to Earth, LEO satellites must travel at high speeds so that the Earth's gravity will not pull them back into the atmosphere. Satellites in LEO travel at 17,000 miles (27,359 kilometers) per hour, circling the Earth in about 90 minutes.

Because LEOs are in such a low orbit, their area of coverage (called the footprint) is small, as shown in Figure 10-14. This means that more LEO satellites are needed to provide coverage, compared to MEO and GEO satellites. One LEO system calls for over 225 satellites for total coverage of the Earth.

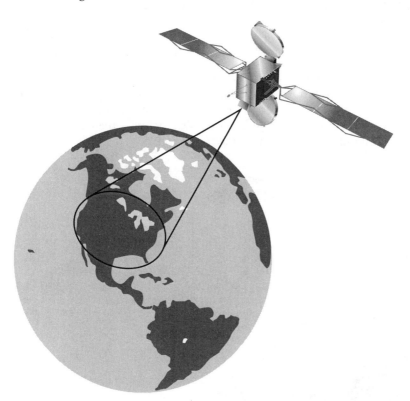

Figure 10-14 LEO footprint

© Cengage Learning 2014

LEO systems have a low latency (delays caused by signals that must travel over a long distance) and use low-powered terrestrial devices (RF transmitters). It takes 20 to 40 milliseconds for a signal to bounce from an Earth-bound station to a LEO, then back to an Earth station.

LEO satellites can be divided into Little LEO and Big LEO groups. Little LEOs provide pager, satellite telephone, and location services. Using a Little LEO satellite, a user can make a phone call from anywhere on Earth. In contrast, cellular telephone services require the user to be within RF range of a transmission tower. Big LEOs carry voice and data broadband services, such as wireless Internet access. Some satellite Internet services provide shared downstream data rates of up to 400 Kbps but require a telephone connection for upstream data to an ISP. Another LEO wireless Internet service provides two-way data services with speeds of up to 500 Kbps. Two-way satellite Internet users need a two-foot by three-foot dish antenna and two modems (one each for uplink and downlink).

In the future, LEOs are expected to be in demand for three markets: rural conventional telephone service, global mobile digital cellular service, and international broadband service. The speeds for wireless access are expected to exceed 100 Mbps.

Today, many companies use satellite technology to reduce line costs. In particular, drugstore and supermarket chains, which usually have stores located in remote towns, use LEO satellites to link these stores with the head office.

Medium Earth Orbit (MEO) **Medium earth orbit (MEO) satellites** orbit the Earth at altitudes between 1,500 and 10,000 miles (2,413 to 16,090 kilometers). Some MEO satellites orbit in near-perfect circles, have a constant altitude, and travel at a constant speed. Other MEO satellites have elongated orbits called highly elliptical orbits (HEOs).

Because they are farther from the Earth, MEOs have two advantages over LEOs. First, they do not have to travel as fast; a MEO can take up to 12 hours to circle the Earth. Second, MEOs have a bigger Earth footprint; thus, fewer satellites are needed, as shown in Figure 10-15. On the other hand, the higher orbit also increases the latency. A MEO signal takes from 50 to 150 milliseconds to make the round trip.

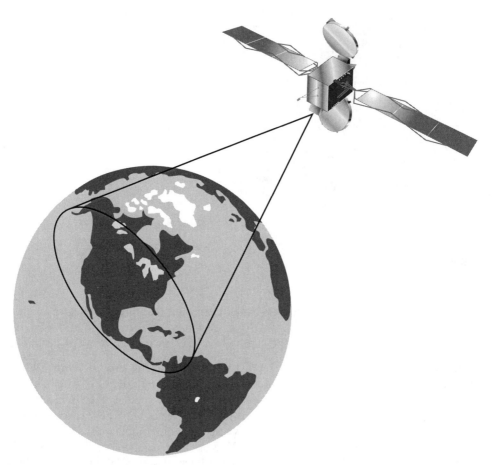

Figure 10-15 MEO footprint

© Cengage Learning 2014

The average orbit characteristics of a HEO satellite are about the same as a MEO. HEO satellites have a high apogee (maximum altitude) and a low perigee (minimum altitude). In addition, HEO orbits can provide good coverage in extreme latitudes. The orbits also typically have a 24-hour period, which means the satellites dwell for a long time at a fixed point over the Earth. This means that with just two satellites in the same orbit, one is always visible from any point on the ground.

Geosynchronous Earth Orbit (GEO) and High Earth Orbit (HEO)

Geosynchronous earth orbit (GEO) satellites are stationed at an altitude of 22,282 miles (35,860 kilometers). A GEO satellite orbit matches the rotation of the Earth and moves as the Earth moves. This means that it remains "fixed" over a given location on the Earth and seems to hang motionless in space. HEO satellites are somewhat rare, but they orbit the planet at a much higher altitude—i.e., above 63,333 miles (101,925 kilometers). Because of their great distance from the surface of the Earth, GEO and HEO satellites can provide continuous service to a very large footprint. In fact, only three GEO satellites are needed to cover the entire Earth (except for the polar regions). Their high altitude causes GEO satellites to have high latencies of about 250 milliseconds and require high-powered terrestrial transmitting devices along with very sensitive receiving equipment. GEO satellites are typically used for global communications—such as TV broadcasting and weather forecasting—but are not normally used for telephony or computer communications because of the one-quarter second delay in round-trip transmissions. The distance of the satellite from the surface of the planet causes this delay, and it affects the performance of computer communications protocols like TCP/IP. Figure 10-16 shows how three GEO satellites can cover the entire planet. HEO satellites have been used to monitor compliance with the nuclear test ban agreements; they are also used in Russia to provide satellite services in the Polar Regions.

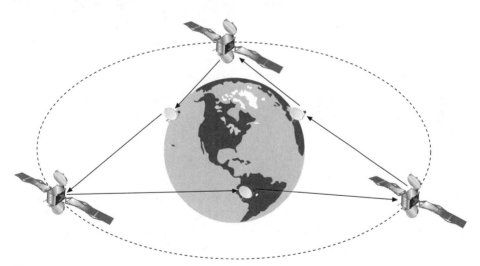

Figure 10-16 Three GEO satellites covering the entire planet

© Cengage Learning 2014

Although GEO satellites are much more expensive to launch, they are an attractive option because of their lifespan of 12–15 years. (The average lifespan of a LEO satellite is only five years.) Also, because their footprints are so large, they are much more efficient compared to LEO satellites. LEO satellites spend a portion of their orbit over sparsely populated areas where continuous coverage may not be needed. The International Telecommunications Union (ITU) regulates GEO usage.

Some HEO satellites, like the ones used for Sirius satellite radio (Radiosat), follow a highly elliptical orbit called Tundra. This orbit is chosen because it allows the satellites to provide better coverage at higher latitudes. Geostationary orbits are only possible around the equator, which would make it difficult to provide service across Canada and the northern part of the United States.

To find how many satellites are in orbit around Earth and operational at any moment, visit *www. ucsusa.org/nuclear_weapons_and_global_security/space_weapons/technical_issues/ucs-satellite-database.html*, where you can download the most current satellite database in either MS-Excel or text format. These two files include the satellite names and provide a wealth of other information about each device. The Apogee column lists the maximum altitude (distance from the planet).

NASA's J-Track 3D Web site lets you see the orbits of all the satellites around Earth in real time and get information on each satellite, such as its purpose, who owns the satellite, the orbital altitude, and current location. Make sure Java is installed on your computer, then visit *science.nasa.gov/realtime/jtrack/3d/JTrack3D.html*. Note that you can also click and hold the left mouse button inside the Java applet window and rotate the planet to view it from any angle.

Table 10-4 summarizes the advantages and disadvantages of the various orbits.

Satellite Orbit	Advantages	Disadvantages
LEO	Low-latency (20–40 milliseconds) Low-power High-speed communications (500 Kbps or higher, depending on application)	Very high orbital speed Average of 225 satellites to cover the entire Earth Small footprint Short life span (average 5 years)
MEO	Medium latency (50–150 milliseconds) Larger footprint than LEO; 24 satellites required to cover the Earth Slower orbital speed; dwells over an area longer; 12-hour orbit Longer life span than LEO (10+ years)	Higher latency than LEO More expensive to replace than LEO
HEO	Similar speed and latency characteristics to MEO; can dwell over an area longer Footprint similar to MEO Can provide good coverage at extreme latitudes (North and South Poles)	Fewer satellites required to cover the Earth than MEO At apogee (high point of orbit), latency increases Highly elliptical orbit, which requires great accuracy and increases cost
GEO	Very large footprint; only three satellites required to cover entire Earth Synchronized with Earth's rotation, allowing for permanent, fixed antennas Very high speeds used for broadcasting Long life span (15+ years)	Very high latency (250 milliseconds); not efficient for two-way IP comm Very expensive to replace Higher power required by greater distance from Earth; more subject to interference Does not provide good coverage at very high latitudes

Table 10-4 Satellite orbit advantages and disadvantages

Experimental Technologies

Satellites are sensitive to disturbances on the surface of our sun and other outer-space phenomena that can cause interruptions in communications or incapacitate a very expensive satellite. The U.S. National Aeronautics and Space Administration (NASA) experimented with ultra-lightweight, solar-powered, unmanned high-flying aircraft in the 1990s (see *www.nasa. gov/centers/dryden/news/ResearchUpdate/Helios/index.html*). The European Space Agency (ESA) has a similar program. The idea behind developing these vehicles is that an aircraft powered by solar cells and using fuel cells as a backup, flying at approximately 100,000 feet, could carry cellular telephone-switching equipment and circle the same area for several days. These aircraft could be used in place of a satellite or ground-based antenna tower infrastructure and would be significantly less expensive to launch and operate than a LEO satellite. The aircraft could also be repaired, which is extremely difficult and expensive to do with a satellite.

Satellite Technology Outlook

The fact that satellites can provide wireless communication service in areas not covered by cellular or WiMAX means that end-users and companies will continue to rely on this technology indefinitely. Today's satellites enable carriers—in combination with airlines, merchant shipping companies, and tourism operators—to offer Internet access and voice calls to passengers and crews across large oceans as well as in high latitudes and remote corners of the Earth. As reliance on communications and data connectivity continues to increase, these companies will continue to look for ways of providing uninterrupted, faster, and lower=cost access for end-users. In addition, satellites can make these services available to unpopulated areas of the planet, such as deserts, large forests, and mountainous regions, where it is not economically viable for any carrier or operator to deploy the required infrastructure.

10

Chapter Summary

- In cellular telephone networks, the coverage area is divided into sections called cells. Each cell includes one or more transmitters with which the mobile devices communicate.

- The transmitters and cellular phones operate at a low level of power, which allows the signals to stay confined to one cell and not interfere with other cells. This means the same frequency can be used in other, nonadjacent cells at the same time. Cellular phones have special codes associated with them that identify the phone, the phone's owner, and the carrier or service provider.

- Some cellular phones use SIM cards to store the user account information and, sometimes, the user's contacts. SIM cards can be moved among different cellular phones, and the phones do not have to be reprogrammed to use the same account and phone number.

- When a cellular phone user moves from a cell to an adjacent cell, the cellular phone will automatically associate with the base station of that cell. This is called a "handoff." If a cellular user moves beyond the coverage area of his cellular network, the cellular phone automatically connects with whatever cellular network is in place in the remote area. The cellular network in the remote area communicates with the one in the home area and verifies that the user has a valid account and can make calls. This connection to a cell outside a user's home area is known as "roaming."

- First Generation cellular technology, known as 1G, uses analog signals, is based on the AMPS standard, operates in the 800–900 MHz frequency spectrum, and uses FDMA. 1G networks use circuit-switching technology and can transmit data at a maximum speed of 9.6 Kbps.

- The Second Generation of cellular technology, known as 2G, can transmit data between 9.6–14.4 Kbps in the 800 MHz and the 1.9 GHz frequency bands and uses circuit-switched networks. 2G systems use digital instead of analog transmissions. 2G systems employ three different multiple access technologies: TDMA, CDMA, and GSM. GSM, developed in Europe, uses a combination of FDMA and TDMA technologies.

- 2.5G networks transmit data at a maximum speed of 384 Kbps. The primary difference between 2G and 2.5G networks is that 2.5G networks use a packet-switched technique to transmit data instead of a circuit-switched technique. Voice calls still use circuit switching. Circuit switching is ideal for voice communications but is not efficient for transmitting data.

- 3G networks provide new and expanded capabilities and data applications features to mobile users. Because the networks are based on purely digital rather than analog technology and can transmit at much higher speeds, they are not limited to circuit-switched voice communications.

- 4G networks achieve data rates that are competitive with wired communications. Long Term Evolution (LTE) technology can achieve data rates as high as 75 Mbps.

- One of the most widely used applications in the world today is Short Message Services (SMS). It allows for the delivery of short, text-based messages between wireless devices such as cellular phones and pagers.

- 3G and 4G cellular phones allow Internet surfing and videoconferencing. HTML-compatible browsers allow cellular phones equipped with color screens to display rich content. Many carriers worldwide are upgrading their networks to LTE at an accelerated pace.

- Java 2 Micro Edition (J2ME) is a subset of Java specifically developed for programming wireless devices. J2ME enables a cellular phone to access remote applications and e-mail and run programs on the cellular phone itself.

- Satellites used for wireless data connectivity employ simple modulation and multiplexing techniques. Satellite systems can transmit point-to-point, point-to-multipoint, and multipoint-to-multipoint.

- LEO satellites orbit the Earth at a low altitude and at high speeds. They have a limited footprint and low latency and use low-powered terrestrial devices.

- MEO satellites orbit the Earth at higher altitudes than LEOs but do not travel as fast as LEOs and have a bigger Earth footprint, requiring fewer satellites. MEOs have higher latency than LEOs.

- GEO satellites orbit at much higher altitudes than MEOs, and their orbits match the rotation of the Earth, so they stay in the same position with reference to a point on the ground. GEO satellites have high latencies and require high-powered terrestrial sending devices. GEO satellites are used for global communications.

Key Terms

2.5 Generation (2.5G)   An interim technology stage between 2G and 3G digital cellular networks in which data is transmitted using packet-switched technology.

3ʳᵈ Generation Partnership Project (3GPP)   A group of six standards organizations from Asia, Europe, and North America that proposed standards for GSM, GPRS/EDGE, HSDPA, HSPA+, and LTE.

8-PSK   A modulation technique in which the phase of the carrier is shifted in 45-degree increments and 4 bits can be transmitted per phase change.

Advanced Mobile Phone Service (AMPS)   The standard used for 1G analog cellular transmissions, based on FDMA. 1G is often simply called AMPS.

CDMA2000 1xEVDO   The 3G digital cellular technology that is a migration from CDMA2000 1xRTT.

CDMA2000 1xEVDV   The 3G digital cellular technology that is a migration from CDMA2000 1xEVDO.

CDMA2000 1xRTT   A 2.5G digital cellular network technology that is a migration from CDMA. ("1xRTT" stands for "1-times Radio Transmission Technology.")

cell   The coverage section of one transmission tower in a mobile network.

compact HTML (cHTML)   A subset of HTML designed for mobile devices.

control channel   A special frequency that cellular phones use for communication with a base station.

Enhanced Data rates for GSM Evolution (EDGE)   A 2.5G digital cellular network technology that boosts GPRS transmissions.

First Generation (1G)   The first generation of wireless cellular telephony, which transmitted at 9.6 Kbps using analog circuit-switched transmission technology.

general packet radio service (GPRS)   A 2.5G network technology that can transmit at up to 114 Kbps.

geosynchronous earth orbit (GEO) satellites   Satellites stationed at an altitude of 22,282 miles (35,860 kilometers) that match the rotation of the planet and therefore appear to be in a fixed position in the sky with reference to a point on the ground.

GSM (Global Systems for Mobile Communications)   One of three multiple-access cellular technologies that make up the 2G digital cellular system; it uses a combination of FDMA and TDMA.

High-Speed Downlink Packet Access (HSDPA)   A packet-switched digital transmission cellular technology that uses 5 MHz W-CDMA (wideband CDMA) channels together with adaptive modulation, MIMO, and hybrid automatic repeat request (HARQ) to achieve data rates between 8 and 10 Mbps.

HSPA+   Also called "evolved HSPA," a technical cellular standard that provides theoretical data rates of up to 168 Mbps (realistically, around 42 Mbps) by combining two HSDPA transmitters, MIMO, and 64 QAM modulation.

i-mode   An Internet access system for digital cellular telephones.

Java   An object-oriented programming language used for general-purpose business programming and interactive Web sites.

Java 2 Micro Edition (J2ME)   A subset of Java specifically developed for programming wireless devices.

LTE (Long Term Evolution)   A digital packet-switched cellular technology that expands on HSPA+ beyond two spatially multiplexed channels, uses OFDM modulation, and also uses 20-MHz-wide channels to achieve data rates of up to 100 Mbps.

LTE Advanced   A proposed standard for broadband cellular communications that expands on LTE by allowing carriers to combine up to five 20-MHz-wide OFDM channels to achieve data rates of up to 1 Gbps.

low earth orbit (LEO) satellites   Satellites that orbit the Earth at an altitude of 200–900 miles (321–1,448 kilometers).

medium earth orbit (MEO) satellites   Satellites that orbit the Earth at altitudes of 1,500–10,000 miles (2,413–16,090 kilometers).

mobile telecommunications switching office (MTSO)   The connection between a cellular network and wired telephones.

roaming   The automatic transfer of the RF signal when moving from one cellular network to another network.

Second Generation (2G)   The second generation of cellular telephony, which uses circuit-switched digital transmission technology.

Short Message Services (SMS)   A delivery system for short, text-based messages sent between wireless devices such as cellular telephones and pagers.

SIM (Subscriber Identity Module) card   Small electronic cards that are used to associate a phone with a user's account.

Third Generation (3G)   Digital cellular wireless generation of cellular telephony, with speeds up to 2 Mbps.

Wideband CDMA (W-CDMA)   The 3G digital cellular technology that is a migration from EDGE.

wireless wide area network (WWAN)   A network that spans a geographical area as large as an entire country or even the entire world.

Review Questions

1. What is the purpose of the SID on a cellular phone or SIM card?

   a.   to identify the user

   b.   to identify the carrier

   c.   to identify the phone

   d.   to identify the area in which the user is located

2. What is the component of a cellular network that connects a base station with a wired telephone network?

   a.   transmitter

   b.   cellular phone

   c.   MTSO

   d.   CDMA

3. Which of the following is not a valid cellular telephone code?

   a. System Identification Code (SID)

   b. electronic serial number (ESN)

   c. digital serial code (DSC)

   d. mobile identification number (MIN)

4. What is it called when a user begins moving toward another cell and the cellular phone automatically associates with the base station of that cell?

   a. roaming

   b. handoff

   c. hunting

   d. multiplexing

5. What is the name given to the special frequency that a cellular phone and base station use for exchanging call-setup information?

   a. W-CDMA

   b. cell tunnel

   c. control channel

   d. GB line

6. What is the main advantage of transmitting voice calls using packet switching vs. circuit switching?

   a. There is no advantage; voice must always be transmitted using circuit switching.

   b. Call setup is faster using packet switching.

   c. The amount of bandwidth used is much larger with packet switching.

   d. The voice call does not tie up the channel 100 percent of the time using packet switching.

7. First Generation (1G) technology is based on Advanced Mobile Phone Service (AMPS). True or False?

8. Division by frequency, so that each caller is allocated part of the spectrum for all of the time, is the basis of TDMA. True or False?

9. Second Generation (2G) systems use digital instead of analog transmissions. True or False?

10. There are two technologies that are used with 2G: W-CDMA and CDMA2000. True or False?

11. The primary difference between 2G and 2.5G networks is that 2.5G networks transmit data using _____.

   a. packets

   b. capsules

   c. DTR

   d. FDMA

12. Which of the following cellular technologies supports MIMO?

    a. CDMA

    b. AMPS

    c. LTE

    d. EDGE

13. In addition to MIMO, what enables HSPA+ to achieve data rates of up to 42 Mbps?

    a. AAS

    b. HARQ

    c. backhauling

    d. spatial multiplexing

14. When does roaming occur in cellular telephony?

    a. when a user is outside her home

    b. when a user connects to another carrier in her home area

    c. when a user is away from her home area

    d. when a user turns off her cellular phone

15. Control information is transmitted as _____ by the _____.

    a. individual frames; MTSO

    b. unicasts; MTSO

    c. TDMA packets; base station

    d. broadcasts; base station

16. What is a femtocell?

    a. a very large cellular area

    b. a small cell supported by LTE Advanced

    c. a GPRS cell

    d. a transmission technique used with OFDM

17. Why are some GEO satellites not usually used for transmitting TCP/IP information?

    a. They cannot transmit a strong enough signal.

    b. Their transmissions do not have a large enough footprint.

    c. They only transmit point-to-point.

    d. The round-trip delay of 250 milliseconds causes protocol problems.

18. Of the following types of satellite, which travels at the highest orbital speed?

    a. LEO

    b. GEO

    c. HEO

    d. MEO

19. Of the following types of satellite, which has the smallest signal footprint?

   a. HEO

   b. MEO

   c. LEO

   d. GEO

20. Of the following types of satellites, which typically has the longest lifespan?

   a. LEO

   b. MEO

   c. Big LEO

   d. HEO

Hands-On Projects

Project 10-1

Conduct research to determine where 4G cellular technologies have been deployed. Include information on what types of technology have been deployed in Asia and South America in addition to the United States and Canada. Write a one-page report on your findings.

Project 10-2

Web sites such as Amazon, eBay, YouTube, and Accuweather display pages in different formats on smartphones as compared to PC screens. If you have use of a smartphone or tablet, access some of these sites from both the mobile device and from the computer. What are some of the differences in the ways these sites display information? What are some of the differences in the way they display buttons and links compared to the way a PC displays them? What are the main reasons for displaying information, buttons, and links in this way? Analyze these differences and write a one-page report on your findings.

Project 10-3

There are several new techniques to increase data transmission speed in satellite technology. Using the Internet and other sources, locate information on these new techniques. Discuss their strengths, weaknesses, and the applications on which they are most often found. How are they implemented if we cannot retrieve the satellites and modify their radios? Write a one-page report on your findings.

Real-World Exercises

The Baypoint Group (TBG), a company of 50 consultants who assist organizations and businesses with issues involving network planning and design, has again requested your services as a consultant. Telecom Argentina is a company that is licensed to provide wired telecommunications services in the northern part of Argentina. The company has contracted TBG to assist it with the selection and implementation of a new field service system. The goal is to provide service technicians with wireless access to the corporate network and a vast electronic library of technical manuals and schematic diagrams, which would reduce or eliminate the need for staff to carry a large number of books and drawings, especially while servicing equipment underground or when climbing on transmission towers. In addition, this means that the technicians would be able to immediately read and update the records for all the equipment, thereby avoiding massive amounts of paperwork as well as potential errors and omissions. However, the company is having trouble deciding on which technology to adopt—handheld cellular, tablets with 3G or 4G access, or notebooks equipped with cellular cards. TBG has asked you to help.

Exercise 10-1

Create a presentation outlining the advantages for Telecom Argentina of using digital cellular handsets or cellular wireless cards. Determine the ability of the smaller cellular handsets (as opposed to notebook computers, which may be difficult to carry everywhere) to display standard PC documents such as Word, Excel, and PDF files, and evaluate how this could help the company. Because the group you will be presenting to is composed of nontechnical managers, be sure your presentation is not too technical. Limit yourself to a maximum of 15 PowerPoint slides.

Exercise 10-2

Jose Riveras, one of the senior executives at Telecom Argentina, was convinced by your presentation. However, he recently heard about 4G cellular and wants to know how this technology will affect the company's plans to purchase equipment now. TBG has asked you to create another presentation for Jose that explains the different generations of cellular technology. Research the status of 4G deployment in Argentina, then create a PowerPoint presentation consisting of 15–18 slides.

Challenge Case Project

CASE PROJECTS

Telecom Argentina is unsure about investing in cellular phones, so it is considering alternatives, including Wi-Fi tablets and notebook computers with the data preloaded onto the devices. Working with three other students, form two teams of two people, with each team selecting one of these technologies. Research in depth the advantages and disadvantages of these respective technologies and how they work. Hold a friendly debate in which each two-person team gives a five-minute talk about the advantages of its technology. After the talk, allow time for the others to ask questions.

chapter 11

Radio Frequency Identification and Near-Field Communication

After reading this chapter and completing the exercises, you will be able to:

- Define Radio Frequency Identification (RFID) and Near Field Communication (NFC)
- Explain the need for RFID
- Describe how RFID and NFC work
- List the components of an RFID or NFC system
- Explain the challenges of RFID

Imagine that you are just making a quick stop at a local supermarket to pick up a few grocery items. As you enter the store, you obtain a bag near the door. Then you walk through the aisles and load the bag with the products you need. When you are finished, you simply walk through an arch-like structure where the cash register should have been, and then you exit the store. There's no need to stop and pay for the products or even to show anyone which products you purchased. You reach for your smartphone, check the receipt, and connect to your bank, instantly verifying that the correct total was deducted from your account.

While driving back home, you stop at a self-serve gas station to fill up the tank. You reach for your smartphone again, activate an application, and bring the phone near the front panel of the pump. The display on the gas pump beeps and authorizes your purchase. When you are finished pumping and replace the gas nozzle, your smartphone beeps again and displays the cost of the fuel. You press a button on the screen, and the smartphone displays the receipt.

Arriving home, you put your purchases in the refrigerator. A display screen on the refrigerator door is automatically updated with the contents, the expiration date of each individual product, and the quantity.

Although this example may sound like a futuristic dream, the standards and technology to make it work are already in use. In fact, there is practically no end to the potential applications of this technology. In this chapter, you will learn about how radio frequency identification works, how it is being used, and some future applications. You will also learn about some of the challenges related to the implementation of such systems.

What Is RFID?

Radio Frequency Identification (RFID) is a technology similar to the barcode labels that are used for almost every single off-the-shelf product anywhere in the world today, the difference being that RFID uses RF waves instead of laser light to read the product code. RFID stores product information in electronic **tags**. A tag is a small component that contains an antenna and an integrated circuit chip. RFID tags can store significantly more information than the bar-code system. This data, held in read-write or read-only memory, can include the date, time, and location where the product was manufactured, the manufacturer name, product serial number, and so on. In comparison, bar-code labels typically include only an item's stock-keeping unit (product code).

RFID technology is not new; it has been in use around the world, in one form or another, for many years. In the late 1930s, the U.S. Army and U.S. Navy introduced a system designated IFF (Identification Friend-or-Foe) that distinguished Allied aircraft from enemy aircraft by use of special codes that could be read by a friendly aircraft at a distance. Likewise, for many years, microchips and antennas inside tiny capsules have been implanted under the skin of household pets. These tags contain a numeric code that gets registered in a centralized database by the company that supplies the tags.

You may also be familiar with a simpler form of RFID that is frequently used in retail stores to prevent theft. After you pay for an item, a small tag attached to the product is run through a powerful magnet at the checkout; the magnet disables the tag, preventing it from activating the alarm as you pass near an antenna located at the store entrance.

What is new about RFID has to do with the standardization efforts of the International Organization for Standardization (ISO) and **EPCglobal Inc.** EPCglobal is an organization entrusted by industries worldwide to establish RFID standards and services for real-time, automatic identification of products in the supply chain of any company anywhere in the world. By publishing a single worldwide set of standards, it is possible for RFID to be implemented and utilized in a global context. EPCglobal adopts the ISO 18000 series of standards for RFID; these define the operating frequencies of the equipment and tags and include all of the other relevant PHY and MAC layer specifications. The EPCglobal specifications concentrate on defining services and higher-layer functions of the standards. In this section, you will learn about the hardware, software, and services that are required to implement RFID. For more information about EPCglobal, visit *www.EPCglobalinc.org*.

RFID System Components

Several components are required to implement an RFID system, connect it with a corporate network, enable integration with existing business software, and ultimately connect with the services that enable worldwide integration of a company's suppliers, manufacturers, distributors, and transportation providers. This section describes the most common components required to implement an RFID system—the tags, antennas, readers, software, and the EPCglobal Network services.

Electronic Product Code (EPC) RFID systems make use of product codes and data formats standardized by EPCglobal Inc. The mission of EPCglobal is to make organizations more efficient by making information about any kind of product available at any time and anywhere. The standards published by EPCglobal enable users to track products from manufacturing through to the end-user and beyond—potentially all the way to the recycling depot or garbage heap. The **Electronic Product Code (EPC)** is a standardized numbering scheme that can be programmed in a tag, which in turn can be attached to any physical product. Think of EPC as the evolution of the barcode or Universal Product Code (UPC), which you can find today in most products.

Each EPC is a unique number or code that is associated with an individual product—a case, box, or pallet, depending on how the owner wishes to tag products so that the items can be identified electronically. EPCs are usually represented in hexadecimal notation. A sample code is shown in Figure 11-1.

01 • 0001B6F • 0000F3 • 00002A9C3

Header   Domain Manager   Object Class   Serial Number

Figure 11-1 96-bit Electronic Product Code (EPC)

© Cengage Learning 2014

The EPC is either 64 or 96 bits long. The 96-bit EPC includes the following fields:

- Header—This 8-bit field identifies the EPC version number.
- EPC Domain Manager—This 28-bit field identifies the manufacturer of the product; it can represent almost 268.5 million different companies.

- Object Class—This 24-bit field identifies a product's stock keeping unit (SKU); it can represent over 16 million different products for each company (e.g., each brand or size of shampoo bottle produced by the same company as a different product).

- Serial Number—This 36-bit field identifies each instance of a product; it can represent over 68.7 billion unique serial numbers.

A 256-bit version of the EPC may be defined in the future. All the EPCglobal specifications for the PHY layer allow for the EPC to be expanded without any changes in the protocol.

The structure of the 64-bit and 96-bit EPCs is shown in Figure 11-2. Whether a manufacturer elects to use a 64-bit or a 96-bit EPC code is dependent on the company's individual needs and that of its clients. The Header field identifies which EPC format is being used, and the software (discussed later in this chapter) translates the tag's data into a format that is compatible with the end-user's business applications. Please note that the diagrams in Figure 11-2 are only intended to show that there can be different formats; it does not go into specific details. Also, these examples are not drawn in the correct scale based on the number of bits in each field.

64-bit Type I	2	21		17		24	
64-bit Type II	2	15	13		34		
64-bit Type III	2	26		13		23	
96-bit	8	28		24		36	

Note: Not to scale

Figure 11-2 Structure of EPC

© Cengage Learning 2014

RFID Tags RFID tags are also commonly known as **transponders**. The word is a combination of "transmitter" and "responder." A typical RFID tag includes an integrated circuit that contains some nonvolatile memory and a simple microprocessor. These tags can store data that is transmitted in response to an interrogation (a transmission) from a **reader**, the device that captures and processes the data received from the RFID tags.

There are two basic types of tags: passive and active. **Passive tags** are the most common type; they are small, can be produced in large quantities at low cost, and do not require battery power. Passive tags use the electromagnetic energy in the RF waves transmitted by the reader's antenna to power the built-in chip and transmit the information stored in its internal memory. Animal-tracking microchip implants, asset management, and access management (access cards for security controlled doors and parking lots) are examples of passive tag applications. Figure 11-3 shows an example of a passive tag.

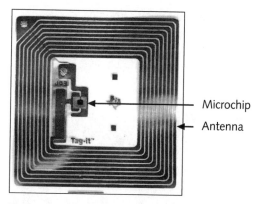

Microchip

Antenna

Figure 11-3 A typical RFID passive tag

© Cengage Learning 2014

Active tags are equipped with a battery to power the microprocessor chip and memory. Having their own power source means that these tags can transmit the signal farther away than passive tags can; however, active tags have a limited life due to the battery. They are also far more expensive ($25 and higher) than passive tags and therefore are used to track only high-value items, such as an entire pallet or container. An example of the application of active tags is to track military supplies shipped around the world; they can also be used for commercial applications, however. Some active tags are called **beacons** because they transmit on a periodic basis without receiving an interrogation from a reader.

A variation of active tags is the **semi-active tag**. This type of tag, also called a semi-passive tag, uses a built-in battery to power the circuit only when a reader first energizes (powers) the tag. The energy transmitted by the reader activates the tag, which then uses the internal battery to power its circuits and respond to the reader. The best example of this type of tag is the devices used for electronic toll collection along highways. The batteries in semi-active tags usually last several years, given that they are only used when the tag is activated by the reader's electromagnetic field.

The size of the memory in a tag varies with the manufacturer and application but is usually between 16 bits (for storing temporary operation parameters) and hundreds of kilobits. The tags are initially programmed with a unique identification code obtained from EPCglobal. The additional memory can be used to record historical information about the product to which the tag is attached, such as the health and vaccination records of cattle, the temperatures that a product has been exposed to during shipping (using a sensor attached to the tag), manufacturing and testing dates, calibration records for test equipment, and so on.

All three types of tags can be produced in flexible packages, also called **smart labels**. Smart labels include an adhesive backing and can be attached to a box, the underside of a product casing, or a pallet. Smart labels can be used to track luggage in airplanes and trains, for example. Because they use RF, the tags are not limited to being placed in a visible area or on the outside packaging of a product. They can be read regardless of their position or orientation, which is one of the major advantages of RFID over bar codes. The ability to read the tags in any position avoids the difficulty store clerks sometimes have of getting the equipment at the counter to read the bar-code labels on products.

11

Tags called **1-bit tags** are passive devices used in some retail stores. They do not contain a unique identification code, a chip, or any memory. They are simply used to activate an alarm to prevent theft. Figure 11-4 shows a 1-bit tag and a passive tag applied to the inside of a product package. These can be used for security, but the passive tag can also be used for inventory control.

Figure 11-4 Passive tag and 1-bit tag used in a product package

© Cengage Learning 2014

An emerging form of RFID is **chipless tags,** also known as RF fibers. Chipless tags do not contain an integrated circuit or memory. Instead, they use fibers or other types of materials that reflect a portion of the reader's signal back; the unique return signal can be used as an identifier. The fibers are made of thin threads, fine wires, or laminates that affect the propagation of RF waves. Chipless tags are typically used in applications in which the tag needs to be hidden and very difficult to reproduce. One example is the card invitations used for high-end events such as the Academy Awards (Oscars).

Chipless tags can be used to identify specific paper-based documents inconspicuously, which means that a person handling the document is not necessarily aware that it is "tagged." Chipless tags also perform far better than other types of tags when attached to a metal surface or to a liquid container. Both cans and bottles present significant problems for most RFID systems because metal surfaces can affect the propagation of RF waves and because most liquids attenuate the signal. Chipless tags can be read at greater distances than 1-bit or passive tags.

Sensory tags, as their name indicates, can be equipped with thermal, gas, smoke, pressure, and a variety of other kinds of sensors to monitor and record environmental conditions, liquid volume levels, or attempts to tamper with a product. They can be produced as passive tags; however, the sensors are not powered until a reader interrogates the tag. Most sensory tags are considerably more expensive than other types of passive tags, come in larger packages, and may be equipped with replaceable batteries that allow them to be used for longer periods of time.

 To learn more about RFID and its applications, including sensory tags, you can watch a short video clip at *www.symbol.com/video/RFID_VNR_Only_1.wmv*. (To view this on a Mac, you will need to install a WMV player such as Flip4Mac.)

The cost of a tag can vary greatly, depending on the type and number of tags purchased over a period of time. In general, passive tag prices range between $0.07 and $0.25 each. As the technology develops and the volumes increase, RFID manufacturers and users expect the cost to fall well below $0.05 per tag. Sensory tags can cost between $25.00 and $100.00 each, depending on the battery life and capabilities.

Table 11-1 compares the tag classes specified by EPCglobal.

Tag Class	Type	Characteristics and Options
Class-1	Passive; identity tags	Includes EPC, tag identifier (ID), and a destroy password (discussed later in the chapter) May include optional password-protected access control and user memory
Class-2	Passive; higher functionality	Includes all features of Class-1 plus: extended tag ID, extended user memory, authenticated access control, and additional features to be defined in Class-2 specification (see EPCglobal)
Class-3	Battery-assisted passive (also called semi-active or semi-passive)	Includes all features of Class-2 plus: a power source May include sensors with optional data-logging capabilities
Class-4	Active	Includes EPC, extended tag ID, authenticated access control, power source, autonomous transmitter (can initiate communications with a reader if the protocol in use permits, but must not interfere with Class-1, Class-2, and Class-3 communication protocols) May optionally include user memory and optional sensors with or without data logging

Table 11-1 **EPCglobal tag specifications**

© *Cengage Learning 2014*

Class-0 tags may still be in use in many locations around the world. However, the Class-0 tag communication protocols are not compatible with the tag classes listed in Table 11-1, and tag types cannot be mixed and used in the same system.

Readers In addition to interfacing with the tags, readers (also called interrogators) connect with the company's network and transfer the data obtained from the tags to a computer. Some readers can also write data onto tags, but those devices are still called readers. Readers that work with passive tags also provide the energy that activates the tags. The read distance is determined by the size and location of the tag and the reader antennas as well as the amount of power transmitted. These specifications are generally limited by national regulations that specify how much power can be transmitted in each frequency. Variations in regulations can result in incompatibilities between the equipment manufactured and licensed for use in different countries.

It is important to keep international standards and regulations in mind when designing and implementing an RFID system that will be used to identify products worldwide; these are generally available from the ISO and EPCglobal.

The frequency ranges and common applications of RFID systems are shown in Table 11-2.

Frequency Band	Common Applications
Low Frequency (LF)—135 KHz	Animal identification, access control, industrial automation
High Frequency (HF)—13.56 MHz	Smart cards, books, clothing, luggage, and various other individual-item-racking applications
Ultra High Frequency (UHF)—433 MHz and 860–930 MHz	Asset tracking, inventory control, warehouse management
Microwaves—2.45 and 5.8 GHz (ISM band)	Electronic toll collection, access control, industrial automation

Table 11-2 RFID frequencies and common applications

© Cengage Learning 2014

Figure 11-5 shows an LF RFID reader used to scan cattle and an LF tag applied to the mock-up of a cattle ear.

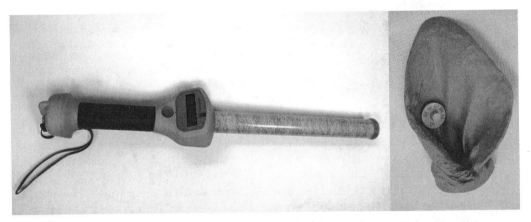

Figure 11-5 LF RFID reader and tag used by cattle farmers to track animals

© Cengage Learning 2014

RFID readers come in as many sizes and types as there are applications for this technology. From left to right, Figure 11-6 shows three examples of RFID readers, each with its own antennas. There is a fixed reader designed to be installed at a retail store entrance, a hand-held reader designed to be plugged into a computer's USB port, and a self-contained, computer-based RFID reader (top right) with tags.

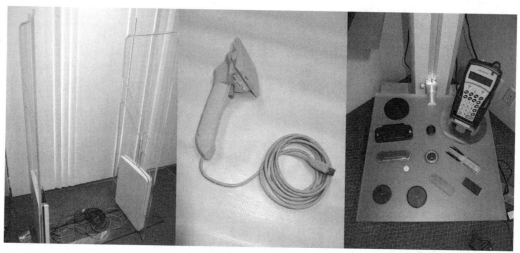

Figure 11-6 RFID readers with antennas

© Cengage Learning 2014

Antennas In Chapter 4, you learned that antennas are responsible for converting the RF energy from the transmitter into electromagnetic waves. The design and location of an antenna can significantly affect the range of the signal and the reliability of the communications. RFID antennas used in tags may be limited in size due to the dimensions of the tag itself. Most tags are small, which allows them to be placed in a variety of different products and packaging.

There are two main types of tag antennas: linear and circular. Linear antennas offer greater range but less accurate reads. Circular antennas have greater read accuracy, especially in applications in which the orientation of the antenna varies due to positioning of the products, but have a more limited range. Some older-style RFID tags sported a large circular antenna that spiraled outward from the center of the tag, where the chip was located. These types of tags are not often used today.

Larger antennas allow the tags to be read at greater distances than smaller antennas. However, remember that, as the frequency increases, the wavelength gets smaller and, consequently, so does the antenna. Higher-frequency antennas can be made relatively small and still allow the tags to be read at greater distances than lower-frequency tags with the same antenna size. Conversely, to detect a higher-frequency signal and minimize attenuation, the antenna needs to be approximately 10–20 microns thick (10 microns = 0.0003937 inches). Lower-frequency antennas can be 2 microns thick. RFID tag design can be quite complex, due to antenna size and thickness, and this can significantly affect read performance. In passive tags, the antenna itself acts as the energy storage device, which supplies electricity to the tag and allows it to respond to a reader. Figure 11-7 shows additional examples of RFID tags.

Reader antennas have to be designed for the specific type of application. Whether the antenna will be located at a retail store entrance for security reasons, near a warehouse shelf, or on a refrigerator door, the type, size, shape, and location of the antenna are critically important to ensure good readability and accuracy. No "typical" style of RFID antenna exists;

Figure 11-7 RFID tags in many shapes and sizes

© Cengage Learning 2014

the variety is huge. To see examples of different RFID reader antenna types, visit *www.inter-mec.com/products/rfid/antennas/index.aspx* or search the Web for "RFID antennas."

You can also search the Web for additional examples of RFID antennas. Always keep in mind, however, that for many specialized RFID applications, antennas may need to be custom designed.

Software The type of software used in an RFID implementation depends on the specific RFID application. Nevertheless, there are three basic categories of software components present in every RFID system: system software, middleware, and business application software.

System software is usually stored in read-only memory (ROM) or flash memory and is present in both the tag and the reader. It is executed by the microprocessor in each device and is used to control hardware functions, implement communication protocols (including collision control, error detection and correction, authorization, authentication, and encryption), and control the flow of data between tags and readers.

Middleware is responsible for reformatting the data from the readers to comply with the formats required by the business applications. It usually runs on a computer that is implemented as a gateway between the readers and the other data-processing equipment at the end-user company. Because each company will likely use different types of business software, RFID middleware allows users to ensure that they can communicate with the RFID equipment. Keep in mind that middleware is not typically sold as prepackaged software, like Microsoft Office or Adobe Acrobat, for example. Instead, each company in the business of providing RFID solutions usually writes its own middleware application software or uses a customizable software package provided by the reader manufacturer.

Business application software is responsible for processing orders, inventory, shipments, invoices, and so on. This type of software also usually relies on database software to store and manage all the transaction records in a typical business period.

EPCglobal Network Services

To use bar codes, a business has to record in a database the item's UPC (bar code), the company's internal product number (SKU), a product description, the manufacturer's name, the price, and the quantity of items in stock. It then has to cross-reference the bar code and SKU so that this information can be accessed by the bar-code readers at the cash register. With RFID, because the EPC already contains a reference to the manufacturer along with a product code, the need for manually entering data for cross-referencing is reduced; the potential for introducing errors when entering this information into the database is lessened as well.

The manufacturer name is used to reorder products when the stock is low or depleted. With EPCs, companies will be able to acquire the manufacturer's name over the Internet using a service from EPCglobal called **Object Name Service (ONS)**. Modeled after the Internet's Domain Name System (DNS), ONS is a mechanism for discovering information about a product and related services. When a reader gets the EPC from a tag, it passes it to the company's servers, which send it to ONS via the Internet. Upon identifying the manufacturer, ONS responds with the URL of the Internet server where the product information is stored. The company's servers can then retrieve all the information about that particular product and can use this for additional data processing.

If you are not familiar with how the Domain Name System (DNS) works, read the information at *http://computer.howstuffworks.com/dns.htm*.

Eventually, trillions of products from millions of companies will likely be included in the ONS database. Like DNS, ONS will be a worldwide-distributed database.

An additional component that will enable companies around the world to exchange information regarding their trade transactions is EPC Information Services (EPCIS). Similar to the Electronic Data Interchange (EDI) specifications that many large companies use to complete paperless transactions, EPCIS will eventually enable large organizations to purchase, invoice, and track product orders over the Internet, eliminating the need to send paper documents by mail or fax. Figure 11-8 shows the five fundamental components of an EPCglobal RFID system—tags, readers, middleware, business applications, and EPCglobal services—and how they are logically connected.

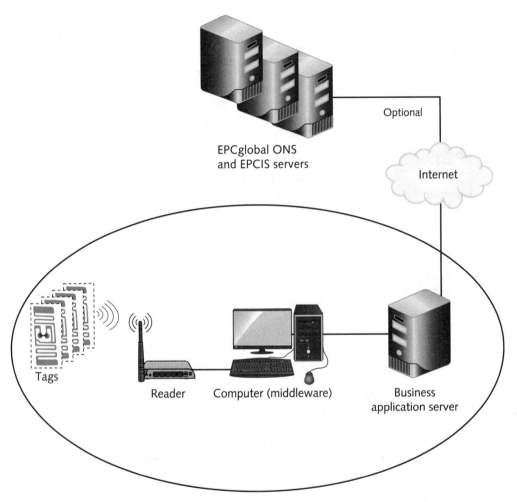

Figure 11-8 Fundamental EPCglobal system components

© Cengage Learning 2014

How RFID Works

Describing how the different RFID tags and readers work would require an entire book, given that these devices use different transmission techniques in each frequency band. This section introduces you to the technical details of how two of the most common types of passive tags and readers transmit and communicate with each other: UHF (400–900 MHz) and HF (13.56 MHz).

PHY Layer

A passive tag, the most common type, only transmits when it receives a signal from the reader. The connection between a tag and a reader is called a **coupling**. RFID primarily uses two types of coupling, depending on the application:

- *Inductive or magnetic coupling*—This type is designed for tags that either touch the surface of the antenna or are inserted in a slot in the reader's case. In these systems, the tags are typically used at a maximum distance of half an inch (just over 1 centimeter) from the antenna. The basic difference between inductive and magnetic coupling is the shape of the antennas.

- *Backscatter coupling*—This type is designed for tags that can be read at distances greater than 3.3 feet (one meter) and up to 330 feet (100 meters) in some cases.

Backscatter is a reflection of radiation. Recall that passive tags are powered by an RF signal sent by the reader. After the reader transmits data (the reader transmission itself supplies power to the tag, so it can receive and decode the reader's transmission), it then begins to transmit a **continuous wave (CW)**, which is an unmodulated sine wave. The CW is captured by the passive tag's antenna, and the tag uses the energy from the CW to supply power to the chip so that the tag can respond to the interrogator. The tag essentially reproduces (reflects) the same wave it receives from the reader, but it modulates this signal with the data by changing the electrical properties and consequently the reflection coefficient of its own antenna. This means that the antenna will transmit with more or less power, affecting the amplitude of the signal reflected.

Backscatter modulation is based on variations of amplitude shift keying (ASK) or a combination of ASK and phase shift keying (PSK), both of which you learned about in Chapter 2. The data is also digitally encoded to ensure that there will be enough transitions between 0 and 1 and vice versa to assist the devices in maintaining synchronization during transmission. (In Chapter 2, see the section titled "Binary Signals.")

The reader has separate transmitter and receiver circuits and antennas; and because it is a powered device, it transmits a much stronger (higher-amplitude) signal than the tags. In order to detect the modulated signal from the tag, the receiver in the reader compares its own strong CW signal with the backscatter. The difference between the two is the data sent by the tag.

Both reader and tag modulate the signal in amplitude by as much as 100 percent or by as little as 10 percent. Ten percent modulation is more sensitive to interference and noise, but the signal can travel farther. One hundred percent modulation is easier for the reader to detect; but during the periods without a CW, the tags are not being powered, so the distance between tag and reader must be significantly reduced. In practice, the signal is modulated somewhere between 10 percent and 100 percent, given that neither of the extremes is very usable. The resulting modulation is a result of the amount of power generated by the reader and the size of the antenna. Figure 11-9 shows a signal modulated at 10 percent and at 100 percent. Note that the signals in the figure are not drawn to scale, in amplitude or in frequency.

Communications between tag and reader are always half-duplex. Interrogators and tags do not transmit and receive data simultaneously. To prevent interference issues from affecting

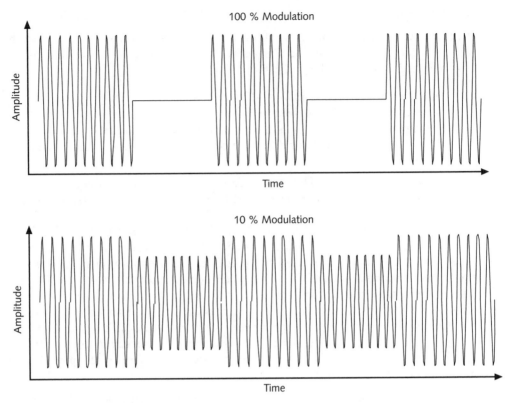

Figure 11-9 ASK modulation

© Cengage Learning 2014

the reliability of RFID systems, and to allow for environments in which multiple readers are installed in the same area (also called dense interrogator environments), the EPCglobal standards also specify the use of frequency hopping spread spectrum (FHSS) and direct sequence spread spectrum (DSSS) transmission. The latter systems are generally only used for advanced active tags.

HF Tag Communication

HF RFID transmission uses a protocol called **Slotted Terminating Adaptive Collection (STAC)**, in which the tags reply within randomly selected positions or time intervals, referred to as slots, which are the reply intervals used in the STAC protocol. The interrogator transmits signals to mark the beginning and end of each slot, depending on the amount of data requested from each tag. Figure 11-10 shows the concept of slots. Note that the slots are not equal in size (the figure is not to scale). The number of slots is regulated by the interrogator and is always a power of two. Some shorter slots may exist when there is no reply from any tags, in which case the interrogator terminates the slot. The maximum number of slots available is 512. The STAC protocol is used to prevent tag collisions in HF, and it is described further in the section titled "Tag Collision Handling in HF." Note that slot F is always present and signals the beginning of the reply intervals. Slot F is the only one with a fixed size. It also ends automatically, meaning that the interrogator does not signal the end of slot F.

Figure 11-10 Reply intervals in the STAC protocol

© Cengage Learning 2014

UHF Tag Communication

UHF readers today support what is called Generation 2 (Gen2) protocols. Gen1 protocols may still be used for tags and readers, but support for Gen1 RFID technology is quickly being discontinued.

The Gen2 protocol defines three techniques for communication between tags and readers. In the first technique, a reader can select tags by transmitting a bit mask that isolates a tag or group of tags. The bit mask works very similarly to the way network masks work in IP addressing, by isolating subnets. In the second technique, a reader can inventory tags by isolating them using a repetitive process (described later in this chapter). In the third technique, once the EPC for a particular tag is known to the system, a reader can alternatively access each tag individually. Gen2 readers may transmit with a lot more power and UHF systems are designed to work at greater distances than HF.

Tag Identification Layer

When an interrogator initiates communication in an RFID system, there must be a way to prevent every tag within range of the reader's signal from responding at the same time. The tag identification layer defines three methods that allow an interrogator to manage the population of tags within reach of its signal: select, inventory, and access.

With the select method, an interrogator sends a series of commands to select a particular segment of the population of tags within its reach. This is done in preparation for an inventory or for the purpose of accessing a specific tag. The selection is based on user-specified criteria, such as a particular category of products from one manufacturer. Tags do not respond to these commands. They simply set internal flags (bits) for responding to later transmissions. In UHF, with the inventory method, an interrogator sends out a series of query commands to get information from one tag at a time. As each tag receives an acknowledgment from the interrogator, it resets the inventory flag and does not respond to further inventory commands in the same round. In HF, the interrogator simply waits for each tag to reply in a different slot. With the access method, the interrogator sends one or more commands to multiple tags or exchanges data with a single tag at a time after uniquely identifying the tag with a command.

The minimum amount of information contained in a tag's memory is the EPC, a 16-bit cyclic redundancy check (CRC), and a destroy password. The **destroy password** is a code programmed into the tag during manufacturing. After the destroy password is transmitted by the reader, the tag is permanently disabled and can never be read or written to again. This tag information structure is shown in Figure 11-11.

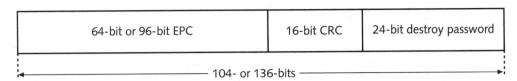

Figure 11-11 Structure of tag information

© Cengage Learning 2014

Tag and Reader Collisions

With a potentially very large population of tags, all tags may respond to a reader at the same time. Depending on whether each product is tagged or not (in warehouses, only boxes or pallets may be tagged), this would result in collisions and would prevent the reader from identifying individual tags. LF tags and readers do not support any collision-handling mechanism; therefore, LF systems can only read one tag at a time. This is not an issue when the application is reading an access card used to open a door or reading cattle tags as the animals pass through a narrow corridor one at a time. However, for RFID to work in a warehouse, in a store, or inside a refrigerator, a better solution is available.

Tag Collision Handling in UHF Because the reader initially may not know which tags are present within the range of its signal, and because new tags may enter the reader's signal field from time to time, the reader may send a VerifyID command. However, if you consider how shelves in a store or warehouse are typically organized, the tags within a certain reader's field belong to certain groups of products. All tags within the reader's field that are the intended recipients of the verification command will reply with their EPC, CRC, and destroy password. If the reader can identify at least one of these tags, it can proceed to select a range of tags by sending a series of commands that instruct the tags about an upcoming inventory. The process repeats until the reader has identified every group of tags within range of its signal. The reader can also tell a tag or a group of tags to be quiet by sending a special command.

This selection process can be compared to a teacher that meets her class for the first time at the beginning of a semester and does not have a list with the names of all the students. To identify each student, the teacher might begin by asking all students to call out their full names. Initially, several students may reply at the same time. The teacher can then ask the students whose last names begin with the letter A to call out their names. Again, she may get more than one reply and not be able to single out a student. Next, she can request that only those students whose last names begin with the letters AA call out their names. This time, the chances of getting multiple simultaneous replies will be much smaller.

By repeating this process and refining the query, eventually the reader will have enough information to be able to communicate with all the tags within a group. It then sends a command to an entire group to set an inventory flag. The next command instructs the tags that the reader will begin an inventory round. During the inventory round, the reader sends an inquiry to each individual tag. Once a tag has replied to an inventory query, it resets its inventory flag and does not reply again until the reader announces the next inventory round.

Tag Collision Handling in HF In HF systems, the reader selects groups of tags based on the STAC protocol. Each tag uses its EPC, CRC, and destroy password to calculate a number that becomes the slot number in which each particular tag will reply. The calculation uses the above parameters along with a random number generator in each tag. The reader then begins an inventory round and waits for each tag to reply in its own time slot, which prevents collisions. The ISO standard assumes that the number of potential collisions in these cases will be less than 0.1 percent. If a collision does occur, thereby preventing the inventory process from finishing correctly, the reader will select a smaller group of tags using the process described earlier, under HF tag communication, and repeat the inventory process.

Reader Collisions Reader collisions may also happen in dense reader environments. If a reader does not receive any replies, it assumes a reader collision has occurred, which means that the tags could not understand the last reader transmission, and backs off for a random period of time before listening for network traffic and attempting to transmit again.

MAC Layer

The RFID MAC layer is responsible for establishing and communicating the transmission parameters—such as transmission bit rate, modulation type, operating frequency range, and frequency hop channel sequence—that are used for communications at the PHY layer. The reader sends commands to the tags establishing the communication parameters for each communications session. The MAC layer parameters for different types of tags—HF, UHF, and others—differ. These variances usually don't pose a problem because it is unlikely that an end-user company will use multiple types of tags in a single environment or application.

Data Rates

As you learned earlier, the amount of data stored in a typical passive RFID tag is relatively small. The lack of a power supply along with low processing power, both of which help keep the tag cost low, means that the resulting data transmission rates for the tags are also low. Some of the EPCglobal standards specify a minimum number of tags per second that a reader should be able to access rather than a specific data rate.

The specifications for HF tags call for readers to be capable of reading 200 tags per second. For tags containing just an EPC, the actual rates will likely be between 500 and 800 tags per second.

The UHF specifications define the tag-to-reader data rate as twice that of the reader-to-tag rate. In North America, the allowed tag-to-reader data rate can be up to 140.35 Kbps. In Europe, due to the RF signal power limitations, the maximum data rate is only 30 Kbps. Conversely, reader-to-tag data rates are 70.18 Kbps in North America and 15 Kbps in Europe. The Gen2 protocol specifications support much faster tag isolation, which results in tag read rates as fast as 1,600 per minute in North America and 600 per minute in Europe.

Near-Field Communications

Now that you have a pretty good understanding of RFID, it's time to find out about Near Field Communications technology. **Near Field Communications (NFC)** is a technology that provides short-range wireless connectivity between devices such as smartphones and tablet computers. NFC is based on the ISO 18092 RFID technology standard along with those of several other organizations.

NFC requires little or no configuration by users, and devices connect automatically as soon as they are brought to within a minimum of 1.6 inches (4 centimeters) of each other. This technology is able to transfer data between devices or read passive tags at rates of between 106 Kbps and 424 Kbps.

NFC originated from and is compatible with FeliCa, a smart card protocol created by Sony that is still in use in parts of Asia, and the MIFARE protocol developed by Philips; both protocols were designed for payment systems. The NFC Forum, founded in 2004 by Nokia, Philips, and Sony, created a set of specifications that builds on RFID and enables contactless two-way data transfer between two powered devices—beyond the typical one-way communication that happens between a smart card and a reader.

NFC can be used with a handheld device for the following:

- MasterCard PayPass transactions and Visa payWave transactions at stores and restaurants
- Electronic discount coupons
- Exchanging business cards, schedules, and maps between handheld devices
- Transferring images, videos, and other types of files between devices or between a device and a printer
- Debit card or prepaid card transactions
- Electronic public transport system tickets
- Airline tickets
- Pairing Bluetooth devices without entering a PIN
- Storing and using secure, encrypted identification numbers, electronic signatures, access codes, and passwords

NFC Operation Modes

NFC-capable handheld devices are typically equipped with a low-power interrogator that can supply power and read tags. The technology uses inductive coupling between two loop antennas. An NFC device can operate in the following modes:

- Listen mode—The initial mode of an NFC device, in which the device essentially acts as a passive tag.
- Poll mode—When an NFC device generates a CW and probes for other devices within its communication range of 1.6 inches (4 centimeters).
- Reader/writer mode—When an NFC device in Poll mode behaves like an interrogator. In this mode, devices can transmit commands to other devices.
- Card emulator mode—When an NFC device in Listen mode behaves like a smart card.
- Initiator mode—When an NFC device in Poll mode changes the communication protocol to talk to another device that only supports half-duplex communications, using the NFC-Data Exchange Protocol (NFC-DEP).
- Target mode—When an NFC device is the target of an initiator that can only communicate in half-duplex mode, using NFC-DEP.

The Initiator and Target modes are a unique characteristic of NFC that differentiates it from RFID in the sense that NFC-capable devices are able to exchange many different types of information with other NFC-capable devices. RFID, on the other hand, is limited to communications between readers and tags. NFC devices can read from and write information to tags when operating as interrogators and can also behave like passive RFID tags.

NFC Tags and Devices

The NFC specifications currently define four types of tags. Each type of tag is designed for a different purpose and has slightly different capabilities, including the amount of memory. Different tag types also communicate using slightly different frame formats, at different speeds, and use different digital encoding (NRZ, NRZ-I, etc.) and different synchronization and modulation methods. Thus, the first thing an NFC-capable device in Poll mode needs to do is identify the type of tag—or tags, given that there may be more than one within range of its magnetic field.

Some tags can be written to only once; others can be protected by a password so that they cannot be written to again unless they are unlocked. The memory on the tag can be used to store URLs, business cards, pictures, brochures in PDF files, etc. This makes NFC far more flexible, useful, and accurate than the Quick Response (QR) codes that are very popular today. Depending on the type, NFC tags can store anywhere from 48 bytes to 32 KB of information. Virtually everyone can purchase NFC tags for as little as $15.00 and, with the right type of application loaded on their phones, program the tags using a smartphone (see *www. tagstand.com*). You can find more information about NFC tags at *kimtag.com/s/nfc_tags*.

NFC technology is still evolving. Although the ISO 14443 specifications have been ratified, the best way to find out which devices currently support NFC, along with the latest news of the industry, is to browse the NFC World Web site at *www.nfcworld.com*.

NFC Communications

11

NFC-capable devices transmit in the 13.56 MHz unlicensed frequency band (the same as for HF RFID) and modulate the signal using ASK or a combination of ASK and PSK over a range of approximately 7–14 KHz of RF bandwidth. Modulation varies between 10 percent and 100 percent, depending on the type of tag. The digital signal is encoded using a method similar to the return-to-zero (RZ) technique you learned about in Chapter 2, which provides enough signal transitions to help ensure good synchronization between wireless devices and between devices and tags.

To transfer data between two smartphones or tablet computers, NFC employs the Data Exchange Protocol (NFC-DEP). A DEP message consists of one or more records. Each record is encapsulated in an RF frame that contains a header and a payload. The header includes the following fields:

- **Identifier**—This optional field is used to define the type of payload carried by the record.

- **Length**—This field can be one octet long for short records but is normally four octets long. A payload length of 0 is used to indicate an empty message (no payload field) and signals the end of the current NFC-DEP communication session.

- **Type**—This field indicates what type of data is carried within the payload and will be used by the receiving device to decide which application will process the data.

For example, pictures are stored in the photo application and URLs are sent to the browser application. An error is generated if the device cannot support the data type specified in this field.

Figure 11-12 shows the components of a DEP message and how they relate to one another.

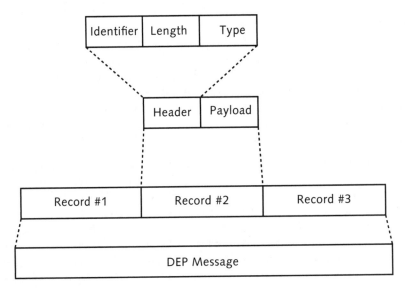

Figure 11-12 Structure of a DEP message

© Cengage Learning 2014

RFID Applications

This section outlines a few of the more interesting RFID applications. These are only the tip of the iceberg, however; the potential uses for RFID are practically unlimited.

 One of the possible applications of RFID is a wireless mouse that doesn't require batteries. The RFID reader is built into a special mouse pad, and the mouse is essentially a passive RFID tag.

Automobile Security

Many new cars are equipped with an antitheft device called an immobilizer. The vehicle's ignition key head contains a tiny Class-1 RFID chip that transmits in the 135 KHz frequency band. A hardware store copy of the key can be inserted in the ignition, but it cannot start the engine. When the original key is inserted in the ignition, a small reader device in the steering column transmits a signal to the key to activate it. The computer that controls the engine only allows the engine to start upon receiving a response from the tag chip in the key. If you lose your key and obtain a replacement from the dealer, you must program the new key in the car. Most vehicles equipped with this type of immobilizer provide in the owner's manual a series of instructions on how to accomplish this.

Health Care

In hospitals, RFID tags in a patient's identification bracelet can provide vital information that cannot be easily misplaced. The tag can contain the patient's admission history, blood type, medications, prescribed dosages, and so on, and it can be read by handheld devices carried by staff. In addition, the EPC on the tag can instantly link the hospital staff with the patient's record in the hospital's database. This feature can prevent errors and also enhance patient comfort and safety.

For elderly and very young patients, the system can sound an alarm if the patient leaves a designated area. Newborn babies and their mothers can wear bracelets that contain matching information, ensuring that the right baby goes to the right mother. Such tags could also prevent babies from being taken out of the hospital by an unauthorized person.

Transportation and Military

RFID tags embedded in standard courier packages and other small boxes can speed up and help automate sorting as well as prevent errors. The wide variety of shapes and sizes of packages today makes it almost impossible to completely automate the process. Humans must still handle the packages and bar-code readers by hand.

During the recent wars in the Middle East and Bosnia, materials officers in the armed forces were faced with having to transport millions of pieces of equipment, ammunition, and replacement parts, often on short notice. With many of these items stored in sealed containers at very large military warehouses all over the United States, coordinating and tracking these shipments is a challenge. Missing or incorrectly stored spare parts and ammunition can put the lives of large factions of the military at serious risk. The U.S. Department of Defense's material goods inventory is valued at over $700 billion, and part of it is composed of perishable or sensitive items—including explosives—that must be protected from extreme environmental conditions.

During Operation Desert Storm, over 40,000 containers were shipped to the Persian Gulf. Because these shipments could not be adequately tracked while in transit, "iron mountains" accumulated in ports and airfields across the United States, which, in many instances, contained redundant materials and supplies. At least two-thirds of these containers had to be opened so that personnel could see what was inside. This can be a dangerous operation when the containers are loaded with explosive items like bullets, missiles, or bombs.

The DoD handles approximately 100,000 ground combat and tactical vehicles, 250,000 wheeled vehicles, 1,000 strategic missiles, 300 ships, and 15,000 aircraft and helicopters. These items are involved in approximately 300,000 shipments per year. When it was initially deployed, the DoD RFID system comprised more than 800 locations with over 1,300 read/write stations used to manage the flow of supplies through the military's In-Transit Visibility (ITV) network.

Sports and Entertainment

RFID tags are used for monitoring tire pressure in racecars. The tiny tags with a built-in sensor and battery are installed right on the tire valve and can be read automatically or manually from inside the car. This technology can also be used in transport trucks and interstate buses; on these vehicles, the tags help save money by controlling tire wear and preventing accidents related to tire condition. Tire pressure monitors are beginning to appear in luxury automobiles as well; these can provide an added measure of safety. Monitoring participants in marathons and triathlons is another common use for RFID tags.

RFID usage is not limited to exotic sports. Common sports such as golf can also benefit from RFID technology. The cost of a high-quality golf ball today can be quite high. Passive tags can be installed inside the balls so that, if they are lost during a game, a pocket reader can help the owner locate the ball in tall grass fields, among trees or fallen leaves, and even under water, depending on the technology employed.

In 2004, the Golden Globe awards used an inconspicuously placed RFID tag in the event invitations to prevent unwelcome paparazzi and other members of the public from entering the event.

People Monitoring, Crowds, and Access

In large amusement parks, parents of children wearing special bracelets containing RFID tags can instantly locate the kids if they become separated from them. Readers installed throughout the park track the location of the youngsters, and parents can go to a kiosk that instructs them how to locate their children, based on information the reader gets from the parent's own RFID tags. Figure 11-13 shows an example of an RFID tag bracelet used to identify people.

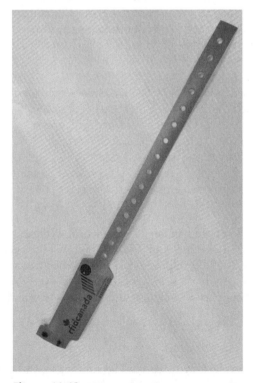

Figure 11-13 RFID tag bracelet

© Cengage Learning 2014

In an application similar to the Golden Globe awards, RFID-tagged concert and sports event tickets can simplify the jobs of security personnel. Even with extensive use of bar codes today, some fans attempt to gain access to a stadium with fake tickets, sometimes trying to take advantage of the volumes of people in order to bypass the gate security. RFID tags embedded in the tickets can make this much more difficult, if not impossible.

Many oil companies, including Shell, Mobil, and Esso, implemented loyalty systems in the 1990s that allow customers to pay for gas at the pump by simply swiping a tiny RFID transponder (held on a key chain) in a specifically marked area at the front of the gasoline pump. Customers sign up for the service, and the charges are automatically made either on the customers' bank accounts or credit cards or to an account where the customers have preloaded funds for fuel. By avoiding the use of credit and debit cards at the pumps, this latter option increases security.

Pharmaceuticals

The pharmaceutical industry is vulnerable to counterfeit drugs that result in monetary loss and can pose a health hazard to consumers. To combat this, individual drug packages are using specialized tags that store the date of manufacture and detailed tracking information that is generated as the packages move through the supply chain. This tracking can help isolate the exact location of the counterfeiting activity by monitoring events at every stop in the supply chain.

Tags in over-the-counter and prescription medication allow vision-impaired people using a special device to listen to a spoken description of their drugs and dosages. This system can be used at home or in a pharmacy.

11

RFID and NFC Challenges

It is not hard to think of a thousand other applications for RFID that have the potential for making life and business easier, safer, and simpler. However, the technology does face some challenges, as you will learn about in this section.

RFID Impact on Corporate Networks

One of the major challenges for the implementation of RFID systems is the impact of the volume of data on a company's network. With manual or bar-code-based inventory control systems, the amount of data that is collected and transmitted across a company's network is usually limited to the on-hand quantities of particular products along with the UPC code for each product. However, RFID systems are usually implemented so that inventory can be counted by simply activating the tags. To ensure that the shelves in a large retail store are always fully stocked with products, for example, the system can direct the readers to interrogate *all* of the RFID tags every 5 minutes or so. This scanning can add a lot of traffic to an organization's network.

To get a sense of the amount of increased traffic on a company's network, consider a scenario in which a large national retailer tags each of the 10,000 individual items in each of its 1,000 stores and then interrogates all of its readers from a central head-office location every 15 minutes. At 17 bytes per product (remember that with the 96-bit EPC, the minimum information from a tag is about 136 bytes), this would generate 170 MB of data for a single read. It would fill a CD-ROM in 1 hour and create 5.44 GB of network traffic in a typical 8-hour business day. In only 1 month, the total volume of traffic would swell to 1.632 terabytes of data. In comparison, the entire collection of 17 million books in the U.S. Library of Congress equals 136 terabytes of data. It would only take 7 years for the library to process that much data through its network. Although most of this data will be processed and the duplicate data discarded, we are still talking about a significant increase in the volume of data on the network.

Network Availability in RFID

Assume that such a system is eventually implemented and that a company relies on it to replenish inventory automatically. In this case, network availability becomes a serious factor in the store's ability to serve its customers. As retailers become dependent on RFID systems to enhance service and reduce costs, greater network bandwidth must be available. The retailer's network must also be reliable—that is, it must remain functional. (Ninety-nine percent availability means that the network is expected to be down for about 80 hours per year.) Any downtime that occurs during business hours can quickly become a serious problem. For most companies, these demands will translate to expanding and adding redundant equipment and communications capabilities to their existing networks, a costly undertaking at best.

In grocery stores and large retail establishments, products are out of stock 7 percent of the time, and some popular items are unavailable 17 percent of the time. This inventory shortfall can represent significant losses for retailers. To combat this problem, many retailers order more products than they need or can sell out of one location. As a result, supermarkets in particular often are forced to discard perishable products, which leads to higher costs for consumers. Item-level tagging for product tracking is a means to reduce or eliminate these types of problems.

Storage Requirements for RFID

Large banks and corporations already are saddled with archiving tremendous amounts of historical data—potentially, tens or even hundreds of terabytes of data for each company. In addition, new laws designed to protect investors and consumers, such as the Sarbanes-Oxley Act, require companies to accumulate and securely store even more information. The huge volume of data that can be generated by RFID systems significantly increases the need to store information accurately and reliably.

 Since 2003, cattle producers in Canada and Europe have been using RFID to track their animals' histories. As of January 1, 2005, each head of cattle in Canada has had to have an RFID tag that stores **NOTE** such information as any health issues, vaccinations, movement (locally or to a new herd), and production of milk and offspring. Records must be kept on slaughtered cattle for many years afterwards.

Device Management

Even without RFID in place, businesses are finding it a challenge to manage the huge numbers of devices on their networks. Network management software does not come at a low price.

Even for small networks with fewer than 1,000 devices, the cost of network management software can easily escalate to well over half a million dollars. As networks expand, the need to remotely monitor and manage servers, routers, switches, and RFID readers from a central location becomes a critical factor in a company's ability to ensure greater network availability. Add to this the task of managing and tracking hundreds, thousands, or even millions of RFID tags and you can imagine the security issues related to wireless RFID transmissions. Managing RFID systems can quickly become a very complex and costly job.

Security Considerations for RFID and NFC

The growth of RFID and the development of relevant worldwide standards have given rise to a large number of security and privacy concerns. There are solutions for RFID-related security issues, but they are not perfect fixes, and challenges still exist. For example, the growth of NFC is still being driven by its application as an electronic wallet that can be used in place of credit and debit cards as well as by its applications in public transportation tickets, passwords, and so forth, and concerns from users are increasing. Recent developments in multi-core processors will no doubt enable the use of more sophisticated encryption algorithms that can help ensure the security and privacy of device users. NFC transmissions are harder to interfere with or capture, due to the short distance between devices; nevertheless, it is theoretically possible to access information from a user's smartphone or tablet if you have a reader that is sensitive enough to capture information from a greater distance. For how an attacker can exploit a security flaw in the the Mifare system, you can watch the YouTube video at *www.youtube.com/watch?v=NW3RGbQTLhE*.

It is possible to read the information from a tag or RFID/NFC-enabled credit card, but financial organizations would not allow these systems to be used by their customers unless there were enough security mechanisms in place to prevent financial loss. At least in North America, it's the financial organizations that have to absorb these losses; as a result, they employ a large variety of tactics to prevent theft. Users are not made aware of these tactics for the simple reason that making this information available would invite additional attempts to defeat the security measures.

In North America, debit and credit card agreement clearly state that customers are not responsible for the charges if their card information is stolen. And even if they were, a thief would need a connection to the financial organization's computer system in order to obtain any other personal information about a customer. The three-digit security code that appears on the back of a credit card is not stored electronically on the magnetic stripe or the RFID/NFC chip. Nor is personal information, such as name, address, and telephone number, although it is stored in a tablet or NFC-enabled cellular phone. All a thief can access is a number, which means that, to obtain your personal information, the thief would need to hack into the financial organization's computer system from your home.

In the United States, the concerns about RFID are centered on privacy. Tag data used for a product after it is purchased could be linked to the consumer and used for targeted marketing. Governments and businesses could then collect that data and use it for a number of applications that would potentially interfere with the consumer's privacy. This is not that different from data being captured from the use of debit and credit cards; the difference is that RFID-generated data could possibly be captured without the user being aware of it. However, to associate this data with a particular person would require obtaining information from debit and credit cards or by following the user home. This is unlikely to happen, because it is the government that creates the privacy laws in the first place. Most of the privacy concerns that people have regarding RFID are due to not having enough information about the technology.

Security related to RFID readers falls under the wired network security policy. Reader-to-tag and tag-to-reader communications have the same vulnerabilities as any wireless network, the only exception being that capturing the tag-to-reader communications may be very difficult. Tag transmissions occur at very low power levels; readers are also transmitting a CW during tag-to-reader communications. Once a tag is installed on a product or packaging, it usually cannot be removed without permanently damaging the tag; however, it is still possible to tamper with the *data* in a Class-1 (read/write) tag by recording over the existing tag data or by adding new data. Powering a mobile reader capable of emitting a high-power CW would require heavy batteries. This could be done from inside a vehicle, but then the mobility of the reader would be severely limited.

Most passive tags do not support authorization or encryption security methods because they lack their own power supply, use chips with low processing power, and are low in cost. Shielding stores and warehouses to prevent RF signals from coming in or going out may solve some of the problems associated with unauthorized access from outside the building, but that is a very expensive proposition. In addition, once consumers take the products to their homes or workplaces, someone using an interrogator nearby may still expose them to privacy violations.

RFID tags do not carry the type of information that would be so critical and useful as to require drastic measures to prevent most anyone from capturing the information contained in the tags' memory storage. In the case of credit and debit cards, there are far easier (but no less criminal) ways to capture the information contained in RFID/NFC chips, so the use of remote sensing equipment, which requires a very complex setup, is unlikely. Nevertheless, both financial institutions and users should continue to be aware of the need to protect against losses and identity theft.

Data in tags can be locked and require a password for the tag to be used again. By using a combination of the EPC, CRC, and built-in destroy password, tags can also be permanently disabled. Locking the tags would make it very difficult to use the information from the tag throughout the distribution channels. Permanently destroying the tag, either by issuing a *kill* command or by physically damaging it, would prevent a retailer from using the tag again if the customer returned the product, limiting the functionality of the RFID system. Physically destroying tags would also prevent the consumer from taking advantage of features like the smart refrigerator application described at the beginning of this chapter.

A **blocker tag** is a device that can be used to simulate the presence of a virtually infinite number of tags. Blocker tags can be used to disable unauthorized readers from accessing the information from a selective group of tags by sending so many responses that an unauthorized reader cannot differentiate between the blocker tag and a legitimate tag. Blocker tags also offer an alternative solution that minimizes some of the issues described earlier in this section, and at a much lower cost. After getting her purchase home, the consumer may optionally destroy the blocker tag so she can continue to use the legitimate tags in, say, her smart refrigerator.

Security for RFID and NFC systems is a complex topic, and there is no single solution that addresses all possible situations. Applications of RFID and NFC far outweigh the potential problems, however. RFID and NFC usage will continue to expand, and eventually these technologies will be present in nearly every aspect of our lives. Educating users and implementing legislation related to data collection and privacy will play a big part in raising consumers' comfort level with the technology, just as it has with the Internet.

Chapter Summary

- Radio Frequency Identification (RFID) stores information about an item's manufacturer and the date and location of production in electronic tags that include an antenna and a chip.

- Standards being published by EPCglobal Inc. will allow RFID to be used worldwide.

- RFID systems are composed of electronic tags, readers, antennas, software, and the EPCglobal network services. The format of the Electronic Product Code (EPC) is defined by the EPCglobal standards. The EPC is either 64 or 96 bits long and includes a code that refers to the manufacturer, a stock keeping unit number, and a serial number.

- RFID tags are also known as transponders. Typical tags include a microprocessor and memory. Tags are accessed by a reader device that captures and processes the data. There are two basic types of tags: passive and active. Passive tags are the most common type. They do not have a power source and rely on the electromagnetic energy in the RF waves transmitted by the reader to power their microprocessors. Active tags are equipped with a battery and can cost upwards of $20. The battery usually limits the life span of active tags. Semi-active tags also include a battery. However, it is only used when the tag is activated by a transmission, which helps the battery last many years.

- Tags can be produced in flexible packages called smart labels with an adhesive backing. They can be affixed to product packaging, pallets, or to the product itself. They are also used to track passenger baggage. Tags are not limited to being placed in a visible area and can be read in virtually any position.

- Retail stores sometimes use 1-bit tags to prevent theft. These tags do not include a unique identification, a chip, or any memory; they are only used to activate an alarm. Chipless tags use fibers or materials that reflect a portion of the reader's signal with a unique pattern that can be used as an identifier.

- Sensory tags are equipped with thermal, smoke, or other type of sensors used to monitor environmental conditions to which a product may have been exposed during shipping and storage. The cost of a tag can vary, depending on the type. Most passive tags cost between $0.07 and $0.25. Class-1 tags are read/write. Some tags can be written to, whereas others are read-only.

- A reader, also called an interrogator, communicates with both the tags and the corporate network. Some readers have the ability to write data to the tags. Readers also provide the energy to activate and power passive tags. Readers and tags operate in one of four frequency bands: 135 KHz (LF); 13.56 MHz (HF); 433 MHz and 860–930 MHz (UHF); and 2.5 GHz and 5.8 GHz (ISM).

- There are two types of tag antennas: linear and circular. Linear antennas have a better range, but circular antennas achieve more reliable reads.

- RFID software includes system software, which controls the functions of the tag and reader hardware; middleware, which is responsible for reformatting the data to meet the requirements of the business applications; and the programs that companies use to process business transactions.

- RFID has a multitude of uses, ranging from health care to entertainment-related applications. The systems are also being used in pharmaceuticals to prevent drug fraud and to assist patients.

- The connection between a reader and a tag is called a coupling. Inductive coupling tags need to be placed within a half-inch of the antenna. Backscatter coupling allows tags to be read at distances of 3.3 feet to 330 feet. Backscatter is a reflection of the reader's signal modulated with the tag data. In order to power the tags, the reader, when not transmitting, sends out a continuous wave. Backscatter modulation is based on variations of ASK and PSK. Communication between tags and readers is always half-duplex.

- In HF RFID, the tags use time slots to communicate with the reader. The number of slots is always a power of two, and the communication is always controlled by the reader. Tags never initiate communications with the reader.

- RFID has the potential for significantly increasing the amount of traffic and storage requirements in the corporate network. With the implementation of RFID systems, network availability and device management become even more critical.

- NFC is a wireless communication technology, based on RFID, that allows enabled devices to communicate at short distances. Unlike RFID, NFC allows devices to transfer files, pictures, videos, URLs, and business cards between smartphones or tablet computers. NFC-enabled devices can also read and write to passive tags. NFC tags typically have greater storage capacity than RFID tags.

- With the implementation of wireless technologies such as RFID and NFC, there are many security and privacy concerns. A tag can be locked or destroyed (electronically or physically), but doing so can limit its functionality. Blocker tags may offer an alternative solution. User and consumer education, along with government legislation, should help raise the comfort level and allow RFID usage to expand.

Key Terms

1-bit tags RFID devices that do not include a chip or memory and cannot store an EPC; they are only used to activate an alarm at retail store entrances as a means of preventing theft.

active tags RFID tags that include a battery.

backscatter The type of modulation used by passive RFID tags, backscatter is a reflection of radiation in which the tag reflects the signal sent by an interrogator while modulating it with the data to be transmitted.

beacons RFID tags that are battery powered and transmit on a periodic basis.

blocker tag A type of Class-1 passive tag that can be used to disable unauthorized readers from accessing the information from a selective group of tags by sending so many responses that a reader cannot differentiate between the blocker tag and a legitimate tag.

chipless tags RFID devices that use embedded fibers to reflect a portion of the RF waves emitted by a reader; the reflected portion of the RF waves is unique and can be used as an identifier.

continuous wave (CW)   An unmodulated sine wave sent by the reader to power the passive tag so that it can transmit a response.

coupling   A connection between a reader and a tag.

destroy password   A code programmed into the tag during manufacturing that can be used to permanently disable the tag.

Electronic Product Code (EPC)   A standardized numbering scheme that can be programmed in a tag and attached to any physical product.

EPCglobal Inc.   An organization entrusted by industry worldwide to establish RFID standards and services for real-time, automatic identification of information in the supply chain of any company anywhere in the world.

Identifier   This optional field is used to define the type of payload carried by the record.

Near Field Communications (NFC)   A short-range wireless technology, based on RFID, that allows the transfer of data between enabled smartphones and tablet computers; it can also read tags.

Object Name Service (ONS)   An EPCglobal Inc. service, modeled after DNS, that can assist in locating information about a product over the Internet.

passive tags   The most common type of RFID tags. They do not include a battery and are powered by the electromagnetic energy in the RF waves transmitted by the reader. Passive tags never initiate a transmission and must wait for a reader to interrogate them.

Radio Frequency Identification (RFID)   A technology that uses electronic, flexible tags equipped with microprocessor chips and memory to identify products. RFID tags can store significantly more information than the current bar-code system.

reader   The RFID device that captures and processes the data received from the tags.

semi-active tags   RFID tags that include a battery that is only used when the tag is interrogated. The batteries in semi-active tags usually last for several years.

sensory tags   RFID tags that include a thermal or other kind of sensor and can record information about the environmental conditions to which a product has been exposed during transportation or storage.

Slotted Terminating Adaptive Collection (STAC)   The communications protocol used by passive RFID tags that work in the 13.56 MHz HF band.

smart labels   Another name for flexible RFID tags that include a microprocessor chip and memory.

tags   Devices that include an antenna and a chip containing memory and can store information about products, such as the manufacturer, product category, and serial number along with date and time of manufacturing.

transponders   Another name for RFID tags.

Review Questions

1. The protocol used to handle collisions in HF RFID is called _____.

    a.   STAC

    b.   Class-1

    c.   Class-0

    d.   blocker

2. Which of the following is true about 1-bit tags?

   a. They store a unique identification code.

   b. They can only be read by a passive reader.

   c. They do not carry any information about the product.

   d. They are also known as RF fibers.

3. One of the main characteristics of sensory tags is that _____.

   a. they can sense the presence of other tags

   b. they can block the signal from other tags

   c. they only respond to the reader if a password is sent first

   d. they can capture information about environmental conditions

4. What is the purpose of an interrogator?

   a. to read information from the tags

   b. to prevent unauthorized access to the tags

   c. to increase the read distance

   d. to store a charge that powers passive tags

5. The function of RFID middleware is to _____.

   a. store information about the types of tags used

   b. convert the data read from the tags into a format that is compatible with that of the business application

   c. control the functions of the reader hardware

   d. control the functions of the tag hardware

6. Reader antennas are sometimes designed for a specific application. True or False?

7. The orientation of the tag's antenna usually does not affect readability. True or False?

8. RFID is not expected to have a major impact on network traffic. True or False?

9. Which of the following is an important characteristic of UHF passive tags?

   a. They have a shorter read distance.

   b. They require less power to be read.

   c. They work at greater distances than most other tags.

   d. They only support very slow communications.

10. What kind of modulation is used with most NFC tags?

    a. OFDM

    b. DSSS

    c. ASK

    d. NRZ-I

11. What type of coupling is used in NFC between a smartphone and a tablet computer?

    a. backscatter

    b. capacitive

    c. physical

    d. inductive

12. To modulate a response signal using backscatter, a tag has to _____.

    a. change the polarity of the incoming signal from the reader

    b. deflect the signal from the transponder

    c. change the characteristics of its own antenna

    d. store the energy from the interrogator

13. Interrogators and tags communicate using _____ communications.

    a. half-duplex

    b. full-duplex

    c. simplex

    d. complex

14. What is the largest amount of memory in an NFC passive tag today?

    a. 2 KB

    b. 8 KB

    c. 16 KB

    d. 32 KB

15. Before an NFC-enabled smartphone can communicate with a tag or another device, what must it do?

    a. read the serial number of the other device

    b. identify the capabilities of the device or tag

    c. receive a reply from all devices within its range

    d. transmit its clock speed

16. One of the ways used by the Gen2 protocol to select tags is by transmitting _____.

    a. a quiet command

    b. a null CW

    c. a bit mask

    d. a higher or lower intensity signal

17. What is one of the most critical challenges associated with RFID system implementation?

    a. the cost of the tags

    b. the fact that tags can be read by anyone with a smartphone

c. the large amount of storage required

d. the encryption protocols

18. Which of the following methods can be used to temporarily or permanently disable a tag? (Select two.)

a. a blocker tag

b. an authentication password

c. a very-high-power pulse

d. the destroy password

19. Which mode must an NFC-capable device be in to behave like a smart card?

a. Poll

b. Listen

c. Initiator

d. Smart card

20. Which of the following RFID technologies does not support reading more than one tag at a time?

a. readers

b. UHF

c. smart labels

d. LF

Hands-On Projects

Project 11-1

Using the Internet, locate suppliers of tags that can be used to track animals. What types and classes of tags are available? What kinds of animals are the tags being used on, other than for tracking herds of cattle? Write a report on your findings.

Project 11-2

As you know, security is an extremely important aspect of any wireless network. There are many security-related issues surrounding RFID, especially with the U.S. government now promoting the use of RFID in passports. Using the Internet, research some of these issues and the organizations involved in creating possible solutions. Focus in particular on what is being done about increasing security and privacy protection. Write a report focused on one of the issues you have identified.

Project 11-3

Many manufacturers and retailers of non-perishable goods already use RFID technology today. Several products come already tagged, and if you have recently purchased a high-value product in a computer store, you may find some tags in the box. Go to several large stores located in a local shopping area and ask the stores' staff whether they are currently using RFID to protect against theft. Do they use it for security only or do they also use it for inventory control? Be conscious of some of the security issues with RFID and identify yourself as a wireless communications student before you ask any questions regarding their use of RFID. Keep in mind that some job opportunities may be available through contacts that you initiate through this project; therefore, be sure to present yourself in a professional manner. If possible, make a list of the types of tags used, such as passive, semi-active, etc. Write a report on your findings.

Real-World Exercises

Exercise 11-1

Instrument Rentals Inc. (IRI) rents electronic test instruments to a variety of heavy industries. The instruments are usually rented for a period of 1 week to 1 year. IRI offers a customer guarantee that its instruments will always be available and calibrated to factory specifications. With 120 locations across the country, the company ships the instruments, checks their calibration upon arrival, and recalibrates them if necessary. It also often services the instruments at the customer's site, which can be in an oil field or inside a mine, to maintain them in top working condition. Finally, it checks every instrument when it is returned at the end of its rental period.

To prevent delays, minimize errors, and avoid Internet access problems, IRI would like to store each instrument's calibration records, its technicians' names, the rental/travel log, and other relevant information stored with the instrument itself. Toward this end, the service-call software that the technicians have in their notebook computers needs to be able to automatically read a record, display it on the screen, and update it on the instrument record storage device. All the instruments are leased by IRI from the manufacturers for a period of 3 years. When a lease expires, IRI wants to be able to look at the records for that particular instrument and make a decision whether to replace it with a new model or extend the lease to prevent interruption of service to its customers. As a well-known RFID and NFC expert, you have been asked to recommend which of these two technologies would be the right solution for its needs.

Prepare a PowerPoint presentation (consisting of 10 to 15 slides) that lists the advantages and disadvantages of RFID and NFC for this type of application, and specify the type of tags and devices that IRI should acquire, should it decide to go ahead with this project.

Exercise 11-2

IRI has decided to go ahead with the project and has asked you to provide a proposal (five pages maximum) specifying all the equipment that will be required to add this technology to

1,000 of its most expensive test instruments. There are two technicians per location, but only one will be equipped to service the equipment in the field. The other technician will be servicing equipment in the office.

Your proposal should include pricing for the tags (including about 100 replacement tags), a portable reader, a fixed reader, middleware, and other equipment. If required, IRI's IT staff will be in charge of reprogramming the middleware to interface with the company's in-house database. Keep in mind that if the project is successful, it may be expanded within 6 months to a year to cover IRI's entire instrument asset base, which consists of more than 10,000 instruments.

Challenge Case Project

The trade union to which the technicians at IRI belong has sent a letter to the company expressing concerns about the privacy of its members, given that the company intends to include the name of the technician who last serviced a particular instrument in its RFID tag. Now, the company has asked you to become involved. A team of three people from IRI will research the union's concern, including checking state regulations. It will then organize a meeting so that all the parties can discuss the matter.

In groups of six, form two teams of three members each—one team representing the union and the other representing IRI. Research the issues just outlined and engage in a friendly debate regarding the union's concerns. The union team may need to do added research so that it is prepared to defend its members' rights.

If you are taking an online course with this text, you can take advantage of collaboration tools such as Google Docs, Google+ Hangouts, Wiggio, or Skype to participate in an online group. Your school may also have its own Learning Management System that allows you to participate in online collaboration groups.

chapter 12

Wireless Communications in Business

After reading this chapter and completing the exercises, you will be able to:

- List the advantages of wireless communications for businesses
- Discuss the challenges of wireless communications
- Explain the steps needed to build a wireless infrastructure

In the early 1930s, a mathematician developed a formula that could be used to make accurate weather forecasts, something that was unheard of. However, because there were no computers or calculators at that time, it took almost three months of hand calculations to come up with the next day's forecast. Obviously, this was far from useful, and many individuals scoffed at such a preposterous solution to weather forecasting. However, with the introduction of computers in the late 1940s, the amount of time needed for the calculations was dramatically decreased. Suddenly, mathematical weather forecasting became very popular, and today it forms the basis for all weather forecasting.

The point is that it sometimes requires vision to see how an idea or technology could be used. This need for vision also applies to new technologies like wireless communications. Whether it is for security reasons or lack of existing knowledge and skills, some IT departments and users still question why we should use wireless technology when the existing wired systems seem to work just fine. But many users find that wireless access to e-mail, Web, and corporate resources does save them time and trouble. They also want to use their own devices—such as tablets and cellular phones—rather than being restricted by those that are supplied by the companies. This has created an entire new set of challenges for IT departments, especially in the area of security.

As you have learned so far, there are many factors to be considered when deploying wireless technologies. Short-range technologies like Bluetooth for headsets and ZigBee for lighting and environmental control can be relatively simple to install and operate, requiring little user intervention after initial setup and configuration. Cellular, Wi-Fi, and WiMAX demand a much higher level of involvement from designers and troubleshooting staff to ensure a reliable and stable environment. Although residential installations usually do not require any specialized skills, deployment in large-business environments can be far more complex. For example, wireless signal propagation presents specific challenges to office buildings, sports stadiums, cruise ships, passenger aircraft, and manufacturing environments.

This textbook cannot possibly cover all the different wireless network design and deployment situations. Instead, this chapter discusses what it takes to convert the potential of wireless technology into a successful business installation. We will take a look at the steps needed to incorporate IEEE 802.11 wireless technology into a business environment, and we'll also look at the challenges that business users adopting this technology must face. The intent is to provide you with a brief introduction to what it takes to achieve a successful wireless installation.

Advantages of Wireless Technology

The advantages of incorporating wireless technology into a business are far-reaching and can positively impact an organization in many ways. In addition to the advantages already discussed in this book—mobile data access, easier network installation, easier office moves, and better disaster recovery—wireless technology provides business-specific advantages, including universal access to corporate data, increased productivity, ability for customers to access their own data, data availability around the clock, and improved information technology (IT) support.

Universal Access to Corporate Data

A major advantage of wireless technology is that it provides access to corporate data from almost any location. This universal access can help a business generate more revenue. For example, a traveling sales representative calling on a customer needs the most current information at his fingertips before he walks in the door. He could review printouts in his hotel room the night before, but these are only as recent as the day they were printed. He could access the company's corporate database from his hotel room that morning, but changes in inventory and sales may occur before his 2:00 P.M. appointment.

But what if the sales representative uses a WiMAX network, a cellular USB Internet stick, his smartphone connected to his laptop, a mobile hotspot, or a tablet with 3G or 4G to access live data, such as the status of the customer's buying history, the product's current inventory, and an up-to-the-minute competitor price list? The information is accessible before he steps out of his car for his appointment—even while he is meeting with the customer. And there is no need to connect to his customer's network. By having universal access to the latest data, the sales representative will be well prepared to make the sale.

Traveling sales representatives are not the only users who can benefit from universal access to corporate data. Anyone who needs to be mobile but also needs access to data can benefit from it. Physicians who move around a hospital can have current data at their fingertips to make decisions, which results in lower costs and improved care for patients. Physicians can also monitor a patient's vital signs from anywhere in the world using a smartphone (see *www.airstriptech.com*). Likewise, factory managers can access data as they check available warehouse storage space for arriving inventory. Wireless technology can also be useful when all parties are in one location. For example, during an intense negotiation session, attorneys, bankers, and their clients can all use wireless laptops to access data or receive SMS messages on their cellular phones, thus helping them make the best decision.

 In 2004, Baycrest, a center for geriatric care in Toronto, Ontario, was one of the first hospitals in North America to implement a computerized physician order entry system. The system lets doctors order tests, exams, and medications directly from a patient's bedside using the WLAN from a handheld device. Physicians can also check the patient's records and charts in the hospital's health information system.

12

Industry experts agree that access to corporate data from almost anywhere is the greatest advantage of wireless technology. This access allows decisions to be made quickly using the most up-to-date information. For a business, these factors translate into increased revenues. Keep in mind that access to corporate data from public networks needs to be properly secured through the use of VPNs, which must make use of the latest encryption methods to ensure the security of the corporation's network as well as compliance with a number of privacy and long-term data storage laws. VPNs and other methods of corporate data access via the Internet are a vast, advanced topic that is well beyond the scope of this text.

Increased Productivity

Having universal access to corporate data leads to increased productivity by employees. As far back as 2001, in a survey commissioned by Cisco, users reported that when using a WLAN they could access data almost two additional hours each day than if they were only using a wired network. This increase occurred when users were away from the computer in their offices but still connected to the WLAN during meetings, conferences, and sales calls. If the additional two hours of connection time translated into 70 minutes of increased productivity (a standard ratio), this means the average user could be 22 percent more productive. For a worker with a salary of $64,000, this means that the annual productivity improvement per wireless user could be worth as much as $7,000 each year to the business. In addition, almost two-thirds of WLAN users reported that the wireless connection improved the accuracy of their everyday tasks. Because more and more companies are now implementing wireless, there are literally dozens of similar surveys that show results just as dramatic or even more so than in the past.

Increased Access to the Customer's Own Data

A key factor in reducing business costs is to shift the burden of accessing a customer's data from the business to the customer. If customers can see data about themselves on the business' computer system, they can make better and more informed decisions. This self-service decreases the use of the business' human resources, which in turn reduces costs and increases revenue for the business.

An example of customers' access to their own data can be seen in the airline and banking industries. Bank clients today can access their account balances, pay bills, and transfer money between accounts from a mobile device. Most airlines have Web sites where customers can view schedules, make reservations, download boarding passes, and check on the current status of their frequent flier miles. These sites generate cost savings for the airlines because they are able to hire fewer telephone reservation clerks. Most airports today offer wireless access for travelers, albeit not always free. Customers can use the WLAN to check their flight information once they enter the terminal, learning their gate number and check-in time. Personal check-in is available for those who have a smartphone, which allows customers to print or sometimes simply display their own boarding passes or a QR code on a smartphone screen, check their baggage at curbside, and access other services. This helps the airline make better use of its staff. In addition, customer satisfaction is increased because travelers spend less time waiting in lines. Increased satisfaction means a repeat customer. All these benefits result from wireless technology that makes the customer's data available from more locations, thereby reducing the burden on the business and thus increasing profits.

Data Availability Around the Clock

Leaving work at 5:00 P.M.—and leaving the work behind—is a thing of the past. Business professionals regularly work evenings, nights, weekends, and holidays to catch up and stay ahead. This means that business users need access to corporate data 24 hours a day, 7 days a week. In the past this required a trip back to the office on weekends or staying late at night to finish that report. However, wireless technology can help make data available from almost anywhere at any time. This means that a business user can still catch her daughter's soccer match or son's music performance without sacrificing productivity. The introduction of RIM's BlackBerry device, and later the Apple iPhone, as well as Android devices represents a paradigm shift in accessibility to e-mail and corporate data. Many business applications have been developed for the smartphones, including software that allows a field technician to update trouble tickets and access technical documents and also allows construction foremen to enter payroll work-hour records while on the job site. There are no limits to how wireless networks can make us more productive and allow us to make better-informed decisions.

Improved IT Support

Wireless technology can help improve the support that information technology (IT) departments provide to users. Two of the most significant advantages for IT departments are easier system setup and decreased cabling costs compared to wired systems. Troubleshooting a wireless network is often simpler than troubleshooting cabling problems, especially for businesses that have large offices with many connection points and hidden cabling infrastructure. Cabling infrastructure issues are frequently overlooked as a potential source of serious network connectivity issues, and troubleshooting and repairing a cable infrastructure can be very labor intensive and time consuming (i.e., expensive).

Other improvements include easier and faster equipment moves, more efficient use of office space, and lower support and maintenance costs. These benefits can lead to lower costs for the business and more time for the IT staff to provide improved support to the users.

Voice over Wireless LAN (VoWLAN)

Consider the cordless telephone you have probably grown to rely on at home. Until 2003, there were few options for businesses that wanted to enable their staff to move around the office while remaining available at their extension numbers. VoWLAN is about to change this, without the high cost of cellular telephone calls. As early as June 2004, there already were approximately 1,600 hospitals in the United States using VoWLAN.

For more information on VoWLAN equipment for hospitals, see *www.vocera.com*. For the latest news about this topic, see *vowlan.wifinetnews.com*.

In many other kinds of workplaces, such as sports facilities, construction sites, and manufacturing plants, some of the staff must remain mobile within the confines of a building or site at all times, which can limit voice communications, given that these people are not always near a phone. Cellular telephones have largely solved this problem, though at a high cost. And although cordless phones are common in homes, business telephone systems do not usually offer good mobility options. WLAN technology allows businesses to go beyond data access and transform the way their staff communicates while performing their daily tasks. The new WLAN standards discussed in Chapter 8, along with 802.11-enabled telephone handsets manufactured by a growing number of companies, means that today's businesses can benefit from the full potential of mobile communications.

VoWLAN takes advantage of voice over IP (VoIP) technology, but instead of using the wired network to carry voice calls, VoWLAN uses the wireless infrastructure to carry both voice and data. **Wireless VoIP phones**, the telephone handsets that connect to a WLAN's access point (AP), enable you to use the WLAN for regular telephone calls while using only a small amount of network bandwidth. Depending on what type of connection a location has with the telephone carrier—either traditional land-based telephone lines or over the Internet—additional equipment may be required to interconnect the wireless network with the phone lines. As more manufacturers and telephone carriers enter the VoIP market, and as more customers sign up for these services, the wireless VoIP handsets will likely become commonplace, eventually replacing cordless phones, thus enabling both data and voice connectivity without wires through a single, common interface.

Keep in mind that regular household telephones, including cordless phones, must never be plugged into an enterprise phone system (a PBX or Private Branch Exchange). These systems are not compatible and use a different voltage than the regular landline phones; also, trying to interconnect them can sometimes damage the phone.

Most newer models of wireless residential gateways and wireless SOHO routers support automatic prioritization of VoIP for Internet calls. Vonage (see *www.vonage.com*) and Skype (see *www.skype.com*) offer adapters that can be plugged into a residential gateway and into a regular cordless phone to enable Internet calls to phone lines. Skype also offers some cordless phones that support their own menu system and can be used to make Skype-to-Skype calls without requiring a computer. (SOHO is an acronym for "small office/home office.")

Making telephone calls using VoIP can save a substantial amount of money in long-distance calls. In addition, most VoIP providers allow a business to have a telephone number that has an area code belonging to a different part of the country, or even the world. This can also generate significant savings when most of a company's business comes from a different region than where the company's offices are located, because it avoids the expense of long-distance calling.

Even some of the major carriers, such as AT&T, have launched VoIP services for business and residential customers. For a current list of VoIP service providers, see *voip.about.com* or *www.voip-info.org*.

Challenges of Using Wireless Technology

Just as there are distinct advantages for a business using wireless technology, there are distinct challenges. These include competing technologies, data security and privacy, user reluctance, and a shortage of qualified staff.

Competing Technologies

Some wireless technologies are clearly based on approved industry standards, such as WLANs following the IEEE 802.11 standards. A business that uses an IEEE standard WLAN is assured that it is investing in a technology that will be the standard for several years to come and can be upgraded, in most cases, by simply loading a new version of the software on the APs and client devices.

However, with other wireless technologies, such as digital cellular telephony, there is no clear indication of what will become the standard and what will fade away. This uncertainty poses a critical decision for businesses. Making the wrong selection may mean investing hundreds of thousands of dollars in a technology that is orphaned in a few years, with dwindling users and support.

As long as technologies continue to compete before one becomes the standard, companies face a certain amount of risk in selecting the right wireless technology. An organization must not only determine which technology is best for it, it must determine which technology will be viable in the future, a task that can be made much easier by having trained staff on board or hiring the right reseller or consulting organization to provide some guidance.

Table 12-1 provides a summary of the wireless technologies discussed in this book, along with some of their applications, pros, and cons.

Wireless Technology	Primary Applications	Pros	Cons
Bluetooth (IEEE 802.15.1)	Cable replacement	Wide availability	Low-speed, limited range
ZigBee (IEEE 802.15.4)	Residential and industrial controls	Low-cost, low-power, mesh networking	Limited security (encryption), low-speed
WiMedia (IEEE 802.15.3c), WiGig, WirelessHD, WHDI	Multimedia distribution, interconnecting consumer entertainment equipment, telephones, and even data	Low-cost, low-power, high-speed, mesh networking with IEEE 802.15.5, QoS	Limited processing power and consequently limited security for some devices; limited range without mesh networking
WLANs—802.11a/b/g/n/ac/ad	Mostly data networking	Established technology; new enhancements to the standards that allow it to support voice, QoS, mesh networking, faster handoffs, multimedia; good security with RADIUS or VPN; LOS required; up to 7 Gbps	Good ability to handle voice and multimedia only for 802.11n; for 802.11b/g/n in the 2.4 GHz band, limited spectrum and limited range without mesh networking; for 802.11a, limited range
WiMAX (IEEE 802.16)	Data, voice, video; fixed or mobile	40 Mbps to 1 Gbps fixed wireless shared-bandwidth with range of up to 35 miles; high-security; 2 Mbps+ for mobile applications; can be overlaid on cellular network; LOS or NLOS	Complex technology
Cellular	Voice, data	Up to 1 Gbps LTE Advanced	High-cost per-minute/per-user
Satellite	Voice, data, video	Covers remote areas not available with other technologies; can achieve 1 Gbps in dedicated connections	Very high cost of deployment; requires high-gain directional antennas for most applications
RFID and NFC	Data for product identification (RFID) or exchanging data between devices up to 1.6 inches (4 cm) apart	Worldwide standard for product identification (RFID) and for exchanging data and payment applications (NFC)	Short range; some security and privacy issues; low processing power and, consequently, limited uses for RFID tags

Table 12-1 Wireless technologies

12

Data Security and Privacy

Wireless technology's greatest strength—allowing users to roam freely without being connected to the network by wires—can also be its greatest weakness, if not addressed properly. Just as a roaming user can receive radio frequency (RF) signals anywhere within a building, so too can an unauthorized user outside the building. Broadcasting network traffic over the airwaves has created a concern for keeping that data secure. Most industry experts agree that opening up a corporate network by adding a wireless component without considering security is far too dangerous. Hardening such systems requires expertise and may significantly increase costs.

User Reluctance

In technology, changes are nearly constant because as standards and technology advance, established vendors continue to improve their products and to make it easier, simpler, and more transparent for users to adapt. Change can be painful for users because it takes time and energy to learn a new system. Unless users can see an immediate benefit to abandoning their comfortable old ways of doing things, they will be reluctant to do so. The human factor in implementing wireless technology is sometimes a significant obstacle.

Shortage of Qualified Staff

Wireless communications technology has touched almost every business in one way or another, including manufacturing, health care, telecommunications, and retail, and it is poised to continue growing, as you have learned throughout this book. As a result of this growth, the need for IT professionals to develop and implement wireless applications and provide support is skyrocketing. However, many schools and training facilities have not yet caught up with the demand for wireless IT workers. Consequently, there is a shortage of qualified IT professionals trained to install, support, and maintain wireless systems.

As technology improves and becomes ever easier to use, the life of a network administrator or a reseller can get more complicated. Users who begin to feel more comfortable with the technology may feel empowered to modify settings, occasionally creating connectivity issues or perhaps exposing the network to security risks. In companies that implement WLANs, network support staff and administrators must not only be aware of these issues, continually monitoring them, but must ensure that their knowledge and training keeps pace with the advances in the IT industry. The latest BYOD (bring your own device) trend is worrying for IT departments, both for reasons of security and because of the user-support headaches it may cause.

Before embarking on building a wireless infrastructure in a business, it is critical to identify the various needs, solutions, and threats and then determine the best way to balance these factors.

Building a Wireless Infrastructure

Once a business has decided to invest in wireless technology, it faces the task of building a new wireless infrastructure. This is much like adding a new network to the organization. In fact, several of the steps necessary to build this new infrastructure are similar to those needed when adding a new wired network. You must also keep in mind that installing APs does require a cable infrastructure. This section looks at the implementation of IEEE 802.11 networks because they are the most common type used in business. Some of the steps required to deploy other types of networks, such as WiMAX and cellular, are similar; however, the process (as well as the business reasons) for deploying these other types is very different, and the cost of the equipment and testing tools is also much higher. This section provides a general overview of the steps and reasoning behind building a wireless network.

Needs Assessment

"Do we really need it?" is a question that must be asked first when deciding whether to add a wireless infrastructure to a business. Sadly, this question is often asked too late in the process. Sometimes, it's enough to make a procedural change or add personnel rather than invest in wireless technology. Evaluating needs involves looking at the organization and the current network, gathering basic information, and determining costs.

Look at the Organization The first step in assessing the need is to step back and examine the organization or business as a whole. Sometimes, users fall into the trap of viewing only their department or unit instead of looking at the entire organization. There are a series of basic yet vital questions that need to be asked, including:

- What is the current size of the organization?
- How much growth is anticipated?
- How do employees in different positions and departments perform their daily activities— meaning, do they need to move around the office and work from different locations?
- How frequently does the company move staff to other offices and need to reconfigure the wiring setup?

Although these questions may seem very basic, they can help focus the thinking on the organization as a whole and away from any one part of it. In addition, they can reveal a great deal in terms of assessing needs and identifying priorities. A company's employees may not be aware of all the implications of implementing a wireless network, such as the need for new security policies and continuous monitoring, not to mention the potential interference problems, which can affect user and application performance and offset the advantages of a WLAN.

12

Employees who work primarily at their desks on a single computer, such as call center/ customer service operators, may not require wireless access. If the room configuration is static, a wired network will provide performance that is more consistent in the long run.

Assess the Current Network The next step in assessing the need for adding a wireless infrastructure is to look at how the organization or business uses its current network. Questions to ask include:

- How does the current network support the organization's mission?
- What are the strengths and weaknesses of the current network?
- How many users does it support?
- What essential applications run on the network?

Different industries have different network requirements. The banking industry needs networks that offer a very high degree of security. The manufacturing industry usually cannot afford any downtime and often needs networks that are completely fault-tolerant. Educational institutions may be able to tolerate a small amount of downtime, but their networks often need to authenticate thousands of new students every few months.

Assessing the current network can help to identify why a new technology may be needed. If the current network can be upgraded or adapted to meet the current needs, then wireless technology may not be necessary at this time. However, if the current network cannot support the anticipated future growth of the business or there is a clear indication that wireless technology can help the business grow, then the investment may be worthwhile.

Documenting the current network in detail can help the assessment. Networks tend to grow in unplanned fashions, as new users or equipment are needed, so documenting the network is necessary to gain a view of the system as a whole. You must always keep in mind that the wired network infrastructure must be able to support the amount of traffic you expect there will be from the new wireless clients. For example, when deploying an 802.11n network, which is capable of transmitting data at 600 Mbps, you must take into account that your wired infrastructure—including cables, switches, and routers—may only support 100 Mbps. Furthermore, to effectively deploy or upgrade to an 802.11ac network and take full advantage of the increased data rates, you may need to replace large portions of the wired network equipment and cabling as well.

Table 12-2 summarizes a sample current network to help you quickly visualize the requirements for a new wireless deployment or upgrade. If the network is complex, a diagram or layout of the network can also help. An example of a simple diagram is shown in Figure 12-1, but keep in mind that an existing network may need to cover several floors of a building, making the task even more challenging.

Description	Data
Number of clients	72
Types of clients	35 using Windows 7 (Ethernet) 20 using MacBook Pro (802.11n 2.4 and 5 GHz, Ethernet) 17 using Apple iOS (9), Android (5), and Blackberry (3); 802.11n; 2.4GHz
Number of servers	1 using Windows 2008
Switches	2 × 48-port
Routers/Subnets	1/1
Type of network	Wired (Ethernet)
Type of cable (medium)	Category 5e; maximum length of 210 ft.
Other devices	5 laser printers (network), 1 wireless 1 scanner

Table 12-2 Sample current network

© Cengage Learning 2014

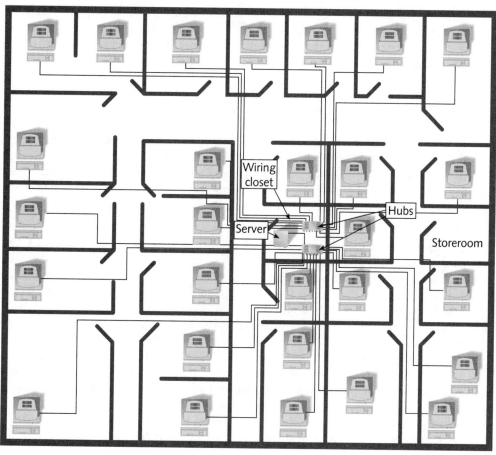

Figure 12-1 Typical network overlaid on a floor plan

© Cengage Learning 2014

12

Gather Information After the organization and the current network have been evaluated and it is determined that wireless technology can fit into the current business strategy, the next step is to gather information. With all the different wireless technologies available and the constant changes taking place in this area, the expertise to gather the information may be beyond that of the current IT staff. Many organizations turn to outside consultants and vendors to help provide information at this point. Some organizations may send out a **request for information (RFI)**. An RFI is a document that seeks information about what vendors may have to offer. RFIs are general in scope. A broad statement such as "The vendor will install a wireless network on the second floor of the building to accommodate 45 users" may be enough to start things rolling. Usually, several vendors are encouraged to respond with information about the particular products they sell.

Once all the RFIs have been returned, the organization can examine each of them in detail. Generally, a pattern will emerge from the RFIs. For example, if four vendors recommend an IEEE 802.11n wireless WLAN whereas one vendor recommends using 80211g, the direction starts to become clear. Evaluate RFIs with caution. Vendors want to sell a product or service, and they may overemphasize the strength of their products while minimizing their weaknesses. Independent research is still needed after the responses to the RFIs have been received.

Perform a Wireless Site Survey

The information you gather about the current network in preparation for implementing a WLAN would never be complete without a proper **wireless site survey**. A wireless site survey consists of measuring the strength and quality of the signal and the resulting transmission speeds and throughput achievable in all the different locations around the office where users will need wireless access to the network. In addition, the site survey helps determine the existence of interference sources, both internal and external, which will establish the susceptibility of the WLAN to environmental factors. The survey helps ensure that the actual performance of the network will meet the needs of all the users.

A simple wireless site survey for a SOHO can be performed using an AP, a wireless adapter card, and the client software provided by the adapter card manufacturer. (The Windows XP or Windows 7 client software is far too simplistic and does not provide enough information.) However, a comprehensive site survey, especially for large office buildings, manufacturing plants, multiple floors of a building, or other complex environments, should be performed using more sophisticated software tools and people who have a level of training and experience that isn't currently available in the organization. The site survey should ideally be performed using the same type and model of equipment that will be installed. The cost of tools and equipment to perform a site survey is fairly high; purchasing them can only be justified if you will be using these tools on a regular basis. There are many prerequisites and steps involved in a site survey. One of the most important is a floor plan, preferably one that includes the location of office furniture items and any large machinery as well. Floor plans assist in the site survey and yield more detailed and complete reports.

A variety of site survey guides and white papers is available on the Internet. To find more information, search for "Wireless Site Survey Guide." A good starting point is *www.wi-fiplanet.com/tutorials/article.php/3761356.*

A wireless site survey will identify a number of additional factors regarding the potential implementation of a WLAN, such as:

- Security features and policies required
- Radio signal range (distance requirements)
- Number of APs and channels required (based on user population, and application load) to provide good coverage and security
- Throughput required
- Location of AP radios and antennas
- Location of fixed client devices
- Location of Ethernet cables for connecting APs
- Type of client adapters (WNICs) and whether external antennas may be required to increase range

- Power (electricity) requirements and type—that is, power over Ethernet or wall sockets
- Growth (expansion) requirements and impact on current design
- Potential interference sources and their locations, how they affect signal quality, and channel selection based on existence of interference sources
- Standards and frequencies to be implemented (802.11a/b/g/n), which may be dependent on the client devices
- Requirements for integration with the company's wired network (additional equipment such as switches, firewalls, authentication servers, Ethernet speed)

These factors will help determine the type and range of equipment that will be needed and will assist in the creation of a request for proposal (RFP, discussed later in this chapter). The wireless site survey may be performed by the company's own technical staff, by a potential vendor, or by a consulting organization, but it should always be done before a vendor provides a final proposal.

Site Survey Tools To perform a proper 802.11 site survey, you will need to have a number of tools available. You can perform a site survey in an existing WLAN—in fact, it is advisable that you do this on a periodic basis, if you suspect interference from nearby WLANs or if equipment, furniture, and people have been moved to different locations around the office. To evaluate the environment for a new deployment, you will need at least one AP of the same model that you intend to install. This is the most essential component of a site survey. A connection to the wired network is not essential, but you will need to supply power to the AP, so be sure to have an extension cord that is long enough to reach the nearest outlet.

The AP will need to be configured to transmit a signal in a channel that is preferably clear of other transmissions. To check the available channels, you can use a tool such as inSSIDer from MetaGeek or any similar tool that can scan the Wi-Fi frequency spectrum that you will be using for this installation and display the presence of nearby WLAN signals. Interference from nearby WLANs will affect the signal quality and, consequently, the maximum throughput of the WLAN you are deploying. There is also a variety of dedicated devices that can do a much better job of checking the Wi-Fi spectrum. One of these is the Fluke Networks AirCheck Wi-Fi Tester, which can also produce comprehensive reports (see *www. flukenetworks.com/enterprise-network/network-testing/AirCheck-Wi-Fi-Tester*). In addition, it can be equipped with an Yagi antenna that helps you locate the direction that a signal is coming from. Figure 12-2 shows a picture of the AirCheck Wi-Fi Tester's home screen.

12

Although you can perform a wireless site survey using simple tools like the manufacturer's client software for a wireless NIC and a laptop computer or even an Android smartphone with a Wi-Fi test application, a large office would require that you make extensive notes at every point to record the data about signal strength and quality. If you will be performing site surveys on a regular basis, there are software tools that allow you to load a floor plan, walk around, and complete a survey in far less time. Two notable options are the Ekahau Site Survey (go to *www.ekahau.com,* click Products, then click Site Survey) and AirMagnet Survey (go to *www.flukenetworks.com,* click Products, WLAN Design and Troubleshoooting, then click AirMagnet Survey). These tools produce extensive graphical and text reports that save time and can help you accomplish a WLAN deployment with optimal performance and security in addition to helping you troubleshoot Wi-Fi signal and coverage issues.

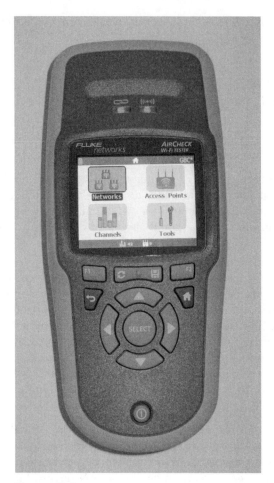

Figure 12-2 Fluke AirCheck Wi-Fi Tester

© Cengage Learning 2014

Other items that will be required for your site survey include:

- A laptop computer compatible with the software you will be using
- A ladder, some wire, packaging tape, or any other means of mounting the AP near the ceiling
- Additional external antennas, if required
- If a floor plan is not available, some means of measuring distances, such as a long tape measure, a laser-measuring device, or a measuring wheel
- Some means of communication, such as a cellular phone or walkie-talkie, for working in teams

You will also need these tools when performing an outdoor site survey. Figure 12-3 shows a picture of a laser-measuring device. These are often the best option because they measure distances up to 167 feet (about 51 meters), cost as little as $100.00, can save you a lot of time, and are accurate to 1/16 of an inch (about 1.6 millimeters).

Figure 12-3 Laser-measuring tool

© *Cengage Learning 2014*

12

Keep in mind that the list of items required for site surveys is by no means complete. Different site surveys may require additional tools or equipment, but the items listed here are the most essential.

Return on Investment

After the company has collected potential solutions from vendor RFIs and conducted independent research, it must determine the project's cost. The cost by itself cannot be the sole basis of the decision. Rather, the company must consider the cost in light of the benefit that the project will provide. It may cost $50,000 to implement wireless technology, which might seem like a high cost. However, if the new technology saves $100,000 per year in other costs and increases revenue by $150,000, then $50,000 may seem very reasonable.

Determining the cost in relationship to the benefit is known as calculating **return on investment (ROI)**. In strict accounting terms, ROI is the profit divided by the amount of the investment. ROI projections are useful when considering the purchase of products or services needed for a business. It is best expressed over a specific period of time.

For example, you might project that a $50,000 wireless network will save a total of $75,000 in 18 months. The trick with ROIs is to determine all the costs as well as all the projected savings.

Upfront costs are ones that are necessary to start a project, such as the cost of installing the wireless technology. As an example, the upfront costs for a WLAN might include APs and wireless NICs for all the devices and computers. The number of APs depends on the coverage area, number of users, and types of services needed. Hardware costs vary, depending on such factors as performance requirements, coverage requirements, and bandwidth.

Upfront costs are not the only costs to be considered. **Recurring costs** are often overlooked when determining final costs. A recurring cost is one that a user continues to pay over an extended period of time. For example, if the company leases a free space optics transceiver or a wireless bridge from a local carrier, the annual lease cost is recurring and should be considered as part of the total cost for the technology over its useful life. The initial cost of equipment is usually amortized (reduced) by a certain percentage every year, but lease and maintenance costs either remain the same or may even increase over time. The installation, projected maintenance, hardware or software maintenance contracts, IT staff training, and user training should all be factored into the total cost of implementation.

A much more difficult task is to determine the savings that can be accumulated. Because the system is not already in place, it may be very difficult to calculate the savings or increased revenue that can result from the implementation of the WLAN. The key here is to be as conservative as possible. Gathering information from other users of the technology can be very helpful.

 Although ROI studies are considered very important, they are not conducted as frequently as they should be. In a recent survey, only 26 percent of the respondents said they had conducted an ROI **NOTE** analysis prior to installing a WLAN system. Almost 25 percent indicated there was "simply no need to," whereas 16 percent said that cost was simply not an issue.

Develop a Plan

Once it has been determined that there is a real need that can be solved by implementing wireless technology, and if the ROI projection is positive, the next step is to create a plan. The adage that "those who fail to plan, plan to fail" is never more true than when considering a new technology. The landscape is littered with projects that were poorly planned and then abandoned after cost overruns escalated astronomically. Developing a sensible, workable plan is perhaps the most critical piece of the entire process. Planning should never be done in a vacuum; instead, the IT staff, users, and consultants should all be asked for their input. Once the plan has been completed, a **request for proposal (RFP)** is sent out to vendors, who respond with a formal cost for the project or equipment. An RFP is a detailed planning document that contains precise specifications for the products and services that the organization intends to buy.

Another type of document often sent to vendors is a request for quotation (RFQ). The difference between an RFP and an RFQ is that an RFP asks the vendor to submit a proposal for the entire project, whereas an RFQ asks vendors for their most competitive prices on specific equipment. RFQs are generally used when the project is designed and implemented by the company's internal staff.

Whom to Involve Making an investment in wireless technology involves the efforts of many people. One of the most important groups is the organization's IT team. The purpose of involving the IT staff is twofold. First, the IT team's members have a broad background in technology and can contribute much to the dialog regarding their experiences and knowledge base. Nothing alienates an IT staff more quickly than when an outside consultant is hired without first tapping the in-house expertise. The second, and most important reason for involving the IT staff, is to make them aware of the proposed project, because they are the ones who will provide technical support and training and will therefore be the strongest promoters of the new technology. If the IT staff is alienated from the planning process, the project will likely be slow to take off or even fail.

Another group to involve in the planning process is the people who will be using the new technology. Generally, it is not practical to involve all users at this early stage. Instead, a representative group should be selected to participate. However, the group should represent a true cross-section of the user base. Too often, only the most technological users, who tend to be enthusiastic about any new technology, are chosen to participate, but that's not a good idea. Instead, the representative group should include both technological users and average users; this will result in more impartial input and more widespread support when the new technology rolls out.

External consultants are the third group to involve in the planning process. By viewing the organization from the outside, they can evaluate its needs from an unbiased perspective. However, a common mistake is to turn an entire project over to consultants and allow them to create the plan, which not only fails to draw on the expertise that users and the IT team can provide but may antagonize those two groups. External consultants should be used as one source of input but not the sole source.

Regular meetings should be scheduled in which the external consultants provide detailed explanations of how the project is moving forward, including a schedule of activities, a list of proposed technologies, and a phased implementation plan—that is, a complete project management plan. This plan should establish priorities and allocate the time needed for the other participants in the process to respond, thereby ensuring that the planning phase stays on target.

Developing a Request for Proposal

Once a plan for wireless technology has been designed, the next step is for the organization to submit a request for proposal (RFP). An RFP might start with a sentence like the following: "The vendor will install an 802.11b WLAN network for 45 users in an area in which users are no more than 275 feet from the access point." It would then include more detailed information, such as a proposed schedule, relevant issues (such as a building that contains certain types of hazardous materials, like asbestos or chemicals, large machinery, a walk-in safe, or a shielded X-ray room in a clinic), and any other information that would assist the vendor in creating its response. Some of the key elements contained in an RFP are:

- Statement of values—This helps vendors understand the organization's philosophy and priorities—for example, whether network performance is more important than the average amount of time it takes the vendor to respond to a problem, or whether the immediate availability of the hardware and software is more important than price. A statement of values assists the vendor in developing its response RFP.

- Description of operations—This includes any future business plans that might affect the RFP, such as a planned expansion in a branch office building.

- Current network and applications—This includes the number of sites, the current configuration, the applications that are currently being used, and the planned additions.

- Timetable—This lists specific dates for each step of the RFP evaluation by the customer. A sample RFP timetable is shown in Table 12-3.

Proposed Date	Activity
May 1	Date RFP is issued
May 15	Last date that written questions must be submitted by vendors
May 30	Date RFP responses are due
June 15	Week that initial cuts will be made
July 1	Week that presentations will be made by the finalists
July 15	Date the contract will be awarded
August 15	Date the contract will be finalized
September 10	Date work will begin
February 12	Date work will be completed

Table 12-3 Sample RFP timetable

© Cengage Learning 2014

Vendors respond to the RFP with their proposals for the project. A vendor's response should contain detailed information regarding what will be installed, suggested timelines, and costs. If a site survey has not yet been performed, it should be included as part of the requirements, so that vendors can provide the cost of the site survey along with their responses. Once all the RFPs have been received and analyzed, the company makes a final decision regarding which vendor to select. Choosing a vendor should be done carefully by checking the vendors' backgrounds and references. Choosing the vendor who submits the lowest cost can often turn out to be a very costly decision.

Performing a Limited Trial

After the RFPs have been received and the vendor has been selected, it is important to perform a limited trial, also known in the industry as a pilot project. It is usually possible to borrow sample hardware and software from the vendor who won the bid. The IT staff should be thoroughly involved in the trial, along with a select group of users. Those users who were involved in the planning process are good candidates.

The new wireless technology should be thoroughly tested. Devices should be connected and then taken offline, the base stations disconnected, and other similar activities performed to see how the technology reacts under both normal and unusual circumstances. Throughput and applications should be tested. This is a time in which the IT department can be introduced to the technology and start learning troubleshooting techniques while dealing with the trial group of users. The security of the new technology should also be thoroughly tested at this point. It is also an opportunity for managers to see the technology in action so that they can begin to understand how it will impact the business.

Training Staff

After the technology has been tested thoroughly, the next step is to begin training. Do not underestimate this step. Training provides users as well as support specialists with the knowledge to effectively operate and support the new wireless technology, and it can save time and costs during the transition. Users need to know how to use the new hardware and software, and the support staff needs to know how to manage the network and diagnose problems. Training will increase the effectiveness of the new technology when it is first installed because users will have less of a learning curve. This, in turn, will minimize the temporary drop in productivity that is normally associated with the installation of a new system. Also, well-trained users will have fewer questions and require less IT support after they start using the new system.

The IT staff must be trained first. This may include on-site training from the vendor, if it was included as part of the RFP, or attending workshops or specialized classes that cover the technology. Once the IT staff has been trained, it can train the users. Because all users learn differently, a variety of training sessions should be offered to accommodate them. The different types of training include:

- Small-group sessions
- Detailed written instructions
- Web-based training
- One-on-one sessions

Rolling Out to All Users

As the training moves toward completion, the final rollout can begin. The most efficient way to do a widespread rollout of a wireless technology is to do it in phases. If possible, start by introducing the wireless technology to just one department or unit of the business. The IT staff will be able to deal with problems more easily if it only has to deal with one department or unit at a time. This also limits the effect of any rollout problems to one department instead of the entire community of users.

On occasion, a project may need to go live before it is entirely debugged and before every feature is added. If this is the case, it is important that the key users understand this, feel comfortable with the temporary state of the new technology, and are aware of the full scale of the project. The key users' leadership among the other users can determine the success of the project.

Once the system is installed and running in a unit, it is a good idea for the vendor and the IT staff to confer and identify any problems before additional units are brought on. IT staff members can also compare notes to determine if the training sessions are meeting the needs of the users based on the type and number of questions that have been received. The training can then be tweaked as the remaining users are trained.

Providing Support

Whereas training is primarily done before the new system is turned on, support continues as users' questions are answered. User-support functions can be carried out in various ways, including:

- Establishing informal peer-to-peer support groups
- Creating formal user-support groups
- Maintaining an internal help desk
- Assigning support to the IT department

Each of these approaches has its strengths and weaknesses. However, an internal help desk is one of the most effective means of support. A **help desk** is a central point of contact for users who need assistance using the technology. It addresses users' problems and provides support services to solve those problems. This can involve providing basic information to users, such as why an FSO connection is slower when it is raining. But the help desk can use the various requests for information to identify areas where improved technology might save the company some money.

Here are some suggestions for running a help desk:

- Have one telephone number for the help desk.
- Plan for temporarily increased call volume after the new network is installed.
- Create a method to track problems effectively.
- Use surveys to determine user satisfaction and to identify any remaining issues.
- Periodically rotate network personnel into the help desk.
- Use information from the help desk to organize follow-up training.

Chapter Summary

- Wireless technology can positively impact an organization in many ways. WLANs allow current data to be accessed quickly from any location. Universal access to corporate data can also lead to increased mobility, productivity, and accuracy by employees.

- VoWLAN uses IP phones and VoIP on the same network the company uses for data. VoWLAN can help to enhance employee availability and customer service. Implementing VoIP may increase the load on the network and require the replacement of some wired network devices, such as switches and routers.

- The challenges related to wireless technology include investing in the correct technology. Unauthorized users outside a building can receive RF signals from an inside WLAN. Some users are reluctant to change to a new technology. The need for information technology (IT) professionals to develop and implement wireless applications and provide support is skyrocketing.

- Once a business has decided to invest in wireless technology, it faces the task of building a new wireless infrastructure. The first step is to evaluate the need for wireless technology by examining the entire organization. Another important step is to look at how the organization uses its current network. If the current network cannot support the anticipated future growth of the organization or there is a clear indication that wireless technology can help the organization grow, then investing in it may be the answer. After the organization and the current network have been evaluated and it is determined that wireless technology can fit into the current business strategy, the organization must gather information, then perform a wireless site survey, which can answer critical questions, such as the number of APs required, types of antennas, interference, and security needs.

- Security needs may increase the cost of the project significantly, given that many other devices, such as additional switches and authentication servers, may be required. Security is always a work-in-progress and must be continually reviewed. New security policies may have to be created and implemented as the result of adding a wireless network.

- There are many sophisticated tools on the market to assist and produce comprehensive site survey reports. Although these reports can be created manually, site surveys can be very time consuming and cost a lot of money. Using the right tools for the job saves both time and money.

- An organization may send out a request for information (RFI). After evaluating the potential solutions suggested by vendor RFIs and independent research, the organization determines the costs of the project. The organization should balance the total cost of implementing a wireless network against the benefits that the project will provide. Determining the cost in relationship to the benefits is referred to as the return on investment (ROI).

- Once it has been determined that there is a real need that can be solved by implementing wireless technology, and if the ROI projection is positive, the next step is to create an implementation plan. Planning should include the IT staff, users, and consultants. Once a plan has been designed, the organization submits a request for proposal (RFP).

- After the RFPs have been received and the vendor has been selected, the company performs a limited trial or pilot project involving a range of users and circumstances. It is usually possible to borrow sample hardware and software from the vendor who won the bid. The IT staff should be thoroughly involved in the trial, along with a select group of users.

- Once the technology has been tested thoroughly, the next step is to begin training. Training provides users as well as support specialists with the knowledge to operate and support the new wireless technology effectively.

- As the training nears completion, the business rolls out the technology to all users in phases.

- After the training is completed, support continues as users' questions are answered. User-support functions can be carried out in a variety of ways, an internal help desk being one of the most effective ways.

Key Terms

help desk   A central point of contact for users who need assistance using technology.
recurring costs   Costs that continue to be paid over a period of time.

request for information (RFI) A document sent to a vendor to gain general information about a vendor's products or solutions to a problem.

request for proposal (RFP) A detailed planning document with precise specifications for the products and services.

return on investment (ROI) The profit or advantage of an action.

upfront costs Costs that are necessary to start a project.

wireless site survey The task of measuring the signal strength and quality in several locations around the office to determine how many APs will be required, how many and which channels will be used as well as what interference sources and security needs there are.

wireless VoIP phones The telephone handsets that connect to a WLAN's AP, permitting use of the WLAN for telephone calls.

Review Questions

1. Of the items below, which one is an important advantage of wireless technology?

   a. universal access to corporate data

   b. lower cost

   c. newer technology

   d. reduced bandwidth

2. A help desk can provide service to users by performing all of the following tasks except _____.

   a. having one telephone number

   b. creating a method to track problems effectively

   c. reporting users' questions to their supervisors

   d. using surveys to determine user satisfaction

3. Using VoWLAN instead of a traditional business telephone system means that the company has _____.

   a. 802.11a technology

   b. 802.11g technology

   c. cordless IP phones

   d. a VoIP router

4. If customers can see data about themselves on the business's computer system, it will enable them to _____.

   a. gain access to secret corporate data

   b. sell this data to other people

   c. reduce the amount of bandwidth needed for their home computers

   d. make better and more informed decisions

5. Which of the following is not an advantage to the IT department of adopting wireless technology?

 a. easier setup

 b. less time-consuming moves of equipment

 c. higher maintenance costs

 d. decreased cabling costs

6. When a business decides to deploy 802.11 wireless technology, it may face problems because _____.

 a. this new technology has not been thoroughly used and tested and is not a mature technology

 b. there is a shortage of qualified staff to deploy and support it

 c. managers are unfamiliar with it

 d. old technology is always easier to work with

7. All wireless technologies are clearly based on approved industry standards. True or False?

8. Wireless technology's greatest strength—that is, allowing access without being connected to the network by wires—is also its greatest weakness. True or False?

9. Using IP phones means that a business must contract to use a VoIP service provider. True or False?

10. "Do we really need it?" is a question that must be asked first when deciding whether to add a wireless infrastructure to a business. True or False?

11. When giving their input on whether to implement a wireless technology, users sometimes fall into the trap of viewing only their own departments or units instead of considering the entire organization. True or False?

12. The banking industry requires networks that have a _____ degree of security.

 a. moderate

 b. high

 c. low

 d. stable

13. Documenting the network in detail can help the task of _____.

 a. decommissioning the network

 b. satisfying the IT department

 c. calming management

 d. assessing the current network

14. A(n) _____ seeks to gain information about what vendors may have to offer.

 a. RFP

 b. TCO

 c. RFI

 d. ROI

15. A determination of a project's cost in relationship to its benefits is known as an _____.

    a. RFP

    b. ROI

    c. RFQ

    d. RFI

16. A _____ cost is one that continues to be paid over an extended period of time.

    a. maintenance

    b. recurring

    c. continuous

    d. spare

17. A _____ should be performed either by the company or by a vendor submitting a proposal for implementation of a WLAN.

    a. wireless site survey

    b. network assessment

    c. plan development

    d. user evaluation

18. Why is it a mistake to turn the entire planning process over to external consultants?

    a. Management will not be involved.

    b. The users will not be serviced properly.

    c. The network may never perform correctly.

    d. Users and the IT staff may not be involved, which might antagonize them.

19. A request for proposal (RFP) should include _____.

    a. a flexible calendar for deployment

    b. a detailed description of similar projects

    c. a description of the current network and applications

    d. an RFI

20. Which of the following will not be recorded in a wireless site survey?

    a. signal quality

    b. location of the data center

    c. suggested location of the AP

    d. recommended type of antenna to use

Hands-On Project

Project 12-1

In this project, you will perform a limited 802.11 site survey. It is assumed that you already know how to install software and configure both a laptop WLAN NIC and an AP to set up a basic WLAN. To complete the project, you will need the following:

- An existing WLAN at your school or an AP or Wireless Residential Gateway.

- A laptop computer equipped with a wireless NIC. You can perform the site survey either using 802.11b, 802.11g, or 802.11n technology at 2.4 GHz or using 802.11a or 802.11n technology at 5 GHz, depending on the equipment available.

- A floor plan or some type of tool for measuring distances. Depending on the size of the facility (this project covers only a single floor), you may use a long tape measure, a measuring wheel, or a laser-measuring device. If the floor is covered with linoleum tiles or carpet tiles, you can also measure the distances by the number of tiles. This will be used to create a drawing of the floor, in case one is not available.

- A copy of Ekahau HeatMapper. This is free software, although it requires you to register on the Web site. Ekahau HeatMapper is not capable of producing detailed reports. However, it will produce a graphic representation of the Wi-Fi signal coverage, and you can do a screen capture on your laptop to save the graph. (Go to *www.ekahau.com*, click **Products**, and then click **HeatMapper**.)

To complete this project:

1. Obtain a floor plan or create your own using the measurement tools. Keep it simple, but be sure to record the measurements you take of the surrounding rooms and hallways as well as the location of any metal cabinets or machinery, such as a photocopier or microwave oven.

2. Download and install **Ekahau HeatMapper**. On the main HeatMapper page, read the information on how to use the program. You will need a JPEG file of the floor plan to load it into HeatMapper. Start the program and, at the top-right of the splash screen, click **I have a map image on**.

3. In the Choose Image dialog box, select the file location of the floor plan, and then click **Choose Image**. HeatMapper will open with the floor map loaded and will quickly display on the left side of the window any information about nearby APs and Wireless Residential Gateways. Figure 12-4 shows a screen capture after the floor plan has loaded. Note that this is a floor plan of a small office, where a site survey would hardly be necessary. However, this office is located in a residential neighborhood and there are a lot of interfering networks around. Your floor plan and results will, of course, be very different.

12

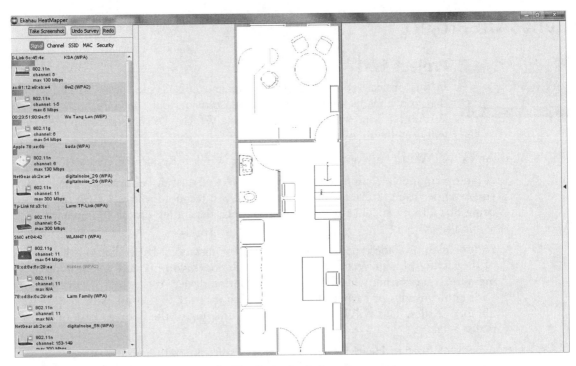

Figure 12-4 HeatMapper showing a small office floor plan before site survey

Source: HeatMapper

4. To begin your site survey, hover the mouse cursor over your current position on the floor plan and click the left mouse button. Then walk around the office and click the left mouse button every 2 to 3 meters at each location. Note that a dashed line extends from your last location to the new one and that a dot shows up at each location where the mouse was left-clicked.

5. When you finish the walk-around, click the right mouse button to display the heat map. You should be able to see all the APs and Wireless Residential Gateways that have been detected. Hover the mouse cursor above each of the APs or Wireless Residential Gateways in the graphic to see the heat map for each one. When you do this, you will also see a Help bubble showing the current signal strength detected at your current location. Do not close HeatMapper yet, as you may have to perform another site survey, depending on whether you are using an existing network or using an AP or Wireless Residential Gateway that you can move around in. Figure 12-5 shows an example of a completed site survey for the small office. The top area of the heat map appears in yellow, indicating a marginal but acceptable signal level. The bottom area appears in a lighter green because it is closer to the location of the AP in the basement. The small, darker area on the right, in the middle, appears in a darker green color, indicating a good signal closer to the opening for the stairs leading to the basement.

Note the APs and Wireless Residential Gateways that have been detected. HeatMapper does not allow you to move the icons for these devices. The full version of Ekahau's Site Survey software allows you to move the AP icons to their actual locations, whereas HeatMapper only guesses the locations of the radios.

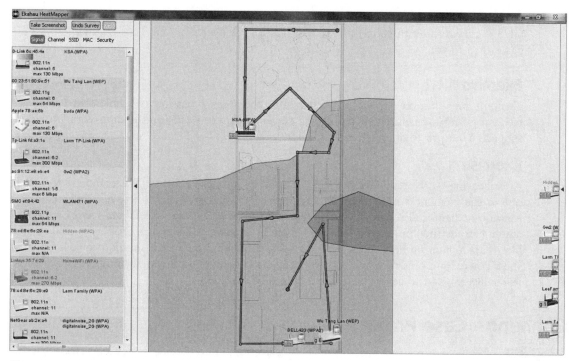

Figure 12-5 Completed HeatMapper site survey

Source: HeatMapper

6. Hover the mouse cursor over your AP or Residential Gateway and click the **Take Screenshot** button on the top-left corner of the HeatMapper window.

7. If you are using Windows 7 or Windows Vista, click the **Start** button on the taskbar, click **All Programs**, click **Accessories**, and click **Windows Paint** to open the application. In Windows Paint, click the **Paste** button to view a copy of your screen capture. If you wish, you can now save this image for later analysis and comparison.

8. After you have finished saving your file, go back to HeatMapper and click the **Undo Survey** button to clear the heat map.

9. Click the first tab on the top-left column of the Paint window, and then click **Save as**. Save the screen capture in JPEG format.

10. If you did not get the results you expected from your site survey and you are able to move the AP, do so and then redo the site survey starting with Step 4 on this project. You may also wish to compare your results with those of other students.

Real-World Exercises

The Baypoint Group (TBG) needs your help with a WLAN proposal. GHS is a chain of sporting good stores that specialize in the sport of soccer. Because GHS has grown in popularity, it now has nine stores in the area. GHS is considering implementing a wireless technology that will link all its stores through wireless broadband service. The chain would install a WLAN in each store and provide its employees with tablet computers for better customer service. GHS is unsure how to start this process. The company has asked TBG for help, and TBG has turned to you.

Exercise 12-1

Create a presentation for GHS that explains the steps necessary to implement a wireless technology infrastructure, beginning with evaluating the needs and ending with providing support. Your presentation should last 20 to 25 minutes. Use PowerPoint to create your slides.

Exercise 12-2

After hearing your presentation, GHS is ready to start the process. The company feels that one of the barriers it must overcome is providing support for its users. It does not have a centralized help desk; instead, employees help each other and the IT staff does a limited amount of instruction (just enough to get the user through his or her problem). GHS would like your opinion on how to set up a help desk and what services it should provide. Create a short PowerPoint presentation about what a help desk does, its advantages and disadvantages, its challenges, and some tips on using a help desk for GHS.

Challenge Case Project

Form a three-person team and, using the Internet, locate news articles and company press releases about each of the following wireless implementations: LAN, MAN, and WAN. Review the challenges that were encountered and some of the expected or resulting benefits of the project. If possible, contact the organizations or vendors and obtain additional information on the challenges and benefits. Your team should then write a one-page report for each implementation and present your analysis to the rest of the class. Allow at least 5 to 10 minutes for the class to ask questions at the end of your presentation and be prepared to answer questions about ROI, technical support, what process and criteria were used to select the vendor, and whether the entire project was handled by internal staff. Your team's report should also include your own conclusions about the project's benefits.

History of Wireless Communications

Studying the history of a topic does not always evoke thrills and excitement. In fact, the question "Who cares about the past?" is often asked when studying history is even mentioned. However, there are several benefits to studying the history of a technology such as wireless communications. First, our current technology wasn't discovered overnight, like stumbling upon a previously unknown island in the ocean. There are always several smaller steps that take place to lead up to the development of the new technology. Tracing the development of these earlier discoveries can help us better understand how the final technology actually functions. Being able to see how a technology was created piece-by-piece, just as the early inventors did, can help us see how each piece fits with the next development and to understand how the technology actually works.

Another advantage of studying the historical development of technology is that it reveals how the device was accepted and used by society. This shows what value society placed on that technology and is a good predictor of how it will be used in the future. In short, studying the past helps us understand where we are headed.

Finally, historical study helps us better appreciate the technology. Some of today's great technological marvels were the result of years of painstaking trial and effort by some of the great minds of earlier days. How they persevered as early trailblazers without knowing exactly where they would end up is a testimony to their character and helps us better appreciate what we have before us today.

Early Developments

The word *telegraphy* comes from a Greek word that means "writing in distance." Telegraphy is a system of communication that is able to transmit signals that represent coded letters and numbers or other signs of writing over long distances. Telegraphy can be divided in acoustic (sound), optical (sight), and electrical transmissions.

Acoustic telegraphy has very ancient origins. Greek historians tell how the Persian king Darius I in 500 BC could send news from the capital city to the outlying provinces of the empire by means of a line of shouting men positioned on hills. This kind of transmission was determined to be 30 times faster than normal couriers carrying the information. Julius Caesar in 50 BC said that the nation of the Gauls could call to war its entire army in only three days just by using the human voice.

Early optical telegraphy consisted of fire at night and smoke or reflections from shiny objects during the day to transmit signals. A device called a hydraulic telegraph was used by the Caraginese around 500 BC. It consisted of two large vases placed on distant hills. The vases were filled with water and had a floating vertical pole at the center with coded letters attached to it. Messages were sent by rising or lowering the pole (by emptying or adding water to the vases) to move the coded letter to a certain point.

An optical telegraph was developed by Claude Chappe in 1792. Coded signals were based on the different positions of three wooden interlinked arms that rotated at the top of a fixed vertical pole. The central arm (called a regulator) was longer than the other two arms (called indicators). The indicator arms could rotate freely around a center and be positioned at 45 degree angles. A book 92 pages long contained 92 different words on each page (for a total of almost 8,500 words). The arms of the optical telegraph were moved to indicate the page number and the word number of the particular word that was to be transmitted. The optical telegraph was officially adopted by the French government and several other European states.

The discovery of electrical current led to the introduction of electrical telegraphy in the early 1880s. Samuel Morse toured Italy in 1830 as a well-known painter. When he was sailing back to the United States, the concept of a telegraph based on *electromagnetism* came to him. Electromagnetism is a magnetic force created by a current of electricity. Morse's first telegraph-receiving instrument was constructed from a wooden clock motor that provided the power to move a paper tape under a pen. The pen was moved by an electromagnet that was driven from a telegraph line. A canvas stretcher from his painting supplies was used as a frame to support the device. Morse received a patent for his telegraph invention in 1838, the same year he completed his last two paintings. In 1844, Morse sent the famous words from the Bible, "What hath God wrought!" on his telegraph from the U.S. Capitol Building in Washington, DC, to Baltimore.

Morse tried without success to obtain European patents for his telegraph. In addition, he invented a code now known as the Morse code for use with his telegraph instrument.

James Maxwell, a Scottish physicist, was also very interested in electromagnetism. In 1861, he developed a mathematical model for a hypothetical medium that consisted of a fluid that could carry electric and magnetic effects. Maxwell theorized that if the fluid became elastic and a charge was applied to it, this would set up a disturbance in the fluid, which would produce waves that would travel through the medium. It was calculated that these waves would travel at the speed of light. Maxwell published his work in 1873.

In 1888, the German physicist Heinrich Hertz made the discovery of radio waves, which are a form of electromagnetic radiation. This confirmed Maxwell's theory. He devised a transmitter that radiated radio waves and then detected them across the length of his laboratory using a metal loop with a gap at one side. When the loop was placed within the transmitter's electromagnetic field, sparks were produced across the gap. This proved that electromagnetic waves could be sent out into space and could be remotely detected. Although people had seen the effects of radio waves before, nobody had realized what they were.

Radio waves were originally called "Hertzian waves."

Radio

Guglielmo Marconi was born in Bologna, Italy, in 1874. By age 21, he had already performed simple experiments that had convinced him it was possible to send signals by using electromagnetic waves. His first successes were at short distances, only about 330 feet (100 meters) between his house and the end of the garden.

Scientists and other experts at that time believed that electromagnetic waves could only be transmitted in a straight line, and then only if there was nothing in the way. They thought that the main obstacle to radio transmission was the curvature of the earth's surface. Marconi was convinced that transmission was possible between two distant points even if they were separated by an obstacle. He placed his transmitter near his house and the receiver almost 2 miles (3 kilometers) away, behind a hill. Overseeing the receiver was Marconi's servant, Mignani, who was holding a rifle. Mignani's responsibility was to fire a rifle shot when the signal was received. From his house, Marconi pushed the key of the transmitter three times and then heard the answer of a distant gunshot. His experiment proved that electromagnetic waves had traveled a distance and overcome an obstacle. With the completion of his experiment in 1895, Marconi had demonstrated that wireless telegraphy, also known as radio communications, was possible.

The word *radio* comes from the term *radiated energy*.

Marconi found little enthusiasm for his invention in Italy. He presented his device to the Italian government, only to be told by an Italian minister that it was "not suitable for telecommunications"! However, in England, where his mother was born, Marconi received support and financial backing and was able to patent his invention. In 1897, the British Ministry of Posts gave him money and technicians to continue his experiments, and the transmission distances gradually became longer, up to 60 miles (100 kilometers).

In 1901, Marconi set up a transmitting station in England, and a receiving station was built on the other side of the Atlantic Ocean on the island of Newfoundland. For three hours every day, a signal was transmitted while Marconi experimented with newer and larger types of antennas suspended from light kites. On December 12, 1901, a signal was received at Newfoundland. For the first time, electromagnetic waves had crossed the Atlantic Ocean, traveling a distance of 2,175 miles (3,500 kilometers). Although Marconi did not know it at the time, the success of his experiment was due to the presence of the *ionosphere*. The ionosphere, a layer of the upper atmosphere (between 40 and 310 miles, or 60 and 500 kilometers), plays a fundamental role in all radio communications. The ionosphere reflects electromagnetic waves like a mirror and allows a radio signal to travel far distances.

The ionosphere was discovered by an English physicist in 1924.

Marconi quickly put his work on wireless telegraphy to practical use. In 1899, for the first time, a distress signal was sent from a shipwrecked boat to a station on land using wireless telegraphy, enabling the passengers to be rescued. Marconi also visited the United States and helped the U.S. Navy set up communications between its cruisers. In 1903, while sailing from England to the U.S., Marconi established the first press agency. News information was flashed to the ship via wireless transmissions. This information was then printed on board the ship as part of a newspaper.

Marconi continued to refine his wireless telegraphy devices. In 1904, he built a rotating device that led to the development of horizontal antennas, which permitted a tremendous increase in the strength of received signals. He later patented this device. In 1934, he demonstrated how a ship, lost in fog, could safely find the entrance of a harbor using wireless signals. In 1935, he performed distant-search experiments that would eventually lead to the invention of radar.

Marconi also studied microwaves, early television technology, and started research on the therapeutic use of radio waves, called Marconitherapy.

Marconi died in Rome in 1937. To remember his great contribution to wireless telegraphy, radios all around the world observed a minute of silence.

In 1909, Marconi was awarded the Nobel Prize for Physics.

Television

The idea of transmitting pictures and sound over distance occupied the minds of dreamers for centuries. Yet unlike radio, television was not created by one individual at one specific point in time. Instead, television evolved over a period of 50 years, based on the discoveries and efforts of many scientists and visionaries.

The basic process of television involves transmitting images by converting light to electrical signals. This is known as *photoelectric technology*. Early attempts to send still images down a telegraph wire, in the mid 1800s, were based on *electrochemical technology*. In 1842, Alexander Bain proposed a facsimile telegraph transmission system based on electrochemical technology. Bain proposed that metallic letters of the alphabet could be transmitted chemically. Electrified metal letters could be scanned by a pendulum device and reproduced at the other end of the telegraph wire by a synchronized pendulum contacting a piece of chemical paper.

Historians normally associate Bain's ideas with the modern day facsimile (fax) machine.

Bain's proposal was improved upon in 1847 when F. Bakewell of Great Britain patented a chemical telegraph. Bakewell replaced the pendulums with synchronized rotating cylinders. By 1861, handwritten messages and photographs could be sent over telegraph lines.

In 1873, Louis May, a British telegrapher, discovered the basics of photoconductivity. He found that selenium bars, when exposed to light, were a strong conductor of electricity. He also found that the conduction of electrical current would vary depending on the amount of light hitting the bars. A later discovery revealed that changes in electrical voltage produced by selenium when scanning a document could magnetically control a pencil at the receiving end of the transmission. By 1881, Shelford Bidwell successfully transmitted silhouettes using both selenium and a scanning system. He called the device the scanning phototelegraph.

The first working device for analyzing a scene to generate electrical signals suitable for transmission was a scanning system proposed and built by Paul Nipkow in 1884. The scanner consisted of a rotating disc with a number of small holes (*apertures*) arranged in a spiral in front of light-sensitive selenium. As the disc rotated, the spiral of 18 holes swept across the image of the scene from top to bottom in a pattern of 18 parallel horizontal lines. This had the effect of dividing the picture into 18 lines of dots or picture elements (*pixels*). For reproduction of the scene, a light source, controlled in intensity by the detected electrical signal, was projected on a screen through a similar Nipkow disc that rotated in synch with the pickup disc.

The Nipkow disc device was capable of transmitting about 4,000 pixels per second.

This was known as the world's first electromechanical television system. However, Nipkow could not build a reliable working system because he was unable to amplify the electric current created by the selenium to drive a receiver. Nevertheless, Nipkow demonstrated a scanning process for the analysis of images by dissecting a complete scene into an orderly pattern of pixels that could be transmitted by an electrical signal and reproduced as a visual image. This became the basis for present-day television.

With improvements in technology, mechanical television later became practical. In 1928, television signals were being sent from London to New York. By 1932, the first home mechanical television sets were available, and over 10,000 sets were sold. These first sets delivered a crude picture consisting of a cloudy 40-line image (compared to 525 lines on today's televisions) on a 6-inch-square mirror. The sets cost between $85 and $135.

North America's first television station, W3XK in Wheaton, Maryland, was started in the 1930s.

Most historians credit Vladimir Zworykin as the "father of television." A Russian immigrant, Zworykin came to the United States after World War I and went to work for Westinghouse. From 1920 until 1929, Zworykin performed some of his early experiments in television. He developed the first practical TV camera tube, known as the *iconoscope*, in 1923. Zworkin's iconoscope (from the Greek for "image" and "to see") consisted of a thin film coated with a photosensitive layer of potassium hydride. His kinescope picture tube formed the basis for subsequent advances in the field. With this crude camera tube and a kinescope as the picture reproducer, Zworkin had the essential elements for electronic television. By 1931, with the iconoscope and kinescope well developed, electronic television was ready to be launched.

A lesser-known early electronic television pioneer was Philo Farnsworth. At age 19, Farnsworth persuaded an investor to fund an all-electronic television system. Farnsworth established his laboratory first in Los Angeles and later in San Francisco. It was in San Francisco, in 1927, that Farnsworth gave the first public demonstration of the television system he had dreamed of for six years. He was not yet 21 years old. Farnsworth was quick to develop several of the basic concepts of an electronic television system and was granted many patents.

By 1939, widespread commercial electronic television broadcasting began in the United States when the National Broadcasting Company (NBC) started regularly scheduled broadcasts in the New York area to only 400 sets. In 1941, the American Federal Communications Authority set the standards for broadcast television. With the start of World War II, however, television production stopped in the United States.

At the end of the war, there was a two-year delay in the development of television as the Federal Communications Authority considered proposals for color television systems. In 1947, all proposals for color television were rejected. Black and white sets, however, were manufactured in large quantities. In 1946, there were only 7,000 televisions in the United States By 1950, there were over 10 million sets.

It took until 1954 for the National Television System Committee (NTSC) to set the standard for color broadcast television. It settled on a system that was compatible with existing black and white TV sets. Color was achieved by inserting the color information inside the black and white signal. The color standard specified 625 lines at 25 frames per second.

By 1970, television had become the primary information and entertainment medium in the world. Today it is estimated that there are 605 million television sets worldwide. However, the standards for television broadcasting are not universal. There are 15 different variations of broadcasting standards used around the world.

Radar

Radar has been hailed as one of the greatest scientific developments of the first half of the 20th century. Although radar is usually associated with detecting airplanes in the sky or ships on the ocean, it actually is used in a variety of different ways. Some of these include:

- Radar is used extensively in weather forecasting and to provide early warning for severe weather. A radar system known as NEXRAD (NEXt Generation Weather

RADar) can gauge the size, intensity, wind speed, and direction of storms, the amount of water vapor in clouds, and can detect high-level circular wind patterns that cause tornadoes.

- Radar is used to help archaeologists excavate ancient sites. Radar can be used from space satellites and airplanes to scan entire regions for possible archaeological sites. The radar waves can penetrate earth, sand, and volcanic ash that cover ancient sites. When the waves strike rock or metal, the echo is reflected back. This helps archeologists determine the best location to dig.

- Radar helps engineers study highway tunnels for potential hidden dangers. Radar can be mounted on a truck and driven through a tunnel that is built under a body of water. Radar can quickly and accurately scan the tunnel for any leaks.

- Located on a space shuttle, radar can be used to locate stagnant pools of water in areas of dense foliage on earth. With this information, the stagnant water, which can harbor insects carrying disease, can be located and drained.

- Radar has also helped provide information about the universe. It is used to locate comets, map stars, and probe planets that cannot be seen with a regular telescope.

"Radar" is an acronym for *RAdio Detection And Ranging*.

Radar is an active remote sensing system that operates on the principle of echoes. When a person in a room yells out, her voice is sent out as sound waves and is reflected back by the walls to the ears of the listener. Instead of sound waves, radars use radio waves because radio waves travel faster, further, and are reflected better than sound waves. Radio waves travel at the speed of light (186,000 miles or 300,000 kilometers per second).

Radar performs three primary functions:

- It transmits microwave signals (called the *pulse*) toward a target.

- After reaching an object, it is reflected back, and the radar receives a return portion of the transmitted signal (called the *backscatter*), as seen in Figure A-1.

- It observes the strength, behavior, and the time delay of the returned signals and produces a "blip" on a screen, as seen in Figure A-2.

A radar display shows a map-like picture of the area being scanned. The center of the picture responds to the radar antenna, and the radar echoes are shown as bright spots on the screen. The distance of the spot from the center of the screen indicates how far away the object is.

The "blips" produced on a screen will vary depending upon the object reflecting the waves. Sophisticated radar can identify not only an airplane in the sky but also its type, manufacturer, and whether it is friend or foe.

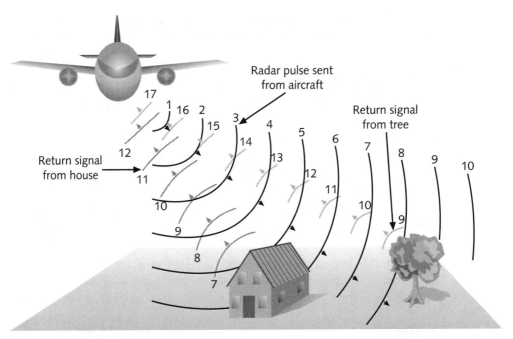

Figure A-1 Radar pulse and backscatter

© Cengage Learning 2014

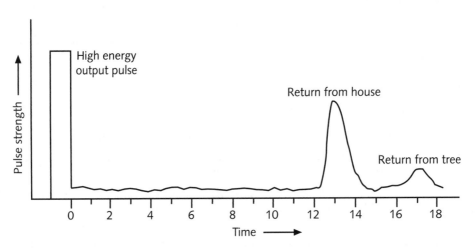

Figure A-2 Radar blips

© Cengage Learning 2014

A special type of radar known as Doppler radar is frequently used today by meteorologists to locate tornados and microbursts, which are downdrafts of air traveling at very high speeds. Doppler radar takes advantage of the *Doppler Effect*. The Doppler Effect is when the frequency of an electromagnetic wave is changed as the wave hits a moving object. Unlike regular radar, Doppler radar sends out waves at multiple sets of frequencies. Upon striking the target, the wave is reflected back at a different frequency than the transmitted wave. The radar compares the frequency of the returned echo with that of the transmitted wave. When the difference is calculated, the speed of the object, which caused the shift in frequency, can be calculated. Wind patterns are shown on the radar display in different colors. The faster a wind is moving, the brighter its color.

Doppler radar is also used by law enforcement agencies to locate speeding motorists. Most police radar guns have a split-screen display window, which shows both the speed of the target and the speed of the patrol vehicle.

The development of radar dates back to the discoveries of the 1860s and 1870s, when James Maxwell developed the equations that outlined the behavior of electromagnetic waves and Heinrich Hertz discovered radio waves. Several years later, a German engineer named Christian Huelsmeyer proposed the use of radio echoes to avoid collisions in marine navigation. The first successful radio range-finding experiment occurred in 1924, when the British scientist Edward Appleton used radio echoes to determine the height of the ionosphere.

The first practical radar system was produced in 1935 by the British physicist Robert Watson-Watt. By 1939, England had established a chain of radar stations along its southern and eastern coasts to detect aggressors in the air or on the sea. About the same time, two British scientists were responsible for the most important advance made in the technology of radar during World War II. Henry Boot and John Randall invented an electron tube that was capable of generating high-frequency radio pulses with large amounts of power.

Satellites

A *satellite* is any object that orbits or revolves around another object. For example, the moon is a satellite of the earth, and the earth is a satellite of the sun. Man-made satellites provide communications capabilities around the world, transmitting television signals, telephone calls, faxes, computer communications, and weather information. Satellites can be sent into space through a variety of launch vehicles.

The theory of satellites dates back to 325 years before the first man-made satellite was ever launched. In the 1720s, Sir Isaac Newton was probably the first person to conceive the idea of a satellite. Newton illustrated how an artificial satellite could be launched from the earth. He pictured the earth with a high mountain and a cannon on top of the mountain firing shots parallel to the ground. Each time the cannon was fired, more gunpowder was used and the shot went farther before striking the ground. Because the earth is round, the shots would curve around it. According to Newton's theory, with enough gunpowder, a shot could eventually go fast enough to circle the earth completely and come back to the mountaintop.

During the Second World War, the German military made great strides in the development of rocket technology. However, even the best rocket technology of that day could not achieve an earth orbit. In 1945, Arthur C. Clarke, a science fiction author, wrote an article that envisioned a network of communications satellites. Three satellites could be placed into space at 22,000 miles (35,400 kilometers) so as to orbit the planet every 24 hours. These satellites would be able to transmit signals around the world by transmitting in a "line of sight" with other orbiting satellites. At the time of Clarke's writing, the idea was not well received.

Satellites of today that follow this same orbit are said to reside in the "Clarke Belt."

The economic feasibility of satellites in the early days was hotly debated. At a cost of over one billion dollars for a satellite, there were serious questions regarding its return on investment.

On October 4, 1957, the Soviet Union launched Sputnik 1. Sputnik 1 was described as "a radio transmitter in a 23-inch polished aluminum ball." Sputnik was equipped with transmitters to broadcast on two different frequencies, and it circled the globe every 90 minutes. After 18 days, its battery was exhausted and the transmitting ceased; and almost three months later, Sputnik 1 was incinerated as it fell from orbit back into earth's atmosphere. A month after Sputnik 1, the Soviets launched Sputnik 2 and its passenger, Laika, a dog who has the distinction of being the first living creature to enter outer space.

The United States followed with its own launch of Explorer 1 in early 1958. The first communications satellite was launched later that same year. The Signal Communication by Orbital Relay (SCORE) satellite broadcasted a Christmas message from President Dwight Eisenhower of "Peace on earth, good will toward men" as the satellite orbited the earth for 12 days until its batteries failed. A succession of Soviet and American launches resulted in larger and more sophisticated satellites reaching orbit. In 1961, Yuri Gegarin became the first man in orbit.

The United States and Soviet Union launched six satellites in 1958, 14 in 1959, 19 in 1960, and 35 in 1961. In 1962, the United Kingdom and Canada launched satellites of their own, along with the 70 satellites launched by the United States and Soviet Union.

After the initial launches, the benefits and prestige associated with satellite communications made satellites a popular item. The National Aeronautic and Space Administration (NASA) confined itself to experiments with "mirrors" or passive communications satellites while the U.S. Department of Defense was responsible for "repeater" or active satellites, which amplified the received signal at the satellite and provided a much higher quality of communications. In 1960, NASA launched Echo 1, a passive reflector satellite with no amplification possibilities. The Echo satellites were basically large metallicized balloons that served as passive reflectors of radio signals. At the time of its launch, it was thought that passive reflector satellites could serve a purpose in communications, but the technology was soon abandoned because the reflected signal was so weak.

In 1960, the American Telephone and Telegraph Company (AT&T) filed a request with the Federal Communications Commission (FCC) for permission to launch an experimental communications satellite. The U.S. government reacted with surprise because there had never been such a request and there was no policy in place to regulate satellites. AT&T designed, built, and even paid for the launches with its own funds, reimbursing NASA for its use of the rockets. The Telstar I and II spacecraft were prototypes for a constellation of 50 medium earth orbit (MEO) satellites that AT&T was working to put in place. Telstar was the first modern communications satellite to be placed in orbit. However, when the U.S. government later decided to give the monopoly on satellite communications to a consortium, AT&T's satellite project was halted.

The first words transmitted over satellite were not as memorable as Alexander Bell's "Watson, come here I need you!" or Samuel Morse's "What hath God wrought?" The first transmitted words were "Will everybody please get off this line?" So many people were trying to be the first to hear the transmission that the circuit was being overloaded!

In 1964, an international organization known as INTELSAT (INternational TELecommunications SATellite Organization) was formed. A consortium of over 130 governments and organizations. Intelsat launched a series of satellites with the goal of providing total earth coverage (excluding the North and South Poles) by satellite transmission. This was achieved by 1969. Today, Intelsat has 19 satellites in orbit that are open to use by all nations. Intelsat owns the satellites, but each nation owns its own earth receiving stations.

INTELSAT completed its global coverage just days before the first men walked on the moon in 1969, enabling one half billion people around the world to watch the landmark event.

NASA led the next wave of communications satellite technology with the launch of Advanced Communications Technology Satellites (ACTS) in 1993. ACTS pioneered the use of several new developments, such as on-board storage and processing and all-digital transmission, which make satellite transmission more reliable.

The explosive popularity of cellular telephones advanced the idea of always being connected, no matter where you were located on earth. Several companies committed themselves to providing a solution by using satellites in low earth orbit (LEO). The most ambitious of these companies was Iridium, sponsored by Motorola. Iridium planned to launch 66 satellites into polar orbit at altitudes of about 400 miles (650 kilometers). Iridium's goal was to provide communications services to hand-held telephones around the world in 1998. However, Iridium declared bankruptcy in 1999. The total cost of the Iridium system was in excess of three billion dollars.

Iridium originally planned to have 77 satellites and thus was named after the 77th element in the periodic charts. However, when the plans were scaled back to only 66 satellites, the name Iridium continued to be used because Element 66 has the less pleasant name Dysprosium.

Cellular Telephones

In the 1930s and 1940s, two-way car radios were installed and used by police, utility companies, government agencies, and emergency services. However, these two-way car radios had several disadvantages and were not very convenient to use. In 1946, in St. Louis, AT&T and Southwestern Bell introduced the first American commercial mobile radio-telephone service to private customers. "Mobiles," as they were called, used the newly issued vehicle radio-telephone licenses granted to Southwestern Bell by the FCC. They operated on six channels. However, interference soon forced Bell to use only three channels.

In a rare exception to the Bell System common practice, subscribers to this first system could actually buy their own radio sets and not use AT&T's equipment.

With two-way car radios, a central transmitter with one antenna could serve a wide area. This is illustrated in Figure A-3. However, this system could not be used with mobiles. The reason is that car-mounted transmitters were not as powerful as the central antenna, and thus their signals could not always be transmitted all the way back. To overcome this limitation, smaller receivers with antennas were placed on the tops of buildings and on poles around the city, creating smaller *cells*, or ranges of service areas. When people were using their mobiles, the conversations, that they heard were transmitted on one frequency by the central transmitter to their moving cars. When they spoke on their mobiles, however, that transmission was sent on a separate frequency that the nearest receiver antenna picked up. In other words, messages were received on one frequency from the central transmitter but messages were sent to the nearest receiver on a separate frequency. When the car moved from one cell to another that was served by a different receiver, the switch between cells was known as a *handoff*. This is illustrated in Figure A-4.

As innovative as mobiles were, there were still several serious limitations. The first limitation was a lack of available frequencies. Mobiles required two frequencies to make a transmission, one frequency to transmit on and one to receive. A single radio-telephone call took up as much frequency space as a radio broadcast station. In the late 1940s, there was very little unused transmission space available. And because the FCC gave priority to emergency services, government agencies, utility companies, and services it thought helped the most people, this left only a tiny amount of frequencies available for mobiles. Most mobile telephone systems could not accommodate more than a total of 250 users, with only a handful actually being able to transmit at one time.

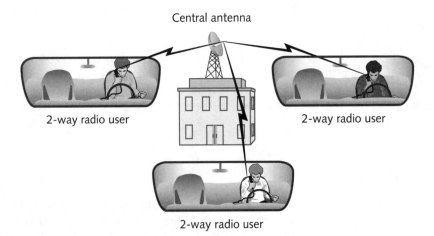

Figure A-3 2-way car radio

© Cengage Learning 2014

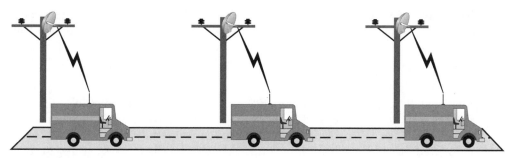

Figure A-4 Mobiles using cells

© *Cengage Learning 2014*

At this time, the technology for the mobiles was not refined, and they actually required six times the amount of frequency that would be needed today.

The second limitation was that waves at lower frequencies travel great distances (sometimes hundreds of miles) when they skip across the atmosphere. Although high-powered transmitters gave mobiles a wide operating range, the signals could also be detected in adjacent cities. Telephone companies could not reuse their channels in nearby cities due to this potential interference; they required at least 75 miles between mobile systems.

Despite the limitations, mobile service was highly desired. Every city that offered mobiles had lengthy waiting lists. By 1976, only 545 customers in New York City had Bell System mobiles but 3,700 customers were on the waiting list. Some individuals were on waiting lists for up to 10 years. Although allocating more frequency would have solved the problem, the FCC did not do so. Even as late as 1978, all mobile carriers nationwide had just 54 channels.

The first modern cellular telephone systems, in the early 1980s, used 666 channels.

Although mobiles had limitations and were used by very few people, they nevertheless launched the basic concept of cellular phones. Designers realized that by using small cells they could use lower-powered transmitters. They also determined that if they could have each cell use a different frequency, then by reusing these frequencies they could substantially increase the traffic capacity of mobile phones. At that time, however, the technology to do so did not exist. Nevertheless, the concepts of using cells and of frequency reuse laid the foundation for cellular telephones 50 years later.

In 1969, the Bell System developed a commercial cellular radio operation using frequency reuse. The unusual setting for this venture was on trains running from New York City to Washington, DC, using pay telephones. Passengers could make telephone calls onboard while the trains were moving at 100 miles an hour. Six channels were reused in nine zones along the 225-mile route. A computerized control center in Philadelphia managed the system. Thus the first cellular phone was a pay phone.

In July of 1978, AT&T and Illinois Bell started a pilot project in Chicago of analog-based cellular telephone service. Ten cells covering 21,000 square miles made up the Chicago system. This first equipment test began using 90 Bell System employees, and after six months it was opened to the general public. This early cellular telephone proved that a large cellular system could work.

Advanced Mobile Phone Service (AMPS) began setting up analog cellular telephone operations in other parts of the world. An 88-cell system in Tokyo began in December 1979, and a system in Mexico City with one cell started in August 1981. Europe saw cellular service introduced in 1981, when the Nordic Mobile Telephone System began operating in Denmark, Sweden, Finland, and Norway. This was the first multinational cellular system.

Initially U.S. cellular telephone development did not keep up with the rest of the world. The most significant reason was the breakup of the Bell System by the U.S. federal court system and the FCC's 1981 regulations that required the Bell System or a regional operating company, such as Bell Atlantic, to have competition in every cellular market. However, the popularity of cellular soon began to spread across the nation, along with the development of an analog cellular infrastructure.

Roaming from one city or state in the United States was easy because the U.S. system was based on an analog cellular system. In contrast, it was almost impossible to roam in Europe. During the 1980s, a plan was launched to create a single Europe-wide digital mobile service with advanced features and easy roaming. This network started operating in 1991. In the United States, there was no such movement because the analog system was working well.

Today cellular telephone deployment is worldwide, but development remains concentrated in three areas: Scandinavia, the United States, and Japan. As of this writing, there are approximately 6 billion cellular phone subscriptions worldwide, creating about $1 trillion in annual revenues.

Glossary

1/3 rate Forward Error Correction (FEC) An error correction scheme that repeats each bit three times for redundancy.

1-bit tags RFID devices that do not include a chip or memory and cannot store an EPC; they are only used to activate an alarm at retail store entrances as a means of preventing theft.

2.5 Generation (2.5G) An interim technology stage between 2G and 3G digital cellular networks in which data is transmitted using packet-switched technology.

2/3 rate Forward Error Correction (FEC) An error correction scheme that uses a mathematical formula to add extra error correction bits to the data sent.

3G (third generation) A digital cellular technology that can send data at up to 21 Mbps over the cellular telephone network.

3rd Generation Partnership Project (3GPP) A group of six standards organizations from Asia, Europe, and North America that proposed standards for GSM, GPRS/EDGE, HSDPA, HSPA+, and LTE.

4G (fourth generation) A digital cellular technology that can transmit and receive data at theoretical speeds up to 20 Mbps when users are moving fast and up to 150 Mbps (theoretically) when users are moving slowly or are stationary.

6LoWPAN The protocol that implements IPv6 on WPANs. Also the name of an IETF working group that defines how the Internet protocols—IPv6, in particular—are applied to the smallest devices so that they can participate in the "Internet of Things."

802.11 standard An IEEE standard released in 1997 that defines wireless local area networks at a rate of either 1 Mbps or 2 Mbps. All WLAN features are confined to the PHY and MAC layers.

8-DPSK A simple method of phase shift keying that uses eight degrees of phase to encode tribits. This method of modulation is very sensitive to co-channel and inter-symbol interference.

8-PSK A modulation technique in which the phase of the carrier is shifted in 45-degree increments and 4 bits can be transmitted per phase change.

A

access control list (ACL) A list of addresses of other devices from which the device that maintains the list expects to receive frames.

access point (AP or wireless AP) A device that receives the signals and transmits signals back to wireless network interface cards (NICs).

acknowledgment (ACK) A procedure used to reduce collisions by requiring the receiving station to send an explicit packet back to the sending station, provided that the received transmission had no errors.

active antenna A passive antenna with an amplifier built-in.

active mode A state in which the Bluetooth device actively participates on the channel.

active scanning The process of sending frames to gather information.

active tags RFID tags that include a battery.

ad hoc mode A WLAN mode in which wireless clients communicate directly among themselves without going through an AP.

adaptive array processing A radio transmission technique that replaces a traditional antenna with an array of antenna elements.

adaptive frequency hopping (AFH) A feature added by Bluetooth version 1.2 that further improves compatibility with 802.11b by allowing the master in a piconet to change the hopping sequence so that it will not use the frequency channel occupied by 802.11b in the piconet area.

adjacent channel interference When signals from two adjacent channels interfere with each other.

advanced antenna system (AAS) An antenna that can transmit multiple simultaneous signals in different directions to stations that fall within the range of each of the antennas.

Advanced Encryption Standard (AES) The latest encryption standard, developed by the National Institute of Standards and Technology (NIST) to replace the Data Encryption Standard. *See* Data Encryption Standard.

Advanced Mobile Phone Service (AMPS) The standard used for 1G analog cellular transmissions, based on FDMA. 1G is often simply called AMPS.

alternate MAC/PHY (AMP) A feature added in version 3 of the Bluetooth specification that makes it possible for Bluetooth radio manufacturers to add a second radio that uses 802.11 to transmit data at speeds of up to 24 Mbps. Compatible Bluetooth devices use FHSS to establish communications with each other and exchange commands and control information, while using the secondary radio for data transfers only.

American National Standards Institute (ANSI) A clearinghouse for standards development in the United States.

American Standard Code for Information Interchange (ASCII) An arbitrary coding scheme that uses the numbers from 0 to 255.

amplifier A component that increases a signal's intensity.

amplitude The height of a carrier wave.

amplitude modulation (AM) A technique that changes the height of a carrier wave in response to a change in the height of the input signal.

amplitude shift keying (ASK) A digital modulation technique whereby a 1 bit is represented by the existence of a carrier signal, whereas a 0 bit is represented by the absence of a carrier signal.

analog modulation A method of encoding an analog signal onto a carrier wave.

analog signal A signal in which the intensity (amplitude or voltage) varies continuously and smoothly over a period of time.

antenna A copper wire, rod, or similar device that has one end up in the air and the other end connected to the ground through a receiver.

antenna diversity A technique that uses two antennas to improve the range of 802.11 and transmits a signal through the antenna that received the strongest signal during the last transmission.

antenna pattern A graphic that shows how a signal radiates out of an antenna.

antenna polarization An indication of the horizontal or vertical orientation of the sine waves leaving an antenna.

associate request frame A frame sent by a client to an AP that contains the client's capabilities and supported rates.

associate response frame A frame returned to a client from the AP that contains a status code and client ID number.

association The process for a device to join a wireless network. In 802.11, association is the process for a client device to join a BSS. *See also* Basic Service Set.

asynchronous connectionless (ACL) link A packet-switched link that is used for data transmissions.

attenuation A loss of signal strength.

authentication A process that verifies that the client device has permission to access the network. In Bluetooth, authentication is the process that verifies that the device asking to join the piconet should be allowed to join.

automatic retransmission request (ARQ) An error-correction scheme that continuously retransmits until an acknowledgment is received or a timeout value is exceeded.

B

backhaul A company's internal infrastructure connection.

backscatter The type of modulation used by passive RFID tags, backscatter is a reflection of radiation in which the tag reflects the signal sent by an interrogator while modulating it with the data to be transmitted.

bandpass filter A filter that passes all signals that are between the maximum and minimum threshold.

bands Sections of the radio frequency spectrum.

bandwidth The range of frequencies that can be transmitted.

Barker code (chipping code) A bit pattern used in a DSSS transmission. The term "chipping code" is used because a single radio bit is commonly referred to as a "chip."

base station (BS) The transmitter connected to the carrier network or to the Internet.

baseband A transmission technique that treats the entire transmission medium as only one channel.

Basic Service Set (BSS) A WLAN mode that consists of at least one wireless client and one AP.

baud A change in a carrier signal.

baud rate The number of times that a carrier signal changes per second.

beacon A frame that signals the beginning of a superframe and contains information about the type and number of time slots contained in the superframe.

beacons The name given to RFID tags that are battery powered and transmit on a periodic basis.

beamforming A technique that enables the transmitting device to use multiple radios and multiple antennas to maximize the signal amplitude at the receiver location.

binary phase shift keying (BPSK) A simple digital modulation technique that uses four phase changes to represent two bits per signal change.

binding The process of establishing a relationship between endpoints in a ZigBee network.

biphase modulation Modulation that uses a half-cycle positive analog pulse to represent a 1 and a half-cycle negative analog pulse to represent a 0.

bit A binary digit; an electronic 0 or a 1 based on the binary number system.

bits per second (bps) The number of bits that can be transmitted per second.

blocker tag A type of Class 1 passive tag that can be used to disable unauthorized readers from accessing the information from a selective group of tags by sending so many responses that a reader cannot differentiate between the blocker tag and a legitimate tag.

Bluetooth A wireless standard that enables devices to transmit data at up to 721.2 Kbps over a typical maximum distance of 33 feet. Bluetooth can transmit data farther, but devices that can use this capability are rare.

Bluetooth radio module A single radio transmitter/receiver (transceiver) that performs all the necessary transmission functions.

broadband A transmission technique that sends multiple signals at different frequencies.

BSSID In an infrastructure WLAN, the BSSID is the MAC address of the AP. In a peer-to-peer network, the BSSID is the MAC address of the first station to be turned on and configured to establish the ad hoc WLAN.

buffering The process that the AP uses to temporarily store frames for clients that are in sleep mode.

burst A transmission containing data to or from a single SS or a broadcast transmission from the BS.

burst profiles A profile negotiated between the BS and the SSs that specifies the number of time slots allocated to the SSs to maintain QoS.

byte Eight binary digits (bits).

C

cable modem A technology used to transmit data over a television cable connection.

carrier sense multiple access with collision avoidance (CSMA/CA) A device-access mechanism in which, before transmitting, a device must listen to the medium to determine if the channel is free.

carrier signal A signal of a particular frequency that is modulated to contain either analog or digital data.

carriers Telephone, cable TV, and other communication providers that own the wires and transmission towers that carry voice, video, and data traffic.

CDMA2000 1xEVDO The 3G digital cellular technology that is a migration from CDMA2000 1xRTT.

CDMA2000 1xEVDV The 3G digital cellular technology that is a migration from CDMA2000 1xEVDO.

CDMA2000 1xRTT The 2.5G digital cellular network technology that is a migration from CDMA. ("1xRTT" stands for "1-times radio transmission technology.")

cell The coverage section of one transmission tower in a mobile network.

certificate authority An organization that supplies security keys and authenticates users.

challenge-response strategy A process used to check if the other device knows a shared identical secret key.

channel The frequency or range of frequencies used by a particular technology to transmit and receive data.

In Bluetooth, a channel consists of all the frequencies in a hop sequence.

channel access methods The different ways of sharing resources in a network environment.

channel time allocation (CTA) Periods of time allocated by the PNC to a specific device for prioritizing communications in a WPAN. *See also* management channel time allocation (MCTA).

channel time allocation period (CTAP) The component of a superframe used for communications between the PNC and other devices.

child piconets Separate piconets with their own IDs; the child PNC is a member of the original or parent piconet.

chipless tags RFID devices that use embedded fibers to reflect a portion of the RF waves emitted by a reader; the reflected portion of the RF waves is unique and can be used as an identifier.

circuit switching A switching technique in which a dedicated and direct physical connection is made between two transmitting devices—for example, between two telephones during a call.

co-channel interference Interference between two devices configured to use the same frequency channel.

Code Division Multiple Access (CDMA) A technique that uses spread spectrum technology and unique digital codes to send and receive radio transmissions.

collision The scrambling of data that occurs when two computers start sending messages at the same time in a shared medium.

compact HTML (cHTML) A subset of HTML designed for mobile devices.

Complementary Code Keying (CCK) A table containing 64 8-bit code words used for transmitting at speeds above 2 Mbps. This table of codes is used instead of the process of adding a Barker code to the bit to be transmitted.

consortia Industry-sponsored organizations that have the goal of promoting a specific technology.

constellation diagram A graphical representation that makes it easier to visualize signals using complex modulation techniques such as QAM. It is generally used in laboratory and field diagnostic instruments and analyzers to aid in design and troubleshooting of wireless communications devices.

contention access period (CAP) A mechanism used to communicate commands or any asynchronous data that may be present in a superframe. The CAP is also used to allow devices that are not yet part of a piconet to send a request to the PNC to join the piconet.

continuous wave (CW) An analog or sine wave that is modulated to eventually carry information, becoming a carrier wave. The term is also used in RFID to describe the continuous wave sent by a reader to power the passive tags so they can transmit a response to the reader.

control channel A special frequency that cellular phones use for communication with a base station.

control frames MAC frames that assist in delivering the frames that contain data.

coupling A connection between a reader and a tag.

crosstalk Signals from close frequencies that may interfere with other signals.

CTS-to-self Short for "clear-to-send-to-self," a coordination method used by 802.11g devices that prevents 802.11 and 802.11b devices that do not "understand" OFDM from attempting to initiate a transmission while the 802.11g device is transmitting data.

customer premises equipment (CPE) The WiMAX devices that are installed in a customer's office or home.

cycle An oscillating sine wave that completes one full series of movements.

cyclic redundancy check (CRC) A common technique for detecting data transmission errors.

D

Data Encryption Standard (DES) The encryption standard used in the United States until the adoption of AES. *See* Advanced Encryption Standard.

data frames MAC frames that carry the user information to be transmitted to a device.

data link layer The layer responsible for the transfer of data between nodes in the same network segment; it also provides for error detection.

dB dipole (dBd) The relative measurement of the gain of an antenna when compared to a dipole antenna.

dB isotropic (dBi) The relative measurement of the gain of an antenna when compared to a theoretical isotropic radiator.

dBm A relative way to indicate an absolute power level in the linear watt scale.

DCF Interframe Space (DIFS) The standard interval between the transmission of data frames.

de facto standards Common practices that the industry follows for various reasons.

de jure standards Standards that are controlled by an organization or body.

decibel (dB) A ratio between two signal levels.

decimal number system A numbering system that has a base number of 10 and uses the digits 0–9.

denial-of-service (DoS) A type of security attack on a networked device in which the attacker sends so many frames to a single device that the device is unable to communicate with other devices.

destroy password A code programmed into the tag during manufacturing that can be used to permanently disable the tag.

detector A diode that receives a light-based transmission signal.

device discovery The process of querying other devices on the network to identify their locations and how many of them there are.

dibit A signal unit that represents two bits.

diffused transmission A light-based transmission that relies on reflected light.

digital certificates A special message signed by a certification authority that is used for security and authentication.

digital convergence The power of digital devices such as desktop computers and wireless handhelds to combine voice, video, and text-processing capabilities as well as to be connected to business and home networks and to the Internet.

digital modulation A method of encoding a digital signal onto an analog carrier wave for transmission over media that does not support direct digital signal transmission.

digital signal Data that is discrete or separate.

digital subscriber line (DSL) A technology used to transmit data over a telephone line.

dipole An antenna that has a fixed amount of gain over that of an isotropic radiator.

direct sequence spread spectrum (DSSS) A spread spectrum technique that uses an expanded, redundant code to transmit each data bit.

directed transmission A light-based transmission that requires the emitter and detector to be directly aimed at one another.

directional antenna An antenna that radiates the electromagnetic waves in one direction only, focusing all the energy from the transmitter in that direction. This results in an effective increase in the gain of a passive antenna, and it can help reduce or eliminate the effect of multipath distortion if there is a clear line of sight between the two antennas.

directional gain The effective gain that a directional antenna achieves by focusing RF energy in one direction.

disassociate frame A frame sent by the new AP to the old AP in an ESS to terminate the old AP's association with a client. Disassociation frames are transmitted from one AP to another over the wired network only, not via the wireless medium.

disassociation A procedure used by devices to leave (i.e., disconnect from) a network.

distributed coordination function (DCF) The default channel access method in IEEE 802.11 WLANs, designed to avoid collisions and grant all devices on the WLAN a reasonably equal chance to transmit on the selected channel.

D-WVAN A secondary wireless video area network that operates in a different frequency channel and is formed when two devices require additional bandwidth but there is no bandwidth available in the current frequency channel.

dynamic rate selection A function of an AP that allows it to automatically select the highest transmission speed based on the strength and quality of the signal received from a client NIC.

E

eighth-wave antenna An antenna that is one-eighth of the wavelength of the signal it is designed to transmit or receive.

electromagnetic interference (EMI) Interference with a radio signal; also called noise.

electromagnetic wave (EM wave) A signal composed of electrical and magnetic forces that in radio transmission usually propagates from an antenna and can be modulated to carry information.

Electronic Product Code (EPC) A standardized numbering scheme that can be programmed in a tag and attached to any physical product.

emitter A laser diode or a light-emitting diode that transmits a light-based signal.

encryption The process of encoding communications to ensure that the transmission, if intercepted, cannot be easily decoded, which discourages many hackers.

enhanced data rate (EDR) A feature of the Bluetooth version 2.0 specification that allows it to support data rates of 2 Mbps and 3 Mbps (by adding two modulations) while remaining fully backward compatible with Bluetooth versions 1.1 and 1.2.

Enhanced Data rates for GSM Evolution (EDGE) A 2.5G digital cellular network technology that boosts GPRS transmissions.

EPCglobal Inc. An organization entrusted by industry worldwide to establish RFID standards and services for real-time, automatic identification of information in the supply chain of any company anywhere in the world.

European Telecommunications Standards Institute (ETSI) A standards body that develops telecommunications standards for use throughout Europe.

Extended Service Set (ESS) A WLAN mode that consists of wireless clients and multiple APs using the same SSID, extending a WLAN seamlessly beyond the maximum range of an 802.11 transmission.

Extensible Authentication Protocol (EAP) A collection of protocols used by IEEE 802.1X for network authentication between a wireless device, an AP, and a RADIUS server.

F

Federal Communications Commission (FCC) The primary U.S. regulatory agency for telecommunications.

filter A component that is used to either accept or block a radio frequency signal.

First Generation (1G) The first generation of wireless cellular telephony that transmitted at 9.6 Kbps using analog circuit-switched transmission technology.

fixed wireless A wireless last mile connection.

fragmentation The division of data to be transmitted from one large frame into several smaller frames.

frame A data link layer packet that contains the header and trailer required by the physical medium.

free space loss The signal loss that occurs as a result of the tendency of RF waves to spread, resulting in less energy at any given point as the signal moves away from the transmitting antenna.

Free Space Optics (FSO) An optical, wireless, point-to-point, line-of-sight broadband technology.

frequency A measurement of radio waves that is determined by how frequently a cycle occurs.

frequency division duplexing (FDD) A mechanism that uses one frequency for uplink and another for downlink. *See* time division duplexing.

Frequency Division Multiple Access (FDMA) A radio transmission technique that divides the bandwidth of the frequency into several smaller frequency bands.

frequency hopping spread spectrum (FHSS) A spread spectrum technique that uses a range of frequencies and changes frequencies during the transmission.

frequency modulation (FM) A technique that changes the number of wave cycles in response to a change in the amplitude of the input signal.

frequency shift keying (FSK) A digital modulation technique that changes the frequency of the carrier signal in response to a change in the binary input signal.

Fresnel zone An elliptical region spanning the distance between two directional antennas that must not be blocked more than 40 percent to prevent interference with the RF signal.

full-duplex transmission Transmissions in which data flows in either direction simultaneously.

full-function device A device used in 802.15.4 (ZigBee) networks that can connect to other full-function devices and has the capability of routing frames to other devices in a ZigBee network. It can also connect to endpoint or child devices. Full-function devices can maintain a connection to multiple devices and can become coordinators.

full-wave antenna An antenna that is as long as the length of the wave it is designed to transmit or receive.

G

gain A relative measure of increase in a signal's power level.

general packet radio service (GPRS) A 2.5G network technology that can transmit at up to 114 Kbps.

geosynchronous earth orbit (GEO) satellites Satellites stationed at an altitude of 22,282 miles (35,860 kilometers) that match the rotation of the planet and therefore appear to be in a fixed position in the sky with reference to a point on the ground.

Gigahertz (GHz) 1,000,000,000 Hertz.

greenfield A mode of operation of 802.11n in which only HT-capable devices are supported.

ground-plane A metal disc or two straight wires assembled at 90 degrees, used to provide a reflection point for monopole antennas that are not mounted on or near the surface of the ground.

GSM (Global Systems for Mobile Communications) One of three multiple-access cellular technologies that make up the 2G digital cellular system; it uses a combination of FDMA and TDMA.

guaranteed time slot (GTS) A reserved period for critical devices to transmit priority data.

guard band The unused frequency space between two adjacent channels.

guard interval (GI) An added 800 nanosecond delay at the end of each 802.11 frame that allows all reflected signals to arrive at the receiver's antennas before another symbol is transmitted.

H

half-duplex transmission Transmission that occurs in both directions but only one way at a time.

half-wave antenna An antenna that is half as long as the wavelength of the signal it is designed to transmit or receive.

handoff In an ESS, when a WLAN device re-associates with an AP on the network and disassociates with the one to which it was previously connected.

harmonics Stray oscillations that result from the process of modulating a wave and that fall outside the range of

frequencies used for transmission. Harmonics also occur when a signal goes through a mixer and must be filtered out at several points before the signal is finally fed to the antenna for transmission.

help desk A central point of contact for users who need assistance using technology.

Hertz (Hz) The number of cycles per second.

high-pass filter A filter that passes all signals that are above a maximum threshold.

High-Speed Downlink Packet Access (HSDPA) A packet-switched digital transmission cellular technology that uses 5 MHz W-CDMA (wideband CDMA) channels together with adaptive modulation, MIMO, and hybrid automatic repeat request (HARQ) to achieve data rates between 8 and 10 Mbps.

hold mode A state in which the Bluetooth device can put slave units into a mode in which only the slave's internal timer is running.

hopping code The sequence of changing frequencies used in FHSS.

horn antenna A two-dimensional directional antenna typically used for microwave transmission; it resembles a large horn with the wide end bent to one side.

HSPA+ Also called "evolved HSPA," a technical cellular standard that provides theoretical data rates of up to 168 Mbps (realistically, around 42 Mbps) by combining two HSDPA transmitters, MIMO, and 64 QAM modulation.

H-WVAN The home or parent WVAN of a D-WVAN. *See* Wireless Video Area Network.

HyperText Markup Language (HTML) The standard language for displaying Web pages.

I

IBSS *See* ad hoc mode.

IEEE 802.11a Developed in 1999, a standard for WLAN transmissions at speeds of up to 54 Mbps.

IEEE 802.11b An amendment to the IEEE 802.11 standard for WLANs that added two higher speeds, 5.5 Mbps and 11 Mbps, and is also known as Wi-Fi, a name given by the Wi-Fi Alliance to technology that has been certified for interoperability with equipment from different manufacturers.

IEEE 802.11e A standard for WLAN applications that implements QoS for WLANs and provides for improvements in their capabilities and efficiency.

IEEE 802.11g A standard for WLAN transmissions at speeds of up to 54 Mbps using the ISM band.

IEEE 802.11i An enhancement to 802.11 that deals with security weaknesses of the original standard and supports the use of network-based authentication servers running software such as RADIUS.

IEEE 802.16 The IEEE standard for wireless broadband metropolitan area networks.

IEEE 802.1X A set of recommendations for increasing the security of IEEE 802 LANs that is also applicable to 802.11 WLANs.

i-mode An Internet access system for digital cellular telephones.

impedance The opposition to the flow of alternating current in a circuit. Represented by the letter "Z" and measured in ohms, impedance is the combination of a circuit's resistance, inductance, and capacitance.

impulse modulation A digital transmission technique employed by UWB in which the polarity of a single analog pulse (one-half of a sine wave) represents a binary digit 1 or 0.

Independent Basic Service Set (IBSS) A WLAN mode in which wireless clients communicate directly among themselves without using an AP. *See also* ad hoc mode and peer-to-peer mode.

Industrial, Scientific and Medical (ISM) band An unregulated radio frequency band approved by the FCC in 1985.

infrared light Light that is next to visible light on the light spectrum and that has many of the same characteristics as visible light.

infrastructure mode *See* Basic Service Set.

inquiry procedure A process that enables a device to discover which devices are in range and determine the addresses and clocks for the devices.

Institute of Electrical and Electronics Engineers (IEEE) 802.11n-2009 A set of standards that allows WLAN computers to transmit data at speeds ranging from 1 Mbps to a maximum of 600 Mbps. 802.11n (or 802.11n-2009, as the specification is now called) can also make use of the 5 GHz band in addition to the 24 GHz band.

Institute of Electrical and Electronics Engineers (IEEE) A standards body that establishes standards for telecommunications.

Institute of Electrical and Electronics Engineers (IEEE) 802.16 Fixed Broadband Wireless A set of standards, some established and some still under development, for fixed and mobile broadband wireless communications that allows computers to communicate at up to 75 Mbps and at distances of up to 35 miles (56 km) in a point-to-point configuration. This set of standards also allows the use of both licensed and unlicensed frequencies.

Integrated Services Digital Networks (ISDN) A technology that transmits data over telephone lines at a maximum of 256 Kbps.

interframe spaces (IFS) Time gaps used in CSMA/CA to allow devices to finish receiving a transmission and checking for errors before any other device is allowed to transmit.

intermediate frequency (IF) The output signal that results from the modulation process.

International Organization for Standardization (ISO) An organization to promote international cooperation and standards in the areas of science, technology, and economics.

International Telecommunication Union (ITU) An agency of the United Nations that sets international telecommunications standards and coordinates global telecommunications networks and services.

Internet Architecture Board (IAB) The organization responsible for defining the overall architecture of the Internet, providing guidance and broad direction to the IETF. The IAB also serves as the technology advisory group to the Internet Society and oversees a number of critical activities in support of the Internet.

Internet Engineering Task Force (IETF) A standards body that focuses on the lower levels of telecommunications technologies.

Internet Society (ISOC) A professional-membership organization of Internet experts that comments on policies and practices and oversees a number of other boards and task forces dealing with network policy issues.

intersymbol interference (ISI) Interference caused when the beginning of a symbol arrives at the receiver antenna while multipath reflections from the previous symbol are still reaching the antenna.

isochronous A time-dependent transmission that must occur every frame or every so many frames to maintain the quality of the connection.

isotropic radiator A theoretically perfect sphere that radiates power equally in all directions; it is impossible to construct one.

J

Java An object-oriented programming language used for general-purpose business programming and interactive Web sites.

J2ME (Java 2 Micro Edition) A subset of the Java programming language designed for use in portable devices such as PDAs and smartphones.

jitter The maximum delay variation between two consecutive packets over a period of time.

K

Kilohertz (KHz) 1,000 Hertz.

L

last mile connection The link between the customer's premises and the telephone company, cable TV company, or ISP.

latency The amount of time delay that it takes a packet to travel from source to destination device.

license exempt spectrum Unregulated radio frequency bands that are available in the United States to any users without a license.

light spectrum All the different types of light that travel from the Sun to the Earth.

line of sight The direct alignment as required in a directed transmission.

link budget The process of calculating the signal strength between the transmitter and receiver antennas to ensure that the link can meet the receiver's minimum signal strength requirements.

link manager Special software in Bluetooth devices that helps identify other Bluetooth devices, creates the links between them, and sends and receives data.

Local Multipoint Distribution Service (LMDS) A fixed broadband technology that can provide a wide variety of wireless services.

Logical Link Control (LLC) One of the two sublayers of the IEEE Project 802 data link layer.

loss A relative measure of decrease in a signal's power level.

low earth orbit (LEO) satellites Satellites that orbit the Earth at an altitude of 200–900 miles (321–1,448 kilometers).

low-pass filter A filter that passes all signals that are below a maximum threshold.

LTE (Long Term Evolution) A digital packet-switched cellular technology that expands on HSPA+ beyond two spatially multiplexed channels, uses OFDM modulation, and also uses 20 MHz-wide channels to achieve data rates of up to 100 Mbps.

LTE Advanced A proposed standard for broadband cellular communications that expands on LTE by allowing carriers to combine up to five 20-MHz-wide OFDM channels to achieve data rates of up to 1 Gbps.

M

management channel time allocation (MCTA) Time periods used for communication between the devices and the PNC.

management frames MAC frames that are used, for example, to set up the initial communications between a client and the AP.

man-in-the-middle A type of security attack in which a hacker uses software installed in a computer to duplicate the behavior of an enterprise AP, capture frames, alter them, and then retransmit the modified frames to the intended receiver or to another device on the network.

master A device on a Bluetooth piconet that controls all the wireless traffic.

Media Access Control (MAC) One of the two sublayers of the IEEE Project 802 data link layer.

medium earth orbit (MEO) satellites Satellites that orbit the Earth at altitudes of 1,500–10,000 miles (2,413–16,090 kilometers).

Megahertz (MHz) 1,000,000 Hertz.

mesh networking A network topography in which each device connects to all other devices within range.

message integrity check A process of adding certain encrypted random data, consisting of both variable and static data, to each communications session so that the receiver can verify that the message has not been tampered with after being transmitted.

message integrity code (MIC) A code composed of a subset of the data, the length of the data, and the symmetric key; used by the receiving device to verify that the data has not been tampered with during transmission. This code is used in the process of message integrity check. *See also* message integrity check.

microbrowser A tiny browser program that runs on a WAP or WAP2 cellular phone.

microwaves The part of the radio frequency spectrum from 3 to 30 GHz.

Mini PCI A small card that is functionally equivalent to a standard PCI expansion card used for integrating communications peripherals onto a notebook computer but that is much smaller.

mixer A component that combines two inputs to create a single output.

mobile telecommunications switching office (MTSO) The connection between a cellular network and wired telephones.

modem (MOdulator/DEModulator) A device used to convert digital signals into an analog format, and vice versa.

modulation The process of changing a carrier signal.

modulation index The amount that the frequency varies.

monopole antenna An antenna built of a straight piece of wire, usually a quarter of the wavelength, with no ground point or reflecting element.

motes Remote sensors used for collecting data from manufacturing equipment or for scientific research, which can communicate using wireless technology.

multiband orthogonal frequency division multiplexing (OFDM) A transmission technique in which the frequency band is divided into a number of frequencies (called sub-frequencies or channels) that do not interfere with one another.

Multichannel Multipoint Distribution Service (MMDS) A fixed broadband wireless technology that transmits at 1.5 Mbps over distances of 35 miles (56 kilometers).

multipath distortion What occurs when the same signal reflects and arrives at the receiver's antenna from several different directions and at different times.

multiple-input and multiple-output (MIMO) A technology that uses multiple antennas (usually three or four) and reflected signals (multipath reflections) to extend the range of the WLAN by attempting to correctly decode a frame from multiple copies of it received at different times.

N

narrow-band transmissions Transmissions that use one radio frequency or a very narrow portion of the frequency spectrum.

Near Field Communications (NFC) A short-range wireless technology, based on RFID, that allows the transfer of data between enabled smartphones and tablet computers; it can also read tags.

neighbor piconets Separate piconets that have their own PNC but that depend on the original piconet's PNC to allocate a private block of time when their devices are allowed to transmit.

Network Interface Unit (NIU) A device that connects an LMDS modem to a LAN or telephone system.

noise Interference with a signal.

nomadic user A user that moves frequently but does not use the equipment while in motion.

non-line of sight (NLOS) When the transmitter antenna cannot be seen from the receiver end, or vice versa.

non-return-to-zero (NRZ) A binary signaling technique that increases the voltage to represent a 1 bit but provides no voltage for a 0 bit.

non-return-to-zero level (NRZ-L) *See* polar non-return-to-zero.

non-return-to-zero, invert-on-ones (NRZ-I) A binary signaling technique that changes the voltage level only when the bit to be represented is a 1.

null data frame The response that a client sends back to the AP to indicate that the client has no transmissions to make in PCF.

O

Object Name Service (ONS) An EPCglobal Inc. service, modeled after DNS, that can assist in locating information about a product over the Internet.

official standards *See* de jure standards.

offset quadrature phase shift keying (O-QPSK) A transmission technique in 802.15.4 that uses two carrier waves of the same frequency but with a phase difference of 90 degrees between them. This technique modulates even-numbered chips in the in-phase wave and odd-numbered chips in the other phase (Q-Phase), using quadrature amplitude modulation, before combining the waves for transmission.

omnidirectional antenna An antenna that sends out the signal in a uniform pattern in all directions.

one-dimensional antenna A straight length of wire or metal connected to a transmitter at one end.

Orthogonal Frequency-Division Multiple Access (OFDMA) A multiple access technique, based on OFDM, that divides the frequency channel into 1536 orthogonal data subcarriers.

oscillating signal A wave that illustrates the change in a carrier signal.

P

packet A smaller segment of the transmitted signal.

packet switching Data transmission that is broken into smaller units.

paging procedure A process that enables a device to make an actual connection to a piconet.

pairing A two-step process for establishing a connection between a Bluetooth master and slave devices.

PAN coordinator The 802.15.4 device that controls access to the piconet and optionally the timing as well.

parabolic dish antenna A high-gain directional antenna that emits a narrow, focused beam of energy and is used for long-distance outdoor links.

park mode A state in which the Bluetooth device is still synchronized to the piconet but does not participate in the traffic.

passband A minimum and maximum threshold that spells out which range of frequencies will pass through a filter.

passive antenna The most common type of antenna. Passive antennas can only radiate a signal with the same amount of energy that appears at the antenna connector.

passive scanning The process of listening to each available channel for a set period of time.

passive tags The most common type of RFID tags. They do not include a battery and are powered by the electromagnetic energy in the RF waves transmitted by the reader. Passive tags never initiate a transmission and must wait for a reader to interrogate them.

patch antenna A semi-directional antenna that emits a wide horizontal beam and an even wider vertical beam.

peer-to-peer mode *See* ad hoc mode.

personal digital assistant (PDA) A handheld computer device used for taking notes, making appointments, creating to-do lists, and communicating with other devices.

phase The relative starting point of a wave, in degrees, beginning at zero degrees.

phase modulation (PM) A technique that changes the starting point of a wave cycle in response to a change in the amplitude of the input signal. This technique is not used in analog modulation.

phase shift keying (PSK) A digital modulation technique that changes the starting point of a wave cycle in response to a change in the binary input signal.

physical layer (PHY) The layer that is responsible for converting the data bits into an electromagnetic signal and transmitting it on the medium.

pi/4-DQPSK A method of modulation that uses two different frequencies exactly 90 degrees apart, which therefore do not interfere with each other.

piconet A Bluetooth network that contains one master and at least one slave that use the same channel to exchange data with one another.

piconet coordinator (PNC) A device that provides all the basic communications timing in an 802.15.3 piconet.

pizza box antenna A small antenna used for MMDS systems.

PN code Pseudo-random code; a code that appears to be a random sequence of 1s and 0s but actually repeats itself. Used in CDMA cellular telephone technology.

point coordination function (PCF) The 802.11 optional polling function.

point-to-multipoint wireless link A link in which one central site uses an omnidirectional antenna to transmit to multiple remote sites, which may use omnidirectional antennas or directional antennas to maximize the distance and the quality of the signal.

point-to-point The most reliable link between two antenna sites, using directional antennas to maximize the distance and the signal quality.

polar non-return-to-zero (polar NRZ) A binary signaling technique that increases the voltage to represent a 1 bit but drops to negative voltage to represent a 0 bit.

polling A channel access method in which each computer is asked in sequence whether it wants to transmit.

power management An 802.11 standard that allows the mobile client to be off as much as possible to conserve battery life but still not miss out on data transmissions.

power over Ethernet (PoE) A technology that provides power over an Ethernet cable.

pre-shared key A 128-bit key used by WPA; it is called "pre-shared" because it is manually configured in each WLAN device before connections can be established.

privacy Standards that ensure transmissions are not read by unauthorized users.

probe A frame sent by a client when performing active scanning.

probe response A frame sent by an AP when responding to a client's active scanning probe.

profiles Sets of predefined WiMAX connection parameters that include the frequency channel, bandwidth of the channel, and transmission mechanism (OFDM, OFDMA, etc.).

protocol adaptation layers (PALs) A set of protocol implementation rules based on the 802.15.3 standard that enables, among other possible protocols, wireless USB at 480 Mbps.

pseudo-random code A code that is usually derived through a number of mathematical calculations as well as practical experimentation.

public key infrastructure (PKI) A unique security code that can verify the authenticity of a user.

Q

QoS (quality-of-service) A resource reservation enhancement to the 802.11 MAC layer that enables prioritization of traffic and is most often used to support delivery of voice, video, and audio frames between WLAN devices. QoS is also used in personal area networks (PANs) to allow devices to request more channel access time in order to prioritize high-volume, time-sensitive traffic, such as a voice stream.

quadbit A signal unit that represents four bits.

quadrature amplitude modulation (QAM) A combination of phase modulation with amplitude modulation to produce 16 different signals.

quadrature phase shift keying (QPSK) A digital modulation technique that combines quadrature amplitude modulation with phase shift keying.

quarter-wave antenna An antenna that is one quarter of the wavelength of the signal it is designed to transmit or receive.

R

radio frequency (RF) communications All types of radio communications that use radio frequency waves.

radio frequency identification (RFID) A technology that uses electronic tags equipped with microprocessor chips and memory to identify products. RFID tags can store significantly more information than the current bar-code system. The data about the product can then be transferred directly to an information-processing system for inventory control, location tracking, and item counting.

radio frequency spectrum The entire range of all radio frequencies that exist.

radio modules Small radio transceivers built onto microprocessor chips and embedded into Bluetooth devices, which enable them to communicate.

radio wave (radiotelephony) An electromagnetic wave created when an electric current passes through a wire and creates a magnetic field in the space around the wire.

reader The RFID device that captures and processes the data received from the tags.

reassociate request frame A frame sent from a client to a new AP asking whether it can associate with the AP.

reassociate response frame A frame sent by an AP to a station indicating that it will accept its re-association with that AP.

re-association The process of a client disconnecting from one AP and reestablishing a connection with another AP.

recurring costs Costs that continue to be paid over a period of time.

Reduced Interframe Space (RIFS) A 2-microsecond interframe space that can be used in 802.11n networks working in greenfield mode to help reduce overhead and increase throughput.

reduced-function device (RFD) In ZigBee networks, a device (such as a light switch or lamp) that can only connect to one full-function device at a time and can only join the network as a child device.

repeater A device commonly used in satellite communications that simply "repeats" the signal to another location.

request for information (RFI) A document sent to a vendor to gain general information about a vendor's products or solutions to a problem.

request for proposal (RFP) A detailed planning document with precise specifications for the products and services.

request-to-send/clear-to-send (RTS/CTS) An 802.11 protocol option that allows a station to reserve the network for transmissions.

return on investment (ROI) The profit or advantage of an action.

return-to-zero (RZ) A binary signaling technique that increases the voltage to represent a 1 bit, but the voltage is reduced to zero before the end of the period for transmitting the 1 bit, and there is no voltage for a 0 bit.

roaming The automatic transfer of the RF signal when moving from one cellular network to another network.

Robust Security Network Association (RSNA) A grouping of several security functions to protect data frames by providing mutual authentication between client devices and access points, controlled access to the network, establishment of security keys, and key management.

RSA An encryption algorithm that uses a large integer composed of smaller numbers that are multiplied by each other. It is based on the idea that it will be difficult to figure out each of the smaller numbers that are used to arrive at the large integer.

S

satellite radio A pay-for-service radio broadcast system that transmits digital programming directly from satellites to a network of ground-based repeaters and that holds the signal regardless of the listener's location. Users must purchase special receivers and pay a monthly subscription fee to listen to commercial-free music channels. Because the digital transmission is decoded at the receivers, the sound quality is also much better than conventional FM radio.

scatternet A group of piconets in which connections exist between different piconets.

scintillation The temporal and spatial variations in light intensity caused by atmospheric turbulence.

Second Generation (2G) The second generation of cellular telephony, which uses circuit-switched digital transmission technology.

semi-active tags RFID tags that include a battery that is only used when the tag is interrogated. The batteries in semi-active tags usually last for several years.

sensory tags RFID tags that include a thermal or other kind of sensor and can record information about the environmental conditions to which a product has been exposed during transportation or storage.

sequential freshness The process of assigning a sequential number to each frame to ensure that it is not transmitted on the same network more than once.

service discovery The process of sending a query to other devices on the network to identify their capabilities.

Service Set IDentifier (SSID) A unique network identifier assigned to an AP during configuration. In an ESS, all APs will be configured with the same SSID.

Short Interframe Space (SIFS) A time period used to allow a receiving station to finish receiving all signals, decode them, and check for errors.

Short Message Services (SMS) A delivery system for short, text-based messages sent between wireless devices such as cellular telephones and pagers.

sidebands The sum and the differences of the frequency carrier that serve as buffer space around the frequency of the transmitted signal.

signal-to-noise ratio (SNR) The measure of signal strength relative to the background noise.

SIM (Subscriber Identity Module) card Small electronic cards that are used to associate a phone with a user's account.

simplex transmission Transmission that occurs in only one direction.

sine wave A wave that illustrates the change in a carrier signal.

slaves Devices on a Bluetooth piconet that take commands from the master.

sleep mode A power-conserving mode used by portable, battery-powered devices in a WLAN.

slotted terminating adaptive collection (STAC) The communications protocol used by passive RFID tags that work in the 13.56 MHz HF band.

smart antennas A new type of antenna that uses a signal processor and an array of narrow beam elements to track the user and send most of the RF energy in the direction of the mobile receiver in order to prevent interference and avoid wasting RF energy.

smart labels Another name for flexible RFID tags that include a microprocessor chip and memory.

smartphone A device that combines a cellular phone with the capabilities of a personal digital assistant (PDA). These devices provide the user with the ability to enter appointments in a calendar, write notes, send and receive e-mail, and browse Web sites, among other functions.

sniff mode A state in which the Bluetooth device listens to the piconet master at a reduced rate so that it uses less power.

spatial diversity The sending of parallel beams during free space optical transmissions.

spatial multiplexing A transmission technique that uses multiple radios and multiple antennas to send different parts of the same PHY frame simultaneously, thus increasing the data rate.

spectrum conflict The potential for technologies using the same frequency bands to interfere with one another to the extent that they sometimes perform poorly when used within close range of one another.

spread spectrum transmission A technique that takes a narrow signal and spreads it over a broader portion of the radio frequency band.

subnets Subsets of a large network that use a different group of IP addresses belonging to the same domain IP address. Subnets are separated from other subnets by routers.

subscriber station (SS) In a WiMAX network, either a CPE device that attaches to a LAN or a laptop computer.

super high frequency (SHF) The part of the radio frequency spectrum from 3 to 30 GHz.

superframe A mechanism for managing transmissions in a piconet. The superframe is a continually repeating frame containing a beacon, contention access periods, channel time allocation periods, and management time allocation periods. Using the superframe is optional in 802.15.4 WPANs.

switching Moving a signal from one wire or frequency to another.

symbol A data unit that can represent one or more bits. A symbol in data communications is also known as a baud.

symmetric encryption key A string of characters, numbers, or both used to encrypt the data within a frame. When all devices in a single network use the same encryption key, they are called "symmetric."

synchronous connection-oriented (SCO) link A symmetric point-to-point link between a master and a single slave in the piconet; it functions like a circuit-switched link by using reserved slots at regular intervals.

system profile A combination of the basic WiMAX profile and one of the transmission profiles.

T

T1 A technology used to transmit data over special telephone lines at 1.544 Mbps.

tags Devices that include an antenna and a chip containing memory and can store information about products, such as the manufacturer, product category, and serial number along with date and time of manufacturing.

Telecommunications Industries Association (TIA) A group of more than 600 companies that manufacture or supply the products and services used in global communications.

temporal key integrity protocol (TKIP) A security protocol used in WPA that provides per-packet key-mixing

Third Generation (3G) Digital cellular wireless generation of cellular telephony with speeds up to 2 Mbps.

time division duplexing (TDD) A mechanism that divides a single transmission into two parts: an uplink part and a downlink part. *See* frequency division duplexing.

Time Division Multiple Access (TDMA) A transmission technique that divides the bandwidth into several time slots.

time slots The measurement unit in a PLCP frame.

traffic encryption key (TEK) The security key used to encrypt the data in a WiMAX network.

traffic indication map (TIM) A list of the stations that have buffered frames waiting at the AP. The TIM is sent in the beacons by the AP.

transponders Another name for RFID tags.

tribit A signal unit that represents three bits.

triple-play The support of transmission of video, voice, and data on the same network.

truck-rolls Visits to a site by support technicians.

two-dimensional antenna An Antenna, such as a dish or patch, that has both height and width. In omnidirectional antennas, the thickness of the pole or wire is not considered a second dimension.

two-level Gaussian frequency shift keying (2-GFSK) A binary signaling technique that uses two different frequencies to indicate whether a 1 or a 0 is being transmitted.

U

Ultra Wide Band (UWB) A wireless communications technology that allows devices to transmit data at hundreds of megabits or even gigabits per second at short distances— up to 6 feet (2 meters) at the higher speeds and up to 150 feet (50 meters) at lower speeds.

ultra-wideband transmission A radio transmission that consists of low-power, precisely timed pulses of energy that operate in the same frequency spectrum as low-end noise, such as that emitted by computer chips and TV monitors.

Unlicensed National Information Infrastructure (U-NII) An unregulated band approved by the FCC in 1996 to provide for short-range, high-speed wireless digital communications.

unregulated bands *See* license exempt spectrum.

upfront costs Costs that are necessary to start a project.

V

virtual private network (VPN) A secure, encrypted connection between two points over a public or private network.

Voice over Internet Protocol (VoIP) A technology that allows voice telephone calls to be carried over the same network used to carry computer data.

Voice over WLAN (VoWLAN) A term used to describe the transmission of telephone calls on WLANs.

voltage Electrical pressure.

W

wake superframe The superframe designated by the PNC in which devices that are in power-saving mode wake up and listen for frames addressed to them.

wavelength The length of a single RF wave, measured from the starting point of the sine wave to the starting point of the next sine wave or from any point in a wave (usually the peak) to the same point on the next wave.

Wideband CDMA (W-CDMA) The 3G digital cellular technology that is a migration from EDGE.

Wi-Fi A certification label awarded to IEEE 802.11 WLAN-compatible wireless devices that pass all interoperability tests performed by an organization called the Wi-Fi Alliance. The acronym is often thought to stand for Wireless Fidelity, but this is a misconception. The name was chosen by the alliance purely for marketing reasons and is not an acronym at all.

Wi-Fi Protected Access (WPA) and WPA2 A security enhancement and interoperability certification introduced by the Wi-Fi Alliance in advance of the 802.11i standard to deal with the security flaws in WEP.

WiGig An alliance of companies involved in developing a common wireless specification for connecting computers, communication, and entertainment devices over short ranges, using the 60 GHz band at multi-gigabit speeds.

WiMAX Worldwide interoperability for microwave access.

WiMAX Forum An industry organization dedicated to promoting the implementation of 802.16 by testing and certifying equipment for compatibility and interoperability.

Wired Equivalent Privacy (WEP) The IEEE specification for data encryption between wireless devices to prevent an attacker from eavesdropping.

wireless application protocol (WAP or WAP2) A standard for transmitting, formatting, and displaying Internet data on cellular phones. WAP can display only text. WAP2 supports HTML and can display color and pictures.

wireless bridges A networking component that connects two wired networks or extends the range of a WLAN.

wireless communications The transmission of user data without the use of wires between devices.

wireless controller Devices that make it much easier to manage large WLANs by implementing most of the functions of an AP and controlling the operation of local or remotely connected radios.

Wireless High-Speed Unlicensed Metro Area Network (WirelessHUMAN) A WiMAX specification based on OFDM that is specifically designed for use in the 5 GHz U-NII band.

wireless local area network (WLAN) A local area network that is not connected by wires but instead uses wireless technology. Its range extends to approximately 100 meters and has a maximum data rate of 600 Mbps, by current standards. Today's WLANs are based on IEEE 802.11a/b/g/n standards.

wireless metropolitan area networks (WMANs) A group of technologies that provide wireless connectivity across a substantial geographical area, such as a large city.

wireless network interface card (wireless NIC) A device that connects to a PC to transmit and receive network data over radio waves. It includes an antenna for wireless communication between networked devices.

wireless personal area network (WPAN) A very small network that typically extends to 33 feet (10 meters) or less. Due to its limited range, WPAN technology is used mainly as a replacement for cables. *See also* piconet and UWB.

wireless residential gateway A combination of several technologies that permit home users to have wireless capabilities and also allow Internet and printer sharing and provide better security than connecting a computer directly to the Internet.

wireless site survey The task of measuring the signal strength and quality in several locations around the office to determine how many APs will be required, how many and which channels will be used, as what interference sources and security needs there are.

wireless video area network (WVAN) The name given to a network in WirelessHD that is dedicated to transmitting multimedia files, usually in an uncompressed format, to a television or similar type of display device. WVANs may also include audio-only devices, such as stereo systems.

wireless VoIP phones The telephone handsets that connect to a WLAN's AP, permitting use of the WLAN for telephone calls.

wireless wide area network (WWAN) A network that spans a geographical areas as large as an entire country or even the entire world.

WirelessHART A wireless sensor network protocol based on the highway addressable remote transducer protocol (HART), designed for interfacing manufacturing equipment and machines.

WirelessHD A specification for the wireless transmission of high-definition video (HD), multichannel audio, and data between consumer devices such as televisions, stereo systems, and Blu-ray players, using the 60 GHz frequency band.

WirelessMAN-SC (single carrier) A WiMAX specification that uses a single carrier and is intended for point-to-point connections in the 10–66 GHz bands.

WPA2 A security specification and interoperability certification introduced by the Wi-Fi Alliance that includes support for AES encryption as well as support for 802.11i and 802.1X.

Y

yagi antenna A directional antenna that emits a wide, less-focused beam and is used for medium-distance outdoor applications.

Z

ZigBee Alliance An organization that creates protocols and specifications for devices used to wirelessly control lighting, as well as security and energy systems, for home and industry. The ZigBee Alliance is essentially an association of manufacturers and interested organizations that promote a global standard for wireless devices used in monitoring and control applications.

Index